IBM® Cognos® Business Intelligence 10: The Official Guide

Dan Volitich
Gerard Ruppert

New York   Chicago   San Francisco
Lisbon   London   Madrid   Mexico City
Milan   New Delhi   San Juan
Seoul   Singapore   Sydney   Toronto

The McGraw·Hill Companies

Cataloging-in-Publication Data is on file with the Library of Congress

McGraw-Hill books are available at special quantity discounts to use as premiums and sales promotions, or for use in corporate training programs. To contact a representative, please e-mail us at bulksales@mcgraw-hill.com.

IBM® Cognos® Business Intelligence 10: The Official Guide

1234567890   DOC DOC   1098765432

ISBN   978-0-07-177593-9
MHID   0-07-177593-5

Sponsoring Editor	**Copy Editor**	**Composition**
Wendy Rinaldi	Lisa Theobald	Cenveo Publisher Services
Editorial Supervisor	**Proofreader**	**Illustration**
Patty Mon	Paul Tyler	Cenveo Publisher Services
Project Manager	**Indexer**	**Art Director, Cover**
Anupriya Tyagi, Cenveo Publisher Services	Karin Arrigoni	Jeff Weeks
Acquisitions Coordinator	**Production Supervisor**	
Ryan Willard	George Anderson	

Contents at a Glance

About the Authors

Dan Volitich is president and owner of John Daniel Associates, which he cofounded in 1996 to serve the business intelligence market. Dan's extensive experience with business intelligence (BI) began in the mid-1980s (before the market coined the term "BI") at a large commercial real estate firm in Fairfax, Virginia. As the company's IT director, he successfully delivered enterprise BI solutions, streamlining mission-critical business functions for every department in the company.

Upon his return to Pittsburgh in the early '90s, Dan again found himself chartered with empowering end users. Dan's background has given him tremendous insight into the value of empowering end users with business-critical data, and that insight is invaluable in the delivery of BI solutions to John Daniel clients today.

With more than 24 years of experience in planning and delivering successful BI solutions to Fortune 500 and mid-market companies, Dan believes superior product knowledge and outstanding customer support are essential components to maintaining a leadership role in the BI market. That combination has been a significant factor in the continued growth of John Daniel Associates. Dan is a Penn State graduate with a bachelor's degree in accounting with heavy emphasis in IT.

Gerard Ruppert is director of technology at John Daniel Associates. Prior to joining John Daniel in 2000, Gerard spent 12 years as a software developer and systems analyst in the public utility and education industries. While developing a data warehouse and investigating BI solutions, Gerard was introduced to IBM Cognos and John Daniel Associates. Being extremely perceptive, Gerard recognized a good thing when he saw it, and immediately gave his resume to Dan. The rest is history. Gerard received his bachelor's degree in computer science from the University of Pittsburgh, followed by a Master of Public Management degree from Carnegie Mellon University.

Contents

Acknowledgments

This is the second IBM Cognos book written by John Daniel Associates. The only experience that we can compare this to is drinking (too much) tequila for the *second* time. Live and learn. The first book, *IBM Cognos 8 Business Intelligence: The Official Guide*, started out as a new, exciting adventure. None of us had written a book, so when Dan posed the question, "How hard can it be?" we all bought in. About nine months later, when the last round of editing was returned to McGraw-Hill, we all swore that we would never do *that* again. As time goes by, however, the memory of first experiences fade, and we convinced ourselves that *this time* it will be different. The writing of this book *was* different from the first experience in some ways, because we were faced with helping readers understand the "new" Cognos 10 while resisting the temptation to reuse much of the previous book's content. We believe that we've succeeded.

Both our first book and this book are the result of a team effort. While Dan and I share the author credit on this book, there is no way this volume would have been completed without the extraordinary efforts of the entire John Daniel Associates team and the support of our families.

A sincere thank you to the following individuals on the John Daniel Associates team: Bryan (and Lauren) Townsend, Alicia (and David) Scappe, and Erin (and Nick) Dunmire. Erin, Bryan, and Alicia are Business Analytics Specialists who have devoted countless hours to writing, editing, and capturing screenshots for this book. They have poured their own experience into the chapters they authored, which is why this book is as good as it is. Thank you also to Mark Mizner, one of John Daniel Associates' Business Analytics Reporting Specialists, and Mary Gido, Support Specialist, for their contributions to multiple chapters. Thank you to Janet Amos Pribanic, executive VP of sales, for staying on top of the constant change that is IBM Cognos, helping us to keep things in perspective, and playing "den mother" to us all.

The biggest thank you goes to our wives, Cricket and Joni. Their support through all of our "little projects" is done with grace that is beyond comprehension.

IBM is a first-class organization. We have been working with this technology for more than 17 years, and we have been an exclusive partner with Cognos for more than 15 years. We wish to thank the Cognos executive team that has supported this effort and trusted us as a partner to deliver this book. Susan Visser and Krista Colby-Wheatley, thank you for your close work with McGraw-Hill in getting this project off the ground. To all of the technical reviewers at Cognos—Trevor MacPherson, Sobia Hameed, Michael McGeein, Paul Glennon, Mike Norris, Wassim Hassouneh, Mike Armstrong, Joe Pusztai, Andrew MacNeil, Karen Recoskie, Dean Browne, Chris McPherson, and Scott Masson—thank you for your expertise and input to help make this an excellent product. A special thanks to Armin Kamal, Proven Practices Advisor at IBM Cognos in Ottawa, Ontario. Over the years, Armin has been a tremendous source of insight into the technology, and he has been a great friend as well.

Special thanks to Tim Casey and Doug Fitzsimmons of Allegheny HealthChoices, Inc. Tim and Doug gave me a crash course in how a real organization uses SPSS statistics on a daily basis. Thank you guys.

Having the privilege to work with the individuals at McGraw-Hill again was a pleasure. Wendy Rinaldi did a great job of keeping us on task and guiding us forward. I know we tried her patience on more than one occasion. Patty Mon, the editorial supervisor; Lisa Theobald, our copy editor; and Anupriya Tyagi, the project manager at Cenveo Publisher Services—all of you did a great job in taking our rough diamond of a manuscript and turning it into the polished gem that it is. All we can say is thank you.

Introduction

Choosing the direction for this book was a challenge. The direction for the first book was clear, as Cognos 8 was brand new and no one had ever written a general user guide. Because IBM Cognos 10 consists of completely new functionality mixed with enhancements to existing functionality, we had some interesting choices to make. Should we rewrite the entire book? No, that was a bad idea since so much of the core functionality in Cognos 10 came from Cognos 8. So what do we add, what do we remove, what should be rewritten, and what can be left as is? Nothing was left as is: every chapter has something new. Completely new chapters on IBM Cognos Business Insight (Chapter 7), Cognos Business Insight Advanced–Relational (Chapter 8), and Cognos Business Insight Advanced–Dimensional (Chapter 9) were added; a review of statistical reporting (Chapter 13) was also added. A new chapter on how to use IBM Cognos Framework Manager (Chapter 16) was added, and the chapter on metadata modeling with Cognos Framework Manager (Chapter 17) completely rewritten. It is our opinion that these changes have made this a stronger technical guide. We hope you agree.

Chapters from the Cognos 8 edition that are not included in this book include "Planning, Budgeting, and Forecasting," "Self-Service Query Authoring" (IBM Cognos Query Studio), and "Analytics Using Analysis Studio" (IBM Cognos Analysis Studio). The exclusion of these chapters is not an attempt to cast them in a negative light or diminish their value. A "Planning, Budgeting, and Forecasting" chapter, though critical components of the solution, is not included in this book, because its content would be extensive and is best served in a separate guide. McGraw-Hill will be publishing a book dedicated to this subject. The user experiences with Cognos Query Studio and Cognos Analysis Studio in Cognos 10 are very much the same as the experience in Cognos 8. For that reason, we refer you to the Cognos 8 edition for that content.

Who Should Read This Book?

The audience for this book includes end users of the IBM Cognos 10 solution, power users, administrators, and even executives who are stakeholders in a performance management or business analytics initiative. If you are new to Cognos 10 as a user or administrator, it is a great time to be coming on board. If you are a client using previous versions of the software and considering migration to Cognos 10, it is a great time to be coming on board.

This book does not, in any way, replace any formal training offering on the Cognos solution. It will, however, augment your knowledge and present real examples and context of applicability with Cognos 10 inherent with the experiences we have had with the solution.

Approach and Organization of the Book

This book is organized a little differently from some of the technology books we have read. The approach was to lay the foundation for an introduction to Cognos 10 and the definitions of performance management and business analytics so that you, the reader, would have that understanding up front while moving through subsequent chapters of the book.

Cognos 10 functionality is defined by user roles, and as such, those roles increase in technical depth and functionality. The user roles in Cognos 10 are defined by a user's need, leveraging specific studios that enable that role. Our intent is to enable you to progress through the content of the book and increase the functionality extended in the solution as you go along. For example, we discuss performance management concepts early on so that you can gain insight into the purpose of a performance management initiative within your organization. Furthermore, the book focuses on aspects that an organization might need to consider when taking on such an endeavor by way of people, process, and technology.

Many of our clients ask us how best to deploy Cognos 10 for their organization. It is our hope that you will find value in the tips and techniques that we have learned along the way with our clients, and we hope that it will have value to you in your Cognos 10 deployment.

The Cognos 10 technology leads this industry in delivering better decision-making tools for its users. But, no doubt about it, it requires smart, diligent people and a cohesive plan and commitment to that plan. Your technical expertise and business insight are both solid requirements for successful deployment of Cognos 10. Whether you're an IT administrator responsible for the delivery of the Cognos Framework Manager model or an end user who is performing analytics for your organization through Cognos Business Insight Advanced, this book will help you elevate your skills and leverage this powerful technology for the betterment of your organization.

Following is a glimpse at what's inside this book.

Part I: Introduction to Business Analytics and IBM Cognos 10

In Part I, the definitions of *performance management* and *business analytics* are discussed, as well as the various perspectives of business analytics. IT administrators play a critical role in this solution. We discuss the IT perspective in such an initiative. The business user's role is empowered by use of effective information in the Cognos 10 solution. Whether consuming a report as a Cognos 10 consumer or performing analytics as a business analyst, the Cognos 10 user roles provide flexibility for information delivery. In addition, we describe the difference between a scorecard and a dashboard, so that you can understand the part each solution can play in your business. We provide insight into and definition of the roles and studios within Cognos 10. These definitions will help identify *how* and *what* to deploy to *whom*.

Part II: Accessing and Using IBM Cognos 10

We move into the access and use of IBM Cognos 10 BI in Part II. The IBM Cognos Connection portal helps you organize information for your business. We share insight about Cognos Connection and how users run reports using filters, options, and settings for report properties. We also provide information for creating a portal page and viewer options. Cognos 10 brings brand-new functionality to the stage by way of IBM Cognos Business Insight, which gives Enhanced Consumers the ability to reuse existing content in their own dashboard environments. The Cognos 10 integration with Microsoft Office through Microsoft Office Solutions is discussed.

Introduction to Business Analytics

IBM Cognos 8 Business Intelligence: The Official Guide devoted a great deal of space to the progression of Business Intelligence (BI), including the value of performance management. The book discussed moving from the use of reports and online analytical processing (OLAP) to the integrated enterprise tying performance measurement to business objectives by incorporating insight to forecast information. The role of the office of finance was expanded, and the information from that natural extension extended enterprise-wide insight to performance. Those concepts are still part of the vision for many organizations, yet many have made significant strides in executing BI and comprehensive performance management strategies. Companies that are successful in implementing performance management strategies are delivering on the promise of BI—that is, fact-based decision-making, better business outcomes, and competitive advantage.

With the introduction of IBM Cognos Business Intelligence v10.1, the business intelligence, to performance management, to business analytics (BA) progression is still about solving the one big challenge for most enterprises: How do we use the information we have—information about our markets, our suppliers, our customers, our employees, and so on—and leverage that information to create a better performing company? Adoption of the technology, the processes, and the people to plan and implement these solutions is a journey. The most successful companies embrace this journey and see it as part of their standard business practices. We have seen companies successfully embrace BA and weather the economic storm much better than competitors who failed to do so—if their competitors made it at all. The "win" that this journey offers an organization really is that powerful.

Businesses gather enormous amounts of data. Business users churn through those enormous piles of data, providing tremendous value from their BI reporting, query, dashboard, and scorecard solutions. Making this information available to the business user so that effective and accurate business decisions can be made offers clear advantages to the organization that masters these concepts and processes first.

BI has historically provided analytics capabilities—after all, that is why OLAP was born and why we all fell in love with the ease of the "slice-and-dice," "drag-and-drop," and "drill-down" functions. However, business is different now, and financial crises, economic challenges, and the need to keep up with the emerging technologies to address these impacts makes our desire to dig deeper and learn more—quicker, better, and faster—even more important. Let's face it: analysts need to be able to identify trends, predict performance outcomes, and stay ahead of their competition to survive. Those who leverage the use of BA successfully will win that battle and their companies will outperform others, leaving behind underperforming competitors.

The benefit to organizations committed to BA versus those that have not yet adopted analytics is great according to *Source: Analytics: The New Path to Value, a joint MIT Sloan Management Review and IBM Institute of Business Value study* (Massachusetts Institute of Technology, 2010). This study states that companies that use analytics perform three times better than those just beginning to adopt it. It also points out that top performers are 5.4 times more likely to use an analytic approach over an intuitive one. The use of analytics is optimized when coupled with solid business processes.

Business analytics is not a new concept. In traditional performance management practices, we have been able to answer the questions, "How are we doing?", "Why?", and "What should we be doing?" Cognos Business Intelligence v10.1 delivers a broad spectrum of analysis solutions, and we will address and narrow the definitions and benefits of those ideals in this book. And, most importantly, we'll guide you through best practices—and strongly suggested practices—for successful deployment.

Types of Business Analytics

The different areas of BA address various needs within the business. In all cases, the type of information required within any user scenario will depend on the user's role within the organization and how that person chooses to access critical information. So, with that, let's talk about the four types of BA:

- Analytical reporting (drill-down)
- Trending (slice and dice)
- Scenario modeling (what-if)
- Predictive modeling (what might be)

Analytical Reporting

A typical consumer of analytical reporting is a business user who prefers well-formatted, regularly delivered reports that provide some guidance on what areas need the user's attention. These users typically need a "top-down" view of their functional area of the business. For example, a typical user within this realm may want to look at product performance or customer revenues, and will want to access this information in a "self-service" fashion. This user may also want to drill down to related reports to gain additional insight or detail, such as the specific product lines performing below expected or forecasted levels. A business user of analytical reporting typically wants to operate autonomously from IT, in a self-service fashion. Lastly, for the user who is interested in, or needs, multidimensional reporting, the reporting solution may be delivered from an OLAP source, which provides the flexibility of analytic reporting and drill functionality, while enabling IT to control what this user should or should not see.

Trending

A business user who performs analysis on a regular basis can be said to "slice and dice" data. In most cases, analytical reporting is not sufficient for a user (typically a business analyst) who wants more freedom to explore the information. A typical example is a user who desires to view performance over different time periods as well as multiple or different perspectives of the same information to confirm hunches or theories. Every organization has at least a few of these users and, in some cases, a large number of them. For clients without a standard Business Intelligence platform, we find that these users invariably resort to Microsoft Excel to manipulate data exactly the way they want.

As we evolve to Cognos Business Intelligence v10.1, we assess that users with more demanding analysis needs have (likely) been dumping information into sophisticated spreadsheets that demand hours of manual manipulation. Those users realize capable business insight to things such as top and bottom analyses and are responsible for delivering answers to complex questions within their enterprises. They are typically the target user audience for BA, and for a solution that will provide them "trending," specifically.

Scenario Modeling

When businesses want to determine the impact of a new business approach by evaluating alternative business scenarios, they require a BA capability called *scenario modeling*. In scenario modeling, business users can develop "what-if" analyses on the fly. It offers users the flexibility to model scenarios against large data sets, to reorganize and compare scenarios within the business. For example, a user might want to understand the impact to the company's customer base if a price increase is introduced on a product within a specific product line (sensitivity analysis): What if we increase pricing by 10 percent, 20 percent, and so on? How many customers are affected by that price increase in our market?

The scenario modeling capabilities found in Cognos Business Intelligence v10.1 provide information that is highly strategic to the business and typically leveraged by fewer users than other forms of analysis. These users are looking for financial analysis, profitability analysis, and other types of analyses and are able to adjust the analysis model without having to reload or re-request the data. The benefit to their business is real scenario comparison, based on a data model that enables analysis with what-if capabilities.

Predictive Modeling

Cognos Business Intelligence v10.1 is the first release in which the concept and functionality of *predictive modeling* is introduced as part of the solution platform. This is where businesses are interested in "what might be" within their data. Since the publication of our last book, IBM has acquired this technology, formerly known as SPSS. The technology allows clients to drive better business outcomes and yield the ability to do the following:

- Attract and retain more profitable customers.

- Detect and prevent fraud.

- Improve resource allocation.

These are just a few examples of the proposed value proposition for organizations seeking predictive analytics.

Business users ask the question, What should we be doing?, because they need the foresight to intervene, allocate resources, and set targets. Further, to understand the answers to this question, business users must be able to try to predict future activity by leveraging three key BA capabilities:

- "What-if" scenario planning to understand potential outcomes
- Predictive modeling to generate prescriptive, real-time, pattern-based strategies within a situational context
- Planning and budgeting to improve visibility, insight, and control over the levels of revenue, expense, capital, workforce, and operational performance

Think back just five or ten years (for those readers in the industry that long) when the benefit of predictive modeling in areas such as fraud prevention was not as important as it is today. An organization looking to apply the full breadth of predictive analytics would have looked elsewhere. The ability to optimize data collection, statistics, data mining, and predictive modeling and deployment services is now within the BI platform.

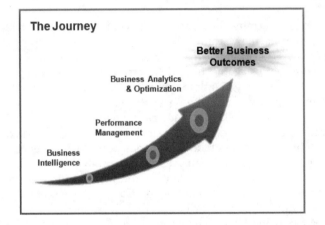

Cognos Business Intelligence v10.1 incorporates the evolution of BA by bringing key categories together in one BA portfolio with the focus of helping clients achieve better business outcomes.

Starting the Business Analytics Journey: Solid Business Intelligence

As you read this book, keep in mind that the concept of BA is a mature perspective, and your options for leveraging benefit from that analysis are greater due to the flexibility of Cognos Business Intelligence v10.1. BI has laid the groundwork for many companies to provide better reporting, better analytics through self-service, and solid web-enabled solutions. But technology alone will not get you where you need to go.

Businesses interested in pursuing BA will expand their business perspective for a more "complete" view, will facilitate collaboration, and will respond to growing user communities and demands for faster performance and more data. The journey to accomplish this task successfully, and the natural extension of BI with BA, will require that an organization establish and agree upon a process and solid strategy.

As companies dig through data to look for answers, to gain insight from enhanced analysis or reporting, they will realize that they need the means to understand and measure their goals and progress. Selecting some cool technology that yields great graphs and highly formatted reports will not necessarily solve this problem, however. We have learned through 16 years of experience that such tools are only part of the solution. Many companies make the mistake of thinking the tools themselves will solve all their data problems, when, indeed, the single largest challenge is not the tools, infrastructure, or data, but the people within the organization.

In that regard, organizations need to ask the following questions:

- Do people truly understand our business and are they willing to make fact-based (not intuitive) decisions? Does the company culture support this?
- Does the company have the process and methodology that will take what we learn from our BI and apply that to new business decisions and processes?
- Will our culture enable, embrace, and execute change?

Answers to these questions require executive input, executive direction, and a commitment to the plan for execution. More importantly, if the answer to any of these questions is no, then your organization might want to reconsider this journey. Should that be your choice, however, you must know that your competition is likely figuring out how to make this work to gain competitive advantage through insights to their markets, their customers, and, ultimately, their profits.

The IT Perspective of BI

From an IT perspective, you must consider the costs associated with implementing and maintaining a host of different tools. It requires investment, time, and human capital, and such duplication results in significant inefficiencies. There is no sharing of resources or report objects, and a help desk is necessary for multiple tools and classes of users.

Business users often rely on assistance from IT to "find the answers" to problems, make something easy to use, and assure them that the answers are correct. Users often want a "big button" that will get them what they want. So IT gets a new project, begins to evaluate tools, writes up the RFP, sends it out to vendors, and then, several months later, claims they have done what they were asked to do. The business users, meanwhile, have not adopted the solution and find themselves still using those disparate spreadsheets. The project is deemed successful by IT but deemed a failure by the business, because users still use the same manual processes and spend exorbitant amounts of time trying to solve the same problems that were present prior to IT's solution. How does this happen? Let's break it down a bit.

We can recall countless experts who have made statements on the value of BI in the marketplace and how "good data" is required to make BI successful. The IT department has been tasked with participation in a BI solution because the mounds of data the company has collected needs to be organized in a manner that can be presented to the business. But is it really about IT and the technology it brings with it? The answer, at least in part, is yes. IT has been responsible in most global and small and medium business (SMB) markets for gathering operational data. It has built sophisticated systems that enable organizations to collect information about most aspects of their businesses, and we've evolved from legacy systems to sophisticated enterprise resource planning (ERP) systems to help our businesses make use of that data to increase knowledge and profitability.

Because IT organizations are best equipped with resources that collect this data, IT has historically been viewed by the business as the group that "owns" the data. And because those who collect the data must be knowledgeable about the organization of that data, they have built and taken ownership of the systems that keep that data. Although significant talent and resources are necessary to make that happen, we now have a business unit whose business is data. But how do we know that the data IT is collecting can tell us what we need to know to improve our performance for tomorrow, or next quarter, or next year, or five years from now? More important, have we provided insight into *how* we collect that data so that it can be transformed into usable information by typically nontechnical business users? The challenge underlying this question is that IT often doesn't understand why the business can't understand the information IT made available.

Because BI solutions bring use of information together with business performance, we need some sort of bridge that lets IT know that the information they are gathering for the business is accurate and provides the business with the confidence that the information can be used easily to make important decisions. And to use that information, IT must do the following:

- *IT must provide "good data."* We have all heard the saying "garbage in, garbage out," and this is very true in this case. IT must adhere to strict data planning and data management that provides, for example, a common definition of "customer," and clean delivery of that definition as defined with the business. While at a client site recently, for example, we were charged with the deployment of a data warehouse for sales and market forecasting for a textiles company. When we pulled the data from its point of sale (POS) system, we noted multiple instances of customer names, misspelled customer names, and varying opinions about whose responsibility it would be to clean this up. Important to note here is that this client knew that multiple instances of a customer name existed in the system, but a manual process of correcting that in a spreadsheet versus in the data source masked the insight to the business that was needed to make informed decisions about product mix.

- *IT must work with the business to understand the benefit of its role in the BI journey.* This is not a "we versus they" undertaking. If you attack it that way, the project will fail. Don't take it personally if the business requires that you change a field or add a field in the database, or if your DBA is asked to adjust access "rights" to the data. Be prepared going in that you'll need to "clean up" your data along the way, and make a solid plan to do so: it will benefit the organization as a whole—and, who knows, you might become an IT hero along the way.

- *IT staff must educate themselves and ask for help from a trusted source who has embarked on this journey before.* Our company has implemented the Cognos solution for 16 years, and when getting new resources up to speed, we have a saying: "It is always easier the tenth time." That doesn't mean that it always takes us ten tries to get it right for a client; it simply means that we have found a few techniques along the way that are better than others, and our clients benefit by our having tested and tried functionality with the Cognos solution before we get there.

The Business Perspective of BI

Because we work with so many organizations, we have unique visibility into how information needs are actually addressed in organizations. The reality is that in many of the organizations we work with, finding answers to the three questions is a manual process that uses a mix of different tools and interfaces. Because of that, business users across the organization will pull together different versions of the same numbers. Different users will likely make slightly different assumptions, use different calculations, and perhaps even use different definitions for terms such as "customer" and "revenue." They might use different interfaces, different time periods, and even different data sources.

The result for the business users is sometimes disappointing, because they will sit down in a meeting and spend the most time talking about where the numbers came from as opposed to *what to do* with the numbers. This slows down the decision-making processes that drive performance.

We have simplified this process by focusing on organizing the users into user groups and leveraging best practices when using multiple data sources. Imagine your organization and the cumbersome and time-consuming efforts that are happening now to satisfy business users' information requirements. You can appreciate the complex environment this creates for IT to support and optimize. That *need* for information cannot be dismissed. Business users are going about using their own means of organizing data so that they can make the necessary adjustments to the business as needed. Perhaps inventory levels need adjusted from one facility to another due to a new client's requirements. Perhaps profitability is lagging with the largest client while revenues have increased. The answer to why these things are happening and how we adjust our business to accommodate them lies in a well-planned and well-delivered BA deployment.

The Pursuit of Business Analytics

Whether you are seeking a solution to uncover insights for specific industries (such as financial services, public sector, distribution, industrial, or communications) or to deliver insights for cross-industry solutions (such as financial performance, customer relations, human capital, advanced case management, supply chain, or asset optimization), BA solutions and associated best practices will provide you with optimized decision-making within your business.

The following discussion covers the progress and requirements that you should consider when committing your organization to a performance-based organization. Becoming a BA lead organization will move your organization from "obstructed" in its view to "aware," or from a "fragmented" organization to an "aligned" organization. It changes organizations from rigid to agile, and, perhaps most important, it can remove the reactive tendencies that many of us live with day-to-day to enable a proactive approach to our performance.

BA, and performance management before that, are strategic endeavors that demand support from senior management. Many performance management initiatives are led by the CEO and/or CFO. We have seen too many initiatives at some of our customer sites fall by the wayside or get lost in budget shuffles or turf wars due to a lack of commitment from the top. On the opposite end of that spectrum, we have had terrific success with companies that have truly changed the way they do business by leveraging the IBM solution to their strategic and competitive advantage with senior executives who were committed to fact-based and analytical decision-making. In one of our most successful clients, the CEO presented his information strategy, which included a BI initiative, and stated to his entire staff that "you are either on this bus with me, or the door is that way." He attributes 20 percent bottom-line growth directly to the success of his BI initiative. To date, it has been an eight-year journey.

In conclusion, you must recognize that your measurement of each deliverable is key in building the next segment of your BA journey. Your investment in strategy and planning is as important as the solution you select. To realize the full benefit of the Cognos Business Intelligence v10.1 solution, start by considering initial smaller projects that will build a successful foundation for your enterprise deployment.

Monitoring Performance Using Dashboards and Scorecards

As businesses continue to look for ways to improve performance and manage the most critical aspects of their business, they look to business analytics to present a standardized view of both "good" and "bad" news. They are looking for visibility into information that will help them see the key performance indicators (KPIs) clearly, understand what is happening, understand why it is happening, and plan a course of action. They seek answers to questions such as "Are we performing better or worse than our targeted sales forecast?" and "Where are we leading/lagging?"

For businesses that have identified KPIs, and the individuals responsible for managing them, dashboards and scorecards in IBM Cognos 10 provide a fast and simple mechanism for interacting with KPIs. This chapter shows you several options for dashboard creation, depending on the requirements of your business users.

Cognos 10 introduces a brand-new environment called *IBM Cognos Business Insight* that lets end users create their own personalized dashboards by leveraging information objects already defined by other authors. Using Cognos Business Insight, a nontechnical user can easily assemble information objects for consumption to serve their specific needs in a way that makes sense to them. This puts the end user in control of presentation, with the content author in control of data integrity. Scorecards, on the other hand, are best delivered via functionality created in IBM Cognos Metric Studio.

Monitoring performance can be a daunting task, but it is a necessary one. Once your organization's vision is established and all objectives have been communicated, most of your management time will be spent monitoring to ensure that the objectives are on track. You need to be immediately aware of critical shortfalls and other related objectives, and you must focus your energies on objectives that most need to be addressed.

Performance monitoring becomes difficult when your data is inconsistent and hard to obtain. Do you use multiple applications, each having its own data structure and architecture? Do you need to switch back and forth between applications to grasp the big picture? Can you easily access the information that you need to understand the pulse of your organization? Each of these issues can be addressed using Cognos 10's measuring and monitoring mechanisms, dashboards and scorecards.

Many organizations are unclear about the differences between dashboards and scorecards. Often, they hear words and phrases from users that might indicate the use of dashboards or scorecards, when what they actually need is a report. Dashboards and scorecards are very different solutions, and each solves different problems. Simply put, a scorecard is like a report card that measures a student's achievements against a target or goal. In our case, it also involves the Balanced Scorecard methodology and strategy mapping when we're deploying to end users. A dashboard is like the dashboard in your automobile. It tells you how your car is performing now, not how you plan for your car to perform at some point in the future.

This chapter explains the differences between dashboards and scorecards and provides the information that will help you decide how to meet your goals and deliver insight to performance against those goals. It also offers hints you can use to achieve success with your dashboard or scorecard implementation.

Dashboards Show Current Information

In today's challenging economic times, visibility to your business and an easy to understand visual of key attributes of your business can give you the picture of performance that you need. Dashboards provide at-a-glance summaries of critical information that is captured during an established time period using sophisticated graphical data representations, such as graphs, charts, gauges, maps, and so on. From these graphical images, you can drill-up or drill-down to see either the bigger picture or essential data. The visualizations are personalized—*you* determine what information is shown and in what format. They are fairly easy to create and are not subject to rules and regulations for creation.

Let's think about an inventory example to demonstrate how dashboards are used. Effectively managing inventory for any organization is paramount in a challenging economy. In fact, visibility and insight to inventory management is vitally important in any economy. Inventory is equal to cash to every organization, and having the right inventory and inventory levels in the right location can represent millions in savings. Inventory that must be shipped from a location that delays on-time delivery or incurs additional shipping fees due to poor inventory management results in costly shipping expenses and customer service issues resulting from delayed shipment or additional fees.

A dashboard can provide regular, timely insight into inventory management to help business users and executives understand whether the business is actually aligned with inventory objectives. If business analytics are used to provide a trend of projected business performance coupled with what actually happened, you can leverage that insight to plan for current inventory needs. You can then see where inventory resides and where shipments were actually made to gain insight into ways to implement corrective or planning actions. (Note, however, that a dashboard alone will not yield corrective action.) An organization's inventory management process, and the ultimate efficiency of that process, coupled with visibility, should yield reduced inventory and better order fulfillment through timely shipments and better customer satisfaction.

Corporate executives, sales directors, and parts and inventory managers each need a different view of perhaps the same information. Each also benefits from having vital information at his or her fingertips via dashboards. Dashboards communicate complex information using graphs and charts. They translate information from various corporate systems and other supplemental data into visually rich presentations that show and compare multiple results so that you can compare and contrast data from different core areas of your business, such as sales, finance, HR, inventory, logistics, and distribution, to view a complete, multidepartment picture.

When our customers ask us to create a dashboard, we first ask them to explain their vision. We must understand what they are looking for to determine the best deployment options. Some customers envision hundreds of numbers on a dashboard that contains links to other dashboards also containing hundreds of numbers. This vision is not a dashboard, however; instead, it is a series of reports linked together. If you have to work hard to understand the contents of a dashboard, it is probably not designed properly, or it is not a dashboard at all.

On the dashboard of your car, you see a variety of gauges and images that visually display instrumentation data from your car, including the measurement of gasoline remaining in your tank, your engine's temperature, and the speed at which you are traveling. Each status is current. You see how fast you are going now, not how fast you drove last month. You see how much gas you have now, not how much gas you had yesterday. You see immediately whether your car is performing as expected. What would happen if each of those graphical representations on your car's dashboard were precise numerical values? Gasoline remaining would be shown in gallons, engine temperature would be in degrees Fahrenheit (at what temperature does the car overheat?)—and wait, how many tire revolutions equals 60 miles per hour? Understanding the state of your car would become much more difficult. What if this information didn't exist at all? Driving your car could be disastrous!

TIP *Cognos 10 offers an offline interactive dashboard that delivers fast, self-contained business intelligence (BI) to reach more users. Using IBM Cognos Active Reports, you can leverage a disconnected reporting application for self-contained, interactive content. This is easy to consume and key for mass deployment.*

Take a look at the Employee Satisfaction dashboard, shown in Figure 2-1, which is part of the installed Cognos 10 demo. This dashboard has three regions. At the upper left, a scatter chart shows the results of an employee survey with indications of satisfaction across a variety of topics. At a glance, you can see that the majority of the employees indicate that communication and feedback needs to improve. At the upper right, the same survey results are charted against industry norms and corporate targets. Again, communication is shown as an area needing improvement, and this affects the employee's overall satisfaction. Finally, the table shows the actual rankings as percentages and how these rankings reflect employee attrition. All provide valuable information when you're evaluating the health of an organization.

So what makes a dashboard valuable? A valuable dashboard is personalized to the needs of an individual user. Some users will want to see all the details that the charts and graphs hide. These users absolutely hate charts and graphs, and that's okay. But keep in mind that delivering a dashboard that they will not use does not usually lead to performance improvement.

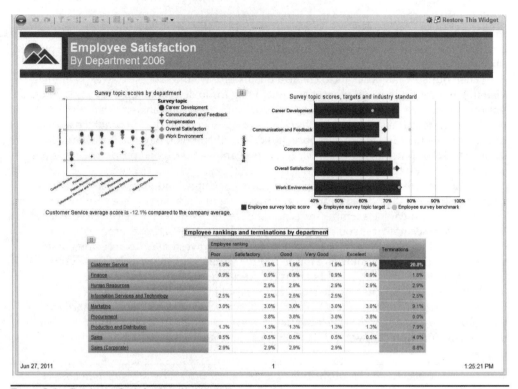

Figure 2-1   Employee Satisfaction dashboard

Viewing Metrics with Scorecards

Scorecards display performance metrics to determine company health. They show visual representations of actuals, targets, and variances and can provide the same drill-through to the details that are used with dashboards. Most likely, you will need to use scorecards or dashboards during your Cognos 10 implementation.

A scorecard tracks performance against strategic and operational objectives using metrics. In Cognos 10, we are able to provide clients with the following:

- Scorecarding capabilities including strategy maps, impact diagrams, and watch lists
- Support for strategy management methodologies such as the Balanced Scorecard or Six Sigma
- The ability to view all scorecard information in dashboards

All companies measure success in large part by how well they meet financial expectations. Company financial data generally reflects past accomplishments (or the lack thereof). They use forecasting to predict the future and budgeting to control expenditures. In many companies, actual, budget, and forecast data is held in disparate systems and stored in many different systems or forms, such as enterprise resource planning (ERP), customer relationship management (CRM), spreadsheets, legacy data, and so on. To calculate metrics on this data, executives and managers are forced to spend time gathering and trying to understand the validity of the results, instead of actually being able to use the data immediately to manage performance. And there can be difficulty in understanding where the problems are located and who is responsible for resolving them—if everyone can agree that the problems exist at all. This can result in your company making strategic business decisions based on gut feelings and best guesses.

Enter scorecards, a proven approach for monitoring, measuring, and managing performance at a tactical and strategic level within the entire organization. Their development is based on a proven methodology for managing and enhancing performance. Automated scorecards gather data from the disparate sources and organize it using metrics. The metrics tell you three fundamental things: your actual measurement (current), the target you want to achieve (budget or forecast), and the actual-to-target variance. If linked with analytics and reports, scorecards can provide visibility and accountability for performance problems that can span multiple departments or functional areas at all levels. Scorecards are always on, always current, and always factual, insofar as they provide a tamper-proof conduit for corporate data and predetermined business calculations.

Figure 2-2 depicts a typical scorecard. Color-coded indicators on the scorecard show how the metrics are performing currently and whether the metric is on an upward or downward trend.

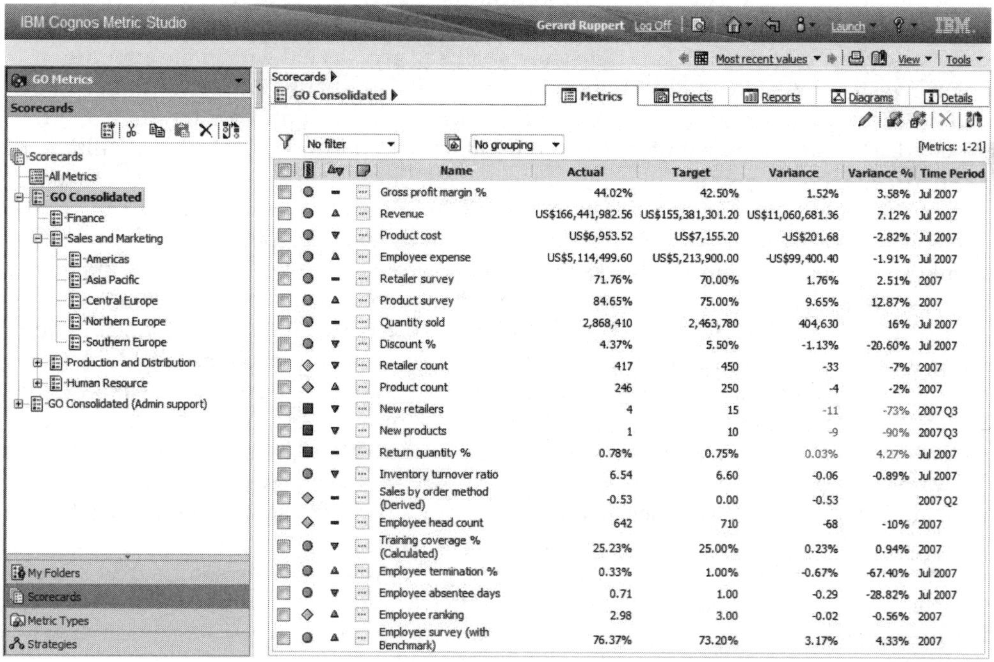

FIGURE 2-2   Typical scorecard

Scorecards provide consistency, which is achieved when everyone agrees to and works toward accomplishing the same goals. Along with identifying the goals, all parties must agree to a consistent view of what actually denotes organizational success. With scorecards, goal-driven metrics can be delivered to each desktop, so that everyone in the organization—from managers to CFOs—can see how their performance and decisions are impacting the company's goals. Users can see at a glance whether their performance is trending up, down, or remaining stable based on color schemes and/or graphics used.

Implementation of a scorecard is more of a business challenge than a technical challenge. Executives or business stakeholders need to identify which metrics should be tracked to provide visibility into the company's performance. Metrics are not one-size-fits-all, and they can change over time. The implementation can take several trials to get right—which is perfectly normal. Companies can start small by identifying key metrics and applying indicators to those metrics. From there, additional metric attributes, such as impacted/impacting relationships, can be added.

Cognos 10 creates scorecard metric relationships of the same metric type automatically. For example, if your scorecard has a corporate sales metric, Cognos 10 can provide tracking to allow the VP of sales to view how divisional and branch sales have impacted corporate sales. Sales managers reviewing the metrics for these relationships can see how their efforts impact those above them in the organization. The VP of sales may also want to see how other metrics impact corporate sales. For instance, if the product quality is poor or if shipments are not sent when expected, the VP might notice a drop in sales. Members of the Business Manager role are able to add these relationships to the scorecard.

Let's look at a scorecard example. Suppose a company spent a significant amount of money implementing a critical business software application. The users were extremely satisfied with the performance of this application and the time savings it provided for their daily tasks. Several months later, users were unable to access vital data in the application. Upon investigation of the problem, the database administrator, the network administrator, and the server administrator all verified that their pieces of the application were working as expected. The three administrators worked in different departments and possibly different locations, all reporting up to different managers and, unfortunately, that was how they were being monitored. The database was running, the network was up, and the server was operable—three green indicators. From their three individual perspectives, the application should have been operable. But it was not working. From an application standpoint, the scorecard was measuring the wrong things or not enough things.

Coordination and alignment among all the responsible parties in the vertical organization makes a Cognos 10 application effective. In this example, your task would be to find the metric that provides that alignment, which is the availability of the critical application. The scorecard for this application should be flagged with the highest priority—a huge red indicator—until the problem is resolved and the users are once again productively using the application. The software being down impacts the users' ability to perform their jobs, which impacts the company's ability to ship products to fill orders. An aligned organization works together to resolve issues, which results in better overall performance.

Scorecards allow you to ensure accountability down to a single-person level by keeping a finger on the pulse of your business. They identify where your company is currently and where it is going. Managers and executives can use scorecards to access the information they need, when they need it, to make the best decisions.

Value of a Balanced Scorecard

The key to a Balanced Scorecard is insight to accountability. The Balanced Scorecard methodology lets business users better understand what will be their future financial performance. It provides the means for employees at all levels and across multiple departments to manage their own performance. What makes this methodology unique and different from forecasting is that it is accomplished without a "crystal ball."

The Balanced Scorecard methodology was created by Drs. Robert Kaplan and David Norton, and an article describing it was published in the *Harvard Business Review* in 1992. Kaplan and Norton write that the interplay between people and processes are dynamics that, when aligned with company strategy, can be measured using metrics.

Let's take a look at the value that a Balanced Scorecard brings to an organization. A Balanced Scorecard includes four major perspectives: financial, customer, internal, and learning and growth. All four perspectives are dependent upon each other. The real trick is to figure out what to monitor today so that next week or next month your financial performance is somewhat guaranteed or predictable.

All companies report and analyze *financial* data. This data is represented in Figure 2-3 in the Finance segment. Depending on how quickly your organization closes its books and

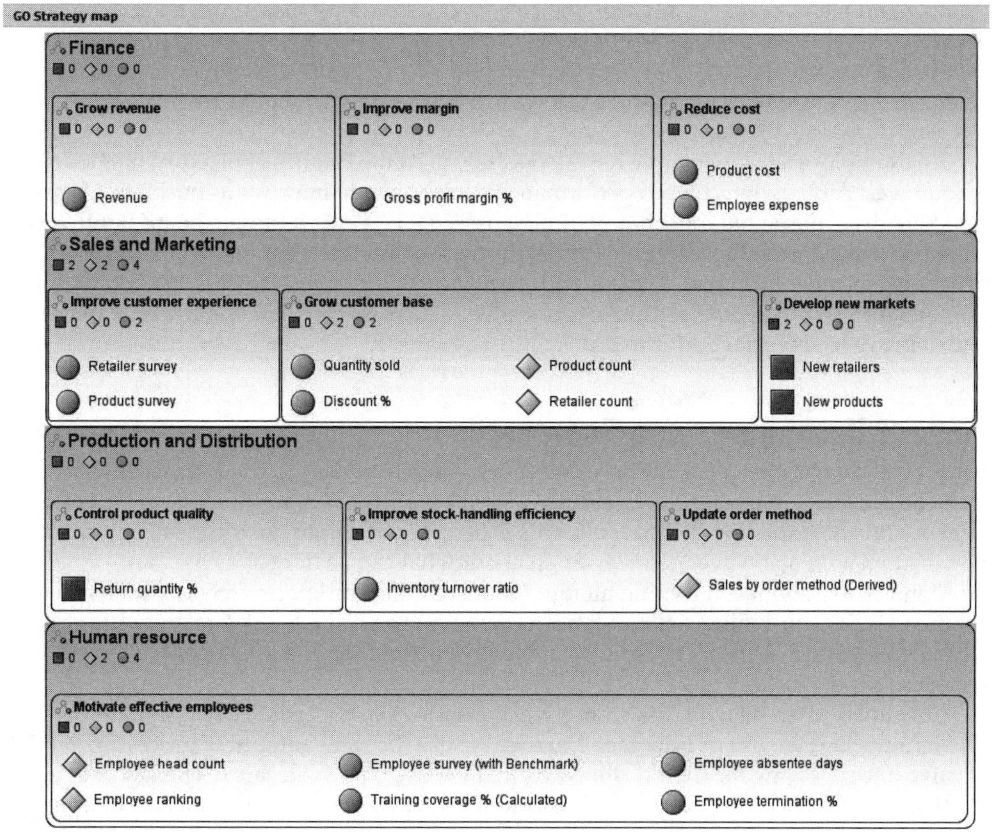

Figure 2-3 Strategy map

publishes financial information, the information you see may be several days old. Financial data is generally backward-looking, providing a view of the past. The challenge for all companies is how to prepare today for solid financial performance tomorrow.

The *customer perspective* is a view of your company as your customers see it and is represented in the Sales and Marketing segment of Figure 2-3. Satisfied customers are a critical component of financial success. If you ensure that your customers are happy today, then next week or next month you should have customers paying their invoices and making repeat orders, which leads to good financial performance. As you begin considering a scorecard initiative, keenly remember that although strategy is important, it is the execution that counts!

How do you make certain your customers are happy today to ensure good financial performance tomorrow? You do this by monitoring your internal perspective. The *internal perspective* is how you view and measure yourselves, which is shown in the Production and Distribution segment in Figure 2-3. Are you shipping on time today? Are you shipping complete orders on time? Do you have in stock what your customers want to buy? You can see where this is going. If you manage your internal perspective (operations) today, then next week or next month your customer satisfaction will be high and the following week or month your financial performance will be on target.

Learning and growth are the foundations of the entire process. This perspective includes training and mentoring new and existing employees. Investing in your team, making sure everyone is trained to perform his or her job, and making sure that workers understand safety measures assures internal perspective performance next week, which assures customer satisfaction the following week, which assures financial performance after that. HR is often responsible for this task, as Figure 2-3 depicts.

An example of a company that has successfully used the Balanced Scorecard methodology is Southwest Airlines, which used performance perspectives to improve its business. Company representatives measured the amount of time passengers were waiting to board Southwest planes and recognized this as a potential performance improvement that would provide a benefit to customers. The airline instituted a new procedure to reduce the turnaround time at the gate. As a result, Southwest Airlines was able to increase its ridership, fly more planes, and improve its financial performance.

Planning for Dashboards and Scorecards

Some businesses have a difficult time determining what metrics to use to create their scorecards. During our interview processes, we often pick some metrics, put in some simple targets, and show the clients the result. This is usually enough to get the creative juices flowing and spur some lively conversation about what can be done.

Don't worry about conquering all four Balanced Scorecard perspectives initially. If your company is like most, financial and internal data will be available to you. Use what you have to get started. Your organization can build upon this sample to plan and align the scorecard for the future.

Customers often seek our assistance when creating dashboards. They don't know what graphs and charts to use or how many to use. We use the same interview process to get the creative juices flowing for their dashboards that we use with scorecards. The key is to get started, because once you "see" your business, or a segment of your business, represented in a dashboard, further development is inevitable because of the ease of digesting such information.

Once you have some ideas about what information would be helpful to monitor, gather all of the users of the application to help you determine the amount of information to be displayed on the dashboard, its purpose, and your goals for implementation. Understanding what metrics provide a clear picture of the performance of your entire organization allows scorecards to be developed. For an implementation to be successful, involvement is needed across the entire corporation, from executives, to middle management, to the IT staff, to the distribution center. A well-executed, well-thought-out plan provides the tools needed to be agile in the face of danger.

Understand Your Needs

Your needs will determine whether you implement a dashboard, a scorecard, or perhaps both. They will also help you to understand how current the information needs to be. The responses provided to questions posed in the initial interview are valuable to help design your Cognos 10 implementation.

NOTE *Cognos 10 provides the tools you need to implement what you want to see. It does not provide turnkey metrics or magic buttons that gather and display the information. You must have a clear understanding of what information will help you manage your company's performance.*

Corporate executives provide valuable information and insight into the company's inner workings. At the beginning of your project, engage the top executives in a meeting to help you understand the needs and direction of the organization. Extend your interviews to the directors and managers reporting to the executives to identify the information they need to see to manage effectively. Some example questions to ask during your interviews include the following:

- What is important to monitor?
- What is your goal?
- What numbers interest you?
- What information helps you to manage?
- What are your targets?
- How do you calculate to reach your target?
- What corrective actions do you take when problems exist?
- What departments impact or are impacted by your ability to meet your goals?
- Who is impacted by your performance?
- How frequently do you need this information?

When all of your interviews are complete, you will understand the information to be gathered, which will help you to determine whether to produce a dashboard or a scorecard.

Choose Metrics

Suppose you've decided to implement a scorecard. For your scorecard to be successful, you need to select the appropriate metrics to be evaluated, and you need to be ready to react to what the metrics tell you. The metrics provided by the application may do the following:

- **Identify weaknesses in your organization down to the person or task creating the weakness.**
  Business case   One organization measured the productivity of all similar machines located in geographically disbursed factories. The indicator on the scorecard for one particular machine was red. The manager initially thought this indicator was wrong because all of the machines were recently serviced. Upon investigation, the manager discovered that workers had reduced the speed of a machine, which affected the productivity of the machine and the group and caused the red indicator to display.

- **Cause an organizational change to take place.**
  Business case   When the Cognos 10 implementation at one company went live, it showed one of the company's distribution centers had more than $1 million in excess inventory that had been carried over for several months. Upper management went on a fact-finding trip to verify the accuracy of this number. An action plan was decided and entered into the actions area of Cognos Metric Studio to improve the metric by reducing excess inventory.

- **Change over time.**
  Business case   An equipment manufacturer understood that its business was cyclical. During winter months, its product sales dropped. Using a scorecard, the business owner monitored the situation closely and changed the metrics to reflect the current sales trend.

The phrase "What gets measured, gets improved" applies. What gets done can be positive or negative, depending on how the measurement is implemented. One company that was concerned about invoices being sent in a timely manner added metrics that measured the amount of time from the last client contact until the invoice was sent. After the company received more red indicators than were desired, the employees found a way to "touch" the account and thereby avoid the red indicator. The company needed to change the metric to enforce the invoice rule. The moral of this story is this: If what you measure can be manipulated, expect it to be manipulated unless you put the right amount of protection in place. Everyone implementing metrics runs into this scenario at least once during the life of a project. Do not be surprised when this happens. It is human nature to try to avoid being caught in a negative spotlight.

If the performance captured by metrics falls below a certain threshold, people are alerted and can take immediate action. They can review additional reports and collaborate with others in their organization to find the solution. If performance measurements are in the red, and they remain red, change needs to occur. On the other hand, if a department's metrics are always green, perhaps bonuses, pay raises, or promotions are appropriate for the workers in that department.

Help Available for Metrics

If you are unsure of which metrics to use to evaluate your business, help is available. You can order the book *The Performance Manager: Proven Strategies for Turning Information into Higher Business Performance,* by Roland Mosimann, Patrick Mosimann, and Meg Dussault (Cognos Incorporated, 2007), online from Cognos or from a bookseller. The book provides an incremental approach to building a scorecard. It describes decision areas within the major functional areas of a company and identifies the goals, metrics, and dimensions that allow you to review information from various standpoints. The book takes into account the need to understand data and to plan and monitor performance.

Every decision-making cycle depends on finding the answers to three main questions:

1. *How are we doing?* Monitor your business using dashboards and/or scorecards.

2. *Why?* Use reports and metrics to measure history against the future to see and understand both anomalies and trends.

3. *What should we be doing?* Review budgets, plans, and forecasts to see a reliable view of the future and to respond to changes happening in your business.

The Performance Manager provides helpful insight into applying performance perspectives in your organization along with examples and case studies of successful implementations.

Benefits of a Successful Implementation

Your application is always running, always current, and offers visibility into your company's operations. It provides an easy way to drive performance by allowing you to measure, monitor, analyze, and plan for optimal organizational behavior. This is accomplished by the following:

- Focusing on key issues that affect financial stability

- Providing immediate access to reliable, consistent, and current data from disparate sources

- Using dashboards or scorecards to show at-a-glance views of performance

- Evaluating business processes, interdepartmental relationships, and strategic goals against target values

- Allowing drill-through to reports providing details of trouble areas

- Facilitating visibility, accountability, and collaboration between and within departments

- Encouraging continuous review of the company's strategy and goals

What should you take away from this chapter? Our goal was to provide enough information about dashboards and scorecards so that, regardless of whether you are a business user or an IT implementer, you are able to communicate with others using the same language. You know what dashboards and scorecards are, and you know which studio to use in Cognos 10.

The main ingredient in a successful Cognos 10 implementation is communication. Business users need to explain their needs clearly in terms of the amount of graphical information versus numerical information to be presented. Implementers need to listen to the business users to understand their needs without any preconceived ideas. Do not get caught in the trap of implementing what you *thought* you heard. Remember, for example, that business user requirements may contain the word *metrics*, but what they actually need is a *report*.

When should you use a dashboard? Dashboards provide a graphical view of the state of the organization at a point in time. Use them when you want to review status at a glance. What about using scorecards? When you are ready to begin your journey into creating a balanced scorecard, follow the methodology put in place by the Balanced Scorecard methodology, and use scorecards to view metric measurements and relationships to other metrics that encourage alignment and coordination across your organization.

Introduction to IBM Cognos 10 Business Analytics

With the introduction of IBM Cognos 10, user licenses and roles have changed only slightly. It remains true that after installing Cognos 10, users often ask two questions: "What do these roles mean? And what can I (or my users) do with them?" This chapter tries to answer these questions.

Successfully implementing Cognos 10 begins with an understanding of the core user roles and responsibilities, as well as the various Cognos 10 studios. Cognos 10 users will have the permissions to interact with Cognos 10 and studios based on the roles and the privileges assigned to them. This chapter describes the user roles and the studios.

NOTE *For information on defining roles and permissions, refer to Chapter 19.*

An organization's employees typically comprise executives, financial accounting staff, IT architects, IT developers, sales managers, part/product managers, and others. Each employee has a specific role in a specific segment of the organization and needs to access data to support that role. Sometimes, the employee may need to view data from within and across organizational segments to make decisions, understand trends, or view performance statistics. Certain data is privileged, such as financial data, and only those with a need to know are granted access.

When you implement your Cognos 10 application, you must keep users' needs in mind. Does the user need to interact with the data or is a static view of the data sufficient? Will the user review the same information month after month, or does the user need to create ad hoc reports during the month to keep track of the company's progress? The answers to these questions determine how you will configure the Cognos 10 license roles in which you have invested.

These questions also help you to determine which Cognos 10 role will be made available to the user. If a user reviews information monthly and does not need to create reports, for example, you can assign the user the Enhanced Consumer role, which allows the user to view or execute reports created by another member of the organization. If a user requires authoring or additional detail, then some of the more advanced roles and functionality will be leveraged for that user.

Cognos 10 User Roles

If you are in the process of implementing user roles and are confused, do not be alarmed. Each of the roles described in this section has a specific set of access permissions, but there is some amount of overlap among roles. You can use predefined roles or create roles of your own.

NOTE *For more information on customizing roles and security, refer to Chapter 19.*

Here, we group the Cognos 10 user roles according to the capabilities the user is granted in the application. The first grouping, *non-author roles*, allows users to access reports generated from Cognos 10 via various mechanisms, such as e-mail, IBM Cognos Connection, or even an iPad or mobile device. The second grouping, *author roles*, allows users to create reports using one or more studios. Also discussed within author roles are the *administration roles* of BI Professional and BI Administrator.

Non-Author Roles

In Cognos 10, six non-author roles let users view stored reports, and Enhanced Consumers can also run reports:

- Remote Recipient
- Recipient
- Active Report Recipient (casual disconnected use)
- Consumer
- Mobile Consumer (pure mobile device access)
- Enhanced Consumer (building block for higher level roles)

Remote Recipient
A Remote Recipient can receive personalized report outputs (other than active reports) that have been generated by Cognos 10 and distributed to the user via e-mail, the Web, or similar means. A Report Recipient must view reports without directly accessing the Cognos BI server.

Recipient
A Recipient has access to the Cognos Connection portal to select and view stored or pre-executed reports. This user can also set the default language, time zone, and other personal preferences in Cognos Connection. The following example shows a typical view of a Recipient's Cognos Connection screen. In Cognos Connection, a blue arrow in the Actions column on the right, or next to the report icon on the left, means "run with options."

Because no blue arrows appear here, you know that the recipient cannot execute any reports; the user can only view reports that have already been executed.

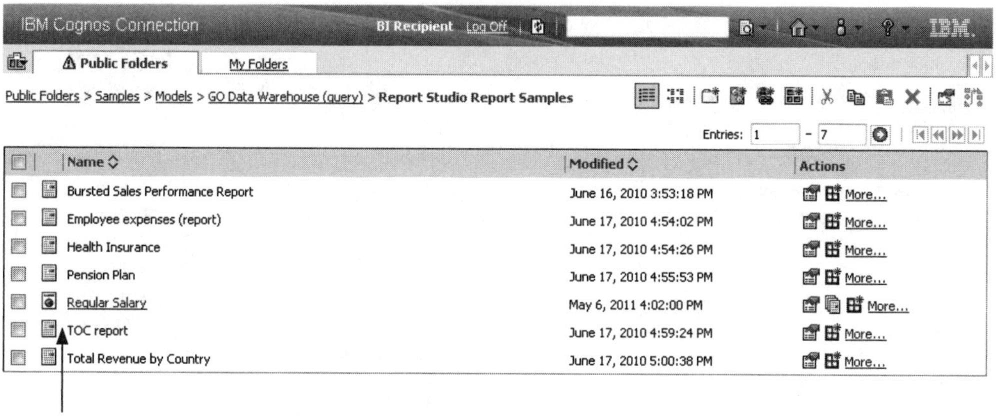

The Recipient can only view these reports; no blue arrow appears, indicating that the recipient cannot execute reports.

NOTE *For more information about Cognos Connection, refer to Chapters 5 and 20.*

Active Report Recipient

Active Report Recipients can receive active reports or other personalized report outputs that have been generated by Cognos 10 and distributed to the user via e-mail, the Web, or similar means. An Active Report Recipient must view reports without directly accessing the Cognos BI server.

Consumer

A Consumer can access the Cognos Connection portal to select and view stored report outputs, to schedule and run reports, and to respond to prompts. This user role can also consume reports output inside the Microsoft Office environment with IBM Cognos for Microsoft Office. This lets the user access BI content directly from a Microsoft Office document. Consumer users can receive IBM Cognos Event Studio notifications (such as status changes, updates about priority customers, and so on). And they can set preferences and create folders in the Cognos Connection portal.

The next example shows a typical view of a Consumer's Cognos Connection screen. Unlike the Recipient's screen, the Consumer's Cognos Connection screen shows "Run With" options displayed in the Actions column for each applicable report. This lets the user execute reports using a variety of options.

Run With option

NOTE *For more information about Cognos Connection, refer to Chapter 5.*

Mobile Consumer

The Mobile Consumer role is for users who require access to Cognos BI only via the optimized applications developed for mobile devices. This role provides rights to access Cognos BI via applications delivered with or supported by the IBM Cognos Mobile server, to consume IBM Cognos Active Report outputs, and use to all of the rights defined for the Cognos BI Consumer role to the degree these functionalities are supported by mobile applications.

Enhanced Consumer

This role is the main report/dashboard consumption license and is the building block for the higher level authoring roles. It is targeted for users who need to view scheduled reports interactively through the Cognos Connection portal and need to use the IBM Cognos Business Insight module and Cognos search functionalities. Enhanced Consumers can use all capabilities available to Consumers, and they are permitted to use the Cognos Business Insight module, Cognos Mobile applications, and Cognos Active Report outputs. In addition, Enhanced Consumers may also use the Cognos Connections software provided with Cognos BI.

Author Roles

Cognos 10 includes many author roles that offer users varying levels of access to functionality. Seven author roles give users access to Cognos Business Insight Advanced (BIA), IBM Cognos Query Studio, IBM Cognos Report Studio, Cognos Event Studio, IBM Cognos

Metric Studio, and IBM Cognos Analysis Studio. The following sections provide a brief description of each of the following roles and to what studios each role has access.

- Business Author
- Business Analyst
- Business Manager
- Advanced Business Author
- Professional Author
- BI Professional
- BI Administrator

Business Author

The Business Author role is designed for business users who need fast answers to business questions. It has all of the capabilities of the Consumer role but also includes ad hoc query and reporting capabilities using Cognos Query Studio. Users can create simple queries or access and edit existing queries. All queries and analysis can be saved in folders in Cognos Connection. Business Authors also have access to the Cognos Business Insight module.

The next example shows a typical view of a Business Author's Cognos Connection screen. Notice that any query that the Business Author can modify displays the Cognos Query Studio action in the Actions column.

Open with Query Studio to modify display

Business Analyst

A Business Analyst has the same rights as the Consumer. This role also has access to the Cognos Business Insight module and Cognos Analysis Studio. Users with this role can also see trends and identify anomalies to help keep an organization ahead of the competition.

The following example shows a typical view of a Business Analyst's Cognos Connection screen and Launch menu.

Business Manager

The Business Manager role is designed for business managers who need a cross-functional view of the business in the perspective of key performance indicators. Business Managers have the same rights as Consumers and have access to Cognos Metric Studio and Cognos Metric Designer and all of their functionality to set up and manage scorecards and scorecard security. Business Managers also have access to the Cognos Business Insight module.

The next example shows a typical view of a Business Manager's Cognos Connection screen and Launch menu.

Advanced Business Author

This role is aimed at business users who need to view scheduled reports, run reports interactively, and create new reports. It includes all the functionality of the Enhanced Consumer, plus the use of the Cognos Query Studio and the Cognos Analysis Studio module and functionality. It provides use of the Cognos Business Insight module and

Cognos BIA. The next example shows a typical view of an Advanced Business Author's Cognos Connection screen and Launch menu.

Professional Author

Professional Authors are generally people who create reports for others to consume. They have a greater requirement for professional quality output. A Professional Author has the same rights as the Consumer, plus access to Cognos Query Studio for creating ad hoc queries and editing saved queries, and Cognos Report Studio for creating and testing new reports, editing existing reports, and publishing the reports for consumption by the organization. As an added level of quality assurance and quality control, the Administrator can require that two Professional Authors publish a report whereby the first Professional Author creates the report and the second audits and publishes the report. Finally, different Professional Authors may be granted access only to the reports pertinent to their department. For example, one Professional Author may access only financial reports, while another may access only sales reports. Again, with Cognos 10, this role grants access to the Cognos Business Insight and Cognos BIA modules.

The next example shows a typical view of a Professional Author's Cognos Connection screen and Launch menu.

BI Professional

The BI Professional spends a great deal of time creating BI content for the rest of the organization to use. A Professional has access to all five studios: Cognos Query Studio, Cognos Report Studio, Cognos Analysis Studio, Cognos Metric Studio, and Cognos Event Studio, as well as Cognos Metric Designer, IBM Cognos Transformer, and all deployed packages. This role has nearly the same abilities as the Administrator with the exception of IBM Cognos Framework Manager and IBM Cognos Map Manager. A Professional can create reports and scorecards, perform analysis, or set up notifications. Typically, an organization has only one or two Professionals. This role also enables access to the Cognos Business Insight and Cognos BIA modules.

The next example shows a typical view of a BI Professional's Cognos Connection screen and Launch menu.

BI Administrator

A BI Administrator has access to all five studios. In addition, this role can access Cognos Framework Manager to model metadata and publish packages, and Cognos Map Manager to create maps, add attributes to maps, and manage maps. The BI Administrator is the creator and manager of how Cognos 10 collaborates with BI content.

The next example shows a typical view of a BI Administrators' Cognos Connection screen and Launch menu.

NOTE *Users assigned the Administrator and Professional roles are licensed for each of the five studios. This can be useful for running a pilot on one of the studios that has not yet been deployed. For example, if scorecarding is not deployed in your organization, one person can have access to Cognos Metric Studio to create a mock-up scorecard. When the decision makers see the value in scorecarding, you can purchase additional Business Manager licenses for the people who would need to access Cognos Metric Studio to consume the scorecards.*

Cognos Connection and Cognos 10 Studios

All of the roles discussed in this chapter, with the exception of the Active Report Recipient, provide access to Cognos Connection. The studios to which users have access depend on the roles the users have been assigned. As discussed, each role allows different access rights. Using Cognos Query Studio, Cognos Report Studio, Cognos Event Studio, Cognos Metric Studio, and Cognos Analysis Studio, you can create ad hoc reports, detailed reports, and notifications based on data, and you can monitor and analyze your data. Table 3-1 provides a graphical depiction of what roles have access to Cognos Connection and the respective studios.

Cognos Connection

Cognos Connection is the web portal by which users access Cognos 10 and the studios. Depending on the role that you have been assigned, you can use the Cognos Connection portal to retrieve, view, publish, manage, and organize your organization's reports, scorecards, and agents. The Administrator also uses the Cognos Connection portal to establish roles and user permissions and manage the Cognos Connection content.

	Active Report Recipient, Remote Recipient, and Mobile Consumer	Recipient*	Consumer	Enhanced Consumer	Business Author	Business Analyst	Business Manager	Professional Author	Advanced Business Author	BI Professional	BI Administrator
Cognos Connection		X	X	X	X	X	X	X	X	X	X
Cognos Query Studio					X			X	X	X	X
Cognos Report Studio								X		X	X
Cognos Event Studio										X	X
Cognos Metric Studio							X			X	X
Cognos Analysis Studio						X				X	X
Cognos Business Insight				X	X	X	X	X	X	X	X
Cognos Business Insight Advanced								X	X	X	X
Cognos Framework Manager											X

* Recipient role does not have execute privileges, but the Consumer role does.

TABLE 3-1   A Matrix of Roles and How They Relate to Cognos Connection and the Studios

All Cognos Connection users can personalize how Cognos Connection displays for them. Users can modify personal preferences, such as the language and regional settings. They can also change the format (PDF, Excel, HTML) in which they receive content, such as queries, reports, and analyses.

Cognos Business Insight

Cognos Business Insight provides a workspace (canvas) where users can create their own dashboard using any object already authored in Cognos 10 content. All content that the user is permitted to view is presented as objects that can be easily dropped onto the workspace, allowing the user to create a fully personalized dashboard. A full description of Cognos Business Insight can be found in Chapter 7. The Cognos Business Insight workspace is shown next:

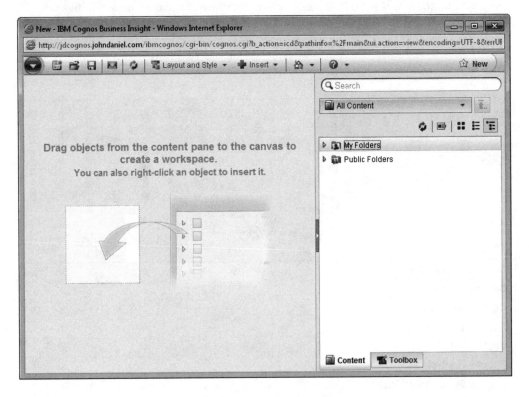

Cognos Query Studio

Cognos Query Studio, shown next, is an easy-to-use authoring tool with which you can quickly create simple queries from the data stored in your database without having the skills of a professional report writer. With a few clicks of the mouse, you can view, filter, sort, and format the data; modify the query layout; and add charts. Finally, you can save and share the queries you created with other people in your organization.

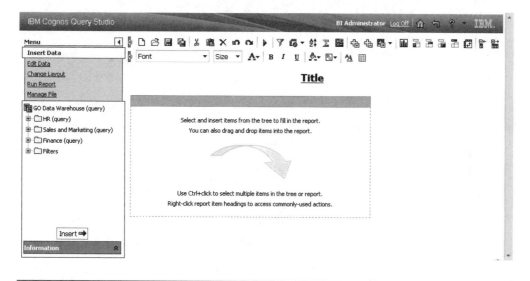

NOTE *For more information about Cognos Query Studio, refer to Chapter 8.*

Cognos Analysis Studio

Cognos Analysis Studio, shown next, helps business users get fast answers to business questions so the organization can better understand product, customer, and organizational needs to react swiftly and stay ahead of the competition. Cognos Analysis Studio is best for exploring information in multiple dimensions and for deep comparative analysis.

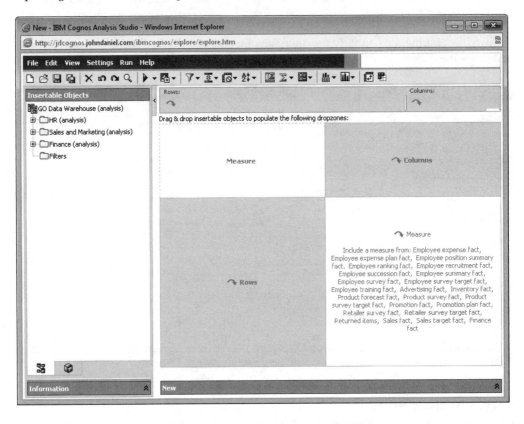

NOTE *For more information about Cognos Analysis Studio, refer to Chapter 11.*

Cognos Business Insight Advanced

Cognos Business Insight Advanced, new to Cognos 10, is a module that combines Cognos Query Studio and Cognos Analysis Studio. It provides a more robust authoring environment for business people who were limited by Cognos Query Studio and Cognos Analysis Studio. The following illustration shows Cognos BIA:

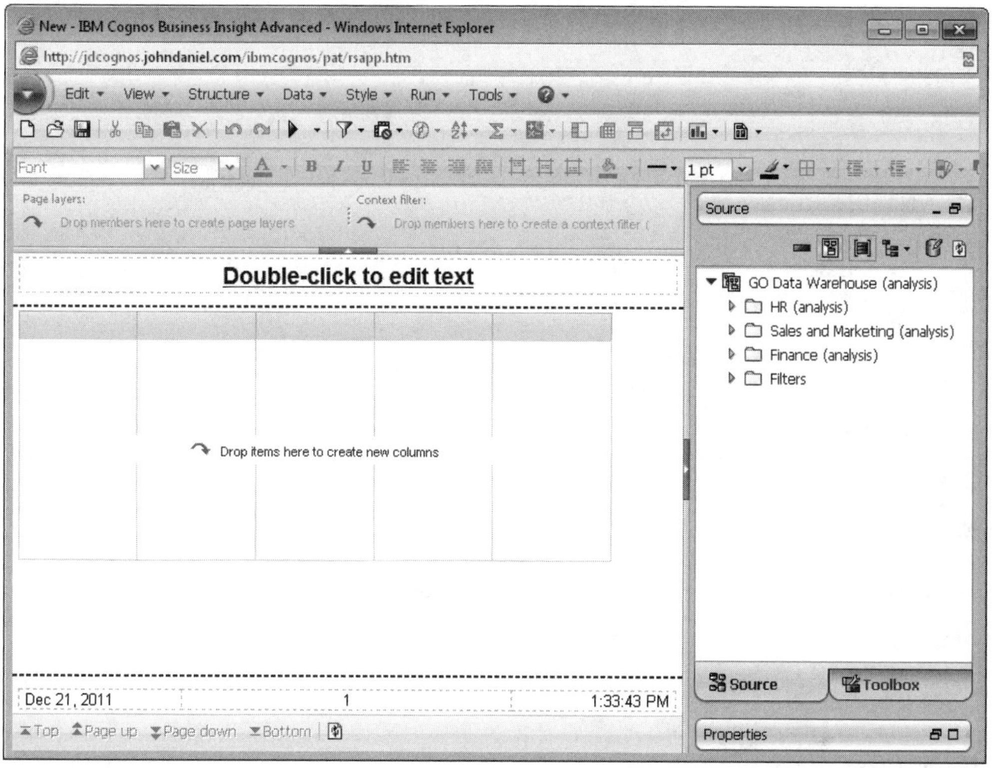

TIP *If you are new to Cognos and Cognos 10, consider kicking off your deployment with Cognos BIA and minimize the use of Cognos Query Studio and Cognos Analysis Studio.*

Cognos Report Studio

With Cognos Report Studio, shown next, you can easily create pixel-perfect reports. You can create charts, maps, lists, repeaters, or any other available report type using static data from relational or multidimensional data sources. When you're authoring reports (report writing), you'll find that Cognos Report Studio is the most robust authoring environment. Chapters 10–12 provide in-depth detail on report authoring.

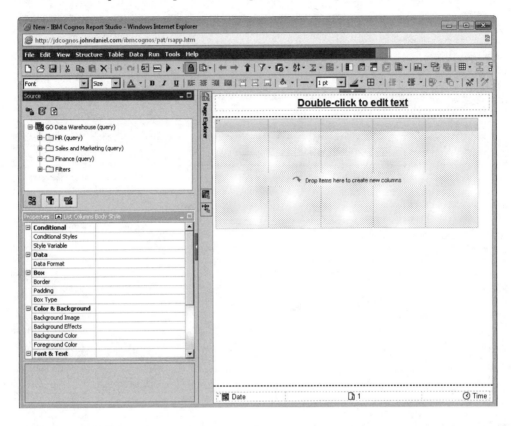

Cognos Event Studio

With Cognos Event Studio, shown next, you can establish a threshold or assign a specific event that sends a notification to the decision makers in your organization. You create agents that monitor your thresholds or event, and when the threshold is reached or the event occurs, the agent sends the notification. Notifications can include e-mails, adding information to the portal, or running reports.

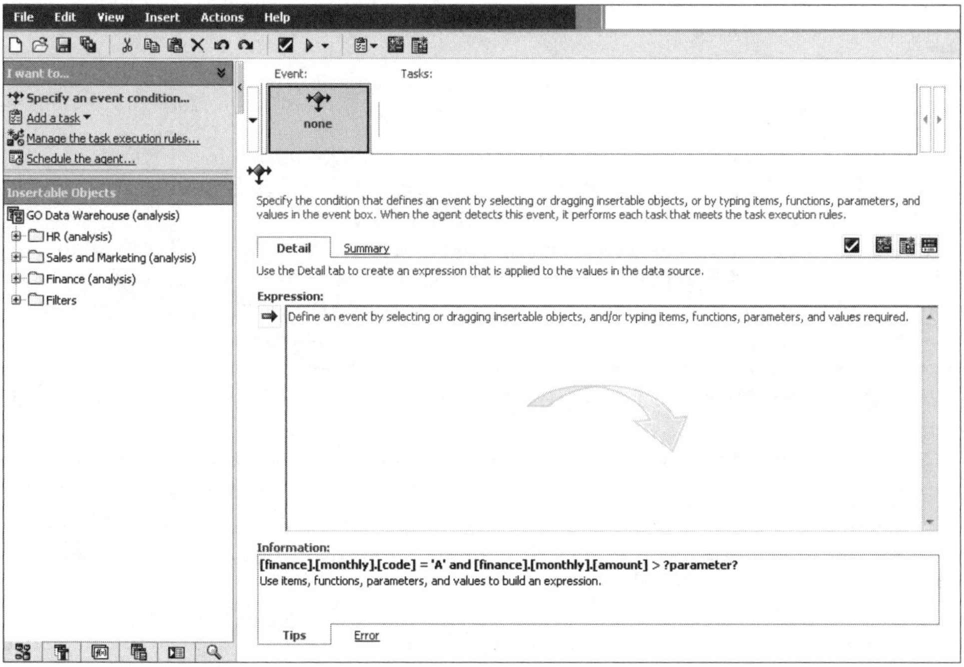

NOTE *For more information about Cognos Event Studio, refer to Chapter 14.*

Cognos Metric Studio

With Cognos Metric Studio, shown next, you can monitor and analyze your organization's business metrics by creating a scorecarding environment. Cognos Metric Studio allows you to establish criteria and then monitor your organization to see how it is responding as the criteria changes.

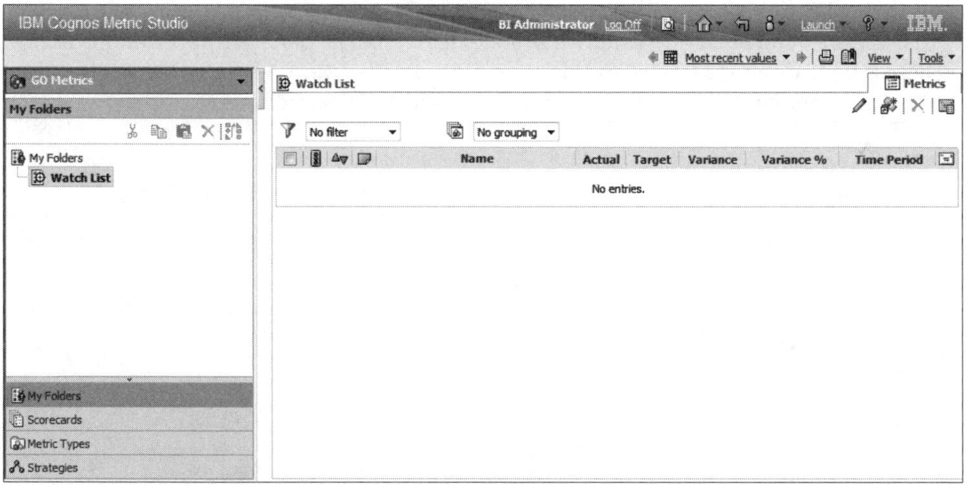

NOTE *For more information about Cognos Metric Studio, refer to Chapter 15.*

IBM Cognos Mobile

Starting with Cognos 10, use of the Cognos Mobile server was added to the standard license. This means that you can now deliver your Business Analytics to a variety of mobile devices without needing to purchase an additional license.

One of the major challenges for decision makers today is dealing with the availability of their business data and the speed at which they receive this information. These are critical factors in determining how fast they can respond to resolve issues, realign resources, or simply monitor sales of high profile customers. The ability to take action more quickly can give businesses a competitive edge. With the onslaught of mobile devices, whether it is an Android device, an iPhone, or a tablet computer, information can be available 100 percent of the time.

As a decision maker, having 24/7 access to the data that drives your business decisions can be invaluable. You no longer have to wait for critical information to help you make decisions that drive your company's success. Business information can be available almost as fast as it arrives through smartphone devices and tablet computers. Cognos Mobile can help businesses maintain their competitive edge.

Cognos Mobile also allows users to access reports from their existing Cognos environment using devices such as iPhones, iPads, Android devices, Blackberry devices, Symbian devices, and Microsoft Windows mobile devices. Users will be able to navigate through content in public folders to which they have access, as well as information in their personal folders. They can run reports, use prompt and drill-through features, and schedule reports to be sent to their device.

Accessing IBM Cognos Mobile

The following examples cover the Cognos Mobile user interface, how to run reports, and how to e-mail reports. You will need to have Cognos Mobile installed and configured in your environment. Cognos Mobile now includes a native iPad application that lets users access their IBM Cognos content.

Blackberry, Symbian, and Windows Mobile devices all have native applications that let you access your Cognos Mobile environment. iPhone, iPad, and Android devices can use web browsers on the device to access your Cognos Mobile environment.

For this example, we are using the Safari web browser on the iPad.

1. Turn on your iPad device, and tap the Safari web browser app. This will open and display the web browser.

Safari (web browser)

2. Type the URL to your Cognos Mobile environment, which should be supplied by the Administrator. After you've entered the URL, you'll see a logon screen for you Cognos Mobile environment, as shown next:

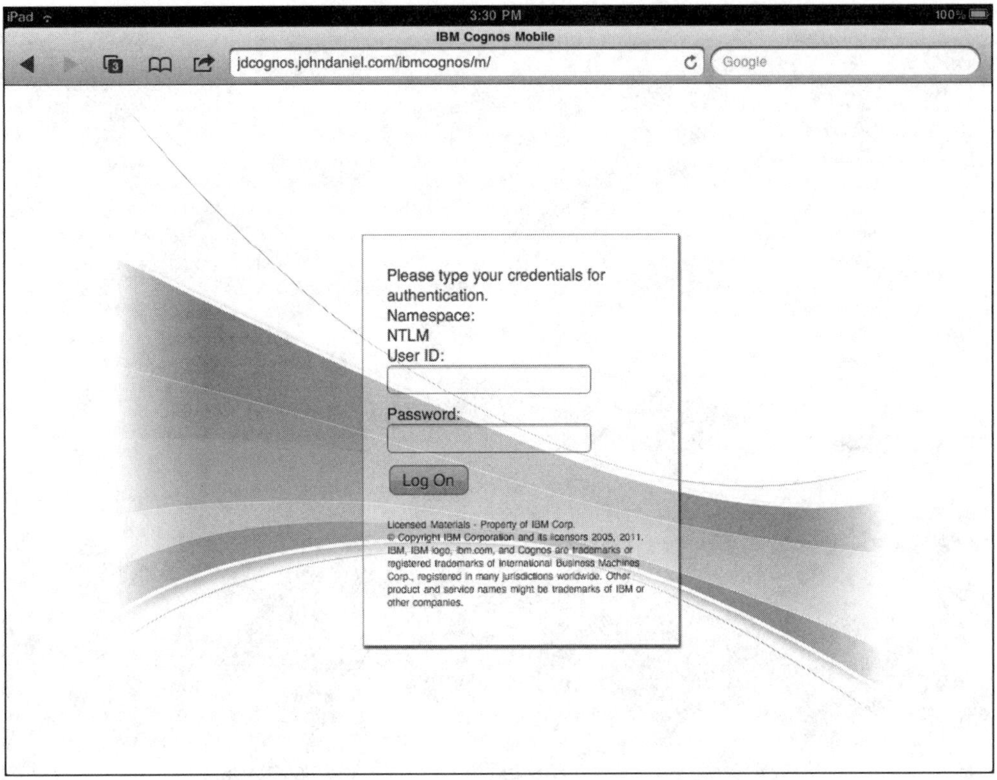

3. Enter your credentials, and tap Log On to open the Cognos Mobile interface.

Tab Bar

The tab icons included in the tab bar are shown in Table 3-2.

Icon	Name	Description
	Home	Personal Home Page
	Favorites	List of reports you have marked as favorites
	Recently Run Reports	List of recently run reports
	Browse	Public Folders and My Folders from your IBM Cognos environment
	Search	Search for reports within your IBM Cognos environment
	Log On/Log Off	Log on and log off of your IBM Cognos environment

TABLE 3-2 iPad Tab Bar Icons

Run a Report

You can run a report by simply tapping a report name within Public Folders. If a report contains prompting and drill-through features, those features are also available within reports run using the IBM Cognos Mobile interface.

1. From the IBM Cognos Mobile Home Page, tap the Browse tab and you'll see the Public Folders area of the IBM Cognos Mobile environment, shown next:

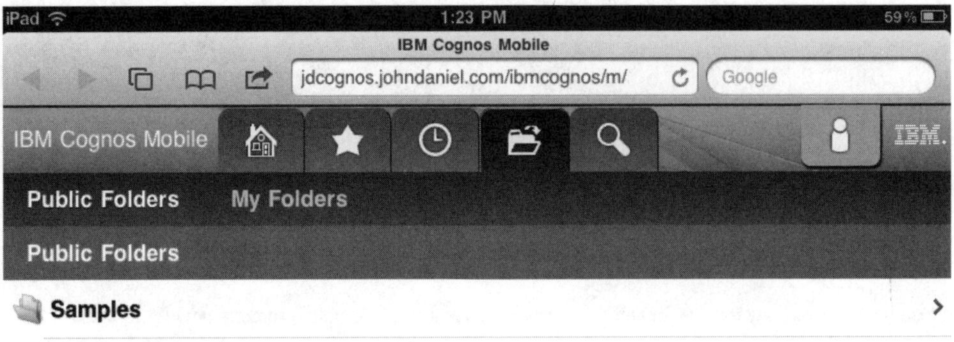

2. Navigate to the report you want to run, and tap the report title to run the report. The selected report is displayed:

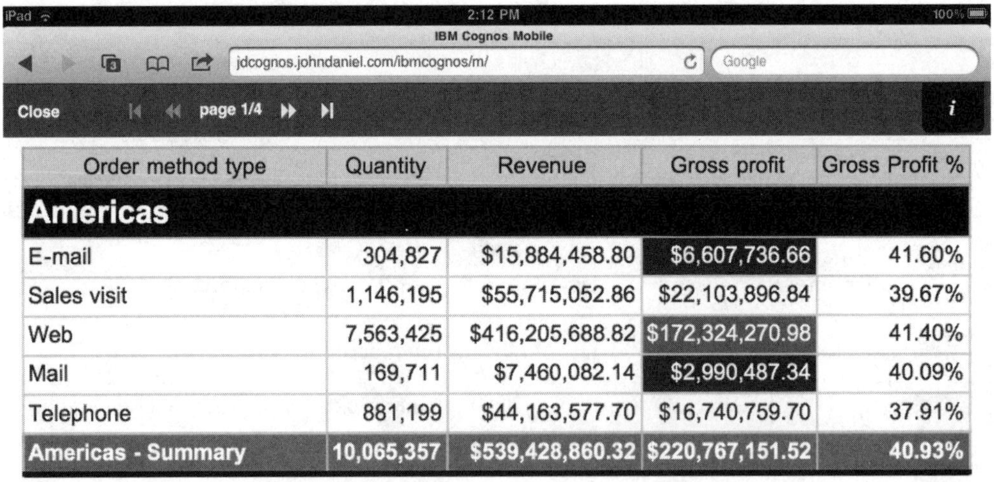

Order method type	Quantity	Revenue	Gross profit	Gross Profit %
Americas				
E-mail	304,827	$15,884,458.80	$6,607,736.66	41.60%
Sales visit	1,146,195	$55,715,052.86	$22,103,896.84	39.67%
Web	7,563,425	$416,205,688.82	$172,324,270.98	41.40%
Mail	169,711	$7,460,082.14	$2,990,487.34	40.09%
Telephone	881,199	$44,163,577.70	$16,740,759.70	37.91%
Americas - Summary	**10,065,357**	**$539,428,860.32**	**$220,767,151.52**	**40.93%**

To close the report, tap the Close link in the upper-left corner of the report.

Add a Report to Home Page and/or Favorites

Eventually, you will find some reports that you like to check on a regular basis. Having links to these reports on your Home Page or Favorites list can be a time saver.

1. Tap the Browse tab and Navigate to the report you want to add to your Home Page and/or Favorites. Run the report. After the reports displays, tap the Information icon. The Favorite and Welcome check box options are displayed.

Information

Americas				
E-mail	304,827	$15,884,458.80	$6,607,736.66	41.60%
Sales visit	1,146,195	$55,715,052.86	$22,103,896.84	39.67%
Web	7,563,425	$416,205,688.82	$172,324,270.98	41.40%
Mail	169,711	$7,460,082.14	$2,990,487.34	40.09%
Telephone	881,199	$44,163,577.70	$16,740,759.70	37.91%
Americas - Summary	10,065,357	$539,428,860.32	$220,767,151.52	40.93%

2. From the Information drop-down, tap the Favorite check box to add the report to the Favorites tab. Tap the Welcome check box to add the report to the Home Page tab. Tap the Information icon to minimize the Information drop-down.

3. Tap the Home tab to view the report we just added.

4. Tap the Favorites tab (the star tab) to view the report we just added.

Remove Reports from Favorites or Recently Run Reports

If you no longer want to see certain reports on the Favorites tab and the Recently Run Reports tab, you can remove them. The steps are the same for both tabs.

1. Tap the Favorites tab, and then tap Edit in the upper-right corner. Each report on your Favorites tab now displays with a red X to the right of the report.
2. Tap the red X to remove the report from that tab.

Search for Reports

Users can also search for a report within the IBM Cognos environment. By using the Search feature within the IBM Cognos Mobile interface, users can easily find reports that are buried within several layers of folders.

1. Tap the Search tab to access the Search feature.
2. In the entry box, enter a keyword to search for a report. In this example we search for the word "Conditional." After you've entered the keyword, tap the Search button. All reports containing the word "Conditional" are displayed:

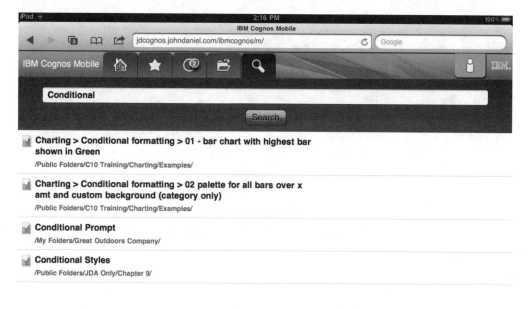

IBM Cognos Mobile for iPad App

The IBM Cognos Mobile for iPad app is a new feature with the release of IBM Cognos Mobile 10.1.1. It is available for download from the Apple App Store. Using the Cognos Mobile iPad app, users can navigate and run reports from their existing Cognos environment. The highlight feature allows users to bring attention to sections of a report. After a section has been highlighted, users can e-mail the report with the highlighted sections.

After downloading and installing the Cognos Mobile for iPad App from the Apple App store, you can launch the app:

1. Tap the app icon from the iPad screen.

IBM Cognos Mobile App

2. The first time you launch the Cognos Mobile for iPad app, you will be prompted to enter the URL of your Cognos environment. Your administrator should supply this to you. Enter the URL and tap the Log On button.

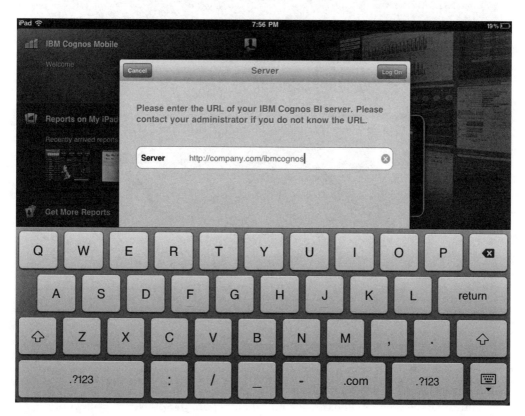

3. In the Log On screen, enter your credentials and tap OK. The main screen of the Cognos Mobile for iPad App is displayed:

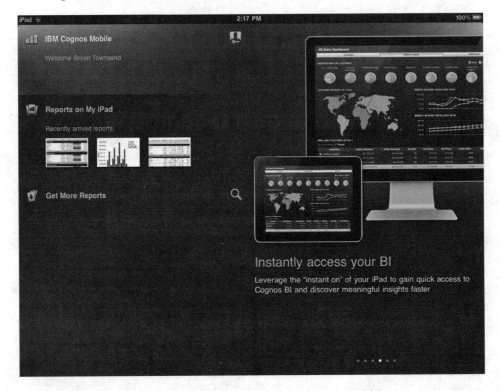

Run a Report

After launching the program you can begin running reports as you would from your computer:

1. From the main screen, tap Get More Reports. This displays My Folders and Public Folders, as shown here:

2. Navigate to a report, and tap that report name. In this example, we tapped the Conditional Styles report. You'll see the View button at the lower-right corner, as shown next:

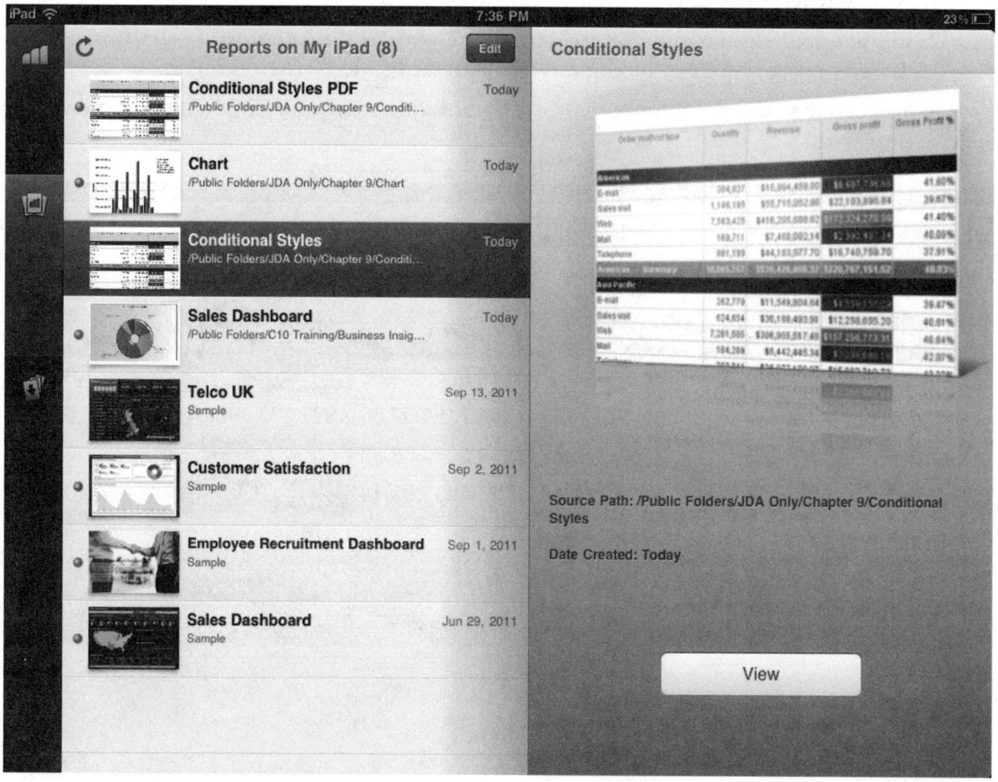

3. Tap View to run the report. The report is displayed:

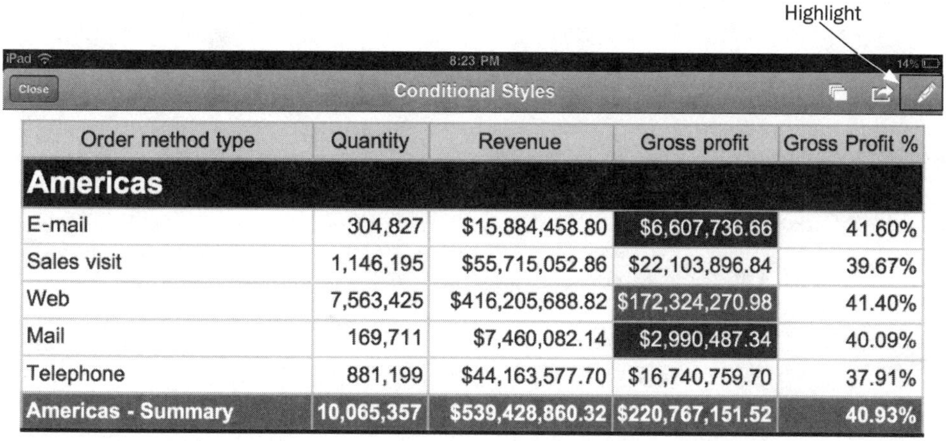

Order method type	Quantity	Revenue	Gross profit	Gross Profit %
Americas				
E-mail	304,827	$15,884,458.80	$6,607,736.66	41.60%
Sales visit	1,146,195	$55,715,052.86	$22,103,896.84	39.67%
Web	7,563,425	$416,205,688.82	$172,324,270.98	41.40%
Mail	169,711	$7,460,082.14	$2,990,487.34	40.09%
Telephone	881,199	$44,163,577.70	$16,740,759.70	37.91%
Americas - Summary	**10,065,357**	**$539,428,860.32**	**$220,767,151.52**	**40.93%**

Highlight a Report

Highlighting a section of a report allows you to bring attention to an area of concern.

1. Navigate to a report, and run the report.

2. In the upper-right corner tap the Highlight icon. At this point, you can draw directly on your report, noting any areas that need to be highlighted.

3. You can then discard your notes (tap Discard) or e-mail your highlights to a co-worker (tap Email).

Order method type	Quantity	Revenue	Gross profit	Gross Profit %
Americas				
E-mail	304,827	$15,884,458.80	$6,607,736.66	41.60%
Sales visit	1,146,195	$55,715,052.86	$22,103,896.84	39.67%
Web	7,563,425	$416,205,688.82	$172,324,278.98	41.40%
Mail	169,711	$7,460,082.14	$2,990,487.34	40.09%
Telephone	881,199	$44,163,577.70	$16,740,759.70	37.91%
Americas - Summary	10,065,357	$539,428,860.32	$220,767,151.52	40.93%
Asia Pacific				

Enhanced Analytics

The success of BI over the past two decades has led to the demand for a wider range of data-analysis tools. Twenty years ago, a business analyst asked to create a report could spend weeks, even months, compiling data from multiple sources—pulling data from spreadsheets, paper forms, annual reports, multiple databases, slips of paper, and napkins. The opportunity for human error was (and in many cases, still is) enormous. You would often see numbers transposed, entered multiple times, or missed entirely. The techniques used in BI have helped to reduce the time required to create reports and increased the reliability of those reports.

Not long ago, a client of ours was responsible for producing a quarterly sales and production report, which consisted of production data from 17 plants, sales information from 8 regions, and operating expenses from across the organization. The final report was sourced from more than 30 spreadsheets, a dozen flat files, statements from utility companies, and various databases. This report consumed one person's life for two and a half months every quarter. Using various BI tools and methods, we were able to help the client produce a more accurate report weekly. In less than one year, if the report was not published at the expected time, business users would grumble because of the delay.

This anecdote demonstrates the ever-rising expectations of your business users. The demand for data, and the means to turn that data into actionable information, is never-ending. Not long ago, BI was the goal. If you were able to provide analysis through OLAP cubes or drilling from report to report, you probably had a successful BI implementation. Yesterday's success with BI has created today's demand for a deeper understanding of the factors that are driving your business. Business analytics is the response to this demand.

In this chapter, we'll take a look at how the data-analysis tools in IBM Cognos BI V10.1 provide an enhanced version of business analytics.

Business Analytics—Enhanced

Business analytics (BA) is a collection of tools, concepts, and processes aimed at improving how your organization turns data into information, shares that information, and allows the business user to analyze that information. When implemented properly, all levels of the business benefit from the ability to make decisions based on considered facts as opposed to "gut feelings" or suppositions.

The term "analytics" can mean wildly different things to different people. For some, looking at a line chart showing actual sales compared to forecast sales over the past 12 months would be an analysis. For others, examining the factors that are impacting sales through statistical methods would be an analysis. In all fairness, both activities are BA.

While examining a line chart will give you an indication of how sales are trending, the line chart will not give you any insight into why sales are trending in that direction. *Enhanced analytics* gives the business user the tools to examine the factors impacting sales, to understand the relationships between those factors, and, ultimately, to predict how a change in those factors will impact sales, or any area of the business. The opportunity to understand and predict the underlying factors that are impacting your business is enhanced analytics.

Elements of Enhanced Analytics

Among our customers, BI is still the primary component of BA. Some customers also use the financial and planning components of IBM Cognos BI, some go outside the Cognos tool set for statistical analysis, and some go to Microsoft Excel to perform analysis in a familiar tool set. Observing our customers' use of these tools has led us to the conclusion that the users who want to understand what is driving their business are looking for the following:

- The ability to perform statistical analysis of their data
- The ability to view their data how they want to and when they want to
- The ability to receive meaningful information while away from the office
- The ability to examine their data with Microsoft Office tools

Let's look at why the business users need these abilities and how Cognos 10 delivers them.

Statistical Analysis

The statistical analysis of data has played a role in most areas of our lives ever since R. A. Fisher formalized the core statistical methods in the early 1900s. Political campaigns try to understand how groups of people will respond to their candidate's position on an issue. Process and quality control are monitored through statistical methods. Marketing companies test a new slogan on a sample of people before investing in a larger effort. The examples could go on for pages. One thing that all of these uses have in common is the need for extensive training in statistical methods before being able to realize the benefits of the tools.

Cognos 10 drastically reduces the amount of training required before you can start gaining benefits from some of the most frequently used statistical tools. The IBM SPSS Statistics Engine gives report authors the ability to add sophisticated statistical analyses to their reports in a drag-and-drop interface.

Be assured, report authors will still require some training in statistical methods before they will be comfortable with the statistical tools. However, a careful study of the Cognos 10 documentation will most likely give report authors enough of an understanding of the tools to add meaningful information to their reports.

The business analyst will always need to provide decision makers with the list reports, charts, and graphs they have become accustomed to receiving. The differentiator—the enhancement—comes when the business analyst can provide mathematical proof that the list reports, charts, and graphs are accurate and reflect reality.

In Chapter 13, we will discuss the various types of statistical analyses available in IBM Cognos Report Studio. For now, here is a brief overview of the types of statistical tools available:

- **Descriptive statistics**   This tool provides a concise review of a set of data. The review contains the more common statistical measures, such as mean, variance, standard deviation, and so on.

- **Means comparisons**   This set of tools is used to compare multiple sets of data. The tools help you identify differences between two or more groups.

- **Correlation and regression**   These tools help you identify and understand which items are related to each other and how a change in one item can affect other items.

- **Control charts**   Primarily used to monitor manufacturing processes in Six Sigma organizations, these charts help you monitor the quality, or "health," of a process.

Self-Service

BA can provide value for any level of your business. The challenge has been in getting that information to the users, regardless of their technical skill level, in a format that is meaningful to them.

As an example, suppose that a user who has no interest in computers requests a report in list format. After receiving the report, the user decides that seeing the data in a chart would be more intuitive. So, the request is sent back to the report author, and the cycle begins again. These back-and-forth exchanges between the technically savvy user and the nontechnical user are common, necessary, and (typically) challenging for all involved.

The trend in BA has been to move report and other content generation from the IT department to the business user. IBM Cognos Business Insight and IBM Cognos Business Insight Advanced, introduced in Cognos 10, provide new levels of self-service for business users of any technical level.

With Cognos Business Insight, any business user can easily access report objects and manipulate them with nothing more than mouse clicks. Business users no longer need to concern themselves with the source of the data, such as whether it's from a relational database, a star-schema data warehouse, or OLAP. The users only need to select the object they are interested in, drop it into the work area, and decide how they want to view it.

Let's return to our example of a nontechnical user who has a list report, which looks something like this:

To see the data in a chart (or another format), the user simply right-clicks the object and selects the new layout.

Now the data is displayed as a chart.

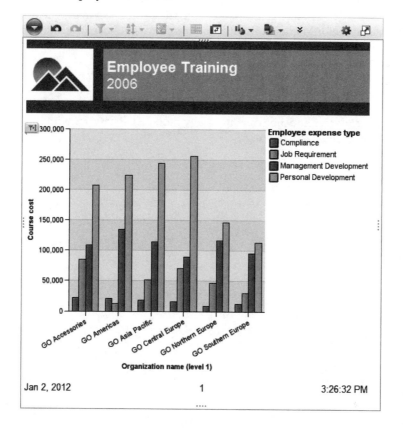

By using the self-service features of Cognos Business Insight, the user has modified the report display without assistance from the IT department or from the author of the content.

Cognos Business Insight Advanced, as the name implies, provides more functionality to business users and, coincidentally, does require additional skill. The self-service features provided by both of these tools are discussed in more detail in Chapters 7, 8, and 9.

Mobility

The demand for high-quality BA is not restricted to the office, and it is not limited to the hours of 9 to 5. The proliferation of smartphones, iPads, and other mobile devices has made accessing business information at any place and at any time the rule, not the exception.

IBM Cognos Mobile delivers BA to your mobile device with many of the same features that you have on your computer at the office. You can drill up and down, answer prompts, and receive the same reports authored for the desktop.

Analytics with Microsoft Excel

Some users will always be more comfortable with Microsoft Excel than with any other tool. IBM Cognos Analysis for Microsoft Excel allows those users to benefit from many of the same features that are found in the various IBM Cognos Studios. Excel users can access the secured data sources found in IBM Cognos Connection. They can perform, save, and share explorations and analyses. They can even open those explorations and analyses in IBM Cognos Report Studio.

In order to use Cognos Analysis for Microsoft Excel, your data must be in OLAP form or, if it is relational data, it must be dimensionally modeled. Analytics with Microsoft Excel will be discussed in detail in Chapter 6.

Accessing and Using
IBM Cognos 10

IBM Cognos Connection

IBM Cognos Connection is a web-based portal that allows users (such as executives, sales associates, finance managers, IT departments, and consumers) to run reports, queries, metrics, and analyses; perform administrative functions; and access other IBM Cognos content. Cognos Connection gives users a single access point to application-specific data available in IBM Cognos for their corporation. Cognos Connection is also the gateway to IBM Cognos applications available to users, such as IBM Cognos Business Insight, IBM Cognos Report Studio, IBM Cognos Metric Studio, and so on.

Users can customize Cognos Connection and the appearance of entries in a variety of ways—by organizing content within folders, selecting separators in list view, setting a default home page, and changing the default language, to name a few. In this chapter, you will learn how to set and use these and other Cognos Connection options.

NOTE *If you do not have access permissions to a specific location, contact your IBM Cognos administrator.*

Getting Started with IBM Cognos Connection

Executives, managers, associates, consumers, and others access their company's data (such as packages, reports, dashboards, scorecards, and so on) using Cognos Connection. Users interact with Cognos Connection by clicking commands, folders, and links to perform various actions.

IBM Cognos Connection Welcome Page

By default, the Welcome page appears at the beginning of each IBM Cognos Connection session. The Welcome page provides a quick and easy way to access public content, the area you have set as your "home," as well as any IBM Cognos application accessible to you. The IBM Cognos Content link directs you to the Public Folders tab. The My Home link directs you to the area in Cognos Connection set as your home, or simply to the Public Folders tab if you have not set a home view; the My Workspaces link provides access to a new or existing workspace within Business Insight; the My Inbox link directs you to your My Inbox area within Cognos Connection.

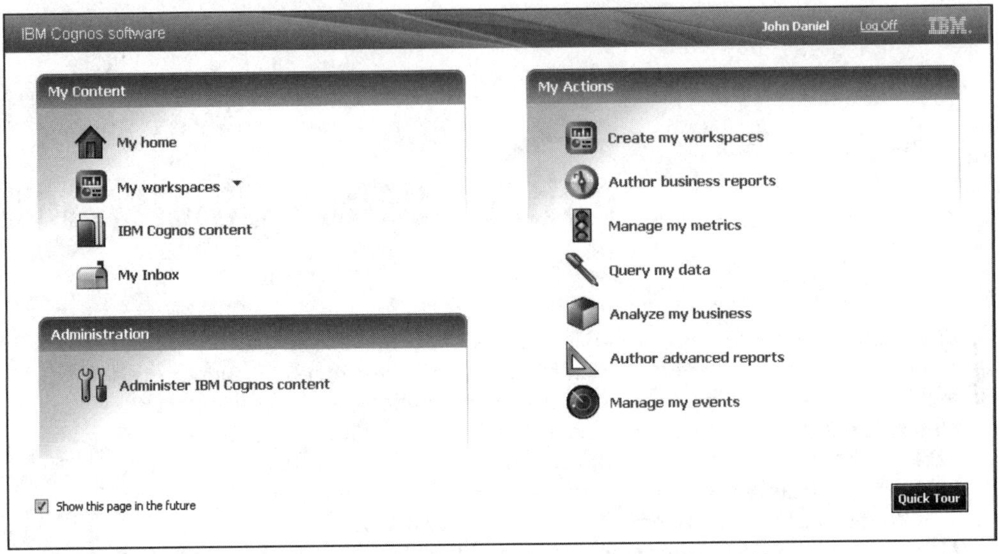

NOTE *The Welcome page is optional. You can choose not to have it appear if you prefer to go directly to Cognos Connection. Refer to the "My Preferences" section later in this chapter for directions on disabling the Welcome page.*

IBM Cognos Connection Interface

At the top of the Cognos Connection interface, in the bar with your Cognos username shown in the following illustration, are commands that you can use for these tasks:

- Log out of the application
- Refresh the screen
- Perform searches
- Set and return to a home page
- Set personal preferences
- View and manage your activities
- Launch studios
- Access online help

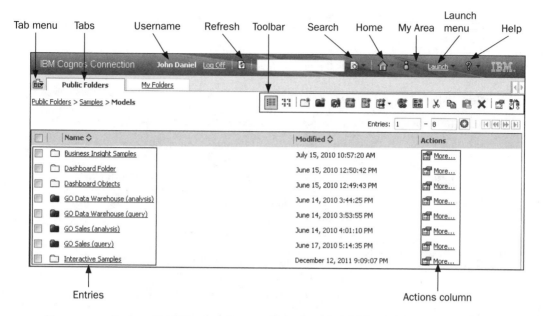

You can navigate within Cognos Connection using the Public Folders and My Folders tabs. The Public Folders tab is a public area that is accessible by many users, while the My Folders tab is a private area accessible only by you. From the Tab menu, you can add tabs, remove tabs, and reorder the tabs.

The entries list contains links to all of the items to which you have access, such as packages, folders, and reports. Entries within Cognos Connection are displayed in a list format by default. Packages are indicated by a blue folder icon and are sources used to build content such as reports. Folders are indicated by a yellow folder icon and are used for organizing other entries.

IBM Cognos Connection Toolbar

You can use the buttons on the Cognos Connection toolbar to perform tasks such as the following:

- Create and order folders
- Set a view
- Create new jobs or pages
- Set properties
- Perform basic cut, copy, paste, and delete actions

Table 5-1 describes the functions available from the Cognos Connection toolbar.

Icon	Name	Description
	List View	Show the name, modified date, and actions of entries
	Details View	Show the name, description, modified date, and actions of entries
	New Folder	Create a new folder
	New Workspace	Create a new workspace in Cognos Business Insight
	New Job	Create a new group of objects that can be scheduled to run as a set
	New URL	Create a new URL to link to an external file or web site
	New Page	Create a new page to group different types of information into a single view
	Cut	Cut an entry to move it to another location
	Copy	Copy an entry to move it to another location while keeping the original entry intact
	Paste	Paste an entry to its new location after cutting or copying
	Delete	Delete an entry from its current location
	Set Properties	Specify general properties and permissions for an entry
	Order	Set a specific order for entries

TABLE 5-1 Cognos Connection Toolbar Buttons

Performing Actions

The Actions column in Cognos Connection provides access to common functions available for each entry. The More link in the Actions column provides access to all actions available for an entry.

Setting Properties

Every entry in Cognos Connection has properties associated with it. Properties allow you to change the appearance, behavior, and metadata of entries. You can modify items such as the name (for example, change a name from *Sales* to *Sales Forecasting*), description, language, and permissions for an entry. You can also edit the number of occurrences and the duration for the run history and report output versions of entries.

There are general properties that are available for every entry, and there are also properties that are specific to certain types of entries. For example, report entries allow you to specify properties such as the default action of the entry link, the default format of the report, and prompt values. For job entries, you can specify properties such as the steps of the job and the order in which the steps are executed.

To set properties for an entry, follow these steps:

1. In the Actions column of the entry whose properties you want to set, click Set Properties, as shown here:

		Name ◇	Modified ◇	Actions
☐	⬤	Bursted Sales Performance Report	January 16, 2012 4:06:15 PM	🖼 🖸 ▶ ◬ ① 🗓 🖼 More...
☐	▦	New page	January 16, 2012 5:15:27 PM	🖼 🖸 More...
☐	▤▶	Percentage Calculation (by year)	January 16, 2012 1:55:00 PM	🖼 ▶ ◬ ① 🗓 🖼 More...
☐	⬤	Recruitment Report	January 16, 2012 8:48:56 PM	🖼 🖸 ▶ ◬ ① 🗓 🖼 More...

Set properties

2. Select the appropriate tab for the properties you wish to specify.

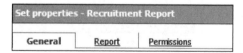

Set properties - Recruitment Report		
General	Report	Permissions

3. Make the desired modifications, and then click OK.

***

NOTE *Some of the most common properties are discussed in the following sections.*

General Properties

The General tab is available for every entry and includes basic properties.

Set properties - Recruitment Report   Help ✕

| General | Report | Permissions |

Specify the properties for this entry.

Type: Report   Location: Public Folders > Samples >
                                                       Models > Interactive Samples   ▦ View the search path, ID and URL
Owner: Gerard Ruppert   Make me the owner
Contact: None   Set the contact ▾   Created: October 1, 2007 3:03:54 PM

☐ Disable this entry   Modified: January 16, 2012 8:48:56 PM

☐ Hide this entry   Icon: ▦ Standard Edit...

                                                    Indexed: December 11, 2011 11:16:49 AM   View indexing details

The name, screen tip and description are shown for the selected language.

Language: Remove values for this language
English   ▾

Name: **Description:**
Recruitment Report   This report contains features that allow users to interact with the
                                                   report. It provides context sensitive links to documentation that
Screen tip: explains how certain features were authored.

Run history: **Report output versions:**
Setting the number of occurrences to zero   Setting the number of occurrences to zero
(0) saves an unlimited number of   (0) saves an unlimited number of
occurrences.   occurrences.
◉ Number of occurrences: 5   ◉ Number of occurrences: 1
○ Duration: [   ] Day(s) ▾   ○ Duration: [   ] Day(s) ▾

Package:
GO Data Warehouse (analysis)   Link to a package...

[OK]   [Cancel]

The settings on the General tab can include the following:

- **Type**   Type of entry
- **Owner**   Owner of the entry (by default, the owner is the creator of the entry)
- **Contact**   Individual responsible for the entry
- **Location**   Location of the entry within IBM Cognos Connection
- **Created**   Date the entry was created
- **Modified**   Date the entry was most recently modified
- **Icon**   Icon for the entry
- **Disable This Entry**   When disabled, an entry is unavailable to users without write permissions to it; users with write access will see the disabled icon next to disabled entries, as in the following illustration.

- **Hide This Entry**   Hide entries to prevent unnecessary use or to organize views
- **Language**   Language for the individual entry
- **Name**   Name of the entry

NOTE *To change the title displayed on a report, you must edit the report in the studio in which it was created.*

- **Screen tip**   Optional description of the entry that appears on mouse-over
- **Description**   Description of the entry
- **Package**   The package to which the entry is linked

CAUTION *When changing the package an entry is associated with, you should understand the consequences of linking a report to a different package. The data in the underlying model must match the query items in the report.*

Report Properties

You can set properties specific to reports, such as the default output format, the default behavior of the report link, and prompt values. For example, you can set the link to open the report in Cognos Report Studio instead of running the report in IBM Cognos Viewer. Modifications made to the properties of a report set the defaults for the report and apply to all users.

Cognos Connection provides several output formats for reports to accommodate users with different viewing requirements. For example, the CEO may want to view a report in PDF format, while the sales manager may want to see the same report in Excel format.

Each output format displays with a unique icon in Cognos Connection.

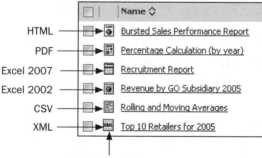

Report Format icon

When you click the Set Properties button in the Actions column of the report whose properties you want to change, select the Report tab. The Report tab displays options for the report.

The settings on the Report tab include the following:

- **Default Action**   Action you want to occur when the report link is clicked. Three options are available:
  - **View Most Recent Report**   Opens the most recent saved version of a report, given that a saved version exists
  - **Run the Report**   Runs the report in real time
  - **Open with Report Studio**   Opens the report in Cognos Report Studio

---

NOTE *In IBM Cognos Connection, a blue arrow located to the right of a report format icon indicates that the report link runs the report in real time.*

- **Override the Default Values** Check this box to specify report options other than the defaults section expands:

> **Report options:**
> ☑ Override the default values
> **Format:**
> | HTML ▼ |
> **Accessibility:**
> ☐ Enable accessibility support
> **Language:**
> | English (United States) ▼ |
>
> **PDF options:**
> No options saved
> Set...

- **Format** Default output format of the report; the report will default to this format when it is run

- **Accessibility** Check this box to enable any accessibility support features in this report each time it is executed

- **Languages** Default language of the report

TIP *The Set link under PDF Options allows you to specify options such as orientation, paper size, and password-protected security for the PDF format. Setting the PDF options here applies these settings as the default PDF settings for the report every time it is run.*

- **Prompt Values** Select the Prompt for Values check box to set default prompt values for the report

- **Run as the Owner** Select this check box to set the owner's credentials to be used when the report is run

- **Advanced Options** This link provides the following options:

> **Number of rows per Web page in HTML reports:**
> | 20 ▼ |
>
> ☑ Enable selection-based interactivity in HTML reports
> ☑ Enable alerts about new versions
> ☐ Enable enhanced user features in saved output versions
> ☐ Enable comments in saved output versions
>
> **Report cache:**
> ☐ Refresh the report cache:
> A report cache is used to optimize the performance of prompt pages. The cache is refreshed automatically when a report runs interactively and the cache is expired. You can also clear the cache at any time.
> **Cache duration:**
> | | Day(s) ▼ |

> **NOTE** *Permissions are also accessed within an entry's properties. Please refer to the Permissions section later in this chapter for more information.*

Running Reports

Reports can be set to retrieve the latest information from the data source when executed or to display a pre-generated version of the report. The icon to the left of the report title indicates the report's settings.

If a blue arrow is displayed to the right of the report format icon, the report executes and retrieves the current data from the data source. If a blue arrow is not displayed to the right of the report format icon, this indicates a saved report. A saved report displays the output from the last execution of the report.

To run a report, click a report link (as seen in the following illustration).

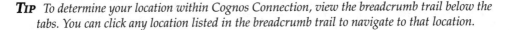

> **TIP** *To determine your location within Cognos Connection, view the breadcrumb trail below the tabs. You can click any location listed in the breadcrumb trail to navigate to that location.*

The Run with Options action allows you to specify how you want to run and receive a report. You can receive a report in a different format than the report's default format or save the report after it runs. For example, a salesperson may want to output the report to an Excel format to use during a customer visit, whereas a sales manager may want to save the report in PDF format after running it for quick and easy retrieval.

Advanced options are also available through the Run with Options action. These allow you to specify settings such as multiple output formats, delivery methods, and languages, as well as the date and time the report is run.

To run a report with options, follow these steps:

1. In the Actions column of the report, click the Run with Options button.

Run With options

The Run with Options screen appears.

```
Run with options - Recruitment Report                                    Help  ⊗

Select how you want to run and receive your report.

Format:                                    💡  To specify a time to run the report, or for additional
  HTML              ▼                          formats, languages, or delivery options, use advanced
                                               options.

Accessibility:
  ☐ Enable accessibility support

Language:
  English (United States)        ▼

Delivery:
  ◉ View the report now
  ○ Save the report
  ○ Print the report:
    Printer location:
    [                        ]   Select a printer...
  ○ Send the report to my mobile device

Prompt values:
No values saved
  ☑ Prompt for values

  [  Run  ]   [  Cancel  ]
```

2. In the Format drop-down list, select the desired format.

3. Select the Enable Accessibility Support check box to allow any accessibility support features in this report for this execution.

4. In the Language drop-down list, select the language in which you want the report to display.

5. In the Delivery area, select the applicable delivery method. You can choose View the Report Now, Save the Report, or Print the Report. If you select the Print the Report option, specify a printer in the Printer Location text box.

NOTE *By default, consumers can save items only in My Folders.*

6. In the Prompt Values area, select the Prompt for Values check box for the report to prompt you if applicable. Alternatively, make sure this option is unchecked if you want the report to use the default prompt values.

7. Click the Advanced Options link. The Run with Advanced Options screen appears.

8. In the Time and Mode area, you can select the Run in the Background option, which allows you to set a specific date and time to run the report, as well as select multiple formats, delivery methods, and languages. When the options available for Run in the Background appear (shown next), select the desired output format(s) and delivery options.

Options

Formats:

☑ HTML   ▼

Number of rows per Web page:

20   ▼

☑ Enable selection-based interactivity

☐ PDF

No options saved
Set...

☐ Excel 2007

☐ Excel 2002

☐ Delimited text (CSV)

☐ XML

Accessibility:

☐ Enable accessibility support

Languages:
English (United States)   Select the languages...

Delivery:
Select at least one delivery method. For burst reports, the email recipients are determined by the burst specification.

☑ Save:

◉ Save the report

◎ Save the report as a report view   Edit the options...

...> Report View of Recruitment Report

☐ Print the report

Printer location:

Select a printer...

☐ Send the report by email   Edit the options...

0 recipients

☐ Send the report to mobile recipients   Select the recipients...

0 recipients

PART II

TIP   *The Set link associated with the PDF format allows you to specify options such as orientation, paper size, and password-protected security. Setting PDF options here only applies to this execution of the report.*

   9. Click the Run button to run the report with the selected options.

Viewing Output Versions

You can view any saved versions of reports. Reports are saved to create a report archive. Having an archive for a report allows you to access saved reports quickly and easily. You can access different versions of a report for as far back as is defined, as well as in different formats and languages for each version. For example, a sales manager may want to compare sales figures in the current month's report to the sales from the previous month's report. He can view the output versions of the report to access both versions of the report. Viewing the output versions also provides access to any other formats in which the report may have been saved.

   If a report has saved versions, a View the Output Versions button is present in the Actions column of the report.

NOTE   *If there is no blue arrow next to the report format icon, this indicates that there is a saved version of the report and that the default action of the report link is to open the most recent saved version.*

To view a version of a saved report, follow these steps:

1. Click the View the Output Versions button in the Actions column.

		Name ◇	Modified ◇	Actions
☐	📰	Bursted Sales Performance Report	January 17, 2012 12:52:33 PM	🖼 📋 ▶ 📐 ⊕ 🗂 🗐 More...
☐	📰▶	Percentage Calculation (by year)	January 16, 2012 1:55:00 PM	🖼 ▶ 📐 ⊕ 🗂 🗐 More...
☐	🔘▲	Recruitment Report	January 16, 2012 8:48:56 PM	🖼 📋 ▶ 📐 ⊕ 🗂 🗐 More...

No blue arrow indicates report link
opens the most recent saved version

View the output versions

2. From the Versions pane, select the version of the report you wish to view.

NOTE *The number of output versions available is set within the properties of the report.*

View report output versions - Recruitment Report   Help ⊗

Current	Archived versions

Select an output version to view by clicking on a Format hyperlink.

Entries: [1] – [3] ⊙ ⏮ ⏪ ⏩ ⏭   Entries: [1] – [3] ⊙ ⏮ ⏪ ⏩ ⏭

☐ Versions ◇
☐ January 17, 2012 3:06:15 PM
☐ January 17, 2012 3:01:16 PM
☐ January 16, 2012 8:48:55 PM
Delete

Formats	Languages ☑	Actions
🔘 HTML	English (United States)	
📰 PDF	English (United States)	📋
📊 Excel 2007	English (United States)	📋

Close

Download

3. In the Formats pane, click the link of the format you want to view the report. The formats available depend on the formats in which the report was saved.

TIP *You can also click the Download button in the Actions column to download the report and save it locally.*

Creating Report Views

Report views are created from a report so that all of the specifications of the report are used, but properties such as prompt values, output formats, and schedules can be different. Having only one actual report to maintain is much easier than managing reports for every branch in a division, for example. You can preset the prompt values and add a job to execute the report views. This can save time by avoiding the need to create many schedules, while also maintaining the integrity of the report.

Within the properties of the report view, the source report for the report view can be determined, and there is a link directly to the properties of the source report.

To create a report view, follow these steps:

1. Click the Create a Report View button in the Actions column of the source report.

		Name ◇	Modified ◇	Actions
☐	▦	Bursted Sales Performance Report	January 17, 2012 12:52:33 PM	🖻 📋 ▶ ◣ ① 田 🗐 More...
☐	▦ ▶	Percentage Calculation (by year)	January 16, 2012 1:55:00 PM	🖻 ▶ ◣ ① 田 🗐 More...
☐	◙	Recruitment Report	January 17, 2012 3:17:57 PM	🖻 📋 ▶ ◣ ① 田 🗐 More...

Create a report view

2. To modify the default name, enter a name into the Name text box.

Specify a name and description - New Report View wizard   Help ✖

Specify a name and location for this entry. You can also specify a description and screen tip.

Name:

Report View of Recruitment Report

Description:

Screen tip:

Location:
Public Folders > Samples > Models > Interactive Samples
Select another location...   Select My Folders

| Cancel | < Back | Next > | Finish |

---

3. Optionally, provide a description and screen tip for the report view.

4. Under Location, click the Select Another Location link to specify a location for the report view that is different from the location of the source report. Alternatively, click the Select My Folders link to save the report view in your My Folders directory.

5. Click Finish. The new report view is created. The report format icon will now have a report view indicator as part of the icon.

Report Format icon with
Report View indicator

Scheduling Reports

You can schedule reports in Cognos Connection to run at a specific time or a recurring date and time by choosing frequency options, such as by day, week, month, year, or trigger. For example, if you have a large report that takes more than a minute or two to run, you can schedule the report to run during nonworking hours to utilize faster performance times. You can specify output formats like PDF, HTML, or Excel. You can also choose a delivery method for the scheduled report, such as saving it to a specific location or e-mailing the report.

NOTE *Each entry in Cognos Connection can have only one schedule.*

The settings for a schedule include the following:

- **Disable the Schedule** This setting disables the schedule without losing the specified settings.

- **Priority** The default priority value is 3. Schedules with a higher priority will be placed ahead of schedules with a lower priority in the queue. If schedules contain the same priority setting, the entry placed in the queue first runs first.

- **Frequency** This provides options to set the frequency of the schedule (for example, to run by week on every Monday and Thursday).

- **Start/End** These options specify when the schedule starts and ends. The calendar can be used to select the date.

- **Options** These settings specify format(s), language(s), and delivery option(s) different from the defaults.

- **Prompt Values** This option allows you to set prompt values on the schedule so that the report runs without user interaction.

To schedule a report, follow these steps:

1. In the Actions column of the entry you wish to schedule, click the Schedule button.

Schedule

2. Specify the frequency of the schedule.

3. Select the start and end dates of the schedule.

4. Under Options, check the Override the Default Values check box to specify format(s), language(s), and delivery option(s) other than the defaults.

5. Under Prompt Values, check the Override the Default Values check box to specify prompt values for the schedule.

6. Click OK. The schedule is created and will run at the next scheduled date and time.

Performing Other Actions

While the most common entry actions are accessible directly in the Actions column, the More link in the Actions column provides access to all actions available for an entry. Actions available to entries include the following:

- **View My Permissions**   Display the permissions you have for the entry
- **Open with Studio**   Open an entry in the studio(s) available to it
- **New Schedule**   Create a new schedule for the entry; indicates a schedule does not exist for this entry

- **Modify the Schedule**   Modify the schedule of an entry; indicates that the entry has an existing schedule
- **Remove the Schedule**   Delete the schedule entirely from the entry
- **View Run History**   Display information about the run history of an entry
- **Move**   Move an entry from its current location to a new location
- **Copy**   Create a copy of an entry while leaving the original intact
- **Create a Shortcut**   Create a pointer to an entry in another location
- **Add to Bookmarks**   Create a bookmark for an entry to allow quick access to the entry's default action

Managing Entries

Cognos Connection provides numerous ways that you can manage content to best fit your organization. For example, you can organize your company's content in a way that is meaningful to the business, set permissions on entries so that users have access to only what they need, create jobs to streamline scheduled entries, and create pages to provide customized areas for different groups of users.

Organizing Entries

Keep entries like folders, packages, reports, analyses, agents, and jobs within Cognos Connection organized in a manner so that users can easily find what they need. You may want to group entries by type, frequency of use, or access permissions. Assess the content and arrange entries according to what makes the most sense for the users.

You can copy and paste, move, rename, and delete entries. You may choose to create folders to organize entries. Using meaningful names and detailed descriptions helps identify entries easily.

TIP *The list of entries can be specifically ordered by using the Order button on the toolbar.*

To create a new folder, follow these steps:

1. On the toolbar, click the New Folder button.

2. Enter a name for the folder in the Name text box.

3. Optionally, provide a description and a screen tip for the folder.

4. Under Location, click the Select Another Location link to specify a location for the folder that is different from the location listed, or click the Select My Folders link to save the folder in your My Folders directory.

5. Click the Finish button.

Setting Permissions

The Permissions tab specifies the users who can access an entry and to what extent. By default, an entry acquires its access permissions from its parent. For example, a report within a folder inherits the permissions from the folder. To specify permissions different than those inherited from the parent, select the Override the Access Permissions Acquired from the Parent Entry check box and adjust the permissions as desired.

NOTE *Only users with Set Policy permissions on an entry can view or change the permissions.*

Managing Versions

Within the general properties of a report, the number of report output versions can be set. By default, entries are set to keep one version. Setting the number of occurrences for a report to 0 keeps an unlimited number of versions. You can also specify a number of days or months for which to keep versions, instead of setting a specific number.

Authorized users can delete older versions or versions that contain erroneous data. For example, suppose several reports are run before you notice that they contain incorrect data. You can simply delete these reports to prevent any confusion that might occur if individuals within your organization viewed this data.

To delete saved versions of a report, follow these steps:

1. In the Actions column, click the View the Output Versions button.

View the output versions

2. In the Versions pane, select the check box next to any versions you want to delete.

3. Click the Delete link at the bottom of the Versions pane.

4. Click OK to confirm the deletion.

5. Click the Close button to return to Cognos Connection.

Viewing Run History

Each time an entry runs in the background, information such as request time, start time, completion time, and status are tracked. This high-level information is the run history for an entry. The status indicates whether the run succeeded or failed. You can also view the run history details, which contain more detailed information for a specific entry, such as errors or warning messages, as well as actions that you can take. This information is extremely useful if a report does not complete when expected or if the execution of a report fails.

Tip *You can view the request, start, and completion times to calculate the amount of time it took for a report to run.*

The number of items available in the run history can be set within the general properties of an entry. By default, five items are listed in the run history of an entry. Setting the number of occurrences to 0 keeps an unlimited number. You can also specify a number of days or months for which to keep run history entries, instead of setting a specific number.

To view the run history, follow these steps:

1. In the Actions column of the entry, click the More link.
2. Click the View Run History link.

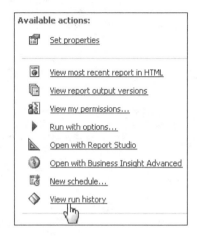

3. View the attributes of the run history.

Request time	Start time	Completion time	Status	Actions
January 16, 2012 4:07:24 PM	January 16, 2012 4:07:24 PM	January 16, 2012 4:07:24 PM	Failed	▶▤
January 16, 2012 11:27:26 AM	January 16, 2012 11:27:26 AM	January 16, 2012 11:27:33 AM	Succeeded	▶▤ ▧
December 12, 2011 8:20:54 PM	December 12, 2011 8:20:54 PM	December 12, 2011 8:20:54 PM	Failed	▶▤
December 12, 2011 8:17:40 PM	December 12, 2011 8:17:40 PM	December 12, 2011 8:17:47 PM	Succeeded	▶▤
December 12, 2011 6:31:07 PM	December 12, 2011 6:31:07 PM	December 12, 2011 6:31:13 PM	Succeeded	▶▤

View Run History details

TIP *From the Status drop-down list in the run history view, select a status to filter the run history entries.*

4. To view more detailed information about a run history entry, click the View Run History Details button in the Actions column.

5. Click Close twice to return to Cognos Connection.

Creating Jobs

A job groups together executable entries in a set, so that they can be executed together, either all at once or sequentially. When a job runs, all entries in the job execute. A job can be scheduled, which can save valuable time because you have one schedule to modify, rather than a schedule for each entry in the job.

For example, suppose you have ten report views that are set to execute every day at 10 A.M. Perhaps they take a lot of time to execute, so you want to change the execute time to 7 P.M., when fewer users are on the system. To do this, you could modify the schedule for each report view separately. However, if you create a job and add the report views to it, you can modify the schedule once.

Job properties include the following:

- **Steps**   This displays a list of steps in the job.
- **Submission of Steps**   This gives you the choice of running the steps all at the same time or in the sequence specified.
- **Defaults for All Steps**   This allows you to set options for all of the steps in the job. Alternatively, you can set different options for each step using the Edit button in the Options and Prompt Values column of the steps.

- **Run History Details Level**   You can choose the level for your job run history details: All or Limited. All saves complete details for the job steps when successful. Limited saves limited details for the job steps when successful. Complete details are saved when a job step fails.

To create a new job, follow these steps:

1. On the toolbar, click the New Job button.

2. In the Name text box, enter a name for the entry.

3. Optionally, provide a description and a screen tip for the job.
4. Under Location, click the Select Another Location link to specify a location for the job that is different from the location listed, or click the Select My Folders link to save the job in your My Folders directory.

5. Click Next to select the steps for the job.

6. Click the Add link to add steps.

7. Under Available Entries, use the breadcrumb trail to navigate to the appropriate location.

8. In the Available Entries pane, select the check boxes of the entries that you want to add to the job.

9. Click the green add arrow to move the entries to the Selected Entries pane.

10. Click OK. The Select the Steps screen displays again, this time with the entries you selected.

11. Under Submission of Steps, select All at Once for the steps to be executed simultaneously, or select In Sequence for the steps to be executed sequentially.

12. Under Defaults for All Steps, set format, language, and delivery options if the same options apply to all steps. Alternatively, set different options for each step using the Edit button in the Options and Prompt Values column of the steps.

13. From the Run History Details Level drop-down list, set the level of detail.

14. Click Next to select how to save and run the job.

15. Select an action from the three choices:

   - The Save and Run Once option saves the job to the specified location and provides options to run the job once.

   - The Save and Schedule option saves the job to the specified location and provides options to set a schedule for the job.

   - The Save Only option saves the job to the specified location only.

16. Click Finish to create the new job.

Creating Pages

Pages allow you to consolidate a variety of content to a centralized location so you can personalize the page, showing only content that relates to one area of business or for which a user or a group of users are responsible. For example, you could create a page displaying reports that the support department accesses on a regular basis. As another example, suppose

Portlet	Description
IBM Cognos Navigator	Access IBM Cognos Connection entries
IBM Cognos Search	Search IBM Cognos Connection entries
IBM Cognos Viewer	View IBM Cognos Content
HTML Viewer	View a web page
RSS Viewer	Insert an RSS feed
Image Viewer	Insert any image to appear on the page

TABLE 5-2 Common Portlets Available within IBM Cognos Connection

your company organizes the sales folders according to year instead of product, and a group of users want to view all the reports for a specific product. You can create a new page with all of the product reports in one location.

Portlets are added to pages to hold the desired content. Portlets allow you to add content and functionality to your page. Table 5-2 shows some of the portlets available in Cognos Connection. For example, you can use an IBM Cognos Navigator portlet to browse folders in one section of your page and an IBM Cognos Viewer portlet to view reports in another, while remaining on the same page.

To create a page, follow these steps:

1. On the toolbar, click the New Page button.

2. In the Name text box, type a name for the new page.

3. Optionally, provide a description and a screen tip for the page.

4. Under Location, click the Select Another Location link to specify a location for the page that is different from the location listed, or click the Select My Folders link to save the page in your My Folders directory.

5. Click Next to set up columns for the page.

6. In the Number of Columns area, select the option for the number of columns to display on the new page.

7. From the Column Width drop-down list, select the width to apply to the column(s).

8. Click the Add link to add portlets to the page column(s).

9. Select the desired portlets from the Available Entries column, and add them to the Selected Entries column.

TIP In the Actions column, click View This Portlet to view what the portlet does and how it will look on the page.

10. Click OK to add the portlets to the column.

11. Repeat steps 8, 9, and 10 to add portlets to any other page columns.

12. Click Next to continue to the screen for setting the page style.

13. Under Title, specify a title for the new page, and choose whether the title is visible.

14. Under Instructions, specify any instructions for the page, and choose whether the instructions are visible.

15. Under Portlet Style, choose to hide the borders of the portlet, hide the title bars of the portlet, and hide the Edit buttons on the title bar by selecting the appropriate check boxes.

16. Click Next to move to the final wizard screen.

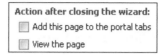

17. Select the Add This Page to the Portal Tabs check box to add the page as a tab in your IBM Cognos Connection account.

18. Select the View the Page check box to see the page after it is created.

19. Click Finish to create the page.

To customize a portlet, follow these steps:

1. Click the page link in Cognos Connection.

2. View the page in Cognos Viewer.

3. Click the Edit button in the portlet title bar.

4. Modify the desired properties, and then click OK.

Customizing IBM Cognos Connection

You can easily customize Cognos Connection to your preferences to help you quickly locate your company's data. All changes that you make take effect immediately. The settings are stored and can be used for future sessions until they are changed again.

Setting Your Home View

By default, the Public Folders tab displays when you log on to Cognos Connection. However, you can set any location in Cognos Connection as your default home view.

To set your home view, navigate to the screen you want to use as your default home page and click Home Options.

Next, click the Set View as Home link. The current location is now set as your default home view.

TIP *To navigate to your home view from anywhere within IBM Cognos Connection, click the Home button.*

Working in My Area

My Area in Cognos Connection is where you manage all of the Cognos Connection properties that are specific to your account. Within My Area, you'll find links to My Inbox, My Watch Items, My Preferences, and My Activities and Schedules. These links enable you to manage tasks, schedules you own, and account preferences.

My Inbox

My Inbox provides an area to manage three types of tasks:

- Approval requests, which are tasks that require approval sent to the inbox of the specified recipients and are created in IBM Cognos Event Studio

- Ad hoc tasks, which are tasks sent to the inbox of the specified recipients and are created from the inbox

- Notification requests, which are notifications about an event sent to the inbox of the specified recipients and can be created in Cognos Event Studio, in the My Inbox area, or from a watch rule

Tasks can be archived to remove unwanted items from your inbox. Tasks are individual items specific to a user, which makes archiving a task apply only to your inbox. Tasks deleted from your archive can still be active, but will no longer be accessible by you.

To view your task inbox, follow these steps:

1. Click My Area, and then select the My Inbox link.

2. Select the Inbox or Archive tab.

3. Apply any desired filters to the list of entries using the Filter drop-down lists along the top of the entries.

The All Types filter has been set to Tasks

4. Click an entry to view the details of the item in the pane at the bottom of the screen.

To create a new inbox task, follow these steps:

1. Click My Area, and then select the My Inbox link.

2. From the New menu, select New Task.

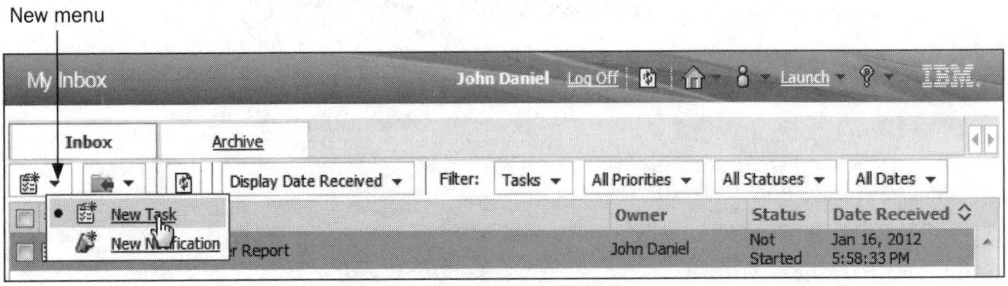

New menu

3. Click the Add/Remove Recipients link, and add the desired recipients.

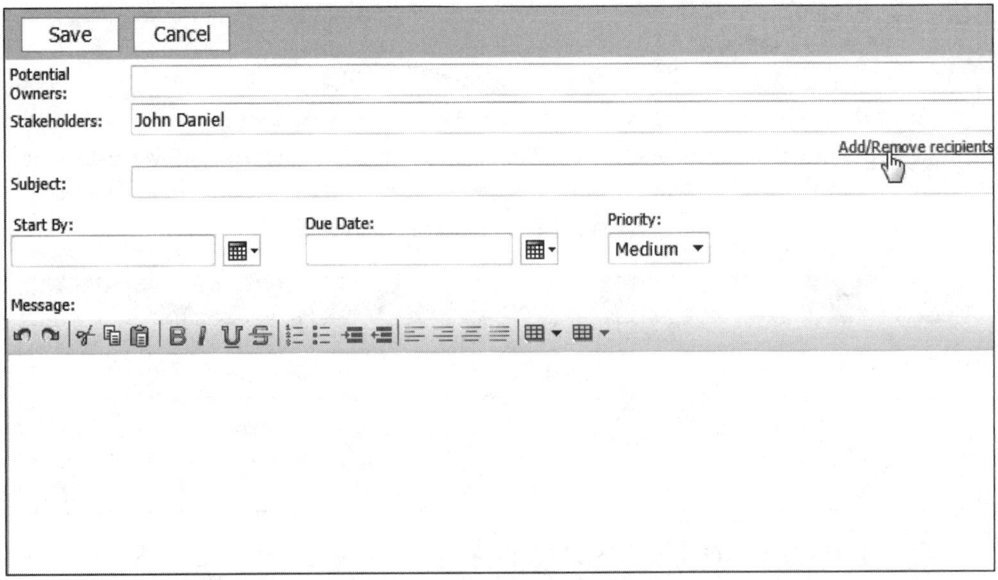

4. Specify a subject for the task in the Subject text box.

5. Optionally, enter the start by and due dates in the corresponding text boxes.

6. Set the priority of the task from the Priority drop-down list.

7. In the Message pane, type the message body for the task.

8. Click the Save button above the recipients.

TIP *Click the Advanced link when setting up the task to specify notification options related to the task.*

To create a new inbox notification, follow these steps:

1. Click My Area, and then select the My Inbox link.
2. From the Task drop-down list, select New Notification.

New menu

3. Click the Add/Remove Recipients link, and add the desired recipients.

4. Specify a subject for the task.
5. In the Message pane, type the message body for the notification.
6. Click the Send button above the recipients.

TIP *Click the Advanced link when setting up the notification to specify options related to acknowledgments of the notification by the recipients.*

My Watch Items

My Watch Items provides you with the ability to oversee information that is important to you. You can create alerts to notify you via e-mail about new report versions. The Alerts tab within your Watch Items shows a list of entries you are subscribed to receiving alerts about. You can create watch rules that use specified conditions to determine whether to deliver a report to you.

When the watch rule is evaluated, the report is delivered if the conditions of the watch rule are met. The Rules tab within your Watch Items displays watch rules you have defined.

My Watch Items	John Daniel Log Off					
Alerts	Rules					

	...> Source	Description	Type
☐	...> Recruitment Report	New versions become available	Email

NOTE *Alerts and enhanced user features must be enabled in the report properties for alerts and watch rules to be available for the report.*

To create an alert, follow these steps:

1. Click the More link in the Actions column of the desired report.
2. Select the Alert Me about New Versions link.

3. Click OK in the message box to create the alert.

To create a watch rule, follow these steps:

1. Open a saved HTML report in Cognos Viewer.
2. Select a value in the report.

	2004		2005		2006		2007	
	Quantity	Revenue	Quantity	Revenue	Quantity	Revenue	Quantity	Revenue
E-mail	1,986,395	$95,402,796.21	968,453	$44,318,886.43	409,049	$23,701,042.57	278,762	$16,420,318.95
Fax	688,786	$28,639,472.14	426,006	$19,896,187.76	249,234	$13,445,559.93	115,988	$8,092,322.18
Mail	488,735	$22,766,850.51	339,635	$16,013,779.49	119,619	$6,905,730.44	5,066	$404,978.53
Sales visit	2,640,065	$101,072,721.10	1,778,941	$79,721,524.37	1,411,468	$73,918,652.38	982,938	$55,481,936.15
Special	340,021	$13,905,918.75	252,429	$10,769,180.34	13,622	$1,006,100.01	30,730	$1,670,121.15
Telephone	3,979,898	$178,793,580.36	2,251,898	$107,160,284.09	684,667	$37,199,842.80	336,381	$17,832,073.81
Web	10,050,830	$473,771,464.65	17,507,323	$881,315,747.68	23,054,131	$1,339,714,172.77	17,846,021	$1,017,434,523.30

3. Click the Watch New Versions link in the Cognos Viewer menu.

4. Select Alert Using New Watch Rule.

5. On the Specify the Rule screen, set the conditions of the rule.

6. Click Next to move to the screen for specifying the alert type.

7. Select the way(s) you want to be notified when the rule condition is met.

8. Click the Edit the Options link(s) to change the defaults of any selected alert types.

9. Click Next to continue to the screen for adding a name and description.

10. Specify a name for the alert.

11. Optionally, provide a description and a screen tip for the watch rule.

12. Under Location, click the Select Another Location link to specify a location for the watch rule other than the My Watch Items area.

13. Click Finish to create the watch rule.

My Preferences

Personalize settings in your Cognos Connection account by modifying your preferences. You can set your preference for the number of entries to display before navigating to another page and the use of grid lines or alternating backgrounds to distinguish between adjacent entries. You can change the look and feel of Cognos Connection by applying a style (Business, Classic, Corporate, Contemporary, Modern, or Presentation). Changes are effective upon submission and remain intact for all future sessions.

To set preferences, follow these steps:

1. Click My Area, and then select the My Preferences link.

2. Select the appropriate tab for the preferences you wish to specify (the tabs are described after these steps).

Set preferences		
General	Personal	Portal Tabs
Specify your settings.		

3. Make the desired modifications and click OK.

The General tab contains preference settings, such as entry formatting, the portal, language, and time zone.

Set preferences   Help ⊗

| **General** | Personal | Portal Tabs |

Specify your settings.

Number of entries in list view: **Report format:**

`15`   `HTML            ▼`

Separators in list view: ☑ Show the Welcome page at startup

`No separator          ▼`

                                            ☑ Show a summary of the run options

Style:

`Corporate    ▼` Preview   ☐ Enable accessibility support for reports I run or schedule

☑ Show hidden entries

Portal

Default view:
- ◉ List
- ◯ Details

Number of columns in details view:

`3 columns  ▼`

Regional options

Product language: **Content language:**
- ◉ Use the default language   - ◉ Use the default language
- ◯ Use the following language: - ◯ Use the following language:

`English            ▼`   `English (United States)          ▼`

Time zone:
- ◉ Use the default time zone
- ◯ Use the following time zone:

`(GMT-05:00) Eastern Time: Ottawa, New York, Toronto, Montreal, Jamaica, Porto Acre    ▼`

`OK`   `Cancel`

The General tab includes the following items:

- **Number of Entries in List View**   This sets the number of items on one page while in list view.
- **Separators in List View**   This offers options for separating entries in list view:

Grid lines:

		Name ◇	Modified ◇	Actions
☐	⚙	Bursted Sales Performance Report	January 17, 2012 12:52:33 PM	🖼 📋 ▶ 📐 🌐 🖽 🖼 More...
☐	📑 ▶	Percentage Calculation (by year)	January 16, 2012 1:55:00 PM	🖼 ▶ 📐 🌐 🖽 🖼 More...
☐	⚙	Recruitment Report	January 17, 2012 3:47:37 PM	🖼 📋 ▶ 📐 🌐 🖽 🖼 More...
☐	📑 ▶	Report View of Recruitment Report	January 17, 2012 3:24:46 PM	🖼 ▶ 🖼 More...

Alternating backgrounds:

		Name ◇	Modified ◇	Actions
☐	⚙	Bursted Sales Performance Report	January 17, 2012 12:52:33 PM	🖼 📋 ▶ 📐 🌐 🖽 🖼 More...
☐	📑 ▶	Percentage Calculation (by year)	January 16, 2012 1:55:00 PM	🖼 ▶ 📐 🌐 🖽 🖼 More...
☐	⚙	Recruitment Report	January 17, 2012 3:47:37 PM	🖼 📋 ▶ 📐 🌐 🖽 🖼 More...
☐	📑 ▶	Report View of Recruitment Report	January 17, 2012 3:24:46 PM	🖼 ▶ 🖼 More...

- **Style**   This sets the template applied to Cognos Connection.
- **Report Format**   This sets your preferred format for reports. This format is applied as the default to new reports you create.
- **Show the Welcome Page at Startup**   Choose whether to display the Welcome page at the start of each session.
- **Show a Summary of the Run Options**   Choose whether to display a summary of the selected run options for reports run in the background.
- **Enable Accessibility Support**   This enables accessibility support by default for reports you run or schedule.
- **Default View**   This provides options for how the Cognos Connection entries are displayed.
- **Product Language**   This sets the language used for your Cognos Connection portal, Cognos Viewer, Cognos Report Studio, and so on.
- **Content Language**   This sets the language used for content such as names, descriptions, and report data.
- **Time Zone**   This sets the time zone used for entries you create and tasks you perform.

The Personal tab includes logon information, groups and roles you are a member of, and capabilities you have within Cognos Connection.

The Portal Tabs tab provides an area to administer the tabs accessible to you in your Cognos Connection portal. From here, you can add, remove, or modify the sequence of tabs.

My Activities and Schedules

My Activities and Schedules provides you with the ability to view your activities as follows:

- Current activities are items that are currently processing.

- Past activities are items that are finished processing.

- Upcoming activities are items that are set to process in the future.

Viewing the schedules shows all of your scheduled entries.

For each option, there is a bar chart divided by status and a list of entries. The entries are listed by name and show properties such as request time, status, and priority. You can filter the entries by a variety of criteria, such as status or type, using the Filter pane. Within the My Activities and Schedules area, you can manage entries by performing activities like setting the priority for current, upcoming, and scheduled entries or re-running failed entries.

To view your activities and schedules, follow these steps:

1. Click My Area, and then select the My Activities and Schedules link.

2. Choose the type of activity or schedules you wish to view from the left-hand pane.

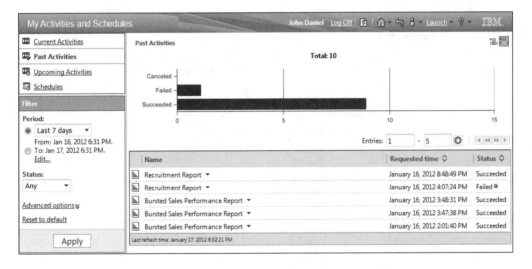

3. Choose any filter options you wish to filter the data on, and then click Apply.

4. View the results in the right-hand pane.

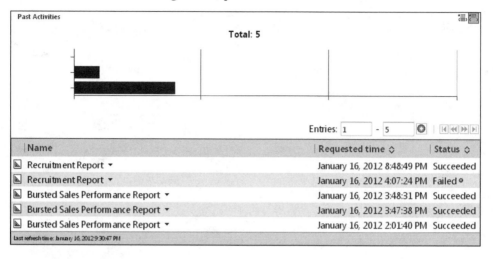

Using IBM Cognos Viewer

IBM Cognos Viewer displays reports run in HTML format. HTML format provides access to all of the interactive content within reports. Table 5-3 describes the features included in Cognos Viewer.

This chapter has touched on the most common ways our customers use Cognos Connection. The time spent investigating how you would like to leverage the many features and functions Cognos Connection is time well spent.

Icon	Name	Description
Keep this version ▼	Keep This Version	Provides options to download or e-mail the report
▶	Run	Runs the report in real time, including any prompt pages that are a part of the report
	Drill Down	When data with the drill-down capability is selected, allows you to drill-down to the children of the selected item
	Drill Up	When data with the drill-up capability is selected, allows you to drill-up to the level of the parent of the selected item
▼	Go To	Allows you to navigate to related links
▼	Format	Lets you choose to view the report in a different format
Add this report ▼	Add This Report	Adds a shortcut to this report to your My Folders or adds the report to your browser favorites
Watch new versions ▼	Watch New Versions	Adds an alert or a watch rule for saved reports or allows you to manage any watch rules associated with the report
Add comments ▼	Add Comments	Lets you add comments to saved reports

TABLE 5-3   IBM Cognos Viewer Features

Microsoft Office Solutions

Whether you need to create a dynamic presentation that incorporates a report containing company sales data, or you just prefer to work in a product that you are more familiar with, IBM Cognos for Microsoft Office and IBM Cognos Analysis for Microsoft Excel may be the tools for you. The IBM Cognos for Microsoft Office add-ins allow you to view Cognos 10 content with Microsoft PowerPoint, Word, and Excel. The IBM Cognos data content within these Microsoft Office documents can be easily updated with current data at the click of a button.

The IBM Cognos Analysis for Microsoft Excel add-in allows you to analyze your Cognos 10 BI content in a flexible spreadsheet application. You can create lists and explorations by applying techniques used in IBM Cognos Report Studio and IBM Cognos Analysis Studio. You also have all of the Excel features and formatting tools available to you for creating your own calculations and working with your data. Once your list or exploration is complete, it can be published to IBM Cognos Connection for user consumption.

In this chapter, you will learn how to use Cognos for Microsoft Office to import Cognos 10 content into an Office application. Cognos Analysis for Microsoft Excel features such as creating list-based reports, creating an exploration, and creating a cell-based analysis will also be discussed in detail.

NOTE *This chapter assumes that the PC you are using has the IBM Cognos for Microsoft Office and IBM Cognos Analysis for Microsoft Excel add-ins installed.*

Getting Started with IBM Cognos for Microsoft Office

How you want to present the content determines which Office application you will use. As an example, let's consider how you could use the same report you created in Cognos Report Studio across all three Office applications.

Suppose that every month you attend a sales meeting with the executives in your organization, and every month they want to know the status of sales. You could print the report you created in Cognos Report Studio and distribute copies to the executives in that sales meeting, providing them with the information that they need, and maybe that was good enough in the past. But now you are on the move, and you want to show them a presentation. It used to be that you needed to create a PowerPoint presentation and laboriously create charts and lists, consuming hours that you did not have. With Cognos for Microsoft Office, you can import the charts and lists quickly and easily, and provide the executives with accurate and timely information.

You don't want to stop with just the presentation, though. You know from past experience that three days after your presentation, one or two of the executives are going to ask follow-up questions that you don't have time to answer. So, you decide to create a handout in Microsoft Word that contains the same data that appeared in your presentation, with brief explanations for each of the charts and lists. You pass these out, and they practically throw the key to the executive washroom at you for your foresight. You have successfully used the same data in two different formats.

But that's not all. You find out an hour before your meeting that the chief financial officer (CFO) is in town and planning to attend the meeting. You know that he likes to see specific financial information, but you do not include this data in your meetings on a regular basis. You don't have time to change your PowerPoint presentation or Word document. Besides, he is a financial person and likes spreadsheets. You create a financial report in Excel and add the calculations that the CFO likes to see, all with time to spare to print copies for everyone. In a few days, you and the CFO will be having a dinner meeting to discuss your career and future advancement.

Will Cognos for Microsoft Office advance your career? That depends on you. It provides the tools that you need to incorporate Cognos 10 content into Microsoft Office documents. The rest is up to you.

There is just one more thing—probably the coolest feature of all. You can reuse the same PowerPoint presentation, Word document, or Excel spreadsheet for a future meeting, because Cognos for Microsoft Office makes that easy, too. Instead of needing to re-create the document or manually entering updated figures, you can refresh your data with the click of the mouse. To help you keep track of your documents, you can publish them to Cognos Connection along with the Cognos 10 content that they reference. You can even store them all in one folder if you like. With Cognos for Microsoft Office, it's easy to create, store, refresh, and reuse a document.

NOTE *Throughout this section, we refer to the IBM Cognos ribbon tab. If you are using a version of Microsoft Office earlier than Office 2007, the tools you need to access can be found in the IBM Cognos toolbar.*

Connecting Microsoft Office to Cognos 10

Before you can begin using the powerful Microsoft Office add-ins, you need to connect your Office products with Cognos 10. The steps for accomplishing this are the same for all three Office products, and you need to take these steps only once. So, you do not need to connect all three Office products individually, and you do not need to do it every time you launch one.

NOTE *The following illustrations feature Microsoft PowerPoint, but the steps are the same for Word and Excel.*

Here's how to connect to Microsoft Office:

1. Launch the desired Office application (PowerPoint in this example). Then click the IBM Cognos ribbon tab, which opens and displays the Cognos 10 add-in components.

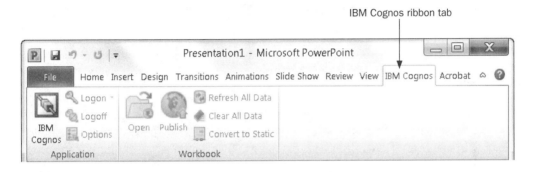

2. Click the IBM Cognos button. PowerPoint displays the IBM Cognos task pane on the right side of the PowerPoint work area.

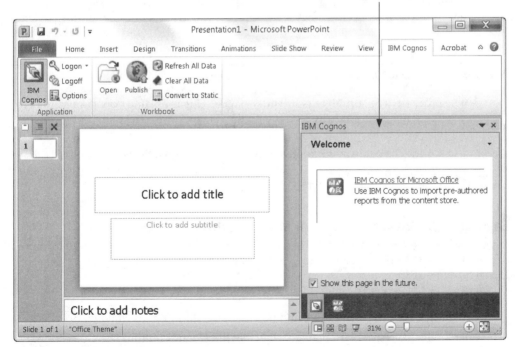

3. From the IBM Cognos ribbon tab, click Options. The Options window displays.

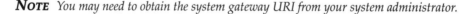

4. The first field to fill in is the System Gateway URI text box in the IBM Cognos Systems area. The system gateway URI is the web address, or URL, required to access the Cognos gateway. In the System Gateway URI text box, enter the gateway location.

NOTE *You may need to obtain the system gateway URI from your system administrator.*

5. The other field to complete is Friendly Name. This is a name you can use to help you to identify the gateway location. In the Friendly Name text box, enter a name for the gateway location.

6. Click Add. The gateway location and the name display in the Systems box.

7. Click OK. Cognos for Microsoft Office is now ready to use existing Cognos 10 content within Microsoft Office.

Logging on to Cognos 10 Through Microsoft Office

If security is applied to the Cognos 10 server, you must be logged on to Cognos 10 to import data into your Microsoft Office documents. You can log on through Cognos 10, or you can log on through Office.

Here's how to log on to Cognos 10 through Office:

1. Launch the Office application, and then click the IBM Cognos ribbon tab.

2. From the IBM Cognos ribbon tab, click the IBM Cognos button. The Office application is activated, and the IBM Cognos task pane is displayed.

3. From the IBM Cognos ribbon tab, click Log On. The Log On dialog displays.

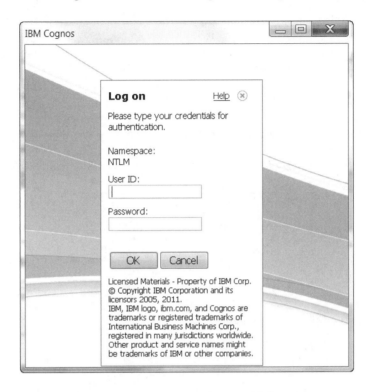

4. If you have more than one authentication provider, from the Namespace list, select a namespace, and then click OK.

5. Enter your IBM Cognos 10 user ID and password in the appropriate text boxes, and then click OK. You are logged on to Cognos 10 and can begin importing Cognos 10 content.

Importing IBM Cognos 10 Content into an Office Application

Importing IBM Cognos 10 content into an Office application is a quick and easy way to use data, charts, and lists. Regardless of the Office application that you use, the steps are the same.

NOTE *The following illustrations feature PowerPoint. The steps are the same for Word and Excel.*

Here's how to import Cognos 10 content into an Office application:

1. Launch the Office application, which opens and displays the IBM Cognos ribbon tab.

2. Click the IBM Cognos ribbon tab, and then click the IBM Cognos button. The IBM Cognos task pane appears.

3. From the IBM Cognos task pane, click the IBM Cognos for Microsoft Office link. Two Cognos content tabs display in the task pane, as shown next. One tab shows the Cognos 10 content residing in Cognos Connection to which you have access. The other tab shows the Cognos content that you have saved locally. Your next steps are dictated by where you select to pull your Cognos 10 content. The more common way is to pull content directly from Cognos 10, so that is covered here.

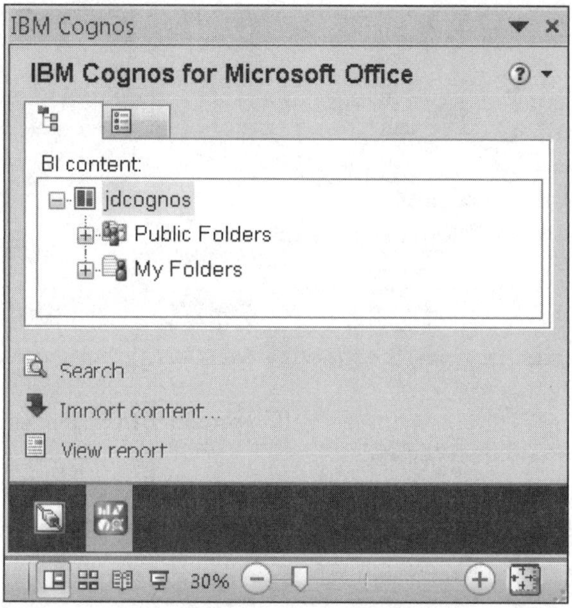

4. From the IBM Cognos for Microsoft Office task pane, click the plus sign to navigate to the Cognos folder in which the content resides, and then select a report to import.

TIP *As an alternative to continuing with step 5, from the IBM Cognos for Microsoft Office task pane, navigate to the content and drag-and-drop the content into your presentation. The report content in its entirety is imported, and you are not presented with the options outlined in steps 5 through 15. If you use this method, skip to step 16.*

5. From the IBM Cognos for Microsoft Office pane, click Import Content. The Import Content screen appears, beginning with the Select Report Properties dialog, with the following settings:

- The Name text box contains the name of the content to be imported.

- The Report Pages area gives you the option of distributing content with multiple pages over multiple slides or having all of the content imported on a single slide.

- The Report Version area gives you the option of running the content prior to importing to have the most current data or importing a version of the content that you have saved.

Import Content

Select Report Properties
Select Version Parameters
Select Report Elements
Page1
    Header
        Image
        FirstPage_ReportTitle2121
        FirstPage_Subtitle1121
    Body
        Combination Chart - survey top
        Text
        Text
        Text
        Combination Chart - survey sc
        Text
        Crosstab1
    Footer
        RunDate1
        Text
        PageNumber
        RunTime1
Finish

Select Report Properties

Set the report properties you want to use during this import.

Name:

Employee Satisfaction 2006

Report pages

◉ Ignore paging

○ Create new slides for report pages

    Insert slides after:

    Slide 1 ▼

    ☐ Respect soft page breaks

Report version

◉ Run the report

○ Select a specific output version

    Version:

    ▼

Cancel   < Back   Next >   Finish

NOTE *The options that appear on the Import Content screen differ slightly for PowerPoint, Word, and Excel, but the concepts are the same across all three products.*

6. From the Report Pages area, select Ignore Paging or Create New Slides for Report Pages. If you select the Create New Slides for Report Pages option, the Insert Slides After drop-down list becomes active, and PowerPoint inserts the slide after the slide you choose from the list.

7. From the Report Version area, select Run the Report or Select a Specific Output Version. If you select the Select a Specific Output Version option, the Version drop-down list becomes active, and PowerPoint imports the version of the content that you choose from the list.

8. Click Next. The Select Report Elements dialog of the Import Content screen displays with a list of the selected content's elements. You can select to import some or all of the elements contained within the content.

9. Clear the check boxes of the elements that you do not want to import. For this example, choose to import only one chart and leave out the header and footer by clearing the Header and Footer check boxes.

10. Click Next. Your next steps depend on the elements that you chose to import. Cognos for Microsoft Office displays a dialog where you define how the selected elements are imported. To continue with the example from step 9, the following illustrations and discussion focus on the steps for importing a chart. In our example, the Chart dialog of the Import Content screen displays with a Name text box, Location list box, and Add New Slide option.

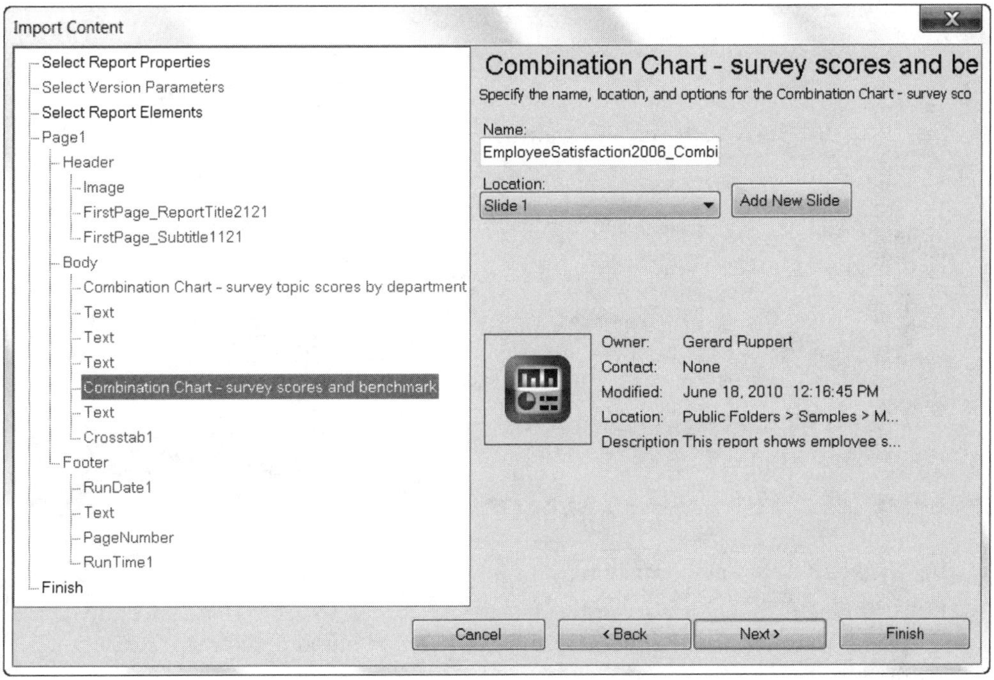

11. Optionally, in the Name text box, enter a new name for the chart to be imported. By default, the chart names are based on the elements of the content.

12. From the Location list, select the slide for which you want the chart to be imported.

13. Optionally, click Add New Slide to import the chart into a new slide.

14. Click Next. In our example, the Finish dialog of the Import Content screen displays. Click Finish to import the chart report object.

15. Once the chart has been imported, you can move and resize the objects, and add a title to enhance the look of the slide.

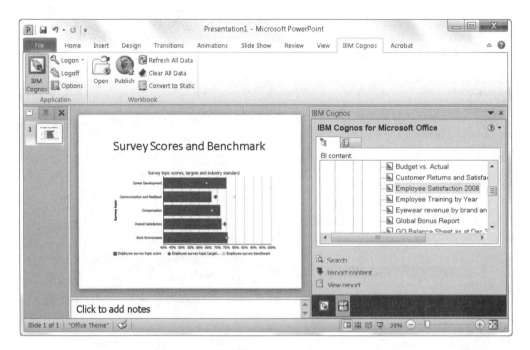

16. To import additional content repeat steps 4 through 15, and then move on to step 17.

17. Save the document in the appropriate format for the Office application that you are using. Your Cognos 10 content is now ready to be shared with others in your organization.

NOTE *If you plan to use this document from month to month, you do not need to re-create it every month. With IBM Cognos for Microsoft Office, you can refresh the data within the document. For more information, refer to the "Refreshing Cognos 10 Content in Microsoft Office" section later in this chapter.*

Using IBM Cognos Analysis for Microsoft Excel

Cognos Analysis for Microsoft Excel allows you to analyze your BI in a familiar spreadsheet application. You can create lists using relationally modeled data, explorations using dimensionally modeled data, or cubes for cell-based analysis from your Cognos 10 installation. In list mode, you can create simple or complex list-style spreadsheets by employing the same drag-and-drop techniques used in Cognos Report Studio. When in list mode, you have the ability to open your spreadsheet in Cognos Report Studio or Cognos Business Insight Advanced. An *exploration* provides a crosstab and tools similar to those used in Cognos Analysis Studio, but it also somewhat restricts the way in which you can create an analysis. A *cell-based analysis* requires that you have a little more knowledge of your data, but it lets you create a more customized analysis.

Accessing IBM Cognos Analysis for Microsoft Excel

Whether you want to use Cognos Analysis for Microsoft Excel to create a list, exploration, or a cell-based analysis, the steps for accessing it are the same.

Here's how to access Cognos Analysis for Microsoft Excel:

1. Launch Excel, which displays the IBM Cognos ribbon tab.

2. From the IBM Cognos ribbon tab, click IBM Cognos. Excel activates the toolbar and displays the IBM Cognos task pane.

3. From the IBM Cognos task pane, click IBM Cognos Analysis. The IBM Cognos
   Analysis task pane displays.

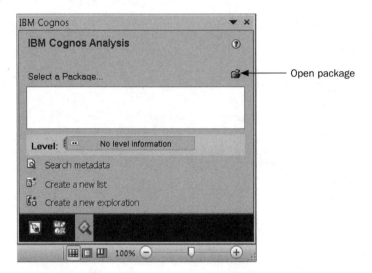

4. From the IBM Cognos Analysis task pane, click the Open Package button. The Select
   Package dialog displays with options for folders in which to retrieve the package. You
   can choose a package from Public Folders, My Folders, or Recently Used packages.

5. Navigate to the folder containing the package that you would like to explore in
   Excel. Select the package, and then click OK.

NOTE *You can select a relationally modeled data source, dimensionally modeled relational data source, or OLAP cube to use IBM Cognos Analysis.*

The source tree for the selected package displays in the IBM Cognos Analysis task pane. The look of the source tree differs based on the type of package selected, as shown next. The source tree of relationally modeled packages is organized using namespaces, query subjects, query items, and measure items. The source tree for dimensionally modeled relational (DMR) and OLAP cube packages is organized using dimensions, hierarchies, levels, and measures.

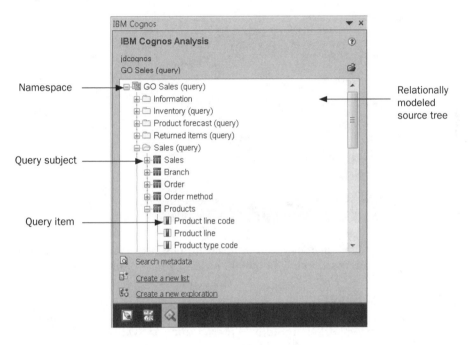

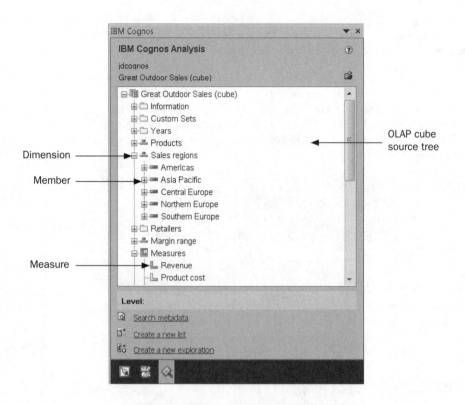

Your next steps depend on whether you want to create a list, exploration, or cell-based analysis. These tasks are discussed in the following sections.

Creating a List-Based Report

A list lets you create a spreadsheet that contains data displayed in tabular format, similar to list reports created using Cognos Report Studio. When creating a new list report in Excel, you have the ability to group data, add filters, and add calculations using options from the IBM Cognos list toolbar. Along with these additional Cognos features, you have all the Excel tools available to you for enhancing the look and feel of your list. Once your list is created, you can publish it to Cognos Connection to make it available to end users.

Creating a New List

To create a new list, group and filter data, and add calculations, follow these steps:

1. Access Cognos Analysis for Microsoft Excel.

2. From the IBM Cognos Analysis task pane, select a package to work with. For this example, select the GO Sales (query) package from the Cognos samples. This displays the GO Sales (query) source tree in the task pane.

3. Click the Create a New List link in the IBM Sales (query). Cognos Analysis creates a new worksheet and displays the list toolbar, overview area, and work area. The overview area shows a list of items that have been added to the exploration and the functions that have been applied. The work area contains a list where you can drag-and-drop items from the source tree to create the list.

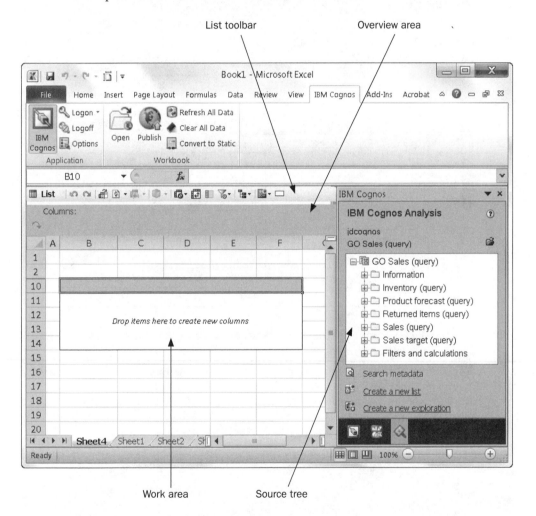

4. Add query item(s) to the list from the source tree by dragging-and-dropping query items onto the list. For this example, add Product Line, Product Type, and Revenue from the Sales (query) folder in the source tree.

5. To group data, from the overview area, click the drop-down list next to the Product Line data item object, and select the Group/UnGroup option. The list is grouped on the product line.

	A	B	C	D
		Product line ▾ **Product type** ▾ **Revenue** ▾		
1				
2				
10		Product line	Product type	Revenue
11		Camping Equipment	Cooking Gear	$272,835,984.18
12			Lanterns	$126,925,660.64
13			Packs	$351,880,402.84
14			Sleeping Bags	$309,172,888.35
15			Tents	$528,221,728.02
16		Golf Equipment	Golf Accessories	$51,514,343.88
17			Irons	$254,814,337.99
18			Putters	$106,184,271.37
19			Woods	$313,898,414.65

6. To filter data, from the list toolbar, click the Filter drop-down and select Edit/Add Filter. The Filter Line dialog is displayed.

7. Expand the GO Sales (query) source tree from the Filter Line dialog. Navigate to the query item that you would like to filter on. For this example, choose Product Line as the item, set the operator to = (Equal), and type **Camping Equipment** as the value. Click OK to add the filter.

Filter Line ✕

Enter your filter criteria

Filter

Product line | = (Equal) ▾ | Camping Equipment

GO Sales (query)

- Products
  - Product line code
  - Product line
  - Product type code

OK   Cancel

8. The filter line is added to the Filter dialog. You have the option to add other filter lines, or you can click OK to apply the filter to the list. In this example, click OK.

▽ Filter	×
Create a filter to limit the number of items in a selected set. Group filters to create custom conditions (AND or OR).	

Filter
⤶ Product line = (Equal) "Camping Equipment"

OK	Cancel

9. The filter is applied to the list. It now shows only the Camping Equipment product line items.

Columns:
| Product line ▼ | Product type ▼ | Revenue ▼ |

	A	B	C	D
1				
2				
10		Product line	Product type	Revenue
11		Camping Equipment	Cooking Gear	$272,835,984.18
12			Lanterns	$126,925,660.64
13			Packs	$351,880,402.84
14			Sleeping Bags	$309,172,888.35
15			Tents	$528,221,728.02

10. To add a calculation, add the Planned Revenue query item to the list, placing it next to Revenue. Next, click the Revenue title and CTRL-click Planned Revenue to select both columns.

11. From the toolbar, click the Insert Calculation drop-down menu and choose %Of(Revenue, Planned revenue). The %Of(Revenue, Planned revenue) calculation is added to the list.

	Columns:				
Product line ▾	Product type ▾	Revenue ▾	Planned revenue ▾	%Of(Revenue , Planned revenue) ▾	

	A	B	C	D	E	F
1						
2						
10		Product line	Product type	Revenue	Planned revenue	%Of(Revenue , Planned revenue)
11		Camping Equipment	Lanterns	$126,925,660.64	$135,242,686.10	94%
12			Cooking Gear	$272,835,984.18	$302,058,230.59	90%
13			Tents	$528,221,728.02	$557,274,647.00	95%
14			Sleeping Bags	$309,172,888.35	$333,438,429.70	93%
15			Packs	$351,880,402.84	$375,110,672.20	94%

Previewing with No Data

When dealing with large sets of data, the refresh time is increased every time you drag a new detailed query item into the list. The Preview with No Data feature allows you to create your detailed list without displaying the data until you have completed the list.

To use the Preview with No Data feature, follow these steps:

1. Click the Create a New List option in the IBM Cognos Analysis task pane.

2. Once the list is added to the work area, click the Run with All Data drop-down list on the toolbar and select the Preview with No Data option. You will notice that the toolbar icon changes from the refresh icon to a blue run arrow.

3. Add several detailed query items to the list. For this example, add Product Line, Product Type, Product, and Quantity to the list. You will see that the list displays only the query item name within the cells of each column.

▦ List				Run with All Data				
Columns:				Preview with No Data				
Product line ▾	Pr ✓						ty ▾	

	A	B	C	D	E
1					
2					
10		Product line	Product type	Product	Quantity
11		<Product line>	<Product type>	<Product>	<#1234#>
12		<Product line>	<Product type>	<Product>	<#1234#>
13		<Product line>	<Product type>	<Product>	<#1234#>
14		<Product line>	<Product type>	<Product>	<#1234#>
15		<Product line>	<Product type>	<Product>	<#1234#>

4. To view the data, select the Run with All Data option from the Run with All Data drop-down list on the toolbar.

Creating an Exploration

An exploration lets you create an analysis in Excel where you are able to interact with data in a way similar to how you interact with data in Cognos Analysis Studio. You can drill-through data, suppress zeros, and nest items. You can perform these functions with data that is pulled directly from Cognos 10. You can also convert this data in Excel formulas, which lets you use the tools available in that application. All these features make creating an exploration a great way to develop financial views of your data.

To create an exploration, follow these steps:

1. Access Cognos Analysis for Microsoft Excel.

2. From the IBM Cognos Analysis task pane, click the Open Package button and select a DMR or an OLAP cube package. For this example, select the Sales and Marketing (cube) package from the Cognos samples.

3. Click the Create a New Exploration option in the IBM Cognos Analysis task pane. Cognos Analysis creates a new worksheet, adds a crosstab object to the work area, and displays the exploration toolbar. The crosstab has a Measure section, Columns section, and Rows section, in which you can drag-and-drop items from the source tree.

NOTE *The toolbar and overview area for an exploration are slightly different than those for a list.*

4. Add a measure to the Measure section from the source tree. Cognos Analysis adds the selected measure to the crosstab, and creates a subtotal column and row for the selected items added to the crosstab. For this example, add Time to the Columns section, Products to the Rows section, and Revenue to the Measure section. As you add items to crosstab, lists are added to the overview area, and you can use these lists to drill-through data and apply filters. Your next steps depend on what you

want to do with your data. The following steps highlight some common ways to work with your data.

	Rows: Products ▾	Columns: Time ▾	Context:			
	A	B	C	D	E	F	G
1							
2							
13		Revenue	2004	2005	2006	2007	Time
14		Camping Equipment	332,986,338.06	402,757,573.17	500,382,422.83	352,910,329.97	1,589,036,664.03
15		Golf Equipment	153,553,850.98	168,006,427.07	230,110,270.55	174,740,819.29	726,411,367.89
16		Outdoor Protection	36,165,521.07	25,008,574.08	10,349,175.84	4,471,025.26	75,994,296.25
17		Personal Accessories	391,647,093.61	456,323,355.90	594,009,408.42	443,693,449.85	1,885,673,307.78
18		Mountaineering Equipment		107,099,659.94	161,039,823.26	141,520,649.70	409,660,132.90
19		**Products**	914,352,803.72	1,159,195,590.16	1,495,891,100.90	1,117,336,274.07	4,686,775,768.85

5. Optionally, drill-through your data to see what is above or below a selected item. Double-click a cell at the top of a column, far left of a row, or at the intersection of a column and row to drill-down. Double-click a subtotal to drill-up.

NOTE *As an alternative, you can use the lists from the overview area to drill-down or drill-up.*

6. To nest an item, select an item from the source tree and drag that item in the work area. Cognos Analysis nests the item in the crosstab. For this example, drill-through Camping Equipment and Cooking Gear to get to the TrailChef Water Bag, and nest the heading "Order method." The results show which sales method generated what revenue for all TrailChef Water Bags that were ordered from 2004 through 2007.

	Rows: Products ▾ Order method	Columns: Time ▾		Context:			
	A	B	C	D	E	F	G	H
1								
2								
13		Revenue		2004	2005	2006	2007	Time
14			Telephone	1,146,240.90	771,239.87	264,678.90	140,644.77	2,322,804.44
15			Sales visit	1,079,374.90	671,631.17	581,665.94	397,871.96	2,730,543.97
16			Web	1,841,524.13	3,883,722.37	5,904,022.84	4,310,295.52	15,939,564.86
17		TrailChef Water Bag	Special	111,085.54	158,680.01		25,603.40	295,368.95
18			Mail	158,511.60	87,595.28	33,594.75		279,701.63
19			E-mail	464,664.68	290,066.06	105,107.79	81,529.43	941,367.96
20			Fax	291,292.82	162,959.50	77,933.88	15,603.45	547,789.65
21			Order method	5,092,694.57	6,025,894.26	6,967,004.10	4,971,548.53	23,057,141.46

7. To swap the positioning of your rows and columns, from the exploration toolbar, click Swap Rows and Columns. Cognos Analysis swaps your rows and columns.

8. You also have the option of converting your Cognos 10 data to Excel formulas. From the exploration toolbar, click Convert to Formulas. By default, the data in your crosstab is pulled from Cognos 10. Cognos Analysis breaks the link between your exploration and Cognos 10 and converts the data in your crosstab to formulas to which you can apply standard Excel formatting.

> **NOTE** *If you choose Convert to Formulas, you will no longer be able to drag-and-drop items from the source tree for this particular exploration.*

9. To create a filter, drag-and-drop an item from the source tree into the Context section of the overview area. For example, you can drag-and-drop the name of a specific country (such as the United States) into the Context section, and the crosstab displays only the items that were sold in that country.

10. Optionally, you can remove empty cells that do not contain data, which is called *suppression*. To suppress zeros, on the exploration toolbar, click the Zero Suppression icon on the toolbar. You are presented with suppression options. From the suppression list, choose one of the following: No Suppression, Suppress Rows Only, Suppress Columns Only, or Supress Rows and Columns.

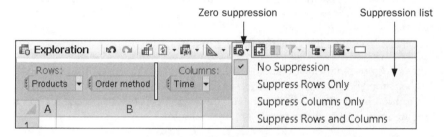

Also, a suppression icon appears in the overview region for the appropriate tag.

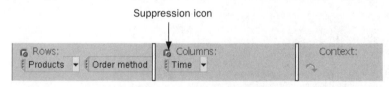

11. You can open your exploration in Cognos Analysis Studio, Report Studio, or Business Insight Advanced, or publish it to Cognos Connection from the exploration toolbar. From the toolbar, click the Open Report in Analysis Studio button, or choose one of the other options from the drop-down list. Cognos 10 prompts you to log on and launches the studio, provided you have access to the selected studio. You can use all of the tools available in the selected studio to work with your data.

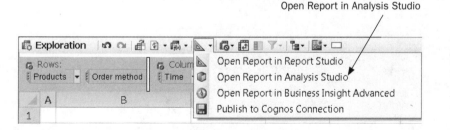

12. From the Excel toolbar, click Save. Excel saves the exploration. You can publish the exploration to Cognos 10. For more information about publishing to Cognos 10, refer to the "Publishing Microsoft Office Documents in Cognos 10" section later in this chapter.

13. Optionally, from the exploration toolbar, click Reset to Blank Exploration to clear your work area and start over.

Creating a Cell-Based Analysis

Like an exploration analysis, a cell-based analysis lets you interact with your data from Cognos 10. However, a cell-based analysis allows you to use specific items from the source tree to build a highly customized analysis without the use of a list or crosstab. You can drill-through your data and use all the tools available in Excel, or you can compare two data sources side by side in the same worksheet. Once you create your cell-based analysis, you can convert it to an exploration.

To create a cell-based analysis, follow these steps:

1. Access Cognos Analysis for Microsoft Excel (see the "Accessing IBM Cognos Analysis for Microsoft Excel" section earlier in this chapter). The Cognos 10 toolbar and work area display, as shown next. The work area provides space for you to drag items from the source tree to create your analysis.

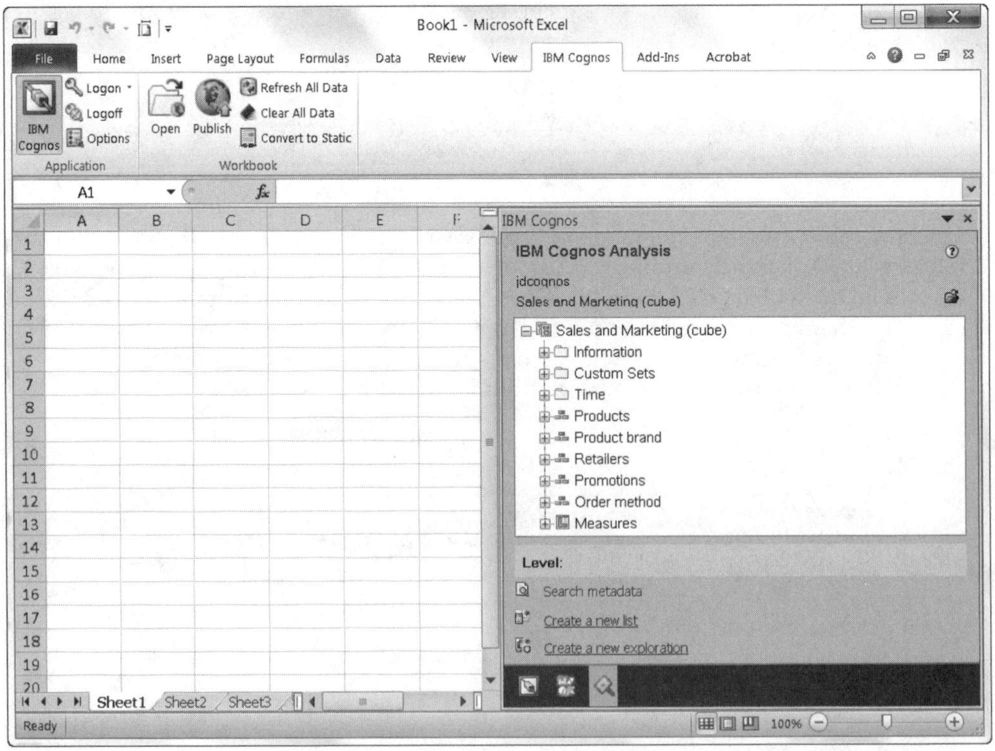

2. Add items for the column(s) from the source tree. Drag your selections to the work area, and then press and hold down the CTRL key as you drag your selections into place. Pressing CTRL while dragging selections over the work area flips selections from rows to columns. Cognos Analysis adds the item(s) as column(s) in your analysis.

TIP *To select noncontiguous items, press and hold down the* CTRL *key while selecting items from the source tree.*

3. Add item(s) for the row(s) from the source tree. Make selections from the source tree, and then drag your selections to the work area. Cognos Analysis adds the item as a row in your analysis.

4. Add a measure from the source tree by dragging an item to the intersection cell directly to the left of your column header and directly above your rows. Cognos Analysis processes the data from Cognos 10 and displays your analysis, as shown next.

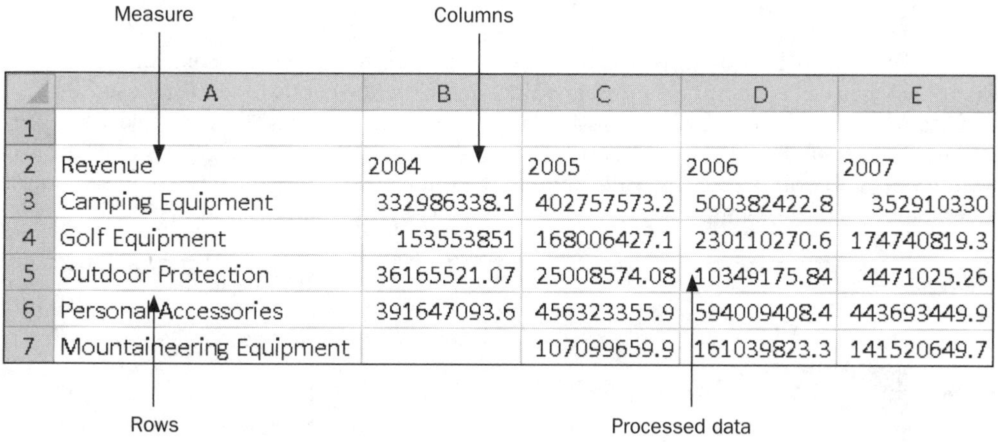

Measure   Columns

	A	B	C	D	E
1					
2	Revenue	2004	2005	2006	2007
3	Camping Equipment	332986338.1	402757573.2	500382422.8	352910330
4	Golf Equipment	153553851	168006427.1	230110270.6	174740819.3
5	Outdoor Protection	36165521.07	25008574.08	10349175.84	4471025.26
6	Personal Accessories	391647093.6	456323355.9	594009408.4	443693449.9
7	Mountaineering Equipment		107099659.9	161039823.3	141520649.7

Rows   Processed data

5. From the Excel toolbar, click Save. Excel saves the analysis. You can publish the analysis to Cognos 10. For more information about publishing to Cognos 10, refer to the "Publishing Microsoft Office Documents in Cognos 10" section later in this chapter.

Expanding and Drilling Through Items

Optionally, you can expand an item to show the components of that item. You can expand an item left, right, up, or down.

Right-click the cell containing the item to be expanded. In the context menu that appears, choose IBM Cognos Analysis Expand. An expand submenu displays. Cognos Analysis inserts the components of the item based on your selection:

- Expand Left inserts the components to the left of the selected item.
- Expand Right inserts the components to the right of the selected item.

- Expand Up inserts the components above the selected item.
- Expand Down inserts the components below the selected item.

The following example shows the results of expanding the Camping Equipment item down.

	A	B	C	D	E
1					
2	Revenue	2004	2005	2006	2007
3	Camping Equipment	332986338.1	402757573.2	500382422.8	352910330
4	Cooking Gear	59761536.5	70843132.06	83917515.27	58313800.35
5	Lanterns	28662904.19	29788923.06	40439357.85	28034475.54
6	Packs	70296289.17	87416758.37	111009558.3	83157796.99
7	Sleeping Bags	65239462.96	77038477.82	98164939.4	68730008.17
8	Tents	109026145.2	137670281.9	166851052	114674248.9

You can also drill-through your data to see what is above or below a selected item. Right-click in a cell containing a number value, and from the context menu, choose IBM Cognos Analysis | Drill. A Drill dialog displays with the detailed data that lies below the item in the selected cell. For example, if you had an analysis with Camping Equipment and 2004 for the year, and you selected to drill-down in the intersecting cell of the two, you would see all of the items under Camping Equipment broken down by quarter, as shown next.

Drill					✕
	Q1 2004	Q2 2004	Q3 2004	Q4 2004	2004
Cooking Gear	$15,273,316.53	$14,787,317.40	$15,039,292.63	$14,661,609.94	$59,761,536.50
Lanterns	$7,043,392.50	$7,166,095.33	$7,420,523.00	$7,032,893.36	$28,662,904.19
Packs	$17,435,846.35	$17,090,027.39	$18,196,405.56	$17,574,009.87	$70,296,289.17
Sleeping Bags	$15,774,778.34	$15,340,855.89	$18,186,089.68	$15,937,739.05	$65,239,462.96
Tents	$26,401,845.50	$25,662,565.81	$29,351,223.12	$27,610,510.81	$109,026,145.24
Camping Equipment	$81,929,179.22	$80,046,861.82	$88,193,533.99	$82,816,763.03	$332,986,338.06

| | | | | | OK |

Comparing Data from Different Data Sources

Another option is to open a new data source to compare data from different data sources on the same analysis. To make such a comparison, follow these steps:

1. From the IBM Cognos Analysis task pane, click Select a Package. The Select Package dialog displays.

2. Navigate to the folder containing the package that holds the data you would like to analyze in Excel.

3. Click OK. The data source replaces the former source tree with one for the selected data source.

4. Drag items in the same way that you did for steps 2 through 4 when creating a cell-based analysis. Cognos Analysis creates the analysis in the same worksheet, using two different data sources.

5. Optionally, insert Excel formulas to compare the data from the two analyses.

6. From the Excel toolbar, click Save to save the analysis.

Viewing an Analysis as an Exploration

To view an analysis as an exploration, right-click in the cell containing the information for which you would like to create the exploration, and then choose IBM Cognos Analysis | Explore. Cognos Analysis creates an exploration in a new Excel worksheet. In the following example, we selected the Camping Equipment and 2004 intersection.

	A	B	C	D	E	F	G
11		Revenue	2004 Q 1	2004 Q 2	2004 Q 3	2004 Q 4	**2004**
12		Cooking Gear	15,273,316.53	14,787,317.40	15,039,292.63	14,661,609.94	*59,761,536.50*
13		Lanterns	7,043,392.50	7,166,095.33	7,420,523.00	7,032,893.36	*28,662,904.19*
14		Packs	17,435,846.35	17,090,027.39	18,196,405.56	17,574,009.87	*70,296,289.17*
15		Sleeping Bags	15,774,778.34	15,340,855.89	18,186,089.68	15,937,739.05	*65,239,462.96*
16		Tents	26,401,845.50	25,662,565.81	29,351,223.12	27,610,510.81	*109,026,145.24*
17		**Camping Equipment**	*81,929,179.22*	*80,046,861.82*	*88,193,533.99*	*82,816,763.03*	*332,986,338.06*

Rows: Camping Equipment   Columns: 2004   Context:

From here, you can work with the data as needed. For more information about explorations, refer to the "Creating an Exploration" section earlier in this chapter. The original analysis is still available from the worksheet on which it was created.

Publishing Microsoft Office Documents in Cognos 10

When you publish Office documents in Cognos 10, you are actually exporting your files. This allows you to share Office documents through Cognos Connection in either Public Folders or My Folders. For example, suppose you create a presentation for a monthly sales meeting with your colleagues and supervisors, and your supervisor wants to use that same presentation for a monthly meeting with the board. Rather than e-mailing him the presentation every month, you can publish it to Cognos Connection, and he will know where to find it.

Here's how to publish Microsoft Office documents in Cognos 10:

1. Launch the Office application for the type of document that you want to export to Cognos 10.

2. Open a saved exploration to be exported.

3. From the IBM Cognos ribbon tab, click Publish. The Publish screen displays with the name of the document in the Name text box.

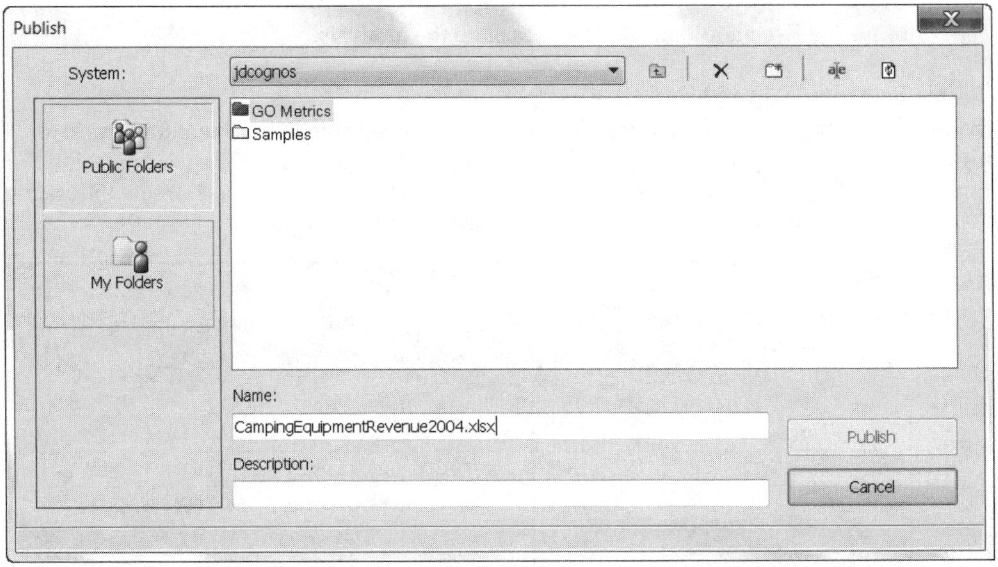

4. Navigate to the location in which you would like to save the Office document.

5. Optionally, in the Name text box, change the name of the document.

NOTE *If you change the name of the document, be sure that you include the period and file extension in the new name. For example, if you change the name of the document from Top Ten Sales Reps in Word.doc to Top Ten.doc, be sure to include the .doc file extension.*

6. Optionally, in the Description text box, enter a description for the document.

7. Click Publish. The document is exported to the selected location in Cognos Connection, as shown next. Other Cognos 10 users with access to the folder in which you saved the document and with the appropriate Office application

installed on their computer can now access the document through Cognos Connection.

Refreshing Cognos 10 Content in Microsoft Office

You have successfully imported all the Cognos 10 data that you need for your Office documents, or you have created a financial exploration using Cognos Analysis for Microsoft Excel for this month. Now, the next month comes and goes, and it is time for you to give your presentation or share your analysis. Cognos Analysis for Microsoft Excel makes refreshing that data simple and easy. As with the other functions mentioned throughout this chapter, the steps to refresh your Cognos 10 content are the same for all three applications.

Here's how to refresh Cognos 10 content in Microsoft Office:

1. Launch the Office application in which you want to refresh your Cognos 10 content. The Cognos 10 toolbar displays.

2. Open the Office document.

3. From the IBM Cognos ribbon tab, click IBM Cognos. The Office application activates the toolbar and displays the IBM Cognos task pane.

4. From the IBM Cognos ribbon tab, click Refresh All Data. Data in your document is updated to reflect your current Cognos 10 content. Your Office document is ready to be shared in less than a minute.

5. Save the document in the appropriate format for the Office application that you are using.

Your Presentation

Now that you have the tools to quickly add Cognos 10 content to the Office application of choice, the quality of your presentations will be enhanced. You will now have the ability to reuse presentations and update content at the click of a button. Now that you are spending less time creating presentations, you can read the rest of this book to enhance your Cognos 10 skills. Can you say "job security"?

IBM Cognos Business Insight

Today's executives, decision makers, and business users require a faster, more efficient way to view, analyze, and act upon key performance indicators needed to make decisions critical to the success of corporate strategies. IBM Cognos Business Insight introduces new functions within a platform that enables easy access to this critical information. It is a web-based, ad hoc tool that gives users the ability to easily create simple or complex dashboards (workspaces) to facilitate the decision-making process and provide users with a competitive edge by bringing this information into a single view for analysis.

In this chapter, you will learn how to use Cognos Business Insight to compile existing lists, crosstabs, and charts from IBM Cognos BI content into a cohesive and interactive dashboard that you can share with other business users. While learning how to create these workspaces, you will become familiar with the application bar, Content pane, content widgets, widget toolbars, and other features within Cognos Business Insight.

Getting Started with IBM Cognos Business Insight

You access Cognos Business Insight from IBM Cognos Connection. Cognos Business Insight opens in a separate web browser window, leaving your Cognos Connection window intact. From there, you can work with the Cognos Business Insight components to create workspaces.

Opening IBM Cognos Business Insight

To open Cognos Business Insight, follow these steps:

1. Log on to Cognos Connection, and navigate to the Public Folders tab.

2. From the Launch menu located in the upper right of the screen, select Business Insight. Cognos Business Insight launches and, by default, the Getting Started page displays.

3. Select which type of workspace you want to work with:

   • The Create New option opens a blank workspace to build on.

   • The Open Existing option allows you to select an already-created workspace from the Cognos BI environment.

   • From Favorites, you can select an existing workspace that has been saved as a favorite.

4. The selected workspace opens within Cognos Business Insight.

TIP *A shortcut to create a new Cognos Business Insight workspace is to click the New Workspace button on the Cognos Connection toolbar.*

From the Getting Started page, you can also access informational videos that provide directions and tips on how to customize your workspace and set your preferences. Please refer to the "Setting Preferences" section later in this chapter for directions on disabling the Getting Started page.

Using the Cognos Business Insight User Interface

The user interface for Cognos Business Insight is made up of several different components, as shown here.

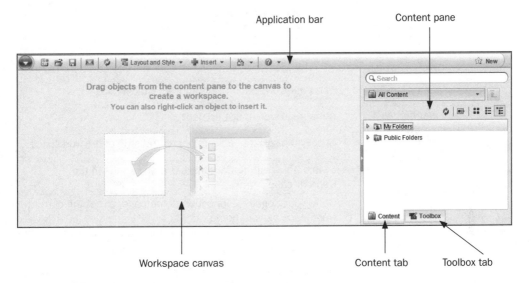

The workspace canvas is the area you will use to compile various objects from the Content and Toolbox tabs, such as tables, charts, images and filters, into a dashboard. The following sections describe the other components of the Cognos Business Insight interface.

Application Bar

The application bar provides quick access to commonly used features. Hovering the pointer over a button on the application bar will provide a tooltip with a short description of the button's function. Some of the functions available from the application bar are listed in Table 7-1.

The Cognos Business Insight Actions menu, available from the application bar, offers the options listed in Table 7-2.

Content Pane

The Content pane displays all of the objects from Cognos Connection that are available for addition to a workspace. Objects inserted into the workspace canvas from the Content pane are displayed in widgets.

From the Content pane, you can add content such as reports, report segments, IBM Cognos PowerPlay Studio reports, URLs, folders, prompt controls, metric lists, individual

Icon	Name	Description
	Actions menu	Access general Cognos Business Insight actions (see Table 7-2)
	New	Create a new workspace
	Open	Open an existing workspace
	Save	Save this workspace
	Email Link	Send the workspace URL to others via e-mail
	Refresh All	Refresh all workspace content
Layout and Style ▾	Layout and Style	Specify the layout of objects or edit the style of the workspace
Insert ▾	Insert	Switch between the Content and Toolbox tabs in the Content pane
	Home	Go to your Cognos Connection home page, or set the current workspace as your home
	Help	Access online help, how-to videos, and other reference information
	Favorites	Tag this workspace as a favorite

TABLE 7-1   IBM Cognos Business Insight Application Bar

Icon	Name	Description
	New	Create a new workspace
	Open	Open an existing workspace
	Save	Save this workspace
	Save As	Save this workspace with an alternate name or in a new location
	E-mail Link	Send the workspace URL to others via e-mail
	Copy Link to Clipboard	Copy the workspace URL to the clipboard, so that you can paste it elsewhere
	Edit Workspace Style	Modify the appearance of the workspace
	My Preferences	Set personal preferences for properties such as language, time zone, whether to display the Getting Started page, and the position of the Content pane
	Log Off	Log off to end your Cognos session (closes the Cognos Business Insight window and logs you off from Cognos Connection)
	Launch	Start IBM Cognos applications
	Refresh All	Refresh all workspace content
	Exit	Exit from Cognos Business Insight

TABLE 7-2   IBM Cognos Business Insight Actions Menu

metrics, IBM Cognos TM1 Websheets and cube views, IBM Cognos Real-time Monitoring objects and filters. Use the Search box to search within the content.

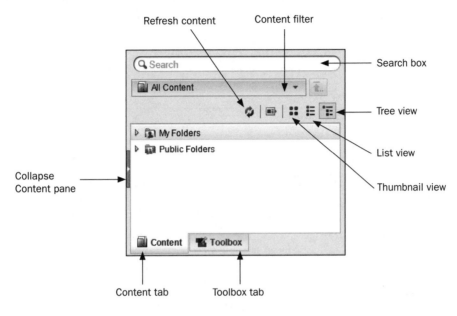

TIP *To hide the Content pane, click the arrow on the side of the Content pane.*

Content Tab

The Content tab within the Content pane provides access to Cognos BI content within Cognos Connection. The My Folders directory contains your personal entries accessible only to you. The Public Folders directory contains public entries accessible to many users. You can change the view of the content by clicking the Thumbnail, List, and Tree buttons.

By default, the Content tab displays all content available within Cognos Connection. You can filter the content by clicking the drop-down list at the top of the Content pane. You have the following filter options:

- **My Favorites**   The objects that you have tagged as favorites
- **My Folders**   The entries within your My Folders directory
- **All Content**   All entries within Cognos Connection that are available to be added to a workspace

The type of widget is determined by the type of content that is being inserted into the workspace. The available content widgets are listed in Table 7-3.

Toolbox Tab

The Toolbox tab contains widgets that allow you to add objects to the workspace, such as text and images. The available toolbox widgets are described in Table 7-4.

Widget	Description
Report	Used when a report or report segment is added to the workspace
IBM Cognos Navigator	Used when a folder is added to the workspace
PowerPlay	Used when a Cognos PowerPlay Studio report is added to the workspace
TM1	Used when a Cognos TM1 Websheet or Cognos TM1 cube is added to the workspace

TABLE 7-3   IBM Cognos Content Widgets

Icon	Widget	Description
▣	Image	Display an image in the workspace
▣	My Inbox	Show tasks and notifications from your Cognos Connection Inbox in the workspace
▣	RSS Feed	Show RSS news feeds in the workspace
▣	Select Value Filter	Filter the data in the workspace by allowing consumers to select values on which to filter
▣	Slider Filter	Filter the data in the workspace by allowing consumers to filter values by choosing a position on a slider bar
▣	Text	Show text in the workspace
▣	Web Page	Show HTML content in the workspace

TABLE 7-4   IBM Cognos Toolbox Widgets

NOTE *The Web Page and Image widgets must refer to a URL that is listed in the Safe Domains list by an administrator.*

Creating a New Workspace

In this section, you will start to use the tools provided by Cognos Business Insight to compile tables and charts into a dashboard that will show gross profit and revenue by country and order method. You will include filters and comments, and learn how to share the final workspace with your team members.

When adding objects from the Content pane to the canvas, data containers called *widgets* are automatically inserted into the workspace to hold these objects. These widgets allow you to modify the content contained within them and allow communication between other widgets in the workspace.

Adding Content

There are several ways to add objects from the Content pane to the workspace canvas:

- Drag objects from the Content pane to the workspace canvas.

- Double-click objects in the Content pane.

- Right-click an object in the Content pane and choose Insert.

The following example demonstrates how to add a crosstab and several reports to the workspace canvas from the Content tab using these methods.

To add objects from the Content tab, follow these steps:

1. In the Content pane, navigate to the object you want to add to the workspace. For this example, within Public Folders, navigate to Samples | Models | GO Data Warehouse (analysis) | Business Insight Source Reports.

2. Drag the desired item to the workspace from the Content pane. For this example, drag Gross Profit to the workspace. The Gross Profit combination chart displays in the workspace.

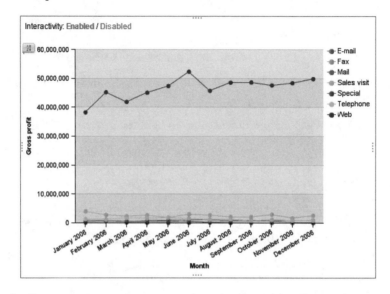

3. In the Content pane, navigate to another object to add to the workspace canvas. For this example, within Public Folders, navigate to Samples | Models | GO Data Warehouse (query) | Business Insight Source Reports | Revenue Data.

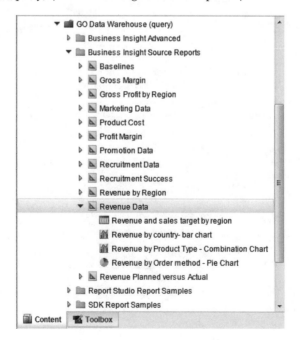

4. Right-click an object in the Content pane and select Insert from the context menu. For this example, right-click Revenue by Order Method–Pie Chart and choose Insert. The pie chart is added to the workspace.

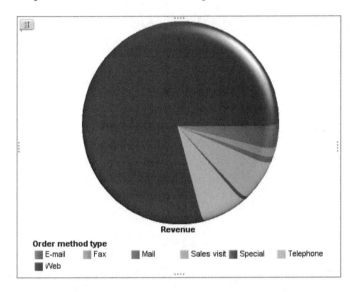

5. To add an item to the workspace canvas with keyboard shortcuts, select an item in the Content pane and press CTRL-SHIFT-ENTER. For this example, insert the Revenue by Country–Bar Chart from the Revenue Data report. The bar chart is added to the workspace.

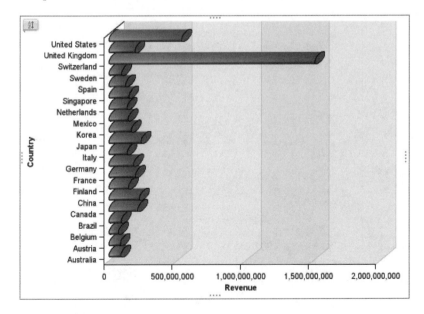

Adding Toolbox Widgets

After placing content widgets on the workspace canvas, you can enhance the functionality of your workspace by adding toolbox widgets. For this example, we will add the Select Value Filter, Slider Filter, and Text widgets.

To add a Select Value Filter widget, follow these steps:

1. In the Content pane, select the Toolbox tab.

2. Drag the Select Value Filter widget to the workspace canvas. A Properties dialog for the widget displays.

3. Select the data item to which the filter will apply. The options available are based on the content widgets within the workspace. For this example, select Order Method Type.

4. Make any necessary changes to the values by modifying the values included or setting a range so that the desired items will be available from the filter widget. For this example, deselect the Special and Fax order methods.

5. Within the Number of Items That Can Be Selected area, choose to allow only one value or multiple values to be selected from the filter.

6. From the Style area, choose how the filter values will look. For this example, select Check Boxes.

7. To add a description to the filter widget, check the Show Descriptive Text box and specify a value. For this example, add the description **Select one or more order methods**.

8. Click OK to close the Properties dialog. The Select Value Filter widget is inserted into the workspace.

9. Make selections within the Select Value Filter widget to filter content widgets within the workspace. The following pie chart is filtered to show just e-mail, sales vist, and telephone orders.

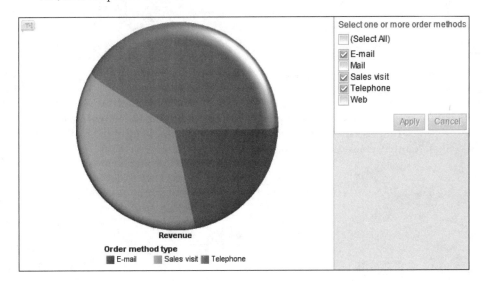

To add a Slider Filter widget, follow these steps:

1. In the Content pane, select the Toolbox tab.
2. Drag the Slider Filter widget to the workspace canvas. A Properties dialog for the widget displays.

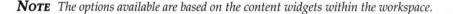

3. Select the data item to which the filter will apply. For this example, select Revenue.

NOTE *The options available are based on the content widgets within the workspace.*

---

4. Make any necessary changes to the values by modifying the values included or setting a range so that the desired items will be available from the filter widget. For this example, choose Lowest Value and Highest Value.

5. From the Style area, choose to allow only one value or a range of values to be selected from the filter. For this example, select Range of Values.

6. Uncheck the Display Values As Filter Labels box for the slider filter to not display labels on each item.

7. To add a description to the filter widget, check the Show Descriptive Text box and specify a value. For this example, uncheck the Show Descriptive Text box.

8. Click OK to close the Properties dialog. The Slider Filter widget is inserted into the workspace.

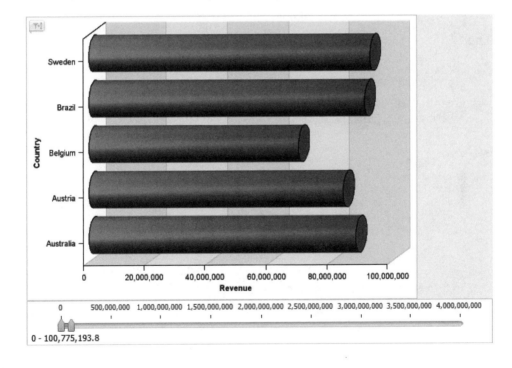

9. Make selections within the Slider Filter widget to filter content widgets within the workspace, as shown in the following example.

To add a Text widget, follow these steps:

1. In the Content pane, select the Toolbox tab.
2. Drag the Text widget to the workspace canvas, and it will be ready for text.

3. Enter the desired text into the widget. For this example, enter the following text to describe how the filter widgets affect the content widgets:

```
The Order Method prompt affects the following widgets:
- Gross Profit combination chart
- Revenue by Order Method pie chart

The Revenue prompt affects the following widgets:
- Revenue by Country bar chart
- Revenue by Order Method pie chart
```

4. To format the text, highlight the text you want to modify and click the More Toolbar Actions button on the widget toolbar, and then make the desired changes.

Rearranging Content

To reposition items in the workspace, follow these steps:

1. In the workspace canvas, click the object you want to move. For this example, select the bar chart.

2. Hover the pointer at the dotted edge of the widget, and the pointer turns into a move pointer.

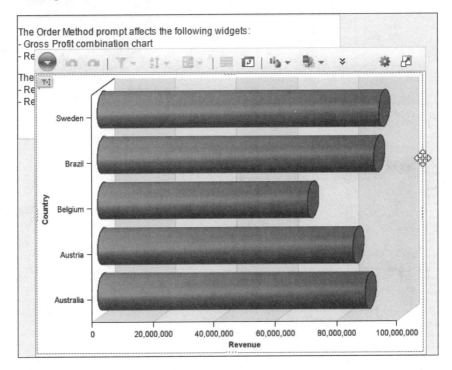

3. Left-click and reposition the selected widget as desired.

4. Repeat steps 1 through 3 as necessary. For this example, rearrange the widgets in the workspace as shown next.

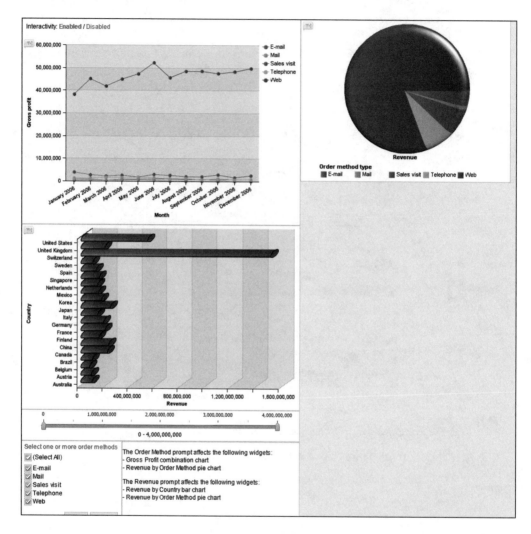

Searching for Content

At times, you may not know the location of the specific data object you need to complete your report, or the data tree might be too large to navigate easily. Cognos Business Insight has full-text search capability that enables you to find an object you are looking for by searching for keywords, phrases, or comments. Results are not case-sensitive, and the search tool will automatically look for variations of your entry. The result set will include only the objects that you have access permissions to view.

NOTE   *Content must be indexed before you can perform a search. If the content has not been indexed, you will see a Cognos Business Insight pop-up stating, "A search index was not yet created. Contact your administrator."*

To search for content, follow these steps:

1. Enter the text to search for in the Search box. For this example, enter **revenue**.

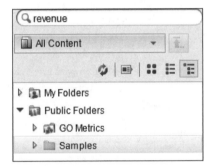

2. Set the content filter to the area you want to search within. By default, the content filter is set to All Content.

3. Click the arrow button in the Search box to perform the search.

4. A list of objects that contain your keywords appears in the Content pane. In addition, your search results are now a selection within the content filter. Also, options to further refine your results appear.

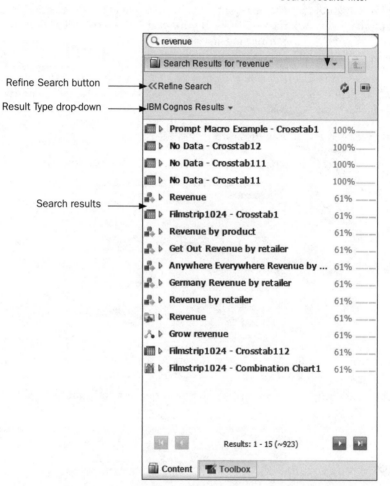

5. To change the type of results, click the Result Type drop-down arrow and choose an option on which to filter.

6. To refine the results, click the Refine Search button. You are offered the following options:

- The Results area is used to hide report parts, show only report parts, or show all results.
- The Type section filters results on a specific object type.
- The Part section filters results on a part type, such as list or bar chart.
- The Creation section filters results to a time period.
- The Owner section filters results by the owner of the entry.
- The Metadata section filters results by a Cognos BI package.

TIP *Make multiple selections within the Refine Search options to filter results by the intersection of the chosen options. To remove a selection, click the Any option under the appropriate section.*

For this example, select Crosstab from the Part section.

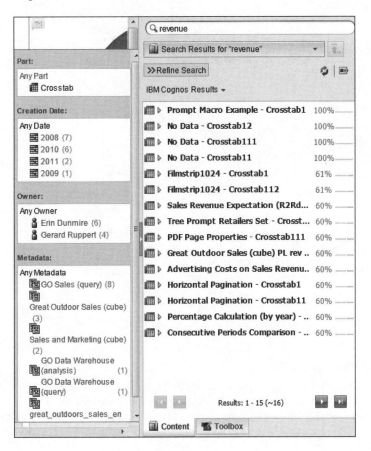

From the Content pane, insert Great Outdoors Sales (cube) PL rev CM to LM – Crosstab 1 on the workspace canvas.

Search for **Total Revenue**, and insert the Crosstab11111 report part of the Total Revenue by Country report, as shown next.

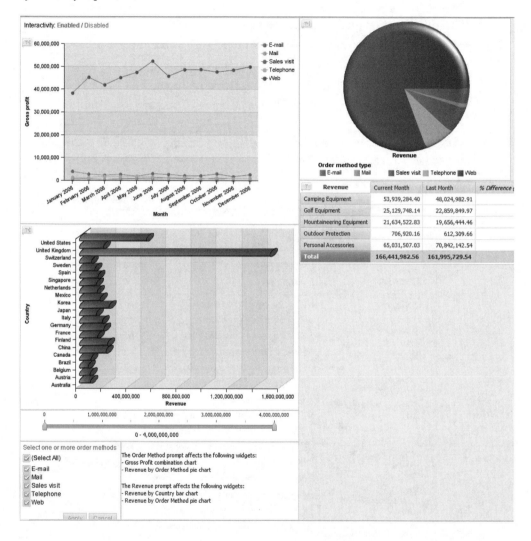

Revenue	Current Month	Last Month	% Difference
Camping Equipment	53,939,284.40	48,024,982.91	
Golf Equipment	25,129,748.14	22,859,849.97	
Mountaineering Equipment	21,634,522.83	19,656,444.46	
Outdoor Protection	706,920.16	612,309.66	
Personal Accessories	65,031,507.03	70,842,142.54	
Total	166,441,982.56	161,995,729.54	

Saving Your Workspace

You should save your workspace periodically throughout the process of creating it so that any modifications made to the workspace during development are not lost. A copy of each widget contained in the workspace is created within the saved version of a workspace. Any modifications made to widgets are saved within the workspace, and they do not affect the original objects.

To save a workspace, follow these steps:

1. From the Actions menu in Cognos Business Insight, select Save As. The Save As dialog opens.

2. Select Public Folders to save the workspace in a public location that others can access, or choose My Folders to save it in a private location that only you can access.

3. Navigate to the directory where you want to save the workspace.

4. In the Name text box, enter a name for the workspace.

5. Click the Save button to save the workspace.

Adding Your Workspace as a Favorite

You can also add a workspace to your list of favorites. The Cognos Business Insight list of favorites is useful when you have access to many workspaces but often reference only a few. Add those that you use most often as favorites to enable quick access to them.

NOTE   *A workspace must be saved before it can be added to Favorites.*

To add a workspace to Favorites, open that workspace in Cognos Business Insight, and then click the Favorites button on the application bar.

The Favorites button star is now yellow to indicate that the workspace is marked as a favorite.

Working with Widgets

In this section, you will explore some of the tools that are available in Cognos Business Insight to work with and customize widgets. First, we'll describe the tools on the widget toolbar, and then we'll cover how to use these tools with your widgets.

Using the Widget Toolbar

Each widget that is added to the workspace canvas contains a toolbar that appears at the top of the selected widget. The widget toolbar contains an Actions menu and toolbar buttons. Table 7-5 lists the actions that are available to all widgets.

The actions available to Report widgets are listed in Table 7-6. Actions available exclusively to Cognos PowerPlay Studio widgets are listed in Table 7-7. Actions available exclusively to Cognos TM1 Cube Viewer widgets are listed in Table 7-8. Along with the Actions menu, the widget toolbar contains the buttons listed in Table 7-9.

Icon	Name	Description
	Remove from Workspace	Delete the object from the workspace
	Listen for Widget Events	Set communication between widgets
	Resize to Fit Content	Alter the size of the widget to fit the content
	Send to Back	Move the selected widget to the back when widgets overlap
	Properties	Set properties for the widget

TABLE 7-5   Actions Available to All Widgets

Icon	Name	Description
	Print As PDF	Print widget content to a PDF document
	Export to	Export the content to PDF, Excel, CSV, or XML format
	Versions	Display saved output versions of the report
	Refresh	Update the content of the widget with the most recent data
	Prompt Again	Display the prompts of the report
	Reset	Reset the content to the most recent version
	Do More	Open the report in Cognos Business Insight Advanced

TABLE 7-6   Actions Available to Report Widgets

Icon	Name	Description
	Export	Export the content to CSV or XLS format
⟳	Refresh	Update the content of the widget with the most recent data
	Show Dimension Viewer	Display the dimension viewer in the widget

TABLE 7-7   Actions Available to IBM Cognos PowerPlay Studio Widgets

Icon	Name	Description
⟳	Refresh	Update the content of the widget with the most recent data
	Reset	Reset the content to the original view
	Restart	Restart a session after a session timeout

TABLE 7-8   IBM Cognos TM1 Cube Viewer Actions

Icon	Name	Description
⟲	Undo	Undo the last modification
⟳	Redo	Redo the last action undone
▼	Filter	Filter a data item within the widget
A↕ ▼	Sort	Sort data within the widget
🧮 ▼	Calculate	Insert a calculation
⊞	Group/Ungroup	Group or ungroup like items
🔁	Swap Rows and Columns	Exchange the items between the rows and the columns of a crosstab
📊	Change Display Type	Set the display type of the widget
🎨	Change Color Palette	Set the color palette of the widget
💬	Comment	Add comments to the widget
⚙	Do More	Open the widget object in Cognos Business Insight Advanced, where you can use advanced customization to enhance the object
⤢	Maximize This Widget	Expand the widget to the full size of the window
⤡	Restore This Widget	Return the widget to regular size after maximizing

TABLE 7-9   Widget Toolbar Buttons

Customizing Widgets

Objects added to a workspace may not always display by default in a meaningful way. You can make a number of modifications to the contents of widgets to get the data to appear exactly how you want it displayed.

Sorting Widget Content

The content in a Report widget may not be in the desired order. You can set items to sort in ascending or descending order.

To sort widget content, follow these steps:

1. Select the item in the widget that you want to sort on. For this example, select the name of a country in the Revenue by Country bar chart.

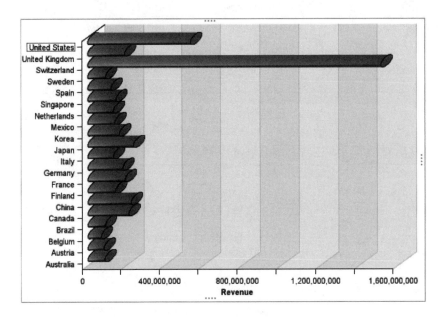

2. Hover the pointer at the top of the widget so that the widget toolbar appears.

3. On the widget toolbar, click the Sort button, and then select the desired option. For this example, select Sort by Label: Country | Descending. The chart regenerates, reflecting the selected option.

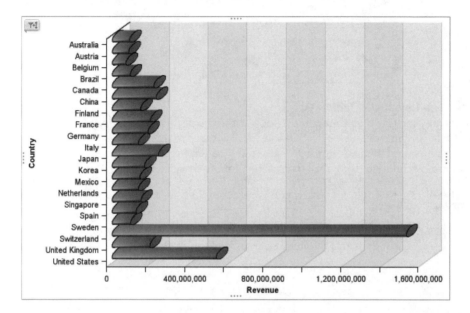

Maximizing and Restoring a Widget

The data contained in a widget may exceed the widget display area. You can take a closer look at the widget content by maximizing the view. For this example, we insert the Crosstab11111 report part from the Total Revenue by Country report located in Public Folders | Samples | Models | GO Data Warehouse (query) | Report Studio Report Samples into the workspace.

To maximize and restore a widget, follow these steps:

1. Select the widget you want to maximize. For this example, select the Total Revenue by Country crosstab.

2. Hover the pointer at the top of the widget so that the widget toolbar appears.

3. Click the Maximize This Widget button to maximize the widget to the full size of the Cognos Business Insight window.

Revenue			Camping Equipment	Golf Equipment	Mountaineering Equipment	Outdoor Protection	
Americas	Brazil	Ao ar livre	2,554,044.39		2,171,110.26	56,302.39	3
		Ar fresco	2,551,975.28		3,882,366.19	180,270.92	5

4. To restore the widget to its place in the workspace, click the Restore This Widget button on the toolbar.

		⚙	🔲 Restore This Widget
Outdoor Protection	Personal Accessories	Total (Product line)	
56,302.39	3,501,023.06	**8,282,480.1**	
180,270.92	5,380,316.96	**11,994,929.35**	
108,891.35	5,516,929.77	**8,256,864.95**	

Deleting an Item from a Table

Objects may include data that you do not want to display. For example, you may add an object that contains details or descriptions unnecessary to the workspace audience. You can remove unwanted items from a list or crosstab in a Report widget.

To remove an item from a list or crosstab, follow these steps:

1. Select the widget for which you want to remove an item. For this example, select the Total Revenue by Country crosstab.

2. CTRL-click any item(s) you want to remove in the list or crosstab. For this example, select the region and retailer in the rows of the crosstab.

		Revenue	Camping Equipment	Golf Equipment	Mountaineering Equipment	Outdoor Protection	P A
Americas	Brazil	Ao ar livre	2,554,044.39		2,171,110.26	56,302.39	3
		Ar fresco	2,551,975.28		3,882,366.19	180,270.92	5
		Armazém do esporte	1,145,731.4	1,485,312.43		108,891.35	5
		Casa do Alpinista	1,961,779.8	1,617,961.38		6,813.54	3
		Esportes Grumari	12,908,332.31	11,256,888.81		665,820.03	8
		Esportópolis	7,365,113.06	719,281.09		371,442.79	
		Galáxia do esporte	2,476,455.78	495,727.77		59,362.27	4
		Lojas do Esportista	2,788,570.61	1,079,903.72		30,643.97	

3. Right-click a selected item and choose Delete from the context menu.

⊞	**Revenue**		Camping Equipment	Golf Equipment	Mountaineering Equipment	Outdoor Protection	Pers Acce
Americas	Brazil	Ao ar livre	⊞ Drill Down		2,171,110.26	56,302.39	3,50
		Ar fresco	⊞ Drill Up		3,882,366.19	180,270.92	5,38
		Armazém do esporte	⊞ Go To ▶	43		108,891.35	5,51
		Casa do Alpinista	⊞ Change Display Type ▶	38		6,813.54	3,21
		Esportes Grumari	Filter ▶	81		665,820.03	8,60
		Esportópoli	Sort ▶	09		371,442.79	92
		Galáxia do esporte	Calculate ▶	77		59,362.27	4,32
			Delete				
		Lojas do Esportista	Group / Ungroup	72		30,643.97	5,1
		Mega Shop do Esporte	⊞ Swap Rows and Columns			8,127	4
		Morro Sports	⊞ Comment ▶	.4		12,686	1,84
		Mundo	⊞ Lineage				
			Glossary			136,104.01	2,93

The selected items are now removed from the crosstab.

Revenue	Camping Equipment	Golf Equipment	Mountaineering Equipment	Outdoor Protection	Personal Accessories	Tot line
Australia	41,935,932.19	19,079,556.43	13,933,120.06	1,140,343.56	33,211,016.9	109
Austria	39,797,963.38	19,122,141.23	11,136,508.85	1,889,515.42	71,763,276.44	143
Belgium	37,097,127.44	16,581,860.49	10,743,999.1	1,612,418.27	46,996,212.33	113
Brazil	44,832,495.18	20,050,048.45	11,325,271.24	2,108,654.19	59,960,209.99	138
Canada	104,205,881.75	46,520,595.34	26,865,510.77	4,991,878.23	123,575,475.3	306
China	110,007,737.38	51,379,804.6	27,244,768.49	5,378,487.26	123,234,113.03	317
Denmark	20,113,303.37	4,046,093.05	3,152,397.32	1,128,100.89	33,573,128.88	62
Finland	70,364,415.98	32,797,545.62	17,980,985.57	3,298,167.13	64,134,195.83	188

Setting the Widget Display Type

Users may find data easier to consume in another format. Report widget content can easily be modified from a table to a chart. When a chart is added to the workspace canvas, it is displayed in the format that the chart was originally authored in, but can be changed to another chart style or even a table. The following display types are supported in Cognos Business Insight:

- Table (list or crosstab)
- Column chart
- Bar chart
- Line chart
- Pie/Donut chart
- Area chart
- Scatter/Bubble/Point chart
- Gauge chart

To change the display type, follow these steps:

1. Select the widget for which you want to change the display type. For this example, select the Total Revenue by Country crosstab.

2. Hover the pointer at the top of the widget so that the widget toolbar appears.

3. Click the Change Display Type button on the widget toolbar.

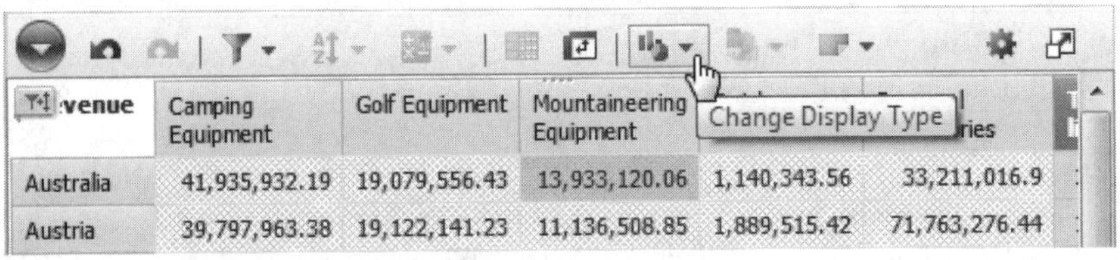

4. Select an option from the display type menu. For a basic display type, choose one of the types listed on the menu. For an advanced display type, select More. For this example, select Pie Chart.

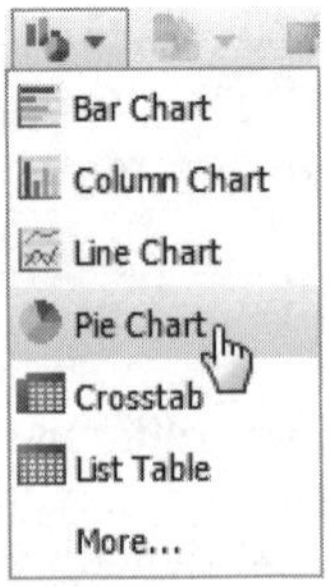

The Total Revenue by Country crosstab now appears as a set of pie charts.

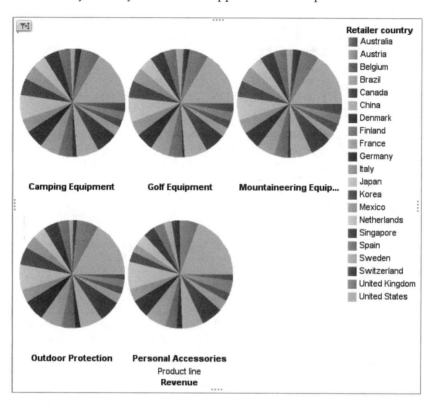

TIP *You can also switch the display type by right-clicking the object and choosing Change Display Type from the context menu.*

Setting Widget Properties

Widgets have general properties associated with them. To provide context to users, you may want to add titles to the widgets in a workspace. You can also set other general properties for Report widgets.

To define a title for a widget, follow these steps:

1. Select the widget to which you want to add a title. For this example, select the widget with the Total Revenue by Country pie charts.

2. Hover the pointer at the top of the widget so that the widget toolbar appears.

3. From the widget toolbar Actions menu, select Properties. The Properties dialog for that widget appears.

Properties - Crosstab11111	⊗

Title	Report

Specify a title for this widget.

Widget title:

Crosstab11111

☐ Use title as default for other languages

☐ Show title on this widget

To modify the widget title setting for all widgets, use the show titles option in the dialog Edit workspace style.

OK	Cancel

4. In the Widget Title text box, specify a title for the widget. For this example, enter **Revenue by Country and Product Line**.

5. To have the title display exactly as defined when viewed in widgets set to another language, select the Use Title As Default for Other Languages check box.

6. To have the title display within the widget, select the Show Title on This Widget check box.

7. Click OK. The widget displays with the changes made.

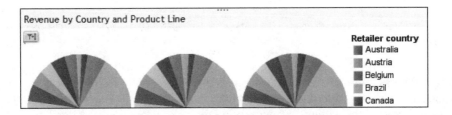

The Report tab of a widget's Properties dialog contains general properties for a Report widget.

To set general properties for a Report widget, follow these steps:

1. Select the widget for which you want to set properties. For this example, select the Revenue by Country and Product Line widget.

2. Hover the pointer at the top of the widget so that the widget toolbar appears.

3. From the widget toolbar Actions menu, select Properties.

4. Select the Report tab.

> **Properties - Revenue by Country and Product L...** (×)
>
> | Title | Report |
>
> Maximum number of rows to show per page:
>
> 20
>
> ☐ Prompt when workspace is opened (prompted reports only)
>
> ☐ Retrieve entire report (saved output only)
>
> View report specification
>
> Location: Public Folders > Samples > Models > GO Data Warehouse
> (query) > Report Studio Report Samples > Total Revenue by Country
>
> OK   Cancel

5. Set any desired properties:

- The Maximum Number of Rows to Show per Page option determines the number of rows shown in a list or crosstab before the paging options are displayed. The default is 20.

- The Prompt When Workspace Is Opened option determines whether prompts display in the widget upon opening the workspace, if the object contains prompts.

- The Retrieve Entire Report option loads the results of the complete report or report object into memory, as opposed to results loading one page at a time. This property applies to saved report output only.

TIP *The View Report Specification link in the Report tab of a widget's Properties dialog displays the XML specification of the report in a new browser window. Beneath the report specification link, the location of the report within Cognos Connection is listed.*

6. Click OK. Modifications to the Report widget are saved.

Modifying Widget Communications

By default, communication occurs automatically between widgets. However, you can disable communication between widgets when it is not wanted. For example, consider a workspace with multiple objects that include data affected by a common item, such as revenue. You may have a pie chart that shows an overall view of revenue by order method that you do not want certain filters to affect.

Widgets sending information are *source widgets*, and widgets receiving information are *target widgets*. If a source widget is a Report widget, a Slider Filter widget, or a Select Value Filter widget, the target is a Report widget. If a source widget is an Image widget, an RSS Feed widget, or a My Inbox widget, the target is a Web Page widget.

To modify widget communication, follow these steps:

1. Select the widget for which you want to modify communication between widgets. For this example, select the Revenue by Order Method pie chart.

2. Hover the pointer at the top of the widget so that the widget toolbar appears.

3. From the widget toolbar Actions menu, select Listen for Widget Events. The Listen for Widget Events dialog appears.

4. Modify the objects the selected widget is listening to. An unchecked object will not affect the selected widget. For this example, deselect the slider filter.

TIP *Expand the plus sign next to an object to specify which components affect the selected widget at a more detailed level.*

5. Click OK when you are finished making modifications. The slider filter in the workspace no longer affects the results of the Revenue by Order Method pie chart.

Viewing the Widget Information Bar

Report widgets contain an information bar that reports of any filters or sorts applied to the content of a widget. By default, the information bar is collapsed.

To view the information bar, follow these steps:

1. Select the widget for which you want to view the information bar. For this example, select the Revenue by Country bar chart.

2. Click the information bar icon located in the upper-left corner of the widget content.

Expand information bar

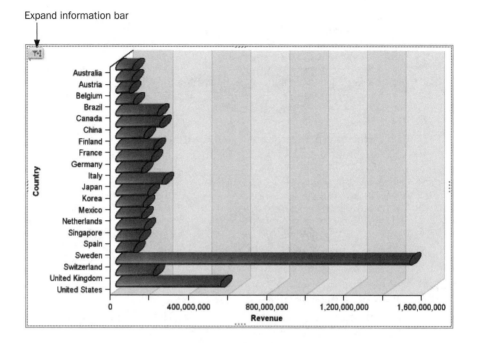

3. The information bar expands, showing any filters or sorts applied to the content.

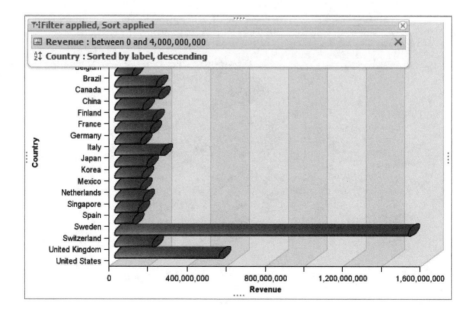

4. To remove a filter or sort from the content, hover the pointer over the item to be removed and click the Delete button.

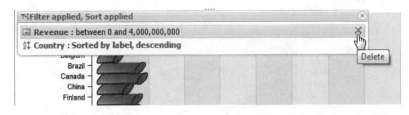

5. To hide the information bar within the widget, click the Collapse button in the title bar of the information bar.

Changing the Widget Color Palette

Options are available to select the color palette for a chart. You may want to modify the color palette to align more closely with company standards or because some data may display better with a different color palette.

To change the color palette of a widget, follow these steps:

1. Select the widget for which you want to change the color palette. For this example, select the Revenue by Order Method pie chart.

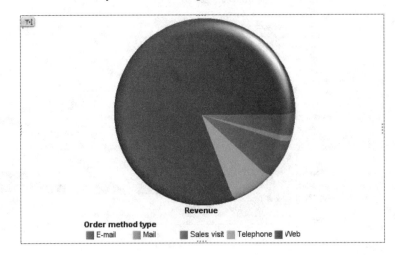

2. Hover the pointer at the top of the widget so that the widget toolbar appears.

3. On the widget toolbar, click the Change Color Palette button, and then select the desired option. For this example, select Dynamic. The chart regenerates with the selected change.

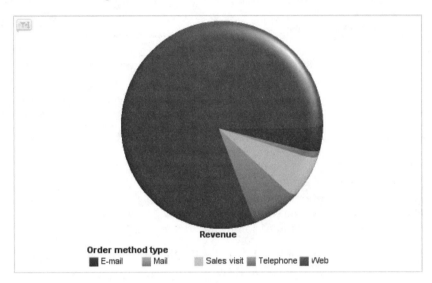

Swapping Rows and Columns

You can switch the position of the rows and columns in a Report widget crosstab to realign how the data is displayed.

To swap rows and columns in a crosstab, follow these steps:

1. Select the widget for which you want to swap rows and columns. For this example, select the Great Outdoor Sales (cube) PL rev CM to LM crosstab.

Revenue	Current Month	Last Month	% Difference (Last Month, Current Month)
Cooking Gear	8,652,732.64	8,012,724.31	7.99%
Lanterns	4,194,349.25	3,890,161.28	7.82%
Packs	12,936,104.39	11,341,955.08	14.06%
Sleeping Bags	11,584,535.24	9,620,748.77	20.41%
Tents	16,571,562.88	15,159,393.47	9.32%
Camping Equipment	53,939,284.40	48,024,982.91	12.32%

2. Hover the pointer at the top of the widget so that the widget toolbar appears.

3. On the widget toolbar, click the Swap Rows and Columns button. The widget regenerates and displays the reformatted crosstab.

venue	Cooking Gear	Lanterns	Packs	Sleeping Bags	Tents	Camp Equip
Current Month	8,652,732.64	4,194,349.25	12,936,104.39	11,584,535.24	16,571,562.88	53,93
Last Month	8,012,724.31	3,890,161.28	11,341,955.08	9,620,748.77	15,159,393.47	48,02
% Difference	7.99%	7.82%	14.06%	20.41%	9.32%	

Resizing a Widget to Fit Its Content

Use the Resize to Fit Content option on the widget toolbar's Actions menu to easily resize a widget to the perfect size for the contained content.

To resize a widget to fit its content, follow these steps:

1. Select the widget that you want to resize. For this example, select the Great Outdoor Sales (cube) PL rev CM to LM crosstab.

2. Hover the pointer at the top of the widget so that the widget toolbar appears.

3. From the widget toolbar Actions menu, select Resize to Fit Content. The widget resizes to the size of the content.

Revenue	Cooking Gear	Lanterns	Packs	Sleeping Bags	Tents	Camping Equipment
Current Month	8,652,732.64	4,194,349.25	12,936,104.39	11,584,535.24	16,571,562.88	53,939,284.40
Last Month	8,012,724.31	3,890,161.28	11,341,955.08	9,620,748.77	15,159,393.47	48,024,982.91
% Difference (Last Month, Current Month)	7.99%	7.82%	14.06%	20.41%	9.32%	12.32%

Adding Comments to Widgets

You may want to add comments to individual widgets to communicate instructions, point out trends, or call attention to specific events.

To add a comment to a widget, follow these steps:

1. Select the widget to which you want to add a comment. For this example, select the Revenue by Country bar chart.

2. Hover the pointer at the top of the widget so that the widget toolbar appears.

3. On the widget toolbar, click the Comment button, and then select Add Comment. A text dialog appears.

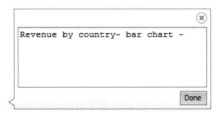

4. In the text box, enter the desired comment.
5. Click the Done button. A comment indicator in the form of a red triangle appears in the upper-right corner of the widget content.

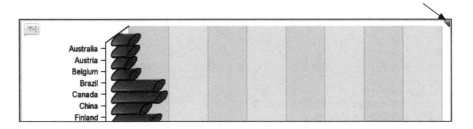

6. Hover the pointer over the comment indicator to view the comment.

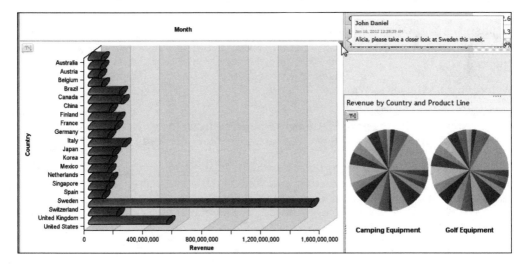

TIP *Click the Comment button again to delete or edit the comment.*

Deleting a Widget

Creating a workspace is often an iterative process. You will not always get it right the first time, and may need to delete widgets from the workspace at some point.

To delete a widget from the workspace, follow these steps:

1. Select the widget that you want to delete.

2. Select Remove from Workspace from the widget Actions menu. A confirmation box appears.

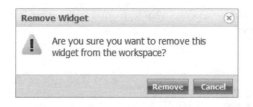

3. Click the Remove button. The widget is deleted from the workspace.

Customizing the Workspace

You can customize your workspace by specifying general layout and style properties. You can also set your preferences for Cognos Business Insight.

Choosing a Workspace Layout

Two automatic layout actions are available from the Layout and Style menu on the application bar:

- **Fit All Widgets to Window**   Proportionally resizes all widgets to fit the workspace window.

- **Arrange All Widgets to Fit Content**   Resizes each of the widgets in the workspace to fit the content, so that the widgets do not contain any white space or scroll bars.

These actions affect all widgets that are included in the workspace. In both cases, the objects on the workspace will be rearranged to best fit the layout chosen. If you want to retain the existing layout, you can resize widgets individually.

Editing the Workspace Style

For your workspace, you can set a background color or image through the style properties. You can also set a background color or image for widgets, and choose whether or not to show widget titles and borders. Widget properties set at the workspace level apply to all objects by default, and they are overridden only if specifically defined at the widget level.

To set workspace style properties, follow these steps:

1. From the Layout and Style menu on the application bar, select Edit Workspace Style. The Edit Workspace Style dialog appears.

2. On the Page tab, set any desired background color or image for the workspace.
3. Select the Widgets tab.

4. Set any desired background color or image for the widgets.

5. To show the titles of all widgets by default, check the Show Titles box, and set the desired properties for the font and size of the titles.

6. To show borders on all widgets by default, check the Borders box, and set the desired border properties.

7. Click the OK button when you are finished making modifications.

Setting Preferences

Cognos Business Insight preferences include language, time zone, whether the Getting Started page displays at startup, and the position of the Content pane.

To set preferences, follow these steps:

1. From the Actions menu on the application bar, select My Preferences. The Set Preferences dialog appears.

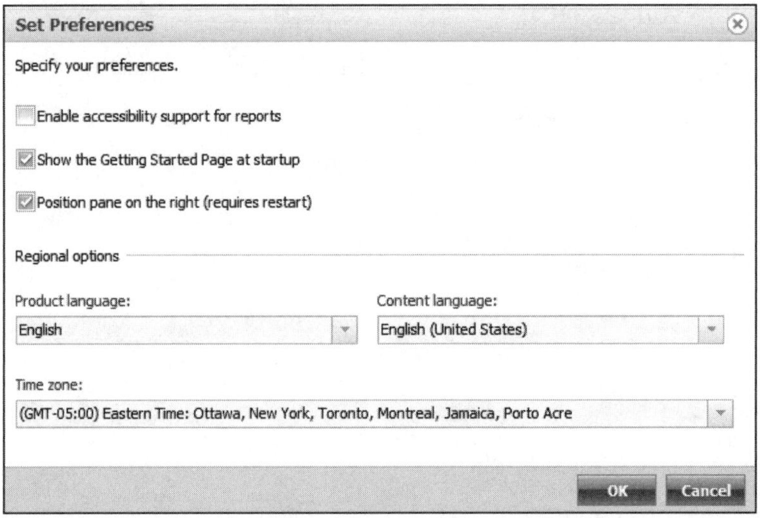

2. Check the Enable Accessibility Support for Reports box to allow accessibility options to be enabled in Report widgets.

3. Check the Show the Getting Started Page at Startup box to enable the welcome page when entering Cognos Business Insight.

4. Uncheck the Position Pane on the Right box to have the Content pane appear on the left side of the Cognos Business Insight interface.

5. Select the appropriate language and time zone options.

6. Click the OK button to accept the changes.

Sharing a Workspace Link

Once you have a workspace created, you may want to put it in a public location for others to access or provide those who may be interested in the workspace a direct link to it. Only users with the proper Cognos access permissions will be able to open a workspace link.

To send a workspace link, follow these steps:

1. In Cognos Business Insight, open the workspace whose link you want to send.

2. Click the Email Link button on the application bar.

3. Your default e-mail editor opens with the workspace URL in the body of the message. Draft the remainder of the message and send it to the desired recipients.

TIP *The Actions menu on the application bar has a Copy Link to Clipboard option. This simply copies the URL to your local clipboard so that you can paste the link into any desired location.*

III PART

Authoring Content with IBM Cognos 10

IBM Cognos Business Insight
Advanced—Relational

Today's business users are looking for quick answers to their business questions. What are my top five selling products this year? How many products were returned last month? Why were they returned? These are the types of questions that can help drive business decisions. The faster managers and executives know which products have been returned and why they were returned, the faster they can react and potentially avert a major issue.

IBM Cognos Business Insight Advanced is a web-based tool that lets you query and analyze data to find answers to your business questions quickly. The easy-to-use interface lets you create simple or sophisticated reports using lists, crosstabs, and charts. Many formatting features are available to make your reports more visually appealing. The page layout features provide a great starting point for creating dashboard reports. You can also build reports in Preview mode, which displays the data while you are creating your report.

Cognos Business Insight Advanced takes advantage of the same report specifications used by IBM Cognos Report Studio. Because of this, you can open Cognos Business Insight Advanced reports in Cognos Report Studio and use the advanced tools in Cognos Report Studio to modify them.

With Cognos Business Insight Advanced, you can create reports from relational or dimensional sources. In this chapter, we will focus on reporting from relational sources using the IBM Cognos samples. You will be introduced to the Cognos Business Insight Advanced user interface and commonly used features.

Getting Started with IBM Cognos Business Insight Advanced

The recommended objects used for reporting from relational sources are lists, crosstabs, and charts. With relational sources, you have access to many commonly used Cognos Business Insight Advanced features, such as grouping, sorting, calculations, and filters. Relational packages are easily identified by the icons in the Cognos Business Insight Advanced Insertable Objects pane (described in the "Using the IBM Cognos Business Insight User

Interface" section of this chapter). Relational packages contain namespaces, query subjects, query items, and measures.

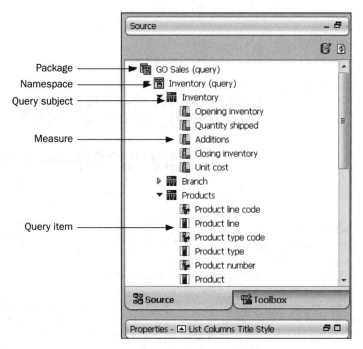

Opening IBM Cognos Business Insight Advanced

To open Cognos Business Insight Advanced, follow these steps:

1. Log on to Cognos Connection and navigate to the Public Folders tab.

2. From the Launch menu located in the upper right of the screen, select Business Insight Advanced. The Select a Package screen displays.

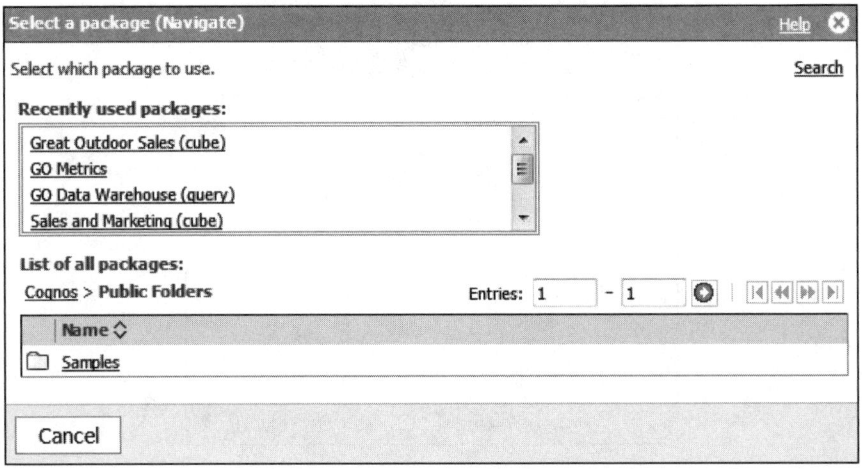

3. Select a package from either the Recently Used Packages area or the List of All Packages area. For the examples in this chapter, use the GO Sales (query) package, which is a relational data source. The Cognos Business Insight Advanced startup page is displayed, as shown next.

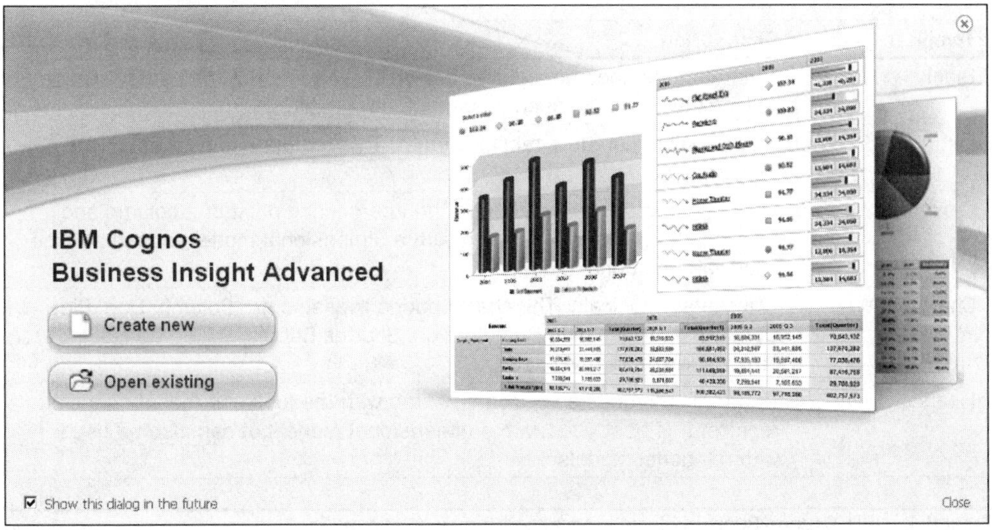

4. Click the Create New button. The New dialog displays, listing the report templates available for use as a starting point for creating reports. Each template is described in Table 8-1.

5. Select the desired template. Click List in the New dialog to create a list report, and then click OK. The Business Insight Advanced user interface displays, which is described in the next section.

Template Style	Description
Blank	This template does not contain any objects. It is up to the user to decide which objects will be used in creating the report.
List	View detailed data in a tabular format. This template is best used with a relational model.
Crosstab	View summarized information at the intersecting point of a column and row. This template is best used with a dimensional model but can also be used with relational models.
Chart	View data graphically. The chart options available are Column, Line, Pie, Donut, Bar, Area, Point, Combination, Scatter, Bubble, Bullet, Gauge, Pareto, Progressive, and Advanced.
Financial	This template uses a stylized crosstab with the look and feel of financial reports. It is best used with a dimensional model but can also be used with relational models.

TABLE 8-1   IBM Cognos Business Insight Advanced Template Styles

Using the Cognos Business Insight Advanced User Interface

The Cognos Business Insight Advanced user interface includes tools for accessing common features, inserting objects, navigating through pages, and setting object properties.

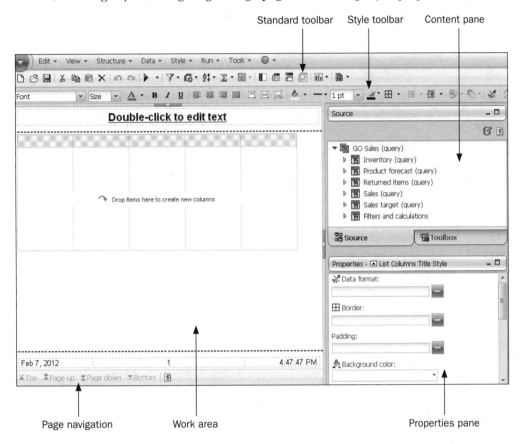

Standard toolbar   Style toolbar   Content pane

Page navigation   Work area   Properties pane

The main interface components are the standard toolbar, style toolbar, Content pane, page navigation, Properties pane, and work area. The following sections describe these components.

Standard Toolbar

The standard toolbar gives users quick access to many commonly used features. Table 8-2 describes some of the functions available from the standard toolbar.

Style Toolbar

The style toolbar gives you quick access to many formatting features offered in Cognos Business Insight Advanced. Table 8-3 describes commonly used functions available from the style toolbar.

Content Pane

The Content pane is made up of two tabs: Source and Toolbox. The Source tab contains the namespaces, query items, and data items that make up the selected package. The Toolbox

Icon	Name	Description
▶ ▾	Run Report	Run a report in HTML, PDF, Excel, CSV, or XML format; access report options.
▽ ▾	Filters	Filter the selected data.
⇅ ▾	Sort	Sort the selected data.
Σ ▾	Summarize	Summarize the selected data.
▦ ▾	Insert Calculation	Create a calculation for the selected data.
▯	Group/Ungroup	Group or ungroup the selected data in a list.
▤ ▾	Page Layout	Select a predefined page layout for the report.

TABLE 8-2   IBM Cognos Business Insight Advanced Standard Toolbar

Icon	Name	Description
A ▾	Foreground Color	Set the color for the selected text.
B	Bold	Make the selected text bold.
♨ ▾	Background Color	Set the background color of the selected object.
— ▾	Border Style	Set the border line style for the selected object.
⊞ ▾	All Borders	Add borders to the selected object.
%#	Data Format	Set the format of the selected data.
▦	Style	Apply a variety of styles to the selected object.

TABLE 8-3   IBM Cognos Business Insight Advanced Style Toolbar

tab contains other objects that can be added to reports. Some commonly used Toolbox objects are listed in Table 8-4.

Work Area
The work area is where you design the layout for your report. You can add data container objects such as lists, crosstabs, and charts. Table objects help organize report layout. You can add other Toolbox objects as needed to aid in your report creation.

Page Navigation
The page navigation is activated when in Preview mode (described in the "Working in Preview Mode and Design Mode" section later in this chapter) and a large number of records are returned. It allows you to page down or up, and jump to the top or bottom page of a report.

Object	Object Description
[ab] Text Item	Add informational text to a report
[::] Block	Container used to help organize a report
⊞ Table	Container used to help with the layout of objects in a report
▦ Query Calculation	Add a calculation to a report
▦ List	Data container for viewing data in tabular format
▦ Crosstab	Data container for viewing data in rows and columns
▪▪▪ Chart	Data container for viewing data graphically

TABLE 8-4   IBM Cognos Business Insight Advanced Toolbox Objects

Properties Pane

The Properties pane shows properties for selected objects in the work area. This allows you to modify properties such as data format, alignment, borders, cell padding, font size, and font color.

Setting View Options

Several options in Cognos Business Insight Advanced let you customize your experience based on your preferences. These features are accessible in the Options dialog, which opens when you select Tools | Options from the menu bar.

In the Options dialog, deselecting the Position Pane on the Right check box changes the interface so that the Insertable Objects pane is displayed on the left, instead of the right (the default), as shown next. This layout may be optimal for Cognos report writers since the Insertable Objects pane in Cognos Report Studio is located on the left.

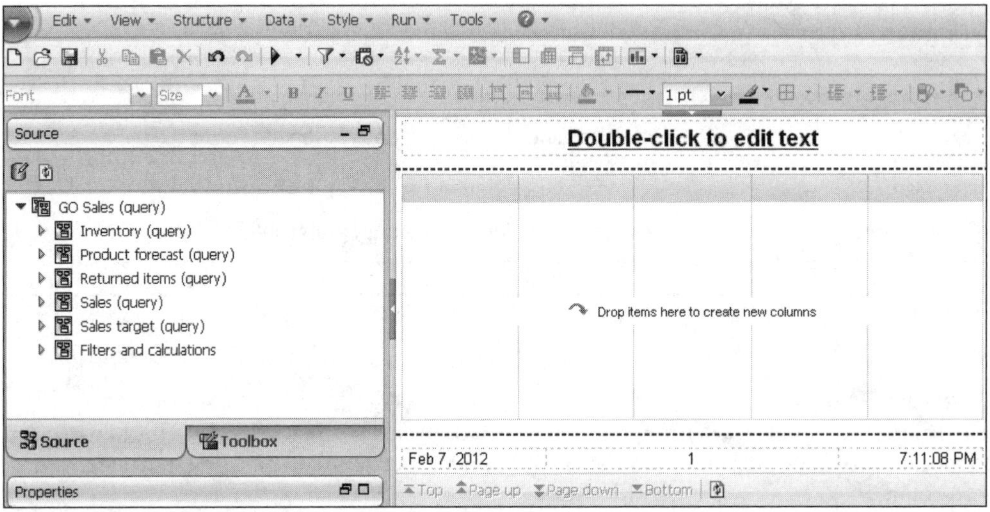

You can turn on rich tooltips by checking the Show Rich Tooltips check box. Tooltips are displayed by hovering the cursor over toolbar buttons. Rich tooltips show the name of the toolbar button and a brief description.

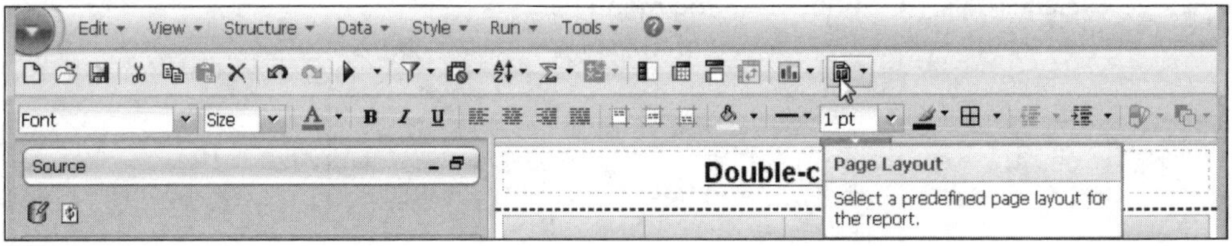

When the Display Report Preview check box is selected, a preview of the report along with the name is displayed when opening saved content.

Working in Preview Mode and Design Mode

In Preview mode, you view live data while creating a report. This allows you to verify results quickly without the added step of running the report to view the data. To switch to Preview mode, select View | Page Preview from the menu bar.

Product line	Revenue
Camping Equipment	$1,589,036,664.03
Golf Equipment	$726,411,367.89
Mountaineering Equipment	$409,660,132.90
Outdoor Protection	$75,994,296.25
Personal Accessories	$1,885,673,307.78
Overall - Summary	**$4,686,775,768.85**

Design mode adds data placeholders to the report while you are creating a report. When in Design mode, you must run the report to see results. To switch to Design mode, select View | Page Design from the menu bar.

Product line	Revenue
<Product line>	<Revenue>
<Product line>	<Revenue>
<Product line>	<Revenue>
Overall - Summary	**<Summary(Revenue)>**

NOTE *When creating a report with large volumes of data, performance can be adversely impacted in Preview mode. Design mode is recommended when dealing with large volumes of data.*

Working with List Reports

To demonstrate a business case using Cognos Business Insight Advanced, we will walk through creating a report showing sales revenue versus planned revenue. This report will include revenue and planned revenue by city and staff members, focusing on 2007 and the United States. The report requirements call for % difference and absolute forecast error calculations to be added. We will use conditional formatting with the % difference calculation to make it easy to identify staff members who are exceeding expectations and those who are below their mark.

Tip *When you create a new report, it is good practice to assign it a name and save it before continuing to build the layout.*

Creating a List Report

List reports display data in tabular format, and they are often used when analyzing detailed data.

To create a list report, follow these steps:

1. Open a new list template in Cognos Business Insight Advanced using a relational package. For this example, select the GO Sales (query) package.

2. From the Content pane, drag a query item to the work area and drop it into the list. For this example, insert the Year query item from the Time query subject of the GO Sales (query) namespace.

3. Add an additional item to the list using the drag-and-drop method. A black flashing bar will appear at the area of insertion, identifying where the item will be placed. For this example, insert the Country query item from the Sales Staff query subject next to Year in the list, as shown next.

4. To add items to the list by double-clicking the item in the Content pane, click within the list to select it, and then double-click the desired item in the Content pane. The item is inserted at the end of the list. For this example, insert City and Staff Name from the Sales Staff query subject.

5. To add multiple items to the list simultaneously, CTRL-click the desired items and then insert them into the list using the drag-and-drop method, or right-click one of the items and choose Insert. Add the Revenue and Planned Revenue measures from the Sales query subject. Your report should look similar to this:

Year	Country	City	Staff name	Revenue	Planned revenue
2004	United States	Boston	Pierre Lavoie	$3,795,932.90	$4,120,702.81
2006	Switzerland	Genève	Caprice Mancini	$4,867,895.33	$4,878,551.33
2005	Austria	Wien	Thomas Schirmer	$7,432,594.57	$7,993,320.21
2006	Canada	Toronto	Samantha Pierce	$3,720,463.21	$3,878,942.24
2005	United States	Seattle	Melanie White	$5,979,668.79	$6,451,385.53

Filtering Reports

Filtering your report allows you to focus the report on a smaller set of data. In this example, we will employ two different ways to use the filter functionality. We will filter the sample report on 2007 and the United States.

To add a filter to a report, follow these steps:

1. From the standard toolbar, click Filters and select Edit Filters from the menu. The Filters dialog displays.

2. From the Filters dialog, click the Add button. The Create Filter dialog displays.

3. In the Create Filter dialog, select the Custom Based On Data Item radio button and choose the desired data item. For this example, select Year from the drop-down list.

4. Click OK in the Create Filter dialog. The Filter Condition dialog displays.

5. In the Filter Condition dialog, for the Condition, select whether the selected values are the only values included or excluded. Choose Show Only The Following Values.

6. From the Values area, choose Specific Values, Comparison, or Range. For this example, select Specific Values from the drop-down list.

7. Within the Values area, set the properties for the filter condition based on the previous selection. Here, add 2007 to the Selected Values list.

8. Click OK to continue. The Filters dialog displays again, this time with the newly added filter.

9. Click OK to add the filter. The data in the work area updates to reflect the filter.

10. To add a filter for a specific item within the report, select the item within the work area. Select United States in the Country column of the list.

11. From the standard toolbar, click the Filters button and select Include [data item] from the drop-down menu. Select Include United States.

12. Click OK. The report is now filtered on both items. The report is filtered on 2007 and United States.

Year	Country	City	Staff name	Revenue	Planned revenue
2007	United States	Los Angeles	Margaret Lewiston	$5,089,417.25	$5,392,405.15
2007	United States	Boston	Eric Carson	$15,139,527.97	$16,116,981.41
2007	United States	Boston	Pierre Lavoie	$10,150,194.30	$10,893,955.11
2007	United States	Miami	Harold Germaine	$5,423,288.56	$5,803,744.78

Grouping Reports

Grouping data makes reports easier to read by breaking up and organizing repeating data items. We will group the data in the sample report by year, country, and city.

To group data in a report, follow these steps:

1. Within the work area, select the item(s) you want to group. Click the Year column, hold down the CTRL key, and click the Country and City columns.

2. From the standard toolbar, click the Group/Ungroup button. The report in the work area updates, and now with the data grouped it is much more visually appealing and easier to read.

Year	Country	City	Staff name	Revenue	Planned revenue
2007	United States	Boston	Eric Carson	$15,139,527.97	$16,116,981.41
			Pierre Lavoie	$10,150,194.30	$10,893,955.11
			Rhonda Cummings	$4,886,101.94	$5,212,489.72
			James Ripley	$5,798,422.20	$6,303,757.92
		Boston - Summary		**$35,974,246.41**	**$38,527,184.16**
		Los Angeles	Margaret Lewiston	$5,089,417.25	$5,392,405.15
			Paula Merkley	$6,694,003.75	$7,242,369.59
			Janice Thomas	$10,573,414.39	$11,156,563.70
			Charles Laurel	$16,835,731.64	$18,178,932.63
		Los Angeles - Summary		**$39,192,567.03**	**$41,970,271.07**
		Miami	Harold Germaine	$5,423,288.56	$5,803,744.78
			Vera Parry	$7,261,110.40	$7,755,506.62
			Karly Millers	$1,247,259.39	$1,317,824.32
		Miami - Summary		**$13,931,658.35**	**$14,877,075.72**

NOTE *Data items can be grouped one at a time or you can select multiple data items and group them together. When grouping multiple items, data items are grouped in the order in which they were selected.*

Summarizing Data

In Cognos Business Insight Advanced, an overall summary line for a report is created automatically. Summary lines are also created automatically for each item that is grouped. You can add summary lines, as well as remove unnecessary summary lines.

NOTE *Notice the summary lines in the example. By default, data in the report is summarized using the summary setting that was specified in the package for that specific data item.*

Adding Summary Lines

The Summarize options, accessed by clicking the Summarize button on the standard toolbar, include Total, Count, Average, Minimum, and Maximum. Let's add an Average summary line to the report.

To summarize data in a report, follow these steps:

1. In the work area, select the item(s) for which you want to create a summarization. Select the Revenue and Planned Revenue columns.

2. From the standard toolbar, click the Summarize button and select the desired summarize option from the menu. Select Average. The summary line is added to the report.

Year	Country	City	Staff name	Revenue	Planned revenue
2007	United States	Boston	Eric Carson	$15,139,527.97	$16,116,981.41
			James Ripley	$5,798,422.20	$6,303,757.92
			Pierre Lavoie	$10,150,194.30	$10,893,955.11
			Rhonda Cummings	$4,886,101.94	$5,212,489.72
		Boston - Summary		$35,974,246.41	$38,527,184.16
		Boston - Average		$8,993,561.60	$9,631,796.04

Removing Summary Lines

Report requirements may specify including only specific summary totals, or after grouping multiple data items, several summary line totals may match for several grouped data items. You can remove summary lines to customize the report as necessary.

In our sample list report, the summary totals for Year, Country, and Overall are the same. We will remove the summary lines for Year and Country. We will also delete the Average summary line added in the previous section.

To remove summary lines, follow these steps:

1. In the work area, select the summary lines you want to remove. Click the United States—Summary line, and then CTRL-click the 2007—Summary line and all the Average summary lines to select them.

2. Click the Delete button on the standard toolbar. This removes the selected summary lines. Only the City and Overall summary lines remain in the work area.

Sorting Reports

Sorting a report enhances the organization and layout of data within the report. Whether you are sorting a data item alphabetically or sorting a measure from highest to lowest value, sorting makes the data within a report easier for end users to find.

The sorting choices, accessed by clicking the Sort button on the standard toolbar, are ascending, descending, or not to sort at all. In our sample report, we will sort the Revenue column in descending order.

To add sorting to a report, follow these steps:

1. In the work area, select the Revenue column.

2. Click the Sort button on the standard toolbar, and select the desired option from the menu. Select Descending from the Sort menu. The Revenue values are now sorted from highest to lowest.

Year	Country	City	Staff name	Revenue▽	Planned revenue
2007	United States	Boston	Eric Carson	$15,139,527.97	$16,116,981.41
			Pierre Lavoie	$10,150,194.30	$10,893,955.11
			James Ripley	$5,798,422.20	$6,303,757.92
			Rhonda Cummings	$4,886,101.94	$5,212,489.72
		Boston - Summary		**$35,974,246.41**	**$38,527,184.16**

NOTE *Alternatively, you can sort a report by highlighting the column, selecting Data | Sort from the menu bar, and picking a sort option.*

The Edit Layout Sorting option on the Sort menu allows you to manage both grouping and sorting within a report. When you select a column in the list, click the Sort button on the standard toolbar and choose Edit Layout Sorting. The Grouping & Sorting dialog is displayed. The following example shows this dialog when the Revenue column in our sample list report is selected.

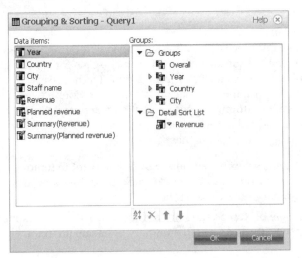

To manage groups, drag-and-drop items from the Data Items pane to the Groups folder in the Groups pane, and then arrange the order of the grouped data items. To manage sorting in your report, drag-and-drop data items to the Detail Sort List folder in the Groups pane, and then sort them by ascending or descending order.

Adding Calculations to Reports

Calculations can enhance reports by adding data that does not exist in the package. In Cognos Business Insight Advanced, you can choose from several predefined calculations or create custom calculations. Access the calculation choices by clicking the Insert Calculation button on the standard toolbar. You can also use the Query Calculation object from the Toolbox to add advanced calculations to reports.

Creating a Custom Calculation

Let's add a custom calculation (% difference) to the sample list report.

To add a custom calculation to a report, follow these steps:

1. In the work area, select the item(s) for which you want to create a custom calculation. CTRL-click the Revenue and Planned Revenue columns.

2. Click the Insert Calculation button on the standard toolbar, and choose Custom from the menu. The Insert Custom Calculation dialog displays.

3. From the Operation drop-down list, choose % Difference.

4. In the Calculation area, make any necessary modifications. Select the % Difference (Revenue, Planned Revenue) radio button.

5. In the New Data Item Name area, choose to use the default name or specify a name for the data item. Select the second radio button, and type **% Difference** as the name for the calculation.

6. Click OK. The calculation is added to the list report.

Year	Country	City	Staff name	Revenue▽	Planned revenue	% Difference
2007	United States	Boston	Eric Carson	$15,139,527.97	$16,116,981.41	6.46%
			Pierre Lavoie	$10,150,194.30	$10,893,955.11	7.33%
			James Ripley	$5,798,422.20	$6,303,757.92	8.72%
			Rhonda Cummings	$4,886,101.94	$5,212,489.72	6.68%
		Boston - Summary		**$35,974,246.41**	**$38,527,184.16**	**7.10%**

NOTE *The order in which the columns for the calculation are selected determines the structure of a predefined calculation. In our example, we selected Revenue prior to selecting Planned Revenue. In a division calculation, Revenue would be the numerator and Planned Revenue would be the denominator. Test this on your own by selecting the measures in a different order, and then choosing a predefined calculation.*

Adding Advanced Calculations to Reports

The Query Calculation object provides access to many functions and list summaries to let you create advanced calculation expressions. We will use it to add an absolute forecast error calculation to our sample report.

To add an advanced calculation, follow these steps:

1. Within the Content pane, click the Toolbox tab to select it.

2. From the Toolbox tab, drag-and-drop the Query Calculation object to the list in the work area. The Create Calculation dialog displays.

3. In the Create Custom dialog, type **Absolute Forecast Error** for the calculation name, and then click OK. The Data Item Expression dialog displays.

4. From the Available Components pane of the Data Item Expression dialog, insert any data items necessary for the calculation to the Expression Definition pane using the Source and the Data Items tabs. Drag-and-drop Revenue and Planned Revenue from the Data Items tab to the Expression Definition pane.

5. From the Functions tab in the Available Components pane, insert any functions necessary for the calculation to the Expression Definition pane. Drag-and-drop the Abs function from the Functions folder to the Expression Definition pane before the data items.

6. Make any other necessary modifications to the expression in the Expression Definition pane. Insert a minus sign between the data items and type a close parenthesis at the end of the expression, as shown next.

7. Click OK in the Data Item Expression dialog. The calculation is added to the list report.

Year	Country	City	Staff name	Revenue ▽	Planned revenue	% Difference	Absolute Forecast Error
2007	United States	Boston	Eric Carson	$15,139,527.97	$16,116,981.41	6.46%	$977,453.44
			Pierre Lavoie	$10,150,194.30	$10,893,955.11	7.33%	$743,760.81
			James Ripley	$5,798,422.20	$6,303,757.92	8.72%	$505,335.72
			Rhonda Cummings	$4,886,101.94	$5,212,489.72	6.68%	$326,387.78
		Boston - Summary		**$35,974,246.41**	**$38,527,184.16**	**7.10%**	**$2,552,937.75**

Formatting Reports

Adding formatting to a report enhances the visual appeal, makes data easier to read, and prepares the report for end user consumption. Many formatting tools are available in Cognos Business Insight Advanced. You can format values to display as dollars or percentages, add borders to objects, and change the font color of text.

We will continue working with our sample revenue list report and add formatting to the data, column titles, and header.

Formatting Data

Data formatting options are available to set properties such as number of decimal places, negative sign symbol, currency symbol, and scale. For this example, we will add currency formatting to the data in the Absolute Forecast Error column of our sample list report.

To set data format for an item in a report, follow these steps:

1. In the work area, select the data item(s) for which you want to specify the data format. Select an item in the Absolute Forecast Error column.

2. Click the Data Format button on the style toolbar. The Data Format dialog displays.

3. From the Format Type drop-down menu, select the Currency format.

4. Within the Properties pane, set any necessary properties. Set the No. of Decimal Places to 0.

5. Click OK to close the Data Format dialog. The list in the work area updates to reflect the changes. The values in the Absolute Forecast Error column are now displayed with a dollar sign and no decimal places.

Year	Country	City	Staff name	Revenue▽	Planned revenue	% Difference	Absolute Forecast Error
2007	United States	Boston	Eric Carson	$15,139,527.97	$16,116,981.41	6.46%	$977,453
			Pierre Lavoie	$10,150,194.30	$10,893,955.11	7.33%	$743,761
			James Ripley	$5,798,422.20	$6,303,757.92	8.72%	$505,336
			Rhonda Cummings	$4,886,101.94	$5,212,489.72	6.68%	$326,388
		Boston - Summary		**$35,974,246.41**	**$38,527,184.16**	**7.10%**	**$2,552,937.75**

NOTE *The summary line values are not affected by the detail data item format changes. The format for the summary line values must be set separately.*

Formatting Column Titles

To add formatting that applies to all of the column titles of a list report, you use the Ancestor feature available from the Properties pane. Now we will format the column titles in our sample report to make them stand out.

To add formatting to all column titles in a list, follow these steps:

1. Select any detail cell within the list.

2. From the Properties pane, click the Select Ancestor button.

3. Select List Columns Title Style from the Ancestor menu. All of the column titles are selected.

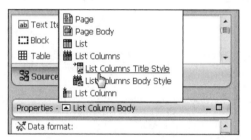

4. Make any desired modifications to the style of the column titles. Click the Bold button on the style toolbar. Now all of the column titles are in boldface text and easier to read.

Year	Country	City	Staff name	Revenue▽	Planned revenue	% Difference	Absolute Forecast Error
2007	United States	Boston	Eric Carson	$15,139,527.97	$16,116,981.41	6.46%	$977,453
			Pierre Lavoie	$10,150,194.30	$10,893,955.11	7.33%	$743,761
			James Ripley	$5,798,422.20	$6,303,757.92	8.72%	$505,336
			Rhonda Cummings	$4,886,101.94	$5,212,489.72	6.68%	$326,388

Formatting the Report Header

By default, headers and footers are added to new reports. The header contains a block and a blank text object, so you can add a title to the report. The footer contains a table with three cells: the first cell contains the date, the second cell contains the page number, and the third cell contains the time. Let's add a title to the header, and add some additional formatting to make the title stand out.

To add and format a title on a report, follow these steps:

1. Double-click the empty text object in the header of the work area. The Text dialog displays.

2. Type **Sales Revenue vs. Planned Revenue** as the name for the title, and then click OK.

3. In the header, click the block object that contains the title to select it.

4. Make any desired modifications to the style of the block containing the title. From the style toolbar, set the background color of the block and click the All Borders button to add borders to the block. The title of the report is now easily distinguishable.

Sales Revenue vs. Planned Revenue

Year	Country	City	Staff name	Revenue▽	Planned revenue	% Difference	Absolute Forecast Error
2007	United States	Boston	Eric Carson	$15,139,527.97	$16,116,981.41	6.46%	$977,453
			Pierre Lavoie	$10,150,194.30	$10,893,955.11	7.33%	$743,761
			James Ripley	$5,798,422.20	$6,303,757.92	8.72%	$505,336
			Rhonda Cummings	$4,886,101.94	$5,212,489.72	6.68%	$326,388
		Boston - Summary		$35,974,246.41	$38,527,184.16	7.10%	$2,552,937.75

Applying a Table Style

The Apply Table Style feature offers several predefined styles that can be applied to lists or crosstab reports. Using these table styles can save you time in the formatting stage of your report.

To use the Apply Table Style feature, click anywhere in your list or crosstab report, and then select click Style | Apply Table Style from the menu bar. In the Apply Table Style dialog that appears, choose a table style that you like, and then click OK.

Apply Table Style		Help (×)

Table styles:

| Default |
| Modern |
| Classic |
| Contemporary |
| Accounting 1 |
| Accounting 2 |

Preview:

xxxxxx	xxxxxx	xxxxxx
xxxxxx	xxxx	###
	xxxxxx	
xxxxxx		

☐ Set this style as the default for this report

Apply special styles to

☑ First column   ☑ Last column

[OK]   [Apply]   [Cancel]

Using Conditional Formatting

Adding conditional formatting to a report lets users quickly identify problem areas as well as areas that are exceeding expectations. In this example, we will apply conditional formatting to the % Difference calculated column. We will use a combination of changing the cell background color and font color to display areas of interest.

To add conditional formatting to a report, follow these steps:

1. Select a cell in the % Difference column.

2. Click the Conditional Styles button on the style toolbar. The Conditional Styles dialog displays.

3. In the Conditional Styles dialog, click the New Conditional Style button, and then select New Conditional Style. The New Conditional Style dialog displays.

4. In the New Conditional Style dialog, choose % Difference, and then click OK. The Conditional Style dialog displays.

5. In the Conditional Style dialog, provide a name for the conditional style.

6. Click the New Value button, enter **.06** to create a threshold, and click OK.

7. Repeat step 6 to add a second threshold value of **.07**.

8. Within the Style column, select a style for each threshold range. A predefined style can be selected from the drop-down menu, or you can click the Edit button (the yellow pencil) to specify a custom style. Choose Poor from the Style drop-down

menu for the top range, Average for the middle range, and Excellent for the bottom range. A preview of the selected styles displays in the Conditional Style dialog.

9. Click OK in the Conditional Style dialog to set the style.

10. Click OK again in the Conditional Styles dialog. The report refreshes with the conditional style applied to the applicable column.

Year	Country	City	Staff name	Revenue▽	Planned revenue	% Difference	Absolute Forecast Error
2007	United States	Boston	Eric Carson	$15,139,527.97	$16,116,981.41	6.46%	$977,453
			Pierre Lavoie	$10,150,194.30	$10,893,955.11	7.33%	$743,761
			James Ripley	$5,798,422.20	$6,303,757.92	8.72%	$505,336
			Rhonda Cummings	$4,886,101.94	$5,212,489.72	6.68%	$326,388
		Boston - Summary		**$35,974,246.41**	**$38,527,184.16**	**7.10%**	**$2,552,937.75**
		Los Angeles	Charles Laurel	$16,835,731.64	$18,178,932.63	7.98%	$1,343,201
			Janice Thomas	$10,573,414.39	$11,156,563.70	5.52%	$583,149
			Paula Merkley	$6,694,003.75	$7,242,369.59	8.19%	$548,366
			Margaret Lewiston	$5,089,417.25	$5,392,405.15	5.95%	$302,988
		Los Angeles - Summary		**$39,192,567.03**	**$41,970,271.07**	**7.09%**	**$2,777,704.04**

Creating Crosstab Reports

Crosstab reports display data in rows and columns, with summarized measures located at the intersecting cells. In this section, we will create a crosstab report from a relational source. To create a crosstab report, follow these steps:

1. Open a new crosstab template in Cognos Business Insight Advanced using a relational package. Select the GO Sales (query) package. The crosstab object displays in the work area, with drop zones for the rows, columns and measures.

2. Insert data items into each of the drop zones of the crosstab from the Content pane. Expand the Sales (query) namespace. From the Order Method query subject, insert Order Method Type to the Rows drop zone. From the Time query subject, insert Year to the Columns drop zone. From the Sales query subject, insert Revenue to the Measures drop zone. Your crosstab report should look similar to this:

Revenue	2004	2005	2006	2007
E-mail	$95,402,796.21	$44,318,886.43	$23,701,042.57	$16,420,318.95
Fax	$28,639,472.14	$19,896,187.76	$13,445,559.93	$8,092,322.18
Mail	$22,766,850.51	$16,013,779.49	$6,905,730.44	$404,978.53
Sales visit	$101,072,721.10	$79,721,524.37	$73,918,652.38	$55,481,936.15
Special	$13,905,918.75	$10,769,180.34	$1,006,100.01	$1,670,121.15
Telephone	$178,793,580.36	$107,160,284.09	$37,199,842.80	$17,832,073.81
Web	$473,771,464.65	$881,315,747.68	$1,339,714,172.77	$1,017,434,523.30

Creating Chart Reports

Chart reports let users view data graphically. Charts usually display data for high-level analysis and are often used in dashboard reports. Cognos Business Insight Advanced offers many different styles of charts. In this section, we will create a clustered column chart using the same data used in the previous examples.

To create a chart report, follow these steps:

1. Open a new chart template in Cognos Business Insight Advanced using a relational package. Select the GO Sales (query) package. The Insert Chart dialog displays.

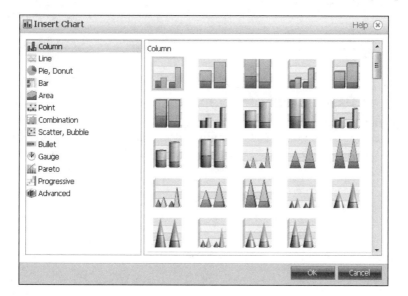

2. Choose the desired chart style, Column, from the left column of the Insert Chart dialog.

3. Choose the desired chart type, Clustered Column, from the right column of the Insert Chart dialog. The chart object displays in the work area. Select the chart in the work area to access the drop zones.

4. Insert items into the drop zones of the chart object from the Content pane. Expand the Sales (query) namespace. From the Order Method query subject, insert Order Method Type to the Categories drop zone. From the Time query subject, insert Year to the Series drop zone. From the Sales query subject, insert Revenue to the Measures drop zone. Your chart report should look similar to this:

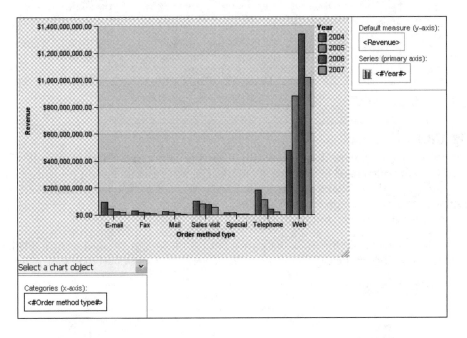

Using Predefined Page Layouts for Reports

Adding a predefined page layout format to a report can help you organize objects within the report. The Page Layout feature is commonly used with dashboard reports. In this example, we will create a dashboard-style report using the chart created in the previous section.

To add a predefined page layout to a report, follow these steps:

1. Open an existing report or create a new report. We'll use the chart report we created in the last example.

2. Click the Page Layout button on the standard toolbar and select the table with two columns and one row from the drop-down. A table is added to the work area, and any existing objects are placed inside the first available cell.

3. Insert any desired report objects into the remaining table cells. For this example, insert a Chart object from the Toolbox tab into the second table column. In the Insert Chart dialog, choose Line for the chart style and Clustereed Line with Circle Markers as the type, and then click OK.

4. Add the desired data items from the Source tab in the Content pane to the new data container. Expand the Sales (query) namespace. From the Retailer Type query subject, insert the Retailer Type query item to the categories. From the Time query subject, insert the Year query item as the series. From the Sales query subject, insert Revenue as the measure.

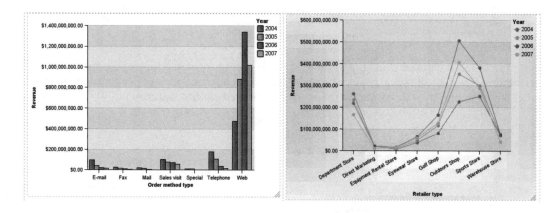

Running Reports

To run a report in Cognos Business Insight Advanced, click the Run Report button on the standard toolbar. Click the downward facing arrow next to the Run Report button to access the Run Report menu. From the Run Report menu, you can choose to run the report in any of the following output options: HTML, PDF, Excel, CSV, or XML.

Also, a Run Options dialog is available from the Run Report menu to specify options associated with running reports.

From the Run Options dialog, you can choose an output format, paper size, paper orientation (the default is portrait), data mode, language, number of rows per report page, whether to prompt for values, and whether to include accessibility features.

IBM Cognos Business Insight Advanced—Dimensional

IBM Cognos Business Insight Advanced allows decision-makers to analyze data quickly to make critical business decisions. When analyzing data, executives or managers need a tool that can accurately answer their most important question. The challenge arises, however, after that initial question is answered, because it always leads to follow-up questions. Rather than bouncing from report to report to find answers, decision-makers must be able to navigate through the data at hand to find the answers to follow-up questions.

Using Cognos Business Insight Advanced with a dimensional source allows users to navigate through data by drilling up or down on hierarchical business attributes known as "dimensions." Suppose, for example, that a retail store manager is in charge of several stores within his region. While looking at a Cognos Business Insight Advanced weekly revenue report, he notices that revenue is down from the prior week. With a simple mouse click on his region in the report, a list of all the stores in his region is displayed. The drill-down feature allows him to determine whether sales are down for all stores, or whether the problem is with a particular store. After determining that one store is having sales issues, he can further evaluate the data for only that store to determine the source of the problem. This quick analysis of data allows the manager to contact the appropriate people and take corrective actions to help boost sales.

Dimensional Data Sources

In this chapter, we will focus on reporting from dimensional sources using the IBM Cognos samples. You will learn about reporting techniques and terminology used when you are working with dimensional sources. You will also learn how to use some of the features within Cognos Business Insight Advanced, such as expanding and collapsing members, suppressing empty cells, creating dimensional calculations, and filtering.

NOTE *Creating workspaces with relational data sources is discussed in Chapter 8.*

The objects you will most often use to report from dimensional sources are *crosstabs* and *charts*. When working with dimensional sources, the source tree contains the package, namespaces, dimensions, level hierarchies, levels, members folders, members, and measures.

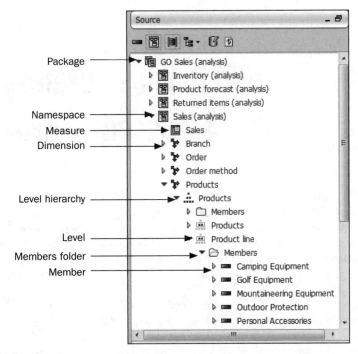

Getting Started with IBM Cognos Business Insight Advanced

To open Cognos Business Insight Advanced, follow these steps:

1. Log on to Cognos Connection, and navigate to the Public Folders tab.

2. From the Launch menu located in the upper right of the screen, select Business Insight Advanced. The Select a Package screen displays.

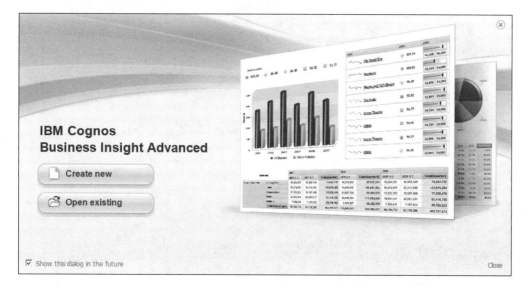

NOTE *You can also access Cognos Business Insight Advanced from the Welcome screen by clicking the Author Business Reports link and then choosing a package.*

3. Select a package from either the Recently Used Packages area or the List Of All Packages area. For the examples in this chapter, we'll use the GO Sales (analysis) package, which is a dimensionally modeled data source. The Cognos Business Insight Advanced startup page is displayed, as shown next:

4. Click the Create New button. The New dialog displays, listing the report templates available for use as a starting point for creating reports.

NOTE *Templates are discussed in detail in Chapter 8.*

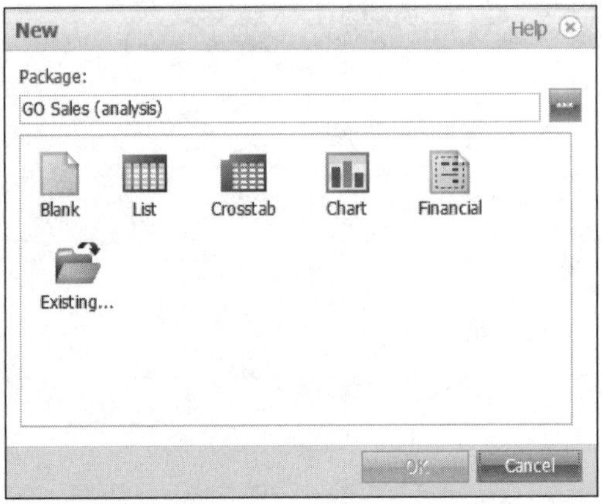

5. Select the Crosstab template, and then click OK. Cognos Business Insight Advanced opens with the crosstab placed in the work area. The user interface contains a Content pane, work area, standard toolbar, Page Layers area, and Context Filter area, as shown next:

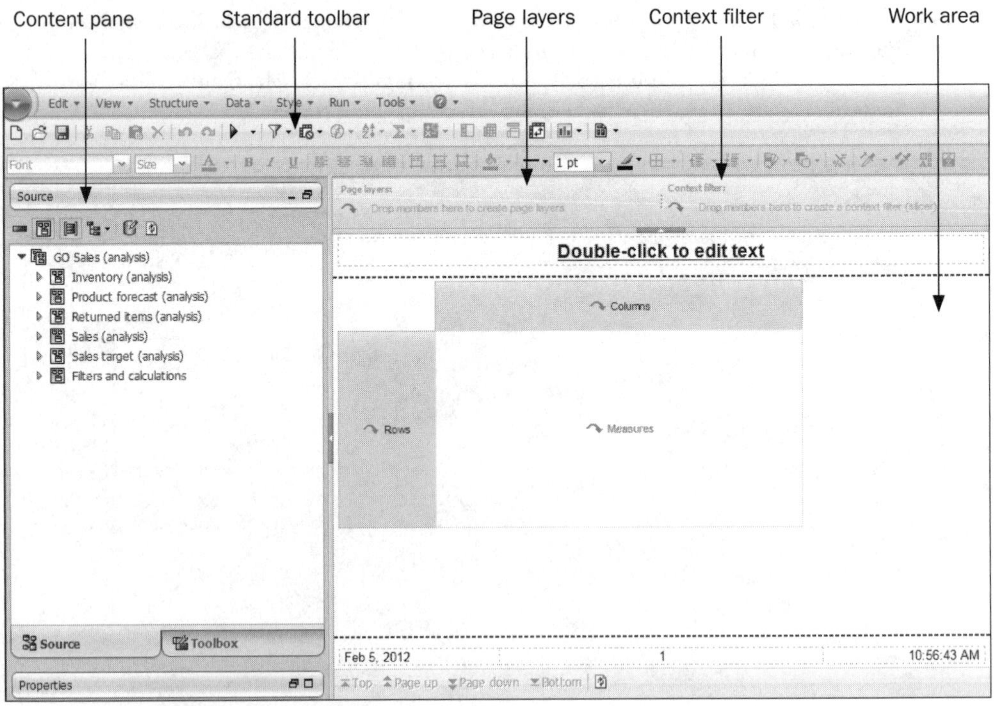

Icon	Name	Description
▶ ▾	Run Report	Run a report in HTML, PDF, Excel, CSV, or XML format; also provides report options
▽ ▾	Filters	Filter the selected data
↕ ▾	Sort	Sort the selected data
Σ ▾	Summarize	Summarize the selected data
🖩 ▾	Insert Calculation	Insert a calculation for the selected data
🖩 ▾	Suppress	Suppress rows and/or columns that have missing values, divide by zero, overflow values, or zero values
⊘ ▾	Explore	Exclude members, move members, edit sets, drill down, and drill up

TABLE 9-1 IBM Cognos Business Insight Advanced Standard Toolbar

- **Work area** Contains the crosstab that will be used to build a report.
- **Standard toolbar** Gives users quick access to many commonly used features. Table 9-1 describes some of the functions available from the standard toolbar.
- **Page layers** Create sections or page breaks for members to display on separate pages.
- **Context filter** Filter your report to allow for a more focused analysis.
- **Content pane** Contains the Source tab that displays the source data to be used in a report, and the Toolbox tab that displays objects that can be used in a report. The Source tab for dimensional reporting contains several features that allow you to customize how the source tree is displayed and how the data is pulled into a report. These features are described in Table 9-2.

Icon	Name	Description
▬	View Member Tree	Display the members tree.
🖽	View Metadata Tree	Display the full package tree.
🖿	Insert Individual Members (currently creating sets) Create Sets for Members (currently inserting individual members)	Toggle between creating sets when inserting multidimensional data items and inserting individual members.
🖿 ▾	Insert Single Member Insert Children Insert Member with Children	Choose the insertion mode for multidimensional data items.

TABLE 9-2 IBM Cognos Business Insight Advanced Content Pane

Generating Crosstab Reports

Crosstab reports display dimensional data in rows and columns and summarized information at the intersecting points of the rows and columns. We will use the GO Sales (analysis) package from the Cognos samples to demonstrate the features and techniques you can use when reporting from a dimensional source in Cognos Business Insight Advanced. You'll learn how to insert hierarchies, members, sets, individual members, and nesting members. We will create a simple crosstab report and describe features such as inserting calculations, adding filters, and summarizing data.

Inserting a Hierarchy

Hierarchies let you quickly add the highest level member or all levels and members of a hierarchy to a crosstab report.

Inserting Root Members   To add root members of a hierarchy to a crosstab, follow these steps:

1. Open a new crosstab template in Cognos Business Insight Advanced using a multi-dimensional package. Choose the GO Sales (analysis) package.

2. On the Source tab in the Content pane, select the View Metadata Tree button.

3. From the Content pane, drag-and-drop a hierarchy on the crosstab in the work area. Expand the Sales (analysis) namespace, then expand the Sales Staff dimension, and then insert the Sales Staff hierarchy into the Rows drop zone of the crosstab. The Insert Hierarchy dialog displays:

4. In the Insert Hierarchy dialog, choose Root Members and click OK.

5. Repeat steps 3 and 4 to insert additional root members. Add the Time hierarchy to the Columns section of the crosstab. Insert Revenue from the Sales Measures namespace in the Measures drop zone of the crosstab. The crosstab in the work area shows the revenue amount for all time and all sales personnel:

Revenue	Time
Sales staff	$4,686,775,768.85

Inserting All Members   To add all members of the hierarchy to a crosstab, follow these steps:

1. On the Source tab in the Content pane, select the View Metadata Tree button.

2. From the Content pane, drag-and-drop a hierarchy on the crosstab in the work area. Insert the Sales Staff hierarchy into the Rows drop zone of the crosstab, replacing the Sales Staff root member. The Insert Hierarchy dialog displays.

3. In the Insert Hierarchy dialog, choose All Members, and then click OK.

4. Repeat steps 1 and 2 to insert additional hierarchies with all members. Insert the Time hierarchy with all members in the Columns drop zone of the crosstab. The crosstab in the work area shows the revenue amounts for all members of the Sales Staff and Time hierarchies.

Revenue	Time	2004	Q1 2004	January 2004
Sales staff	$4,686,775,768.85	$914,352,803.72	$221,704,705.31	$72,741,622.65
Americas	$977,087,880.80	$192,230,456.30	$47,381,351.43	$16,431,525.70
United States	$533,803,961.85	$110,834,974.32	$27,620,520.99	$9,664,986.06
Seattle	$160,000,148.41	$31,601,608.62	$7,875,494.71	$2,769,717.12
Melanie White	$20,429,686.84	$4,271,397.66	$1,011,104.42	$293,536.73
George Harrows	$49,959,770.53	$6,385,764.52	$1,723,128.44	$722,794.57
Audrey Lastman	$46,970,382.48	$11,231,579.80	$2,925,814.77	$822,186.59
Bart Scott	$42,640,308.56	$9,712,866.64	$2,215,447.08	$931,199.23

Inserting a Member   Members can easily be added to a crosstab by dragging and dropping them into the crosstab. You can use several options on the Source tab of the Content pane to change how members are inserted. The Create Sets For Members button lets you choose whether you want to insert members within a set or insert members individually. The Insert Member With Children button provides options to insert a member with children, insert a single member, or insert the children of a member.

Inserting a Member with Children   To insert a member with children in a crosstab, follow these steps:

1. On the Source tab in the Content pane, select the View Metadata Tree button.

2. From the Source tab in the Content pane, select Insert Member with Children as the insertion mode.

3. Drag-and-drop a member from the Content pane to the crosstab. Navigate to Sales (analysis) namespace | Sales Staff dimension | Sales Staff hierarchy | Sales Region level | Members folder, and insert the Americas member on the Rows of the crosstab, replacing the Sales Staff hierarchy from the last section. The Americas member and its children display on the rows of the crosstab.

4. Insert additional members into the crosstab. Navigate to Sales (analysis) namespace | Time dimension | Time hierarchy | Time level | Members folder, and insert the Time member on the columns of the crosstab. The Time member and its children display on the columns of the crosstab.

Revenue	2004	2005	2006	2007	Time
Brazil	$17,566,891.21	$22,580,246.05	$28,939,868.92	$21,447,899.23	$90,534,905.41
United States	$110,834,974.32	$131,677,071.69	$164,986,189.21	$126,305,726.63	$533,803,961.85
Canada	$41,468,882.87	$49,366,410.09	$67,341,094.59	$53,511,041.09	$211,687,428.64
Mexico	$22,359,707.90	$35,589,920.02	$50,770,840.19	$32,341,116.79	$141,061,584.90
Americas	$192,230,456.30	$239,213,647.85	$312,037,992.91	$233,605,783.74	$977,087,880.80

Inserting a Single Member   To insert a single member in a crosstab, follow these steps:

1. On the Source tab in the Content pane, select the View Metadata Tree button.

2. From the Source tab in the Content pane, select Insert Single Member as the insertion mode.

3. Drag-and-drop a member from the Content pane to the crosstab. Navigate to Sales (analysis) namespace | Sales Staff dimension | Sales Staff hierarchy | Sales Region level | Members folder, and insert the Americas member in the Rows drop zone of the crosstab, replacing the current content. The Americas member displays on the Rows section of the crosstab.

4. Insert additional members into the crosstab. Navigate to Sales (analysis) namespace | Time dimension | Time hierarchy | Time level | Members folder, and insert the Time member in the Columns drop zone of the crosstab, replacing the current content. The Time member displays on the Columns section of the crosstab.

Revenue	Time
Americas	$977,087,880.80

Inserting Child Members   To insert children of a member in a crosstab, follow these steps:

1. On the Source tab in the Content pane, select the View Metadata Tree button.

2. From the Source tab in the Content pane, select Insert Children as the insertion mode.

3. Drag-and-drop a member from the Content pane to the crosstab. Navigate to Sales (analysis) namespace | Sales Staff dimension | Sales Staff hierarchy | Sales Region level | Members folder, and insert the Americas member in the Rows drop zone of the crosstab, replacing the current content. The children of the Americas member display on the Rows section of the crosstab.

4. Insert additional members into the crosstab. Navigate to Sales (analysis) namespace | Time dimension | Time hierarchy | Time level | Members folder, and insert the Time member in the Columns drop zone of the crosstab, replacing the current content. The children of the Time member display on the Columns section of the crosstab.

Revenue	2004	2005	2006	2007
Brazil	$17,566,891.21	$22,580,246.05	$28,939,868.92	$21,447,899.23
United States	$110,834,974.32	$131,677,071.69	$164,986,189.21	$126,305,726.63
Canada	$41,468,882.87	$49,366,410.09	$67,341,094.59	$53,511,041.09
Mexico	$22,359,707.90	$35,589,920.02	$50,770,840.19	$32,341,116.79

Nesting Members

Nesting members allow you to group data in a hierarchy. Hierarchies, levels, members, and measures can be nested in the Rows and Columns sections of a crosstab. Nesting can be applied to a set or to an individual member in a set.

Nesting Members Within a Set   You can group data in a hierarchy with nesting members. Nesting can be applied to a set or to an individual member in a set. When inserting items into the work area as sets, the items are grouped together and behave as a unit. When you insert items into the work area that are not members of sets, the items behave individually.

To nest members within a set, follow these steps:

1. Open a new crosstab template using a multi-dimensional package. Choose the GO Sales (analysis) package.

2. From the Source tab in the Content pane, click the Create Sets For Members button, so that the button reads Insert Individual Members (currently creating sets) upon mouse-over.

3. Insert items into the Rows, Columns, and Measures drop zones of the crosstab. Insert the Americas member and its children from the Sales Staff dimension to the Rows section, the Time member and its children to the Columns section, and Revenue into the Measures section.

4. From the Content pane, drag a second item into the Rows or Columns drop zone, inside of the first item, and drop it where the flashing black bar appears. Insert

Products (with children) within the Americas sales region. The product lines are nested within each country in the Americas sales region:

	Revenue	2004	2005	2006	2007	Time
United States	Camping Equipment	$60,143,498.08	$67,317,788.98	$79,318,144.45	$56,492,359.55	$263,271,791.06
	Personal Accessories	$16,332,709.27	$15,719,103.65	$21,964,680.23	$18,508,851.48	$72,525,344.63
	Outdoor Protection	$6,540,425.46	$3,942,571.55	$1,668,409.49	$719,154.19	$12,870,560.69
	Golf Equipment	$27,818,341.51	$27,136,551.74	$36,462,554.70	$27,985,723.39	$119,403,171.34
	Mountaineering Equipment		$17,561,055.77	$25,572,400.34	$22,599,638.02	$65,733,094.13
	Products	**$110,834,974.32**	**$131,677,071.69**	**$164,986,189.21**	**$126,305,726.63**	**$533,803,961.85**
Canada	Camping Equipment	$22,512,613.08	$25,194,281.56	$32,218,644.72	$24,280,342.39	$104,205,881.75
	Personal Accessories	$6,181,816.42	$5,816,967.63	$9,120,131.18	$7,984,647.32	$29,103,562.55
	Outdoor Protection	$2,481,183.06	$1,517,129.56	$690,763.20	$302,802.41	$4,991,878.23
	Golf Equipment	$10,293,270.31	$10,198,203.06	$14,767,791.61	$11,261,330.36	$46,520,595.34
	Mountaineering Equipment		$6,639,828.28	$10,543,763.88	$9,681,918.61	$26,865,510.77
	Products	**$41,468,882.87**	**$49,366,410.09**	**$67,341,094.59**	**$53,511,041.09**	**$211,687,428.64**

Nesting Members Within an Individual Member   To nest members within an individual member, follow these steps:

1. Open a new crosstab template using a multidimensional package. Choose the GO Sales (analysis) package.

2. From the Source tab in the Content pane, click the Insert Individual Members button, so that the button reads Create Sets For Members (currently inserting individual members) upon mouse-over.

3. Insert items into the Rows, Columns, and Measures drop zones of the crosstab. Insert the Americas member and its children from the Sales Staff dimension to the Rows section, the Time member and its children to the Columns section, and Revenue into the Measures section.

4. From the Content pane, drag a second item into the Rows or Columns drop zone, inside of the first item, and drop it where the flashing black bar appears. Insert Products (with children) within United States. The product lines are nested only within the United States:

Revenue		2004	2006	2007	2005	Time
United States	Camping Equipment	$60,143,498.08	$79,318,144.45	$56,492,359.55	$67,317,788.98	**$263,271,791.06**
	Golf Equipment	$27,818,341.51	$36,462,554.70	$27,985,723.39	$27,136,551.74	**$119,403,171.34**
	Mountaineering Equipment		$25,572,400.34	$22,599,638.02	$17,561,055.77	**$65,733,094.13**
	Outdoor Protection	$6,540,425.46	$1,668,409.49	$719,154.19	$3,942,571.55	**$12,870,560.69**
	Personal Accessories	$16,332,709.27	$21,964,680.23	$18,508,851.48	$15,719,103.65	**$72,525,344.63**
	Products	**$110,834,974.32**	**$164,986,189.21**	**$126,305,726.63**	**$131,677,071.69**	**$533,803,961.85**
Canada		$41,468,882.87	$67,341,094.59	$53,511,041.09	$49,366,410.09	**$211,687,428.64**
Mexico		$22,359,707.90	$50,770,840.19	$32,341,116.79	$35,589,920.02	**$141,061,584.90**
Brazil		$17,566,891.21	$28,939,868.92	$21,447,899.23	$22,580,246.05	**$90,534,905.41**
Americas		**$192,230,456.30**	**$312,037,992.91**	**$233,605,783.74**	**$239,213,647.85**	**$977,087,880.80**

Nesting and Stacking Measures Within a Set   To nest and stack measures within a set, follow these steps:

1. Open a new crosstab template using a multidimensional package. Choose the GO Sales (analysis) package.

2. From the Source tab in the Content pane, click the Create Sets For Members button, so that the button reads Insert Individual Members (currently creating sets) upon mouse-over.

3. Insert items to the Rows and Columns drop zones of the crosstab. Insert the Americas member and its children from the Sales Staff dimension to the Rows section and the Time member and its children to the Columns section.

4. From the Content pane, drag a measure into the Rows or Columns drop zone, inside of the first item in the drop zone, and drop it where a flashing black triple-bar appears. Insert Revenue inside of the years in the Columns drop zone.

5. From the Content pane, drag a second measure into the crosstab and drop it next to first measure at the flashing black triple-bar. Insert Planned Revenue next to Revenue within the years in the Columns drop zone. Two measures are now nested within the years of the crosstab:

	2004		2005		2006		2007		Time
	Revenue	Planned revenue	Revenue	Planned revenue	Revenue	Planned revenue	Revenue	Planned revenue	
Brazil	$17,566,891.21	$19,070,291.82	$22,580,246.05	$24,180,719.34	$28,939,868.92	$30,686,354.32	$21,447,899.23	$22,921,132.42	
United States	$110,834,974.32	$120,568,411.49	$131,677,071.69	$141,378,575.06	$164,986,189.21	$175,141,477.19	$126,305,726.63	$135,206,361.01	
Canada	$41,468,882.87	$44,716,732.31	$49,366,410.09	$52,571,115.03	$67,341,094.59	$71,003,308.84	$53,511,041.09	$56,726,735.85	
Mexico	$22,359,707.90	$24,310,371.45	$35,589,920.02	$38,180,499.29	$50,770,840.19	$53,972,558.19	$32,341,116.79	$34,619,340.19	
Americas	**$192,230,456.30**	**$208,665,807.07**	**$239,213,647.85**	**$256,310,908.72**	**$312,037,992.91**	**$330,783,698.54**	**$233,605,783.74**	**$249,473,569.47**	

Adding Filters

Filtering your data lets you focus your report on a smaller set of data. For example, suppose you want to see revenue and planned revenue data for the current year only. In this case, you can add a filter that will include only the current year in the report. When you are using dimensional data with Cognos Business Insight Advanced, you can use several options to focus your data. You can use context filters or create custom filters to narrow the data returned.

Adding a Context Filter

To add a context filter to a crosstab, follow these steps:

1. Create a new crosstab and insert items into the Rows, Columns, and Measures drop zones of the crosstab. Continue to use the crosstab from the previous section.

2. From the Content pane, drag-and-drop an item in the Context Filter section at the top of the work area. Insert the Web member in the Context Filter section.

	2004		2005		2006		2007		Time
	Revenue	Planned revenue	Revenue	Planned revenue	Revenue	Planned revenue	Revenue	Planned revenue	
Brazil	$12,626,914.51	$13,776,598.81	$22,580,246.05	$24,180,719.34	$28,939,868.92	$30,666,354.32	$21,117,462.80	$22,569,932.97	
United States	$37,439,070.14	$40,731,258.49	$79,529,412.44	$85,435,934.54	$146,647,486.63	$155,778,369.49	$105,247,945.44	$112,820,103.34	
Canada	$13,943,278.81	$14,998,240.28	$34,545,686.33	$36,803,266.36	$46,352,355.74	$48,976,323.65	$45,231,844.43	$48,013,460.47	
Mexico	$4,251,899.15	$4,725,643.04	$13,886,304.99	$14,993,981.29	$43,724,327.72	$46,503,617.63	$32,341,116.79	$34,619,340.19	
Americas	$68,261,162.61	$74,231,740.62	$150,541,649.81	$161,413,901.53	$265,664,039.01	$281,924,665.09	$203,938,369.46	$218,022,836.97	

The values in the crosstab are now focused on web orders for the Americas sales region by year. Notice that the context filter (Web) is automatically displayed in the header. This is a visual indicator indicating that there are filters on the report.

3. Add additional context filters. Insert the 2007 member from the Time dimension in the Context Filter section.

	2004		2005		2006		2007		Time
	Revenue	Planned revenue	Revenue	Planned revenue	Revenue	Planned revenue	Revenue	Planned revenue	
Brazil							$21,117,462.80	$22,569,932.97	
United States							$105,247,945.44	$112,820,103.34	
Canada							$45,231,844.43	$48,013,460.47	
Mexico							$32,341,116.79	$34,619,340.19	
Americas							$203,938,369.46	$218,022,836.97	

The crosstab is now focused on web orders for the Americas sales region for the year 2007. With context filters, you will notice that the members that do not meet the filter criteria are not removed from the crosstab.

Suppressing Rows and Columns

In this example, because we have a context filter on 2007, the other year members do not contain any values but remain in the report. To remove the blank cells, you can use the Suppress Rows and Columns feature.

To suppress cells with zeroes or blanks, click the Suppress button on the standard toolbar, and choose Suppress Rows and Columns. This removes the unwanted blank cells:

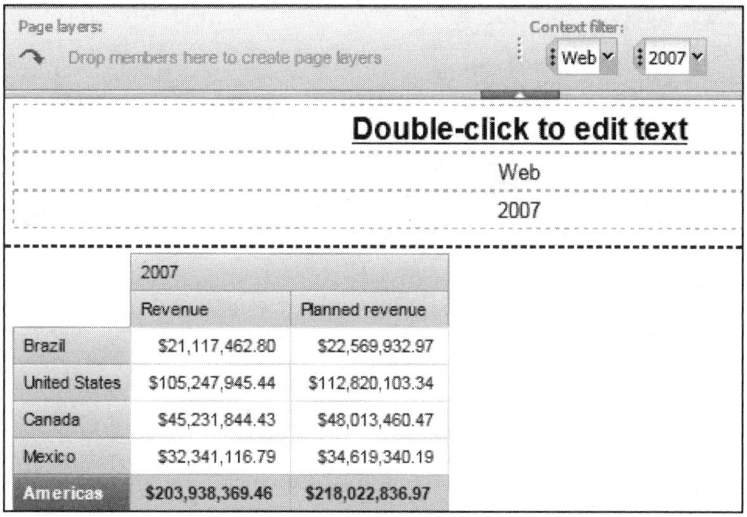

Page layers:			Context filter:	
Drop members here to create page layers			Web ∨ 2007 ∨	

Double-click to edit text

Web

2007

	2007	
	Revenue	Planned revenue
Brazil	$21,117,462.80	$22,569,932.97
United States	$105,247,945.44	$112,820,103.34
Canada	$45,231,844.43	$48,013,460.47
Mexico	$32,341,116.79	$34,619,340.19
Americas	**$203,938,369.46**	**$218,022,836.97**

Deleting a Context Filter

To delete a context filter, follow these steps:

1. Click the downward-facing arrow next to the filter in the Context Filter section of the work area, as shown next:

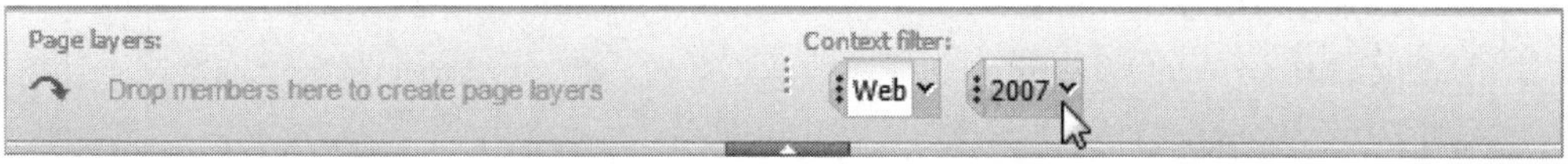

Page layers:	Context filter:
Drop members here to create page layers	Web ∨ 2007 ∨

2. Select Delete from the menu. The context filter is removed. For this example, we removed the 2007 filter from the report.

Creating a Custom Filter

To create a custom filter, follow these steps:

1. In the crosstab, select the item for which you want to create a custom filter. Select the 2007 cell in the columns of the crosstab.

2. Click the Filters button on the standard toolbar, and choose Create Custom Filter from the drop-down menu. The Filter Condition dialog appears:

3. Make any necessary modifications to the filter condition. Add 2006 to the list of selected values so that 2006 and 2007 will be included in the crosstab.

4. Click OK to create the filter:

	2006		2007		Time
	Revenue	Planned revenue	Revenue	Planned revenue	
Brazil	$28,939,868.92	$30,666,354.32	$21,117,462.80	$22,569,932.97	
Canada	$46,352,355.74	$48,976,323.65	$45,231,844.43	$48,013,460.47	
United States	$146,647,486.63	$155,778,369.49	$105,247,945.44	$112,820,103.34	
Mexico	$43,724,327.72	$46,503,617.63	$32,341,116.79	$34,619,340.19	
Americas	$265,664,039.01	$281,924,665.09	$203,938,369.46	$218,022,836.97	

Creating a Calculation

Adding calculations to your reports lets you include additional data in a report that does not exist in the data source. For example, using the Revenue and Planned Revenue measures, you can create Revenue as a percentage of a Planned Revenue calculation to show a manager how close actual revenues come to expected revenues. We continue to use the same sample report created throughout the chapter in this section.

To create a calculation, follow these steps:

1. Select two items in the crosstab for which you want to create a calculation. CTRL-click Revenue and Planned Revenue in the columns of the crosstab.

	2006		2007		Time
	Revenue	Planned revenue	Revenue	Planned revenue	
Brazil	$28,939,868.92	$30,666,354.32	$21,117,462.80	$22,569,932.97	
Canada	$46,352,355.74	$48,976,323.65	$45,231,844.43	$48,013,460.47	
United States	$146,647,486.63	$155,778,369.49	$105,247,945.44	$112,820,103.34	
Mexico	$43,724,327.72	$46,503,617.63	$32,341,116.79	$34,619,340.19	
Americas	$265,664,039.01	$281,924,665.09	$203,938,369.46	$218,022,836.97	

2. Click the Insert Calculation button on the standard toolbar, and choose Custom from the drop-down menu. The Insert Custom Calculation dialog appears:

Insert Custom Calculation   Help ⊗

Operation:

+ (addition)

Calculation

Revenue + Planned revenue

Number:

New data item name

⦿ Use the default name

(Revenue + Planned revenue)

○

OK   Cancel

3. In the Insert Customer Calculation dialog, select the desired action from the Operation drop-down menu. Choose % (percentage) as the operation.

4. In the Calculation area, make any necessary modifications. Select the Revenue As A Percentage Of Planned Revenue radio button.

5. In the New Data Item Name area, choose to use the default name or type a name for the calculation. Click the radio button next to the blank space and type **% Variance**.

6. Click OK to create the calculation. The custom calculation is added to the crosstab:

	2006			2007			Time
	Revenue	Planned revenue	% Variance	Revenue	Planned revenue	% Variance	
Brazil	$28,939,868.92	$30,666,354.32	94.37%	$21,117,462.80	$22,569,932.97	93.56%	
Canada	$46,352,355.74	$48,976,323.65	94.64%	$45,231,844.43	$48,013,460.47	94.21%	
United States	$146,647,486.63	$155,778,369.49	94.14%	$105,247,945.44	$112,820,103.34	93.29%	
Mexico	$43,724,327.72	$46,503,617.63	94.02%	$32,341,116.79	$34,619,340.19	93.42%	
Americas	$265,664,039.01	$281,924,665.09	94.23%	$203,938,369.46	$218,022,836.97	93.54%	

Creating Page Layers

Adding page layers lets you uniformly split a report across several pages. Page layers are also helpful when you are dealing with larger sets of data. We continue to use the same sample report created throughout the chapter in this section.

To create page layers, follow these steps:

1. From the Content pane, drag-and-drop an item into the Page Layers section of the work area. Insert the Products member into the Page Layers section.

Page layers:
Products ∨

Context filter:
Web ∨

Double-click to edit text

Camping Equipment

Web

	2006			2007			Time
	Revenue	Planned revenue	% Variance	Revenue	Planned revenue	% Variance	
United States	$68,908,006.62	$73,133,607.60	94.22%	$47,080,667.44	$50,559,862.23	93.12%	
Canada	$20,836,212.68	$21,999,327.01	94.71%	$21,053,149.96	$22,392,446.58	94.02%	
Mexico	$21,237,845.32	$22,570,176.94	94.10%	$14,460,414.42	$15,530,979.03	93.11%	
Brazil	$14,080,643.24	$14,919,855.17	94.38%	$9,369,955.89	$10,049,347.60	93.24%	
Americas	$125,062,707.86	$132,622,966.72	94.30%	$91,964,187.71	$98,532,635.44	93.33%	

Feb 8, 2012   1   3:16:39 PM

⊼ Top   ⊼ Page up   ⊻ Page down   ⊼ Bottom   🗒

The values in the crosstab have been filtered on the first product line, and the paging buttons in the work area are now enabled. A header (Camping Equipment)

has been added to the title section of the work area to provide a visual aid to what the crosstab contains.

2. Click the Page Down link to see the next page. Golf Equipment displays:

Double-click to edit text

Golf Equipment

Web

	2006			2007			Time
	Revenue	Planned revenue	% Variance	Revenue	Planned revenue	% Variance	
United States	$35,065,878.28	$37,810,664.54	92.74%	$26,062,316.85	$28,493,419.65	91.47%	
Canada	$13,395,471.23	$14,307,397.85	93.63%	$11,261,330.36	$12,080,112.98	93.22%	
Mexico	$10,400,565.58	$11,240,180.22	92.53%	$7,136,064.21	$7,788,170.28	91.63%	
Brazil	$6,185,100.85	$6,669,122.41	92.74%	$4,733,649.19	$5,168,155.60	91.59%	
Americas	$65,047,015.94	$70,027,365.02	92.89%	$49,193,360.61	$53,529,858.51	91.90%	

| Feb 8, 2012 | 2 | 3:16:39 PM |

⊼Top ⬆Page up ⬇Page down ⊻Bottom

Enabling Drill-Down and Drill-Up

Drill-down and drill-up capabilities in a report allow users to navigate through hierarchical data. This flexibility lets users view data at a high level or view more detailed lower level data. By default, Cognos Business Insight Advanced reports do not have drill-up and drill-down capabilities when they are executed by an end user in IBM Cognos Viewer. This feature must be enabled by the report creator. We continue to use the same sample report created throughout the chapter in this section.

To add drill-down and drill-up capabilities to a report, follow these steps:

1. From the Data menu, select Drill Options. The Drill Options dialog displays.

2. In the Drill Options dialog, select the Allow Drill-Up And Drill-Down check box. Click OK.

3. Click the Run Report button on the standard toolbar. The report displays in IBM Cognos Viewer:

Camping Equipment

Web

	2006			2007			Time
	Revenue	Planned revenue	% Variance	Revenue	Planned revenue	% Variance	
United States	$68,908,006.62	$73,133,607.60	94.22%	$47,080,667.44	$50,559,862.23	93.12%	
Canada	$20,836,212.68	$21,999,327.01	94.71%	$21,053,149.96	$22,392,446.58	94.02%	
Mexico	$21,237,845.32	$22,570,176.94	94.10%	$14,460,414.42	$15,530,979.03	93.11%	
Brazil	$14,080,643.24	$14,919,855.17	94.38%	$9,369,955.89	$10,049,347.60	93.24%	
Americas	$125,062,707.86	$132,622,966.72	94.30%	$91,964,187.71	$98,532,635.44	93.33%	

Notice that the items in the rows and columns are now underlined, indicating they are links. This signifies that drill-down and drill-up capabilities are enabled for this report.

4. Click a link in the crosstab to drill-down on the selected item. Click the United States link to drill-down to the Sales Staff cities within the United States.

5. Right-click an item in the crosstab and select Drill Up from the context menu to drill-up one level on the selected item.

Camping Equipment

Web

	2006			2007			Time
	Revenue	Planned revenue	% Variance	Revenue	Planned revenue	% Variance	
Boston	$15,890,615.49	$16,863,916.65	94.23%	$9,607,648.59	$10,304,373.88	93.24%	
Seattle	...718.78	$26,391,501.76	94.15%	$16,213,457.39	$17,424,418.52	93.05%	
Los Angele	...707.87	$23,663,430.58	94.18%	$17,138,826.93	$18,425,412.83	93.02%	
Miami	...964.48	$6,214,758.61	94.66%	$4,120,734.53	$4,405,657.00	93.53%	
United St:	...006.62	$73,133,607.60	94.22%	$47,080,667.44	$50,559,862.23	93.12%	

Drill Down
Drill Up
Go To ▶
Glossary
Lineage

NOTE *The drill-down and drill-up options work only for HTML output reports.*

Creating Custom Groups

You can create custom groups to organize members in a group that might not exist in the data source but that may have value to the business. We continue to use the same sample report created throughout the chapter in this section.

NOTE *This is a new feature in IBM Cognos v10.1.1. It is not available in Cognos v10.1.*

To create a custom group, follow these steps:

1. Select the United States member in the rows of the crosstab.

2. Click the Explore button on the standard toolbar, and choose Edit Set from the drop-down menu. The Set Definition dialog appears.

3. In the Set Definition dialog, click the New button, and select Custom Grouping from the drop-down menu. The Custom Grouping dialog appears:

4. In the Custom Grouping dialog, click the New button. The Custom Group dialog appears.

5. In the Custom Group dialog, specify a name for the new custom group. Enter **North America** in the New Group Name text box.

6. Add items to be included in the group from the Available Members pane into the Members pane. Navigate to the Sales Staff dimension and add the United States, Canada, and Mexico members to the Members pane.

7. Click OK to save the new custom group. The Custom Grouping dialog appears again, now with the new custom group.

8. In the Custom Grouping dialog, choose the behavior for the remaining values. Select the Group Remaining Values Into A Single Group radio button, and enter **South America** in the text box.

9. Click OK to save the changes made to the custom groupings.

10. In the Set Definition dialog, click OK. The new custom groups appear in the crosstab:

Double-click to edit text							
Camping Equipment							
Web							
	2006			2007			Time
	Revenue	Planned revenue	% Variance	Revenue	Planned revenue	% Variance	
North America	$110,982,064.62	$117,703,111.55	94.29%	$82,594,231.82	$88,483,287.84	93.34%	
South America	$14,080,643.24	$14,919,855.17	94.38%	$9,369,955.89	$10,049,347.60	93.24%	
Americas	$125,062,707.86	$132,622,966.72	94.30%	$91,964,187.71	$96,532,635.44	93.33%	

PART III

Report Authoring— Relational Data

T oday's decision makers are looking for quicker, more efficient ways to view their business data for a competitive edge. IBM Cognos Report Studio is a web-based application that gives users the ability to create simple or complex reports that allow decision makers to make quick and intelligent business decisions. Cognos Report Studio grants users the flexibility needed to create lists, crosstabs, charts, and dashboard-style reports. Reports can be grouped, sorted, and formatted in a variety of ways to meet business requirements. Report output options include the industry standards HTML, PDF, and Microsoft Excel. Cognos Report Studio makes it easy to manipulate and present data with a wide array of report-creation tools.

In this chapter, you will learn how to use Cognos Report Studio to create several different styles of reports. While creating these reports, you will become familiar with commonly used toolbar items, menu options, and other features within Cognos Report Studio. As in many IBM Cognos Business Intelligence v10.1 applications, you have multiple ways of accomplishing a task. This chapter details the most commonly used ways to accomplish a single task and references alternative ways to achieve the same goal.

Getting Started with IBM Cognos Report Studio

You access Cognos Report Studio from IBM Cognos Connection. Cognos Report Studio opens in a separate web browser window, leaving your Cognos Connection window intact. From there, you can work with the Report Studio components to create reports.

Opening IBM Cognos Report Studio

To open Cognos Report Studio, follow these steps:

1. Log on to Cognos Connection and navigate to the Public Folders tab.

2. From the Launch menu located in the upper right of the screen, select Report Studio. The Select a Package screen displays.

3. Select a package from either the Recently Used Packages area or the List of All Packages area. The Cognos Report Studio Startup dialog appears.

4. To create a new report, select the Create New button. The New dialog opens.

5. Choose the type of new report you want to create. Report styles are described in Table 10-1.

6. Click OK. Cognos Report Studio opens.

Report Style	Description
Blank	Create an empty template. Unlike the other templates, this template does not contain any objects at all (such as headers, lists, crosstabs, or footers). Use this to create a report from scratch.
List	View detailed information in a tabular format.
Crosstab	View summarized information at the intersecting point of a column and row. For example, when viewing sales figures for each month of the year, the sales staff members could display in the rows, the months could display in the columns, and the sales figures could display at the intersections of the rows and columns.
Chart	View graphically represented data. The available options are Column, Bar, Progressive, Pareto, Line, Pie, Donut, Area, Combination, Scatter, Bubble, Point, Radar, Polar, Gauge, Metrics Range, and Microchart.
Map	Show tabular data in geographical form. For example, a map of the United States could be colored to show revenue for sales territories.
Financial	View data in a financial format. This template contains a crosstab, but it has a style attached to it with a financial look.
Repeater Table	Repeat blocks of data within a report. Repeaters are commonly used to create mailing labels.
Statistics	Use for reports that contain statistical information.
Active Report	Create highly interactive, managed reports for business users to consume offline.
Blank Active Report	Same as Active Report without any objects in the layout by default.
Report Template	Use to build reports. This template is useful for reports that require certain business standards.
Existing	Open a saved report from Cognos Connection.

TABLE 10-1   IBM Cognos Report Studio Report Styles

If you choose to open an existing report, rather than create a new one, you'll see the Open dialog. Navigate to the report that you wish to open, and then click Open to start Cognos Report Studio with the selected report.

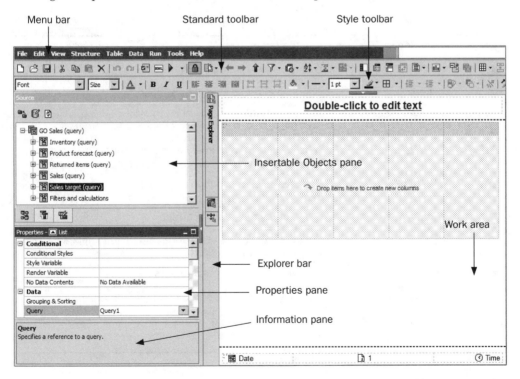

Using the Cognos Report Studio Interface

The Cognos Report Studio main user interface is made up of several sections, as shown next.

The main interface components are the standard toolbar, style toolbar, Insertable Objects pane, Explorer bar, work area, Properties pane, and Information pane. The following sections describe these components.

TIP *You can change the layout of the Cognos Report Studio so that the work area is on the left side of the screen. To make this change, choose Tools | Options from the menu bar, and then select Position Pane on the Right.*

Standard Toolbar

The standard toolbar provides quick access to commonly used features. Hovering the pointer over a button on the toolbar provides a tooltip with a short description of the button's function. Some of the features available from the standard toolbar are listed in Table 10-2.

Style Toolbar

The style toolbar offers options for formatting reports. Some commonly used features available from the style toolbar are listed in Table 10-3.

Icon	Name	Description
▶	Run Report	Run the report
🔒	Lock/Unlock	Lock or unlock page objects
▼	Filters	Open the Filters dialog, where report filters can be added or modified
↕	Sort	Sort the report in ascending or descending order
Σ	Aggregate	Drop-down list of summary functions that can be applied to the report and also allows creating a custom aggregation
	Calculate	Drop-down list of common calculations for the selected item(s) and also allows creating a custom calculation
	Group/Ungroup	Group or ungroup data in a report
	Section	Create sections in a report, with a data item appearing as a heading for the section
	Headers & Footers	Create page headers and footers
	Create Chart	Provides options to insert a chart into the report
	Build Prompt Page	Create a prompt page for the report

TABLE 10-2   IBM Cognos Report Studio Standard Toolbar

Icon	Name	Description
Size ▾	Font Size	Change the size of the selected text
A	Foreground Color	Change the color of the selected text
♨	Background Color	Change the background color of an object
—	Border Style	Select the border style for an object
⌇	Border Color	Select the border color for an object
⊞	All Borders	Add borders to the selected object with the selected style and color
%⁺	Data Format	Specify the format of a data item
▓	Conditional Styles	Apply style(s) to cells depending on a condition

TABLE 10-3   IBM Cognos Report Studio Style Toolbar

TIP *If a toolbar icon has a downward-facing black arrow to the right of it, this indicates the toolbar button has a drop-down list associated with it.*

Insertable Objects Pane
The Insertable Objects pane consists of the following tabs:

- **Source**   Contains the namespace(s), query subjects, and data items that make up the selected package
- **Data Items**   Contains the data items that are being used in the current report
- **Toolbox**   Contains other objects that can be added to reports, as listed in Table 10-4

Explorer Bar
The options on the Explorer bar determine how the work area is used:

- **Page Explorer**   Enables you to manage report pages, prompt pages, and classes
- **Query Explorer**   Enables you to manage queries that are in the report
- **Condition Explorer**   Enables you to manage the variables defined for the report

Work Area
The work area has three different modes:

- In the Page Explorer mode, you insert data items and other Toolbox objects into the work area to create the layout for the report.
- In the Query Explorer mode, you can manipulate the queries, data items, and filters for the report.
- In the Condition Explorer mode, you can edit variables and values for those variables.

Object Type	Object Description
[ab] Text Item	Add informational text to the report
Block	A container to help organize other objects within the page
Table	Organize objects in a table within the report, for which you can specify the desired number of rows and columns
Query Calculation	Create a calculated data item in the report query
Layout Calculation	Create a calculation that is part of the layout of the report and is not in the report query
Image	Insert a referenced image to the report
Singleton	Add a single data item anywhere within the report
Conditional Blocks	Organize objects and apply conditional formatting to them
HTML Item	Include HTML code or JavaScript in the report to use functionality outside Cognos Report Studio
Date	Insert the current date on the report (having the date the report was executed on the report is useful for commonly printed reports)
Row Number	Insert a column that numbers each row (this can be useful when validating data)
Value Prompt	Prompt the user to select values from a list to filter the report results
Date Prompt	Prompt the user to select a date or date range to filter the report results

TABLE 10-4   IBM Cognos Report Studio Toolbox Objects

Properties and Information Panes

The Properties pane lists the properties that you can set for an object in a report. These properties include data format, border, padding, background color, conditional properties, and many other types of settings.

The Information pane lists the description of the item currently selected in the Properties pane.

Object Hierarchy

In Cognos Report Studio, objects are organized in a hierarchy. Parent/child relationships exist between objects. When formatting is applied to an object, it is also applied to all children of that object. For example, a list contains list columns, and each list column has a list column title and a list column body. If you select a list and change the font weight to bold, it will apply to all children of the list object. Formatting on objects lower in the hierarchy overrides formatting on objects higher in the hierarchy.

Within the title bar of the Properties pane, there is a Select Ancestor button, which displays a list of ancestors for the item currently selected in the report. This allows you to easily navigate through the objects on the page or to select objects that are not easily selected from the work area, so that properties can be set for these objects or styles can be applied to them.

Creating List Reports

A *list report* is a report that presents data in rows and columns. List reports are used to show detailed information in a list format.

TIP *When you create a new report, it is good practice to assign it a name and save it before continuing to build the layout.*

To create a simple list report, follow these steps:

1. In Cognos Report Studio, create a new report, choose the List report style, and then click OK.

2. From the Source tab in the Insertable Objects pane, drag a data item to the work area and drop it where you would like to insert it. A flashing black bar displays where you can drop a data item to be added to the list, as shown next. For this example, insert the Sales Region data item from the Sales Staff query subject of the Sales (query) namespace within the GO Sales (query) package.

3. From the Source tab in the Insertable Objects pane, double-click a data item to add to the list. For this example, double-click the Order Method Type data item from the Order Method query subject. The new data item displays to the right of the first data item in the list.

Sales region	Order method type
<Sales region>	<Order method type>
<Sales region>	<Order method type>
<Sales region>	<Order method type>

4. In the Insertable Objects pane, CTRL-click a few data items you would like to add to your list. For this example, select the Quantity, Revenue, and Gross Profit data items from the Sales query subject.

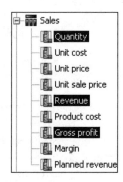

5. Right-click one of the selected items and choose Insert. Your list should now look similar to this:

Sales region	Order method type	Quantity	Revenue	Gross profit
<Sales region>	<Order method type>	<Quantity>	<Revenue>	<Gross profit>
<Sales region>	<Order method type>	<Quantity>	<Revenue>	<Gross profit>
<Sales region>	<Order method type>	<Quantity>	<Revenue>	<Gross profit>

6. On the standard toolbar, click Run Report to view the report in IBM Cognos Viewer.

Sales region	Order method type	Quantity	Revenue	Gross profit
Americas	E-mail	971,240	$44,399,346.51	$18,168,547.90
Asia Pacific	E-mail	642,345	$32,455,838.86	$13,418,365.27
Central Europe	E-mail	1,305,133	$66,296,383.70	$27,043,233.39
Northern Europe	E-mail	266,989	$12,059,800.38	$4,973,086.39
Southern Europe	E-mail	456,952	$24,631,674.71	$10,153,883.59
Americas	Fax	348,171	$14,976,874.45	$6,024,663.85

Cognos Report Studio displays the data in a simple, unformatted state. The sales regions are ordered alphabetically for each order method, but there is a lot of repetitive information in the list. Grouping data items will make this report easier to read.

Grouping Data

Grouping data makes reports more visually appealing and helps the end users to locate and view the data. In this section, we will group data in the sample list report that we just created.

To group data in a list, follow these steps:

1. In the list, select the column(s) on which you want to group. For this example, select the Sales Region column.

2. On the standard toolbar, click the Group/Ungroup button. An icon appears in the list, indicating that the data item is grouped.

Sales region	Order method type	Quantity	Revenue	Gross profit
<Sales region>	<Order method type>	<Quantity>	<Revenue>	<Gross profit>
<Sales region>	<Order method type>	<Quantity>	<Revenue>	<Gross profit>

3. On the standard toolbar, click Run Report to view the changes made to the report. Grouping data in the report has made it easier to read, as shown here:

Sales region	Order method type	Quantity	Revenue	Gross profit
Americas	E-mail	971,240	$44,399,346.51	$18,168,547.90
	Fax	348,171	$14,976,874.45	$6,024,663.85
	Mail	305,257	$12,008,347.94	$4,880,866.71
	Sales visit	2,284,176	$107,417,742.10	$42,455,201.74
	Special	267,679	$10,645,941.64	$4,250,064.10
	Telephone	2,198,641	$99,234,407.27	$38,160,319.72
	Web	12,569,218	$688,405,220.89	$283,787,804.29
Asia Pacific	E-mail	642,345	$32,455,838.86	$13,418,365.27
	Fax	395,803	$20,171,677.79	$8,523,793.11
	Mail	193,660	$12,763,167.65	$5,479,077.12

Filtering Data

Filtering allows you to minimize the amount of data that is returned in the report. Filters can reduce processing time by eliminating unnecessary data. In this section, we will add filters to the sample list report to narrow the focus of the query.

Filtering on an Existing Item

To filter on an existing item in a report, follow these steps:

1. Select a data item in the report. For this example, select the Order Method Type column.

2. On the standard toolbar, click the Filters button and choose Create Custom Filter from the submenu. The Filter Condition dialog displays.

3. From the Condition drop-down list, choose to include or exclude the values. For this example, select Do NOT Show the Following Values.

4. In the Values list, specify the items on which you want to filter. For this example, move Fax and Special to the Selected Values list.

Filter Condition - Order method type		Help ✕

Condition:

Do NOT show the following values: ▾

☐ Prompt for values when report is run in viewer

Values

Keywords:

[   ]   Search ▾

Values:		Selected values:
E-mail		Fax
Fax		Special
Mail		
Sales visit		
Special	➡	
Telephone	⬅	
Web		

Select all Deselect all   ✶ ✕   Select all Deselect all

☐ Include missing values (NULL)

OK   Cancel

5. Click the OK button.

6. Run the report. The result set now excludes the Fax and Special order method types.

Sales region	Order method type	Quantity	Revenue	Gross profit
Americas	E-mail	971,240	$44,399,346.51	$18,168,547.90
	Mail	305,257	$12,008,347.94	$4,880,866.71
	Sales visit	2,284,176	$107,417,742.10	$42,455,201.74
	Telephone	2,198,641	$99,234,407.27	$38,160,319.72
	Web	12,569,218	$688,405,220.89	$283,787,804.29
Asia Pacific	E-mail	642,345	$32,455,838.86	$13,418,365.27
	Mail	193,660	$12,763,167.65	$5,479,077.12
	Sales visit	1,588,658	$70,484,129.49	$27,708,290.76
	Telephone	1,601,540	$80,985,399.09	$33,841,143.57
	Web	12,104,697	$630,140,864.16	$255,702,262.81
Central Europe	E-mail	1,305,133	$66,296,383.70	$27,043,233.39
	Mail	233,141	$10,698,741.87	$4,052,124.52

Creating an Advanced Filter

To create an advanced filter, follow these steps:

1. On the standard toolbar, click the Filters button and choose Edit Filters from the submenu. The Filters dialog displays.

2. Click the Add button to add a new detail filter.

NOTE *Detail filters are used to filter detail-level values within a report. Summary filters are used to filter summary-level values within a report.*

3. In the Create Filter dialog, select Advanced.

4. Click OK. The Expression dialog displays.

Source   Data items   Queries   Functions   Parameters

5. From the Source tab in the Available Components pane, double-click any data items to add them to the filter expression. For this example, add the Year data item from the Time query subject in the Sales (query) namespace to the Expression Definition pane.

6. From the Functions tab in the Available Components pane, add functions to the filter expression. For this example, add the "in" function from the Operators folder to the expression.

TIP *The Tips tab in the Information pane of the Expression dialog supplies information about the selected function, such as a definition, an example, and the syntax.*

7. Add any necessary terms to your expression definition. For this example, select the Year data item again on the Source tab, and then click the Select Multiple Values button.

Add 2005 and 2006 to the Selected Values list, and then click Insert to add them to the expression definition.

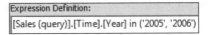

Tip *Alternatively, you can type expressions directly into the Expression Definition pane instead of choosing items from the Available Components pane.*

8. Click OK to return to the Filters dialog.

9. Click OK again to return to Cognos Report Studio.

10. Click Run Report on the standard toolbar to view the changes made to the report. The values are significantly lower than when the report was run without the filter, as shown next.

Sales region	Order method type	Quantity	Revenue	Gross profit
Americas	E-mail	304,827	$15,884,458.80	$6,607,736.66
	Sales visit	1,146,195	$55,715,052.86	$22,103,896.84
	Web	7,563,425	$416,205,688.82	$172,324,270.98
	Mail	169,711	$7,460,082.14	$2,990,487.34
	Telephone	881,199	$44,163,577.70	$16,740,759.70
Asia Pacific	Telephone	703,044	$36,977,100.97	$15,982,719.73
	Mail	104,209	$5,442,445.34	$2,289,686.18

TIP *You can also use Query Explorer mode to add and edit filters. Additionally, you can easily remove all filters from a report by clicking the Filters button on the standard toolbar and selecting Remove All Filters.*

Adding Query Calculations

Adding calculations to a report allows users to view additional data that does not exist in the package. A Query Calculation adds a new data item with a user-defined expression to the query. In this section, we will add a gross profit percentage calculation to the sample list report.

To add a calculation to a report, follow these steps:

1. In the Insertable Objects pane, select the Toolbox tab.

2. Double-click Query Calculation. The Create Calculation dialog displays.

3. In the Name box, type a name for the calculation. For this example, use the name *Gross Profit %*.

4. Click OK. The Expression dialog displays.

5. From the Source tab or the Data Items tab in the Available Components pane, add data items to the expression definition. For this example, add the Gross Profit data item from the Data Items tab.

NOTE *The Data Items tab contains items that are already included in the report query.*

6. From the Functions tab in the Available Components pane, add functions to your expression definition. For this example, insert the divide operator (/) from the Operators folder.

7. Add any other necessary data terms to your expression. For this example, add the Revenue data item from the Data Items tab.

> Expression Definition:
> [Gross profit] / [Revenue]

***

TIP   Alternatively, you can type expressions directly into the Expression Definition pane instead of choosing items from the Available Components pane.

8. Click OK to return to Cognos Report Studio.

9. Click Run Report on the standard toolbar to view the report. The added calculation is formatted in the default style, as shown next.

Sales region	Order method type	Quantity	Revenue	Gross profit	Gross Profit %
Americas	E-mail	304,827	$15,884,458.80	$6,607,736.66	0.41598752
	Sales visit	1,146,195	$55,715,052.86	$22,103,896.84	0.39673115
	Web	7,563,425	$416,205,688.82	$172,324,270.98	0.41403632

By default, calculations use the format of the data items that make up the calculation. You must manually change the format to the appropriate style, if necessary. In our example, the values in the Gross Profit % column should be formatted to display as a percentage.

Formatting Data

You can specify the data format for data items that are not formatted in the desired way. Format properties can be defined for types such as Text, Number, Currency, Percent, and Date. You can also set properties such as the number of decimal points, the currency symbol, the style of a date, and what is displayed when data is missing. For our sample list report, we will format the Gross Profit % column values.

To set the format for a data item, follow these steps:

1. Select the column for which you want to set the format. For this example, select the Gross Profit % column.

2. In the Properties pane, click the Data Format property, and then click the ellipsis. The Data Format dialog displays.

3. From the Format Type drop-down list, select the appropriate type. For this example, select Percent.

Data Format		Help ✕
Format type:	Properties:	
Percent ▼	Percentage Symbol	▲
	Percent Scale (integer)	
	No. of Decimal Places	
	Decimal Separator	
	Scale	
	Negative Sign Symbol	
	Negative Sign Position	
	Use Thousands Separator	
	Thousands Separator	
	Group Size (digits)	
	Secondary Group Size (digits)	
	Maximum No. of Digits	
	Minimum No. of Digits	▼

4. In the Properties pane, set any desired properties for the format type. For this example, set the No. of Decimal Places property to 2.
5. Click OK to save the formatting properties.
6. Click Run Report on the standard toolbar to view the report. The Gross Profit % values are now formatted as percentages.

Sales region	Order method type	Quantity	Revenue	Gross profit	Gross Profit %
Americas	E-mail	304,827	$15,884,458.80	$6,607,736.66	41.60%
	Sales visit	1,146,195	$55,715,052.86	$22,103,896.84	39.67%
	Web	7,563,425	$416,205,688.82	$172,324,270.98	41.40%
	Mail	169,711	$7,460,082.14	$2,990,487.34	40.09%

Summarizing Data

Summary-level data can be added for the entire list report, for one grouped data item, or for multiple grouped data items. In this section, we will add summary lines to the sample list report and the Sales Territory grouped data item.

Adding Summary Lines

To summarize data in a report, follow these steps:

1. Select the column(s) that contain the data you would like to summarize. For this example, select Quantity, Revenue, Gross Profit, and Gross Profit %.

2. On the standard toolbar, click the Aggregate button, and then select Total from the submenu. This adds a total summary line to the report.

Sales region	Order method type	Quantity	Revenue	Gross profit	Gross Profit %
<Sales region>	<Order method type>	<Quantity>	<Revenue>	<Gross profit>	<Gross Profit %>
<Sales region> - Total		<Total(Quantity)>	<Total(Revenue)>	<Total(Gross profit)>	<Total(Gross Profit %)>
<Sales region>	<Order method type>	<Quantity>	<Revenue>	<Gross profit>	<Gross Profit %>
<Sales region> - Total		<Total(Quantity)>	<Total(Revenue)>	<Total(Gross profit)>	<Total(Gross Profit %)>
Overall - Total		<Total(Quantity)>	<Total(Revenue)>	<Total(Gross profit)>	<Total(Gross Profit %)>

3. On the standard toolbar, click Run Report. In this example, the report now contains a summary line for each sales region.

4. Click the Bottom link in the Cognos Viewer window to navigate to the last page of the report to view the summary line for the entire report.

	Mail	58,935	$3,011,530.92	$1,252,323.87	41.58%
	Sales visit	314,292	$15,959,181.82	$6,509,151.91	40.79%
	Telephone	315,707	$14,652,707.97	$6,129,798.86	41.83%
	Web	3,080,968	$168,140,203.51	$68,907,509.17	40.98%
Northern Europe - Total		3,861,289	$205,200,673.60	$84,202,840.49	206.04%
Southern Europe	E-mail	211,704	$11,712,127.15	$4,886,095.64	41.72%
	Mail	14,997	$872,362.43	$399,357.02	45.78%
	Sales visit	268,446	$12,873,125.76	$5,047,957.13	39.21%
	Telephone	336,556	$14,961,187.86	$6,078,828.44	40.63%
	Web	2,845,529	$148,714,147.13	$61,651,940.00	41.46%
Southern Europe - Total		3,677,232	$189,132,950.33	$78,064,178.23	208.80%
Overall - Total		48,525,184	$2,609,969,663.02	$1,073,456,818.60	1,024.51%

Modifying the Aggregation Method

The Aggregation Method property for summary data may need to be adjusted if the results are not what you were expecting. The Aggregation Method property defines the type of aggregation applied to summarized values. In our example, the Aggregation Method property for the Gross Profit % calculated field defaulted to Total because we chose Total as the aggregation for the columns we summarized. This property needs to be changed in order to correctly roll up the Gross Profit % calculation (*[Gross profit]/[Revenue]*) at the summary level.

To change the Aggregation Method property, follow these steps:

1. Select the cell for which you want to modify the Rollup Aggregation Function property. For this example, select <Total(Gross Profit %)> at the <Sales region> - Total level.

2. In the Properties pane, click the Aggregation Method property.

3. Select the appropriate option. For this example, choose Calculated.

4. On the standard toolbar, click Run Report. The summary-level data for the calculated column now displays the average of the detail rows instead of the total.

Sales region	Order method type	Quantity	Revenue	Gross profit	Gross Profit %
Americas	E-mail	304,827	$15,884,458.80	$6,607,736.66	41.60%
	Mail	169,711	$7,460,082.14	$2,990,487.34	40.09%
	Sales visit	1,146,195	$55,715,052.86	$22,103,896.84	39.67%
	Telephone	881,199	$44,163,577.70	$16,740,759.70	37.91%
	Web	7,563,425	$416,205,688.82	$172,324,270.98	41.40%
Americas - Total		10,065,357	$539,428,860.32	$220,767,151.52	40.93%
Asia Pacific	E-mail	262,770	$11,549,804.64	$4,559,157.29	39.47%
	Mail	104,209	$5,442,445.34	$2,289,686.18	42.07%
	Sales visit	624,654	$30,188,493.91	$12,258,655.20	40.61%
	Telephone	703,044	$36,977,100.97	$15,982,719.73	43.22%
	Web	7,261,505	$386,965,517.48	$157,256,773.31	40.64%
Asia Pacific - Total		8,956,182	$471,123,362.34	$192,346,991.71	40.83%

NOTE *Select Automatic Summary from the Aggregate drop-down list on the standard toolbar to create summary lines with the Aggregation Method property set based on the data item.*

Adding Prompts to Reports

You can add prompts to reports to allow user interaction. Prompts act as questions for specific areas of business that narrow the result set, making the report more manageable. Prompts can come in many styles, such as text box prompts, value prompts, search and select prompts, and date prompts. Within each prompt type, a variety of properties can be set to alter its functionality. For example, you can set a value prompt to allow one or multiple items to be selected. Date prompts can prompt for a single date or a range of dates.

In this section, we will add a prompt for product line to the sample list report we have been building in this chapter. With a prompt for product line added to the report, the user can choose which product line(s) display in the report.

To add a prompt to a report, follow these steps:

1. In the work area, select the column that contains the data item for which you want to add a prompt. For this example, select Sales Region.

2. On the standard toolbar, click the Build Prompt Page button. A prompt page is automatically created based on the column you selected, and is now displayed in the work area. The prompt page consists of a title for the prompt and the prompt itself.

3. On the standard toolbar, click Run Report. The prompt page screen displays.

4. From the prompt, make a selection. For this example, select Southern Europe at the Sales Region prompt.

5. Click Finish. The report filters out the values not selected. Therefore, the other sales regions are not displayed in the report.

Sales region	Order method type	Quantity	Revenue	Gross profit	Gross Profit %
Southern Europe	E-mail	211,704	$11,712,127.15	$4,886,095.64	41.72%
	Mail	14,997	$872,362.43	$399,357.02	45.78%
	Sales visit	268,446	$12,873,125.76	$5,047,957.13	39.21%
	Telephone	336,556	$14,961,187.86	$6,078,828.44	40.63%
	Web	2,845,529	$148,714,147.13	$61,651,940.00	41.46%
Southern Europe - Total		3,677,232	$189,132,950.33	$78,064,178.23	41.27%
Overall - Total		3,677,232	$189,132,950.33	$78,064,178.23	41.27%

Cognos Report Studio completed several actions when creating the prompt. To take a closer look, select Query Explorer from the Explorer bar. Cognos Report Studio created the Sales Region query:

By opening the report query (Query1 in this example), you can see a detail filter has been added to filter the query on the selections chosen in the prompt. Double-click the new filter to view the expression in more detail. For this example, the expression definition is as follows:

```
[Sales (query)].[Sales staff].[Sales region] in ?Sales region?
```

The filter is a key component in creating prompts.

Adding a Cascading Prompt

With *cascading prompts*, the values in one prompt are driven by what is selected in another prompt. In this example, the Sales Country prompt is driven by what is selected in the Sales Region prompt. When a region is selected, only countries within that region are included in the Sales Country prompt.

To add a cascading prompt to a report, follow these steps:

1. Create a prompt in your report to be used as the cascading source. For this example, use the Sales Region prompt created in the previous section.

2. With the prompt page selected from the Page Explorer, add another prompt from the Toolbox tab to the work area. The Prompt Wizard dialog displays. For this example, add a Value prompt to the work area below the Sales Region prompt.

3. In the Create a New Parameter box, name the parameter. For this example, name the parameter **Sales country**.

4. Click Next. The Create Filter options display.

5. Click the ellipsis button to the right of the Package Item property.

6. Choose a data item to which you want to link the prompt. For this example, select Country from the Sales Staff query subject in the Sales (query) namespace.

7. Click OK.

8. From the Operator drop-down list, select an operator. For this example, choose the "in" operator.

TIP *The equal sign operator will allow only one item to be chosen at the prompt (the prompt's Multi-Select property is set to No), while the in operator will allow multiple items to be chosen at the prompt (the prompt's Multi-Select property is set to Yes).*

9. Click Next. The Apply Filter options display, where you choose which queries are filtered by the prompt.

10. Select the appropriate check box(es). For this example, select the Query1 check box.

11. Click Next. The Populate Control options display.

12. In the Name text box, enter a name for the query. For this example, name the query **Sales country**.

13. From the Cascading Source list, select the prompt to be used as the source. For this example, select Sales Region.

14. Click Finish.

15. Set any necessary properties of the cascade source prompt from the Properties pane, as shown next. For the Sales Region prompt, set the Multi-Select property to No and the Auto-Submit property to Yes. When you set the cascade source prompt to submit automatically, options appear in the second prompt when a selection is made in the first.

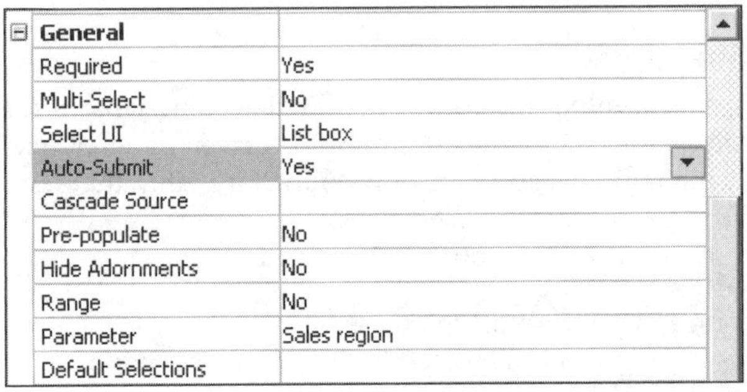

General	
Required	Yes
Multi-Select	No
Select UI	List box
Auto-Submit	Yes
Cascade Source	
Pre-populate	No
Hide Adornments	No
Range	No
Parameter	Sales region
Default Selections	

NOTE *The Multi-Select property defines whether a prompt allows you to select more than one item. The Auto-Submit property allows the prompt to automatically render the selection made, and it can be set to Yes only if Multi-Select is set to No.*

16. Apply any desired formatting to the prompt page. For this example, insert a Block object from the Toolbox tab above the new prompt. Then insert a Text Item with the text **Sales country** inside the block object to create a label for the prompt.

TIP *Inserting items inside blocks makes it easy to format the padding and alignment of the object.*

17. From the standard toolbar, click Run Report. The prompt page screen displays.

18. From the first prompt, make a selection. The second prompt populates with options based on your selection at the source prompt. For this example, choose Southern Europe from the Sales Region prompt. Then at the Sales Country prompt, CTRL-click to select Italy and Spain.

```
Sales region
 *  Americas
    Asia Pacific
    Central Europe
    Northern Europe
    Southern Europe




Sales country
 *  Austria
    Italy
    Spain








                              Select all Deselect all
```

19. Click Finish. The values in the report are filtered on the items that you selected at the prompts. Gross profit is about $20,000,000 less than the results from the previous section.

Sales region	Order method type	Quantity	Revenue	Gross profit	Gross Profit %
Southern Europe	E-mail	211,704	$11,712,127.15	$4,886,095.64	41.72%
	Mail	14,997	$872,362.43	$399,357.02	45.78%
	Sales visit	85,927	$3,664,488.19	$1,401,155.96	38.24%
	Telephone	155,709	$7,906,681.46	$3,156,683.82	39.92%
	Web	2,262,442	$117,284,636.96	$48,421,541.78	41.29%
Southern Europe - Total		**2,730,779**	**$141,440,296.19**	**$58,264,834.22**	**41.19%**
Overall - Total		**2,730,779**	**$141,440,296.19**	**$58,264,834.22**	**41.19%**

Formatting Prompt Pages

Formatting a prompt page can result in a better end user experience. You can increase the efficiency of a prompt page by putting careful thought into the layout. For example, providing a title clues users in to which report they are executing, while placing buttons and prompts themselves in a central location can decrease the time required to navigate to them.

To apply prompt page formatting, follow these steps:

1. Add a title to the prompt page. For this example, title the prompt page **Gross Profit Margin Prompt Page**.

2. Select the page body of the prompt page.

3. In the Properties pane, select Center for the Horizontal Alignment property to place all content at the center of the page.

4. From the Toolbox tab, insert a Block object below the last prompt.

5. With the new block selected, set the Padding property to 15 px at the top and the bottom.

6. Drag the Cancel and the Finish buttons from the bottom of the page to the new block.

7. Delete the page footer, where the Back and Next buttons are located.

8. Set the Select UI property for each prompt to what fits best, considering the items contained and the layout of the page. For this example, change the Select UI property to Drop Down List for the Sales Region prompt.

9. Set the Header Text property for desired prompts to display specific text. For this example, change the Header Text property for the Sales Region prompt to **Select a sales region**.

10. Run the report to see the prompt page screen. The prompt page now has a title and is concise and centralized.

TIP *Organizing prompt page objects in a table provides a lot of formatting capabilities. Tables provide a high degree of control over the placement of items.*

Displaying Prompt Values in Reports

With a report expression, users can see what was selected at prompts. A Layout Calculation allows you to add report functions that are executed in the report layout as opposed to executing with the report query. Now we will add a report expression to the sample report we have been creating throughout this chapter.

To add a report expression to a report, follow these steps:

1. From the Toolbox tab, insert a Layout Calculation object below the title of the report. The Expression dialog displays.

2. In the Available Components pane, select the Parameters tab.

3. Double-click a parameter to add it to the expression. For this example, add Sales Country. The expression *ParamDisplayValue('Sales country')* is added to the Expression Definition pane.

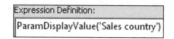

4. Click OK to create the report expression.

5. On the standard toolbar, click Run Report. The prompt page screen displays.

6. From the prompts, make your selections. For this example, again choose Southern Europe, from the Sales Region prompt, and then CTRL-click to select Italy and Spain at the Sales Country prompt.

7. Click Finish. The report displays the items that you selected in the prompt below the title.

Italy, Spain

Sales region	Order method type	Quantity	Revenue	Gross profit	Gross Profit %
Southern Europe	E-mail	211,704	$11,712,127.15	$4,886,095.64	41.72%
	Mail	14,997	$872,362.43	$399,357.02	45.78%
	Sales visit	85,927	$3,664,488.19	$1,401,155.96	38.24%
	Telephone	155,709	$7,906,681.46	$3,156,683.82	39.92%
	Web	2,262,442	$117,284,636.96	$48,421,541.78	41.29%
Southern Europe - Total		2,730,779	$141,440,296.19	$58,264,834.22	41.19%
Overall - Total		2,730,779	$141,440,296.19	$58,264,834.22	41.19%

Formatting Reports

Formatting a report, such as adding a header, changing font size, and applying borders and backgrounds, organizes the data and makes it easier for end users to consume. In this section, we will apply some basic formatting to the sample list report we've built in the previous sections.

Creating a Header

You can add a header to a report to make it easier to read. Now we will convert a column in the sample list report to a header.

To add a header to a list report, follow these steps:

1. Select the list column body in the column for which you want to create a header. For this example, select the Sales Region list column body.

Sales region	Order method type	Quantity	Revenue	Gross profit	Gross Profit %
<Sales region>	<Order method type>	<Quantity>	<Revenue>	<Gross profit>	<Gross Profit %>
<Sales region> - Total		<Total(Quantity)>	<Total(Revenue)>	<Total(Gross profit)>	<Total(Gross Profit %)>
<Sales region>	<Order method type>	<Quantity>	<Revenue>	<Gross profit>	<Gross Profit %>
<Sales region> - Total		<Total(Quantity)>	<Total(Revenue)>	<Total(Gross profit)>	<Total(Gross Profit %)>
Overall - Total		<Total(Quantity)>	<Total(Revenue)>	<Total(Gross profit)>	<Total(Gross Profit %)>

2. On the standard toolbar, click the Headers & Footers button and choose Create Header from the drop-down list. A header is created for the Sales Region column, while the original column is still intact, but no longer necessary.

NOTE *A column must be grouped before it can be made into a header.*

3. With the list column body still selected, from the standard toolbar, click the Cut button. The selected column is removed from the list report.

4. Run the report. For this example, choose Italy and Spain again in the Southern Europe sales region at the prompts. Once rendered, the report shows that the Sales Region column is removed, and the Order Method Type column is now the first in the list.

Italy, Spain

Order method type	Quantity	Revenue	Gross profit	Gross Profit %
Southern Europe				
E-mail	211,704	$11,712,127.15	$4,886,095.64	41.72%
Mail	14,997	$872,362.43	$399,357.02	45.78%
Sales visit	85,927	$3,664,488.19	$1,401,155.96	38.24%
Telephone	155,709	$7,906,681.46	$3,156,683.82	39.92%
Web	2,262,442	$117,284,636.96	$48,421,541.78	41.29%
Southern Europe - Total	2,730,779	$141,440,296.19	$58,264,834.22	41.19%
Overall - Total	2,730,779	$141,440,296.19	$58,264,834.22	41.19%

To emphasize the header, you can modify its style by increasing the font size and changing the background color of the list cell.

Changing the Font Size

You can change the font size of the objects in your report. We will use this feature to increase the font size of the header added to the sample report in the previous section.

To change the font size, follow these steps:

1. In the report, click the object for which you want to modify the font size to select it. For this example, select the Sales Region header.

2. From the style toolbar, select the Size drop-down menu and select the desired font size. The object changes to the selected size. For this example, select 12pt.

TIP *Alternatively, many style properties can be modified by right-clicking an object and selecting the property from the Style submenu.*

Setting a Background Color

You can modify the background color of an object in a report. We will use this feature to add color to the new header in the sample report.

To set the background color, follow these steps:

1. Click the object for which you want to set the background color to select it. For this example, select the Sales Region header.

2. From the style toolbar, select the Background Color drop-down menu and choose a color to apply to the background. For this example, select Navy from the Named Colors tab.

TIP *On the Web Safe Colors tab of the Background Color drop-down menu, move the pointer over a color box to display the hexadecimal value. On the Custom Color tab, you can specify the RGB or hexadecimal values for a color.*

Adding a Border to an Object

Adding borders to objects in reports can provide a visual separation between the groups and the summary levels in reports, or make report headers more prominent. As an example, we will add a border to the summary lines of the sample report.

To add a border to an object, follow these steps:

1. Select the object for which you want to add a border. For this example, click the <Sales region> - Total cell to select it.

2. Use the Select Ancestor button in the title bar of the Properties pane to select the appropriate object. For this example, select List Row. The entire row is now selected.

3. Right-click the object, choose Style, and then choose Border. The Border dialog displays.

4. Select the desired color, style, and width for the borders, and then add the borders to the desired sides of the object. For this example, add a solid line, 1pt, black border to the top of the row.

5. Click OK to save the border changes.

6. On the standard toolbar, click Run Report to view the report.

Order method type	Quantity	Revenue	Gross profit	Gross Profit %
Southern Europe				
E-mail	211,704	$11,712,127.15	$4,886,095.64	41.72%
Mail	14,997	$872,362.43	$399,357.02	45.78%
Sales visit	85,927	$3,664,488.19	$1,401,155.96	38.24%
Telephone	155,709	$7,906,681.46	$3,156,683.82	39.92%
Web	2,262,442	$117,284,636.96	$48,421,541.78	41.29%
Southern Europe - Total	2,730,779	$141,440,296.19	$58,264,834.22	41.19%
Overall - Total	2,730,779	$141,440,296.19	$58,264,834.22	41.19%

Applying Conditional Highlighting

Conditional highlighting allows the end user to quickly identify areas of interest within the business. One way this can be achieved is by changing the background and text color of a data item cell in a report when certain requirements are met or are not met. In our example, we will use several manually created conditions, a predefined condition, and predefined styles for the conditions. We will use the *Gross Profit* column of the sample list report for the conditionally highlighted field. The criteria and results for this example are shown in Table 10-5.

To add a new conditional style, follow these steps:

1. Select the object for which you want to set conditional highlighting. For this example, select the Gross Profit column.

2. On the style toolbar, click the Conditional Styles button. The Conditional Styles dialog displays.

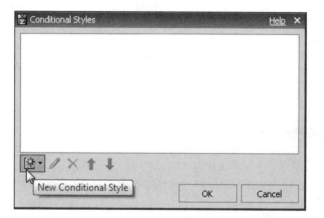

3. Select New Conditional Style from the New Conditional Style drop-down list.

4. Select the data item on which you want to base the condition. For this example, select Gross Profit.

Gross Profit Criteria	Style/Value	Cell Color for Met Criteria	Text Color for Met Criteria
>= $100,000,000	Excellent	Green	White
>= $10,000,000 and < $100,000,000	Average	White	Black
< $10,000,000	Poor	Red	White

TABLE 10-5 Conditions for the Conditional Highlighting Example

5. Click OK. The Conditional Style dialog opens.

6. Click the New Value button at the bottom of the dialog.

7. Enter a value to set a threshold for values. For this example, enter **10000000** (10 million).

8. Repeat steps 6 and 7 for as many thresholds as you want to set. For this example, set one more threshold of **100000000** (100 million).

9. Set the style for each range by choosing a predefined style from the drop-down list in the Style area of the dialog or by defining a custom style (by clicking the pencil icon next to the style setting). For this example, select Excellent for the top range

and Poor for the bottom range. The values in the center range will remain in the default style.

NOTE *Predefined styles define the background and foreground color of items. You can choose the Edit (pencil) button to define custom styles. Customizing a style enables you to set properties such as the background color, foreground color, alignment, border, and margin, as well as advanced properties, such as the background image and visibility.*

10. Click OK, and then click OK again in the Conditional Style dialog.

11. On the standard toolbar, click Run Report to view the report with conditional highlighting.

Order method type	Quantity	Revenue	Gross profit	Gross Profit %
Americas				
E-mail	304,827	$15,884,458.80	$6,607,736.66	41.60%
Mail	169,711	$7,460,082.14	$2,990,487.34	40.09%
Sales visit	1,146,195	$55,715,052.86	$22,103,896.84	39.67%
Telephone	881,199	$44,163,577.70	$16,740,759.70	37.91%
Web	7,563,425	$416,205,688.82	$172,324,270.98	41.40%
Americas - Total	10,065,357	$539,428,860.32	$220,767,151.52	40.93%
Overall - Total	10,065,357	$539,428,860.32	$220,767,151.52	40.93%

NOTE *The conditional style is not applied to the summary level. To show the conditional highlighting at the summary level, you need to create the same conditions for the summary-level cells.*

Formatting Titles

Adding formatting to report titles makes it easier for end users to locate and view data on the report. Now we will add and format a title for the sample list report.

To format titles in a report, follow these steps:

1. Add a title to the report page. For this example, set the report title to **Gross Profit Margin**.

2. Select the page header of the report page.

3. In the Properties pane, select Center for the Horizontal Alignment property to center all content in the page header.

4. In the Properties pane, set the top and bottom padding to 20 px each for the Padding property.

5. Provide a title for any prompt values by inserting a Text Item object before the layout calculation. For this example, insert the text **Sales countries:** before the layout calculation.

Gross Profit Margin

Sales countries: <%ParamDisplay...%>

6. From the style toolbar, set any desired formatting properties, such as Font, Color, and Borders. For this example, set the font weight for the "Sales countries:" label to Bold.

7. Run the report. The example report now has a title and other page header formatting applied.

Gross Profit Margin

Sales countries: Brazil, Canada, Mexico, United States

Order method type	Quantity	Revenue	Gross profit	Gross Profit %
Americas				
E-mail	304,827	$15,884,458.80	$6,607,736.66	41.60%
Mail	169,711	$7,460,082.14	$2,990,487.34	40.09%
Sales visit	1,146,195	$55,715,052.86	$22,103,896.84	39.67%
Telephone	881,199	$44,163,577.70	$16,740,759.70	37.91%
Web	7,563,425	$416,205,688.82	$172,324,270.98	41.40%
Americas - Total	10,065,357	$539,428,860.32	$220,767,151.52	40.93%
Overall - Total	10,065,357	$539,428,860.32	$220,767,151.52	40.93%

Creating Crosstab Reports

Like list reports, crosstab reports show data in rows and columns. However, crosstab reports show data summarized at the intersecting point of the rows and columns. Crosstabs allow you to view more information in a more compact form than in lists.

To create a crosstab report, follow these steps:

1. Open Cognos Report Studio.

2. From the Startup dialog, select Create New.

3. From the New dialog, select Crosstab. Click OK. The template for the crosstab report displays in the work area.

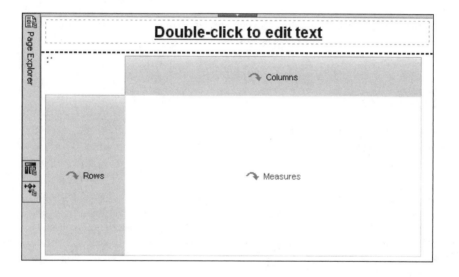

4. From the Source tab in the Insertable Objects pane, drag a data item to the Columns drop zone of the work area. For this example, add the Year query item to the columns from the Time query subject in the Sales (query) namespace of the GO Sales (query) package.

5. From the Source tab in the Insertable Objects pane, drag a data item to the Rows drop zone of the work area. For this example, add the Product Line query item from the Products query subject to the rows.

6. Nest any desired data items within the rows of the crosstab by dragging items from the Insertable Objects pane to the right side of the Rows drop zone in the work area. For this example, drag the Product Type query item from the Products query subject and drop it to the right of Product Line in the Rows drop zone.

7. Nest any desired data items within the columns of the crosstab by dragging items from the Insertable Objects pane to the bottom of the Columns drop zone in the work area. For this example, drag the Quarter query item from the Time query subject and drop it below Year in the Columns drop zone.

8. From the Source tab in the Insertable Objects pane, drag a data item to the Measures drop zone of the crosstab. For this example, insert Quantity from the Sales query subject as the measure. Your work area should look similar to this:

Quantity		<#Year#>		<#Year#>	
		<#Quarter#>	<#Quarter#>	<#Quarter#>	<#Quarter#>
<#Product line#>	<#Product type#>	<#1234#>	<#1234#>	<#1234#>	<#1234#>
	<#Product type#>	<#1234#>	<#1234#>	<#1234#>	<#1234#>
<#Product line#>	<#Product type#>	<#1234#>	<#1234#>	<#1234#>	<#1234#>
	<#Product type#>	<#1234#>	<#1234#>	<#1234#>	<#1234#>

9. On the standard toolbar, click Run Report to display the crosstab report.

Quantity		2004				2005			
		Q1	Q2	Q3	Q4	Q1	Q2	Q3	Q4
Camping Equipment	Cooking Gear	695,847	875,495	691,013	642,765	1,194,456	776,465	710,576	819,832
	Lanterns	267,526	283,761	297,167	261,723	281,193	280,914	263,023	287,668
	Packs	136,061	134,567	136,622	138,653	165,528	155,733	158,334	184,551
	Sleeping Bags	156,332	151,592	199,199	161,396	196,633	173,839	226,256	194,129
	Tents	164,009	157,704	176,179	167,442	208,426	204,910	200,682	220,616
Golf Equipment	Golf Accessories	171,445	164,578	142,097	135,191	229,677	228,908	157,665	175,685
	Irons	18,954	18,459	20,608	20,888	25,188	19,829	20,237	22,228
	Putters	72,567	95,262	77,438	101,105	77,883	68,474	69,848	128,685
	Woods	13,308	12,923	13,717	14,442	20,745	16,791	17,064	18,886

Crosstab reports also allow you to aggregate both the rows and columns. You can add formatting to the report to make it more visually appealing for the end user. For example, you can set conditional highlighting, prompts, dynamic titles, and many of the same options described in the previous sections.

Creating Chart Reports

Charts are a graphical representation of tabular data. With Cognos Report Studio, you can create many chart types, including column, bar, area, line and pie charts. They can be used to quickly identify large numeric data for different areas of business. Charts are commonly used in dashboard-style reports.

To create a simple chart report, follow these steps:

1. Open Cognos Report Studio.
2. From the Startup dialog, select Create New.
3. From the New dialog, select Chart, and then click OK. The Insert Chart dialog displays.

4. On the left side of the dialog, select a chart style. For this example, select Column.
5. Select a type for your chart. For this example, select Column with 3-D Effects.

TIP *Hover the mouse pointer over the chart icons in the Insert Chart dialog for a chart type tooltip.*

6. Click OK. A blank chart appears in the work area. This type of column chart has three drop zones: Default Measure, Categories, and Series. The default measure is the value that you want measured for each category and series. Categories and series can be the areas of business that you want to evaluate.

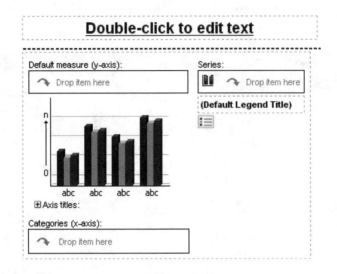

7. From the Source tab in the Insertable Objects pane, drag a data item to the Default Measure drop zone. For this example, drag Revenue to the Default Measure drop zone from the Sales query subject in the Sales (query) namespace of the GO Sales (query) package.

8. From the Source tab in the Insertable Objects pane, drag a data item to the Categories drop zone. For this example, drag the Year query item from the Time query subject to the Categories drop zone.

9. From the Source tab in the Insertable Objects pane, drag a data item to the Series drop zone. For this example, drag the Sales Region query item from the Sales Staff query subject to the Series drop zone.

10. On the standard toolbar, click Run Report. The results graphically show a year-by-year comparison of revenue for each sales region. You can see that Central Europe makes up the largest portion of the revenue.

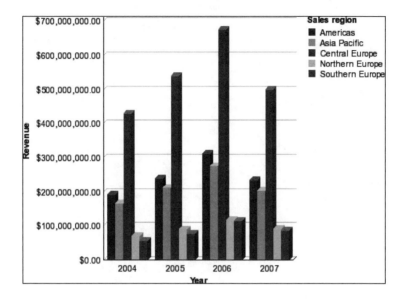

T IP *In a chart, hover the mouse pointer over a bar to see the value for that bar.*

Additional report authoring examples and techniques are discussed in Chapter 12.

Report Authoring— Dimensional Data

IBM Cognos Report Studio offers users many ways of viewing and structuring report data to fulfill report requirements. When you incorporate *dimensional structures* into your reports in Cognos Report Studio, you turn the analysis report into a highly formatted presentation. Chapter 10 discussed reporting using relational data sources. This chapter describes how to use the advanced features in Cognos Report Studio to create effective dimensional reports. You will learn about dimensional structures and their uses and important functions that will help you leverage the dimensional data structures.

Model Types and Dimensional Structure

Two types of models are used in Cognos Report Studio: relational and dimensional models. Relational models and dimensional models present information in different ways. Each type of model offers its own particular advantages.

Relational models organize your data in the same way that a database does—using *flat metadata*. This means that all the query items in a relational query subject are presented at the same level.

Dimensional query subjects typically present their query items in *multiple levels of a predefined hierarchy*. Dimensional models have drill-down capabilities due to the dimensional structures (hierarchies) that are defined. This drill-down capability is available in Cognos Report Studio, but it must be enabled by the report author.

Dimensions contain members that can be structured into hierarchies and levels. Dimensions are the highest level of descriptive data. They tend to deal with the major aspects of the business. From a business modeling perspective, dimensions contain data that answer questions such as who, what, when, where, why, and how.

Below dimensions are *hierarchies*, which provide context to the structured levels of data that they contain. Multiple hierarchies can be used to provide alternative views of the information included in the dimension. Hierarchies can contain several structured levels of information. Each subordinate level in a hierarchy contains increasingly detailed information that relates to the dimension.

NOTE *A hierarchy need not contain any defined levels. A parent-child hierarchy depends on the relationships between members rather than stratifying the members into distinct levels.*

Members are data entities that provide context to cell values. They are made up of a *member key* to identify the member, a *caption* that describes the member, and possibly *attributes* that provide additional information about the member. The following illustration shows an example of a dimensional structure and the data entities that display within that structure. The dimensional structure contains dimensions, hierarchies, levels, members, and attributes:

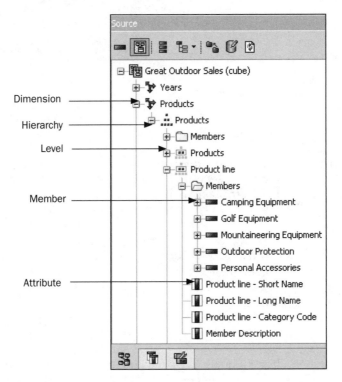

Navigating Dimensional Structures

The top level of the dimensional structure shown in the preceding illustration is the Products dimension. This dimension contains only one hierarchy, which is also named Products. It also contains information at many levels that relate to the products sold within the organization—information about specific products, product lines, and product models.

Below the Products dimension is the Products hierarchy. You can see the hierarchy Members folder and several levels related to the Products dimension, such as Products, Product Line, Product Type, and Product Name. These items represent the core structures that define the gradation of detailed information in the Products hierarchy.

Under the Product Line level is a Members folder and some Product Line attributes. As mentioned, an attribute provides additional details about the members in the Product Line level. In this example, the attribute is a Product Line category code associated with each member. You can tell that this is an attribute by the icon that appears next to the name Product Line–Category Code and by its position in the hierarchy. Attributes appear at the same level as the Members folder. Within the Members folder are several members of the Product Line level. The Members folder contains Camping Equipment, Mountaineering Equipment, Personal Accessories, and more.

Generating a Report from a Dimensional Model

In reports, dimensional structures and relational structures behave differently. When you create reports that contain data from a dimensional structure, a number of unique features and options become available that allow you to input and manipulate data in a report in different ways. This section explains some of the options and features you will encounter when creating a report with a dimensional model.

NOTE   *In general, dimensional data works well in crosstab reports, while relational data works well in list reports.*

Inserting Hierarchies into Reports

When you insert a hierarchy into a report, Cognos Report Studio prompts you with a dialog that appears only when dimensional data is inserted. The Insert Hierarchy dialog allows you to insert Root Members or All Members, as shown next:

If you choose the Root Members option, only the members from the top of the hierarchy that display in the selected level will display in the report. For example, if you insert the Products hierarchy into a report, only the highest level member displays in the report. If you choose the All Members option, the highest level member and all of the child members from each of the levels in the Products hierarchy display in the report.

To insert hierarchies into a report, follow these steps:

1. In Cognos Report Studio, create a new Crosstab style report using a multidimensional package. For this example, use the Great Outdoors Sales (cube) package from the Cognos Business Intelligence v10.1 samples.

2. From the Source tab in the Insertable Objects pane, drag-and-drop a hierarchy into the crosstab.

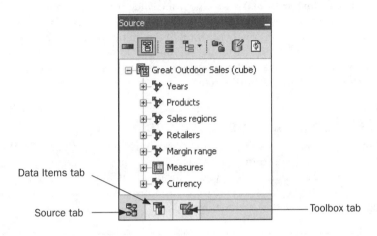

3. From the Insert Hierarchy dialog, select either Root Members or All Members.

4. Click OK to insert the selected dimensional structure into the report. Report Studio inserts the hierarchy into the crosstab.

Attributes in Reports

Attributes can be included in a report to provide additional descriptive data for report users. Adding attributes to a report can be helpful for users who are unfamiliar with the data.

To insert an attribute into a report, follow these steps:

1. In Cognos Report Studio, create a new Crosstab style report using a multidimensional package. For this example, use the Great Outdoors Sales (cube) package.

2. From the Source tab in the Insertable Objects pane, drag-and-drop an attribute into the Rows drop zone of the report. For this example, insert Product Line – Long Name and Product Line – Category Code. The Insert Member Property dialog displays:

3. Select the Insert Property Only option to insert the attribute into the report.

4. Click OK.

5. From the Insertable Objects pane, drag-and-drop a time period into the Columns drop zone of the report, and drag-and-drop a measure into the Measures drop zone. For this example, we use the 2007 member and the Revenue measure.

6. Run the report.

Revenue		2007
Camping Equipment	991	352,910,329.97
Golf Equipment	995	174,740,819.29
Mountaineering Equipment	992	141,520,649.70
Outdoor Protection	994	4,471,025.26
Personal Accessories	993	443,693,449.85

NOTE *Members also contain a descriptor known as the* member unique name *(MUN). A MUN describes a member's position in a dimensional structure and is referenced in the expression definition. If a MUN is changed or altered, any report that references that MUN will no longer render. See the IBM Cognos documentation for information on how to monitor this; it is something that you can avoid.*

Focusing Dimensional Data

Dimensional data offers an extension to relational data structures, providing several ways to view and manipulate data. It is important that you understand how dimensional data structures behave and how to use the tools in Cognos Report Studio to manipulate these structures. This section explains how to use Cognos Report Studio to focus dimensional data to meet the requirements of your reports.

Dimensional Query Behavior

Dimensional queries return all members, whether they have measure values or not. Therefore, large dimensional structures without proper filtering can lead to large, inefficient reports. The key to creating efficient reports is limiting the items rendered in the queries to ensure that users get only the data they need to meet their requirements.

Creating Efficient Dimensional Queries

One way to create dimensional queries that return only necessary data is to add information to a table by selecting individual members directly from the Insertable Objects pane. This can become a tedious task, however, if you want to include many members in a report, and it still might leave information in your reports that you do not need. To ensure that your dimensional queries return the most efficient reports, you need to use Cognos Report Studio options such as Set functions, Filter functions, Except functions, slicers, context filters, page layers, simple prompting, dimensional prompt expressions, and tree prompts. These topics are explained in the following sections so that you can learn how to create efficient and effective reports.

Set Function

The *Set function* is used to gather specific members from within a dimensional structure. For example, if you have a data hierarchy called Diamond Jewelry that contains the members

Bracelets, Earrings, Necklaces, and Rings, and you want to retrieve only Bracelets and Rings, you can use the Set function to create a data item that returns only these two child levels from the parent, Diamond Jewelry.

To create a Set function expression, follow these steps:

1. Create a new Crosstab style report using a multidimensional package. For this example, use the Great Outdoors Sales (cube) package.

2. From the Insertable Objects pane, insert the desired items into the Columns drop zone of the crosstab. For this example, use the Year level.

3. From the Insertable Objects pane, insert the desired measure into the Measures drop zone of the crosstab. For this example, use the Revenue measure.

4. From the Toolbox tab in the Insertable Objects pane, drag-and-drop a Query Calculation into the Rows drop zone. The Create Calculation dialog displays, as shown next:

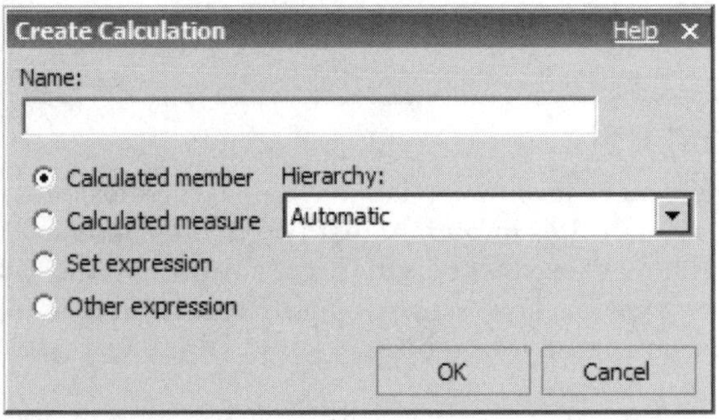

5. In the Name text box, enter a name for the Set function calculation.

6. Select the Set Expression radio button.

7. Select the desired hierarchy from the Hierarchy drop-down menu. For this example, select the Products hierarchy.

8. Click OK. The dialog closes and the Set Expression dialog displays:

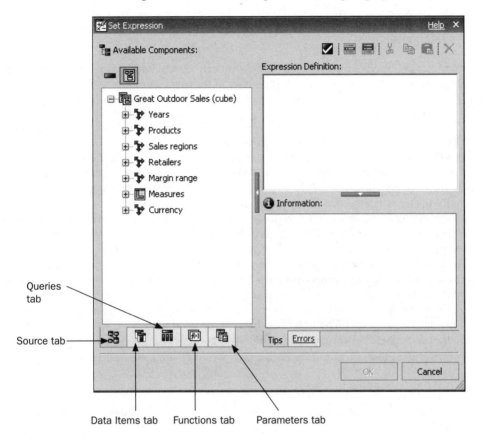

Queries tab

Source tab

Data Items tab   Functions tab   Parameters tab

9. From the Functions tab, expand the Dimensional Functions folder, and then expand the R-Z folder.

10. From the R-Z folder, drag-and-drop the Set function into the Expression Definition pane, or type the calculation in the pane.

11. From the Source tab in the Available Components pane, drag-and-drop the desired members into the Expression Definition pane, and close the expression with a parenthesis. For this example, use the Camping Equipment, Golf Equipment, and Mountaineering Equipment members. The member aliases display in the Expression Definition pane, as shown next:

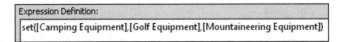

NOTE *When using the Set function, the list of selected members must be from the same hierarchy.*

12. Click OK. The dialog closes and Cognos Report Studio enters the selected members into the report.

Once you define a Set function expression, you can reuse it in other expressions to return the results only for the members that you defined in the expression.

Filter Function

The Filter function and detail filters are used to filter measure values in reports. This section explains how to use the Filter function in reports.

The *Filter function* returns a set of members in a query that is created by filtering a larger set of members based on a Boolean (a yes or no) condition. The Filter function is applied only to the members returned by the expression that you create. The Filter function is especially useful when the data for your reports is sparse, when you may not have measure values for all members, or when the report contains unnecessary data that does not meet the requirements of your report. Including unnecessary information can slow down the rendering of your reports, and they will typically be much larger than necessary.

The following illustration shows an example of an inefficient, unfiltered report. The report includes the Retailer level within the Sales Region level on the rows, the Year level on the columns, and the Revenue as the measure. When a report like this runs without filters, it takes a long time to generate because it returns every member. Additionally, the report contains many zero values. The Filter function can be used to remove zero values and ensure that only useful information is included in the reports.

Revenue		2004	2005	2006	2007
Americas	American Home			32,972.07	
	Asan Department				
	Ausrüstungshaus Globetrotter				
	Beach Beds Pty Ltd.				
	Bergsteiger-Glück				
	Billing's Department Store	147,900.39	674,460.29	1,293,497.51	
	Brambilla				
	CanDepot	656,336.01	2,398,825.40	2,639,775.38	838,474.69
	Chen Yu Enterprise Co.,				
	Chuei Hyakkaten				
	Classens				
	Conception française				

To create a Filter function expression, follow these steps:

1. Create a new Crosstab style report using a multidimensional package. For this example, use the Great Outdoors Sales (cube) package.

2. From the Insertable Objects pane, insert the desired items into the Rows drop zone of the crosstab. For this example, use the Sales Region level.

3. From the Insertable Objects pane, insert the desired items into the Columns drop zone of the crosstab. For this example, use the Year level.

4. From the Insertable Objects pane, insert the desired measure into the Measures drop zone of the crosstab. For this example, use the Revenue measure.

5. From the Toolbox tab in the Insertable Objects pane, drag a Query Calculation into the Rows drop zone to the left of the Sales Region level. The Create Calculation dialog displays.

6. Enter a name for the Filter function calculation in the Name text box.

7. Select the Other Expression radio button.

8. Click OK. The Expression dialog displays.

9. In the Available Components pane, select the Functions tab.

10. Within the functions list, expand the Dimensional Functions folder, expand the D-G folder, and drag-and-drop the Filter function to the Expression Definition pane, or type the calculation in the pane.

11. From the Source tab in the Available Components pane, insert the items that you want to include in the filter into the Expression Definition pane. In this example, select the Retailer level.

12. Type a comma at the end of the expression.

13. From the Data Items tab in the Available Components pane, drag-and-drop a measure into the Expression Definition pane. The measure path displays in the Expression Definition pane. In this example, insert the Revenue measure.

14. Make any other necessary modifications to the expression. For this example, type **is not null and [Revenue] <> 0)** at the end of the expression. The greater than and less than signs translate to "not equal to"; you are asking Cognos Report Studio to return all retailers with revenue that is null and not equal to zero. You can view the complete expression in the Expression Definition pane, shown next:

Expression Definition:
filter([great_outdoors_sales_en].[Retailers].[Retailers].[Retailer],
[Revenue] is not null and [Revenue] <> 0)

15. Click OK to save the Filter function expression.

16. Run the report. When the Filter function is applied to the data used to create the inefficient report, as shown next, the rows with all values of null or 0 are removed from the report.

	Revenue	2004	2005	2006	2007
Americas	American Home			32,972.07	
	Billing's Department Store	147,900.39	674,460.29	1,293,497.51	
	CanDepot	656,336.01	2,398,825.40	2,639,775.38	838,474.69
	Connor Department Store	5,451,503.40	3,210,908.12	2,108,037.32	945,598.89

Except Function

The *Except function* returns the members of one Set function expression that are not in a second Set function expression. This means that the Except function excludes a set of members from a larger defined set. A common use is to combine an Except function with the Top Count function or Bottom Count function, which are discussed later in this chapter.

To create an Except function expression, follow these steps:

1. Create a new Crosstab style report using a multidimensional package. For this example, use the Great Outdoors Sales (cube) package.

2. From the Source tab in the Insertable Objects pane, insert the desired items into the crosstab. For this example, insert the Year level into the Columns drop zone and Revenue into the Measures drop zone of the report.

3. From the Toolbox tab in the Insertable Objects pane, drag-and-drop a Query Calculation into the Rows drop zone. The Create Calculation dialog displays.

4. Enter a name for the Except function calculation in the Name text box.

5. Select the Other Expression radio button.

6. Click OK. The Expression dialog displays.

7. Within the Available Components pane, select the Functions tab.

8. From the functions list, expand the Dimensional Functions folder, and expand the D-G folder.

9. Drag-and-drop the Except function into the Expression Definition pane.

10. In the expression, include the information sources that you want to view in the report.

11. On the Source tab in the Available Components pane, navigate to the level that you want to include in the report.

12. Insert the selected level into the Expression Definition pane. The level path displays in the Expression Definition pane. For this example, select the Product Line level.

13. Place a comma at the end of the expression in the Expression Definition pane.

14. From the Functions tab in the Available Components pane, expand the Dimensional Functions folder and expand the R-Z folder.

15. Drag-and-drop the Set function into the Expression Definition pane.

16. On the Source tab in the Available Components pane, navigate to the level that you selected in step 9.

17. Select the members that you want to exclude from the report.

18. Drag-and-drop the selected members into the Set function in the Expression Definition pane. The members that display in this Set function are the exceptions that will be excluded from the report. For this example, select the members Camping Equipment, Golf Equipment, and Mountaineering Equipment.

19. Close the expression with two closing parentheses. This illustration shows the entire expression:

> Expression Definition:
>
> except([great_outdoors_sales_en].[Products].[Products].[Product line],
> set([Camping Equipment],[Golf Equipment],[Mountaineering
> Equipment]))

20. Run the report. The report displays in IBM Cognos Viewer, and the three items included in the Set function expression are excluded from the report:

Revenue	2004	2005	2006	2007
Outdoor Protection	*36,165,521.07*	*25,008,574.08*	*10,349,175.84*	*4,471,025.26*
Personal Accessories	*391,647,093.61*	*456,323,355.90*	*594,009,408.42*	*443,693,449.85*

Slicer Filter

A *Slicer* filter affects the cell value. Slicers are used to reduce the data included in the measure area. Slicers are applied to the cells of the crosstab, not the row or column edges. This means that slicers are useful if you want some data in a report to be hidden and other data to be visible. You can create more than one slicer to filter across two or more dimensions, but you cannot create two slicers from the same dimension.

NOTE *You typically create slicers from a dimension that is not already referenced in a report. You can create slicers using items from a dimension that is referenced in a report, but often the results will not make sense.*

We will use slicers in an example before diving into the procedure used to apply a slicer. The next illustration contains a crosstab with the Product Line level on the rows, the Year level on the columns, and Revenue as the measure from the Great Outdoors Sales (cube) package:

Revenue	<#Year#>	<#Year#>
<#Product line#>	<#1234#>	<#1234#>
<#Product line#>	<#1234#>	<#1234#>

The report generated from this crosstab shows revenue for all product lines and for all years:

Revenue	2004	2005	2006	2007
Camping Equipment	332,986,338.06	402,757,573.17	500,382,422.83	352,910,329.97
Golf Equipment	153,553,850.98	168,006,427.07	230,110,270.55	174,740,819.29
Mountaineering Equipment		107,099,659.94	161,039,823.26	141,520,649.70
Outdoor Protection	36,165,521.07	25,008,574.08	10,349,175.84	4,471,025.26
Personal Accessories	391,647,093.61	456,323,355.90	594,009,408.42	443,693,449.85

Create a Simple Slicer   We could use a slicer to make this report display only results from certain retailers. The following example describes how you would create such a slicer. For this example, we use American Home and Beach Beds Pty Ltd.

To create a simple slicer, follow these steps:

1. Create a new Crosstab style report using a multidimensional package. For this example, use the Great Outdoors Sales (cube) package.

2. From the Insertable Objects pane, insert the desired items into the crosstab. For this example, insert the Product Line level into the Rows drop zone, the Year level into the Columns drop zone, and Revenue into the Measures drop zone of the crosstab.

3. From the Query Explorer tab, click the Query1 link to modify the query:

4. From the Source tab in the Insertable Objects pane, insert the desired items in the Slicer pane of the work area. For this example, drag-and-drop the members American Home and Beach Beds Pty Ltd. from the Retailer level into the Slicer pane. The members display within a Set function in the Slicer pane:

Data Items	Detail Filters
Product line	
Year	
Revenue	Summary Filters
American Home	
Beach Beds Pty Ltd.	
	Slicer
	set([American Home],[Beach Beds Pty Ltd.])

5. Run the report. You can see that the values are considerably lower than they were before applying the slicer, because the slicer has included data only for the American Home and Beach Beds Pty Ltd. retailers:

Revenue	2004	2005	2006	2007
Camping Equipment		3,780,937.74	7,531,946.20	4,505,365.18
Golf Equipment		1,024,088.68	1,690,507.24	1,422,559.25
Mountaineering Equipment				
Outdoor Protection		238,812.23	56,934.62	350.16
Personal Accessories	1,241,969.60	2,537,662.41	4,017,063.23	3,009,637.72

Create a Compound Slicer   After creating a simple slicer, you might want to move on to create *compound slicers.* A compound slicer contains more than one element in the Slicer pane. We will continue with our simple slicer example.

To create a compound slicer, follow these steps:

1. Insert the desired members into the Slicer pane. For this example, drag-and-drop the years 2005 and 2006.

2. Click Run Report on the standard toolbar. The report displays, as shown next:

Revenue	2004	2005	2006	2007
Camping Equipment		3,780,937.74	7,531,946.20	
Golf Equipment		1,024,088.68	1,690,507.24	
Mountaineering Equipment				
Outdoor Protection		238,812.23	56,934.62	
Personal Accessories		2,537,662.41	4,017,063.23	

You will notice the slicer does not affect the row or column edges appearing in the report, as you can still see all of the members from the Year level, but it affects the data itself and displays null values where no data is returned, years 2004 and 2007.

Context Filter

The Context filter allows you to use a member to filter or focus the data contained in the report. Insert a member into the Context Filter area in the work area of the report layout, and that member and all of its children become available to filter the report.

NOTE *More than one Context filter can be used.*

In the next example, Retailers has been inserted into the Context Filter area. This means that you can filter the report using any of the Retailers available:

To select a member to filter by, follow these steps:

1. Click the down arrow next to the member in the Context filter.

2. Select one of the child members to be used to filter the data.

NOTE *When you select a member in the Context filter, the name of that member displays in the header in the work area. The header is automatically updated when the filters of the report are changed.*

Page Layers

Page layers can be added to a report to create separate pages for each of the included members. In the previous example, the Sales regions member was inserted into the Page Layers area. You can see that "Americas" displays in the header of the work area. Americas is the first child member in the Sales regions member, so it is the first page displayed in this report. You can use the Top, Page Up, Page Down, and Bottom buttons at the bottom of the work area to cycle through each of the pages.

	Americas			
	Department Store			
Revenue	2004	2005	2006	2007
Camping Equipment	31,898,072.03	30,817,555.80	32,921,965.83	16,252,760.30
Golf Equipment	16,620,016.66	16,132,328.74	17,265,979.60	10,268,400.95
Mountaineering Equipment				
Outdoor Protection	3,716,889.85	1,951,775.35	479,017.20	42,178.30
Personal Accessories	5,601,895.90	4,111,228.31	5,831,091.01	3,869,518.94

NOTE *As you change pages, the member displayed in the header of the work area is automatically updated to reflect the page layer you are currently viewing.*

Simple Prompting

Prompting allows users to choose what data is visible and invisible each time the report is run. Enabling prompting is easy. Click the Context Filter list and choose Prompting. In the menu that displays, choose one of the following values:

- **No Prompt**   Selected by default, it will not create a prompt.
- **Prompt On Hierarchy**   Creates a tree prompt in your report.
- **Prompt On Level**   Creates a value prompt that allows you to select values from the level of the assigned member.
- **Single Value**   Allows only one member to be selected from a list. This option is available only once a prompt is selected.

Dimensional Prompt Expressions and Tree Prompts

Dimensional prompt expressions and tree prompts allow you to create reports that prompt the user to select between different sets of data to determine what information will be visible in the report. For example, if your report contained the member Camping Equipment, and you wanted to allow users to generate separate reports that display results for specific brands of equipment, you could create a prompt that allows users to select which brands they want to display in the report.

The most common prompt expressions are based on a level or a hierarchy. The following sections explain how to create prompts using a crosstab report.

Create a Dimensional Prompt Expression   Dimensional prompt expressions allow users to select a member to include in a report.

To create a dimensional prompt expression, follow these steps:

1. Create a new Crosstab style report using a multidimensional package. For this example, use the Great Outdoors Sales (cube) package.
2. From the Insertable Objects pane, insert the desired items into the crosstab. For this example, insert the Year level into the Columns drop zone and Revenue into the Measures drop zone of the report.

3. From the Query Explorer, click the Query 1 link.

4. From the Toolbox tab in the Insertable Objects pane, insert a Data Item into the query. The Expression dialog displays.

5. On the Source tab in the Available Components pane, navigate to the level that you want to use as a prompt for the report.

6. Insert the selected level into the Expression Definition pane. The level path displays in the Expression Definition tab. For this example, select the Product Line level.

7. From the Functions tab in the Available Components pane, insert the -> operator.

8. At the end of the expression, enter a parameter name enclosed in question marks, as shown next. In this example, we enter the following text: **?p_Product_Line?**

> Expression Definition:
>
> [great_outdoors_sales_en].[Products].[Products].[Product line]->?p_Product_Line?

NOTE *If you are using a different data item than Product Line, enter a parameter name that makes sense for the expression, such as the referenced data item name, in the place of p_Product_Line for this step.*

9. From the Expression dialog, click OK.

10. From the Properties pane, name the data item.

11. Using the explorer bar, click the Page1 link to return to the layout of the report.

12. From the Data Items tab in the Insertable Objects pane, add the data item to the report. For this example, add the data item to the Rows drop zone.

13. Run the report. A value prompt displays in IBM Cognos Viewer:

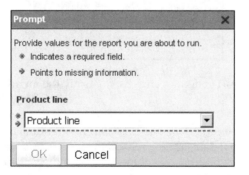

14. From the list in the value prompt, choose a value for the parameter. Notice that you are able to select only one member from the list. For this example, select Golf Equipment.

15. Click OK. The report displays in the IBM Cognos Viewer window.

Revenue	2004	2005	2006	2007
Golf Equipment	153,553,850.98	168,006,427.07	230,110,270.55	174,740,819.29

16. Optionally, manipulate the dimensional prompt expression to enable the selection of multiple prompt expressions.

17. Modify the dimensional prompt expression so that it is inside a Set function, as shown next:

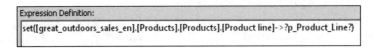

Expression Definition:
set([great_outdoors_sales_en].[Products].[Products].[Product line]->?p_Product_Line?)

18. From the Expression dialog, click OK.

19. Run the report. A value prompt displays that allows you to select multiple members at the prompt, as shown next:

> **Prompt**   ✕
>
> Provide values for the report you are about to run.
> * Indicates a required field.
> ↦ Points to missing information.
>
> **Product line**
>
> *↦ | Camping Equipment
>   Golf Equipment
>   Mountaineering Equipment
>   Outdoor Protection
>   Personal Accessories
>
>   Select all Deselect all
>
> | OK | Cancel

20. Click OK. The report generates and displays only the members that you selected from the prompt.

Create a Tree Prompt   A tree prompt can also be used to filter data on a report. Tree prompts work only with dimensional data, as they rely on the hierarchical structure to build the member tree. A tree prompt returns a set of members and their descendants from within a single hierarchy. The following instructions demonstrate how to create a tree prompt using the Products hierarchy from the example used in the preceding section.

NOTE *The Set function is not mandatory for a tree prompt. If the Set function is omitted, the tree prompt will still be generated, because it is referencing a hierarchy. However, the tree prompt will be only a single-select prompt.*

To create a tree prompt from a dimensional prompt expression, follow these steps:

1. Update the data item expression so that it represents the hierarchy instead of the level. For this example, remove **.[Product line]**, so that the expression refers to the Products hierarchy, and change the parameter name from p_Product_Line to **p_Products** as shown next.

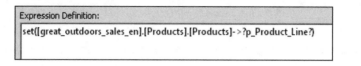

NOTE *If you are using a hierarchy other than Products, enter a parameter name that makes sense for the expression, such as the referenced data item name, in place of p_Products in step 1.*

2. From the Expression dialog, click OK.

3. Run the report. Cognos Report Studio prompts you with a tree prompt control, from which you can select check boxes to determine what data displays, as shown next:

4. Select the check boxes next to data items that you want to include in the report.

5. Click OK. The report displays in IBM Cognos Viewer, containing the data that you selected:

Revenue	2004	2005	2006	2007
Sleeping Bags	65,239,462.96	77,038,477.82	98,164,939.40	68,730,008.17
Tents	109,026,145.24	137,670,281.86	166,851,052.00	114,674,248.92
Irons	54,093,311.24	55,116,575.97	81,997,784.03	63,606,666.75
Putters	29,419,377.82	28,923,250.88	29,695,643.19	18,145,999.48
Mountaineering Equipment		107,099,659.94	161,039,823.26	141,520,649.70

Limit Data Shown in Tree Prompts   You can also limit what users see in tree prompts. This example explains how to restrict what data users can see in a tree prompt.

To limit data shown in tree prompts, follow these steps:

1. From Page Explorer on the Explorer bar, click the Prompt Pages link. A Prompt Pages pane displays in the work area, as shown next:

2. From the Insertable Objects pane, drag-and-drop a Page object into the Prompt Pages pane in the work area.

3. Double-click the newly inserted page within the Prompt Pages pane. The page opens in the work area.

4. From the Toolbox tab in the Insertable Objects pane, drag-and-drop a Tree Prompt object into the work area. The Prompt Wizard Choose Parameter dialog displays, as shown next:

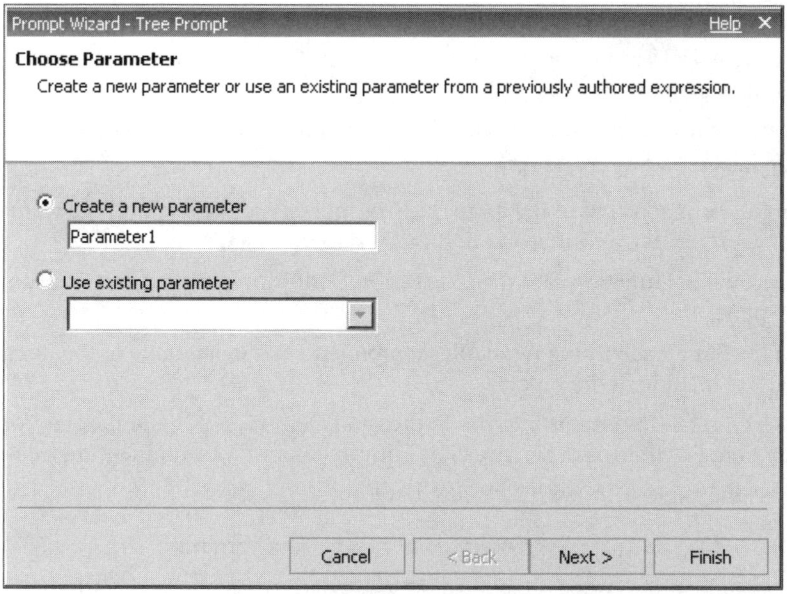

5. Select the Use Existing Parameter option, and choose a parameter from the drop-down list. For this example, we select the p_Products parameter we created in the previous section.

6. Click Next. The Populate Control dialog displays.

7. In the Name text box, enter a name for the Query, or use the default name, as shown next:

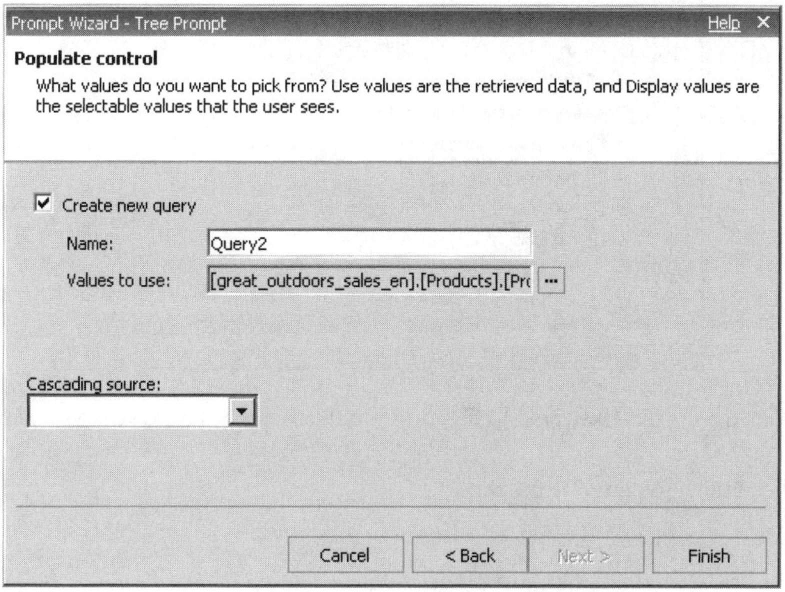

8. Click Finish. The wizard closes and the prompt page displays.

9. From Query Explorer on the Explorer bar, select the new query. The new query displays in the work area.

10. Double-click the data item in the Data Items pane. The Expression dialog displays.

11. Delete the current expression.

12. On the Functions tab in the Available Components pane, expand the Common Functions folder, and then expand the R-Z folder.

13. Insert the Set function into the Expression Definition pane, or enter the text in the pane.

14. On the Source tab in the Available Components pane, navigate to the items that you want to include in the report.

15. Insert the selected items into the Expression Definition pane to the right of the Set function. For this example, use Golf Equipment and Mountaineering Equipment.

16. Close the expression with a closing parenthesis, as shown next, and then click OK:

Expression Definition:

set([Golf Equipment],[Mountaineering Equipment])

17. Run the report. The tree prompt displays, containing only the members specified in the Set function:

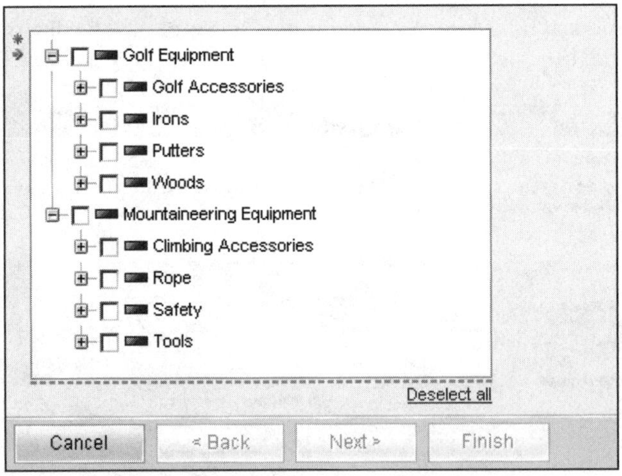

- ☐ Golf Equipment
  - ☐ Golf Accessories
  - ☐ Irons
  - ☐ Putters
  - ☐ Woods
- ☐ Mountaineering Equipment
  - ☐ Climbing Accessories
  - ☐ Rope
  - ☐ Safety
  - ☐ Tools

Deselect all

Cancel   < Back   Next >   Finish

18. Select the check boxes next to the individual items that you want to display in the report.

19. Click Finish to generate the report.

Navigating with Dimensional Functions

Dimensional functions make a report dynamic. You can create reports that prompt users to select a member to be featured in the report, and that member can be used to select other members based on its relationship in the dimensional function. Many dimensional functions are used to navigate through dimensional data in Cognos Report Studio. This section highlights some of the more important family functions, relative functions, and complex functions used to navigate through those structures.

Family Functions

Family functions allow you to navigate through a dimensional data hierarchy both vertically and horizontally to retrieve members that are relative to a selected member. You can use family functions to retrieve members. The functions are *ancestor, children, cousin, descendants, firstChild, firstSibling, lastChild, lastSibling, parent, siblings,* and many others. A variety of family functions are available in Cognos Report Studio. This section will explain parent, children, ancestor, and cousin functions.

The following illustration shows a dimensional structure and the family relationships among the members in the structure. This dimensional structure contains revenue data included in members that represent specific periods of time, such as the year, quarter, and month.

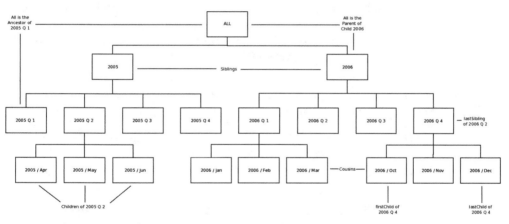

Children and Parent Functions

The *Children* function navigates one level down in the dimensional structure to retrieve the child members of the selected member. For example, imagine that you have a parent member called Camping Equipment, and you want to retrieve the types of equipment that are children to the Camping Equipment member. You can use the Children function to retrieve these Camping Equipment types. If you look at the Insertable Objects pane in the next illustration, you see a member named 2006. If you apply the Children function on member 2006, it will return all the child members at the next level down, or members 2006 Q 1, 2006 Q 2, 2006 Q 3, and 2006 Q 4. Here is the expression: *children([2006]).*

The *Parent* function performs the opposite action of the Children function. You can use the Parent function to retrieve the member one level up in the hierarchy from the selected member. The Parent function is useful if you want to know the context of the data with which you are working or if you need to navigate up a level in the dimensional structure. If you applied the Parent function to member 2006 Q 1 from the preceding illustration, it will retrieve the member 2006. Here is the expression: *parent([2006 Q 1]).*

Cousin Function

The *Cousin* function retrieves a member in the same position relative to a member that you specify in the expression. The Cousin function asks you to enter both the member for which you want to retrieve a cousin and the relative ancestor member from which you want to locate that cousin. For example, imagine that you are browsing through sales information in member 2006/Jun, or June 2006. Now imagine that you want to compare this sales information to that from June of the previous year. You can use the Cousin function to retrieve that data. You would need to enter member 2006/Jun in the first half of the Cousin function expression and enter the relative parent member 2005 in the second half of the expression. This function will navigate through the 2005 parent member and retrieve the cousin member 2005/Jun. Here is the expression: *cousin([2006/Jun],[2005]).*

NOTE *The cousin member is determined based on the position in the collection of descendants from the ancestor at the same level as the selected ancestor member. For example, if your expression was* cousin([2006 Q 1], [2005]) *and 2005 Q 1 was not present in the hierarchy, then 2005 Q 2 would be the cousin (assuming 2005 Q 2 was the first member in the descendants of 2005).*

Ancestor Function

The *Ancestor* function retrieves a parent member several levels up in the hierarchy, based on either the number of levels up or an ancestor level that you specify in the expression. If you applied the Ancestor function to member 2006/Jun in the preceding example, and you specify that the expression is to navigate up two levels, the Ancestor function looks up one level to the yearly quarter member (2006 Q 2), and then looks up again to the year member to return the member 2006. Here is the expression: *ancestor([2006/Jun],2).*

Relative Functions

Relative functions navigate horizontally in a level to retrieve members in the dimensional structure. Relative functions include *currentMember*, *lag*, *lead*, *nextMember*, and *prevMember*. These functions are not bound to the parent-child relationships of the hierarchy as the family functions are.

Lag and *Lead* functions retrieve sibling members that are a specified number of places before (*lag*) or after (*lead*) the selected member. The number of positions before or after the selected member is specified by the report author in the expression. If you applied the Lead function to the member, such as 2005/Apr, and you entered 2 in the Lead function expression, it would return the member 2005/Jun: *lead([2005/Apr],2)*. It does not make sense to use the Lag function on member 2005/Apr because it is the first child element at that level, and there are no members before it to retrieve. The PrevMember and NextMember functions behave similarly to Lead and Lag functions, but they can retrieve only the previous or next sibling member, respectively. This means that you are not required to enter a number of places to move in their expressions.

NOTE *Applying the Lag or Lead function to the first or last respective member of the level won't return any member for the expression.*

Relative Time Functions

Relative time functions are typically used with the time dimension. This group includes functions such as *ClosingPeriod*, *LastPeriods*, *OpeningPeriod*, *ParallelPeriod*, and *PeriodsToDate*.

The *ClosingPeriod* function returns the last sibling of a level, which can optionally be restricted to the descendants of a specified member. In our example, the closing period of member 2006 Q 2, at the month level, would be member 2006/Jun. The OpeningPeriod function behaves in the same way as the ClosingPeriod function, but it returns the first time period in the level. For our example, the opening period of 2006 at the quarter level would be 2006 Q 1. Here is the ClosingPeriod expression definition: *closingPeriod([great_outdoors_sales_en].[Years].[Years].[Month],[2006 Q 2])*.

The *ParallelPeriod* function returns a member from a period in the same relative position as the specified member in the expression. This means that it works similarly to the Cousin function; however, where the Cousin function requires that the new ancestor member be defined explicitly, the ParallelPeriod function allows you to define the new ancestor based on a lag or lead at the same level of the ancestor of a specified member. For comparison purposes, this makes the ParallelPeriod function more dynamic than the Cousin function, as the new ancestor will always be a relative rather than a fixed reference. For example, imagine that you are reviewing sales information in a report at the end of the month of May 2006, and you want to review sales information from May of the year before so that you can get an idea of how sales information changed. You can retrieve this data by creating a ParallelPeriod function expression. Continuing with our example, you will need to create the function and enter the *Years level* as the first part of the expression, enter *2006/May* as the parent member in the expression, and then enter the number *1* as the number of periods to move. This retrieves member 2005/May: *parallelPeriod([great_outdoors_sales_en].[Years].[Years].[Year],1,[2006/May])*.

NOTE *Positive and negative numbers behave differently in the ParallelPeriod function than they do in most other functions. In most functions, a positive number would indicate a movement forward through the members of the level, but in this function, positive numbers move backward, or toward the first period in the level. Negative numbers cause the function to navigate forward to the next period in the level, or toward the last period in the level.*

The *PeriodsToDate* function can be used to retrieve all the descendants of a given member at a level up to a selected member or period. This function is commonly used to define sets such as the months of a "Year to Date," where the individual months are bound by a common ancestor, the year, but do not share a common parent member at the quarter level. For example, if you selected the *Year level*, and the member two levels down named 2006/Apr, the function would retrieve 2006/Jan, 2006/Feb, 2006/Mar, and 2006/Apr (January through April 2006). As you can see from this example, the PeriodsToDate function retrieves sibling members regardless of their parent as long as they are at the same level as 2006/Apr and included underneath the ancestor 2006: *periodsToDate([PowerCube].[Years] .[Years].[Years],[2006/Apr])*.

Complex Functions

You can combine many of the navigational functions mentioned to create *complex navigational functions*. These functions can be used to navigate to and retrieve members that would normally require many steps to locate. The next example explains how to use complex functions and dynamic data to create a report that contains revenue information for a specific month and for the year-to-date up to a selected month. The data item This Year Selected Period can be seen in the first column heading:

Revenue	<#This Year Selected Period#>	<#Last Year Selected Period#>	<#2 Years Ago Selected Period#>	<#This Year YTD#>	<#Last Year YTD#>	<#2 Years Ago YTD#>
<#Product line#>	<#1234#>	<#1234#>	<#1234#>	<#1234#>	<#1234#>	<#1234#>
<#Product line#>	<#1234#>	<#1234#>	<#1234#>	<#1234#>	<#1234#>	<#1234#>

This column contains revenue information for a selected month this year, which is 2006 in this example. Double-click the column heading to display the Expression dialog. In the Expression Definition pane, you can view the expression, as shown next:

Expression Definition:
[great_outdoors_sales_en].[Years].[Years].[Month]->?Selected Period?

NOTE *Syntax instructions display below the Expression Definition pane in the Expression dialog any time you select a function that requires you to add members or additional data to the expression.*

The expression in the preceding illustration creates a single selection prompt that asks the user to supply the month for the report. All the other data items that reference this data item retrieve their information based on the user's selection. This means that This Year Selected Period is a dynamic data item, and it is determined by what is selected in the prompt. For our example, let's assume that September 2006 (2006/Sep) has been selected here.

Now look at the column heading Last Year Selected Period—the second column heading in our example. This column contains revenue information for a selected month last year.

Double-click this column heading to view the expression in the Expression Definition pane of the Expression dialog:

Expression Definition:

parallelPeriod([great_outdoors_sales_en].[Years].[Years].[Year], 1,[This Year Selected Period])

To illustrate complex functions (multiple functions, as well as nesting), we use the expression shown in the next illustration. It returns the same results as the previous expression.

Expression Definition:

cousin([This Year Selected Period],lag(ancestor([This Year Selected Period],2), 1))

This complex expression contains three functions as well as nesting. All of these functions reference the data item This Year Selected Period. Therefore, these functions navigate through the dimensional structure to retrieve certain members based on the prompt selection. As mentioned, for our earlier example, the member 2006/Sep was selected at that prompt.

The function that is nested the deepest in this complex function is the *Ancestor* function. This function tells Cognos Report Studio to give us the ancestor 2006/Sep, two levels up. This returns the year member 2006.

The next function nested in this complex function is a *Lag* function. This function looks back one member from 2006 to the member 2005.

The final function in this complex function is a *Cousin* function. This function retrieves the cousin of 2006/Sep, but for the year 2005. This gives us the member in the same relative position, which is 2005/Sep.

The third column in our report is 2 Years Ago Selected Period. This column contains revenue information for a selected month two years ago. Double-click this column heading to view the following expression:

parallelPeriod([great_outdoors_sales_en].[Years].[Years].[Year],2,[This Year Selected Period])

NOTE *To illustrate complex functions (multiple functions as well as nesting), the following expression was used. It returns the same results:*

cousin([This Year Selected Period],lag(ancestor([This Year Selected Period],2),2))

The 2 Years Ago Selected Period basically works the same way as Last Year Selected Period, except that the lag function has changed from one to two members back (theParallelPeriod function has also been changed from 1 to 2). This means that the Lag function (ParallelPeriod function) returns 2004 and the entire complex function returns 2004/Sep.

Our example also contains three columns that have not yet been discussed: This Year YTD, Last Year YTD, and 2 Years Ago YTD. These columns return an aggregate, or sum, of all of the revenue in their respective year leading up to the dynamic data item selected in This Year Selected Period.

To create an aggregate of each month to populate these YTD columns, you first need to use data items that retrieve all the members leading up to This Year Selected Period. This example shows a Query Explorer screen that contains the data items needed to retrieve this information. The data items are This Year Periods To Date, Last Year Periods To Date, and 2 Years Ago Periods To Date.

Double-click any of these data items to open the Expression dialog. If you double-click This Year Periods To Date, the expression displays in the Expression Definition pane, as shown next:

Expression Definition:

periodsToDate([great_outdoors_sales_en].[Years].[Years].[Years],[This Year Selected Period])

This expression uses the data item This Year Selected Period to retrieve all the members from the beginning of the year through the period selected in the prompt in This Year Selected Period. Last Year Periods to Date and 2 Years Ago Periods To Date use Last Year Selected Period and 2 Years Ago Selected Period, respectively, as follows:

Last Year Periods To Date:

periodsToDate([great_outdoors_sales_en].[Years].[Years].[Years],[Last Year Selected Period])

2 Years Ago Periods To Date:

periodsToDate([great_outdoors_sales_en].[Years].[Years].[Years],[2 Years Ago Selected Period])

These expressions return the entire set of members from the period to date, which is not necessary if you want to view the sum of the revenues up to a particular month in a given year. The aggregate expressions used in the YTD columns solve this problem by rolling these values for each year into a single value.

Double-click one of the YTD column headings to see one of the following expressions:

This Year YTD:

aggregate(currentMeasure within set [This Year Periods To Date])

Last Year YTD:

aggregate(currentMeasure within set [Last Year Periods To Date])

2 Years Ago YTD:

aggregate(currentMeasure within set [2 Years Ago Periods To Date])

In these aggregate expressions, you will notice that the data items This Year Periods To Date, Last Year Periods To Date, and 2 Years Ago Periods To Date are aggregated to create a sum value for all months in the year leading up to the selected period in the year.

NOTE *The Aggregate function relies on the aggregation defined within the cube to determine the rollup type. If the rollup is different from what is required for the report, then the relevant member summary function should be used instead of aggregate. For example, if the rollup type is set to average, you should use the total member summary function.*

Prompt Macro

You can use a prompt macro in conjunction with complex relative time functions and a static choice to filter a report using the relative time periods within the time dimension of a cube. For example, suppose some users want to be able to create a report that reflects the current month without the users having to reselect the prompt selection month after month. However, the users also want the flexibility to run the report ad hoc for any other month available in the cube.

NOTE *Using a prompt macro to filter a report for the relative time period is also extremely beneficial when using Report Views.*

To create a prompt macro, follow these steps:

1. Create a new Crosstab style report using a multidimensional package. For this example, use the Great Outdoors Sales (cube) package.

2. From the Insertable Objects pane, insert the desired items into the Rows drop zone of the crosstab. For this example, use the Product Lines level.

3. From the Insertable Objects pane, insert the desired measure into the Measure drop zone of the crosstab. For this example, use the Revenue measure.

4. From the Toolbox tab in the Insertable Objects pane, insert a Query Calculation into the Columns drop zone. The Create Calculation dialog displays.

5. Enter a name for the Prompt Macro calculation in the Name text box. For this example, name the calculation Selected Month.

6. Select the Other expression radio button.

7. Click OK. The Expression dialog displays.

8. Type the following expression: **#prompt('Current Month','*token*')#**.

Expression Definition:
#prompt('Current Month','token')#

9. Click OK to set the specified expression for the calculation.
10. Click the Build Prompt Page button on the standard toolbar.
11. From the Toolbox tab in the Insertable Objects pane, add a Value Prompt to the Prompt Page.
12. Create a new or use an existing parameter. For this example, select Use Existing Parameter and select Current Month from the drop-down.

13. Click Next to continue within the prompt wizard.
14. Select the ellipsis for the Values To Use property and navigate to the appropriate level. For this example, select the Month level: [great_outdoors_sales_en].[Years] .[Years].[Month]

15. Click OK to set the Values To Use property.

16. Click Finish to create the prompt.

17. Highlight the Value Prompt on the Prompt Page.

18. From the Properties, select the ellipsis for the Static Choices property.

Query	Query2
Use Value	Month
Display Value	
Static Choices	...

19. Click the Add button in the Static Choices dialog.

20. Enter the desired expression for the prompt macro, and click OK. For this example, use the following information:

    In the Use column, enter **linkmember(firstChild([great_outdoors_sales_en].[Years] .[Current Month].[Current Month]->:[PC].[@MEMBER].[Current Month]), [great_outdoors_sales_en].[Years].[Years].[Month])**

In the Display column, enter **Current Month**

21. Click OK to accept the changes to the static choices.
22. Run the report. The prompt that appears should look like the following:

23. Select Current Month. The results are displayed in the following example. You can see that the column shows 2007/Jul, because that is the current month in the cube:

Revenue	2007/Jul
Camping Equipment	53,939,284.40
Golf Equipment	25,129,748.14
Mountaineering Equipment	21,634,522.83
Outdoor Protection	706,920.16
Personal Accessories	65,031,507.03

NOTE *You can use all of the aforementioned relative time functions to create complex functions that reference the prompt macro (Selected Month) to filter a report. This technique is extremely useful when you are creating report views, because the prompt value Current Month can be preselected and the report view can be scheduled to run every time the cube is updated. This eliminates the need to maintain the prompt selection.*

Advanced Report Authoring

In Chapter 10, you learned how to create a report, add filters, group reports, and apply formatting, among other things. In this chapter, you will learn advanced features of IBM Cognos Report Studio, including using a variety of query types, setting variables, and adding HTML items in reports. You will also learn how to create drill-through access, use advanced prompting, and create a table of contents (including entries for particular data items and bookmarks) to make navigating through reports and data easier for the user.

This chapter also discusses several report options. The No Data Contents option displays a message for the user when a report does not have data to display. The Master Detail Relationships option allows you to link separate data containers such as a list, crosstab, or chart within a report, and the Bursting option distributes the contents of a report to specific recipients or groups via e-mail or to a directory in IBM Cognos Connection. The Singleton object allows you to place a single query item anywhere in the report layout. All of these features offer high level of flexibility when you are creating advanced reports. For the samples in this chapter, we use the GO Sales (query) package from the Cognos BI samples.

Create Drill-Through Access

Creating drill-through access within a report makes it easier for you to navigate through large reports or link separate reports containing related information. When you create drill-through access, you can create a bookmark that lets you navigate through a particular dimension of a report or pass a parameter from a source report to a target report. When the drill-through data item value in the source report is selected, the target report opens. The target report is filtered on the parameter that was passed from the source report. This allows you to link separate reports with related information. For the following example, we will set up drill-through access using two separate reports: a target report and a source report.

Set Up a Target Report for Drill-Through Access

The target report opens after you click a data item value in the source report. This report contains related or more detailed information about the source report. In the next section, we create a source report that contains revenue for retailer region, retailer type, and retailer by year. In this section, region is set up as our drill-through text within the target report. When you click the region drill-through text from the source report, the target report opens, displaying revenue for retailers for the region that was selected in the source report. Setting up drill-through access gives the user quick access to detailed information without having to navigate through folders to run another report.

To set up a target report for drill-through access, follow these steps:

1. Create or open a report to use as the target report. For this example, use a crosstab created from the GO Sales (query) package using the Sales (query) namespace. From the Retailers query subject, insert Region into the rows drop zone of the crosstab. From the Retailer Type query subject, nest Retailer Type and Retailer within Region. Add Year from the Time query subject to the columns drop zone, and Revenue from the Sales query subject as the measure.

2. Create an advanced detail filter for the target report that uses the parameter on which you want to filter when drilling through from the source report. For this example, create a filter for Region, as shown next. This filters the report based on which sales region is selected in the source report.

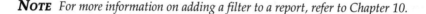

NOTE *For more information on adding a filter to a report, refer to Chapter 10.*

3. Save the target report. For this example, save the target report as **Retailer Revenue by Year**.

TIP *You can run the target report to see that you are prompted for the value correctly to ensure that the filter is defined properly.*

Set Up a Source Report for Drill-Through Access

The source report contains the data item value that a user can click to drill-through to the target report to view more detailed information. To set up the source report to contain the drill-through definition, you need to know the name and location of the target report and the parameter used in the filter of the target report.

To set up a source report for drill-through access, follow these steps:

1. Create or open a report to use as the source report that contains the item you want to use for the drill-through. For this example, use a crosstab created from the GO Sales (query) package using the Sales (query) namespace with Region as the rows, Year as the columns, and Revenue as the measure. Region will be used as the drill-through.

2. In the work area, select the item to be used as the drill-through. For this example, select Region in the rows of the crosstab.

NOTE *To activate the Drill-Through Definitions button on the toolbar, you must first make a selection in the work area.*

3. Click the Drill-Through Definitions button on the standard toolbar. The Drill-Through Definitions dialog displays:

New button

4. Click the New button. The Drill-Through Definitions dialog refreshes, displaying parameters to define a drill-through.

5. Under Report, click the ellipsis to choose the report to which you will drill-through.

6. Select the target report and click the Open button. For this example, select the Retailer Revenue by Year report.

7. From the Action drop-down list, select the action for how the target report will render during drill-through. Commonly used actions are Run The Report, which runs the report and displays the most recent data; View Most Recent Report, which displays the most recent saved output version of the report; or Default, which uses the report action defined in Cognos Connection. For this example, select the Run The Report action.

8. From the Format drop-down list, select the output format for the report when it runs. You can choose HTML, PDF, Excel 2007, Excel 2002, Delimited Text (CSV), XML, and Default, which uses the output format defined in Cognos Connection. In this example, select HTML from the Format drop-down list.

9. To open the target report in a new window when it is accessed from the source report, select the Open In New Window check box. If you do not select this check box, the target report replaces the source report in IBM Cognos Viewer.

10. Click Edit to display the parameters from the target report. The Parameters dialog displays with the details of the parameter(s) in the target report:

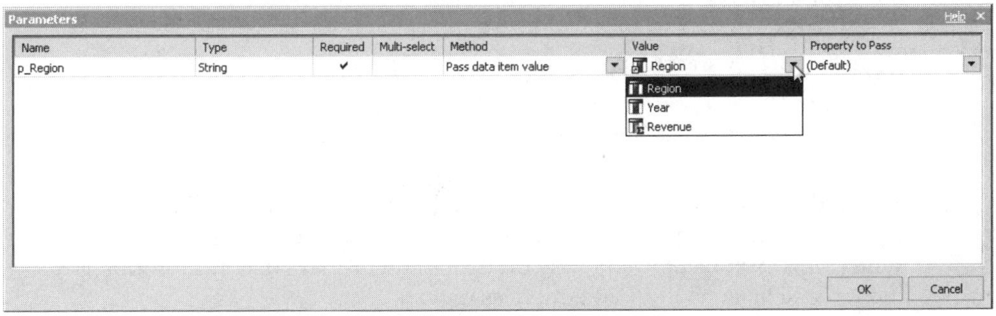

11. From the Method drop-down list, select the method for passing the parameter. You can choose from Do Not Use Parameter, which does not pass the parameter; Pass Data Item Value, which passes a value from a data item within the source report; Pass Parameter Value, which passes a parameter value from the source report; or Default, which does not pass the parameter. For this example, select Pass Data Item Value.

12. From the Value drop-down list, select the data item value from the source report. In this example, use Region.

13. Click OK. The parameter(s) to pass to the drill-through definition display in the Parameters pane in the Drill-Through Definitions dialog.

14. From the Display Prompt Pages drop-down list, select an option for when to display the prompt pages. For this example, use Only When Required Parameter Values Are Missing.

15. Click OK to save the drill-through definition. Cognos Report Studio updates the report. The data item being used as a drill-through object becomes a hyperlink, and the drill-through icon displays, as shown next:

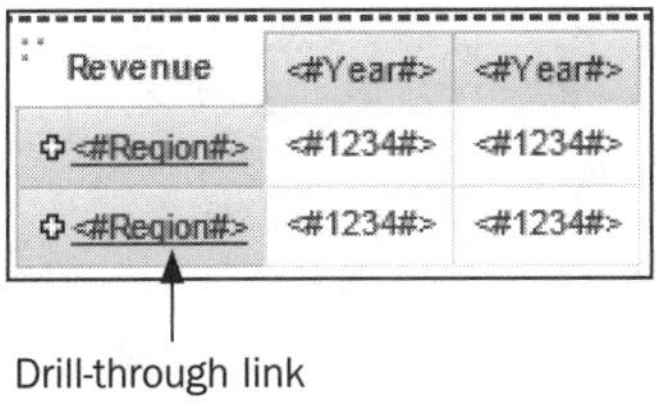

Drill-through link

16. Run the report to test the drill-through. The source report opens in IBM Cognos Viewer and the data items containing the drill-through definition display as hyperlinks that allow you to drill-through to the target report, as shown next:

Revenue	2004	2005	2006	2007
Americas	$292,401,703.35	$353,489,093.90	$458,164,908.61	$334,479,899.34
Asia Pacific	$227,714,548.00	$290,076,956.87	$380,703,219.69	$283,844,454.42
Central Europe	$202,944,732.04	$263,579,333.75	$325,949,572.45	$247,681,932.40
Northern Europe	$100,629,009.61	$132,108,570.75	$168,361,380.74	$129,222,484.71
Southern Europe	$90,662,810.72	$119,941,634.89	$162,712,019.41	$122,107,503.20

17. From the column containing the drill-through definition links, click a hyperlink. The drill-through target report displays with detailed information about the selected item. In this example, the target report opens and displays detailed information about the Retailers within the Americas region.

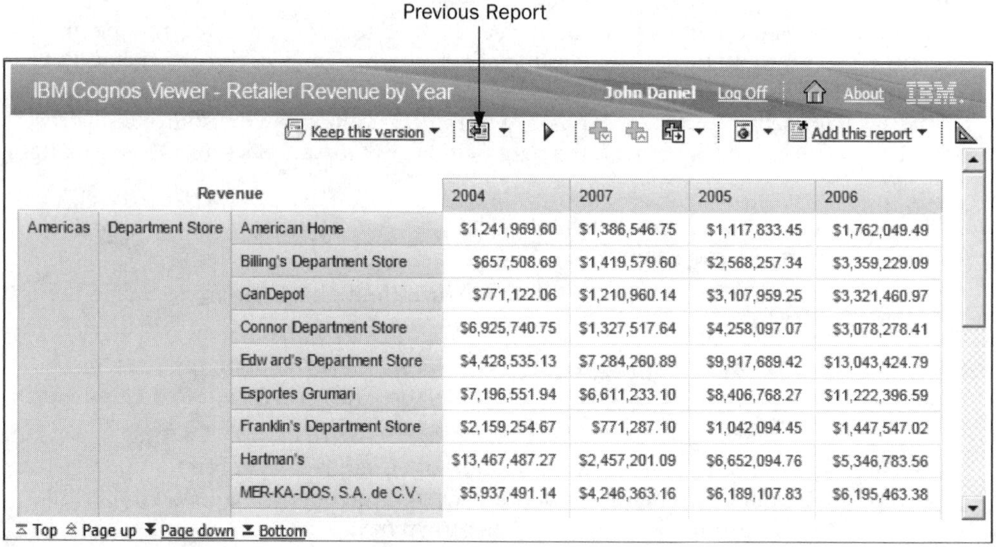

Previous Report

IBM Cognos Viewer - Retailer Revenue by Year   John Daniel   Log Off   About   IBM.

Keep this version ▼ | ▢ ▼ | ▶ | ▤ ▤ ▣ ▼ | ▢ ▼ | Add this report ▼ | ▨

		Revenue	2004	2007	2005	2006
Americas	Department Store	American Home	$1,241,969.60	$1,386,546.75	$1,117,833.45	$1,762,049.49
		Billing's Department Store	$657,508.69	$1,419,579.60	$2,568,257.34	$3,359,229.09
		CanDepot	$771,122.06	$1,210,960.14	$3,107,959.25	$3,321,460.97
		Connor Department Store	$6,925,740.75	$1,327,517.64	$4,258,097.07	$3,078,278.41
		Edward's Department Store	$4,428,535.13	$7,284,260.89	$9,917,689.42	$13,043,424.79
		Esportes Grumari	$7,196,551.94	$6,611,233.10	$8,406,768.27	$11,222,396.59
		Franklin's Department Store	$2,159,254.67	$771,287.10	$1,042,094.45	$1,447,547.02
		Hartman's	$13,467,487.27	$2,457,201.09	$6,652,094.76	$5,346,783.56
		MER-KA-DOS, S.A. de C.V.	$5,937,491.14	$4,246,363.16	$6,189,107.83	$6,195,463.38

≍ Top ≙ Page up ⬇ Page down ≍ Bottom

TIP *To return to the source report, click Previous Report on the IBM Cognos Viewer toolbar and then click the source report link.*

Master Detail Relationship

Master detail relationships link information between two data containers (such as a list, crosstab, or chart) within a report: a master data container and a detail data container. With a master detail relationship, you can use a single report to display information that would normally take two reports. You can also link data from two separate data sources into one report, as long as the data sources are in the same package.

Create a Master Detail Relationship

Master detail relationships can be created for any data container within Cognos Report Studio (such as a list, crosstab, or chart). This section describes the steps required to link three list containers. One list container will act as the master container, and the other two lists will contain detailed data relating to the master container. We will add formatting to the report to make it more visually appealing.

To create master detail relationships, follow these steps:

1. Create a new report, using the desired template. For this example, create a list report.

2. From the Insertable Objects pane, insert data items into the work area to create the parent report. For this example, from the Branch query subject in the Sales (query) namespace, add Branch Code, City, Address 1, and Postal Zone to the list.

3. From the Toolbox tab in the Insertable Objects pane, add a second data container to the work area. For this example, insert a second list object, adding it as a column to the existing list object in the work area. This nests the second list object within the original list object.

4. From the Insertable Objects pane, insert data items into the second data container in the work area, ensuring that one of the data items correlates to the master data container. For this example, add Branch Code, Product Line, Quantity, and Revenue to the nested list.

Branch code	City	Address 1	Postal zone	List			
<Branch code>	<City>	<Address 1>	<Postal zone>	Branch code	Product line	Quantity	Revenue
				<Branch code>	<Product line>	<Quantity>	<Revenue>
				<Branch code>	<Product line>	<Quantity>	<Revenue>
				<Branch code>	<Product line>	<Quantity>	<Revenue>

5. Select the data container that you want to be the child of the relationship to add a master detail relationship between the two data containers. For this example, select the second list object by clicking the three red dots in the corner of the list object.

Select data container

Branch code	City	Address 1	Postal zone	List			
<Branch code>	<City>	<Address 1>	<Postal zone>	Branch code	Product line	Quantity	Revenue
				<Branch code>	<Product line>	<Quantity>	<Revenue>
				<Branch code>	<Product line>	<Quantity>	<Revenue>
				<Branch code>	<Product line>	<Quantity>	<Revenue>

PART III

6. In the Properties pane, click the ellipsis button within the Master Detail Relationships property. The Master Detail Relationships dialog displays, showing the data items that make up the queries linked to the data containers.

7. Click the New Link button to create a link between the two queries. By default, the link is created between the first data items from each query.

8. Select the appropriate items from each query to link. For this example, select Branch Code from both Query1 and Query2.

9. Click OK to set the master detail relationship.

10. Run the report to view the results.

Branch code	City	Address 1	Postal zone	List			
6	Paris	75, rue du Faubourg St-Honoré	F-75008	**Branch code**	**Product line**	**Quantity**	**Revenue**
				6	Camping Equipment	961,712	$55,471,856.14
				6	Golf Equipment	170,100	$24,545,420.57
				6	Mountaineering Equipment	307,880	$12,691,085.32
				6	Outdoor Protection	505,331	$3,179,004.41
				6	Personal Accessories	320,600	$15,406,303.45
7	Milano	Piazza Duomo, 1	I-20121	**Branch code**	**Product line**	**Quantity**	**Revenue**
				7	Camping Equipment	1,128,345	$63,654,611.29
				7	Golf Equipment	223,747	$30,667,801.08
				7	Mountaineering Equipment	432,607	$17,425,641.14

Although the master detail relationship is displaying properly within this sample report, it is a little difficult to digest the data in its current format. To make the report easier to read and to add more value, you can add another list with a master detail relationship and some formatting to this report.

Branch code: 6 | Paris | 75, rue du Faubourg St-Honoré | F-75008

Actuals			Forecast		
Product line	**Quantity**	**Revenue**	**Product line**	**Planned revenue**	
Camping Equipment	961,712	$55,471,856.14	Camping Equipment	$59,563,067.64	
Golf Equipment	170,100	$24,545,420.57	Golf Equipment	$26,733,732.61	
Mountaineering Equipment	307,880	$12,691,085.32	Mountaineering Equipment	$13,328,961.87	
Outdoor Protection	505,331	$3,179,004.41	Outdoor Protection	$3,337,295.73	
Personal Accessories	320,600	$15,406,303.45	Personal Accessories	$16,325,574.68	

Branch code: 7 | Milano | Piazza Duomo, 1 | I-20121

Actuals			Forecast		
Product line	**Quantity**	**Revenue**	**Product line**	**Planned revenue**	
Camping Equipment	1,128,345	$63,654,611.29	Camping Equipment	$68,248,070.52	
Golf Equipment	223,747	$30,667,801.08	Golf Equipment	$33,374,411.16	
Mountaineering Equipment	432,607	$17,425,641.14	Mountaineering Equipment	$18,319,015.84	

Adding a Microchart to a Report

Micocharts are mini charts that can be used for a variety of purposes within a report. It can be useful to embed a microchart within a crosstab to provide additional context of an item. The microchart can graphically represent a row or column, allowing the user to spot trends quickly over a period of time. This can draw an executive's or manager's attention to important data within a report in a shorter period of time, allowing them to make decisions more quickly.

To add a microchart to a crosstab, follow these steps:

1. Create a new report, using the crosstab template.

2. From the Insertable Objects pane, insert data items into the crosstab in the work area. For this example, insert Product Type nested within Product Line on the rows, Year on the columns, and Revenue as the measures from the Sales (query) namespace of the GO Sales (query) package.

3. Right-click within the rows section of the crosstab, and select the Insert Chart for Row Data option from the dialog box. For this example, right-click Product Type in the crosstab. The Insert Chart dialog displays, with the Microchart chart style selected.

4. From the right pane of the Insert Chart dialog, select a microchart type from the available options. For this example, choose column.

5. Click OK to insert the microchart into the work area.

6. Run the report to view the results. The microchart displays within the crosstab, and shows a column for each year within each product type.

Revenue		2004	2005	2006	2007
Camping Equipment	Cooking Gear	$59,761,536.50	$70,843,132.06	$83,917,515.27	$58,313,800.35
	Lanterns	$28,662,904.19	$29,788,923.06	$40,439,357.85	$28,034,475.54
	Packs	$70,296,289.17	$87,416,758.37	$111,009,558.31	$83,157,796.99
	Sleeping Bags	$65,239,462.96	$77,038,477.82	$98,164,939.40	$68,730,008.17

Selecting Ancestors

Ancestors are all the containers that hold the currently selected container. Clicking the Select Ancestor button displays a list of ancestors for the currently selected container. This allows you to navigate quickly through the containers on a page or to select common containers of the page that you are not able to select easily in the work area, so that you can change their properties or apply styles to them.

For example, suppose you have created a report with headings and content that are the same size and font, making it difficult to differentiate the information. You can quickly modify the headings by using the Select Ancestor button to select the appropriate data container. Then you can edit properties of all headings simultaneously to increase font size and perhaps make the heading text boldface, to distinguish the headings from the contents of the report.

To select ancestors, follow these steps:

1. Open a report. Cognos Report Studio displays the report in the work area.

2. Click the work area outside of any containers. The Page Body properties display in the Properties pane.

3. In the title bar of the Properties pane, click the Select Ancestor button. A menu appears, showing the available ancestors for the selected item. In this example, click the Select Ancestor button to display the ancestors for Page Body, as shown next:

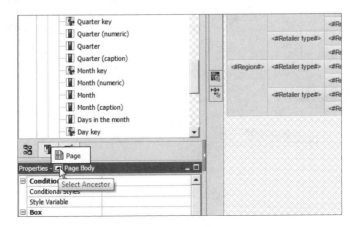

4. Click the desired ancestor from the list. For this example, select Page. The page properties display in the Properties pane.

5. From the Properties pane, set the desired properties. For this example, set the Horizontal Alignment property to Center. The work area displays the settings you selected applied to the report. Here, the contents of the page are centered:

Modify the Style for Multiple Items

You can edit the properties of a style, such as list columns title style, which modifies the style of all instances of that type. This method is faster than changing the style of items individually.

To modify the style of multiple items, follow these steps:

1. Click a cell whose style appears in multiple instances, and then click the Select Ancestor button. A menu displays, showing all available ancestors for the selected item.

2. From the ancestors menu, select the desired item. For this example, select List Columns Title Style.

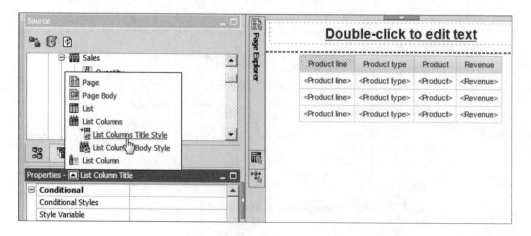

3. Set any desired properties for the selected style. For this example, from the style toolbar click the Bold button, and set the font size to 11pt. The bold style is applied to all column titles.

Double-click to edit text			
Product line	**Product type**	**Product**	**Revenue**
<Product line>	<Product type>	<Product>	<Revenue>
<Product line>	<Product type>	<Product>	<Revenue>
<Product line>	<Product type>	<Product>	<Revenue>

Query Management

A *query* defines the data items and conditions that, when sent to the data source, determine the set of data that is returned for inclusion in the report. A Cognos Report Studio report can contain multiple queries, resulting in multiple sets of data being included in the report. They can be managed using Query Explorer, which gives you a great deal of control over the data that appears in a report.

Queries must be associated to the report layout in order for the data to appear in the report. You can associate your queries to the report layout in several ways. If you create the report by starting with a report template that contains a data container (such as a list, crosstab, or chart), a query is automatically associated with the layout. If you start with a blank report and drag a data container to the work area, a query is created and automatically associated to the layout. At any time, you can change the query that is associated to a data container by changing the Query property of the data container in the Properties pane.

Query Types

Cognos Report Studio provides several types of queries, such as Join, Union, Intersect, and others, which are described in detail in Table 12-1. These give you the flexibility to create complex reports and to create reports using query items from different data sources. The query types listed in the table are accessible by navigating to Queries from the Query Explorer menu.

Creating a Join

Joins link two separate queries. This allows you to perform a calculation between these queries that might not be possible without the join. For example, suppose you have created individual queries for each year, and each returns the revenue for retailers, and you want to measure the rate of growth from year to year for each retailer. Using joins, you can join the

Icon	Description
Query	Add a single query to a report. Single query objects, single query items, and multiple data items can be added within this query to return one subset of data in the report.
Join	Join two separate queries. You can manipulate the relationships between the queries using links.
Union	Link multiple queries into one subset of data. The queries can be from the same data source or from different data sources. Note that the queries must contain the same number of data items, the data types must be compatible (for example, a Date is only compatible with a Date), and the data items must appear in the same order.
Intersect	Take multiple queries and return only the data that intersects in the queries. For example, suppose Query1 contains 100 products and Query2 contains three products. Data item(s) are returned only when a match occurs between the two queries. So if two products in Query1 match two products in Query2, only two products are returned.
Except	Take multiple queries and return the data where no match occurs between the queries. This operation performs the opposite of the Intersect object. Using the example from the Intersect description, 98 products would be returned.
SQL	Write a SQL statement manually or convert a regular query into a SQL query object. This query corresponds to relational models. Note that once a query item is converted into a SQL query object, you cannot pull data from your source model. Any additional data must be added manually.
MDX	Write Multidimensional Expressions (MDX) code manually, which is the underlying SQL for dimensional models. Note that once a query item is converted into a SQL query object, you cannot pull data from your source model. Any additional data must be added manually.

TABLE 12-1   Query Types

query that returns the first year's revenue with the query that returns the second year's revenue and measure the rate of growth between each year in a new query.

To create a join between two queries, follow these steps:

1. Create a new report using the blank template.

2. From the Query Explorer tab, click the Queries link. Currently, no queries are available, so no queries appear in the work area.

3. From the Insertable Objects pane, drag-and-drop a Join object into the work area. The Join object creates Query1, the Join relationship object, and two drop areas for the queries that you want to join, as shown next:

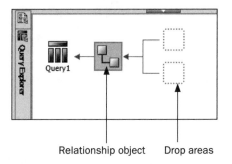

Relationship object   Drop areas

4. From the Insertable Objects pane, drag-and-drop a Query object into the first (upper) drop area in the work area. A shortcut to Query2 displays in the first (upper) drop area, and "Query2" displays on the page in the work area.

5. From the Insertable Objects pane, drag-and-drop another Query object to the second (lower) drop area. A shortcut to Query3 appears in the join relationship and "Query3" displays in the work area.

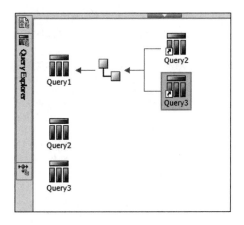

6. Double-click one of the two queries that make up the join and add the desired data items to the query by inserting items from the Insertable Objects pane to the Data Items pane in the work area. For this example, add Retailer, Year, and Revenue to Query3 from the Sales (query) namespace of the GO Sales (query) package.

7. From the Properties pane, set any desired properties for the data items, such as Type, Name, or Label. For this example, set the Name property of Revenue to 2006 Revenue and the Name property of Year to Current Year 2006.

8. Within the Detail Filters pane, create any desired filters. For this example, define a detail filter using the Year data item to limit data retrieved by this query to the year 2006.

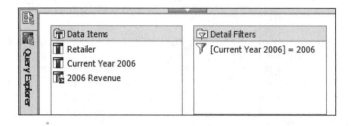

9. From the Query Explorer tab, open the other query that makes up the join, and add the desired data items to the query. For this example, add Retailer, Year, and Revenue to Query2.

10. Repeat steps 7 and 8 to set any properties of the data items or any detail filters for the query. For this example, repeat these steps for Query2, replacing "Current Year 2006" with "Prior Year 2005", and "2006 Revenue" with "2005 Revenue". Set the filter to include only 2005.

11. From the Query Explorer tab, click the Queries link. The available queries display in the work area.

12. In the work area, double-click the Join relationship object. The Join Relationships dialog displays with the data items that make up each query.

As an alternative, from the Properties pane, you can click the ellipsis within the Join Relationships property to launch the Join Relationships dialog.

13. Click the New Link button to create a join relationship between two data items. A link is created, and by default, points to the first data items from each query.

14. Select the data items from each query that you want to link for the join relationship. For this example, the Retailer data item from each query is what we want to link, because Retailer is the common attribute between the queries.

15. In both Cardinality drop-down lists, select the applicable relationship impact setting for the data items. The available options are 1..n, 1..1, 0..n, and 0..1. For this example, select 1..1 so that the report displays the retailers that are the same from both queries.

16. Click OK to save the specified join relationship settings.

17. Double-click the join query, and add the desired data items to the query. For this example, add Retailer, 2005 Revenue, and 2006 Revenue to Query1.

At this point, the join query is complete and can be linked to from a data container in the layout.

18. From the Page Explorer tab, open Page1. A blank template displays in the work area.

19. From the Toolbox tab in the Insertable Objects pane, insert a data container object into the work area. For this example, use a List object to create a list report.

20. In the Properties pane of the data container, set the Query property to the join query. In this example, set the Query property to Query1 for the List data container, as shown next. The data items within the join query are now available for use.

Properties - List	
Conditional	
Conditional Styles	
Style Variable	
Render Variable	
No Data Contents	No Data Available
Data	
Grouping & Sorting	
Query	Query1
Rows Per Page	
Master Detail Relationships	

NOTE *By default, when adding a data container, a new query is created for that container. In this example, Query4 was created when the list was added. When you set the Query property of the List data container to Query1, Cognos Report Studio removes Query4 because it did not contain data items.*

21. From the Data Items tab in the Insertable Objects pane, insert the data items from the join query into the data container in the work area. For this example, add Retailer, 2005 Revenue, and 2006 Revenue to the list.

Data Items	Retailer	2005 Revenue	2006 Revenue
Query1	\<Retailer>	\<2005 Revenue>	\<2006 Revenue>
Retailer	\<Retailer>	\<2005 Revenue>	\<2006 Revenue>
2005 Revenue	\<Retailer>	\<2005 Revenue>	\<2006 Revenue>
2006 Revenue			

22. Add any other items to the report you want. For this example, to show the growth between the two years, create a Query Calculation named "Annual Growth %" that calculates the growth percentage from year to year as the last column in the list, as shown next:

Expression Definition:
([2006 Revenue]-[2005 Revenue])/[2005 Revenue]

23. From the Properties pane, set the desired properties for any data items in the report, such as Source Type, Data Item Value, and Data Format. In this example, for the Annual Growth calculation, set Format Type to Percent and No. of Decimal Places to 1 for the Data Format property.

24. Click Run to run the report and view the output. In this example, the growth between the revenue for each year displays in the Annual Growth % column:

Retailer	Revenue	Revenue	Annual Growth %
1 for 1 Sports shop	$1,841,265.46	$1,715,812.95	-6.8%
4 Golf only	$1,667,634.53	$1,875,229.33	12.4%
Aarhus Sport	$1,214,820.52	$2,506,561.08	106.3%
Accapamento	$1,711,149.20	$2,613,580.91	52.7%
Accesorios Importados, S.A. de C.V.	$1,853,330.86	$2,650,667.17	43.0%
AcquaVerde	$2,084,544.22	$2,881,701.02	38.2%
Act'N'Up Fitness	$3,146,200.50	$5,014,080.59	59.4%

NOTE *By default, the 2005 Revenue and 2006 Revenue column titles display as the original data item name of Revenue.*

25. To set a data item label, click Query Explorer and select Query1.

26. Select the data item in the Data Items pane for which you want to set the column title. For this example, select the 2006 Revenue data item.

27. In the Properties pane, set the label property as desired. For this example, type **2006 Revenue** in the Label property.

Properties - Data Item	_ □
⊟ **Data Item**	
Type	Data Item
Name	2006 Revenue
Label	2006 Revenue
Expression	[Query3].[2006 Revenue]
Aggregate Function	Automatic

28. Repeat steps 26 and 27 for any other data items as necessary. For this example, for the 2005 Revenue data item, set the Label property to **2005 Revenue.**

29. Run the report to view the results.

The titles are now displayed properly in the report:

Retailer	2005 Revenue	2006 Revenue	Annual Grow th %
1 for 1 Sports shop	$1,841,265.46	$1,715,812.95	-6.8%
4 Golf only	$1,667,634.53	$1,875,229.33	12.4%
Aarhus Sport	$1,214,820.52	$2,506,561.08	106.3%
Accapamento	$1,711,149.20	$2,613,580.91	52.7%
Accesorios Importados, S.A. de C.V.	$1,853,330.86	$2,650,667.17	43.0%
AcquaVerde	$2,084,544.22	$2,881,701.02	38.2%
Act'N'Up Fitness	$3,146,200.50	$5,014,080.59	59.4%

Creating a Union

Unions let you link multiple separate queries into one result set. When using the Union object, the queries can come from the same data source or from separate data sources.

NOTE *For the Union to work properly, each query must have the same number of data items, the data types must be compatible, and the data items must appear in the same order.*

For example, suppose the Sales division of a large corporation has multiple territories, with a different number of sales representatives working within each territory. The corporation wants to create a sales report that shows the top five sales representatives and the bottom five sales representatives for all of the territories. To do this, you can create a report that contains two separate queries. One query returns the top five sales representatives, and the other query returns the bottom five sales representatives. The union pulls the two queries into one query to create the sales report.

To create a union between two queries, follow these steps:

1. Create a new report using the blank template.

2. From the Query Explorer tab, click the Queries link. Currently, no queries are available, so no queries appear in the work area.

3. From the Insertable Objects pane, insert the Union object into the work area. The Union object creates Query1, the Union relationship object, and two drop areas for the queries that you want to link together in the work area, as shown next.

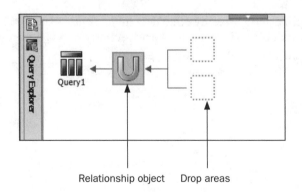

Relationship object   Drop areas

4. From the Insertable Objects pane, insert a Query object into the first (upper) drop area in the work area. A shortcut to Query2 displays in the first (upper) drop area and "Query2" displays on the page in the work area:

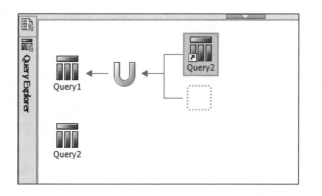

5. From the Insertable Objects pane, insert another Query object to the second (lower) drop area. A shortcut to Query3 displays in the union relationship and "Query3" displays in the work area.

6. Double-click one of the two queries that make up the union and add the desired data items to the query by inserting items from the Insertable Objects pane to the Data Items pane in the work area. For this example, add Sales Region, Staff Name, Year, and Revenue to Query3 from the Sales (query) namespace of the GO Sales (query) package. Also, create a new data item named Rank that calculates sales region rank by inserting a Data Item object from the Toolbox tab in the Insertable Objects pane to the Data Items pane. The rank is sorted in ascending order to determine the bottom sales reps.

7. Edit the expression definitions of any data items you want by double-clicking the data item. For this example, we edit the expression definition of Sales Region, so that additional text is concatenated onto the Sales Region data item in the report. Include a space before Bottom so that a space appears between the name of the region and the word "Bottom" in the report, as shown next.

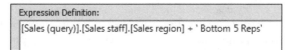

8. Within the Detail Filters pane, create any desired filters. For this example, filter the year data item on 2006 and the rank data item so that it returns the ranks 1 through 5.

9. From the Properties pane, set any desired properties, such as Type, Name, or Label. For this example, set the Application property to After Auto Aggregation for the Rank detail filter, so that the rankings are determined before the filter is applied.

10. Repeat steps 6 through 9 for the other query that makes up the union. For this example, repeat these steps for Query2. Create a Rank data item sorting the rank in descending order to determine the top sales reps, and edit the expression definition of Sales Region to include the text "Top 5 Reps".

NOTE *Query2 must have the same number of data items in the same order and named the same as Query3. The data types must also be compatible.*

11. From the Query Explorer tab, click the Queries link to view the queries in the report.

12. From the Properties pane of the Union operator, set any properties you want. To retain all of the duplicate rows that are returned on the report, set the Duplicates property to Preserve. To change the order of the data items in the queries, set the Projection List property to Manual.

13. Open the union query, and add the necessary data items. For this example open Query1, and add Sales Region, Staff Name, Year, Revenue, and Rank to the query. At this point, the union query is complete and can be linked to from a data container in the layout.

14. From the Page Explorer tab, open Page1. A blank template displays in the work area.

15. From the Toolbox tab in the Insertable Objects pane, insert a data container object into the work area. For this example, use a List object to create a list report.

16. In the Properties pane of the data container, set the Query property to the union query. For this example, set the Query property to Query1 for the List data container. The data items in the union query are now available for use in this list.

NOTE *By default, when adding a data container, a new query is created for that container. In this example, Query4 was created when the list was added. When the Query property is set to Query1, Cognos Report Studio removes Query4 because it did not contain data items.*

17. From the Data Items tab in the Insertable Objects pane, insert the data items from Query1 into the data container in the work area. For this example, add Sales Region, Staff Name, Year, Revenue, and Rank to the list.

18. Make any desired changes to the format of the report. For this example, group Sales Region, insert a total for Revenue, and sort the Rank column in ascending order.

19. Run the report to view the results. In this example, the five top sales representatives and five bottom sales representatives display for each region.

Sales region	Staff name	Year	Revenue	Rank
Americas Bottom 5 Reps	Beatríz Couto	2006	$905,704.48	1
	Morela Castro	2006	$1,533,562.39	2
	Silvia Romero	2006	$2,449,969.65	3
	Karly Millers	2006	$3,392,973.85	4
	Samantha Pierce	2006	$3,720,463.21	5
Americas Bottom 5 Reps - Total			$12,002,673.58	
Americas Top 5 Reps	Charles Laurel	2006	$20,681,527.49	1
	George Harrows	2006	$17,924,373.12	2
	Lucía Reyna	2006	$17,341,182.19	3
	Pascal Lanuit	2006	$17,173,887.86	4
	Eduardo Guimarães	2006	$15,262,238.60	5
Americas Top 5 Reps - Total			$88,383,209.26	
Asia Pacific Bottom 5 Reps	Akira Hashimoto	2006	$1,206,901.22	1
	Jake Cartel	2006	$1,582,666.10	2

A Word of Caution

Creating joins between queries that you create is a very powerful ability. As a wise man once said, with great power comes great responsibility. The reports you create need to be maintainable, efficient, and, above all else, correct. If you find yourself adding joined queries to your reports, especially if it is the same join in multiple reports, ask yourself these questions: Do I fully understand the Cognos Framework Manager package that I am using as the source for my report? If you believe that you do, then ask yourself if the Cognos Framework Manager model is correct.

These are important questions, because when you are working with a complete and correct Cognos Framework Manager package, you should rarely need to create joined queries. Not long ago, we had a new customer who had never used Cognos Report Studio, but they knew everything there was to know about how to write SQL. We spent some time building a Cognos Framework Manager package to meet the customer's reporting needs, and we all got down to work writing reports. A few weeks into the report authoring, the SQL expert was becoming visibly frustrated. The expert's reports ran very slowly, took much longer to develop, and returned inconsistent results.

When we looked at the report causing the problems, we found joined queries—not a few, not a dozen: the report had 32 queries and 16 joins. The report author did not understand how Cognos Report Studio and Cognos Framework Manager work together to remove most of the complexities of report authoring. The point of this story is this: if you find yourself creating more than one or two joined queries in a report, you might not understand the Cognos Framework Manager package, or the Cognos Framework Manager package might need to be revised.

If you are wondering about the 32-query report, it was rewritten with 2 queries, no changes to the Cognos Framework Manager model, and the runtime went from 90 minutes to about 5 seconds. A screen shot of the Query Explorer pane for this report is shown toward the end of Chapter 17.

Specify What Appears When No Data Is Available

When no data is available for a report, you can inform users that no data is available by defining what Cognos Report Studio displays. This can be defined for lists, crosstabs, charts, maps, repeaters, repeater tables, and table of contents objects. If a prompted value returns no data, a more specific message can be displayed for the users by informing them of the values entered that returned no data.

Setting up this feature can provide users with feedback on why they received no data. By default, the No Data Contents option is set to display the text "No Data Available", but you can configure any desired content to appear when there is no data.

To set up the No Data Contents option, follow these steps:

1. Open or create a report. For this example, use a crosstab report with Product Line on the rows, Year on the columns, and Revenue as the measure from the Sales (query) namespace of the GO Sales (query) package. Add a text box prompt on the Year data item to allow users to enter the year on which they want to filter the report.

2. Select the data container in the work area. For this example, select the crosstab.

NOTE *The Select Object option is designated by the three dots in the upper-left corner of a data container.*

3. From the Properties pane, click the ellipsis in the No Data Contents property. The No Data Contents dialog displays.

4. Select the Content Specified In The No Data Tab radio button to set what appears when there is no data to display.

5. Click OK. The No Data Contents tab appears in the work area.

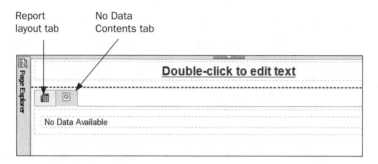

6. From the Insertable Objects pane, insert the items you want to display when no data is available. For this example, use a Text Item and a Layout Calculation. The Layout Calculation is used to include the Year prompt value in the message to the user.

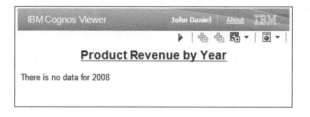

7. Run the report to view the results. For this example, type **2008** in the Year prompt. The report renders in IBM Cognos Viewer, showing a message that there is no data for 2008.

Dynamic Data Formatting Using Variables

By using variables, you can change the format of values displayed in a report depending on what you choose at a prompt. For example, if you choose Quantity at a prompt, you could set the values to display Quantity in numeric form with no decimal places; but if Revenue is chosen, Revenue can be displayed with the values set as currency with two decimal places.

To set up dynamic data formatting in a crosstab using variables, follow these steps:

1. Open or create a crosstab report. For this example, use Product Line for the rows, Year for the columns, and Quantity as the measure.

2. Create a prompt page for the report that prompts the user to select a measure. For this example, use a value prompt with the parameter p_Measure. In the Static Choices property of the value prompt, add Quantity and Revenue as the options.

3. From the Condition Explorer tab, click the Variables link. A Variables pane and a Values pane display in the work area.

4. From the Insertable Objects pane, drag-and-drop a Boolean Variable object into the Variables pane. The Expression dialog displays.

5. Set the expression definition for the variable. For this example, type **ParamDisplayValue('p_Measure') = 'Quantity'**.

6. Click OK to set the expression for the variable. The variable is added to the work area.

7. From the Properties pane, set any desired properties of the variable. For this example, type the Name property as **v_Measure**.

8. From the Query Explorer tab, open the report query. For this example, navigate to Query1.

9. Modify the expression of the measure data item to be dynamic based on the input from the prompt. For this example, use the Quantity data item and set the expression definition to a case statement. The case statement specifies the measure used in the crosstab based on the parameter used for the prompt. If the prompt returns Quantity, the data item is Quantity, and if the prompt value is not equal to Quantity, the data item is Revenue.

```
Expression Definition:

case
  when ?p_Measure? = 'Quantity'
  then ([Sales (query)].[Sales].[Quantity])
  else ([Sales (query)].[Sales].[Revenue])
end
```

10. From the Properties pane, change the Name property of the measure data item to reflect the modifications. For this example, set the name of the data item to **Measure**.

11. From the Page Explorer tab, open the report page.

12. Click a cell in the crosstab to set properties for the Crosstab Intersection.

13. From the Properties pane, set the Style Variable property to the name of the variable you created. For this example, set it to v_Measure.

14. From the Condition Explorer tab, click the Yes value for the variable. The Explorer bar turns green, indicating that conditional formatting is turned on. Any changes that you make while the Explorer bar is green apply only to the variable value.

15. From the Properties pane, set the Data Format property for the Yes value. For this example, set the Format Type to Number and the No. of Decimal Places to 0.

16. From the Condition Explorer tab, click the No value for the variable.

17. From the Properties pane, set the Data Format property for the No value. For this example, set the Format Type to Currency and the No. of Decimal Places to 2.

18. Run the report to view the results. The prompt dialog displays in Cognos Viewer with the specified prompt values. In this example, you can choose Quantity or Revenue from the prompt.

PART III

19. Select a value, and click Finish. For this example, select Quantity. The report displays, showing Quantity values in a numeric format with no decimal places:

Measure	2006	2005	2007	2004
Golf Equipment	1,536,772	1,297,793	1,186,154	1,092,982
Personal Accessories	10,706,015	8,567,357	8,061,994	7,572,339
Outdoor Protection	1,599,585	4,111,058	689,446	5,614,356
Mountaineering Equipment	3,700,262	2,644,713	3,555,116	
Camping Equipment	8,399,156	6,903,764	6,103,176	5,895,053

20. Run the report again, this time selecting a different measure. For this example, select Revenue. The report displays, showing Revenue values in a currency format with two decimal places.

Measure	2006	2005	2007	2004
Golf Equipment	$230,110,270.55	$168,006,427.07	$174,740,819.29	$153,553,850.98
Personal Accessories	$594,009,408.42	$456,323,355.90	$443,693,449.85	$391,647,093.61
Outdoor Protection	$10,349,175.84	$25,008,574.08	$4,471,025.26	$36,165,521.07
Mountaineering Equipment	$161,039,823.26	$107,099,659.94	$141,520,649.70	
Camping Equipment	$500,382,422.83	$402,757,573.17	$352,910,329.97	$332,986,338.06

Dynamic Column Rendering in a List Report Using Variables

By using variables, and the Render property of a list column, you can determine which columns will be displayed in the report output. For example, for a report that contains inventory and sales data, you can give the users the ability to select Sales or Inventory in a prompt page to determine whether sales columns or inventory columns are displayed.

To set up dynamic column rendering in a list, follow these steps:

1. Open or create a list report. For this example, use a list that contains Product Line, Product Type, Product, Opening Inventory, Closing Inventory, Quantity, and Revenue from the Inventory (query) and Sales (query) namespaces of the GO Sales (query) package.

2. Determine the columns in the report you want to conditionally render. For this example, the Quantity and Revenue columns should render if the user chooses "Sales" at the prompt, while the Opening Inventory and Closing Inventory columns should render when "Inventory" is chosen at the prompt.

3. Create a prompt page for the report that prompts the user to select a value based on the columns you want to render. For this example, use a value prompt with the parameter p_Measures. In the Static Choices properties of the value prompt, add Sales and Inventory as the options.

4. From the Condition Explorer tab, click the Variables link. A variable needs to be created so that its condition can evaluate whether columns will render in the report. A Variables pane and a Values pane display in the work area.

5. From the Insertable Objects pane, drag-and-drop the String Variable or Boolean Variable object into the Variables pane. For this example, use a String Variable. The Expression dialog displays.

6. Set the expression definition for the variable. For this example, type **ParamDisplayValue('p_Measures')**, and add the values Sales and Inventory to the Values pane for the string variable.

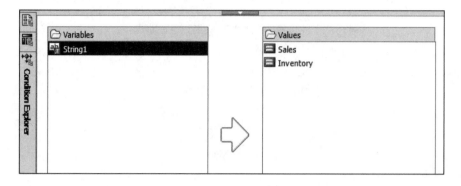

7. From the Properties pane, set any desired properties of the variable. For this example, set the Name property to **v_Measures**.

8. From the Page Explorer tab, open the report page.

9. In the list, select a column for which you want to specify whether it displays or not. For this example, select the Opening Inventory column.

10. From the Properties pane, click the Select Ancestor button and choose List Column.

11. With List Column selected, click the ellipsis in the Render Variable property in the Properties pane. The Render Variable dialog displays.

12. From the Variable drop-down, select the appropriate variable. For this example, select the v_Measures variable.

13. Within the Render For section, set the desired properties. For this example, uncheck the Sales check box so that this column only renders when Inventory is selected at the prompt.

14. Click OK to set the selected render variable properties.

15. With List Column still selected, ensure that the Render property is set to Yes.

16. Repeat steps 9 through 15 for each of the columns in the list that you want to render conditionally. For this example, set the Closing Inventory column so that is renders only when Inventory is selected at the prompt and set the Quantity and Revenue columns to render only when Sales is selected at the prompt.

17. Run the report to view the results. For this example, select Sales from the prompt page. The report renders only the sales-related columns, as shown next.

Product line	Product type	Product	Quantity	Revenue
Camping Equipment	Cooking Gear	TrailChef Canteen	965,723	$11,333,518.65
Camping Equipment	Cooking Gear	TrailChef Cook Set	813,780	$41,184,274.90
Camping Equipment	Cooking Gear	TrailChef Cup	1,812,123	$5,702,502.70
Camping Equipment	Cooking Gear	TrailChef Deluxe Cook Set	442,136	$53,195,154.45
Camping Equipment	Cooking Gear	TrailChef Double Flame	245,559	$34,311,174.84
Camping Equipment	Cooking Gear	TrailChef Kettle	2,336,950	$25,368,496.06
Camping Equipment	Cooking Gear	TrailChef Kitchen Kit	866,669	$19,535,825.83

Bursting Reports

Bursting lets you distribute the contents of a particular report that would be of interest or value to a recipient or group of individuals based on dynamic data. For example, a sales report can have bursting applied for the individual sales representatives and the report can be distributed through e-mail, showing only their individual sales; or the report can apply bursting to the sales representatives by territories, showing their sales according to territory. A report can also be distributed to a directory, and only those individuals who have access to that directory or report are able to access the report.

NOTE *For bursting to work properly, a recipient or group on which you want to burst the report (such as a territory or the individual users) must be specified in the report.*

To set up bursting in a report, follow these steps:

1. Open or create a new report. For this example, use a list report with Sales Region, Staff Name, Product Line, and Revenue from the Sales (query) of the GO Sales (query) package.

2. From the Query Explorer tab, open the query that retrieves the data you want to distribute.

3. From the Toolbox tab in the Insertable Objects pane, drag-and-drop a Data Item object into the Data Items pane to add a recipient to receive the report. The Expression dialog displays. For this example, the report will burst to a group of Cognos users. Do the following:

   - From the Security tab in IBM Cognos Administration, open the Cognos namespace to view the groups within the Cognos namespace.
   - In the Actions column, click the Set Properties button for the Consumers group.
   - From the General tab, click the View The Search Path, ID And URL link.

View the search path, ID and URL	Help ⊗

Search path:

CAMID(":Consumers")

ID:
xOkNvbnN1bWVycw__

Default action URL:
None

Close

   - Copy the text in the Search Path text box to insert into the expression definition in Cognos Report Studio.
4. In Cognos Report Studio, set the expression definition for the recipients of the report. For this example, paste the Consumers group Search Path into the Expression Definition text box. Add single quotes around the expression.

Expression Definition:
'CAMID(":Consumers")'

5. Click OK to save the expression definition for the new data item.

6. From the Properties pane, set any desired properties for the data item. For this example, set the Name property to **BurstRecipients**.

7. From the File menu, select Burst Options. The Burst Options dialog displays.

8. Select the Make Report Available For Bursting check box.

9. From the Query drop-down list in the Burst Groups area, select the query that you are using. For this example, select Query1.

10. From the Label drop-down list, select the data item to be used to label each burst report. For this example, use Sales Region.

11. Click the Edit (pencil) button beneath the Groups area to specify the groups upon which the burst reports are based. The Grouping & Sorting dialog displays.

12. From the Data Items area, double-click the applicable data item by which you want the reports grouped, and then click OK. For this example, select Sales Region so that the reports are grouped by each region.

13. In the Burst Recipient area of the Burst Options dialog, from the Query drop-down list, select the query to use for the recipients. For this example, select Query1.

14. From the Data Item drop-down list, select the data item that you created for the recipients of the burst report(s). For this example, select BurstRecipients.

15. From the Type list, select the applicable option to send the report. The available options are Automatic, Email Addresses, and Directory Entries. For this example, select Directory Entries.

16. Click OK to save the specified burst options.

17. From the standard toolbar, save the report. The report is ready for bursting.

18. In IBM Cognos Connection, navigate to the saved report and click Run With Options from the Actions column of the entry to run the burst report manually.

19. On the Run With Options screen, click the Advanced Options link. The advanced options appear on the screen.

20. From the Time And Mode area, select the Run In The Background option to access the bursting option.

21. From the Bursting area, select the Burst The Report check box.

22. Click the Run button, and then click OK. Cognos Connection runs the report in the background.

23. From the Actions column of the burst report entry, click the View The Output Versions button. The output versions display by the group specified in the burst options in Cognos Report Studio. In this example, the report displays by sales region (Americas, Asia Pacific, Central Europe, and so on).

24. Click the report format link of a group. For this example, select the HTML link for the Americas region. The report displays in IBM Cognos Viewer with the items from the selected group.

Sales region	Staff name	Product line	Revenue
Americas	Eric Carson	Personal Accessories	$5,713,176.83
Americas	Drina Delgado	Mountaineering Equipment	$164,487.56
Americas	Donald Chow	Mountaineering Equipment	$4,904,718.69
Americas	Elaine Varney	Personal Accessories	$56,701.06
Americas	Alexandre Pereira	Camping Equipment	$16,906,320.08
Americas	Rhonda Cummings	Mountaineering Equipment	$264,862.74

NOTE *Bursting cannot be applied to a crosstab report by itself. You can do this, however, if you drag a crosstab report into a list report and then link the two reports using master detail relationships. For more information on master detail relationships, refer to the "Master Detail Relationship" section earlier in this chapter.*

Advanced Prompting

An *inline prompt* is a prompt embedded within a report. The user is not prompted at runtime with an inline prompt, but has access to the prompt from the report results. For example, a sales report that displays the top five sales representatives for each region by default can contain a prompt within the report so that the number of representatives displayed for each sales region can be defined by the user. The user can simply change the value in the text box prompt, submit the change, and the requested number of sales representatives displays. The user does not have to exit the report to change the value.

To set up a report with an inline prompt, follow these steps:

1. Open or create a new report. For this example, use a list report with Sales Region, Staff Name, and Revenue from the Sales (query) of the GO Sales (query) package. Add a query calculation named Rank that calculates the rank for each sales region by revenue. Group the list on Sales Region, add a total to the Revenue column, and sort the Rank column in ascending order.

Expression Definition:
rank([Revenue] for [Sales region])

2. From the Toolbox tab in the Insertable Objects pane, add two block objects to the left of the data container.

3. From the Toolbox tab, add a Text Item object to the first block in the work area. The Text dialog displays.

4. In the text box, enter instructional text for the prompt being created. For this example, enter **Specify the Number of Rankings to View**.

5. From the Toolbox tab, insert a Text Box Prompt object to the second block in the work area. The Prompt Wizard displays.

6. In the Create A New Parameter text box, enter a name for the parameter. For this example, enter **p_Rank**.

TIP *It is good practice to preface the names of parameters with p_, such as* p_rank. *This helps you organize and identify your parameters.*

7. Click Finish to close the Prompt Wizard. The text prompt is added to the second block in the work area.

NOTE *Inline text prompts require a prompt button to submit changes. Value prompts contain an option in the properties to submit the selection in the prompt automatically when it is altered.*

8. From the Toolbox tab, insert a Prompt Button object to the right of the text prompt in the work area.

9. In the work area, click the prompt button to select it.

10. From the Properties pane, change the Type property to Reprompt so that the button re-runs the report when clicked. The new Reprompt prompt button displays in the work area.

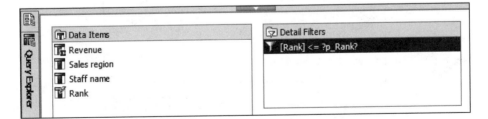

11. In the work area, click the Text Box Prompt object to select it.

12. From the Properties pane, set any desired properties for the Text Box Prompt object. Set the Required property to No so that the user is not prompted before the report runs. For this example, set the Numbers Only property to Yes and specify the number 5 for the Default Selections property.

13. From the Query Explorer tab, open the query to which you want to add a detail filter for the prompt value.

14. Add the applicable detail filter that includes the parameter created for the prompt. For this example, add a detail filter for the Rank parameter:

15. From the Properties pane, set any desired properties for the detail filter. For this example, set the Application property to After Auto Aggregation so that rank is determined before the filter is applied.

16. Run the report to view the results. The report displays in IBM Cognos Viewer with the Reprompt text box and button. In this example, the five top sales representatives for each region display, with their corresponding Revenue values and Rank order:

Top Reps by Sales Regions

Specify the Number of Rankings to View

* 5   [Reprompt]

Sales region	Staff name	Revenue	Rank
Americas	Charles Laurel	$59,406,874.73	1
	George Harrow s	$49,959,770.53	2
	Eduardo Guimarães	$48,839,028.63	3
	Janice Thomas	$48,547,731.47	4
	Lucía Reyna	$47,438,275.14	5
Americas - Total		$254,191,680.50	
Asia Pacific	Chang-ho Kim	$59,422,592.32	1
	Fei Meng	$51,005,700.69	2
	Akemi Takahashi	$49,285,152.87	3
	Fang Chan	$47,820,429.34	4
	Xiangyong Wang	$45,167,539.44	5
Asia Pacific - Total		$252,701,414.66	

17. In the prompt text box, enter a value to reprompt the report, and click the Reprompt button. For this example, type **3**. The report displays the top three reps within each region.

Top Reps by Sales Regions

Specify the Number of Rankings to View

* 3   [Reprompt]

Sales region	Staff name	Revenue	Rank
Americas	Charles Laurel	$59,406,874.73	1
	George Harrow s	$49,959,770.53	2
	Eduardo Guimarães	$48,839,028.63	3
Americas - Total		$158,205,673.89	
Asia Pacific	Chang-ho Kim	$59,422,592.32	1
	Fei Meng	$51,005,700.69	2
	Akemi Takahashi	$49,285,152.87	3
Asia Pacific - Total		$159,713,445.88	

HTML Items

You can add HTML items to your reports that allow you to insert anything that your browser can execute, such as images, links, multimedia, tooltips, or JavaScript. An HTML item is a container in which you can insert HTML code. For example, HTML items allow you to apply formatting to a page to maintain consistency with other pages in IBM Cognos Connection (for example, displaying the same styles, borders, and so on) or to add JavaScript to a page to provide the user with interactivity, such as a tooltip that displays when the user moves the mouse pointer over an item on the page. In this example, we will add JavaScript to an HTML item to set the current date as the default for a date prompt.

NOTE *HTML items appear only when the report is run in HTML format.*

To add an HTML item to a report, follow these steps:

1. From the Insertable Objects pane, insert the HTML Item object into the work area. The HTML Item displays in the work area where inserted, as shown next. This is the container in which HTML, or JavaScript, code can be inserted.

2. In the work area, double-click the HTML Item. The HTML dialog box displays. As an alternative, in the Properties pane of the HTML item, click the ellipsis in the HTML property.

3. Enter the HTML code in the dialog. For this example, enter the following code to make a date prompt display the current date:

```
<script language="javascript">

//sets the current date

var curDate = new Date();

curDate.setDate(curDate.getDate());
pickerControlCurrentDate.setValue(getFormatDate(curDate, 0, 'YMD'));

</script>
```

4. Click OK to close the dialog.

5. Run the report and view the results. In this example, the prompt page displays in IBM Cognos Viewer with the current date in the date prompt:

```
Select Order Date
 *  Feb 19, 2012              ▦▾
```

Singleton

A *singleton* object lets you insert a single data item anywhere in a report. Inserting a single data item is beneficial when you want to display a value that is independent from the rest of the values in the report or when an item will be used repeatedly. You can also include multiple singleton items in a report that are from the same query. For example, suppose your sales department creates a report for the highest earning product and another report for the lowest earning product. The marketing director wants to view each of these in her Forecasting report. Using the singleton object, these two items can easily be added to her Forecasting report.

Insert a Singleton Object

You can add a singleton to a report in Cognos Report Studio in two ways: by inserting the singleton object from the Toolbox tab in the Insertable Objects pane into the work area or by inserting a data item directly into the work area. In this example, we are using a crosstab report with Product Line, Product Type, and Product nested in the rows, Year as the columns, and Revenue with as the measure.

To insert a singleton object, follow these steps:

1. From the Toolbox tab in the Insertable Objects pane, insert a block object where you want to add the singleton to the report. For this example, insert the block to the right of the block object that contains the title.

2. From the Toolbox tab, insert a singleton object into the newly added block. The empty singleton data container is added to the report, as shown next.

3. From the Insertable Objects pane, insert a data item into the singleton container in the work area. For this example, insert the Revenue data item from the Source tab.

4. To add context to the singleton object, insert a Text Item object from the Toolbox tab of the Insertable Objects pane with descriptive text. For this example, type **Highest Revenue:** as the text.

Edit a Query Associated with a Singleton Object

By default, a new query is created when you add the singleton object to a report. A singleton object displays the appropriate item in the first row of data the query returns. If the query associated with the singleton object returns multiple rows, you may need to filter the data that is retrieved by the query to see what you want. For this example, we will edit the query associated with the singleton object by adding a filter to retrieve the maximum Revenue for 2006.

To edit the query associated with the singleton object, follow these steps:

1. From the Query Explorer tab, open the query the singleton object created. The data items associated with the query display. For this example, open Query2 and see the Revenue data item in the query.

2. From the Insertable Objects pane, add the desired data items to the query in the Data Items pane. For this example, add Product and Year from the Source tab. Create a new data item called Maximum Revenue that returns the revenue for the highest grossing product, as shown next:

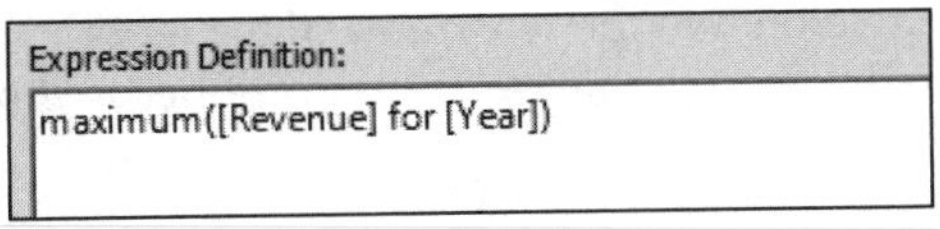

> Expression Definition:
>
> maximum([Revenue] for [Year])

3. Add any detail filters to the singleton query. For this example, to see the product with the maximum revenue for the year 2006, two filters are needed:

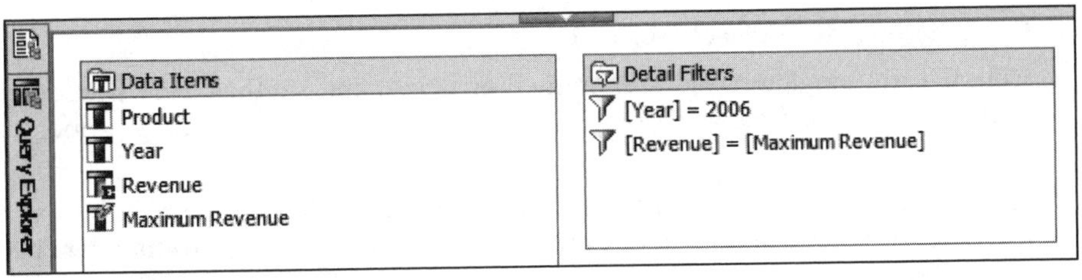

Data Items	Detail Filters
Product	[Year] = 2006
Year	[Revenue] = [Maximum Revenue]
Revenue	
Maximum Revenue	

TIP *To view the underlying data when editing a query, from the Query Explorer tab, right-click the applicable query, select View Tabular Data, and then click OK. A tabular view of the data for the query displays in IBM Cognos Viewer.*

4. Run the report to view the results. The report displays in IBM Cognos Viewer with the singleton. In this example, the Revenue singleton displays under the header, as shown next:

Product Revenue by Year
Highest Revenue: $363,575.08

Revenue			2004	2006	2005	2007
Camping Equipment	Lanterns	EverGlow Double	$579,888.23	$813,432.32	$606,853.40	$563,229.99
		EverGlow Butane	$1,683,295.87	$2,442,683.32	$1,766,632.34	$1,666,289.17
		Firefly 4	$1,812,359.60	$2,537,509.47	$1,834,826.30	$1,808,817.32
		Firefly Lite	$1,781,675.71	$2,513,168.60	$1,904,895.40	$1,749,763.67
		Firefly Extreme	$1,932,015.22	$2,741,418.22	$2,022,956.70	$1,901,257.12

Associate Multiple Singletons to One Query

In some cases, you might need multiple singleton items displayed on a report. You can associate the singletons with the same query, if possible, to maintain the best performance for the report.

To associate multiple singletons to one query, follow these steps:

1. Open or create a report with a singleton. For this example, use the report created in the last two sections.

2. Insert a second singleton into the work area of the report. For this example, insert a singleton before the text item below the report title, as shown next.

3. Click the singleton object to select it.

4. With the new singleton selected, in the Properties pane, set the Query property to the query of the first singleton. For this example, change the Query property to Query2.

5. From the Data Items tab in the Insertable Objects pane, insert a data item from the query to the second singleton object. For this example, add the Product data item to the second singleton object.

6. To add context to the singletons, modify or add any necessary Text Item objects with descriptive text. For this example, modify the existing Text Item object by typing **has the highest revenue for 2006:**

7. Run the report and view the results. The report displays in IBM Cognos Viewer with both singletons. This example shows the Product singleton and the Revenue singleton, with descriptive text in between:

Product Revenue by Year						
Star Lite has the highest revenue for 2006: $363,575.08						
Revenue			2004	2005	2006	2007
Camping Equipment	Lanterns	EverGlow Double	$579,888.23	$606,853.40	$813,432.32	$563,229.99
		EverGlow Butane	$1,683,295.87	$1,766,632.34	$2,442,683.32	$1,666,289.17
		Firefly 4	$1,812,359.60	$1,834,826.30	$2,537,509.47	$1,808,817.32
		Firefly Lite	$1,781,675.71	$1,904,895.40	$2,513,168.60	$1,749,763.67
		Firefly Extreme	$1,932,015.22	$2,022,956.70	$2,741,418.22	$1,901,257.12

Table of Contents

The Table of Contents object lets you create a report booklet of a PDF report, which contains a table of contents page with hyperlinks to the different pages within the report. The table of contents provides a navigation method that helps the user quickly view a specific page within a multiple-page report. For example, suppose the CEO of a large production company receives a report booklet of more than 100 pages. Instead of having to sort through each page in the report, she can easily navigate to her desired location using the hyperlinks in the table of contents within the PDF file.

You can also add bookmarks to the pages within the report booklet for navigation purposes. This is useful to be able to navigate back to the table of contents in a lengthy report. All of these options are discussed in the following sections.

Set Up the Table of Contents

When a report contains multiple entries, adding a table of contents to a report booklet makes viewing the entries easier for the user, because links to the entries can be displayed in one location.

To set up a table of contents in a report, follow these steps:

1. From the Page Explorer tab, click the Report Pages link and add pages from the Insertable Objects pane for each page you want in the report. These pages are the report pages to be used in the table of contents.

2. Rename the pages, naming the first **Table of Contents**. In this example, name the pages as shown next:

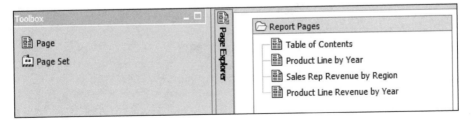

3. Add content to each page in the report. For this example, create a crosstab for the Product Line by Year page, a list for the Sales Rep Revenue by Region page, and a chart for the Product Line Revenue by Year page.

4. From the Page Explorer tab, open the Table of Contents page.

5. From the Toolbox tab in the Insertable Objects pane, insert a Table of Contents object into the work area.

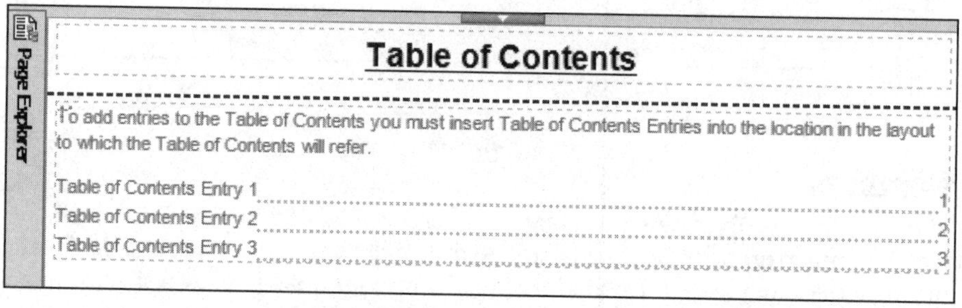

6. From the Page Explorer tab, open a report page. For this example, open the Product Line by Year page.

7. From the Toolbox tab in the Insertable Objects pane, insert a Table of Contents Entry object into the work area so that it is the first item on the page, as shown next.

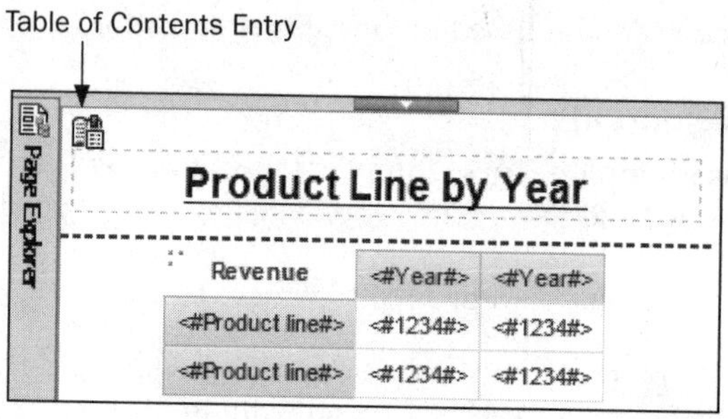

8. Repeat steps 6 and 7 for the remaining pages in your report. For this example, repeat these steps for the Sales Rep Revenue by Region and the Product Line Revenue by Year pages.

9. From the Page Explorer tab, open the Table of Contents page.

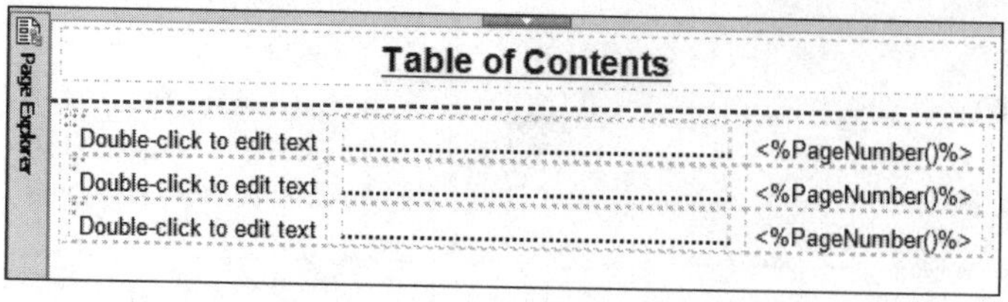

10. Add the page names for each page by double-clicking in each Double-Click To Edit Text box. For this example, type these names: **Product Line by Year**, **Sales Rep Revenue by Region**, and **Product Line Revenue by Year**, as shown next:

11. From the Run menu, select Run Report–PDF to run the report in PDF format and view the output. The report booklet displays in Adobe Reader in an IBM Cognos Viewer window with a descriptive Table of Contents that contains hyperlinks to the report pages within the PDF:

Add a Table of Contents Entry for a Particular Data Item

You can add a table of contents entry that is specific for a particular data item within the report. This is useful when a single report spans many pages to be able to navigate to the parts of the report quickly. For example, suppose a company's product report contains pages for its entire product line (Glasses, Plates, Silverware, and so on), and the details of each of these product lines spans multiple pages. In the report, a table of contents entry can be created for each product line, making the product lines easy to navigate to by users.

Continuing with the example from the last section, we will now add a table of contents entry for particular data items in the report.

To add a table of contents entry for a particular data item, follow these steps:

1. From the Page Explorer tab, open the page within the report that contains the item for which you want to set up a table of contents entry. For this example, open the Sales Rep Revenue by Region page.

2. From the standard toolbar, click the Unlock button.

3. From the Toolbox tab in the Insertable Objects pane, insert a Table of Contents Entry object into the cell for which you want the table of contents to link. For this example, insert the Table of Contents entry in the Sales Region cell in the list.

4. From the Page Explorer tab, open the Table of Contents page. The table of contents now has an additional data item included. In this example, <Sales region> displays in the table of contents.

5. Format the table as desired. For this example, modify the Sales Region cell so that the Padding property of the item is indented 20 pixels from the left of the table and the font is set to gray.

6. From the Run menu, select Run Report–PDF to run the report in PDF format and view the output. The report booklet displays in Adobe Reader in an IBM Cognos Viewer window with a hyperlink for each data item. In this example, a hyperlink displays for each region in the Sales Rep Revenue by Region report.

Add Bookmarks to the Table of Contents

Bookmarks take the user from their current location within the report booklet back to the Table of Contents page. This lets the user quickly navigate through the report instead of having to scroll through all of the pages within the booklet.

Continuing with the example from the last section, let's add bookmarks to the report booklet.

To add bookmarks to the table of contents, follow these steps:

1. From the Page Explorer tab, open the Table of Contents page.

2. From the Toolbox tab in the Insertable Objects pane, insert a Bookmark object above the header in the work area.

3. Click the Bookmark object to select it.

4. From the Properties pane, set the Label property to an appropriate name for the Table of Contents page. For this example, type **Return to TOC**.

5. From the Page Explorer tab, open a page within the report. For this example, open the Product Line by Year page.

6. From the Toolbox tab in the Insertable Objects pane, insert a Block object under the crosstab data container in the work area to add a hyperlink that returns the user to the bookmark on the Table of Contents page.

7. From the Toolbox tab in the Insertable Objects pane, insert a Text Item object into the new block object in the work area. The Text dialog displays.

8. In the text box, enter descriptive text for the action, and then click OK. For this example, type **Return to Table of Contents**:

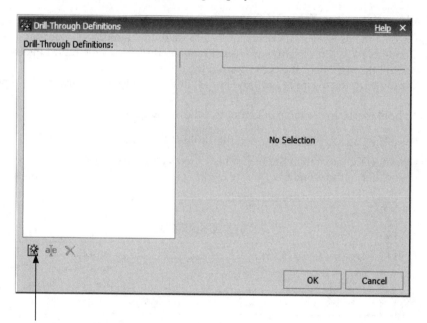

9. Right-click the text item, and from the context menu select Drill-Through Definitions. The Drill-Through Definitions dialog displays.

New Drill-Through Definition button

10. Click the New Drill-Through Definition button.

11. In the Drill-Through Definitions dialog, select the Bookmark tab.

12. From the Source Type list, select Text. A text box displays under the Source Type list.

13. Click the ellipsis to the right of the Text box. A Text dialog displays.
14. Enter the Label that was used for the Bookmark object on the Table of Contents page you created in step 4. For this example, type **Return to TOC**.

NOTE *The Label name must be the same name that was used for the bookmark.*

15. Click OK. The text item is now a hyperlink.

16. Click the block object to select it.
17. From the standard toolbar, click the Copy button.
18. Navigate to the other pages in the report where you want to insert the link, and after clicking the page to select it, click the Paste button on the standard toolbar to insert the block with the link.
19. From the Run menu, select Run Report–PDF to run the report in PDF format and view the output. The report booklet displays in Adobe Reader in IBM Cognos Viewer with the hyperlinks for the report.

20. Click a report hyperlink to view the table of contents entry. For this example, click the Product Line by Year link. The Return to Table of Contents hyperlink displays in the report, as shown next. When clicked, this hyperlink returns the user to the Table of Contents page.

Active Reports

An active report is a type of portable and highly interactive report output that can be created in Cognos Report Studio. Active reports are saved with the interactivity built into them, so they are especially useful for offline users, who can take the reports with them and open them anywhere.

The layout and the data in an active report are defined by active report controls, which can be found on the Toolbox tab of the Insertable Objects pane and are described in Table 12-2. Most controls have a static version that is hard-coded to a specific item and a dynamic version that is data driven. Variables are used in active reports to pass information from one control to another.

Icon	Name	Description
	Variable Text Item	Use a variable for text. For example, you can use a variable to display a chosen prompt value as a title.
	Row Number	Show a number for each row in the report.
	Deck	Use a deck to conditionally display one of a number of static options, such as a list or a crosstab, depending on what is chosen in another control. You define the number and type of the options.
	Data Deck	Use a data deck to conditionally display one of a number of data-driven options. The number of options and which options are displayed is determined by the data.
	Tab Control	Show multiple pages for an area within an active report divided by tabs you define.

TABLE 12-2 Active Report Toolbox Items

	Data Tab Control	Show multiple pages for an area within an active report divided by tabs driven by data.
	Button Bar	Include a group of buttons you define.
	Data Button Bar	Include a group of buttons defined by data.
	Toggle Button Bar	Include a group of buttons you define that change appearance when clicked.
	Data Toggle Button Bar	Include a group of buttons defined by data that change appearance when clicked. Users can select one option.
	Radio Button Group	Insert a group of radio buttons with static options.
	Data Radio Button Group	Insert a group of radio buttons with options defined by a data item. Users can select one option.
	Check Box Group	Insert a group of check boxes with static options. Users can select any number of the options.
	Data Check Box Group	Insert a group of check boxes with options defined by a data item. Users can select any number of the options.
	Drop-Down List	Insert a drop-down list of static options. Users can select one option.
	Data Drop-Down List	Insert a drop-down list of options defined by a data item. Users can select one option.
	List Box	Insert a list of static options. Users can select any number of the options.
	Data List Box	Insert a list of options defined by a data item. Users can select any number of the options.
	Iterator	Enable the navigation of another control by clicking defined buttons, such as previous and next.
	Data Iterator	Enable the navigation of another control by clicking buttons defined by a data item.
	Discrete Values Slider	Insert a slider bar with static options to provide users the ability to filter values.
	Data Discrete Values Slider	Insert a slider bar with options defined by a data item to provide users the ability to filter values.
	Continuous Values Slider	Insert a slider bar for numeric values with a minimum and maximum you define to allow users to filter values.
	Button	Insert a single button into the report.

TABLE 12-2 Active Report Toolbox Items

TIP *An existing report can be converted to an active report by opening the report in Cognos Report Studio and choosing File | Convert to Active Report.*

NOTE *Regular Toolbox items such as lists, crosstabs, charts, tables, text items, and so on, can also be used in active reports and are also considered controls when used in active reports. Two additional tabs are present in the Insertable Objects pane when you are working with active reports:*

- *Active Report Controls* *This tab provides a list and access to all controls used in the current active report.*

- *Active Report Variables* *This tab provides a list and access to all variables used in the currrent active report.*

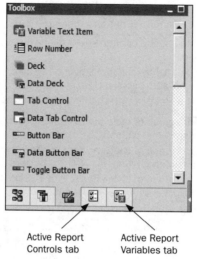

Active Report   Active Report
Controls tab   Variables tab

Create an Active Report

The following example shows how to start an active report. For the purposes of the example, we add only one list control to the report. The following examples used throughout this section will show you how to add more controls and configure interactivity between them.

To create an active report, follow these steps:

1. Open Cognos Report Studio and select a package which you want to use to create the report. For this example, select GO Sales (query).

2. From the Welcome dialog, select Create New.

3. In the New dialog, select Blank Active Report or Active Report.

NOTE *The Active Report and Blank Active Report types provide the same functionality and controls with which to create an active report. The difference is that the blank version does not have any of the default layout components, such as background images and page numbers, that are included in the Active Report type.*

4. From the Insertable Objects pane, add the desired controls to the report. For this example, insert a list with the Product Line, Product Type, Year, and Quantity data items from the Sales (query) namespace:

You have created an active report with a simple list. Active reports feature a layout and queries exactly like other Cognos Report Studio reports. Many of the features and functions of regular reports can be used with active reports. Continue following the examples in this section to create functionality exclusive to active reports.

Add a Control with Static Data

You can insert controls that require static data when you want to specifically define the data used for the control. For example, you might want to set specific time periods to be selectable, such as a 5-year range, instead of all 12 years available in a data source.

To add a static control, follow these steps:

1. Within an active report, insert the desired static control into the work area in Cognos Report Studio. For this example, continue using the list created in the last section. Insert a Discrete Values Slider control before the list in the work area:

2. Click the Definition button to specify the properties of the control. The Slider Values Definition dialog opens.

3. In the Slider Values Definition dialog, set the properties of the control as necessary. You can change the Label value, specify names for values, insert additional values, define what displays for each card in a deck, and so on. For this example, change the label to Year and add names for the Year options:

4. Click OK. The values are saved within the control.

Add a Control with Dynamic Data

You can insert controls that require dynamic data when you want the data to define what items are used for the control. For example, you might want to enable users to filter values on a product line. If you specify the values manually, the control will require modification if a new product line is introduced or a product line name is changed. However, if the control is set up to retrieve the product lines from the data, the options will update automatically.

To add a dynamic control, follow these steps:

1. Within an active report, drag-and-drop the desired dynamic control to the work area in Cognos Report Studio. For this example, continue to work with the example from the last section. Insert a Data Check Box Group control before the Slider control in the work area.

2. Insert the appropriate data item from the Insertable Objects pane to the main Drop Item Here area. For this example, insert Product Line as the main item.

3. To specify an image for the control, insert a data item in the Drop Item Here area under Icon, if available.

4. To specify an item on which to filter the main item, insert a data item in the Drop Item Here area under Values. This is useful to set up a cascading prompt scenario. For example, a product line control could be linked to a product type control so that the product types shown correspond with the selected product lines.

Add Interactivity to Controls

You now have added controls to an active report, but how do they communicate with each other? A filter control does not know what data it is to filter unless it is configured. You can set up communication between controls when you want the actions in one control to affect another control.

To add interactivity to controls, follow these steps:

1. Within an active report, click the Create A New Connection button in one of the controls you want to link. For this example, continue using the report from the last section.

2. In the Create A New Connection dialog, set the Source Control property to the control in which you want to perform the actions that will affect the target control. For this example, set Source Control to Data Check Box Group1.

3. Under Source Control, set the Data Item property to the item from the source that will affect the target. For this example, set Data Item to Product Line.

4. Set the Target Control property to the control whose behavior you want the actions of the source control to affect. For this example, set Target Control to List 1.

5. Under Target Control, set the Data Item value to the item from the target that will be affected by the source. For this example, set Data Item to Product Line.

6. In the center of the Create a New Connection dialog, set the Behavior of the connection. The Select option will select the values in the target, and the Filter option will filter on the values in the target. For this example, use Filter.

7. Choose to Create A New Variable or Reuse An Existing Variable. If creating a new variable, specify the name and data type for the variable. For this example, set the Name **Product line** as a string data type.

TIP *Create A New Variable is the only option available if there are no existing variables in the active report.*

---

8. When you have finished setting all properties, click the Connect button to create the connection.

9. Hover the pointer over the Interactive Behavior button to see a summary of the connections set up for the control, as shown next.

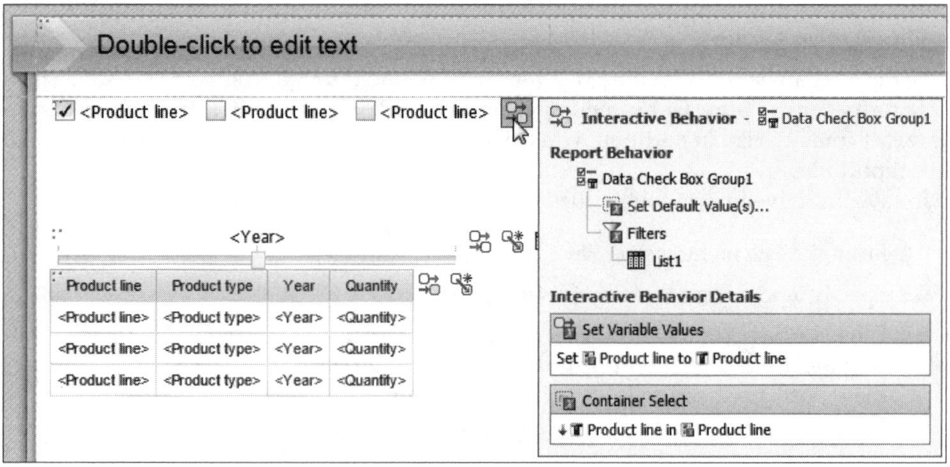

10. Repeat steps 1 through 9 to set up interactivity for any other controls. For this
    example, create another connection between the Year slider control and the list:

Save an Active Report

Active reports can be consumed by two methods: online through Cognos Connection in
HTML format or in a browser by opening a downloaded MIME HTML (MHT) file, regardless
of Internet connectivity. In addition, you can add an access code to an active report to secure
active report files.

To save an active report, follow these steps:

1. From the File menu, select Save As.

2. Specify a name and location for the report.

3. Click the Save button. You have saved the active report to Cognos Connection to
   provide users access to the report to run it in a browser in HTML format or to access
   the report specification for future modification.

4. From the Run menu, select Download Active Report.

5. When prompted, save the report as an MHT file. This saves the report as an external
   file that can be transported from the saved location to any necessary users.

To secure an active report, follow these steps:

1. From the File menu, select Active Report Properties.

2. In the Access Code text box of the Active Report Properties dialog, type a password for the active report.
3. Click OK.
4. Save the active report to embed the access code into the report specification.

Statistical Reporting Overview

I n this chapter, you will learn how to use IBM Cognos Report Studio to add statistical analyses to your reports. Using IBM Cognos Statistics, the report author can access a variety of powerful statistical tools without the need to export data to an external application. While working through this chapter, you will become familiar with the three basic types of statistical analyses available through Cognos Report Studio: data distribution, data analysis and testing, and statistical process control.

Reports created in Cognos Report Studio can provide a wide array of views into your business: for example, *list reports* can give you every detail about a set of data as well as aggregating values by groups, *charts* provide a graphical representation of your data, and *crosstabs* provide a basic analytical tool. At times, your business will require additional insight into what the collected data actually means and what it implies for the future, and these tools will help you quickly answer questions like the following, with less effort, and with a high degree of confidence: Has a new marketing campaign resulted in increased revenue? Will increasing the marketing budget increase future revenues? Has there been a decrease in accident reports since adding monthly safety training classes? In which areas can we expect to see future problems? Has there been a change in the age and genders of our customers? If so, in what direction is the change headed?

Basic Concepts

All statistical analyses in IBM Cognos Business Intelligence v10.1 consist of *variables* and *cases*. In the context of the SPSS tools, a variable is any attribute in your data that is of interest and a case is a unique set of these variables. Variables in Cognos Statistics are usually divided into three groups: analysis, measure, and case variables. An *analysis* variable is a query item about which we will be asking qualifying questions. A *measure* variable is a query item that has a meaningful numeric value. A *case* variable is a query item that can be used to identify uniquely all the other variables in a single set and usually does not have any business value.

NOTE *To be successful with the statistical analysis tools available in Cognos 10, the report author must understand the statistical methods being used and the data being analyzed. If you are new to statistical analysis or would like more detailed descriptions of the concepts presented here, you can refer to the IBM Cognos documentation or search the Internet for any topic of interest.*

Variable Types

Statistical variables are of four types: nominal (also called categorical), ordinal, interval, and ratio. Each type of variable has its own measurement scale, and each scale imparts different levels of information.

A *nominal* variable does not have a numerical meaning; it can only be used to place items into specific categories, or "buckets." Nominal variables do not provide any directional or quantitative information; they cannot tell us whether a variable is increasing or decreasing, and they cannot tell us if a variable is bigger or smaller than some other value. Examples of nominal variables include gender and color.

An *ordinal* variable is a number that provides ordering or ranking information for the variable. These values let us know the position that a variable holds in the set. Examples of ordinal variables are the placing of runners in a foot race—Joe came in first, John was second, Bob was third. Another example is the seeding of teams in a tournament. Suppose in a junior hockey league that the Peewee Hotshots are first seed, the Slapshot Shooters are second seed, and so on. The values 1 and 2 have no mathematical meaning; in this case, 2 is not twice as many as 1 and 1 + 2 does not equal 3. However, knowing that the Peewee Puckers are a "1 seed" tells us that the team is ranked the best in its class.

An *interval* variable is a value that has mathematical meaning in that the measurement between two values has meaning and the value has directional meaning. So, for example, a temperature of 10 degrees Celsius is 10 units of measure greater than a temperature of 0 degrees Celsius, and 10 degrees Celsius is "more" temperature than 0. However, 10 degrees Celsius is not twice as warm as 0 degrees Celsius. Zero degrees Celsius does not mean there is no temperature; it just means that the temperature is between −1 and 1.

A *ratio* variable has all of the attributes of the interval variable, but the value 0 in a ratio variable does mean there is none of the variable. Speed is an example of a ratio variable; 25 miles per hour is half as fast as 50 miles per hour, and 0 miles per hour means that there is no speed at all.

This chapter is meant to expose you to the statistical functionality available in Cognos Report Studio, not to teach statistics. Many statistical concepts are not covered in this book, but they are available in Cognos Report Studio, such as samples, populations, skewness, and kurtosis, to name a few. We assume the reader is familiar with these concepts.

Statistical Analyses

Cognos 10 provides five types of statistical tools for use in Cognos Report Studio: descriptive statistics, means comparison, nonparametric tests, correlation and regression, and control charts. Each type and its functions are described in the following sections.

Descriptive Statistics

Descriptive statistics provide basic quantitative summarizations of your data. The functions in this statistical tool include both numeric and graphical summarizations that give you a feel for the shape of your data, such as the number of cases in your sample; the mean, median, and standard deviation of your measure; and descriptive graphical representations of your sample. For example, descriptive statistics can show whether your data is normally distributed—a key assumption of many statistical tests.

Several functions are used with descriptive statistics.

Basic Descriptive Statistics   This function generates a table that displays three sets of information: central tendency (mean, count, sum, and median), dispersion (standard deviation, variance, standard error of mean, range, minimum, and maximum), and distribution (skewness and kurtosis).

Histogram   A histogram is a graphical representation of the frequency distribution of your data using the width of the graph's bars to represent the variable values and the height to represent the frequency. The following example shows a histogram that indicates that about 50 employees have a salary range from $0 to $10,000 and about 100 employees earn more than $88,000.

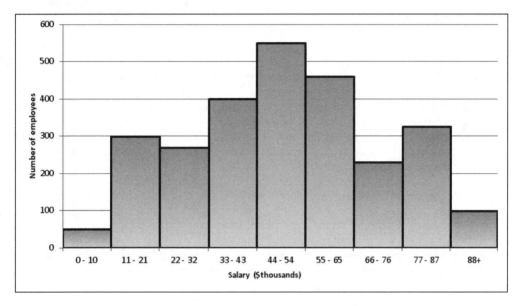

Boxplot   The boxplot is a graphical representation of the five-number summary of descriptive statistics. The five-number summary consists of the minimum (the lowest value in the sample), the first quartile, the median (the middle value in the sample), the third quartile, and the maximum (the largest value in the sample). This graph also displays values that might be outliers or extreme values.

Q-Q Plot   The Q-Q (quantile-quantile) plot is a graphical comparison of the quartiles of two probability distributions. This graph is a more advanced version of the histogram in that it allows you to compare the distribution of your data against a second set of observed data or against a theoretical set of values.

Means Comparison
Means comparison, also called comparison of two means, is used to analyze the similarities between two sets of normally distributed data. Means comparisons can be performed against your sample data and a known value or against a set of sample data.

One-Sample t-Test   The one-sample t-test is a comparison of means used to test two sets of data, where one set is your sample and the other is a known value. This test can be used to determine whether your sample data, on average, differs significantly from a known value.

One-Way ANOVA   The one-way ANOVA (analysis of variance), such as the one-sample t-test, is a comparison of means; however, the one-way ANOVA allows you to compare two or more samples. This test can be used to determine whether two or more separate populations have any significant relationships.

Nonparametric Tests

Up to this point, all of the statistical tests we have discussed assume that the data being examined is normally distributed. When your data does not fall under a normal distribution, however, you need a different set of tools to perform your analysis. The functions in this section allow you to analyze these types of samples.

One-Way Chi-Square Test   The one-way chi-square test, also called the chi-square goodness-of-fit test, is used to compare the actual observed values in your data against an expected value for a single category. For example, suppose your company makes balloons in four colors: red, orange, green, and blue. Your marketing department says that each package of 100 balloons has 25 red, 25 orange, 25 green, and 25 blue. To test this claim, you can use the one-way chi-square test to determine whether the packages really do include 25 of each color, within a given margin of error.

Two-Way Chi-Square Test   The two-way chi-square test, also called the chi-square test of independence, is similar to the one-way chi-square test, except the two-way test allows you to test two categories at a time. Continuing with the balloon example, suppose your marketing department wants to know what gender and age groups are buying your product. You can take a sample of people buying your product, collect their age and gender, and use the two-way chi-square test to determine whether gender is a contributing factor in who is buying your balloons.

Correlation and Regression

Correlation is used to determine whether a relationship exists between two variables, and if a relationship exists, how strong is it.

Regression is used to examine the relationship between dependent and independent variables. Regression lets you predict how a dependent variable will change when you change one or more of the independent variables.

Basic Correlation   Basic correlation measures the relationship between two variables and shows to what extent the two variables are proportionally related. For example, you can determine whether a positive or negative correlation exists between sales of jewelry (variable 1) and sales of women's clothing (variable 2). A +1 correlation indicates a perfect positive relationship, and −1 indicates a perfect negative relationship between the variables.

Linear Regression   Linear regression is used to analyze the relationship between dependent and independent variables. Graphically, the relationship can be represented by a straight line, often called the best fit line. Various linear functions can then be used to find the best fit line for the sample data. Once the function that best represents your data is found, you can use that function to calculate predictive values.

Curve Estimation   A curve estimation is a form of regression analysis—the key difference between linear regression and curve estimation is that nonlinear equations are used in curve estimation to calculate the best fit line for your sample data.

Control Charts

Control charts are commonly used to monitor a business or manufacturing process to determine whether the process being monitored is behaving as expected. Control charts are a key component to quality control processes in most industries.

X-Bar   X-bar charts plot a series of mean values that have been calculated from groups of samples. For example, suppose you work in a steel mill producing steel beams used in construction. Your process manufactures beams in batches of 10, and you can run 100 batches per shift. For quality control purposes, you need to ensure that the average width of the beams in each batch is between 5.98 and 6.02 inches. If you measure each beam in a batch, calculate the average width (mean) for the batch, and plot the mean for each batch on a chart, you will have created an X-bar chart.

R   The R chart (range chart) behaves similarly to the X-bar chart, except that R charts plot the range values of the sample rather than plotting the mean values of the sample.

S   The S chart (standard deviation) behaves similarly to the X-bar and R charts, except S charts plot the standard deviations of the sample as opposed to plotting the mean or range values of the sample.

Moving Range   The moving range chart calculates the difference between the values of the current case and the previous case. The resulting value is plotted as an individual point on the chart.

Individuals   Individuals are control charts that plot the individual value associated with each case in your sample. These charts are useful when you have the ability to measure each item in your sample.

p, np (Cases Are Units) and p, np (Cases Are Subgroups)   P charts (proportion of nonconforming sample charts) plot the proportion of samples that do not meet a true/false test. Instead of plotting each value in the sample, the p chart plots those samples that do not pass the specified test. P charts allow you to plot the values as individual values, or grouped values.

Np charts (number of nonconforming sample charts) are similar to p charts, except that np charts plot the actual count of samples that do not pass the specified test as opposed to the proportion of samples that do not pass the test. These charts assume that the population size used for each count is the same.

c, u (Cases Are Units) and c, u (Cases Are Subgroups)   C charts and u charts (count charts) also plot a count of nonconforming samples. Unlike p and np charts, in which the value is either pass or fail, c charts and u charts plot the number of times a case fails within a given situation.

Business Scenario: Shampoo pH Levels

As an introduction to Cognos Statistics, let's look at the Shampoo pH sample data that comes with Cognos 10 (Figure 13-1). This data contains the results of pH tests conducted on samples of shampoo taken during the manufacturing process.

FIGURE 13-1
Shampoo pH
sample metadata

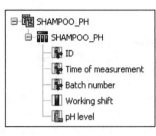

In our sample data, each query item in the SHAMPOO_PH query subject is a variable. The query item "ID" is the case variable, because it uniquely identifies a single row, or case, in the query subject. "pH level" is the measure variable; it contains the numeric data of interest. In this case, the measure variable contains the results of the pH test conducted on the shampoo samples. "Time of measurement," "Batch number," and "Working shift" are analysis variables; these are query items that can be grouped to describe the case.

Using this data, we will work with the following business scenario: To ensure the quality of the shampoo, the company wants to use statistical analysis to gain insight into the consistency of its product. The pH level is a critical ingredient of the shampoo and must fall within a specific range. The pH scale is the logarithmic measure of the acidity or alkalinity of a solution; pure water has a pH level of 7, battery acid has a pH level of 0, and lye has a pH level just under 14. The shampoo company knows that its product works best when the shampoo pH level is 5, but a level between 4 and 6 is acceptable.

Creating a New Statistics Analysis

The statistical tools in Cognos 10 are accessed from Cognos Report Studio. Start Report Studio, select the SHAMPOO_PH package, and create a new report. You will be prompted to select a report template; if your installation of Cognos 10 includes the statistical package, you'll see the template icons shown in the following illustration. If you do not see the Statistics icon, speak to your Cognos BI administrator.

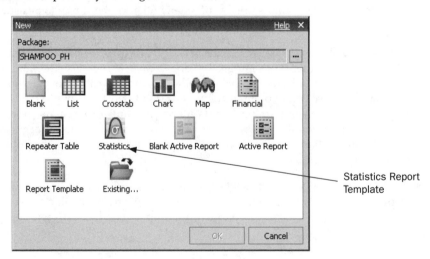

Basic Descriptive Statistics

After you click the Statistics icon in the New dialog, you will be prompted to select the type of statistics you would like to run. To help you get familiar with our sample data, let's start with the Basic Descriptive Statistics using the Report Wizard.

1. From the Descriptive Statistics options, select Basic Descriptive Statistics. Then click OK.

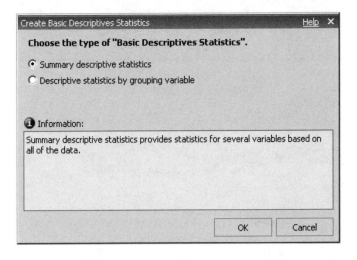

2. Select Summary Descriptive Statistics, and then click OK.

NOTE *Most of the statistical functions in Cognos 10 can be run either for individual cases or for cases that have been grouped.*

3. Select pH level as the analysis variable (drag-and-drop it onto the Analysis Variables box) and click Next.

4. Select ID as the cases variable and click Next.

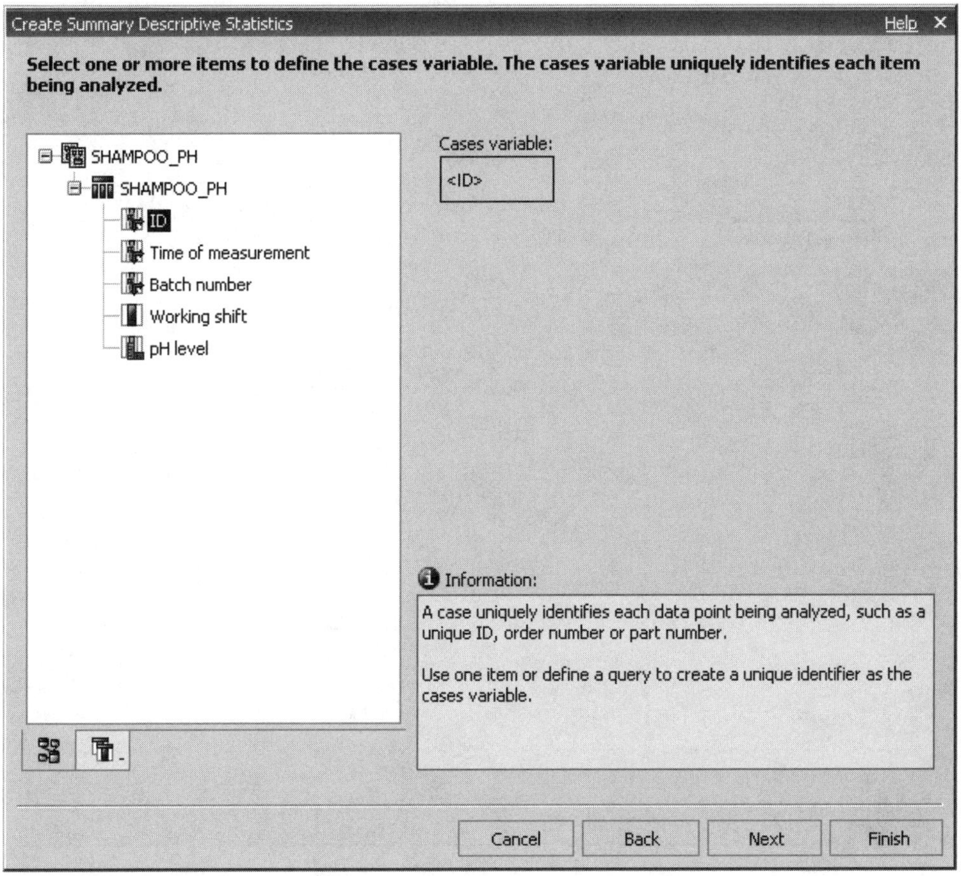

Create Summary Descriptive Statistics	Help ✕

Select one or more items to define the cases variable. The cases variable uniquely identifies each item being analyzed.

- ⊟ SHAMPOO_PH
  - ⊟ SHAMPOO_PH
    - ID
    - Time of measurement
    - Batch number
    - Working shift
    - pH level

Cases variable:

<ID>

ⓘ Information:

A case uniquely identifies each data point being analyzed, such as a unique ID, order number or part number.

Use one item or define a query to create a unique identifier as the cases variable.

Cancel   Back   Next   Finish

NOTE *Most of the statistical functions found in Cognos 10 include a number of optional statistics. The type and number of optional statistics will vary based on the type of statistical analysis being run.*

5. Select any additional statistics that you want to include in the basic descriptive statistics table.

The report definition window will look like the following:

Here's the result output with the default settings:

Descriptive Statistics	
	pH level
Mean	4.99
Std. Deviation	.256
N	240
Median	4.98
Minimum	4
Maximum	6

NOTE *Once a statistical function has been added to a report, you can modify the settings of the analysis in the Cognos Report Studio Properties window.*

6. To add functions to the descriptive statistics, click the statistical object (pH level in the Insertable Objects pane) in the report window and make the modifications you need. In this example, we will add all the additional calculations available.

Data	
Query	Query1
Master Detail Relationships	
Miscellaneous	
Name	Summary Descriptive Statistics1
General	
Plug-in name	Statistic
Command	Summary Descriptive Statistics
Edit in wizard	
Central Tendency	
Mean	Yes
Mean Type	Arithmetic (standard)
Median	Yes
Count (N)	Yes
Sum	Yes
Dispersion	
Standard Deviation	Yes
Standard Error of Mean	Yes
Variance	Yes
Range	Yes
Maximum	Yes
Minimum	Yes
Distribution	
Skewness	Yes
Kurtosis	Yes

The report output now includes the additional values, as shown next:

Descriptive Statistics	
	pH level
Mean	4.99
Std. Deviation	.256
N	240
Median	4.98
Std. Error of Mean	.016
Range	1
Variance	.065
Kurtosis	-.266
Std. Error of Kurtosis	.313
Skewness	-.006
Std. Error of Skewness	.157
Sum	1,198
Minimum	4
Maximum	6

Histogram

Looking at the minimum and maximum values from the basic descriptive statistics might make you wonder about the distribution of the test sample values that fall between 4 and 6. The histogram will display the frequency distribution of our test samples.

To add a histogram to the current report, follow these steps:

1. Locate the Statistics icon in the Insertable Objects pane, and drag-and-drop the object onto your report.

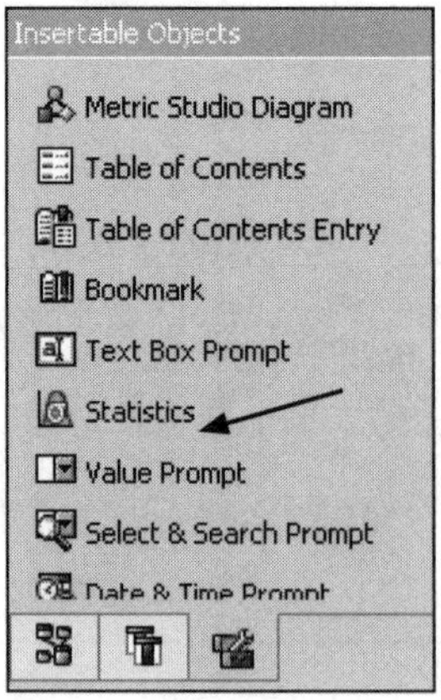

2. Select the Histogram option from the Descriptive Statistics menu and click OK.

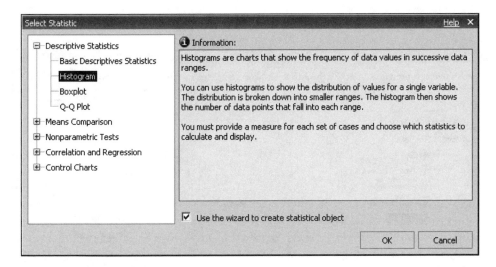

3. Drag-and-drop the analysis variable that you want to see plotted into the Analysis Variable box (pH level), and then click Next.

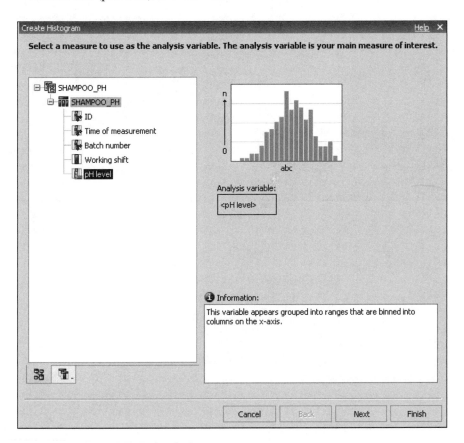

4. Drag-and-drop the cases variable (ID) to the Cases Variable box. Then click Next.

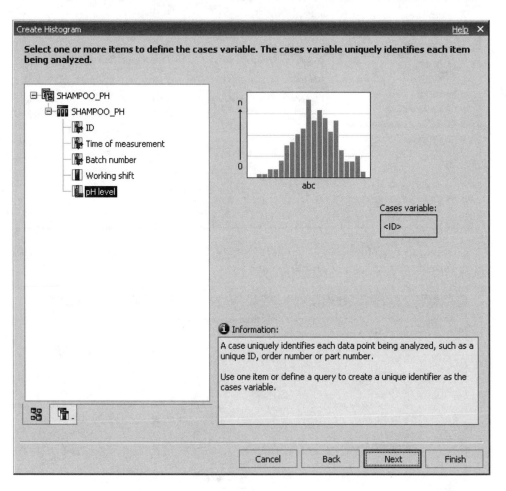

5. Add the optional Titles and Footnotes information and click Finish.

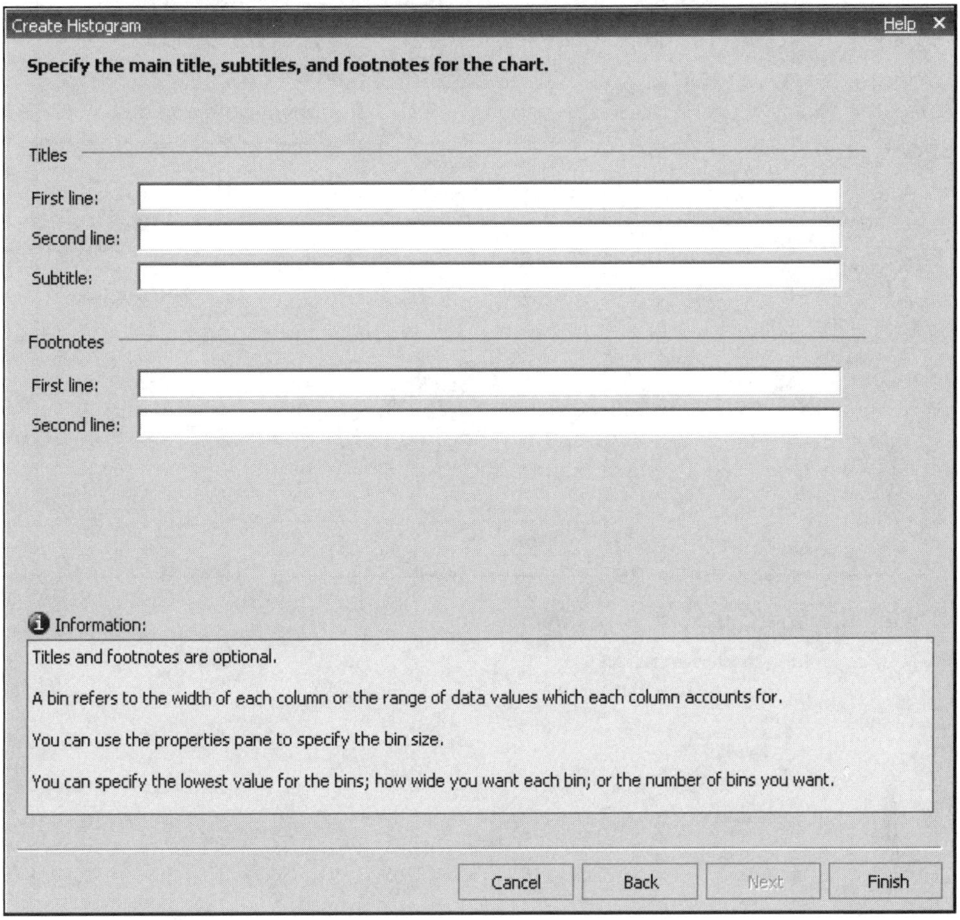

```
Create Histogram                                                    Help  ✕

  Specify the main title, subtitles, and footnotes for the chart.


  Titles

  First line:    [                                                    ]

  Second line:   [                                                    ]

  Subtitle:      [                                                    ]

  Footnotes

  First line:    [                                                    ]

  Second line:   [                                                    ]



  ⓘ Information:

  Titles and footnotes are optional.

  A bin refers to the width of each column or the range of data values which each column accounts for.

  You can use the properties pane to specify the bin size.

  You can specify the lowest value for the bins; how wide you want each bin; or the number of bins you want.



                              [ Cancel ]   [ Back ]   [ Next ]   [ Finish ]
```

The new report definition window looks like this:

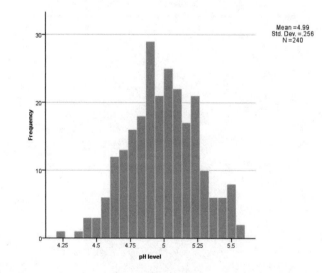

And here's the report output:

Descriptive Statistics

	pH level
Mean	4.99
Std. Deviation	.256
N	240
Median	4.98
Std. Error of Mean	.016
Range	1
Variance	.065

One-Sample t-Test

The basic descriptive statistics have provided some helpful information, but we would like to start doing some analysis. From our business case, we know that the target pH level we want is 5. A one-sample t-test will give us a deeper insight into how well the sample values match the expected values.

1. In the Insertable Objects pane, drag-and-drop the Statistics icon onto your report.

2. Select One-Sample t-Test from the Means Comparison group and click OK.

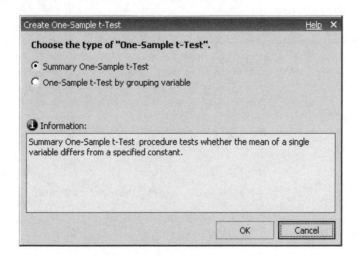

3. Select the Summary One-Sample t-Test, and then click OK.

4. Drag-and-drop the analysis variable (pH level) into the Analysis Variables box. Then click Next.

5. Drag-and-drop the cases variable (ID), and click Next.

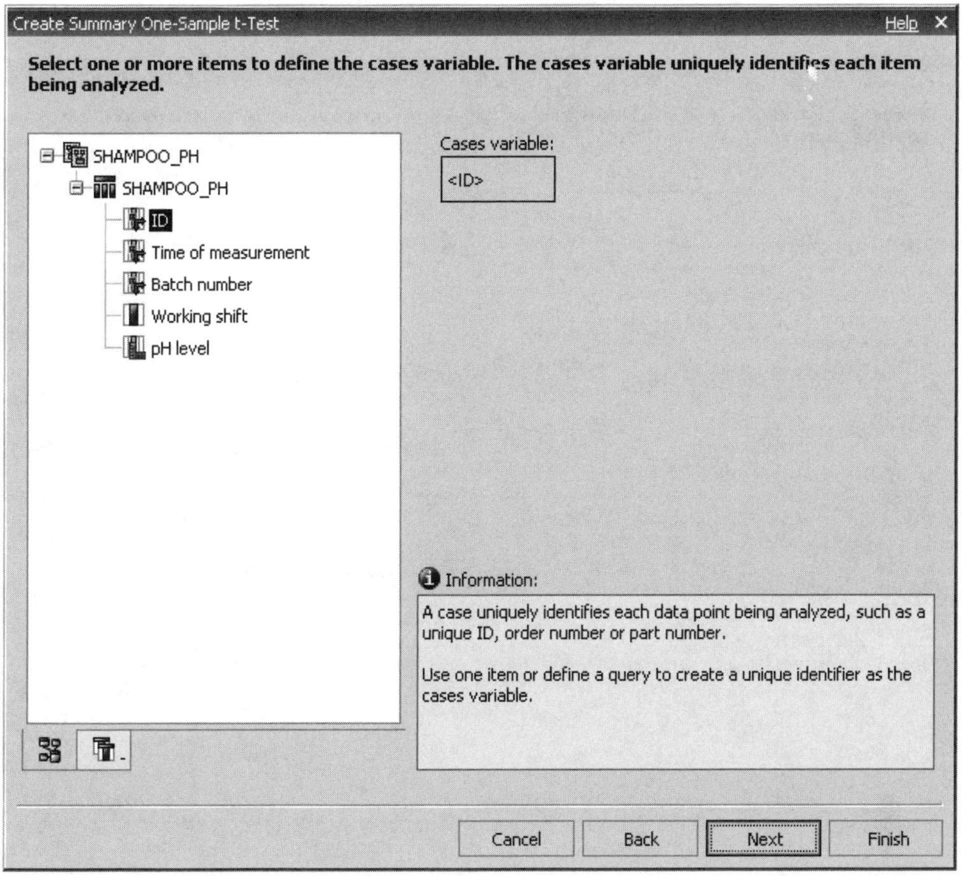

Create Summary One-Sample t-Test — Help ✕

Select one or more items to define the cases variable. The cases variable uniquely identifies each item being analyzed.

- SHAMPOO_PH
  - SHAMPOO_PH
    - ID
    - Time of measurement
    - Batch number
    - Working shift
    - pH level

Cases variable:

<ID>

ⓘ Information:

A case uniquely identifies each data point being analyzed, such as a unique ID, order number or part number.

Use one item or define a query to create a unique identifier as the cases variable.

Cancel   Back   Next   Finish

6. For this test, we will need to provide information in the Test Value box; in this case the value is 5 (the ideal pH level). Accept the defaults for all other fields. Then click Finish.

Like the basic statistics, the one-way t-test provides a numerical result:

One-Sample Statistics

	N	Mean	Std. Deviation	Std. Error Mean
pH level	240	4.99	.256	.016

One-Sample Test

	Test Value = 5					
	t	df	Sig. (2-tailed)	Mean Difference	95% Confidence Interval of the Difference	
					Lower	Upper
pH level	-.513	239	.609	-.008	-.04	.02

The One-Sample Statistics table is an optional view that includes the basic statistical values for the sample being tested. These numbers are the same as those found in the default Basic Descriptive Statistics.

One-Way Chi-Square Test

We can use the one-way chi-square test to check our hypothesis against the actual observations. Suppose we hypothesize that all three shifts in our shampoo factory run the same number of tests per shift, and if they don't, our test of pH levels is not valid. We can use the one-way chi-square test to check our assumption against the actual observations.

1. In the Insertable Objects pane, drag-and-drop the Statistics icon onto your report.

2. Select the One-Way Chi-Square Test from the Nonparametric Tests group and click OK.

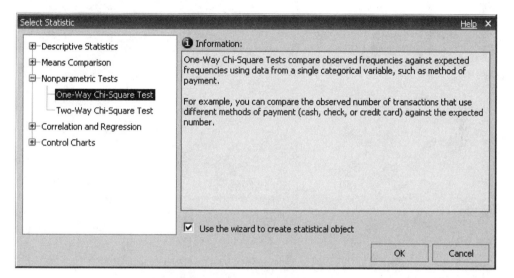

3. Select the One-Way Chi-Square option and click OK.

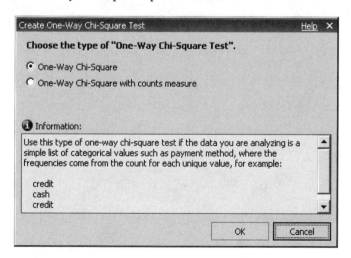

4. Drag-and-drop Working Shift into the Analysis Variable box, and then click Next.

5. Drag-and-drop ID into the Cases Variable box, and then click Next.

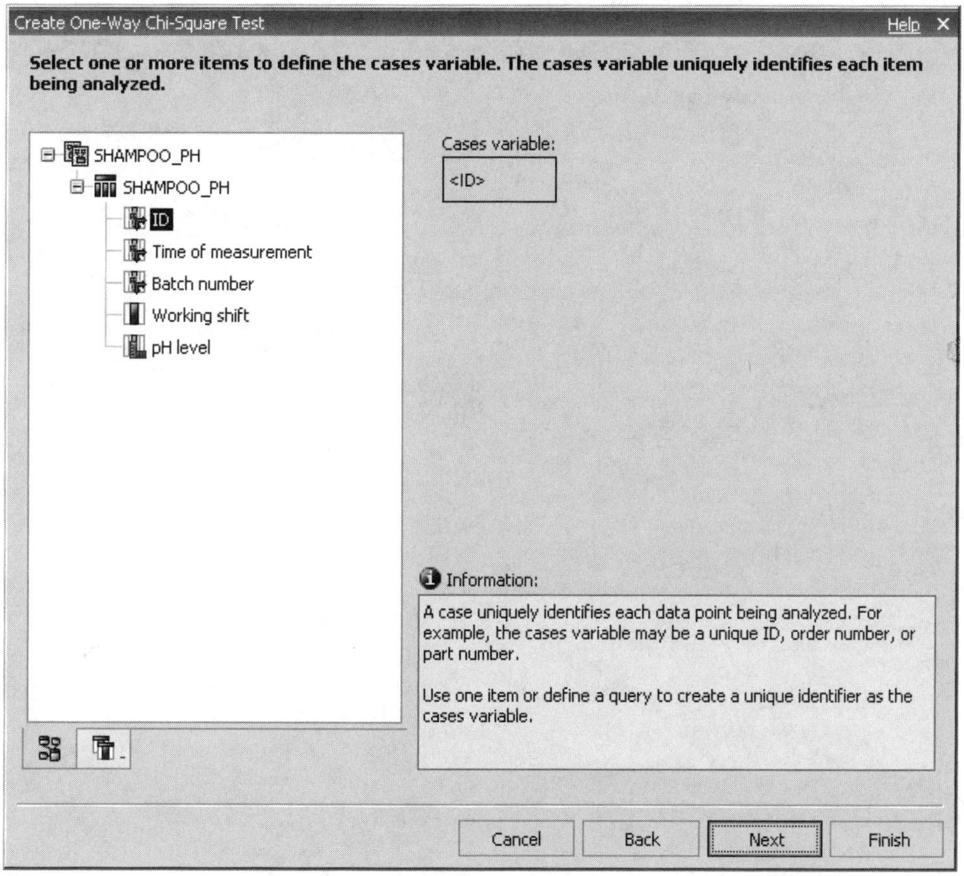

A screenshot of the "Create One-Way Chi-Square Test" dialog box. The dialog title bar reads "Create One-Way Chi-Square Test" with a "Help" link and close button (X).

Select one or more items to define the cases variable. The cases variable uniquely identifies each item being analyzed.

Tree structure on the left:
- SHAMPOO_PH
  - SHAMPOO_PH
    - ID
    - Time of measurement
    - Batch number
    - Working shift
    - pH level

Cases variable:
<ID>

Information:

A case uniquely identifies each data point being analyzed. For example, the cases variable may be a unique ID, order number, or part number.

Use one item or define a query to create a unique identifier as the cases variable.

Buttons: Cancel | Back | Next | Finish

6. Customize the output by selecting Show Quartiles and/or Show Frequencies. In this case, accept the default, Show Frequencies. Then click Finish.

```
┌─────────────────────────────────────────────────────────────────────┐
│ Create One-Way Chi-Square Test                              Help   X │
│  Specify the customized output to display.                           │
│                                                                      │
│                                                                      │
│  Customize output ─────────────────────────────────────────────     │
│     ☐ Show quartiles                                                 │
│     ☑ Show frequencies                                               │
│                                                                      │
│                                                                      │
│                                                                      │
│                                                                      │
│                                                                      │
│                                                                      │
│                                                                      │
│                                                                      │
│  ⓘ Information:                                                       │
│  ┌────────────────────────────────────────────────────────────────┐ │
│  │ For more information, click the Help link in the top right corner.│ │
│  │                                                                  │ │
│  │                                                                  │ │
│  └────────────────────────────────────────────────────────────────┘ │
│                                                                      │
│                          ┌────────┐ ┌────────┐ ┌────────┐ ┌────────┐ │
│                          │ Cancel │ │  Back  │ │  Next  │ │ Finish │ │
│                          └────────┘ └────────┘ └────────┘ └────────┘ │
└─────────────────────────────────────────────────────────────────────┘
```

The Chi-Square result of 2.100 tells us that the frequency of samples in our analysis variable is not identical. The asymptotic significance (Asymp. Sig.) greater than 0.05 tells us that there is no statistical significance in the test samples.

Chi-Square Test

Frequencies

Working shift

Working shift	Observed N	Expected N	Residual
Night	90	80.0	10.0
Morning	78	80.0	-2.0
Afternoon	72	80.0	-8.0
Total	240		

Test Statistics

	Working shift
Chi-Square	2.100[1]
df	2
Asymp. Sig.	.350

[1] 0 cells (.0%) have expected frequencies less than 5. The minimum expected cell frequency is 80.0.

Correlation and Regression

Because correlation and regression statistics are about analyzing the impact of one measure on another, we will step away from our pH level sample with only a single measure and use the Bank Loan sample data for this discussion. This data includes information about loan applications being made at a multiple-branch bank. The data includes customer age in years, household income, level of education, credit card debt, and a number of other items.

Suppose you work at the bank where we gathered our sample data, and your manager wants to know if a relationship exists between a customer's household income and his or her credit card debt. The basic correlation chart can be used to plot the relationship between these two variables, show the basic descriptive statistics, and show the correlations numerically.

1. Open a new report using the BANKLOAN_CS samples. Click the Statistics template icon.

2. From the Correlation and Regression group, select Basic Correlation and click OK.

PART III

Select Statistic   Help X

- Descriptive Statistics
- Means Comparison
- Nonparametric Tests
- Correlation and Regression
  - Basic Correlation
  - Linear Regression
  - Curve Estimation
- Control Charts

ⓘ Information:

Basic correlation measures the strength of relationship between two variables.

☑ Use the wizard to create statistical object

OK   Cancel

3. Drag-and-drop Household Income In Thousands into the Analysis Variable 1 box, and then click Next.

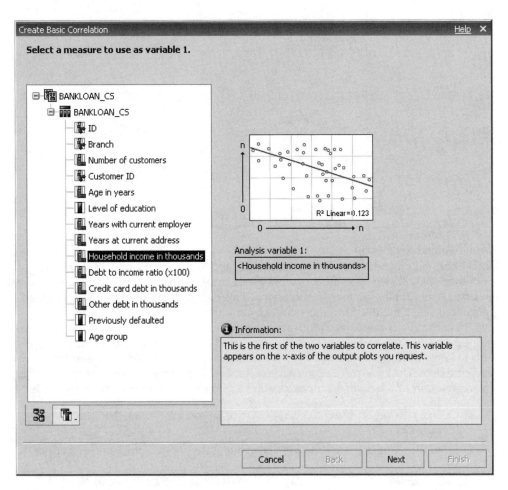

4. Drag-and-drop Credit Card Debt In Thousands into the Analysis Variable 2 box, and then click Next.

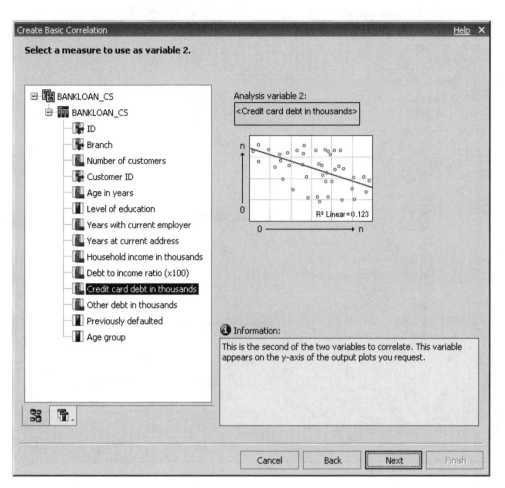

5. Drag-and-drop ID into the Cases Variable box, and then click Next.

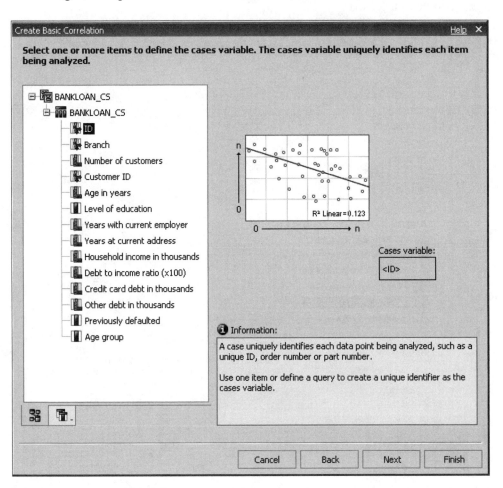

6. Customize the correlation output by specifying the type of correlation coefficient, significance test, and how to handle missing values. In this example, you'll accept the defaults by clicking Next.

Create Basic Correlation   Help ✕

Specify the correlation coefficient to compute, the type of test of significance, and how to handle missing values. You can also specify the customized output to display.

Correlation coefficients

- ○ Kendall's tau-b
- ○ Spearman
- ⦿ Pearson
    - ☐ Show means and standard deviations
    - ☐ Show cross-product deviations and covariances

Test of significance

- ⦿ Two-tailed
- ○ One-tailed

☑ Flag significant correlations

Missing values

- ○ Exclude cases listwise
- ⦿ Exclude cases pairwise

Customize output

☑ Show chart

ⓘ Information:

Use Pearson correlation for parametric data, Spearman correlation for nonparametric data, or Kendall's tau-b for binary or ordinal data.

Cancel   Back   Next   Finish

PART III

7. Add Titles and Footnotes and click Finish, or click Finish to accept the defaults.

The finished report should look like this:

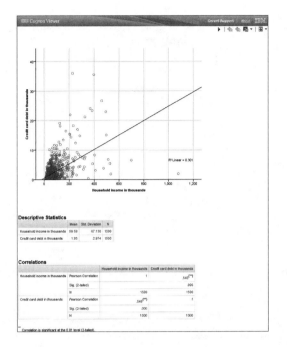

Based on the chart, it appears that a strong correlation exists between household income and credit card debt. However, a perfect correlation would be either 1 or –1, and no correlation at all would be 0. In our data, we see that the Pearson correlation is 0.549, which indicates a moderate relationship between the two measures.

Control Charts

Cognos 10 comes with a variety of control charts, each of which is visually and functionally similar to the other. We will look at the X-bar chart in this example, but it is possible that one of the other control charts would be a better fit for your specific analysis.

Going back to our shampoo example, we are interested in monitoring pH level changes during the production process. The X-bar will plot the mean value of each batch over time.

1. In the Insertable Objects pane, drag-and-drop the Statistics icon onto your report.

2. From the Control Charts group, select the X-Bar option and click OK.

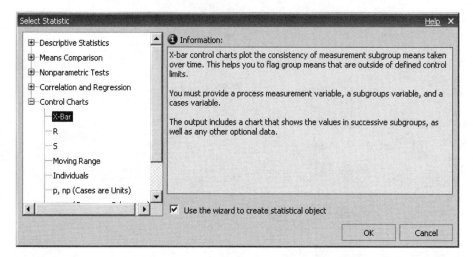

3. Drag-and-drop pH level into the Process Measurement Variables box, and then click Next.

4. Drag-and-drop the Batch Number into the Subgroups Variable box, and then click Next.

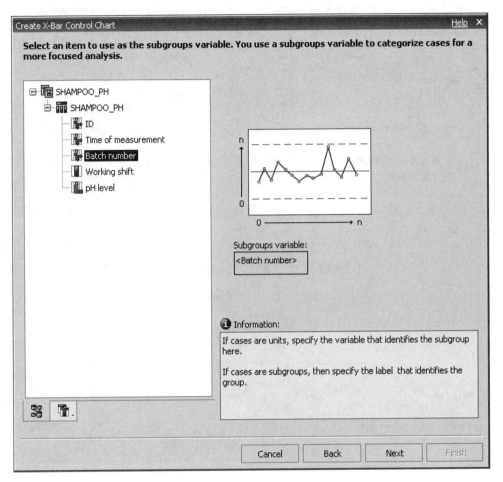

5. Drag-and-drop ID into the Cases Variable box, and then click Next.

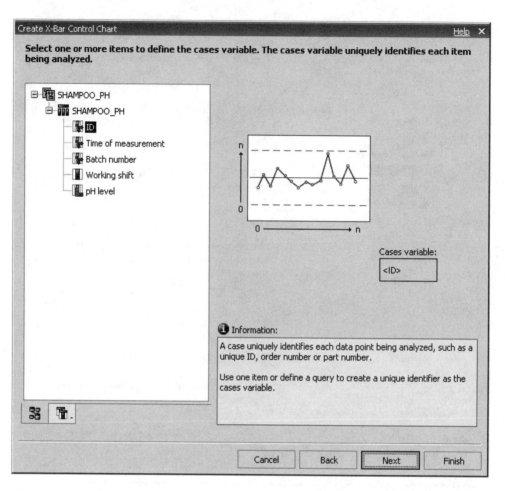

6. Customize the chart by selecting the number of standard deviations, subgroup size, and control rules. In our sample, we'll use the default settings. Then click Next.

7. You can further customize the X-bar chart by defining specification limits and including capability and process performance tables. In our sample, we'll accept the defaults by clicking Next.

8. The last screen allows you to define Titles and Footnotes for the chart. Add these, or leave them blank, and then click Finish.

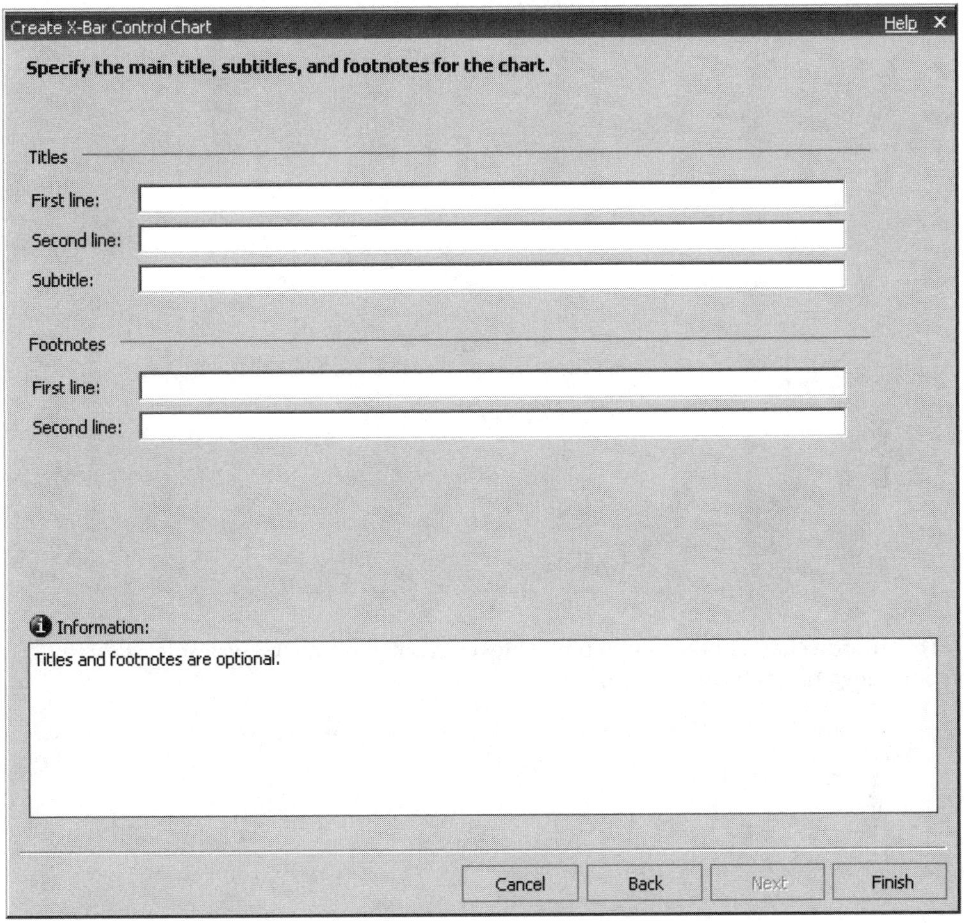

Create X-Bar Control Chart — Help ✕

Specify the main title, subtitles, and footnotes for the chart.

Titles
First line:
Second line:
Subtitle:

Footnotes
First line:
Second line:

ℹ Information:

Titles and footnotes are optional.

Cancel   Back   Next   Finish

The resulting X-bar chart for our shampoo process looks like this:

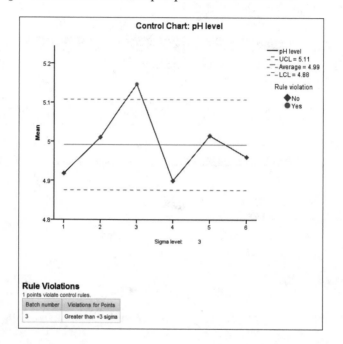

This control chart shows us that the pH level in batch number 3 was at least three standard deviations above the mean.

Event Management

Many organizations require up-to-date notification of data changes to drive business decisions. For these organizations, the information must be delivered promptly so that decisions can be made in a timely manner to enhance the value of the business. With IBM Cognos Business Intelligence, event notifications can be sent based on business rules that define areas in need of attention. IBM Cognos Event Studio enables you to create *agents* that identify critical information and quickly deliver it to the business.

With Cognos Event Studio, your organization can be alerted to events when they happen to make effective and timely business decisions. Cognos Event Studio is driven by agents that look at data you specify to detect specific events that might occur within your business. An *event* is triggered when specific actions occur or when data conditions previously defined are met. You specify the event condition (to test for the change in data), and when the agent detects this change, Cognos Event Studio performs a set of tasks, such as sending an e-mail notification, adding information to a portal, running reports, or triggering a job.

Suppose, for example, that you are part of the sales team at a sporting goods company. You want to be the sales manager for a specific product line, but before that can happen, you must prove that you can sell. A new product is about to hit the market and you think it's a great one. In fact, you believe this is the product that will help you get the promotion you want. You tell your manager that if you can sell $1 million worth of this product every month for the next three months, you want the promotion. Your manager agrees, and off you go. You do all the things a good salesperson does, and you wait for the monthly sales results to arrive.

In this example, the event of interest to you, the ambitious salesperson, is the monthly sales reports—specifically the numbers for your product. The condition is this: Did my product produce at least $1 million in sales this month? Finally, the task will be to send an e-mail to the manager when sales reach $1 million or more.

The business uses for event management can differ not only among businesses, but also among departments within a business. For example, the quality assurance manager at a manufacturing company might want to receive a notification e-mail any time the number of defective parts being produced reaches a specified threshold. Within the same company, an HR manager might want to have a report sent to her every Monday if there are employees who have not submitted their time cards for the previous week. These are two very different events, but the actions that make the events trigger are the same: new information is added to a data source, expressions are checked, results are evaluated, and an action either does or does not occur.

In your organization, the events, conditions, and tasks that you create for an agent will depend on what is important to you. No matter what that is, once you understand the basics, you will find that Cognos Event Studio is a flexible tool that assists in monitoring your data effectively.

What Is an Event?

A business event is a change that occurs in a business context. A business event is often represented by one or more individual events, typically as a pattern, at the technology level. When you contact a call center, for example, the Interactive Voice Response (IVR) application generates an event for the incoming call. Consider the opportunity of being able to detect that the incoming call represents the third time the same customer has called within the last two days. Thinking back to our ambitious salesperson example, the salesperson might want to be alerted to understand whether the reason for the customer's call would impact a pending sale.

Within Cognos Event Studio, business events, or simply events, are the driving force behind the agent; events represent conditions in the data that meet the criteria required for an action to occur. When a condition is met, the event tells the agent to trigger the list of actions defined within the agent.

Events are made up of event instances, an event list, an event key, and task execution rules. An *event instance* is a row of data that meets the criteria of the event condition. An *event list* consists of the event instances that have been processed by the agent and are categorized by the following statuses:

- **New**   This is the first time event instances have been returned.
- **Ongoing but changed**   Event instances have been returned before, but the results are different this time.
- **Ongoing and unchanged**   The current event instances are the same as those returned the previous time.
- **Ceased**   No event instances were returned.

An *event key* is a unique combination of fields from your data source that is used to identify the status of an event. The *task execution rules* define for which event status(es) each task is executed.

When an agent executes, it looks at the data for any event instances. The agent uses the event key at runtime to compare the most recent event instances to the event instances from the previous run. From the comparison, the agent allocates a status to each event instance and stores the event instance in the event list. The task execution rules then determine which tasks are executed based on the event list.

Creating an Agent

An *agent* is an IBM Cognos Connection entry created with Cognos Event Studio. Agents contain one event condition, any number of tasks, and all the properties associated with the condition and tasks. When an agent runs, it checks the data for occurrences of the event and, if detected, performs the tasks using the task execution rules. Tasks can be run at the same time or in the order that you have specified.

Agents can be set to accept *prompts*, which provide the flexibility to reuse an agent for multiple users or business cases. Prompt values can be provided through the schedule or by passing in the values of a source item from the events of another agent.

Within Cognos Connection, you can create a view of an agent. *Views* are used to share the specifications of an agent to be used in another agent. With an agent view, different prompt values or an alternative schedule can be set.

The *source* for a Cognos Event Studio agent is a package published in your Cognos BI environment. Cognos Event Studio uses the package, whether it is relational, dimensionally modeled relational (DMR), or a cube, to specify the event condition with data from the source, and then this data is monitored by the agent. Items from the source can also be used to define calculations and parameters to be included in the event condition.

NOTE *Cognos Event Studio looks at data sources from your Cognos BI application. If you use a cube data source, Cognos Event Studio results will be triggered only after the data is refreshed in the source.*

Opening Cognos Event Studio

You access Cognos Event Studio from Cognos Connection. Cognos Event Studio opens in a separate web browser window, leaving your Cognos Connection window intact.

To open Cognos Event Studio, follow these steps:

1. Log on to Cognos Connection, and navigate to the Public Folders tab.

2. From the Launch menu located at the upper-right of the screen, select Event Studio. The Select A Package dialog displays.

3. Click a package link. Cognos Event Studio opens.

TIP *You can also launch Cognos Event Studio from the Cognos Connection Welcome page by clicking Manage My Events.*

Navigation in Cognos Event Studio

The Cognos Event Studio interface is split into four areas: the I Want To pane, the Insertable Objects pane, the summary area, and the content area:

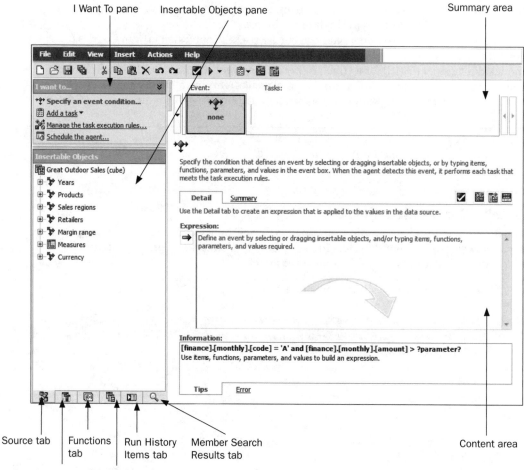

The I Want To pane shows the tasks and functions available when you are creating an agent. You can choose to specify an event condition, add tasks, manage the task execution rules, schedule the agent, and reorder tasks from this area.

The Insertable Objects pane has six tabs: Source, Data Items, Functions, Parameters, Run History Items, and Member Search Results. The tabs are similar to those in Cognos Report Studio and contain the following:

- **Source tab**   Displays a hierarchical list of the items, relational or dimensional, available in the selected Framework Manager package.

- **Data Items tab**   Provides a quick reference to a list of the data items and calculations contained in the agent.

- **Functions tab**   Provides a list of functions, such as operators and summaries, that you can use in event conditions and to create calculated data items.
- **Parameters tab**   Displays a list of any parameters used in the event condition.
- **Run History Items tab**   Lists system environment variables that you can include in event conditions defined for when errors occur. These items include the date/time of the error, the person who ran the task, and other information.
- **Members Search Results tab**   Shows search results for any items searched on the Source tab. The search utility displays at the bottom of the tree on the Source tab when a level has more members than can be displayed due to space constraints.

The summary area shows an overview of the sequence for your agent, consisting of the event and the tasks to be executed when the event condition is met.

The content area displays the details of the item selected in the summary area. When specifying an event condition, the expression entered displays here. When viewing a task, the details of the selected task display in this area.

Specify a Condition

In the following example, you will specify an event condition for an agent. To specify the event condition, you can use a combination of data items, functions, calculations, parameters, and run history items.

To specify an event condition, follow these steps:

1. In Cognos Event Studio, select Specify An Event Condition in the I Want To pane.

2. Select either the Detail or the Summary tab in the content area. Choose Detail if you are defining an event condition that applies to individual values in the data source. Choose Summary if you are defining an event condition that applies to aggregate values. For this example, we select the Detail tab.

3. In the Expression text box, create a query expression by dragging items from the Insertable Objects pane or by typing directly in the Expression text box. For this example, **[Revenue] > 1000000** is defined as the expression.

TIP *To select from a list of values for the selected item, click the Select Values button. Move the values you want from the Pick Items box to the Selected Items box, and then click OK.*

4. To test that the event condition is defined properly, click the Validate button on the toolbar in the content area.

5. To check the event list to ensure that you have specified the event condition correctly, select Preview from the Actions menu.

6. To view the number of event instances for the event condition you have specified, select Count Events from the Actions menu.

TIP *To create an expression for a cell (or an intersect) in a dimensionally modeled or OLAP data source such as a PowerCube, use the* `value(tuple([member_name],..,[measure_name]))` *syntax for the expression. Example:* `value(tuple([Americas],[Camping Equipment], [Revenue])) > 1000000`

Define a Parameter

Parameters can be used within an event condition. A parameter is a variable. When the agent is manually run, the user will be prompted to enter a value for the parameter. When a schedule is set up to run the agent automatically, you define the prompt value(s) and save them into the schedule. Parameters can also be used to accept the results from a previous agent.

To define a parameter, follow these steps:

1. Click the New Parameter button on the toolbar in the content area. The Define The Parameter pane displays.

Define the parameter	Help ✕
Specify a name for this parameter.	
Parameter name:	

OK   Cancel   Apply

2. In the Parameter Name text box, type a name for the parameter.
3. Click OK to save the parameter.
4. Click the Parameter tab in the Insertable Objects pane to access the new parameter.

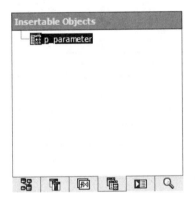

Define a Calculation

A calculation uses multiple data items to derive a single value.

To define a calculation, follow these steps:

1. Click the New Calculation button on the toolbar in the content area. The Define The Data Item pane displays.

Define the data item	Help ✕

Specify a name and expression.

Name:

Expression: ☑ ▦

Information:

total ([distinct] expr [auto])
total ([distinct] expr for [all | any] expr { , expr })
total ([distinct] expr for report)
Returns the total value of selected data items.

| Tips | Error |

| OK | Cancel | Apply |

2. In the Name text box, type a name for the calculation. For this example, type the name **Gross Profit %**.

3. In the Expression text box, define the calculation by dragging items and/or functions from the Insertable Objects pane or by typing directly in the Expression text box. For this example, define the expression for the calculation as Gross Profit divided by Revenue:

Name:

Gross Profit %

Expression: ☑ ▦

➡ [great_outdoors_sales_en].[Measures].[Gross profit]/[great_outdoors_sales_en].[Measures].[Revenue]

TIP *Click a function in the Insertable Objects pane to view its meaning in the Information box.*

4. Click OK to save the calculation.

5. Click the Data Items tab in the Insertable Objects pane to access the new calculation. You can include the calculation when specifying an event condition or task. For this example, we add the Gross Profit % calculation to the event condition, as shown next:

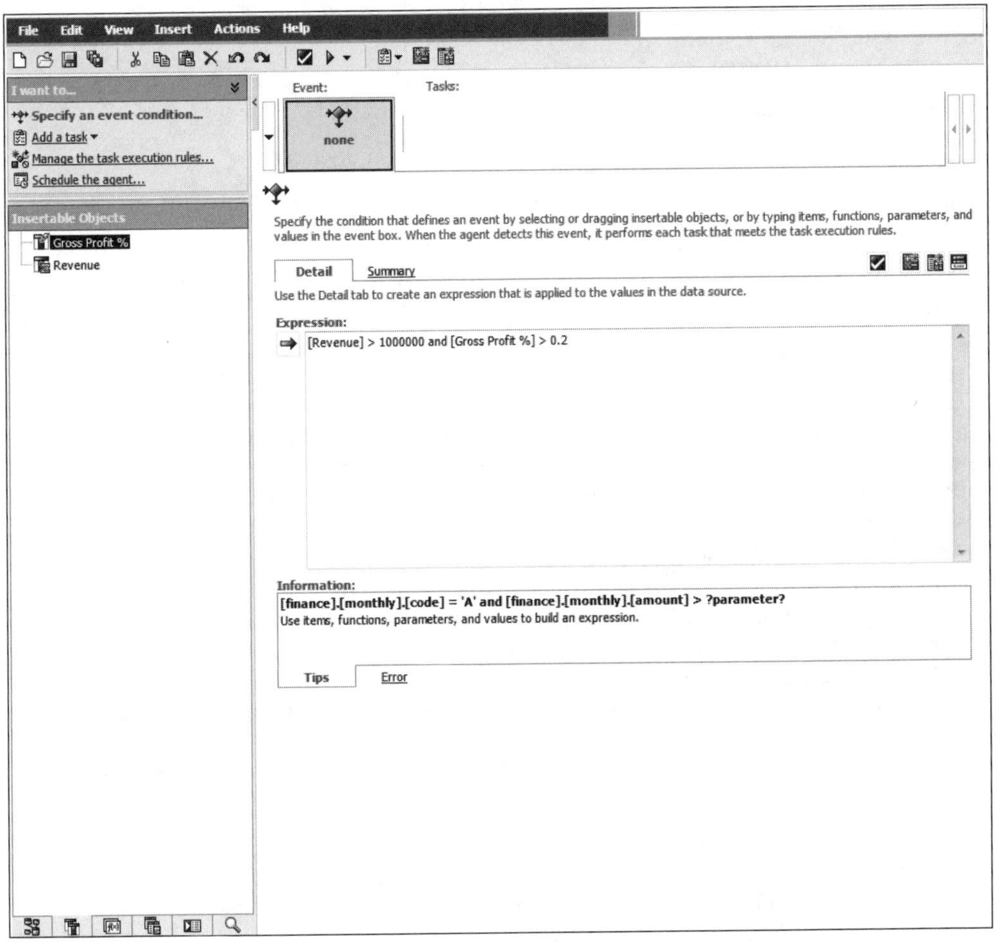

Adding a Task

Once the condition has been specified, you can add tasks to be completed when the condition is met. While only one condition can be defined per agent, an agent can have multiple tasks. Tasks can be used for things such as sending a notification to the business as data changes, providing automation to workflow, or running administrative tasks.

The list of tasks assigned to an agent displays in the summary area. Tasks can be set up to perform in sequence or all at once. The following tasks are available:

- Send an email
- Publish a news item
- Run a report

- Run a job
- Run an agent
- Run an approval request
- Run a notification request
- Update a database
- Call a web service
- Run an export
- Run an import
- Run an index update
- Run a content maintenance task
- Run a metric task
- Run a migration task

As you set up tasks and specify the event condition, it is important that you keep in mind how often tasks are performed. Most of the tasks are performed once, such as "Run a report" and "Run an approval request". The "Update a database" and "Call a web service" tasks occur once per event instance. The "Run a migration task" and "Send an email" tasks vary depending on the criteria of the event.

The most commonly used items within Cognos Event Studio are notifications, which are used to alert people to the results of an agent. An e-mail can be sent directly to recipients or a news item can be published to a folder frequently viewed by people who need the information. The notification you select should contain all relevant information regarding the event and should be visible to your audience.

An important feature of notifications is that they can contain dynamic information; data items from the package can be inserted directly into notifications. The values are not retrieved until the agent is run. You can include any level of detail you find necessary for the recipients.

NOTE *The dynamic content in e-mail notifications can be applied to the list of recipients, the subject, and the body of the message. The dynamic content in news item notifications can be applied to the headline, the screen tip, and the text.*

E-mail notifications can be used through the "Run a report" task or the "Send an email" task. The "Run a report" task sends a single report that is built separately from the agent, while the "Send an email" task sends a text based e-mail that can include dynamic content from your package. Dynamic content cannot be included in the "Run a report" task.

NOTE *To receive a report on a regular predictable basis, the best method is to set up a schedule through Cognos Connection. Cognos Event Studio is best used if the report should only be delivered based on certain criteria.*

When using e-mail notifications with dynamic content, the outcome of the e-mail will differ depending on the number of event instances that are within the agent. Data items serve as placeholders for the content. When the agent is run, the placeholders turn into data. If the agent detects several events that satisfy the event condition, the size of the message can increase, or when the subject or the address lines contain data items, multiple e-mails may be generated. If the data items appear only in the message body, then a single e-mail is sent with the information for all of the details. A dynamic subject will generate an e-mail for each different subject, and a dynamic recipient list will generate an e-mail for each different e-mail address.

News items are published as a headline within a folder. The content in the folder is viewable in your Cognos Connection portal page. When the user clicks a news item headline, he or she can open Cognos BI content or view a web page.

NOTE *A migration task is also available to migrate Cognos Series 7 content to the current environment.*

Send an Email

Add an e-mail task to an agent to send an e-mail regarding an important business event. E-mail tasks let you send an e-mail with the content you want to the appropriate recipients. You can also include dynamic content in the "Send an email" task.

To add a "Send an email" task, follow these steps:

1. In the I Want To pane, click Add A Task.

2. Select Send An Email. The details of the task display in the content area:

3. In the To text box, enter the main recipients of the e-mail using one of three methods:

   • Drag data items from the Insertable Objects pane.

   • Click the Select the Recipients link to choose users.

   • Type the address(es) directly into the text box.

4. To specify recipients for the Cc field, enter recipients in the Cc text box.

5. To specify recipients for the Bcc field, click the Show Bcc link and then enter recipients in the Bcc text box.

6. In the Subject text box, type the subject of the e-mail. You can also drag items from the Insertable Objects pane to create a dynamic subject. (Example: *[Customer_Count]* customers responded to *[Promotion_Name]*; where *Customer_Count* and *Promotion_ Name* are referencing items on the Data Items tab.)

7. In the Body text box, enter the body of the e-mail by typing in the text box or dragging data items from the Insertable Objects pane.

TIP *To change the message from HTML to plain text or vice versa, click the Change To Plain Text link or the Change to HTML Format link.*

8. To include the event list in the message, click the Attach link and then select Attach The Event List.

9. To include links to Cognos BI content, click Add Links.

10. Click Save on the Cognos Event Studio toolbar. The agent is saved with an e-mail task. When the e-mail task is executed, the agent retrieves values for any source items and sends the e-mail to the selected recipients.

Publish a News Item

Add a news item task to an agent to publish a headline to a folder in Cognos Connection. To add a "Publish a news item" task, follow these steps:

1. In the I Want To pane, click Add A Task.

2. Select Publish A News Item. The details of the task display in the content area:

3. In the Headline text box, type the headline for the news item. You can also drag items from the Insertable Objects pane to the text box.

4. To provide a description for the Cognos Connection entry, enter text in the Text box.

5. To provide a screen tip for the Cognos Connection entry, enter text in the Screen Tip box. This text box has a 100-character limit.

6. In the Link To area, select the option for the item that you want to appear when the user clicks the headline:

   - **Event List**   The headline will link to the list of events that meet the event condition.

   - **Entry**   The headline will link to a selected Cognos Connection entry.

   - **URL**   The headline will link to a web address.

7. In the News List Location area, click the Select A Location link to specify where the headline will publish.

8. Click Save on the toolbar. The agent is saved with a news item task. When the news item task is executed, the agent publishes the headline to the location specified.

Run a Report

Add a report task when you want a report to run dependent upon an event. For example, if an event condition is "January sales > 1,000,000", the sales manager might want a report that lists the sales of each product by sales representative.

To add a "Run a report" task, follow these steps:

1. In the I Want To pane, click Add A Task.

2. Select Run A Report. The Select The Report dialog displays:

Select the report (Navigate)		Help
Navigate the folders or search to find the report, query, analysis, or report view to include in the agent.		Search

Cognos > **Public Folders**

Entries: 1 - 4

Name ◇
GO Metrics
GO Sales (analysis)
GO Sales (query)
Samples

| OK | Cancel |

3. Navigate to the appropriate report, and select the radio button next to the report name.

4. Click OK.

5. Click Save on the toolbar. The agent is saved with a report task. When the report task is executed, the agent runs the report and delivers it according to the default delivery options.

Customize a Run a Report Task   The report that you associated with an event might not have the default settings that you need—for example, the report defaults to HTML format, but you would like the format to be PDF. You can customize the report settings specifically for your task.

To customize a "Run a report" task, follow these steps:

1. In the summary area, click the report task that you want to customize. The details of the task display in the content area:

Specify the report to run.

Select a report, its options, and its prompt values if any. The agent will run this report when it detects events and determines that the task execution rules are met.

Report:
Pension Plan
Select the report...

Options:
Default
Set...

Prompt values:
Specify the prompt values used to satisfy the parameters of this task, if any. Select to use a literal value or an item from the event list. Select to specify values to override the default values.

Parameter	Type	Required	Multi-select	Method	Value

No entries.

---

2. Under Options, click the Set link. The Select The Report Options dialog displays with the default values for the report:

Select the report options - Pension Plan   Help ✕

Select the run options to use for the task.

☐ Override the default values

   Formats:
   Default

   Languages:
   Default

   Delivery:
   Save the report

OK	Cancel

---

3. Select the Override The Default Values check box.

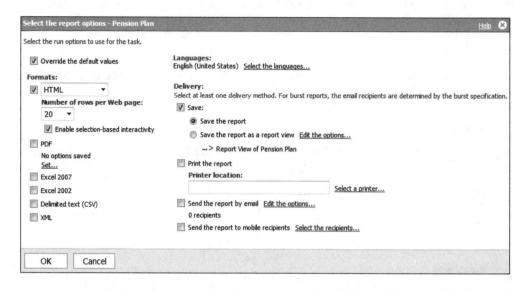

4. Make any modifications to the report options.

5. Click OK to save the report options you have set.

6. Under Prompt Values, specify the prompt values used when the task is executed for any prompts associated with the report.

7. When you have finished customizing the report task, click Save on the toolbar. The agent is saved with the customized report task. The next time the report task runs it will use these settings.

Run a Job

Add a job task whenever you want the agent to run a job. A *job* is a group of executable entries, such as reports, that are executed as a batch.

To add a "Run a job" task follow these steps:

1. In the I Want To pane, click Add A Task.
2. Select Run A Job. The Select The Job dialog displays:

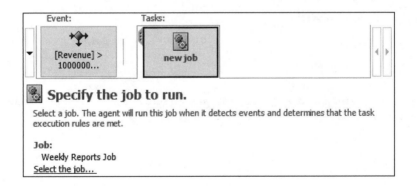

3. Navigate to an existing job that you want to run and select the radio button next to the job.
4. Click OK. The details of the task display in the content area:

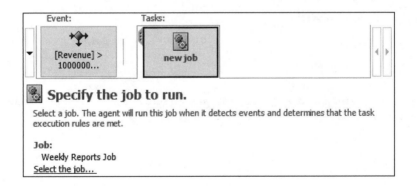

5. Click Save. The agent is saved with a job task. When the task is executed, the job will run.

Run an Agent

Add an agent task when you would like the agent to run another agent. Running more than one agent in sequence allows the output from one agent to be used as the input for another agent. An agent task can also be used to allow agents pulling from different data sources to interact. For example, when an agent detects that the same customer has called three times in the past two days, you could then run a second agent that does an additional check to determine whether that customer has a deal pending and notify the related salesperson. This approach offers greater control of the database access and allows for reuse of agents.

To add a "Run an agent" task, follow these steps:

1. In the I Want To pane, click Add A Task.

2. Select Run An Agent. The Select The Agent dialog displays.

3. Navigate to the saved agent that you want to run and select the radio button next to the agent.

4. Click OK. The details of the task display in the content area:

5. If the agent has any parameters, click the Specify Values link under Prompt Values to define the values the task will use.

6. Click Save on the toolbar. The agent is saved with an agent task. When the task is executed, the agent that you specified runs.

Run an Approval Request

Include an approval request when you want an event to be dependent upon the approval of defined individuals. The owner of the task responds to the request through their My Inbox area in Cognos Connection. If other tasks appear after the approval request task within the agent, those tasks will not be completed until the request has been approved. If the approval is denied, the tasks in the agent after the denied approval request are not completed.

To add a "Run an approval request" task, follow these steps:

1. In the I Want To pane, click Add A Task.

2. Select Run An Approval Request. The details of the task display in the content area:

3. Click the Select The Recipients link and add the desired recipients to the Potential Owners and the Stakeholders properties.

NOTE *Only one of the recipients needs to respond to the request. A task needs to be defined for each person required to respond to an approval request.*

4. In the Subject text box, type the subject of the approval request. You can also drag items from the Insertable Objects pane to create a dynamic subject.

5. In the Body text box, enter the body of the approval request by typing in the text box or dragging data items from the Insertable Objects pane.

TIP *To change the message from HTML to plain text or vice versa, click the Change To Plain Text link or the Change To HTML Format link.*

6. To include the event list in the message, click the Attach link and then click Attach The Event List.

7. To include links to Cognos BI content, click Add Links.

8. To set deadlines for the approval request, specify the properties under Due Dates.

9. Under Icon, drag an item from the Insertable Objects pane to set a custom icon for the request.

10. Under Priority, set the priority of the approval request by selecting an option from the drop-down list or dragging an item from the Insertable Objects pane.

11. Under Task Owner Action, specify whether the task owner simply approves or rejects all tasks *or* chooses which of the remaining tasks in the agent will execute.

12. Under Options, specify when My Inbox notifications are sent to the owners and stakeholders of the task.

13. Click Save on the toolbar. The agent is saved with an approval request task. When the task is executed, the agent sends an approval request to the My Inbox of the defined recipients.

Run a Notification Request

Include a notification request in an agent when you want an event to prompt a My Inbox update to the specified recipients.

To add a "Run a notification request" task, follow these steps:

1. In the I Want To pane, click Add A Task.

2. Select Run A Notification Request. The details of the task display in the content area:

3. Click the Select The Recipients link and add the desired recipients to the To and the Cc properties.

4. In the Subject text box, type the subject of the notification request. You can also drag items from the Insertable Objects pane to create a dynamic subject.

5. In the Body text box, enter the body of the notification request by typing in the text box or dragging data items from the Insertable Objects pane.

6. Under Priority, set the priority of the approval request by selecting an option from the drop-down list or dragging an item from the Insertable Objects pane.

7. Under Options, specify when My Inbox notifications are sent to the owners and stakeholders of the task.

8. Click Save on the toolbar. The agent is saved with a notification request task. When the task is executed, the agent sends a notification to the My Inbox of the defined recipients.

Update a Database

Add a database task to update the information in a database by executing an existing stored procedure that is part of the database. Databases that have a package in the Cognos BI environment based on them are available for this task. Stored procedures must be marked as a data modification stored procedure in Cognos Framework Manager to be available in Cognos Event Studio.

To add an "Update a database" task, follow these steps:

1. In the I Want To pane, click Add A Task.

2. Move your pointer over Advanced. When the Advanced submenu displays, select Update A Database. The details of the task display in the content area.

3. From the Package drop-down list, select the Framework Manager package that contains the stored procedure that you want to use.

4. From the Data Modification Stored Procedure drop-down list, select the stored procedure to use.

5. Select Use A Value or Use An Item from the Method drop-down list for each argument.

6. Specify the value or item for each argument.

7. Click Save on the toolbar. The agent is saved with a database task. When the task is executed, the agent executes the stored procedure with the values set, updating the database.

Call a Web Service

Add a web service task to run applications on either internal or external web servers using standard Internet protocols.

TIP   *An agent can have a simple event condition such as 1=1, and then contain a web service task to have a web service task run through Cognos Connection.*

To add a "Call a Web service" task, follow these steps:

1. In the I Want To pane, click Add A Task.

2. Move your pointer over Advanced, and when the Advanced submenu displays, select Call A Web Service. The details of the task display in the content area:

3. In the Web Service URL text box, enter the URL to the web application that you want to run.

TIP   *Any external web service referenced must be listed in the valid domains list in the configuration tool.*

4. Click Retrieve to display a list of parameters that the web application requires.

5. Enter the applicable information.

6. Click Save. The agent is saved with a web service task. When the task executes, the web service is used.

TIP *If your web service takes complex types—for example, if the web service is "wrapped"—the complex type information must be available to Web Services Invocation Framework (WSIF). A buildws script is available in the Cognos bin directory that will process the Web Services Description Language (WSDL) URL and build the appropriate support classes.*

Run an Export

You can use an agent to run a saved content export process. This is useful when different installations of Cognos BI are used for your development and production environments and you want an export to be deployed dependent upon a specific event.

To add a "Run an export" task, follow these steps:

1. In the I Want To pane, click Add A Task.

2. Move your pointer over Advanced, and when the Advanced submenu displays, select Run an Export. The Select The Export dialog displays:

3. Navigate to the name of the saved export that you want to deploy and select the radio button next to the export.

4. Click OK. The details of the task display in the content area:

5. Click Save on the toolbar. The agent is saved with an export task. When the task executes, the export is deployed.

Run an Import

The import task goes hand-in-hand with the export task. You can use an agent to run a saved import task; this will move migrated content from an export file into the target environment.

NOTE *The agent will not physically move an export file from one server to another server. The Content Administrator is responsible for performing this task.*

To add a "Run an import" task, follow these steps:

1. In the I Want To pane, click Add A Task.

2. Move your pointer over Advanced, and when the Advanced submenu displays, select Run An Import. The Select The Import dialog displays:

3. Navigate to the name of the saved import that you want to transfer and select the radio button next to the import.

4. Click OK. The details of the task display in the content area:

5. Click Save on the toolbar. The agent is saved with an import task. When the task executes, the specified file is imported.

Run an Index Update

Include an index update task in an agent when you want an already defined index update to execute contingent upon an event. For example, you could set up an agent to update the Cognos BI search index when new product lines are added to your data set.

To add a "Run an index update" task, follow these steps:

1. In the I Want To pane, click Add A Task.

2. Move your pointer over Advanced, and when the Advanced submenu displays, select Run An Index Update. The Select The Index Update dialog displays:

3. Navigate to a previously saved index update task and select the radio button next to the task.

4. Click OK. The details of the task display in the content area:

5. Specify the scope of the index update.

6. Click Save on the toolbar. The agent is saved with an index update task. When the task executes, the index is updated with the specified scope.

Run a Content Maintenance Task

You can use an agent to run a content maintenance task previously defined in Cognos Administration. Content maintenance tasks perform maintenance such as consistency checks and report upgrades.

To add a "Run a content maintenance" task, follow these steps:

1. In the I Want To pane, click Add A Task.

2. Move your pointer over Advanced, and when the Advanced submenu displays, select Run A Content Maintenance Task. The Select The Content Maintenance Task dialog displays:

3. Navigate to a previously saved content maintenance task and select the radio button next to the task.

4. Click OK. The details of the task display in the content area:

TIP *Select a mode for consistency check maintenance tasks: Find Only locates user information in the content store that no longer exists in the namespace, and Find And Fix locates this information and cleans up any discrepancies.*

5. Click Save. The agent is saved with a content maintenance task. When the task executes, the specified content maintenance task runs.

Run a Metric Task

Add a metric task if you want a metric maintenance task to run dependent upon an event. To add a "Run a metric" task, follow these steps:

1. In the I Want To pane, click Add A Task.

2. Move your pointer over Advanced, and when the Advanced submenu displays, select Run A Metric Task. The Select The Metric Task dialog displays:

3. Navigate to the metric task that you want to use and select the radio button of the metric task.

4. Click OK. The details of the task display in the content area:

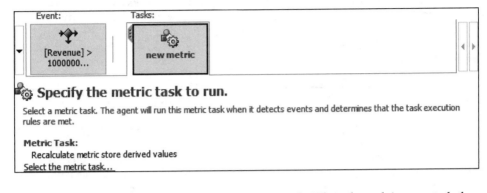

5. Click Save. The agent is saved with a metric task. When the task is executed, the specified metric maintenance task runs.

Test an Agent

It is a good idea to test your agent as it is being developed. Testing often allows you to find and fix any errors while they can still be isolated to the segment of the agent that you have been modifying. If you develop the entire agent and then test it, you could spend a lot of time trying to locate problems.

Two types of errors are common: logic and syntax errors. Validating will check the syntax of the agent. This test confirms that keywords are spelled and used correctly, all necessary attributes are specified, and required properties are defined. Testing the logic can be performed by choosing Preview All from the Actions menu. This link displays the steps that the agent will take and what the outcome would be if it were run. It is up to you to determine whether the steps taken are logical or not.

To test an agent, follow these steps:

1. From the Actions menu, select Validate. If any syntax errors are found in the agent, they display in the View The Validation Results dialog after the validation is complete.

View the validation results	Help ⊗
ⓘ No Errors.	
OK	

2. From the Actions menu, select Preview All. A new window displays each task in the agent. Examine the steps to determine whether they are correct.

Specify the Task Execution Rules

Task execution rules define the event status for which each task is executed. By default, tasks are executed for all new and all ongoing instances of events. You can modify this behavior through the Manage The Task Execution Rules option in the I Want To pane. This option allows you to define whether a specific task will or will not run based on the status of the event instance.

NOTE *Task execution rules can be modified only one task at a time.*

An event key is a combination of items that uniquely identifies each event instance and is used to determine the status of each event instance. The status is set by comparing the event keys detected in each execution of the agent with those from the previous run. The event list is then analyzed against the task execution rules for each task in the agent, and any tasks are executed that meet the defined criteria.

Using our salesperson example, an agent has been created to provide the salesperson feedback on sales of her product. The event condition is set so the cumulative monthly revenue is greater than $1 million for her product. The event key for the agent is the product number and the date of the last day of the month. Each time this agent executes, the event key is used to determine the status of the event. The task execution rules are set to execute the task if the status of the event is New. The agent is scheduled to run on the first of each month.

For example, the first time the agent is executed, on February 1, the event key is 107113:20120131, which consists of product number 107113 and the date of January 31, 2012. The event status is New. If the agent is executed on February 2, the event key is 107113:20120131, because only one event meets the condition. This event status is Ongoing but unchanged. When the agent executes as scheduled on March 1, the event key is 107113:20120229 and the event status for this event is New. Now two events meet the event condition. In the event list, the first is categorized as Ongoing but unchanged and the second is categorized as New.

The agent checks the status of the event and performs the task if the execution rules are met. The salesperson is interested in receiving an e-mail only when the event key is New, so we select only New Events within the task execution rules.

To specify task execution rules, follow these steps:

1. In the I Want To pane, select Manage The Task Execution Rules. The Set The Task Execution Rules dialog displays:

2. From the Task drop-down list, select the task for which you want to modify the execution rules.

3. Within the Select When To Perform This Task area, choose one of the following options:

   - **For Selected Events**   Select this option to specify under what circumstances to perform the task.

   - **When The Agent Or Any Of Its Tasks Fail**   Select this option to perform the task when the agent or a task fails.

4. If you selected For Selected Events, select or clear the check boxes for the following options to specify the situation(s) in which to perform the task:

   - **New Events**   Execute task for events occurring for the first time.

   - **Ongoing Events**   Execute task for events occurring before (either with same or different results).

   - **Ceased Events**   Execute task for events that occurred before but are not occurring now.

- **When The Following Item Is True For Selected New, Ongoing, And Ceased Events**   Execute task when a specified evaluation is true.
- **No Events**   Execute task when no events meet the condition.

TIP   *When the For Selected Events option is chosen, most users typically select the New Events and Ongoing Events check boxes, along with the All Ongoing Events option in the Ongoing Events drop-down list.*

5. Click the Event Key tab. The Event key dialog displays, where you can specify the item(s) that uniquely identify the event:

6. Select the items to include in the event key by choosing one of the following:

- **Include All Items (Default)**   Choose this option to include all items referenced in the event condition for the event key.
- **Include Only Selected Items**   Choose this option to specify selected items for the event key.

TIP   *When you are first setting the event key, start with the Include All Items (Default) option. You can modify the key later if the default does not meet your needs.*

7. Click OK to set the task execution rule settings. Cognos Event Studio displays the event and tasks for the agent.

8. Click Save on the toolbar. The agent is saved with the task execution rules as set.

Preview the Data

You can use the Preview option in Cognos Event Studio to see the event instances that would meet the condition if you were to run the agent (the event list). The Preview All option shows you the event list and an overview of each task that meets the task execution rules.

Choose Preview on the Actions menu to view the event list. Choose Preview All on the Actions menu to view the event list and get a preview of each task in the agent. The Cognos Viewer window displays, as shown next. When you are finished examining the results, close the results window.

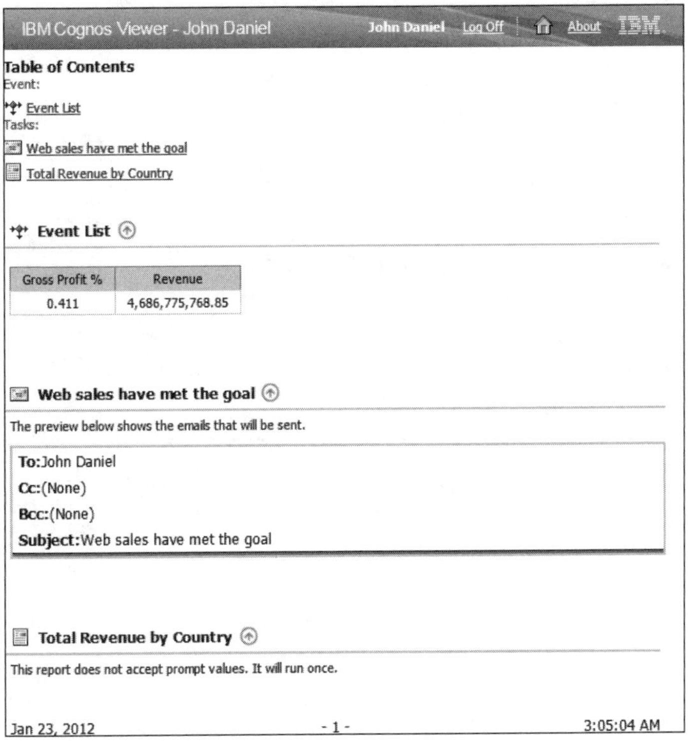

Save an Agent

You should save your agent periodically throughout the process of creating it so that any modifications made to the agent are not lost.

To save an agent, follow these steps:

1. From the File menu, select Save As. The Save As dialog opens.

2. In the Name text box, enter a name for the agent.

3. Under Location, click the Select Another Location link to specify a location for the agent that is different from the location listed, or click the Select My Folders link to save the report view in your My Folders directory.

4. Click OK. The agent is saved.

Scheduling an Agent

Setting a schedule for an agent allows you to set the agent to run at a later date and time or on a recurring basis. The agent monitors data and performs tasks according to its schedule and does not need to be run manually. Only one schedule can be associated with an agent.

To schedule an agent in Cognos Event Studio, follow these steps:

1. In the I Want To pane, select Schedule The Agent. The schedule pane displays:

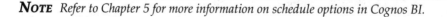

2. Set the schedule according to your needs.

3. Click OK. The agent is scheduled.

4. Click Save. The agent is saved along with the schedule.

NOTE   *Refer to Chapter 5 for more information on schedule options in Cognos BI.*

Maintaining an Agent

Requirements for your agent can change over time. The event condition might need to be updated or additional tasks might need to be removed from the agent. Listed here are steps for some of the most common actions performed for an already created agent.

Modify an Event Condition

It is likely that an event condition may change, especially early in the life of a new agent. You might find that a logical condition is not quite what you thought or that the threshold on a condition is set too high or too low. In this case, you can update your condition.

To modify an event condition, follow these steps:

1. Open the agent that you want to change in Cognos Event Studio.

2. Select the event in the summary area. The event details display in the content area:

Event: Tasks:

none   Web sales high   This is the headline

Specify the condition that defines an event by selecting or dragging insertable objects, or by typing items, functions, parameters, and values in the event box. When the agent detects this event, it performs each task that meets the task execution rules.

Detail	Summary

Use the Detail tab to create an expression that is applied to the values in the data source.

Expression:

[Order method type] = 'Web' and [Quantity] > 10000

3. In the Expression text box, update the condition.

4. Click Save on the toolbar. The agent is saved with the updated event condition.

Modify a Task

When you want to make changes to a task, you can open the agent and make any necessary modifications to the task. For example, you might need to update the recipient list in an e-mail task or change options on a report task.

To modify a task, follow these steps:

1. Open the agent that you want to change in Cognos Event Studio.

2. In the summary area, select the task that you want to modify.

3. Change any applicable options as needed.

4. Click Save. The agent is saved with the task modifications.

Delete a Task

If you no longer want or need a task within an agent, you can simply delete it.

To delete a task, follow these steps:

1. Open the agent that you would like to change in Cognos Event Studio.

2. In the summary area, select the task that you want to delete.

3. Click the Delete button on the toolbar or select Delete from the Edit menu.

Change the Order in Which Tasks Run

In an agent, you can either run tasks all at the same time or in sequence. You can define the order in which tasks are run only when you set them to run in sequence. You should specify tasks to run in sequence whenever a task in the sequence is dependent upon the outcome of a task earlier in the sequence or to be mindful of the use of system resources. For example, if you have a database update task that changes the information that will be included in a report, you would want that task to execute completely before the report task executes.

To change the order in which to run tasks, follow these steps:

1. In the I Want To pane, select Reorder The Tasks. The Reorder The Tasks dialog displays:

2. In the Submission Of Tasks area, select the All At Once or In Sequence option.

3. Move the tasks into the appropriate order by highlighting each task and then clicking the Up, Down, To Top, and To Bottom links.

4. Click OK. The tasks are listed in the specified order in the summary area.

5. Click Save. The agent is saved.

Specify Default Options for Tasks of an Agent

You can control the default behavior of report and import options for all tasks of an agent. When set in this location, these options apply to the defaults for any report or import tasks created in the agent.

Specify Default Options for Report Format

You can set the output format (such as PDF, HTML, or Excel) and define delivery options (for example, send to a printer, e-mail, save, and so on) for all report tasks within an agent. Report options can also be set individually on each report task.

NOTE *Refer to Chapter 5 for more information on the report options available in Cognos BI.*

To specify default options for report tasks, follow these steps:

1. From the Actions menu, select Set Default Options For All Tasks. The Select Default Options screen displays:

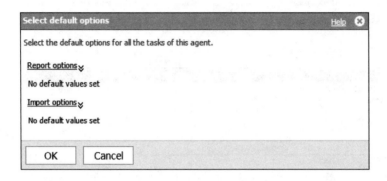

2. Click the Report Options link to expand the options.

3. Select the Specify Default Values For All The Reports Of This Agent check box. The options expand:

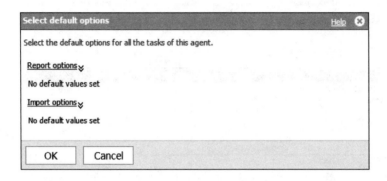

4. Set any desired report options.

5. Click OK. The specified report options are set as the default options for any report task created in this agent.

6. Click Save. The agent is saved with the specified report options set as default.

Specify Default Options for Import Tasks

You can define to how to handle report specification upgrades and content store IDs for all import tasks created in the agent.

To specify default options for import tasks, follow these steps:

1. From the Actions menu, select Set Default Options For All Tasks. The Select Default Options screen displays.

2. Click the Import Options link to expand the options.

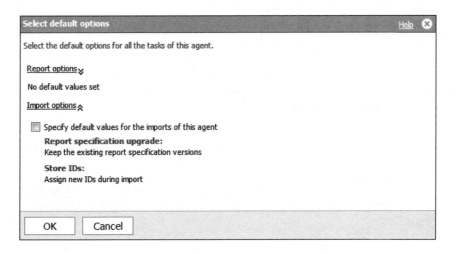

3. Select the Specify Default Values For The Imports Of This Agent check box. The available options expand.

4. Set the desired report specification upgrade option.

5. Set the desired store IDs option.

6. Click OK. The specified import options are now set for any import tasks added to this agent.

7. Click Save. The agent is saved with the specified import options set as default.

Using Agents in Cognos Connection

Common Cognos Connection actions such as cut, copy, paste, delete, set properties, run, and schedule can be performed on agents.

Run an Agent Manually

Once an agent has been saved, you can run it either manually or on a schedule within Cognos Connection. Running an agent manually can be helpful in verifying that it runs properly.

To run an agent manually, follow these steps:

1. In Cognos Connection, navigate to the saved agent.

2. In the Actions column of the agent you want to run, click the Run With Options button. The run options display.

3. Select the time at which you want to run the agent.

4. Click Run. The agent runs at the next occurrence of the selected time.

Schedule an Agent in Cognos Connection

Most agents should run on a schedule, because the events that you are checking for might happen only once a day or once a month.

To schedule an agent from Cognos Connection, follow these steps:

1. In Cognos Connection, navigate to the saved agent.

2. In the Actions column of the agent you want to schedule, click the Schedule button. The schedule options display.

3. Set any properties for the schedule you want.

4. Click OK. The agent runs at the next occurrence of the selected date and time.

NOTE *Agents can also be scheduled from within Cognos Event Studio by selecting Schedule The Agent from the I Want To pane. Refer to Chapter 5 for more information schedule options in Cognos BI.*

Create an Agent View

An agent view can be created of an agent to share the agent specification. This can be useful when you want agents with the same event condition and tasks set with different sets of prompt values or set on varying schedules.

To create an agent view, follow these steps:

1. In Cognos Connection, navigate to the saved agent for which you would like to create an agent view.

2. In the Actions column of the agent, click the Create An Agent View Of This Agent button.

Create an agent view

3. Type a name for the agent view.

4. Optionally, provide a description and screen tip for the agent view.

5. Under Location, click the Select Another Location link to specify a location for the agent view that is different from the location of the source agent, or click the Select My Folders link to save the report view in your My Folders directory.

6. Click OK. The agent view has been created in the specified location.

Tip *You can now create a schedule for the agent view separate from any schedule associated with the source agent.*

PART III

Scorecards and Metrics

IBM Cognos Business Intelligence v10.1 provides the mechanisms for you to gather, load, and consume key performance indicators, also known as metrics, with the use of IBM Cognos Metric Designer and IBM Cognos Metric Studio. You can use Cognos Metric Designer to gather metrics from data sources and prepare them for use in Cognos Metric Studio. Cognos Metric Studio enables users to monitor the performance of the business using metrics to track relevant measurable goals aligned with a broader strategy, such as a Balanced Scorecard. You can read about the Balanced Scorecard methodology in Chapter 2.

NOTE *Metric store data can be sourced for other Cognos BI uses, such as reports and workspaces.*

Cognos Metric Studio

Cognos Metric Studio provides an area where you can monitor and analyze metrics for your business. *Metrics* are performance indicators that track actual results, planned results, and the variance between the two over time for areas important to your business. Metric status and trend indicators help you quickly assess the performance of your business to identify areas of concern that require action.

NOTE *IBM Cognos BI Metric Server must be installed before Cognos Metric Studio will be available from the Launch menu. Also, if a metric package has not been configured, Cognos Connection will prompt you to create a metric store when opening Cognos Metric Studio.*

Opening Cognos Metric Studio

To open Cognos Metric Studio, follow these steps:

1. Log on to IBM Cognos Connection, and navigate to the Public Folders tab.

2. From the Launch menu, select Metric Studio. The Select A Package screen displays.

3. Select a metric package from either the Recently Used Packages area or the List Of All Packages area. Cognos Metric Studio opens to your Watch List by default:

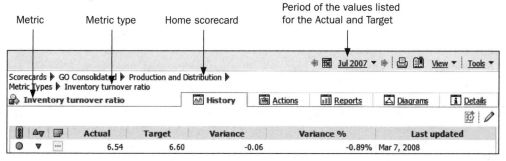

> **TIP** *Alternatively, Cognos Metric Studio can be opened by clicking the Metric Package entry's link in Cognos Connection if the default action is set to Open With Metric Studio within the properties of the package.*

Accessing Metrics

Metrics can be accessed using any of the four navigation buttons in the bottom of the left pane in Cognos Metric Studio: My Folders, Scorecards, Metric Types, and Strategies. To access information about a metric, simply click the metric name in the Name column in the right pane.

Each metric is assigned a home scorecard. When you are viewing a metric, at the top left of the right pane, you will see the metric's home scorecard with a "breadcrumb trail" and the metric type of the metric. The home scorecard indicates where the metric is loaded, but you can create a shortcut to a metric on any scorecard.

At the top of each tab within a metric is a table that displays the actual results of a metric in comparison to the planned value for the selected period. At the top-right of the pane (above the tabs) is the period with which the values are associated. Click this link to choose another period to view.

History

The History tab of a metric shows a trend chart of the metric's historical values. The metric history chart reflects the actual results as blue dots connected by a line, the planned values (target) as green diamond shapes, and the range in which the metric is acceptable (tolerance) as vertical yellow lines. A metric's history chart makes it simple to identify the status and trend of a metric. This is also the location in Cognos Metric Studio where you can manually enter values for a metric or simply view the individual values by year. Click the Enter Values button (the yellow pencil icon) in the upper-right corner to access the values for a metric.

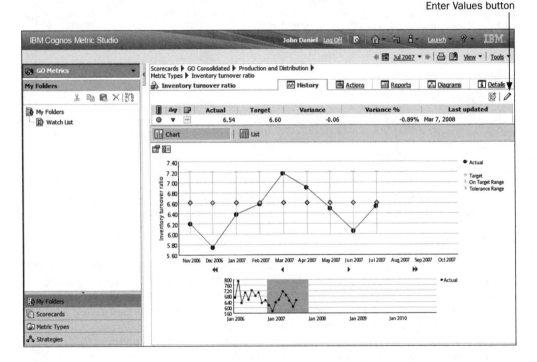

Actions and Projects

Users can create actions to define short-term goals for a metric by specifying the goal and progress marks such as dates to start and finish the goal. Projects can be created using metrics on a scorecard to define long-term goals for a set of metrics. Actions are a collection of goals for one metric defined at the metric level, while projects are a collection of goals for metrics on a scorecard defined at the scorecard level.

Reports

The Reports tab provides an area to associate information that may provide additional insight into the performance of a metric. Reports can be attached to several Cognos Metric Studio items such as metrics, scorecards, metric types, and strategies. You can link a Cognos BI report or any other report accessible by a URL. Multiple reports can be associated with an item, while one is set as the default. The report set as the default will display when you are accessing the Reports tab, and you can access any associated additional reports from the bottom of the Reports tab.

Diagrams

In the Diagrams tab, you can see diagrams that visually represent a metric's performance. *Custom diagrams* can include maps or other bitmaps to help illustrate the context of the metric. *Impact diagrams* illustrate the influence of metrics on each other. You can specify which items impact another and how they do so. Diagrams can be created for Cognos Metric Studio items such as metrics, scorecards, and metric types. Items referenced in a diagram provide a direct link to that item. Relationships in diagrams can link to strategy elements, metrics, other diagrams, and projects. Items referenced in another item's impact diagram will show that relationship on the item's own diagram.

You might, for example, have a diagram for a Revenue metric, showing that it is impacted by a Product Cost and a Quantity Sold metric, as shown next:

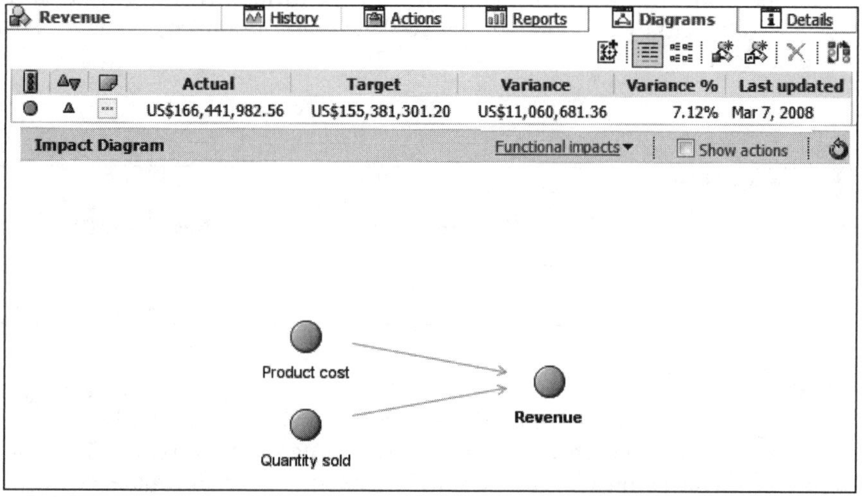

When you view the diagram for Product Cost, you will see that the metric impacts Revenue, as shown next:

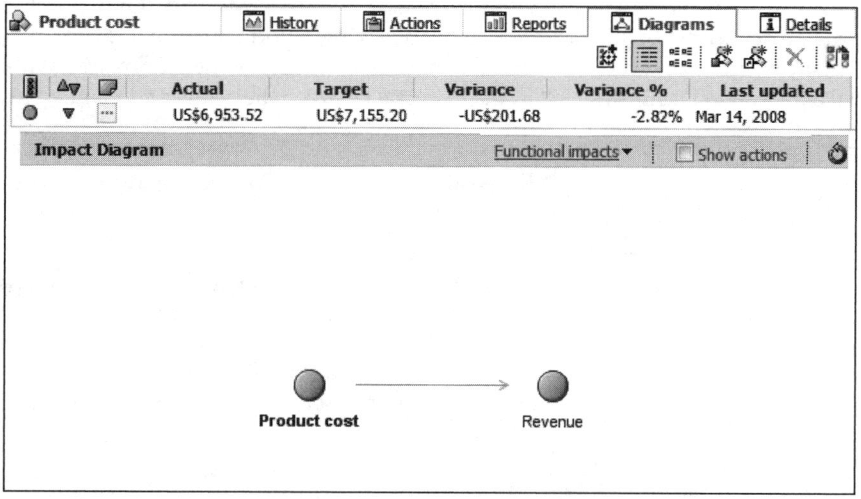

Details

In the Details tab, you can specify general properties and information associated with an item. Details can be specified for Cognos Metric Studio items such as metrics, scorecards, metric types, and strategies. The name, description, language, owner, and permissions for an item are defined in this tab, as well as other properties specific to the type of item.

My Folders

The My Folders area within Cognos Metric Studio lets you keep an eye on any metrics of interest to you. This area will automatically include an "accountability" scorecard, a list of metrics that you own. It also includes a watch list of metrics you choose to watch. Adding metrics to your watch list creates a shortcut to the metrics. From here, you can also set up e-mail notifications for any metrics for which you are the owner. You can quickly add a metric to your Watch List by clicking the Add To Watch List button (shown next) within any of the tabs of a metric.

Add To Watch List button

Scorecards

Metrics can be grouped, organized, and secured using scorecards. Scorecards group together metrics that are relevant to a particular group of users or part of the business. To see more information about a metric on a scorecard, simply click the metric link in the Name column. The Projects, Reports, and Diagrams tabs provide areas to specify long-term metric goals and include additional information associated with a scorecard.

For example, you could create a "Finance" scorecard for your accounting department with metrics such as "Gross Profit Margin %," "Revenue," "Product Cost," and "Employee Expense" to provide the department with indicators of the business important to them. The Metrics tab of this Finance scorecard, shown next, would show an overview of the four metrics with values for actual and planned results as well as the variance between the actual and planned results:

Metric link

Each metric is loaded onto a home scorecard, but any number of scorecards can be created to suit your business needs, and any number of shortcuts can be made for a metric and added to your scorecards.

NOTE *A metric must have a home scorecard.*

To add a metric shortcut to a scorecard, follow these steps:

1. In Cognos Metric Studio, navigate to the scorecard for which you want to add a metric shortcut.

2. On the Metrics tab of the scorecard, click the Add Shortcuts To Metrics button on the toolbar:

Add Shortcuts To Metrics button

Actual	Target	Variance	Variance %	Time Period
44.02%	42.50%	1.52%	3.58%	Jul 2007

3. In the Select Metrics dialog, find the metric you want to add to the scorecard using one of the following methods:

   • Use the Navigate tab to locate the desired metric by its home scorecard or its metric type.

   • Use the Search tab to search for the desired metric by name, description, or owner.

4. Select the check box next to the metric(s) you want to add.

5. Click the OK button. The metric shortcut is added to the scorecard.

To order metrics on a scorecard, follow these steps:

1. In Cognos Metric Studio, navigate to the scorecard for which you want to order the metrics.

2. Open the Metrics tab of the scorecard, and click the Order Metrics button on the toolbar:

Order Metrics button

Metrics	Projects	Reports	Diagrams	Details

[Metrics: 1-4]

Actual	Target	Variance	Variance %	Time Period
44.02%	42.50%	1.52%	3.58%	Jul 2007

3. In the Order Metrics dialog, select a metric name and choose Up, Down, To Top, or To Bottom to move the metric to the desired position:

Order Metrics - Finance

Explicitly set the order of the metrics for this scorecard.

Gross profit margin %
Revenue
Product cost
Employee expense

Up Down To Top To Bottom

4. Repeat step 3 until all the metrics are rearranged in the desired order.

5. Click the OK button. The metrics are reordered as specified.

Metric Types

A *metric type* specifies the properties for a group of metrics that are of a similar type. Metrics of the same metric type share similarities such as performance pattern, definition, and tolerance type. In conjunction with the target for a metric, performance pattern and tolerance determine the area in which a metric qualifies as Excellent (green), Average (yellow), or Poor (red). A metric must have a metric type. A metric type can have any number of metrics associated with it, but a metric can have only one metric type.

For example, a business may have a "Quantity sold" metric for each of five regions within the organization, and an overall "Quantity sold" metric for the entire organization. All six of these metrics would be of the same metric type, because they would share properties such as the performance pattern (above the target is positive—higher quantities sold are good!) and tolerance type (percentage of target).

To create a new metric type, follow these steps:

1. In Cognos Metric Studio, click Metric Types at the bottom of the left pane.

2. Click the New Metric Type button at the top of the left pane.

3. On the General tab, in the Name text box, specify a name for the metric type.

4. Optionally, specify a Description and/or Technical Description for the metric type.

5. Change any of the other desired General properties from their defaults:

- **Language**   Language in which the metric type will display
- **Owner**   User responsible for the metric type
- **Identification Code**   Unique identifier for the metric type
- **Calendar Details**   Level at which values will be stored and displayed; Month is the most commonly used setting
- **Unit**   Whether the values of the metrics for this type will be in dollars, as a percentage, or as a generic number

6. Click the Columns And Calculations tab.

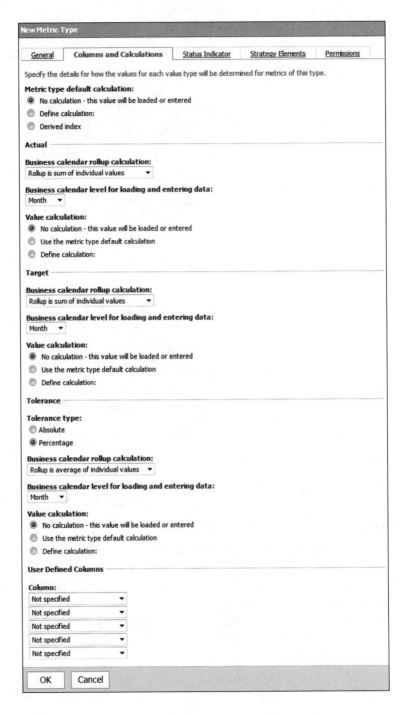

7. Change any of the desired Columns And Calculations properties from their default values:

- **Metric Type Default Calculation**   Whether the values for this metric type will be loaded (either from flat files or from Cognos Metric Designer extracts), defined by a calculation you specify, or derived from other metrics

- **Business Calendar Rollup Calculation**   How the values are calculated for segments of the business calendar that are not loaded (usually quarters and years). For example, suppose an Employee Count metric has values of 11 for January, 9 for February, and 10 for March. The Quarter 1 rollup would be 30 if rollup is set to Sum, 10 if set to Average, 9 if set to Minimum, 11 if set to Maximum, 11 if set to First, and 10 if set to Last. If set to Supplied By Client, Cognos Metric Studio will use the rollup defined in the metric load.

- **Value Calculation**   How the actual, target, or tolerance is calculated. This property determines whether values are not calculated by Cognos Metric Studio (loaded or manually entered), the same as the Metric Type Default Calculation, or use their own calculation.

- **Tolerance Type**   Tolerance is the range from the target that a metric qualifies as average (yellow). This property determines whether the tolerance is defined by a general number (absolute) or a percentage. For example, if the target for a metric is 10 and the tolerance is defined as 10, the Excellent (green) zone for the metric is between 0 and 20 if set to Absolute or between 9 and 11 if set to Percentage (10 percent of the target is 1).

- **User Defined Columns**   Include additional values for comparison with the metric.

8. Click the Status Indicator tab.

9. Select the performance pattern from the following options:

- **Above Target Is Positive**   Higher values are more favorable than lower values; values above the target or highest threshold are Excellent (green), values below the tolerance or lowest threshold are Poor (red), and values within the tolerance or the two thresholds are Average (yellow). For example, a "Revenue" metric would be set to Above Target Is Positive.

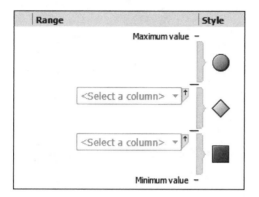

- **Below Target Is Positive**   Lower values are more favorable than higher values; values below the target or lowest threshold are Excellent (green), values above the tolerance or highest threshold are Poor (red), and values within the tolerance or between the two thresholds are Average (yellow). For example, a "Number of Returns" metric would be set to Below Target Is Positive.

- **On Target Is Positive**   Values within half the tolerance range on either side of the target or in the middle of set thresholds are Excellent (green), values one tolerance range outside of the green zone or between the first set of thresholds and a second set are Average (yellow), and values outside the tolerance range or the second set of thresholds are Poor (red).

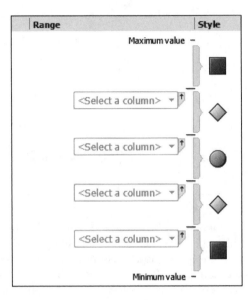

10. Optionally, change the score calculation so that target boundaries can be set with user-defined columns.

11. To specify strategy elements included with the metric type, use the Strategy Elements tab.

12. To specify permissions for the metric type other than the default (Everyone), use the Permissions tab.

13. When finished defining all properties, click the OK button. The metric type is created and appears in the Metric Type list in the left pane.

TIP *To modify metric type properties for an existing metric type, navigate to the Details tab of the metric type and click the Set Properties button.*

Strategies

Use strategies to organize metrics in meaningful ways for your business and to determine whether strategic objectives are being met. Strategy elements group metrics with similar goals, and a strategy groups together all the pieces of the strategy elements beneath it. Strategies can be accessed from the menu in the left pane in Cognos Metric Studio. Strategies and strategy elements are created and organized in the left pane in Cognos Metric Studio, while the metrics and metric types that are part of strategy elements are defined in the right pane.

The following illustration shows the metrics of the strategy elements (Grow Revenue, Improve Margin, and Reduce Cost) that are a part of the Finance strategy element. In this example, the Finance strategy element was chosen from the GO Strategies strategy in the left pane of Cognos Metric Studio.

Strategies ▶ GO Strategies ▶							
Finance ▶				Metrics	Projects	Reports	Details

No filter ▼							
Finance						■ 0 ◇ 0 ● 4 ⌃	
Grow revenue						■ 0 ◇ 0 ● 1 ⌃	
	A▽		**Name**	**Actual**	**Target**	**Variance**	**Variance %**	**Time Period**
●	▲	···	Revenue	US$166,441,982.56	US$155,381,301.20	US$11,060,681.36	7.12%	Jul 2007
Improve margin						■ 0 ◇ 0 ● 1 ⌃	
	A▽		**Name**	**Actual**	**Target**	**Variance**	**Variance %**	**Time Period**
●	—	···	Gross profit margin %	44.02%	42.50%	1.52%	3.58%	Jul 2007
Reduce cost						■ 0 ◇ 0 ● 2 ⌃	
	A▽		**Name**	**Actual**	**Target**	**Variance**	**Variance %**	**Time Period**
●	▽	···	Product cost	US$6,953.52	US$7,155.20	-US$201.68	-2.82%	Jul 2007
●	▲	···	Employee expense	US$5,114,499.60	US$5,213,900.00	-US$99,400.40	-1.91%	Jul 2007

Metric Security

Within Cognos Metric Studio, security can be set for a number of items, such as scorecards, metric types, strategies, and metrics, so that information is displayed to the appropriate users. Security is applied by setting the permissions on the Permissions tab accessed through the Details of an item.

Cognos Metric Designer

Cognos Metric Designer is a client application with which you can define and organize metrics to load them into Cognos Metric Studio. Cognos Metric Designer can help you achieve automation with your organization's metrics by providing the tools to create metrics extracts and publish them to Cognos Connection. A *metrics extract* is a set of specifications for a metric, including scorecard mappings, time period(s) for which the metric will be populated, the metric type, and definitions for the actual, target, and tolerance settings.

Once published to Cognos Connection, metrics extracts can be scheduled similarly to other Cognos Connection entries, which means you can set them up to execute on a regular basis so that updating metrics does not require manual intervention.

Create a Cognos Metric Designer Project

To create a new Cognos Metric Designer project, follow these steps:

1. Open Metric Designer. The Welcome page displays:

2. Click the Create A New Project link in the Welcome page.
3. In the New Project dialog, type a name for the project.

4. Optionally, change the location of the new project from the default.
5. Click the OK button.

6. Log on with your IBM Cognos credentials, and then click OK:

7. In the Create Metric Package Reference dialog, specify the metric package you want to link to the project:

8. Click OK to set the metric package for the project.
9. Click the No button to deny launching the Metrics Extract wizard. You now have a new Cognos Metric Designer project.

Import Sources

Import sources provide a link between metrics extracts and the data used to load the metrics. Packages in Cognos Connection (relational or dimensional) and Impromptu Query Definitions (IQDs) can be used as import sources. For IBM Cognos PowerCube import sources, time mappings must be made between the dates in the cube and the dates in the metric store.

To create an import source for a package, follow these steps:

1. Within a Metric Designer project, right-click Import Sources in the left pane. Then select Create | Package Import Source.

2. Specify a name for the import source.

TIP   *It is useful to name the import source the same as the package so that it is easily identifiable.*

3. Click Next.

4. Select a package from Cognos Connection for the import source.

5. Click Finish. The new import source is now listed in the left pane.

To set up time mappings for a cube package import source, follow these steps:

1. In Cognos Metric Designer, right-click a cube package import source, and select Edit Metric Studio Time Mappings.

2. In the Time And Currency Mappings pane, map the years, quarters, and months between the cube and the metric store by click the ellipsis buttons in the Data Mapping column:

Time and Currency Mappings		☒
Specify business calendar mappings		

Specify the data mappings for each business calendar level.

Business calendar levels:

Year
Quarter
Month

Dec 31, 2010   [▦▾] [◁][◁◁][▷▷][▷]

Business calendar members:

Name	Data Mapping	
2006 (Jan 1, 2006 - Dec 31, 2006)	**2006**	···
2007 (Jan 1, 2007 - Dec 31, 2007)	2007	···
2008 (Jan 1, 2008 - Dec 31, 2008)		···
2009 (Jan 1, 2009 - Dec 31, 2009)		···
2010 (Jan 1, 2010 - Dec 31, 2010)		···

Up   Down   To top   To bottom   Remove   Remove all

☑ Automatically update the time mappings when new times are added to the cube.

[Cancel]   [< Back]   [Next >]   [Finish]

3. Check the Automatically Update The Time Mappings When New Times Are Added To The Cube check box so that when new months, quarters, or years are added to the cube they are automatically mapped to the next period in the metric store.

4. Click Next.

5. Set the currency mappings for the cube.

6. Click Next.

7. Select the dimensions you want to display as reports in Cognos Metric Studio.

8. Click Finish. The time mappings have been set for the import source.

Create a Metrics Extract from a Cube Package Source

To create a metrics extract from a cube, follow these steps:

1. Within a Cognos Metric Designer project, right-click the metric package reference in the left pane and select Create, and then Metrics Extract, as shown here:

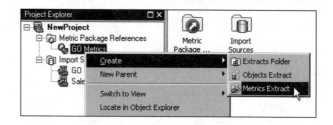

2. Specify a name for the metrics extract. For this example, type **Revenue by Retailer**.

3. Click Next.

4. Select the cube import source you want to use to create the metrics extract. For this example, choose the Sales and Marketing cube from the IBM Cognos v10.1 samples.

5. Click Next. The Scorecard Mapping dialog displays:

![Create Extract - Scorecard Mapping dialog]

6. Drag items from the Available Objects pane to the New Scorecard Levels pane to create the scorecard hierarchy. For this example, we insert the different levels of retailers from the Retailers dimension in the cube:

The attribute values are filled in automatically based on values in the cube. Identification code values are based on category codes for the corresponding items as specified in the Cognos Transformer cube model.

NOTE *The identification code for each Cognos Metric Studio scorecard must be unique and cannot be used anywhere else in the metric store. When you load metrics, you must use consistent, predictable, and repeatable identification codes for scorecards so that each metric is loaded to the correct scorecard.*

7. Select a Parent Scorecard for the hierarchy you have defined if it is beneath another scorecard in Cognos Metric Studio. For this example, we select GO Consolidated (Admin support).

8. Click Next. The Time Periods Filtering dialog displays:

9. Select a time period for which you want to load data into the metric store from the metrics extract:

   - **Use All Time Periods** All time periods mapped between the cube and the metric store are populated.

   - **Use The Current Time Period** Only the current time period (based on the system date) is populated.

   - **Use The Last Completed Period** Only the time period one period before the current is populated.

   - **Use The Selected Time Periods** Manually select the time periods you want to populate. This option is useful for loading history when you do not want to use all periods mapped between the cube and the metric store.

10. Click Next. The Metric Mappings screen displays:

11. From the cube's Measures dimension in the Available Objects pane, drag the measure you want to use for the extract to the Metric Mappings pane. For this example, drag the Revenue measure from the cube. In the Metric Attributes pane, the path to the measure appears in the Value column of the Actual attribute.

TIP *To modify the expression for any of the attribute values, click the ellipsis button in the row for the value you want to modify. You can create calculations to populate metrics with values that do not exist in the cube.*

12. From the Metric Type drop-down list, select the metric type associated with the extract. For this example, choose Revenue By Retailer.

13. Define a value for the Target attribute by inserting a measure or clicking the ellipsis and defining an expression. For this example, insert the Planned Revenue measure from the cube.

14. Define a value for the Tolerance attribute by inserting a measure or clicking the ellipsis and defining an expression. For this example, set the tolerance to 0.1, so that it is 10 percent of the target.

15. Select a value for the Aggregate Function attribute to determine how the detail values will aggregate. For this example, choose Automatic.

16. Select a value for the Rollup Aggregate Function attribute to determine how the summary values will aggregate. For this example, choose Summarize.

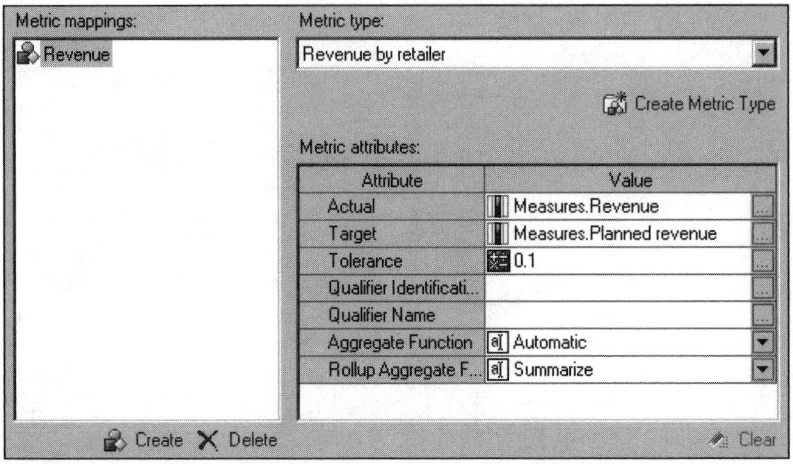

Attribute	Value
Actual	Measures.Revenue
Target	Measures.Planned revenue
Tolerance	0.1
Qualifier Identificati...	
Qualifier Name	
Aggregate Function	Automatic
Rollup Aggregate F...	Summarize

17. To apply a filter to the values returned by the definitions specified above, click the Create link under Metric Filters, and then specify an expression. For example, it is possible to limit Revenue By Retailer metrics to the three most popular order methods by creating a metric filter.

18. Click Next. The Filter Data dialog displays, as shown here:

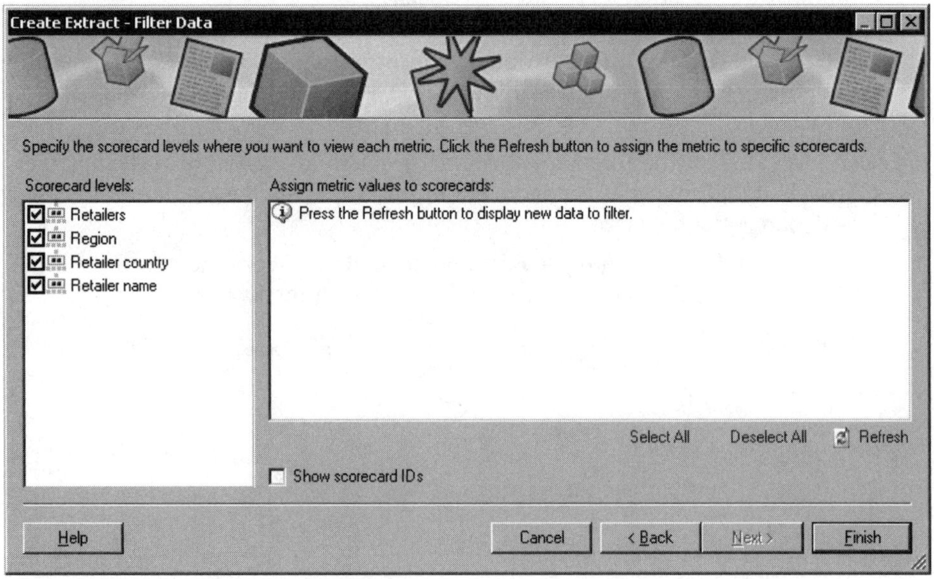

19. To view the scorecards that will be populated by the metrics extract, click the Refresh link.

```
Assign metric values to scorecards:
⊟ ✓ ▼ 🖿 Retailers
   ⊟ ✓ ▼ 🖿 Americas
      ⊞ ✓ ▼ 🖿 United States
      ⊞ ✓ ▼ 🖿 Canada
      ⊞ ✓ ▼ 🖿 Mexico
      ⊞ ✓ ▼ 🖿 Brazil
   ⊞ ✓ ▼ 🖿 Asia Pacific
   ⊞ ✓ ▼ 🖿 Northern Europe
   ⊞ ✓ ▼ 🖿 Central Europe
   ⊞ ✓ ▼ 🖿 Southern Europe


                              Select All    Deselect All    ⊘ Refresh

☐ Show scorecard IDs


              Cancel      < Back      Next >      Finish
```

TIP *Check the Show Scorecard IDs check box to make the scorecard identification codes appear next to the scorecard names. This is useful to help you ensure that the scorecard IDs are what you expect.*

20. To exclude any of the items, click the green check mark next to the item.

TIP *You can exclude lower level values from building metrics while still including the values in totals by selecting Hide Metric Value But Include In Totals from the drop-down menu on an item.*

21. Click Finish.

22. To validate the extract, choose Yes.

23. If no errors are found, click OK. If errors are found, address the issues and revalidate. The extract is created:

```
Project Explorer                      ☐ ✕
⊟ 🖺 NewProject
   ⊟ 📁 Metric Package References
      ⊟ 📦 GO Metrics
         └ 📊 Retailer by Revenue
   ⊟ 📁 Import Sources
      ├ 📊 GO Sales (query)
      └ 📊 Sales and Marketing (cube)
```

Create a Metrics Extract from a Relational Package

To create a metrics extract from a relational package, follow these steps:

1. Within a Cognos Metric Designer project, right-click the metric package reference in the left pane and select Create, and then Metrics Extract.

2. Specify a name for the metrics extract. For this example, use Gross Profit Margin.

3. Click Next.

4. Select the package import source you want to use to create a metrics extract. For this example, choose the GO Data Warehouse (Query) package.

5. Click Next. The Scorecard Mapping dialog displays.

6. Drag items from the Available Objects pane to the New Scorecard Levels pane to create the scorecard hierarchy, or create the hierarchy manually. The value used for the identification code should be the unique identifier for the scorecard to which you want the metrics to map. The value used for the name should be the name of the scorecard to which the metrics map. For this example, create two levels and manually specify the values for each level so that the scorecards are populated correctly.

New scorecard levels:		Level attributes:	
New Level		Attribute	Value
New Level1		Identification Code	'FINANCE_SC'
		Name	'Finance'
		Description	
		Language Code	
		Owner	
		Owner Namespace	
		Append Scorecard ...	Yes
			Clear

TIP *The identification code for an existing scorecard can be found on the Details tab of the scorecard in Cognos Metric Studio. It is useful to verify the scorecard ID in this location if you are manually entering the identification code in the extract.*

7. Select Yes for the Append Scorecard attribute to concatenate scorecard levels together.

NOTE *The identification code for each scorecard must be unique and cannot be used anywhere else in the metric store. When you load metrics, you must have consistent, predictable, and repeatable identification codes for scorecards so that each metric is loaded to the correct scorecard.*

8. Select a Parent Scorecard for the hierarchy you have defined if it is beneath another scorecard in Cognos Metric Studio. For this example, do not specify a parent scorecard.

9. Click Next. The Time Hierarchy Mapping dialog displays.

10. Enter a value for the attributes that you want to load data into from the metrics extract. You can use a date from the package or use a date function to calculate a date. For this example, use the current_date function for the Month attribute to load values for current period.

11. Click Next. The Metrics Mapping dialog displays.

12. From the Available Objects pane, drag the data item to the Metric Mappings pane you want to use to create the definition of the Actual. For this example, we use the Gross Margin measure from the package. The path to the measure appears in the Value for the Actual attribute.

TIP   To modify the expression for any of the attribute values, click the ellipsis button in the row for the value you want to modify. You can create calculations to populate metrics with values that do not exist in the package.

13. From the Metric Type drop-down menu, select the metric type associated with the extract. For this example, choose Gross Profit Margin %.

14. Define a value for the Target attribute by inserting a measure or clicking the ellipsis and defining an expression. For this example, enter **0.425**.

15. Define a value for the Tolerance attribute by inserting a measure or clicking the ellipsis and defining an expression. For this example, enter **0.025**.

16. Select a value for the Aggregate Function attribute to determine how the detail values will aggregate. For this example, choose Average.

17. Select a value for the Rollup Aggregate Function attribute to determine how the summary values will aggregate. For this example, choose Average.

18. To apply a filter to the values returned by the definitions specified above, click the Create link under Metric Filters and specify an expression.

19. Click Next. The Filter Data screen displays.

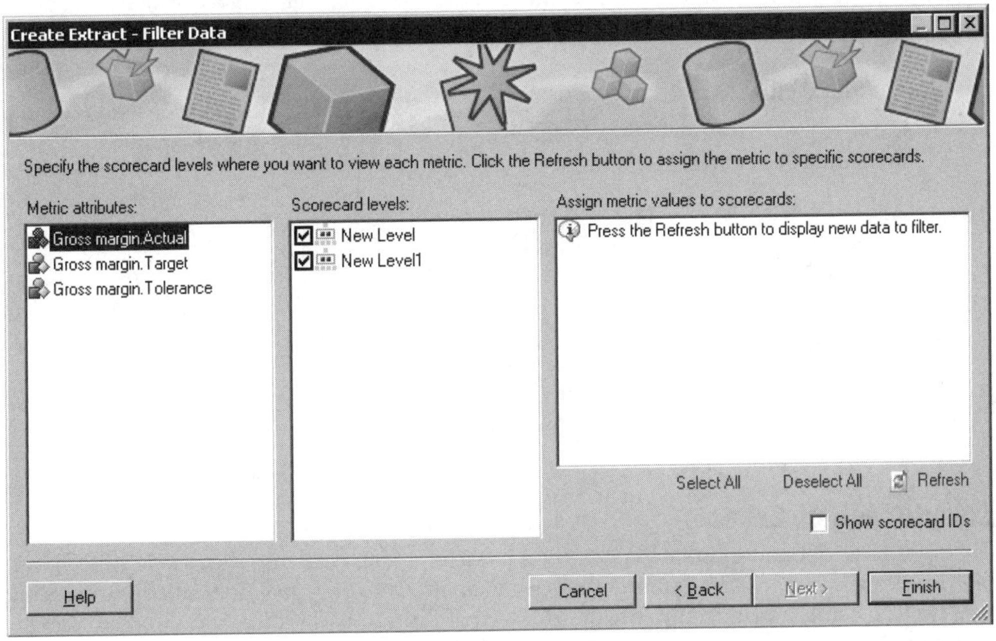

20. To view the scorecards that will be populated by the metrics extract, click the Refresh link.

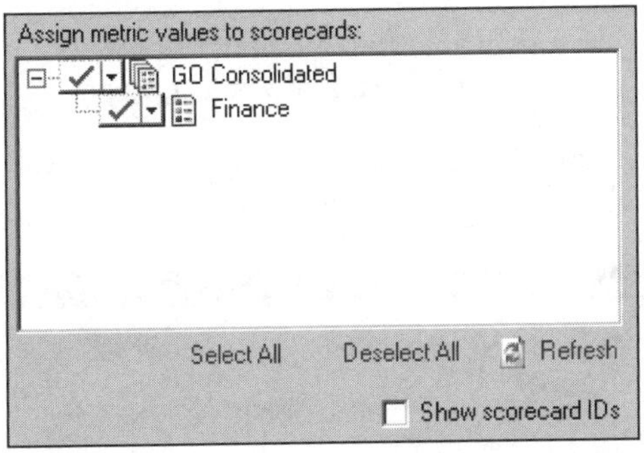

TIP *Check the Show Scorecard IDs check box for the scorecard identification codes to appear next to the scorecard names. This is useful to ensure that the scorecard IDs are what you expect them to be.*

21. To exclude any of the items, click the green checkmark next to the item.

TIP   *You can exclude lower level values from building while still including the values in totals by selecting Hide Metric Value But Include In Totals from the drop-down menu on an item.*

22. Click Finish.

23. To validate the extract, choose Yes.

24. If no errors are found, click OK. If errors are found, address the issues and revalidate. The extract is created:

Execute Metrics Extracts

Once you have defined metrics extracts, you need to get the data into the metric store. Metrics extracts can either be written directly to an intermediary location called the "staging area" before being transferred to the metric store or written to flat files that can then loaded to the staging area. After metrics have been loaded to the staging area, you must transfer them into the metric store through Cognos Connection metric maintenance.

When extracts are written to flat files, you can see the data that is created by the extract or have access to the data for modification. For example, you might have created a calculation for the Actual attribute in the extract definition. You can write the results to a flat file to view the results to ensure that you formulated the calculation correctly.

To execute an extract to the staging area, follow these steps:

1. Within a Cognos Metric Designer project, right-click the extract you want to execute and choose Execute. The Execute Extract dialog displays.

2. Under Options, select Write To Metric Staging Area.

3. Click OK.

4. If the execution is successful, click OK. If errors are found, address the issues and execute again.

To execute an extract to flat files, follow these steps:

1. Within a Cognos Metric Designer project, right-click the extract you want to execute and choose Execute.

2. Under Options, select Write To Files.

3. Specify the location for the files to be created.

4. Click OK to execute the extract.

5. If the execution is successful, click OK. If errors are found, address the issues and execute again.

6. Navigate to the location of the files, and open the CMV file in a text editor.

The CMV file is a specially formatted tab-delimited text file. The number of tabs between values indicates which properties the values are loaded into in the metric store. "A" indicates an actual, "O" indicates a tolerance, and "T" indicates a target.

NOTE *Tab-delimited files can be manually created and then loaded into Cognos Metric Studio to populate values. Routines can be written to output data from systems in an acceptable tab-delimited format and saved in an import source location. Metric maintenance tasks can then be used to import the data into the metric store. Please refer to the Cognos Metric Studio user guide for more information.*

Publish to Cognos Connection

To automate metrics extracts to update regularly, you must publish extracts to Cognos Connection. Once an extract definition is in Cognos Connection, it can be scheduled like other Cognos Connection entries. From Cognos Connection, users have web access to extracts, so that they can be executed manually if necessary without accessing Cognos Metric Designer. For example, a data update might have occurred during the week for an extract that is scheduled to execute only on Sundays. A user can manually execute the extract through Cognos Connection, without requiring access to Cognos Metric Designer.

To publish an extract to Cognos Connection, right-click on the extract in Cognos Metric Designer and select Publish To Content Store. By default, extracts publish within the metric package in Cognos Connection.

Published metrics extracts

Ensure that Scorecards Have Unique ID Codes

If you discover that newly transferred metric data is not displayed on the intended scorecard, nine times out of ten, the problem lies with the identification code. The identification code must be unique, predictable, and repeatable. If it is not, you will run into problems such as metrics not populating the expected scorecards and new scorecards with unpredictable names.

To ensure unique scorecard IDs, within the extract definition, you can set the scorecards to append the identification codes for the higher levels. This does not ensure predictability, however. Predictability is best executed by creating a clear, meaningful schema of identification codes for your scorecard hierarchies, and then ensuring that this schema is utilized when loading metrics.

Choose the Best Time Setting

When creating a metric extract from a cube package source, you are asked to identify what time period of data to gather. Although the choices seem obvious, you might not always get what you expect unless you understand what the various choices mean. The following descriptions should help you determine which to select.

Use All Time Periods

All time periods mapped between the cube and the metric store are populated. This setting is great for loading historical data quickly. The caveat is that you might get too much data. A metric store always includes all periods for the current year. If the cube includes periods beyond the current period, and they are mapped to the metric store in the import source, metrics will populate for each of these periods. For example, suppose it is March and you want to load metric data only through March, but your cube contains data through December. With All Time Periods selected, metrics will be built and populated through December. By default, Cognos Metric Studio displays the most recent period for a metric, so the December metric is what will appear on scorecards, which is not the desired result.

Use the Current Time Period

The current time period is based on the system date. The Current Month category from the PowerCube is not used as you might expect. Cognos Metric Studio uses the time period in which the system date falls. This setting is useful for metrics that correlate with real time, such as Employee Count.

Use the Last Completed Period

The last completed period is the period prior to the current time period (as defined in the preceding section). This setting is useful for metrics that do not have real-time value because they require an entire completed period for relevance. Financial information usually requires a completed period for the values to make sense. For example, if a Revenue metric at the month level builds on the 3rd of the month for the current period, the actual value will include only three days of revenue, which would be far less than the other months' values, as they would reflect entire months.

Use the Selected Time Periods

Use this setting if you need to specify the time periods for metrics to load. You can use this setting for troubleshooting or loading specific time periods. For example, in April you decide you want to change the target for the current year for a metric that usually builds only the current period. This option allows you to select the four months of the year so far to reload the values. This setting is generally not used for production, because it is not dynamic.

Metric Maintenance

In Cognos Metric Studio, a number of maintenance tasks can be performed for metrics. Metric maintenance tasks can be accessed from Cognos Connection inside the metric package folder or from the Tools menu in Cognos Metric Studio.

You can perform the following metric maintenance tasks:

- **Import Data From Files Into Staging Area**   Imports data from flat files to the staging area. The location(s) from which files are imported are defined within

Import Sources, available from the Tools menu in Cognos Metric Studio. Tab-delimited files either manually created or written from Cognos Metric Designer are copied into an import source location, and then you run this task to load the files to the staging area.

- **Transfer Data From Staging Area Into Metric Store**   Transfers the data loaded into the staging area into the metric store. When extracts are executed or data is imported from files, the data is in the staging area. This task moves the data from the intermediary staging area to the metric store.

- **Import And Transfer Data From Files Into Metric Store**   This task combines the previous two tasks.

- **Recalculate Metric Store Derived Values**   Forces the scores, derived values, and summary values to compute again. This task needs to be executed after manually entering values or after data is loaded.

- **Synchronize Metric Store Users With External Namespaces**   Updates the metric store with user information from the external namespaces configured for Cognos BI.

- **Update Search Engine Index**   Updates the index used for searching Cognos Metric Studio. After new items are loaded, you should run this task so that the new items are indexed.

- **Clear Staging Area Rejected Data Logs**   Metric data that has been rejected ends up in designated tables in the metric store. Rejects do not get cleared automatically. It is a good idea to run this task after loading a number of new metrics or after troubleshooting.

- **Clear Metric History Data Only**   Clears the actuals, targets, and user-defined columns for all metrics in the selected metric store. This option clears all values but leaves the metric store calendar intact.

- **Clear Metric History And Calendar Data**   Clears the actuals, targets, and user-defined columns for all metrics in the selected metric store as well as any calendar data. This option completely resets the metric store. You should run this task only when you want to start from scratch.

Be Careful When Clearing Metric Data

The Clear Metric History Data Only and the Clear Metric History And Calendar Data tasks delete *all* of the metric data in the selected metric store. When you select either of these functions, IBM Cognos does not display an "Are you sure?" prompt. Imagine how catastrophic it would be to click this link and delete all of your work with no Undo command! We recommend that you disable these functions or change their permissions to avoid loss of information.

To disable an entry, follow these steps:

1. Click the Set Properties button in the Actions column of the entry you want to disable.

2. On the General tab, select the Disable This Entry check box.

3. Click OK.

Administration
of IBM Cognos 10

IBM Cognos Framework Manager Fundamentals

Many people new to IBM Cognos Framework Manager think of it as nothing more than a GUI tool used to map source database columns to query items for presentation to the business user. This misconception is especially strong among database administrators, database designers, and anyone else familiar with relational databases—based on direct, painful, and personal experience. It took some time to understand that Cognos Framework Manager is more about educating the query engine on how to structure the query than about modeling based on the data that is in the database. Although Cognos Framework Manager is used to perform mappings, organize metadata, and present that metadata to the business user, as important as those tasks are, they are a small fraction of what Cognos Framework Manager is intended to do.

The proper use of Cognos Framework Manager is critical to the success of your business intelligence (BI) effort. In our nearly 20 years of consulting with IBM Cognos and business analytics (BA), one situation will always, without exception, cause a BA initiative to struggle. That situation occurs when the business user loses confidence in the accuracy of the data they are receiving. A poorly designed Cognos Framework Manager model can produce incorrect or inconsistent results, either of which will shake the confidence of the business user—and that confidence is fragile to begin with. As such, the importance of understanding how to use Cognos Framework Manager properly cannot be overstated.

We are making the assumption that the modeler reading this chapter is starting from zero, that you have not been exposed to Cognos Framework Manager at all. Based on that assumption, the goal of this chapter is to introduce the mechanical concepts and processes that a Cognos Framework Manager modeler needs to understand to begin effectively using the tool. To discuss all of the features available in Cognos Framework Manager would require a book of its own. This chapter will get your modeler comfortable with the core concepts needed to build a solid model and package. If you are an experienced modeler, we encourage you to skim through the chapter to reinforce the fundamental tasks involved in working with Cognos Framework Manager.

NOTE *The authors are interested in hearing about your experiences with Cognos Framework Manager. If you would like to share those, send an e-mail to Book@JohnDaniel.com.*

A Crash Course in Model Design Accelerator

Prior to IBM Cognos Business Intelligence v10.1 (Cognos BI v10.1), the only way to start a new Cognos Framework Manager project was from a completely empty model. Version 10 introduced the Model Design Accelerator (MDA), a wizard that can jumpstart a new project. The MDA guides you through creating a single-fact star-schema model, with the additional benefit of automatically creating all the elements needed for a well-designed project.

Let's jump right in by creating a simple model using the MDA. In our sample model, Order Details will provide the facts and Branch, Product, Time Dimension, and Order Header will be our query subjects or dimensions. When we are done, we will have created an example of how a well-designed Cognos Framework Manager project should look. Throughout the chapter, we will discuss how to create similar objects manually.

1. Start Cognos Framework Manager and click the Create A New Project Using Model Design Accelerator link.

Model Design Accelerator link

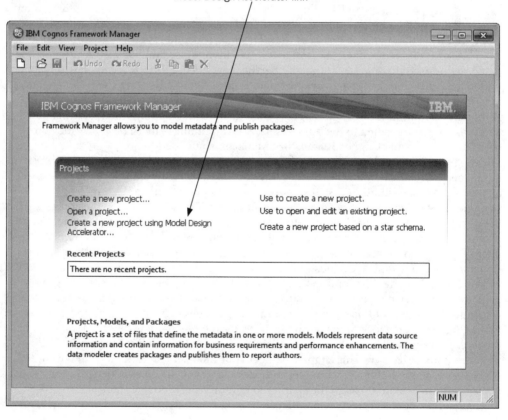

The New Project dialog opens:

2. Enter **MDA** as the Project Name and click OK. A Creating Project dialog is displayed, followed by the Select Language dialog:

3. Select the desired language and click OK. You'll see the Model Design Accelerator application followed by the Metadata Wizard – Select Data Source dialog.

4. Select the great_outdoors_sales sample data and click Next. The Metadata Wizard–Select Objects dialog will open.

5. Expand the GOSALES database and the Tables folder, and then click the check boxes to the left of BRANCH, ORDER_DETAILS, ORDER_HEADER, PRODUCT, and TIME_DIMENSION. Then click the Continue button.

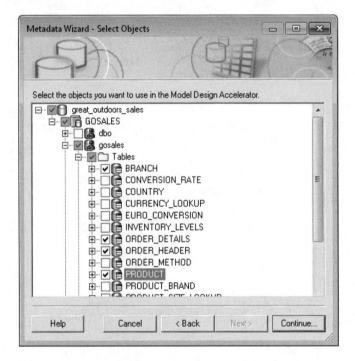

The Model Design Accelerator displays the imported metadata in the Explorer Tree and a star-schema template in the Model Design Accelerator window. The template shows a Fact Query Subject in the center, with four New Query Subjects surrounding the Fact Query Subject.

NOTE *MDA will always create four New Query Subject templates regardless of the number of tables imported. You can add or delete the templates as needed.*

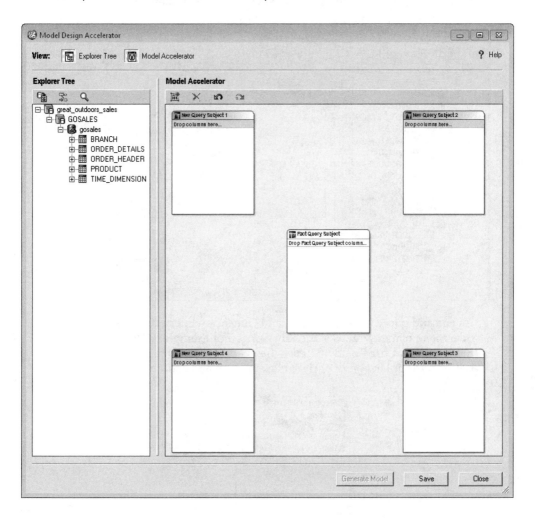

6. To add the facts to the model, open the ORDER_DETAILS table in the Explorer Tree, select the measures QUANTITY, UNIT_COST, UNIT_PRICE, and UNIT_SALE_PRICE. Drag-and-drop these items onto the Fact Query Subject.

7. As you add query items to the Fact and Dimension query subjects, replace the query item names with user-friendly names. For example, UNIT_COST can be renamed Unit Cost. To do this, click the query item to rename and press the F2 button on your keyboard; or right-click the item and choose Rename.

NOTE *When the wizard is complete, the names you provide will be used in the Business and Presentation Views, while the original names will be retained in the Database View.*

8. Add columns from the BRANCH table to the first Query Subject by right-clicking the BRANCH table and selecting Copy To New Query Subject 1. You can also select the fields you want in the query subject and drag-and-drop them, as you did in step 6.

Once the columns are in the New Query Subject, the MDA will automatically create a new relationship between the Fact Query Subject and the New Query Subject just modified.

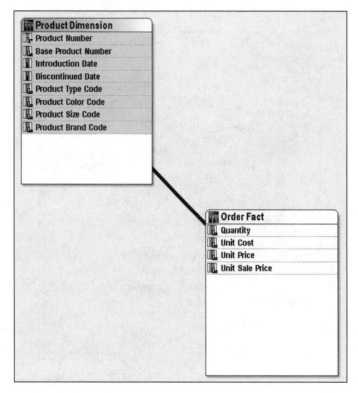

9. Add the ORDER_HEADER, PRODUCT, and TIME_DIMENSION tables to the remaining New Query Subject templates. Another way to add these is to click and

drag-and-drop the table name from the Explorer Tree to the New Query Subject template. Your model should look like the following:

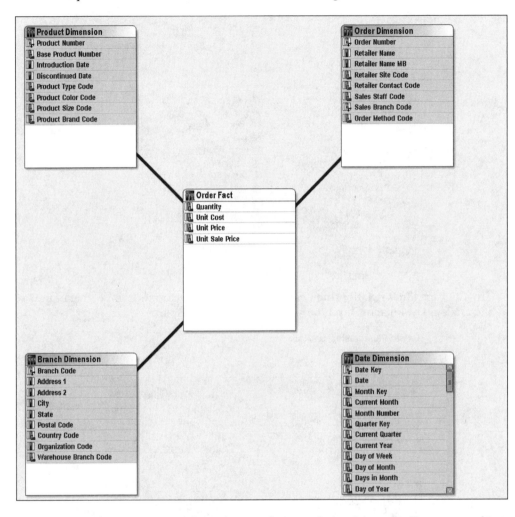

Notice the Date query subject does not have a relationship to the Fact query subject. Because there are no links in the database between the TIME_DIMENSION table and the ORDER_DETAIL table, MDA cannot know what the relationship should be. Next, you will manually add a relationship to fix this.

10. Double-click the New Query Subject template that is missing a join—the New Query Subject 3 template. The Query Subject Diagram dialog will open.

11. Click the Enter Relationship Creation Mode link in the upper-right corner of the dialog. The Relationship Editing Mode dialog will display.

Create Relationship icon

12. Click the DAY_DATE column of the TIME_DIMENSION table, and then CTRL-click the SHIP_DATE column of the ORDER_DETAILS table. Then click the Create Relationship icon at the upper-left corner of the dialog. The Modify The Relationship dialog will display.

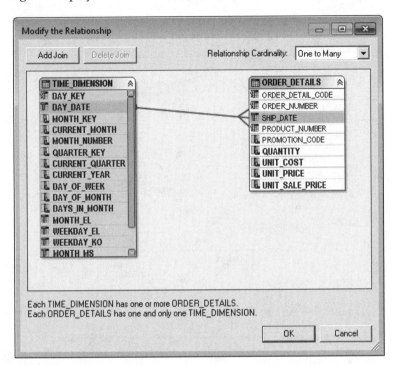

In this case, the relationship is defined correctly. If it were not defined correctly, you could change the cardinality, add joins, or delete unwanted joins.

NOTE *You can change the cardinality notation from the default, simplified crow's foot, to standard crow's foot or Merise by right-clicking anywhere on the dialog and selecting Options.*

PART IV

13. Click the OK button to return to the Relationship Editing Mode dialog, which will show the new join.

14. Click OK again to return to the Query Subject Diagram dialog.

15. Close the Query Subject Diagram by clicking the close box (the red X) in the upper-right corner, to return to the Model Design Accelerator window. Notice that the Branch Dimension table is joined directly to the Order Fact table. If you are familiar with the tables, you know that there is no direct join from Branch to Order Details. To see what is going on, look at the relationship created by the MDA.

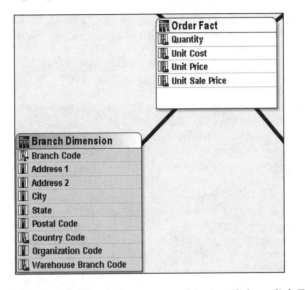

16. Double-click the Branch Dimension query subject, and then click Enter Relationship Creation Mode at the upper-right corner of the dialog to open the Relationship Editing Mode dialog:

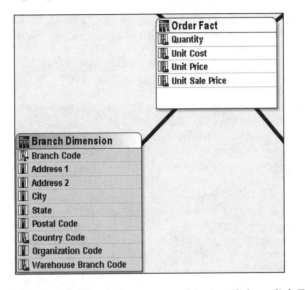

Notice two things in this illustration: The ORDER_HEADER table (renamed Order Dimension in our diagram) has been placed between the BRANCH and ORDER_ DETAILS tables. The MDA was able to determine that no direct join exists between ORDER_DETAILS and BRANCH, but it did find the BRANCH to ORDER_HEADER to ORDER_DETAILS join path. Also, the cardinality between the dimension tables BRANCH and ORDER_HEADER is one-to-many. In our modeling practice, we strongly recommend that joins between dimension tables be one-to-one or zero-to-one, because the use of "n's" (many) in a dimensional relation can result in ambiguous joins later on.

17. To alter the cardinality of a join from the Relationship Editing Mode dialog, double-click the join you want to modify to open the Modify The Relationship dialog.

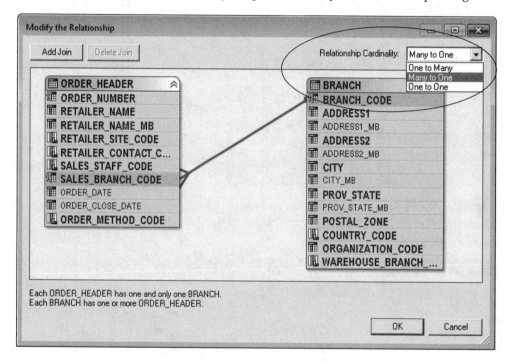

18. From the Relationship Cardinality drop-down menu, select One To One. Click the OK button to close the dialog. The join will now be one-to-one.

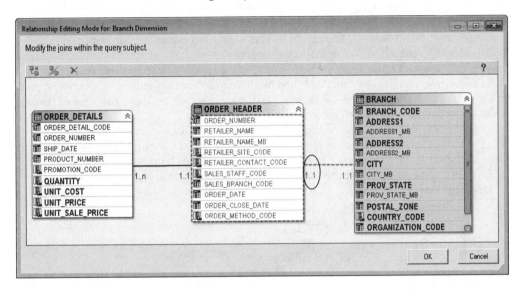

19. Click the OK button to exit the Relationship Editing Mode dialog and click the close box to close the Query Subject Diagram dialog.

20. If you have not already done so, rename the query subjects by right-clicking the header and typing a user-friendly name. For example, Fact Query Subject can be named Order Facts, New Query Subject 1 can be named Branch, New Query Subject 2 can be named Order Header, and so on.

21. Click the Generate Model button found at the bottom of the Model Design Accelerator window. You will be asked if you want to continue: click Yes.

The MDA will create and open the model.

NOTE *You can save your work at any time by clicking the Save button at the bottom of the Model Design Accelerator window. Resume your work by opening the saved Cognos Framework Manager project, clicking Tools, and then clicking Run Model Design Accelerator.*

The Results of the MDA

We do not like to use the term "best practice" because it carries a tone of finality. Although we may be splitting hairs, we prefer to say, Based on what we know about how this works as of right now, this is how we should do it. That sentiment expresses our response to the model created by the MDA. All of the key elements that we have found in successful Cognos Framework Manager projects are found in the model created by the MDA.

For example, one proven practice when modeling metadata is the use of a three-layered model of the data: Physical View, Business View, and Presentation View. All three of these views are in the model and are created for you by the MDA.

The Physical View creates a namespace for the data source used in the model. The usage values of the dimension query items are set to Attribute. If you made the query item name changes recommend earlier in the chapter, these name changes will be reflected in the Business View while the original names will be maintained in the Physical View. The Presentation View, created using shortcuts back to the Business View, is presented to the authors of IBM Cognos content.

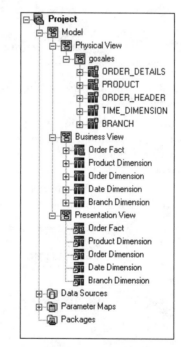

The remainder of this chapter will discuss the key elements of a successful Cognos Framework Manager project as well as how to create and maintain the model manually.

Building the Model by Hand

We quickly ran through the process of creating your first model. Granted, you cannot do much with it, but it does introduce you to some basic concepts. Now let's slow down and look at how we can perform many of the same tasks manually. As with any new endeavor, a learning curve is involved: we start climbing this one by introducing terms and concepts that you will see throughout this book. With a flood of new terms and concepts coming at you, to quote Douglas Adams, "Don't Panic." Read all the sections, and if you have to go back and read something again, that is OK. The model we created with the MDA will serve as a good reference for the rest of this chapter.

Metadata

For the Cognos Framework Manager modeler, metadata information is used to describe the structure of the database or any data store that holds data in which the business user is interested. *Metadata* is an IT term for a set of data that describes and gives information about other data. Metadata consists of descriptions of primary and foreign keys, indexes, relationships, and entity-relationship (ER) diagrams.

Table and column names might be meaningful, such as "SalesTable" and "Sales_Amount," or they could just as easily be "TB1002" and "FS0A1." Business users will not know that "TB1002" is the table that holds the sales history for your business. They do not care if the primary index on "TB1002" is unique or not. The modeler needs to understand and care about these things.

The Cognos Framework Manager modeler must provide the business content authors (anyone who uses IBM Cognos Studios to produce output) with a view of the metadata that makes sense to the business user and returns accurate and predictable results. So what has to happen to accomplish this? IT language must be translated into business language via *metadata modeling*.

Metadata Modeling

Metadata modeling consists of pulling the IT-level metadata from the data source(s) into Cognos Framework Manager. The metadata will be contained in a *query subject*, which is a collection of query items. The initial query subject will have the same name as the table from which it came. *Query items* represent fields in the query subject.

NOTE *The relationships defined between query subjects is the most important concept to understand in this chapter. This relationship determines how the IBM Cognos 10 query engine will build the SQL used to query the data sources.*

Next, we define the relationships between query subjects. These relationships define how the IBM Cognos 10 query engine will build the SQL used to query the source database. This is where we ensure that the results seen by the business users are correct and predictable. This chapter will devote a fair amount of space to this concept.

Finally, the metadata is renamed and organized so that the business user does not need to speak IT or even have a translator handy. At this point "TB1002" becomes "Sales History" and "FS0A1" becomes "Sales Amount."

Metadata mapping is one of the key elements of a successful Cognos Framework Manager project, and the MDA does it for us as long as we perform the initial renaming within the wizard.

Components of a Framework Manager Project

A new Cognos Framework Manager project has five components that appear in the Project Viewer: the Project itself, a namespace called Model, Data Sources, Parameter Maps, and Packages:

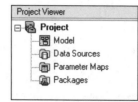

The Project is the container for all the components used by Cognos Framework Manager. These components are stored in a folder on the computer's file system. The Model namespace will contain all of the metadata and modeling needed to translate IT language into business language. The Data Sources folder contains references back to the data sources defined in IBM Cognos Connection. Parameter Maps are substitution tables that are populated when the package is published. Parameter Maps provide flexibility in customizing the behavior of your model. You can think of the Parameter Maps folder as a container for any substitution tables you might have. Finally, Packages are collections of metadata that we are going to publish in Cognos Connection for use by the business users.

Architecture

You can take many approaches to modeling metadata when using Cognos Framework Manager. Some factors can influence your approach, such as the source of the raw data, how many tables will be included in the final project, how the finished package will be used, and so on. Despite the various factors and the many ways you can design your model, years of experience with a wide range of data sources has consistently shown that a three-tiered, or layered, model works best.

The MDA handles the creation of the three layers automatically. Each of the layers is discussed in the following sections.

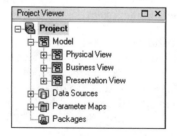

Views and Namespaces

Views, also called *layers*, in the context of a Cognos Framework Manager model, are a logical collection of query subjects, relationships, filters, folders, and other objects that are stored in a namespace. A *namespace* is a physical object that uniquely qualifies the elements within it. This allows for name reuse from one namespace to the next. Views are used to represent a specific state of your metadata.

NOTE *A view or layer is a conceptual object as opposed to a physical one. Unlike the namespace, there is no object in Cognos Framework Manager called a "view" or "layer".*

Continuing with the translation analogy, the first view of our translation, the Physical View, is the raw IT language—remember "TB1002"? The second view, the Business View, is where we translate the IT language to business language. This is where we declare that the "TB1002" table is the same as the "Sales History" table. The final view is the Presentation View. This view provides a shortcut to the "Sales History" query subject found in the Business View.

Physical View   The first view in our model is the Physical View. This view is used to hold the query subjects and relationships used to build the model. The query subjects in this view should be unmodified views of the source tables. This ensures that simple select statements are sent to the database, which prevents additional metadata calls at runtime.

Business View   The second view is the Business View. This view contains query subjects that have been optimized for use by the business user. This is where items are renamed, folders are created for organizational purposes, query subjects are consolidated, and, when necessary, query subjects are merged.

Presentation View   The final view is the Presentation View. As the name implies, this is the view of the model that will be presented to the business user. The query subjects in this view are organized to make sense for the business user.

Star Schema and Snowflake

A *star schema* is a database design optimized for reporting. The design is based on a central *fact* table that is surrounded by *dimension* tables. The name comes from the star-like shape of the ER diagram when you focus on a single fact table and its related dimensions. Star schemas are a key element of a successful Cognos Framework Manager project, and the MDA does a good job of creating them for us.

In the following illustration, you can see the fact table (ORDER_DETAILS) in the middle of the diagram. The fact table is surrounded by dimension tables that provide descriptions of the central facts. Technically, this is a variation of a star schema; it's called a *snowflake*, because it contains a dimensional query subject (BRANCH) that is not directly joined to the central fact table.

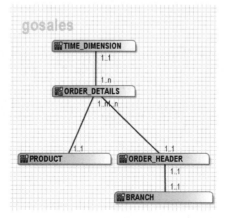

Star schemas combined with conformed dimensions play an important role in our overall model design approach. We discuss this topic in more detail in Chapter 17.

Fact Table

In its simplest terms, a fact table contains measures that will be aggregated in a report or some other tool. In a database, a fact table is used to hold transactional data and the keys to the attributes that describe those transactions. For example, a Sales fact table could include columns for the facts of a sale, such as the number of items sold, the price for which each item sold, and the cost of each item sold. These are all facts or measures and will be numeric values. The Sales fact table will also have key columns that join to the dimensional data for a given fact.

Dimension Tables

A dimension table, again in simplest terms, is a table that does not contain any measures. In a database, a dimension table holds attributes, or descriptive values, that can be applied to one or more fact tables. A given row in our example Sales fact table will have a column for the transaction date, store location, sales rep, item number, and so on. Each of these columns represents a dimension; each dimension typically represents a single table in the database.

In general, you will find three types of dimension tables in your models: nonconformed, conformed, and role-playing. All three types of dimension tables are simply tables in a database; how they are used in your model will determine to which type they belong.

Conformed and Nonconformed Dimensions   When a dimension can be used by more than one fact table with consistent and correct results, it is known as a *conformed dimension*. Conformed dimensions allow you to build queries that use measures from more than one fact table without overstating values. In short, the data in a conformed dimension applies to all of the fact tables in a given query.

For example, a part dimension, such as one found in a manufacturing company, is likely to be a conformed dimension because Part Number Z100-N means the same thing to a sales representative as it does to an inventory manager: Part Z100-N is always a "red widget."

An example of a nonconformed dimension depends on how the data is being used in the query. For example, if we look at a query using Sales fact, Sales Targets, and the Part dimension, the Part is conformed because Part applies to both Sales and Sales Targets. However, if we add the Order Method dimension to this query, we will see that Order Method is not conformed, because Order Method applies to the Sales fact table but it does not apply to the Sales Target table.

Role Playing (Aliases) Tables

At some point during your use of relational databases, you will need to use a single table for multiple tasks. When a single table is used to provide different dimensional information based on a join or filter, that table is said be a "role playing" or "alias" table. A common example of this is an employee dimension. An employee of a manufacturing company, for example, can fill multiple roles. A single employee can be a sales representative and a store manager at the same time, but only one record in the employee dimension exists for that individual. If a Sales fact table has a key for a sales representative and a key for the store manager, you cannot use a single instance of the employee query subject to fill both roles. Likewise, if the Sales fact table has a key for the sales representative and a different fact table—say, a Store Performance fact—has a key for the store manager again, you cannot use the same employee dimension to fill both roles.

SQL Generation

When you're modeling metadata in Cognos Framework Manager, your primary task is to be sure that any Cognos Studios using your model will always return the correct results. That statement may seem self-evident, but we state the obvious because it is possible to build a Cognos Framework Manager model that does not always return the correct results.

Incorrect SQL generation can occur for a number of reasons, and all of those reasons go back to breaking modeling rules. The Cognos query engine is deterministic when building SQL statements. Specific conditions in the model will result in specific SQL being generated and then sent to the source database. Modeling your metadata according to the rules will result in consistent SQL, which translates to correct results for the business user.

Minimized SQL

When SQL is being generated, we usually prefer that the code contain only the tables and joins needed to return the data we are seeking. This is called *Minimized SQL* and is desirable because of its impact on query performance. As a rule of thumb, less SQL is faster SQL, and faster is better.

A number of factors can disable the creation of minimized SQL. Creating joins between model query subjects, as opposed to data source query subjects, can override the minimized setting in the query subjects. Adding determinants to and merging model query subjects can also disable minimized SQL. The common thread here is model query subjects. As a result, we strongly recommend that you check the SQL generated by your model query subject to ensure the SQL is either minimized or non-minimized, depending on your needs.

Creating Components

Now that we've covered an overview of the concepts and terminology we will be using, let's get into the mechanics of creating a Cognos Framework Manager project. We'll start with the basics of creating common objects and progress to more complex actions.

For this section, we will be using the Cognos 10 GO Sales sample database, and we will name our project SampleProject.

NOTE *The Cognos 10 GO Sales database is a sample relational database that comes as part of your Cognos installation. This database is more complex than a star schema but is not so complex as to be intimidating.*

Projects

A Cognos Framework Manager project consists of a set of files located on a computer's file system. The actual project filename will use a .cpf extension and the folder contents will look something like the following:

Name	Date modified	Type	Size
archive-log.xml	1/18/2012 5:52 PM	XML Document	1 KB
customdata.xml	1/18/2012 5:52 PM	XML Document	1 KB
IDLog.xml	1/18/2012 5:52 PM	XML Document	21 KB
log.xml	1/18/2012 5:52 PM	XML Document	107 KB
mda_engine_project.xml	1/18/2012 5:52 PM	XML Document	31 KB
mda_metadata.xml	1/18/2012 5:52 PM	XML Document	12 KB
model.xml	1/18/2012 5:52 PM	XML Document	141 KB
NewProject.cpf	1/18/2012 5:52 PM	CPF File	2 KB
Preferences.xml	1/18/2012 5:52 PM	XML Document	1 KB
session-log.xml	1/18/2012 5:52 PM	XML Document	106 KB
session-log-backup.xml	1/18/2012 5:52 PM	XML Document	1 KB

The following ten steps are similar to the initial steps found in the "A Crash Course in Model Design Accelerator" section earlier in the chapter.

To create a new project, follow these steps:

1. Open the Cognos Framework Manager client tool from the Windows Start menu by opening to the IBM Cognos 10 folder and clicking the IBM Cognos Framework Manager link.

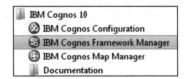

The first time Cognos Framework Manager runs, you will see the following screen:

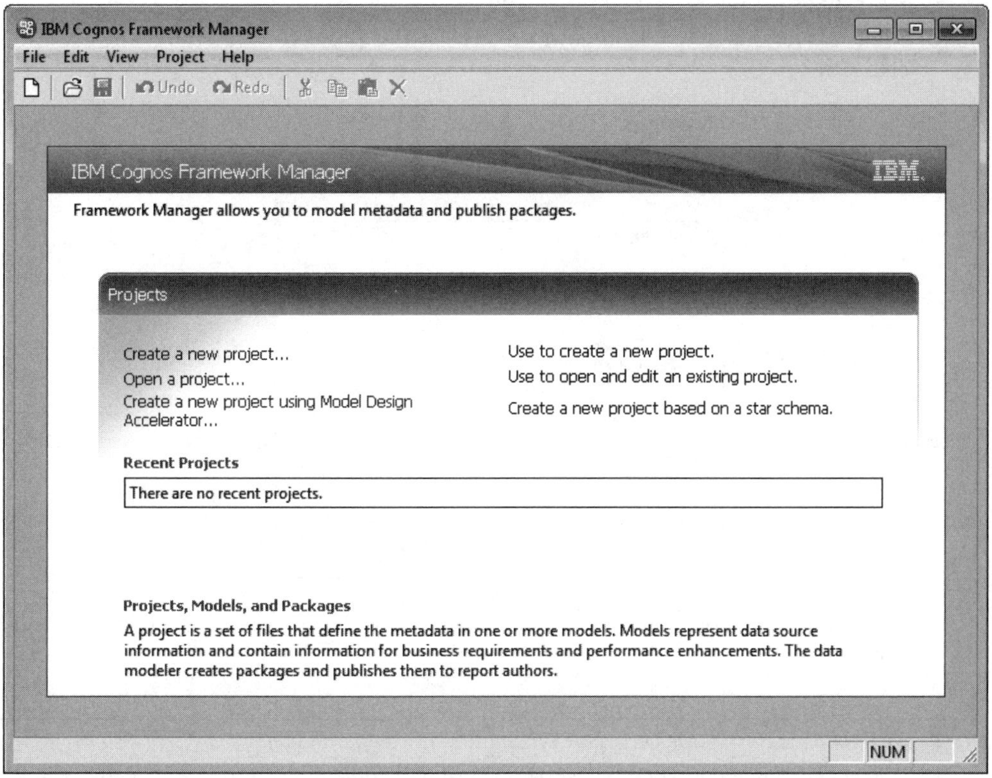

2. Start a new project by clicking the Create A New Project link to open the New Project dialog.

3. Change the Project Name by typing **SampleProject** and set the Location to an appropriate location on your file system.

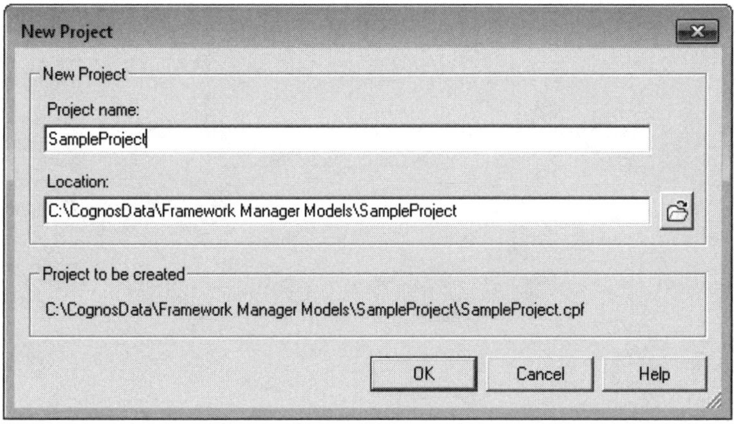

4. Click the OK button to create the project. If anonymous login has been disabled, you will be prompted to enter a username and password.

5. Select the language to use in your project; for this project, choose English. Then click OK.

6. Select the source for the metadata to be used in the project. Select Data Sources and click OK.

NOTE *We recommend using the Metadata Wizard to bring data into your model. We also recommend that you import entire tables, as opposed to individual fields from a table. Importing whole tables makes maintenance easier and helps performance by reducing the need for meta reads from the data source.*

7. You will see the Select Data Source dialog with a list of available data sources. Click the great_outdoors_sales data source and click Next.

The exact contents in the Select Objects dialog that opens next will depend on the relational database management system (RDBMS) being used. The following dialog is based on Microsoft SQL Server.

8. The Tables folder contains a list of the database tables available for use in the model. You can select one or more tables at this point. If the table you are importing already exists in the model, Cognos Framework Manager will ignore it unless you select the Import And Create A Unique Name option. You can also expand a table to pull individual columns from a table, but we advise against that practice.

In this example, we will be creating the relationships manually. Check the box to the left of the PRODUCT, BRANCH, ORDER_HEADER, ORDER_DETAILS, and TIME_DIMENSION tables and click Next. This will display the Generate Relationships dialog.

9. The selections you make in this dialog determine how Cognos Framework Manager defines the relationships between the objects being imported. In our experience, the modeler is better served by defining the relationships manually for two reasons: First, by manually examining each relationship, the modeler will have a better understanding of how the model is designed. Second, even though the relationships created by the wizard will reflect the relationships and cardinality from the data source, your reporting needs might require adjustments to those relationships and

cardinality. For these reasons, we suggest that you uncheck the Use Primary And Foreign Keys check box. This will disable the rest of the dialog. Then click Import.

The results of the import are displayed:

10. Click Finish and the new Project will be displayed:

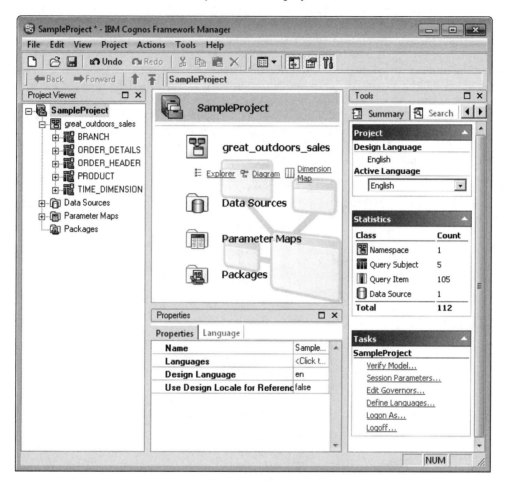

Relationships

The relationships between query subjects, as defined by the modeler, are critical components of a successful Cognos Framework Manger model. A relationship has two parts: the *join* and the *cardinality*. (We will use the terms "join" and "relationship" interchangeably.) Now that we have imported the first group of tables into our model, we need to define the relationships and cardinality between database tables.

NOTE *Although we prefer to create relationships between query subjects by hand, there are times when we allow the Metadata Wizard to create the joins and cardinality automatically. We will discuss that topic in more detail in Chapter 17.*

Joins

Joins are the definition of which query item(s) in one query subject are directly related to the query item(s) in a second query subject. For an example, we will look at the Great Outdoors sample data that you just imported. We start with the BRANCH and ORDER_HEADER query subjects. If you wanted to know how many orders a specific branch took, you could count the number of orders in the ORDER_HEADER query subject, then group the rows by the SALES_BRANCH_CODE query item found in the ORDER_HEADER query subject. However, if you also want to know details about the branches invoiced in the orders, you have to join the ORDER_HEADER query subject to the BRANCH query subject. In this example, the join is easy to identify because the ORDER_HEADER query subject has a query item named SALES_BRANCH_CODE and the BRANCH query subject has a query item, set as an Identifier, named BRANCH_CODE.

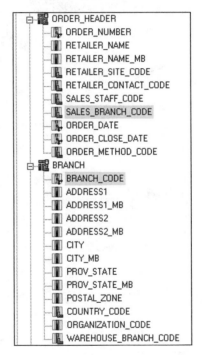

Joins are not always as easy to identify as this example might lead you to believe. Database column names do not always clearly identify the nature of the data being stored, and some joins require more than one query item to ensure that the correct relationship is defined. If you do not know which query items are used to join the query subjects, ask your DBA for help in identifying them. The wrong join will return incorrect results to the business users.

Cardinality

The second component of a relationship is *cardinality*. Cardinality can be explained in excruciating mathematical detail, and for that, we will direct you to the Internet. For now, you can think of cardinality as an indicator of how the number of rows in one query subject relate to the number of rows in a second query subject when looking at the join between the two.

NOTE *Cognos Framework Manager can display cardinality using Merise or crow's foot notation.*

When discussing the cardinality of a join, such as the join just discussed, we might say: that it is a one-to-many. Using Merise notation, we would represent the one-to-many cardinality as 1..1 to 1..n. The first number in the Merise notation denotes whether the relationship is optional or required: 0 = optional, 1 = required. The second number in the notation denotes whether it is a one or a many cardinality. Basically, cardinality has two components: the optionality and whether it is on the one or the many side.

Cardinality is determined by the number of rows retrieved from a given query subject for a specific key value. If we select all the rows from the BRANCH query subject using the key query item BRANCH_CODE = 30, we will get exactly one row returned:

BRANCH_CODE	ADDRESS1	ADDRESS1_MB	ADDRESS2	ADDRESS2_MB	CITY
30	Avenida Paulista, 333	Avenida Paulista, 333	CJ 231 2o. Andar	CJ 231 2o. Andar	São Paulo

When we select all the rows from the ORDER_HEADER query subject using the same branch code as a filter, many rows are returned:

SALES_STAFF_CODE	SALES_BRANCH_CODE	ORDER_DATE	ORDER_CLOSE_DATE	ORDER_METHOD
10406	30	Jan 12, 2004 12:00:00 AM	Jan 19, 2004 12:00:00 AM	1
10406	30	Jan 12, 2004 12:00:00 AM	Jan 20, 2004 12:00:00 AM	1
10098	30	Jan 12, 2004 12:00:00 AM	Jan 21, 2004 12:00:00 AM	1
10406	30	Jan 12, 2004 12:00:00 AM	Jan 28, 2004 12:00:00 AM	1
10098	30	Jan 12, 2004 12:00:00 AM	Jan 19, 2004 12:00:00 AM	1
10098	30	Jan 12, 2004 12:00:00 AM	Jan 19, 2004 12:00:00 AM	2
10406	30	Jan 12, 2004 12:00:00 AM	Feb 2, 2004 12:00:00 AM	2
10406	30	Jan 12, 2004 12:00:00 AM	Jan 19, 2004 12:00:00 AM	5
10098	30	Jan 12, 2004 12:00:00 AM	Feb 8, 2004 12:00:00 AM	5
10098	30	Jan 12, 2004 12:00:00 AM	Jan 19, 2004 12:00:00 AM	5
10406	30	Jan 13, 2004 12:00:00 AM	Jan 20, 2004 12:00:00 AM	6
10098	30	Jan 12, 2004 12:00:00 AM	Jan 19, 2004 12:00:00 AM	5

NOTE *The cardinality of a query subject determines whether Cognos Framework Manager will treat the query subject as a fact table or as a dimension table. The result of that determination has a major impact on the SQL generated by the Cognos query engine.*

Create a Relationship

As with most of the tasks in Cognos Framework Manager, there is more than one way to create a relationship. You can choose Actions | Create | Relationship. Or you can right-click the namespace that contains the query subjects for which you want to create a relationship, and choose Create | Relationship.

In this example, we will be using the BRANCH and ORDER_HEADER query subjects to demonstrate a third way to create relationships. If these query subjects are not already in the model, they should be imported into the Physical View.

1. From the Physical View, expand the ORDER_HEADER and BRANCH query subjects:

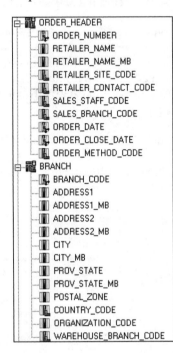

2. Click the BRANCH_CODE query item from the BRANCH query subject, and then CTRL-click SALES_BRANCH_CODE.

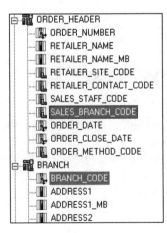

3. Right-click one of the highlighted query items and choose Create | Relationship:

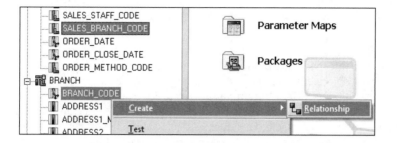

The Relationship Definition dialog is displayed.

4. If there is only one link required between the query subjects, and the cardinality is one-to-many (reading from left to right), you are done creating the relationship. If additional joins are required, or if the cardinality needs to be modified, you can perform those tasks at this time as well.

You will need to create relationships between ORDER_HEADER and ORDER_DETAILS, PRODUCT and ORDER_DETAILS, and TIME_DIMENSION and ORDER_DETAILS to bring this model into alignment with the one created using the MDA.

Namespaces

As noted earlier, namespaces are uniquely identified containers that are used to store and help organize all of the objects found in your model. Because the namespace is unique, objects with the same name can be used in different namespaces. For example, the namespace called "Physical View" can have a query subject called "PRODUCT," while another namespace called "Business View" can also have a query subject called "PRODUCT." When referring to the lowest level objects, you will need to use the fully qualified name. To reference the PRODUCT object in the Business View, the syntax would be *[Business View].[PRODUCT]*. To access the Database View PRODUCT, you would use *[Database View].[PRODUCT]*.

Initially, a project will have a single namespace that defaults to the name of the data source used the first time you load metadata. In our example, that name is great_outdoor_sales. If you have more than one data source in your model, we suggest that you create a separate namespace for each data source in the Physical View. This will help keep your metadata organized and allow you to use tables of the same name but sourced from different databases.

The reuse of names among namespaces provides the modeler with semantically meaningful objects throughout the modeling process. The use of consistent naming conventions on all three tiers of the model makes the model easier to understand and maintain. Another use of namespaces is in the creation of start schema groupings, which will be discussed a little further on in this chapter.

Rename a Namespace

Because the initial namespace created by Cognos Framework Manager inherited its name from the data source used to create it, you will probably want to rename it. This namespace will hold all of the folders and other namespaces of the model; as such, it should a meaningful name.

1. From the Project Viewer, select the namespace you want to rename—in this case, great_outdoors_sales.

2. Select the Name value and replace it by typing **GO Sales Reporting**:

NOTE *If you do not see the Properties window, it has probably been closed. To reopen the window, click the Properties icon in the menu bar of Cognos Framework Manager.*

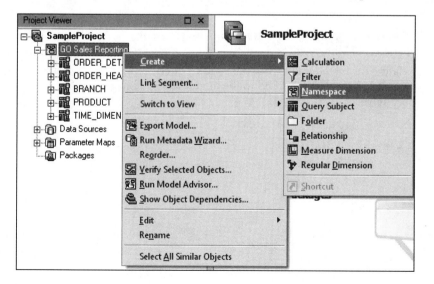

Create a New Namespace

You can place a new namespace inside of the initial namespace, inside folders, or inside other namespaces. Let's create the Database View namespace.

1. Right-click the namespace that will be the parent of the new namespace—in this case, right-click Go Sales Reporting, and choose Create | Namespace.

Cognos Framework Manager will create a new namespace, called New Namespace:

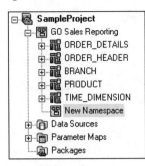

2. Select the new namespace and type **Database View** for the Name value in the Properties window.

3. Move the Data Source query subjects into the new namespace.

NOTE *To move objects between namespaces, click the objects, and then drag-and-drop them into the target namespace or folder.*

Query Subjects

A query subject is usually classified as one of two main types: a *model query subject* or a *data source (or table) query subject*. A third type, a *stored procedure query subject*, is rarely used.

Data Source Query Subjects

A data source query subject is defined by the source table metadata. These are the types of query subjects created when you run the Metadata Wizard. As noted, we recommend that data source query subjects contain all of the metadata for the table being imported for two reasons:

- Full table data source query subjects do not have any negative impact on the generation of Minimized SQL.

- Updating the metadata of a full data source query subject can be done through a one-click wizard, as opposed to the manual effort required for field-specific query subjects.

The PRODUCT table that we included in our initial model creation is an example of a data source query subject. A full table data source query subject will have a SQL definition similar to the one found in the PRODUCT query subject we imported:

Running the Metadata Wizard and pulling just the PRODUCT_NUMBER from the PRODUCT table will give us a data source query subject with the following definition:

We always follow one rule when working with data source query subjects: Do not touch the SQL in a data source query subject. We follow this rule for two reasons. First, the select * data source query subject provides better performance than a field-specific query. Second, maintenance of a select * is much easier than maintaining a changing database table.

Along with our one rule, we do have a few suggestions:

- Review all of the relationships in the Database View.
- Do not add calculations to data source query subjects.
- Review, and when needed, define determinants in data source query subjects.
- Do not rename any query items in the Database View.
- Set the query item attributes in the Database View.

If you look back at the model created by the MDA, you will see that all of these recommendations are performed by the wizard when a new model is created.

Create a New Data Source Query Subject   Continuing with our model, we realize that the report authors need two additional query subjects: PRODUCT_LINE and PRODUCT_TYPE. Again, we use the Metadata Wizard to create new data source query subjects. The Metadata

Wizard that you see when adding a new data source query subject is the same wizard used during the initial creation of the project.

1. Right-click the namespace that will hold the new data source query subject and choose Run Metadata Wizard.

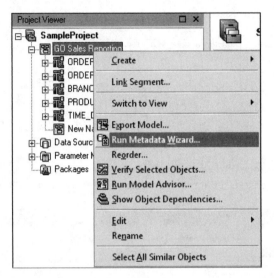

The Select Metadata Source dialog will open:

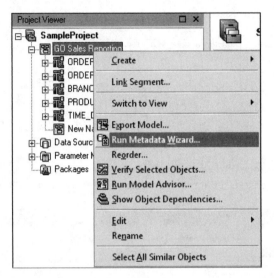

2. Select the data source and click Next. The Select Data Source dialog opens:

3. Click the great_outdoors_sales data source and then click Next. The Select Objects dialog opens.

4. Check the PRODUCT_LINE and PRODUCT_TYPE objects, and then click Next. The Generate Relationships dialog opens:

5. For these tables, we will allow Cognos Framework Manager to create the joins for us by choosing the Use Primary And Foreign Keys check box. Click Import, and the Finish dialog will display the results of the import:

6. Click Finish and you will see the newly imported data source query subject. In our models, we prefer to set the cardinality between dimensional query subject to be 1..1 to 1..1—in this case, the Metadata Wizard has set the cardinality to 1..n to 1..1.

7. Double-click the join between PRODUCT_TYPE and PRODUCT_LINE, and change the PRODUCT_TYPE cardinality to 1..1. Then click OK.

8. Join the PRODUCT_TYPE to the PRODUCT dimension on the PRODUCT_TYPE_ CODE and click OK.

The updated diagram will look like the following:

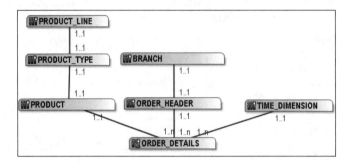

Model Query Subjects

Model query subjects are made of elements from one or more data source query subjects. The Business View, the second tier of the three-tier data model, will have most of the model query subjects in your Cognos Framework Manager project.

NOTE *Unless otherwise specified, when we refer to a "query subject," we are referring to a model query subject.*

Create a New Model Query Subject   The majority of your model query subjects will be sourced from a single data source query subject, some will be a merging of two or more complete data source query subjects, and some will be a combination of individual query items from any number of data source query subjects. In this example, we will use the PRODUCT data source query subject to create a new model query subject. Now would be a good time to create your Business View namespace by following the steps mentioned earlier.

To create a new model query subject from a single data source query subject, follow these steps:

1. Right-click the Business View namespace that will hold the new query subject, and choose Create | Query Subject.

2. In the New Query Subject dialog, enter the name of the new query subject, select the Model radio button, and click OK.

3. From the Query Subject Definition dialog, navigate to the source for the new query subject, and click (and hold) on the PRODUCT data source query subject.

4. Drag-and-drop the PRODUCT model object to the Query Items And Calculations box on the right. The source query subject will expand automatically. Then click OK.

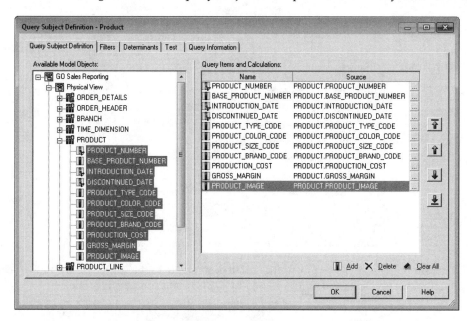

You will see a new query subject, Product, in the Business View namespace:

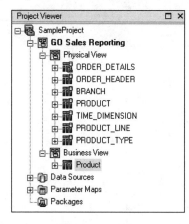

You can also use this method to modify an existing model query subject by combining items from multiple query subjects.

Create a New Merged Model Query Subject   You can create a merged model query subject by combining two or more query subjects, or by combining query items from two or more query subjects into a single model query subject. In order for a merging of query subjects to be successful, you must first verify that the relationships between all of the source query subjects have been defined and that those relationships are correct. Relationships between query subjects will be discussed shortly; for this example, we assume that our relationships have been defined and validated.

Merged query subjects allow the modeler to bring logically related objects from separate query subjects into a single query subject. This merging of objects is part of the IT-to-business translation. (Seeing product information split into Product, Product Type, and Product Line tables will make perfect sense to a database administrator. For a typical business user, seeing product information that clearly belongs together, split into three different tables, does nothing more than reinforce the user's belief that all IT people are simply bizarre.)

For this example, we will merge three data source query subjects into a single model query subject.

1. CTRL-click the Data Source query subjects to be merged (PRODUCT, PRODUCT_LINE, and PRODUCT_TYPE):

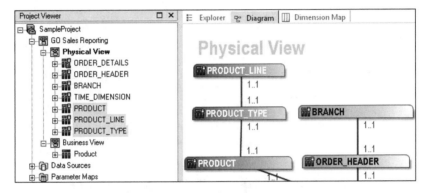

2. Right-click the selected query subjects and choose Merge In New Query Subject.

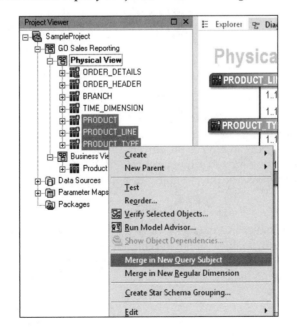

PART IV

Cognos Framework Manager will present the following dialog:

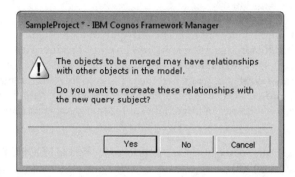

3. If any of the individual query subjects involved in the merge have relationships to query subjects outside of those being merged, and you want the newly merged query subject to have the same relationship, click Yes; otherwise, click No. We recommend clicking No and manually creating any relationships you need. Click No in the dialog box and the new merged query subject will be created:

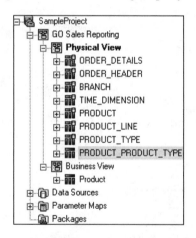

The default name of the new query subject will be the combination of the names of the first and last data source query subjects selected for the new merged query subject. In this case, the new query subject can replace the current Product query subject in the Business View. Delete the Product query subject, rename the PRODUCT_PRODUCT_TYPE query subject "Product," and move the query subject from the Physical View to the Business View.

Query Items

Query subjects are like tables in a database. By extending that analogy, we can think of query items as columns in a table. Unlike the columns in a table, query items give the data modeler a high degree of flexibility in how the metadata is presented to the business user and in how the underlying data behaves when accessed by the business user.

Most query items come from data source query subjects, model query subjects, and stored procedure query subjects. Query items can also be derived from calculations, database functions, and environment variables.

Adding New Query Items

At some point you will need to derive information that is not available in the source data. The new query item could be something as simple as combining first and last name query items into a full name query item or adding credit and debit to calculate a balance. Calculated query items can also be very complex, including conditional logic and advanced mathematical functions.

NOTE *Calculated query items can have a dramatic impact on the performance of your SQL queries. It is strongly recommended that calculated query items use database-only functions or are incorporated directly into the database when possible.*

As an example, suppose we expect a 10 percent increase of all production costs and we want to provide the new production cost as a query item for our business users. Here's how it's done:

1. Right-click the model query subject where the new query item is to be created and choose Edit Definition.

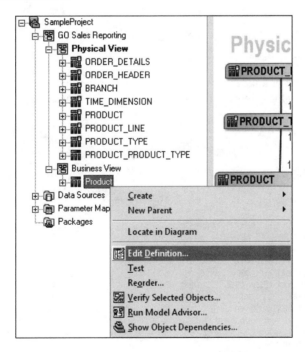

The Query Subject Definition dialog displays:

2. Click the Add link located at the bottom right of the dialog and the Calculation Definition dialog opens. Rename the query item to "Increased Production Cost."

3. Locate the PRODUCTION_COST query item from the Product query subject, then drag-and-drop it into the Expression Definition window.

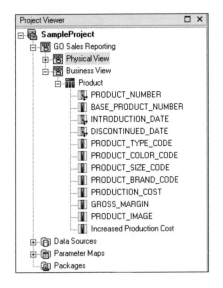

4. Complete the calculation by adding **(Production Cost * 0.10)** to the current Production Cost. The final expression should look like this:

5. Click OK, and the new query item will be added to the Product query subject.

Test a Query Subject

To check the results of the new query item, follow these steps:

1. Right-click the modified query subject and choose Test.

Create ▶
New Parent ▶
🖾 Edit Definition...
Test
Reorder...
🖼 Verify Selected Objects...
🖼 Run Model Advisor...
🖳 Show Object Dependencies...
Merge in New Query Subject
Merge in New Regular Dimension
Create Star Schema Grouping...
Remap To New Source
Edit ▶
Rename
Select All Similar Objects
🖼 Launch Context Explorer

This will open the Test Results dialog:

2. Click the Test Sample link at the bottom of the dialog. A small sample of the data for the query subject will be displayed:

Test Results					
					Test Query Information

☐ Auto Sum

Test results

ODE	PRODUCTION_COST	GROSS_MARGIN	PRODUCT_IMAGE	Increased Production Cost
	15.93	0.28	P03CE1CG1.jpg	17.523
	78.55	0.28	P20CE1SB3.jpg	86.405
	2	0.6	P91OP4SS16.jpg	2.2
	5	0.28	P04CE1CG1.jpg	5.5
	1	0.5	P16CE1TN2.jpg	1.1
	34.97	0.3	P05CE1CG1.jpg	38.467
	85.11	0.28	P06CE1CG1.jpg	93.621
	9	0.25	P09CE1CG1.jpg	9.9

▶ Test Sample   Total Rows   Options

Close   Help

Renaming Query Items

If you look at the preceding image, you will notice that the query item names have defaulted to the name of the columns from the original metadata source. This automatic naming works nicely with database tables that have well-defined column names. Sadly, most tables do not have well-defined column names.

Renaming query items is essentially the same as renaming any object in Cognos Framework Manager: Click the object to rename, locate the Name property in the Properties window, and type a new user-friendly name for the object.

Query Item Usage, Aggregation, and Other Attributes

For this discussion you will need to add a new query subject to your model. Following the steps defined earlier in this chapter, add ORDER_DETAILS from the great_outdoors_sales data source. When you are done, you should have a new query subject in your Physical View called ORDER_DETAILS; it should look like this:

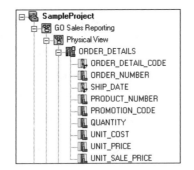

When a business user interacts with a model, the behavior of the data will be determined by how the properties of the query item are set. For example, when the business user adds a query item that references a numeric value to a report, will the value be totaled or will it be averaged? Maybe nothing will happen. Cognos Studios determine the proper behavior for the data referenced by a query item by looking at the usage of the query item being referenced.

Query Item Usage Property   The query item usage is found in the Properties window of Cognos Framework Manager:

Properties		☐ ✕
Properties	Language	
Name		ORDER_DETAIL_CODE
Description		
Last Changed		2012-01-18T19:04:05
Last Changed By		
Model Comments		
Screen Tip		
External Name		ORDER_DETAIL_CODE
Is Hidden		false
Usage		Identifier
Format		<Click to edit.>
Currency		
Data Type		Int32
Precision		0
Scale		0
Size		4
Is Nullable		false
Display Type		Value
MIME Type		
⊞ **Prompt Info**		
Regular Aggregate		Count
Semi-Aggregate		Unsupported
Is Unsortable		false

Usage Property ——→ Usage

A query item can have one of four usage types: Identifiers, Attributes, Facts (measures), or Unknown. Each of the types can be identified by its associated icon. The query item types and their icons are shown in Table 16-1.

TABLE 16-1
Query Item Icons

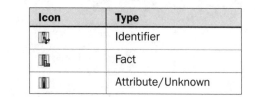

Icon	Type
▦	Identifier
▦	Fact
▥	Attribute/Unknown

The usage is determined by Cognos Framework Manager when the metadata is initially loaded into the model. The following rules are used to decide what the usage should be for a query item:

- **Identifiers**   If the source column is a database key or date/datetime, the query item usage will be set to an Identifier.

- **Facts**   If the source column is a numeric value or a time interval, the query item usage will be set to Measure.

- **Attributes**   If the query item is not an Identifier or a Measure, the query item usage will be set to Attribute.

NOTE *Cognos Framework Manager is reasonably accurate when determining the usage of a query item, but it is not foolproof. You must verify and correct the Usage property for all of the Items in a query subject to ensure accurate results.*

Because the rules used to set the Usage property of a query item to Fact are very general, Cognos Framework Manager can sometimes get it wrong. The most common misclassification occurs on columns that contain numerical codes, or keys. For example, look at the ORDER_NUMBER query item in the ORDER_DETAILS data source query subject. You can see by the icon and the Usage type that Cognos Framework Manager has decided this item is a Fact. But it is not actually a Fact; it is an Attribute. During the import process, Cognos Framework Manager examined the properties of the database column and did not find any keys on the ORDER_NUMBER, which ruled out an Identifier. When Cognos Framework Manager then examined the data type and found a numeric field, the rules determined this item to be a Fact. There is no way for the Cognos Framework Manager import logic to determine that, even though the source field is numeric, the values it holds are not measures. The sum of the order numbers is meaningless.

In this example, the data modeler will need to modify the Usage property from Fact to Attribute. Other query items will need to be modified as well: PRODUCT_NUMBER and PROMOTION_CODE should also be Attributes as opposed to Facts. The good news is that Cognos Framework Manager allows you to modify multiple attributes at one time. To change the Usage property of all the query items incorrectly set to Fact, you can do the following:

1. CTRL-click the query items to change.

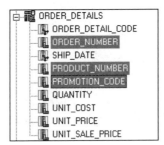

The Properties window in Cognos Framework Manager will change to show only the selected items.

	Name ⟳	Descri ⟳	Last Chan ⟳	Last C ⟳	Model ⟳	Screen ⟳	External N ⟳	Is Hidden ⟳	Usage ⟳	Format
ORDER_NUMBER	ORDER_NU...		2012-01-18T...				ORDER_NU...	false	Fact	‹Click to edit.›
PRODUCT_NUMBER	PRODUCT_...		2012-01-18T...				PRODUCT_...	false	Fact	‹Click to edit.›
PROMOTION_CODE	PROMOTION...		2012-01-18T...				PROMOTION...	false	Fact	‹Click to edit.›

2. Scroll to the Usage column, click the first cell in the column, click the down arrow, and select Attribute from the list.

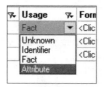

3. Click and hold on the small down arrow that appears at the bottom right of the cell.

4. Drag the arrow to the bottom of the cell and release the mouse button.

All of the Usage properties will now be set to Attribute.

The click-and-drag method for changing multiple attributes on a query item can also be used on the Format and Is Hidden properties as well as the Usage property.

NOTE *The properties of a data source query item are preserved when the item is used in a model query subject. Therefore, we recommend setting all of the query item properties, except the Name, in the Physical View of your model. You must do this right away; if you change these after a model query subject is using them, the changes made in the Physical View will not be propagated to the Business View.*

Regular Aggregate   The Usage property is important because of the impact that the property has on the aggregation setting of a query item. The Regular Aggregate property, as with all the other properties, is set during the initial metadata load. This property determines how the values of a query item will be calculated when a summarization is applied to those values.

When a query item is determined to be an Identifier or an Attribute, the Regular Aggregate property will be set to Count. This means that if a business user applies a summary to a column of Identifiers or Attributes, the value displayed in the summary cell will be a count of the rows returned by the report or query. If the query item is an Attribute or an Identifier, and the data type is a Date, the Regular Aggregate defaults to Unsupported. Applying a summarization to a query item with an Unsupported Regular Aggregate property will have no effect on the data.

When a query item is determined to be a Fact, the Regular Aggregate property will be set to Sum. In this case, applying a summarization to a column of Facts, the value displayed in the summary cell will be the total of all the values added together.

There are a number of aggregation types to choose from; Table 16-2 shows the complete list. Selecting the correct aggregation type will depend on your understanding of the data and how the business user will be using that data.

NOTE *Refer to the "IBM Cognos Framework Manager User Guide" for additional details on when to use a specific aggregation type.*

Aggregation Type	Result
Average	Divide the sum of the values by the count of the rows.
Automatic	Use the aggregation rules from the data source.
Calculated	Sum the values of the dataset after applying order of precedence rules.
Count	Count the number of rows in the column.
Count Distinct	Count the distinct number of values in the column.
Count Non-Zero	Count the number of values in the column that are not equal to zero.
Maximum	Display the maximum value from all the values in the column.
Minimum	Display the minimum value from all the values in the column.
Median	Display the median value for the column.
Standard Deviation	Display the standard deviation for the values in the column.
Sum	Add all the values in column together.
Variance	Display the statistical variance of the values in the column.
Unknown	None.
Unsupported	None.

TABLE 16-2 Regular Aggregation Types

Other Attributes of Interest Although the Usage and Regular Aggregate properties of a query item are the most important when it comes to accurate data for the business user, some other properties are also worthy of note:

- **Description** Provides documentation for other modelers and for users through the Lineage and Properties features of Cognos 10.

- **Screen Tip** Provides a brief pop-up description of the query item. If null, the value defaults to the query item name.

- **Format** Defines the format for the data associated with the query item, such as display values as currency or percent, specify the date format, and so on.

- **Prompt Info** A collection of properties used to define how the query item should behave when it is being used in a prompt.

Folders

A folder in Cognos Framework Manager is similar to any other folder in an application. Folders are used to help the modeler organize all of the objects in the project. Unlike namespaces, folders do not have any impact on how a query item is accessed. Two types of folders can be used: query item folders and model folders. The primary difference between these is where they are found. Query item folders are found inside of query subjects, and model folders are found in namespaces and are used to help organize your model.

Create a New Folder

For this example, suppose that in your model you have the namespace and query subject: [Business Layer].[Product]. You decide to place all of the Product Code fields into a folder called Codes. You can do the following:

1. CTRL-click to select all the desired query items:

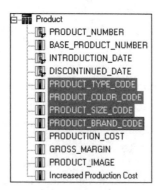

2. Right-click the selected items, and choose New Parent | Query Item Folder.

This will place the selected items into a new folder called New Query Item Folder. The new folder will be selected and ready to rename immediately.

3. Rename the folder. Name it Codes.

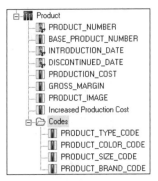

Once you publish the model and access the query items that have been placed in the folder, the fully qualified path to the query item (called an *expression*) will have no reference to the folder. If you added PRODUCT_TYPE_CODE to a report, the expression would be [Business View].[Product].[PRODUCT_TYPE_CODE].

NOTE *Query item folders are not preserved when you create a model query subject from a data source query subject, and as such, we suggest that you use query item folders only in Business View.*

Shortcuts

Shortcuts are, in essence, pointers from one object to another that allow the reuse of one object multiple times. Query subjects and relationships are the most common objects to be used in shortcuts. Over the years, we have seen a number of clients use shortcuts in various ways and with varying degrees of success. Based on our experiences to date, the only place we use shortcuts is in star-schema groupings in the Presentation View.

Star-Schema Groupings and the Presentation View

The only model layer that will have shortcuts is the Presentation View. Our Presentation View consists of *star-schema groupings*, are collections of a single fact query subject and the regular (or dimension) query subjects that support the fact query subject. Many of your fact query subjects will be reusing the same dimension query subjects, and that makes them ideal candidates for shortcuts.

Once again, the model created by the MDA automatically creates the first star schema for us:

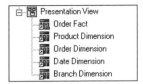

If you are not using the MDA model, you will need to create your Presentation View namespace at this time.

Creating Star-Schema Groupings   Star-schema groupings are created by selecting a fact query subject and the dimension query subjects that support it.

1. Open the Business View of your model and CTRL-click the fact query subject and the dimension query subjects that support it. CTRL-click Order Details, Branch, Product, and Order Header to select them all.

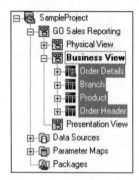

2. Right-click one of the selected query subjects and choose Create Star Schema Grouping.

The Create Star Schema Grouping dialog is displayed. The Available Objects area lists the query subjects you selected for the star-schema grouping.

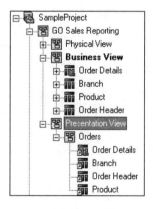

3. Accept the default criteria for creating the grouping. Enter **Orders** in the Namespace Name text box, and then click OK. A new namespace will be created in the Business View.

4. Drag-and-drop the Orders namespace you just created from the Business View into the Presentation View.

If you open the new star-schema grouping, you will see that all of the query subjects you selected are now represented by shortcuts in the Presentation View. When using shortcuts, any change made to a query subject in the Business View is reflected in the Presentation View automatically.

Modifying a Star-Schema Grouping   Over time, your star-schema grouping may change, and you might want to add or remove shortcuts to various query subjects. This can easily be accomplished with a few clicks of the mouse.

In this case, we will remove Product. Right-click the query subject shortcut you want to remove, and choose Edit | Delete.

The shortcut has been removed and the original query subject is intact.

To add a shortcut to an existing star-schema grouping, follow these steps:

1. Right-click the query subject (let's use Product again) that will be the target of the shortcut from the Business View, and choose Edit | Copy.

2. Right-click the target star-schema grouping, and choose Edit | Paste Shortcut. A shortcut to the Business View query subject will be created with the name of the original query subject preceded by "Shortcut to".

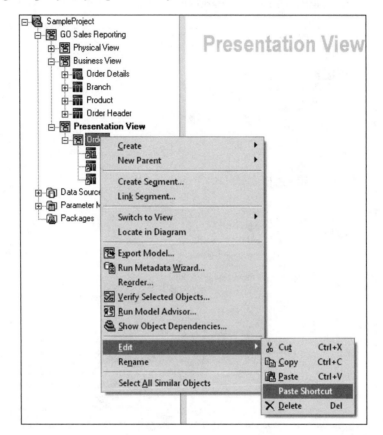

3. Rename the new shortcut. In most cases, you can remove the "Shortcut to" from the name.

***

NOTE *You can manually create star-schema groupings by creating your own namespace, and then pasting shortcuts from the Business View into the star-schema grouping namespace you created.*

Packages

Now that we have content ready for the business user in the form of star-schema groupings, we are ready to publish the Presentation View in a package. *Packages* are collections of star-schema groupings and other model objects that are published from Cognos Framework Manager into Cognos Connection. The blue folders in Cognos Connection represent the published packages.

TABLE 16-3 Package Object States	

☑	Selected
⬚	Hidden
☒	Unselected

A single model can contain multiple packages, which reduces the total number of Cognos Framework Manager projects that you will need to manage. Multiple packages are common in models containing a large number of fact query subjects. In most organizations, not every business user has access to all of the data available in a model. There are multiple ways of dealing with this challenge; a simple one is to exclude sensitive information from the package altogether.

The first time you create a new package, Cognos Framework Manager will select every object in the project for inclusion in the package. However, we do not want the Physical or Business Views in a package to be accessible by the business users.

Each object in package can be set individually to be selected for inclusion in a package, hidden from the user while still in the package, or unselected so that it is not included in the package at all. The green check mark indicates that the object will be included in the package and will be both visible and accessible to the business users. Clicking a green check mark will change the mark to a red X and the object, along with all of its children, is excluded from the package. Click the red X and the object will become hidden, which means that it will be included in the package, will be available for use in reports, but will not be visible to the business user (Table 16-3).

NOTE *Child objects inherit their parents' Selected, Hidden, or Unselected status.*

Create a New Package

Package creation is a straightforward task of selecting the objects to include, exclude, or hide in the package. We can now create a package that includes all of the objects in the Presentation View and hides the Physical and Business Views.

1. Right-click the Packages folder in the Project Viewer, and choose Create | Package.

The Create Package – Provide Name dialog displays:

2. Enter **Orders** in the Name text box, and click Next. The Create Package – Define Objects dialog is displayed:

3. Click the green check mark next to the Physical View two times. The first click will toggle the object from Selected to Unselected, and the second click will toggle the object from Unselected to Hidden.

4. Click the green check mark next to the Business View two times. Your package should look like the following:

5. Click Next. The Create Package – Select Function Lists dialog displays:

By default, the function sets for all supported databases are included in the package. You need to include only the function set for the source database. You can also define the function sets in the Project menu; that way, all future projects will have the function set you define.

6. SHIFT-click all the function sets to select them, and then click the left-pointing green arrow to remove all of the function sets from the package.

7. Select the database function set for your database, and click the right-pointing arrow to add it back to the package.

8. Click Finish and you will prompted to run the Publish Package wizard.

9. Click Yes and the Publish Wizard – Select Location Type dialog will be displayed.

The Select Location Type dialog has two settings that require attention: the Folder Location In The Content Store box determines exactly where the package being published will reside. For this example, we will use the default Public Folders. The Enable Model Versioning check box allows the modeler to maintain multiple versions of the model within the Cognos content store.

10. Accept Public Folders as the package location, uncheck Enable Model Versioning, and then click Next. The Publish Wizard – Add Security dialog will be displayed.

11. Accept the defaults and click Next. (Security is covered later in the book.) The Publish Wizard – Options dialog is displayed.

The Externalized Query Subjects section of the Options dialog lets you publish the package as a collection of files on a network drive. This is how to generate Impromptu Query Definition (IQD) files used by IBM Cognos Transformer. (We encourage our customers to use Cognos Report Studio reports as the data sources for Cognos Transformer; therefore, we do not use externalized query subjects very often.)

The other item on the Options screen is the Verify The Package Before Publishing check box. We strongly recommend leaving this checked. The verify process checks for model consistency prior to being published, and this can save you a lot of aggravation by catching syntax errors before the package is published.

12. Click the Publish button and the package will be published to the specified location. If no errors were encountered during the publish process, you will see the Publish Wizard – Finish dialog.

13. Click the Finish button.

Analyze Publish Impact

Before long, your Cognos Framework Manager model will change, as objects are added, removed, or renamed. Adding content to an existing model will not have any negative effects on existing reports. However, removing or renaming objects can cause any reports referencing those objects to fail.

You can identify objects that have changed in your package and see how those changes will affect existing reports by running the Analyze Public Impact tool. For this example, first create a simple Cognos Report Studio report that includes [Product].[Product Number].

Then, in the Business View of the model, rename [Product].[Product Number] to [Product]
.[The Product Number]. Then follow these steps:

1. Right-click the Orders package and choose Analyze Publish Impact.

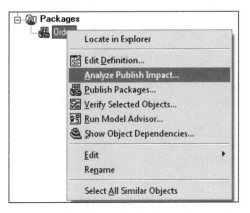

The Analyze Publish Impact dialog displays:

In this example, you can see the object renamed The Product Number is shown as
Modified in the Change column. The Change Details For area shows the property
values before and after the change.

2. To see the reports directly affected by the rename, click the check box to the left of the object, and then click the Find Report Dependencies link. The Report Dependency dialog displays:

3. Click the Search button. The Impacted Reports section of the Report Dependency dialog will list any reports affected by the object changes. In this dialog, you click the report to edit it immediately, you can save the results to a text file, or you can send the results to a printer.

Tools

Cognos Framework Manager contains various tools that you can use for help in creating a correct model and maintaining that model. The Tool menu is context-sensitive, which means that you will see different options in the menu list depending on where the focus is set when you open the tool menus.

The tools you'll probably use most often are the Model Advisor and Update Objects. The Model Advisor will scan the model you have created and identify any possible issues. The Update Objects tool synchronizes the query subjects in the model with the metadata from the database source.

Model Advisor

As your model becomes more complex, it becomes easy to miss the details that can have a major impact on the performance and accuracy of your model. Some examples include: incorrect cardinality causing ambiguous joins between query subjects, missing determinants causing inflated totals, multiple join paths between query subjects causing loops, and so on.

The Model Advisor will check for these types of issues and provide information on how to correct them. Often, the issues raised by the Model Advisor are not truly problems, but simply items that appear suspect. Use your own experience and judgment before making the changes suggested by the advisor.

Run the Model Advisor

Running the Model Advisor during the development of your model can help you catch potential issues early; the old software developer adage, "Test early, test often," applies to model development as well. At the very least, you should run the Model Advisor before you publish a package. To run the Model Advisor, follow these steps:

1. Right-click the model namespace in the Project Viewer of Cognos Framework Manager, and choose Run Model Advisor.

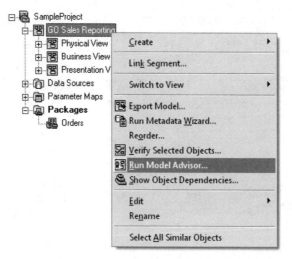

2. A dialog box displays with information about running the Model Advisor. Click Yes to continue.

SampleProject - IBM Cognos Framework Manager

You are attempting to perform model advisor on a container that in turn contains namespaces and or folders. We advise that you perform model advisor in the following three key use cases:

1. As a diagnostic test on a new import of metadata. This would be performed on a physical layer / folder or namespace.
2. Verifying that specific issues are resolved. For example multi-select objects and running a query (testing a query)
3. Validation of a package before publishing.

Do you want to continue?

Yes   No

3. The Model Advisor displays a list of criteria to use in the evaluation of the model:

4. Select the criteria to use (we suggest selecting all of them), and then click Analyze.

The time required to analyze your model will depend on its size and complexity. When the analysis is complete, the results display in the Model Advisor tab of the dialog. Again, the results you receive will depend on the state of your model.

Our sample model generates a few issues that we will examine one at a time.

The first issue lets us know that Cognos Framework Manager will treat ORDER_DETAILS as a fact when SQL is generated, because all of the joins to the ORDER_DETAILS query subject are on the many (or "n") side of the join.

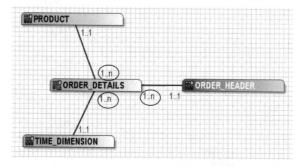

This is not an issue, because ORDER_DETAILS is a fact, and we want it to behave as such. If we saw this same issue on a query subject that we knew was not a fact, we would need to verify and correct, if necessary, the cardinality of the joins.

The second issue tells us that we have three query subjects that could behave as facts or dimensions, as shown here:

Issue 2: Query subjects that can behave as facts or dimensions		

This query subject can behave as a fact or a dimension. It is recommended that you evaluate this query subject in the context of the model to ensure queries will not be split improperly or unnecessarily. More information about ambiguous cardinality...

Object Name	Problem Description	Action
PRODUCT	The query subject PRODUCT is referenced by relationship ends of different cardinalities.	
PRODUCT_TYPE	The query subject PRODUCT_TYPE is referenced by relationship ends of different cardinalities.	

When Cognos Framework Manager tries to determine whether a query subject is a fact or a dimension, it checks the cardinality. If all of the joins on a query subject are "n" (many), then the query subject always behaves as a fact. If all of the joins on a query subject are "1" or "0," then the query subject always behaves as a dimension. If a query subject has both "n" and "1" on it, the cardinality is ambiguous, and that can cause inconsistent query results.

NOTE *The cardinality in Cognos Framework Manager is not intended to reflect the cardinality of the source database. The intent of cardinality in Cognos Framework Manager is to instruct the query engine on how to build SQL.*

Look at the PRODUCT and PRODUCT_TYPE join in our model, and you can see the ambiguity:

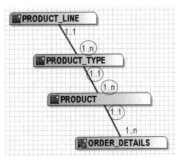

The cardinality shown is, from an entity relationship perspective, correct. However, from a Cognos Framework Manager perspective, the cardinality does not provide clear instructions on how to build the SQL when these query subjects are accessed in a report.

This is a concern due to the potential for inconsistent results from our queries. The fix is to modify the cardinality so that non-fact query subjects do not have any "n" joins, as shown here:

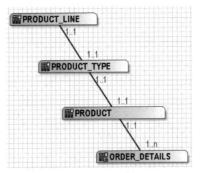

The third issue lists objects that could cause Minimized SQL generation to fail:

Issue 3: Factors that will override the Minimized SQL setting

A query subject has attributes that will override the SQL Generation type setting of Minimized. Relationships between model query subjects, determinants on model query subjects and data source query subjects with modified SQL will override the Minimized SQL Generation type. More information about minimized SQL...

Object Name	Problem Description	Action
PRODUCT_PRODUCT_TYPE	There may be problems generating minimized SQL for object PRODUCT_PRODUCT_TYPE.	
	This object is set to use minimized SQL.	

As noted in the Model Advisor result, model query subjects with relationships, model query subjects with determinates, and data source query subjects with modified SQL will cause the SQL generated by Cognos to override the Minimized SQL setting. The loss of minimized SQL can cause serious performance issues and inconsistent results.

Update Objects

The Update Objects menu option is available from the Tools menu after you've selected one or more query subjects in your model. If you are working with an established database, you will not use this tool often, since the database definitions are not likely to change. If you are working with a database that is in development and the tables are changing, you will use Update Objects quite often.

Update a Query Subject

Suppose you are developing a new database application, and you believe the database is complete. You then start the Cognos Framework Manager modeling process and you get your model working nicely. As you are about to click the Publish button, you realize that the Product table is missing a critical field. Adding the field to the database is not difficult, and adding a field to a query subject is even easier.

In this example, you will add a new column to the Product table in great_outdoors_sales called NEW_IMPORTANT_COLUMN. You will add the column to the model using the Update Objects tool. Follow these steps:

1. Click the query subject to update—in this case, the PRODUCT query subject in the Physical View of your model.

2. From the Cognos Framework Manager menu bar, choose Tools | Update Object.

3. A message dialog will display. When the dialog closes, open your query subject to see the update:

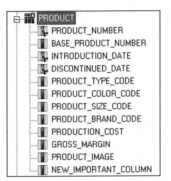

The Update Objects tool will also update all of the query item attributes of the target query subject.

Context Explorer

As your model grows in size and complexity, you'll find yourself using one tool more and more often. The Context Explorer tool lets you quickly see which query subjects are related to any other query subject you choose, assuming the query subject you choose has joins.

To access the Context Explorer for our PRODUCT data source query subject, follow these steps:

1. Right-click the PRODUCT data source query subject in the Physical View of your model, and choose Launch Context Explorer.

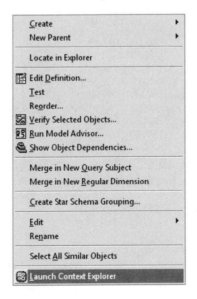

You'll see the Context Explorer window, which shows all of the query subjects that are directly related to the PRODUCT query subject:

2. Select another query subject in the Context Explorer diagram. To see all of the joins on that query subject, click the Show Related Objects button.

The Context Explorer window now looks like this:

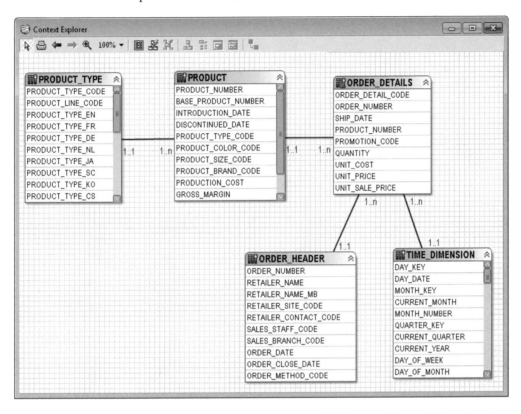

You'll find many useful features in Cognos Framework Manager. More of these features are discussed in the next two chapters. For more information, refer to your IBM Cognos 10 documentation, or make a copy of your model and just poke around for fun!

Queries, Relationships, and Determinants in IBM Cognos Framework Manager

In Chapter 16, you were introduced to the mechanics of building a Cognos Framework Manager model. In this chapter, we discuss how various modeling practices affect queries generated by Cognos Framework Manager. To demonstrate the key concepts of this discussion—query subjects, relationships, and determinants—we will be using a simplified example.

As you have probably learned, there is usually more than one way to accomplish any given task when working with IBM Cognos Business Intelligence v10.1 (Cognos BI). This makes it difficult to talk about "the right way" versus "the wrong way" of performing tasks in Cognos BI. Nevertheless, when you're modeling data with Cognos Framework Manager, there usually is a "best way" of performing a task. In this chapter, we will show you how we currently approach various tasks, such as defining determinants, choosing cardinality, creating joins, and so on. In some cases, we will show what happens when you choose not to follow the preferred approach.

NOTE *The data set used in the examples for this chapter is available for download on the John Daniel Associates web site (http://www.JohnDaniel.com/Cognos10Book).*

Remember that metadata modeling is a large topic with many facets. We cannot possibly cover all the approaches and situations related to the task. The intent of this chapter is to present the basic tools and concepts you'll need to begin building sound metadata models with Cognos Framework Manager. As you gain more experience with modeling and with IBM Cognos, you might come back to some part of this chapter and think, "Well, that's one heck of an oversimplification." If that happens, then we have done our job, because that means you have grown beyond the fundamental concepts that follow.

NOTE   *The IBM Cognos developerWorks web site (http://www.ibm.com/developerworks/data/ products/cognos/) is an outstanding resource for additional information.*

Car Rental Example

We have found, when learning something completely new, that starting with a simple example works best. When instructing new customers in modeling metadata with Cognos Framework Manager, we often use a simple car rental scenario. The remainder of this chapter will use that example to teach you some of the lessons we have learned.

Although this example might appear trivial, it does represent a common data scenario. At a high level, this example scenario involves multiple fact tables, each with measures at different levels of granularity (levels of detail). For example, budget and forecast amounts are often recorded at a monthly level, while actual sales are usually recorded at the daily level. Granularity is not limited to the date dimension; we can expect to see budget and forecast amounts at product line levels, sales region levels, or at any other grouping the data supports.

The challenging question report authors, and by extension data modelers, face is this: "How do we accurately, and easily, report measures of different granularity in a single report?" The question has many answers, including this one: "We can export data to a spreadsheet, update it, load it into a local database application, write some SQL functions to massage the data, export the results to a spreadsheet, apply formatting, and e-mail the results." Although that answers part of the question, it ignores the "accurately, and easily" portion. A properly modeled Cognos Framework Manager model can provide the complete answer; in this case, the answer is as easy as "drag-and-drop the data you want from the Cognos Framework Manager model into your report."

NOTE   *We have used Microsoft SQL Server 2008 R2 for all of the examples in this chapter.*

Business Rules

Let's look at the business rules used to manage our car rental business.

1. Any vehicle may be rented zero, one, or more times in one day.

2. Every occurrence of a rental, and its revenue, is stored as one row in the Rental Income table.

3. Any vehicle may undergo repairs zero, one, or more times in one month.

4. Every occurrence of a repair, and its cost, is stored as one row in the Equipment Repairs table.

5. A manufacturer may or may not have a monthly repair budget associated with it.

Sample Data

The sample data for this scenario consists of five tables used to manage our fictional car rental company. We have two dimension tables: Date Dimension with day, month, and week levels, and Equipment Dimension with a unique identifier, manufacturer, model, year, and color for each vehicle in our fleet. We have three fact tables: Rental Income Fact, which contains the income associated with renting a given vehicle on a given date; Equipment Repairs Fact, which contains the expense associated with repairing a given vehicle on a given date; and Manufacture Repair Budget Fact, which contains the budgeted amount allocated to the repair of vehicles of a given manufacturer during a given month.

The tables and data are shown in Figure 17-1.

Date Dimension

Date	YYYYMM	Year	Holiday	Month
2009-01-01 00:00:00.000	200901	2009	Y	Jan-09
2009-01-02 00:00:00.000	200901	2009		Jan-09
2009-01-03 00:00:00.000	200901	2009	NULL	Jan-09
2009-01-04 00:00:00.000	200901	2009	NULL	Jan-09
2009-01-05 00:00:00.000	200901	2009	NULL	Jan-09
2009-01-07 00:00:00.000	200901	2009	N	Jan-09
2009-01-08 00:00:00.000	200901	2009	NULL	Jan-09
2009-02-01 00:00:00.000	200902	2009	NULL	Feb-09
2009-02-02 00:00:00.000	200902	2009	NULL	Feb-09
2009-03-01 00:00:00.000	200903	2009	NULL	Mar-09
2009-03-02 00:00:00.000	200903	2009	NULL	Mar-09
2009-03-03 00:00:00.000	200903	2009	NULL	Mar-09
2009-04-01 00:00:00.000	200904	2009	NULL	Apr-09
2009-05-01 00:00:00.000	200905	2009		May-09

Equipment Dimension

VIN	MAKE	MODEL	YEAR	COLOR
1234ASDF	Ford	Taurus	2008	White
1234JKLM	Chevy	Truck	2005	Green
5678ASDF	Ford	Mustang	2008	Yellow

Rental Income Fact

VIN	R_DATE	R_INC
1234JKLM	2009-01-02 00:00:00.000	2000
1234ASDF	2009-01-07 00:00:00.000	2300
1234JKLM	2009-05-01 00:00:00.000	4000
1234ASDF	2009-04-01 00:00:00.000	3000
5678ASDF	2009-03-02 00:00:00.000	2000
1234ASDF	2009-01-07 00:00:00.000	1000
5678ASDF	2009-01-07 00:00:00.000	1500

Equipment Repairs Fact

VIN	REP_DATE	REP_AMT
1234ASDF	2009-01-01 00:00:00.000	500
1234ASDF	2009-02-01 00:00:00.000	500
1234JKLM	2009-03-01 00:00:00.000	500
5678ASDF	2009-01-02 00:00:00.000	250
1234ASDF	2009-01-07 00:00:00.000	1000
1234ASDF	2009-01-07 00:00:00.000	1000
1234ASDF	2009-01-07 00:00:00.000	1000
1234ASDF	2009-01-07 00:00:00.000	1000
1234ASDF	2009-01-07 00:00:00.000	1000
1234ASDF	2009-01-07 00:00:00.000	1000
1234ASDF	2009-01-07 00:00:00.000	1000
1234ASDF	2009-01-07 00:00:00.000	1000
1234ASDF	2009-01-07 00:00:00.000	1000

Manufacture Repair Budget Fact

MAKE	MONTH	BDGT
Chevy	200901	100
Ford	200901	100
Ford	200902	100
Ford	200903	100

FIGURE 17-1 Sample Rental Data

PART IV

Building an IBM Cognos Framework Manager Project

We are assuming that you have read Chapter 16 or you have some experience using Cognos Framework Manager to create projects and models. As such, we will not detail every step in creating a project. Instead, we will focus here on the metadata modeling that occurs when you're creating a new project and model.

Importing the Metadata

After creating a new project, you'll need to run the Metadata Wizard to pull in the data source query subjects that you need. In this case, you'll pull in the Date Dimension, Equipment, Rental Income, Equipment Repairs, and Manufacturer Repair Budget tables. Once the wizard is done, the diagram should resemble the following:

In this example, during the Metadata Wizard import, turn off the Use Primary And Foreign Keys To Detect Relationships feature; this results in the lack of joins appearing in the diagram. When modeling metadata with which you are very familiar, or when the metadata is sourced from an existing star schema such as a data warehouse, the Use Primary And Foreign Keys To Detect Relationships feature can be a great time-saver. The joins and cardinality resulting from the Metadata Wizard import will always match the joins and cardinality found in the source database. However, that does not mean that they will match your intended model design. As a result, after a Metadata Wizard import, you should always verify that the joins and cardinality are what you expect.

We belabor this point because we believe that the single most important concept in modeling metadata is this: The cardinality of the relationships in Cognos Framework Manager is used to educate the Cognos query engine on how to build SQL. As such, the importance of the cardinality cannot be overstated.

If you are not very familiar with your metadata, or if your model will have a large number of database tables, we recommend building your model one small piece at a time. Although it is possible to use the Metadata Import Wizard to bring all of the tables and joins from your source database into the model, we strongly advise against doing so.

NOTE *The cardinality of the relationships in Cognos Framework Manager is used to educate the Cognos query engine on how to build SQL.*

Creating the Relationships

Now that we have the data source query subjects imported, we can start defining, or verifying, relationships. This is the point at which most novice modelers start down the wrong path, even when dealing with a small number of query subjects.

To reiterate, the purpose of relationships and cardinality in Cognos Framework Manager is to educate the query engine on how to build SQL. You might end up making changes to the imported cardinality in Cognos Framework Manager, and that is all right, because the cardinality in your model is not required to match the cardinality in the source database system.

Before we start building our relationships, here is a quick reminder of two key concepts from Chapter 16: First, a fact query subject contains one or more measures. For this discussion, think of *measures* as numeric values that will be aggregated. In a Cognos Framework Manager model, any query subject that only has "n's" on it will be treated as a fact query subject by the query engine.

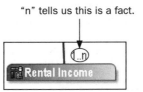

The second concept is that a dimension query subject does not contain any measures. In a Cognos Framework Manager model, any query subject with a "1" or "0" is treated as a dimension by the query engine.

The cardinality, and what it means to the query engine, is important because of how the query engine builds the SQL requested by the report. Although there are numerous ways to build a query, you need to understand only a few concepts to model metadata with Cognos Framework Manager:

- The types of query statements that will be found in your SQL
- When each type of query is created
- How each type of query interacts with the others
- How the cardinality defined in Cognos Framework Manager impacts which type of query is generated.

These concepts will be discussed throughout this chapter.

Building the First Model: Mistakes, Traps, and Determinants

To be honest, we struggled with the best way to introduce you to the concepts that our experience has shown to be the most important in building a sound Cognos Framework Manager model. We do not like to give negative examples—that is, examples that we know would end with a bad model. However, because we have seen customers fall into the same trap over and over, and because we also found ourselves in the same bad model trap when we first began modeling with Cognos Framework Manager, we have decided to show you practices that lead to the bad model trap. These negative examples are clearly marked; we want to lead you away from the traps, not into them.

The 99.9 Percent Mistake

We do not keep statistics on how many models go bad for the same basic reasons; however, based on experience, 99.9 percent of first attempts at building Cognos Framework Manager models by modelers coming to the tool from impromptu catalog building or relational database modeling make the same mistake. In short, they build their Cognos Framework Manager models as they would build an impromptu catalog or model a normalized relational database. So, for the sake of example, let's do that with our rental data and see where it leads.

The information of interest to the business is Rental Income, and starting from there we expand the query subjects to see the query items. Then we decide to start our model with the tables: Rental Income, Equipment, and Dates.

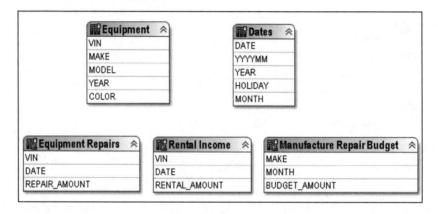

TIP *Placing fact query items in a row below the dimensional query items in the Cognos Framework Manager diagram can help you identify shared dimensions as well as questionable joins, such as fact-to-fact joins.*

Rental Income has a query item called VIN (which stands for Vehicle Identification Number) that also exists in Equipment; we know VINs are unique, so we create a relationship from the Equipment table to the Rental Income table. Looking at the sample data, we see the

DATE query item in the Rental Income table is a full date, which matches the DATE query item from the Dates dimension. We create a join on those fields.

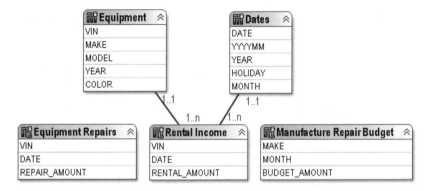

Equipment Repairs also has VIN and DATE query items, so we use those fields to join to the Dates and Equipment tables. The diagram is starting to take shape, and it looks correct.

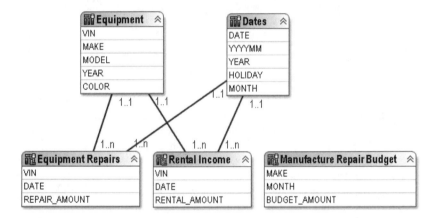

The Trap

This is where we face "The Trap." What do we do with the Manufacture Repair Budget query subject? This fact query subject is at a different granularity than the other facts. At this point, the modeler has four options:

1. The modeler will join the Manufacture Repair Budget query subject to the Equipment query subject on MAKE and to the Dates query subject on YYYYMM, and believe they are done.

2. The modeler will decide that the Manufacture Repair Budget query subject simply will not work with the Rental Income and Equipment Repairs query subjects because of granularity issues. The modeler will either ignore the query subject altogether, or, if the modeler has the access, he or she will create summary tables for the Equipment Repairs and Rental Income and use those in a different Cognos Framework Manager model.

3. The modeler will include the Manufacture Repair Budget and Equipment query subjects in the model with no join between the query subjects. This pushes the problem back to the report author.

4. The modeler will leverage the power of Cognos Framework Manager and allow the tool to generate the proper SQL.

Because option one is the most common approach, that is the one we will go with here. The diagram, after creating the joins discussed in option one, will look like the following:

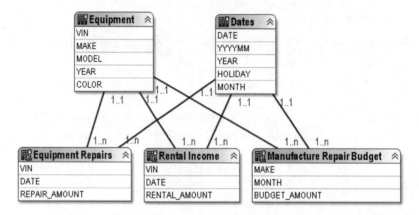

You might look at the Dates to Manufacture Repair Budget join and think, "Wait, the [Dates].[YYYYMM] to [Manufacture Repair Budget].[YYYYMM] join is not a one to many! It has to be many to many because YYYYMM is going to be repeated about 30 times a month." A great deal of shouting, table pounding, and even salty language is usually tossed around when we first show this model to database administrators. But, remember, as we have said before, that the cardinality seen in a Cognos Framework Manager model is meant to represent the reporting requirements of the model. The database cardinality may, or may not, meet that requirement, hence the need for metadata modeling. The illustrated cardinality is meant to instruct the query engine on how to build consistent SQL statements. Cognos Framework Manager will allow you to create a many-to-many (1..n-to-1..n) join. However, as a rule, you should avoid many-to-many relationships in Cognos Framework Manager, simply because you have yet to understand fully what the query engine will do with a many-to-many relationship.

For now, you will have to take our word and publish the model. For a sanity check, we use IBM Cognos Report Studio to check the totals of each of the three fact query subjects.

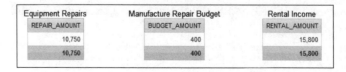

The totals for each fact query subject are correct, which is not a surprise because the totals are coming from single tables. For a slightly more realistic report, we add [Dates].[DATE] and [Equipment].[VIN] and rerun the report:

Rental Income

DATE	VIN	RENTAL_AMOUNT
Jan 2, 2009 12:00:00 AM	1234JKLM	2,000
Jan 7, 2009 12:00:00 AM	1234ASDF	3,300
Jan 7, 2009 12:00:00 AM	5678ASDF	1,500
Mar 2, 2009 12:00:00 AM	5678ASDF	2,000
Apr 1, 2009 12:00:00 AM	1234ASDF	3,000
May 1, 2009 12:00:00 AM	1234JKLM	4,000
		15,800

We make a new list report to check the BUDGET_AMOUNT with the following query items: [Equipment].[MAKE] and [Manufacture Repair Budget].[BUDGET_AMOUNT]. The resulting "Make, Budget Amount" report looks like this:

MAKE	BUDGET_AMOUNT
Chevy	100
Ford	600
Overall - Total	700

In this report, the BUDGET_AMOUNT total is nearly doubled the correct value of $400. The inflated value occurred because of how the query engine built the SQL used to retrieve the requested data, and because the query engine used the metadata we provided in the Cognos Framework Manager model.

Ta-da! That is the trap. Even though it appears we have done everything correctly, we are getting incorrect results. The values are incorrect because we did not give the query engine all the information it needed to build the proper SQL.

To understand what happened in this case, let's look at the SQL used to generate the above results. To view the SQL for this report, follow these steps:

1. From Cognos Report Studio, choose Tools | Show Generated SQL/MDX.

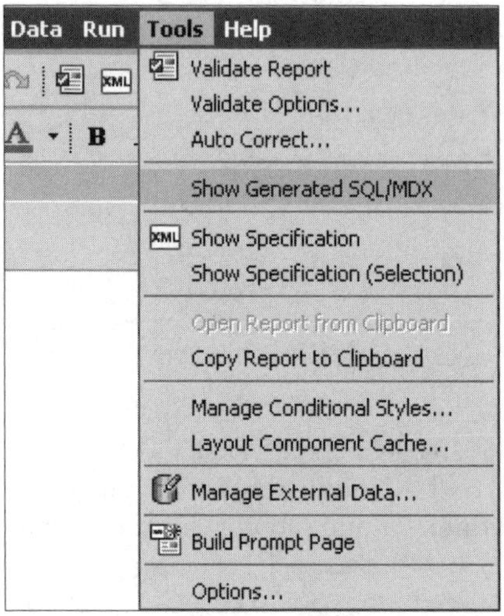

The Generated SQL/MDX dialog will display, showing the Native SQL:

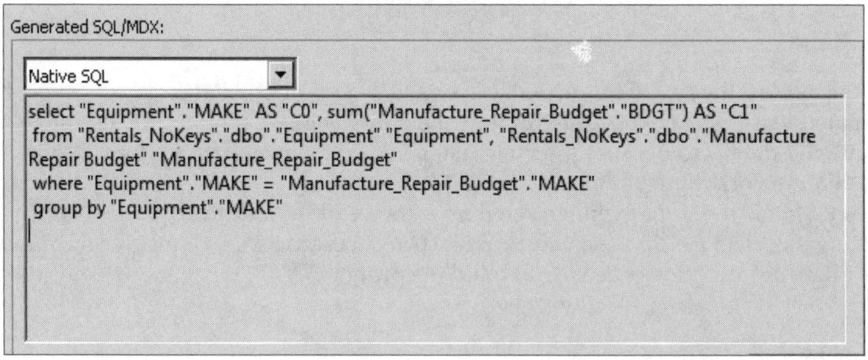

Generated SQL/MDX:

Native SQL

```
select "Equipment"."MAKE" AS "C0", sum("Manufacture_Repair_Budget"."BDGT") AS "C1"
from "Rentals_NoKeys"."dbo"."Equipment" "Equipment", "Rentals_NoKeys"."dbo"."Manufacture
Repair Budget" "Manufacture_Repair_Budget"
where "Equipment"."MAKE" = "Manufacture_Repair_Budget"."MAKE"
group by "Equipment"."MAKE"
```

2. To see the IBM Cognos SQL, click the drop-down menu and select IBM Cognos SQL.

Generated SQL/MDX:

Native SQL

Native SQL
IBM Cognos SQL

The Native SQL selection displays the actual SQL statements that were sent to your source database. (This SQL is database-specific and may look slightly different depending on your database system.) The IBM Cognos SQL selection displays the SQL used by Cognos Report Studio to process the data returned from the native query.

```
Generated SQL/MDX:

  IBM Cognos SQL          ▼

 select
     Equipment.MAKE  as  MAKE,
     XSUM(Manufacture_Repair_Budget.BDGT  for Equipment.MAKE )  as  BUDGET_AMOUNT,
     XSUM(XSUM(Manufacture_Repair_Budget.BDGT  for Equipment.MAKE )  at Equipment.MAKE )
 as  Total_BUDGET_AMOUNT_
 from
     Rental.Rentals_NoKeys.dbo.Equipment Equipment,
     Rental.Rentals_NoKeys.dbo."Manufacture Repair Budget" Manufacture_Repair_Budget
 where
     (Equipment.MAKE = Manufacture_Repair_Budget.MAKE)
 group by
     Equipment.MAKE
```

NOTE *This discussion of SQL generation is at a very high level. For a detailed discussion of how SQL is generated, refer to the "IBM Cognos Framework Manager Guidelines for Modeling Metadata" documentation that comes with your IBM Cognos installation.*

If we clean up the Native SQL a bit and take another look at the tables involved in the query, the problem becomes clear:

Manufacture Repair Budget				Equipment				
MAKE	MONTH	BUDGET_AMOUNT		VIN	MAKE	MODEL	YEAR	COLOR
Chevy	200901	100		1234ASDF	Ford	Tarus	2008	White
Ford	200901	100		1234JKLM	Chevy	Truck	2005	Green
Ford	200902	100		5678ASDF	Ford	Mustang	2008	Yellow
Ford	200903	100						

```
SELECT  "Equipment"."MAKE"                                      AS "C0",
        SUM("Manufacture_Repair_Budget"."BUDGET_AMOUNT") AS "C1"
FROM    "Rentals"."dbo"."Equipment" "Equipment",
        "Rentals"."dbo"."Manufacture Repair Budget" "Manufacture_Repair_Budget"
WHERE   "Manufacture_Repair_Budget"."MAKE" = "Equipment"."MAKE"
GROUP   BY "Equipment"."MAKE"
```

If you are not familiar with SQL, here is a brief explanation: The SQL is instructing the database to get the values from the MAKE field of the Equipment table and find all the matching MAKE values and BUDGET_AMOUNT values from the Manufacture Repair Budget table. The database will examine the first row in the Manufacture Repair Budget

[Equipment].[MAKE]	[Manufacture Report Budget].[MAKE]	[Manufacture Report Budget].[BUDGET_AMOUNT]
Ford	Ford	100
Ford	Ford	100
Ford	Ford	100
Ford	Ford	100
Ford	Ford	100
Ford	Ford	100
Chevy	Chevy	100

TABLE 17-1   Interim SQL Results

table, consider the MAKE value for that row, and look for a matching value in the MAKE field of the Equipment table. If the values from both tables match, the database will set aside those two rows. This same process is repeated for every row in the Manufacture Repair Budget table. The results at this point might look like those shown in Table 17-1.

The results from Table 17-1 are then grouped on MAKE and the BUDGET_AMOUNT for the individual rows are totaled, as shown in Table 17-2.

Determinants: "Get Out of the Trap Free" Card

In all fairness to the database, it returned the exact data we asked for. The over-counting occurred because the instructions defined in Cognos Framework Manager were incomplete. In our first model, we either did not know about, or did not understand, determinants.

There is one aspect of determinants that you should always keep in mind. The definition of a determinant is either right or it is wrong. In many parts of Cognos BI, you can be creative in how you solve a problem. Determinants are *not* one of those areas.

Determinants are used by Cognos Framework Manager to instruct the query engine on how to resolve granularity differences between multiple query subjects. Determinants work by identifying the query items within a query subject that result in a unique combination of data for a join. Many multidimensional data modelers like to think of determinants as levels in a hierarchy, and although that view is not technically correct, it can help you visualize how determinants are configured.

[Equipment].[MAKE]	[Manufacture Report Budget].[MAKE]	[Manufacture Report Budget].[BUDGET_AMOUNT]
Ford	Ford	600
Chevy	Chevy	100

TABLE 17-2   Final SQL Results

A determinant has three components: the determinant itself, the key for the determinant, and the attributes associated with the key.

The determinant itself can be one of two types, as shown in the illustration: Uniquely Identified or Group By. To qualify as uniquely identified, the key for the determinant must represent a unique row in the query subject. For example, in a date dimension, the date field would be a uniquely identified determinant key. In our Equipment table, the VIN would be a uniquely identified determinant key, because a VIN can be assigned to one vehicle exactly. The attributes of a determinant key consist of the query items that are also unique for the key. In the case of uniquely identified keys, every query item (with the exception of the key query items) is an attribute of the key. During the Metadata Wizard import of a new data source query subject, Cognos Framework Manager will automatically create a uniquely identified determinant for each unique index found.

NOTE *If you see a uniquely identified determinant with a multipart key, do not panic. That is a normal and acceptable occurrence.*

A group by determinant's key is at a higher level of granularity than the uniquely identified key, and its key query items are usually a part of a join to another query subject.

Looking at the Equipment data source query subject again, we can see that Cognos Framework Manager has created VIN, a uniquely identified determinant for us.

Unlike uniquely identified determinants, group by determinants cannot be created automatically by Cognos Framework Manager, because the query engine does not have the information it needs to identify them. We have a saying at John Daniel Associates: "You can't just know." When working with data, and how that data is to be grouped and summarized, the query engine (and every other application) must be instructed on how to handle every detail. Group by determinants provide the query engine with the instructions it needs to group and summarize data properly. Like uniquely identified determinants, group by determinants consist of a key and attributes. For a group by determinant, the key consists of one or more query items that identify a unique row in the query subject that is at a higher level of detail than the uniquely identified key.

Using our Equipment data source query subject as an example, the VIN query item has already been set by Cognos Framework Manager as the uniquely identified determinant because the VIN is a unique key in the database. The MAKE query item is used in a join to the Manufacture Monthly Budget query subject at a higher granularity than the VIN query item. Because of that, the MAKE query item needs to be the key in a group by determinant. We will also need to define a determinant on the Dates data source query subject. The [Dates].[YYYYMM] query item is at a higher granularity than the [Dates].[DATE] query item; as such, we need to define a group by determinant.

Once the determinants have been set and the package republished, the query engine will have all the information it needs to build the proper SQL for the "Make, Budget Amount" report. When we run the report, the query engine now sees that the join between Equipment and Manufacture Budget Repair has a determinant defined on the MAKE query item. Because of the determinant, the query engine will instruct the database to group by the Equipment data on the MAKE query item before retrieving the measure data from the Manufacture Repair Budget table.

The new SQL from the "Make, Budget Amount" report will look like the following:

```
SELECT  "Equipment3"."MAKE"                              AS "C0",
        SUM("Manufacture_Repair_Budget"."BUDGET_AMOUNT") AS "C1"
FROM    (SELECT "Equipment"."MAKE" AS "MAKE"
         FROM    "Rentals"."dbo"."Equipment" "Equipment"
         GROUP  BY "Equipment"."MAKE") "Equipment3",
        "Rentals"."dbo"."Manufacture Repair Budget" "Manufacture_Repair_Budget"
WHERE   "Manufacture_Repair_Budget"."MAKE" = "Equipment3"."MAKE"
GROUP   BY "Equipment3"."MAKE"
```

Compare this SQL to the original SQL; you should notice that the FROM statement has changed. The original FROM statement is a standard inner join:

```
FROM    "Rentals"."dbo"."Equipment" "Equipment",
        "Rentals"."dbo"."Manufacture Repair Budget" "Manufacture_Repair_Budget"
```

The new FROM statement is a nested query:

```
FROM    (SELECT "Equipment"."MAKE" AS "MAKE"
         FROM    "Rentals"."dbo"."Equipment" "Equipment"
         GROUP  BY "Equipment"."MAKE") "Equipment3",
        "Rentals"."dbo"."Manufacture Repair Budget" "Manufacture_Repair_Budget"
```

In this SQL, the Equipment group by query is performed first, which results in a unique list of MAKE values named "Equipment3." The result of adding the group by determinant is shown when we rerun the "Make, Budget Amount" report:

MAKE	BUDGET_AMOUNT
Chevy	100
Ford	300
Overall - Total	400

Because we have covered a lot of information, a quick review might be helpful. To fix the over-counting in our "Make, Budget Amount" report, we first had to identify what was causing the inflated results. We found that the problem was caused by the join between the Equipment query subject and the Manufacture Repair Budget query subject using a query item, MAKE, which is at a higher granularity in the Equipment query subject than it is in the Manufacture Repair Budget query subject. Finally, we found that by adding a group

by determinant to the Equipment query subject, the query engine could create SQL that
returned the correct results.

Setting Determinants   If this is your first exposure to determinants and you find yourself
rereading parts of this discussion, do not be concerned. The good news is setting up a
determinant is much easier than understanding how they work. Once you have identified
the group by determinant (or determinants) for a query subject, you can set the determinant
by following these steps.

    1. Open Cognos Framework Manager and locate the query subject to modify.

    2. Right-click the data source query subject and choose Edit Definition

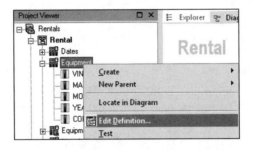

    3. From the Query Subject Definition dialog, click the Determinants tab

In this case, we already have the uniquely identified determinant called VIN that was created for us by Cognos Framework Manager.

4. To add a new determinant, click the Add link located in the middle-right of the determinant screen:

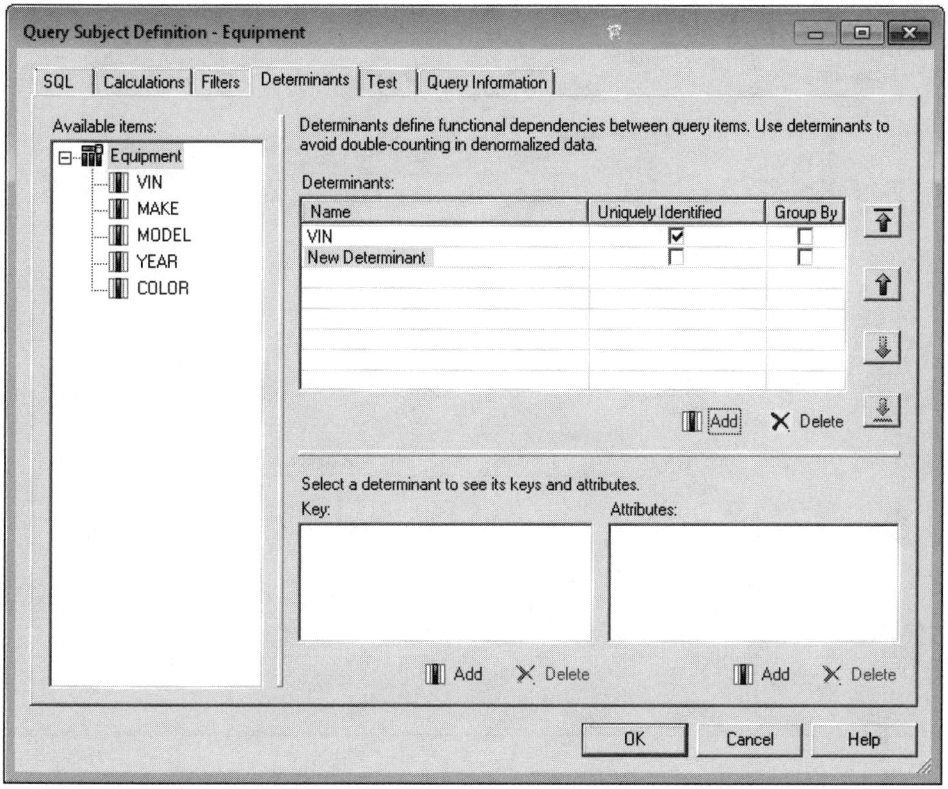

This will add a new determinant at the bottom of the Determinants list. To rename the new determinant, click the name, press F2, and type in a new name.

5. Click the Group By check box for the new determinant to identify it as a Group By. Then click the name of the determinant to reselect and click the Move Up arrow on the right.

NOTE *The order of the determinants in the list is important. Because determinants are evaluated serially, from top to bottom, uniquely identified determinants should be at the bottom of the list. The group by determinants are placed above the uniquely identified determinants in order of granularity from the finest level of detail up to the largest level of detail. For example, from bottom to top, the order of determinants in our sample Date query subject would be: Date (uniquely identified), YYYYMM (group by), and Year (group by).*

6. With the MAKE group by determinant selected, click the key query items in the Available Items pane on the left—in this case, that is the MAKE query item. Then click the Add link under the Key pane:

7. Lastly, from the Available Items pane, select any query item that is an attribute of the determinant group by key. In this case, there are no attributes for this key.

8. Click OK and republish the package.

There is no doubt that your data source query subjects will be much more complex than the examples used in this chapter. However, the same rules apply regardless of how complex your metadata.

When Do I Need a Determinant? Without knowing your data, you have no guaranteed way to identify the need for determinants. Nevertheless, you can look for a few signs that usually indicate the need for determinants:

- Inflated measures, which we just discussed, are one of the signs. If a report author adds a query item to a report and the measures "blow up," you might need a determinant.

- If you have a dimensional query subject joined to a fact query subject on a key that repeats, you might need a determinant. For example, a single Month key in a fact table will repeat once for every day of the month in the dimension table. Although the Month key itself uniquely identifies the month, because it is joined to a table that repeats, you can end up with double counting.

- If you have blob data, you will need determinants. A determinant on a blob is needed to allow quick access to the rows for the blob data without the need for a full scan of that field, which is very expensive in database terms.

Using the car rental example, let's look at the date dimension. The Dates query subject joins to the Rental Income query subject on DATE, but it also joins to the Manufacture Repair Budget on YYYYMM. This is an example of a query subject with a join on a column that does not have unique values at the given level. The determinant for the Dates query subject would look like the following:

Notice that this group by determinant does have an attribute for the key. We added this because the MONTH query item is at the same level of detail as the YYYYMM query item.

Building Relationships to Build SQL

Up to this point, you have seen how to build a Cognos Framework Manager model using a few simple tables. Now we are going look behind the curtain to see how the relationships and cardinality defined in the Cognos Framework Manager model affect the queries generated by the query engine.

Star Schemas

In Chapter 16, we talked about star schemas and how to create them. In this chapter, we will discuss why we use them. We use star schemas in our models because they work. When your data is modeled as a star schema, and determinants are set where needed, you will find the SQL generated by the query engine to be consistent and correct.

NOTE *Star schemas are not strictly required by Cognos Framework Manager. However, in our experience, using the star-schema metadata modeling approach has resulted in accurate and consistent results from our Cognos Framework Manager models and reporting.*

Consistent and correct are reason enough, but star schemas have the added benefit of being easy to understand from a modeling perspective, and they are recognized as a proven practice by industry leaders. Star schemas work well because of how the query engine generates SQL.

Query Types

As you begin to study the SQL generated by the query engine, you will notice three types of queries: *single table queries, single fact–single grain queries,* and *multiple fact–single grain queries.* You will also find multiple fact–multiple grain queries, which, for our conversation, we treat the same as multiple fact–single grain queries, except that determinants would be applied to prevent any double-counting.

Single Table Queries

The queries found in your reports will range from extremely simple to insanely complex. On the simple end of the spectrum are single table queries. These queries select one or more fields from a single table and are often used to explore dimensional data and to create simple lists, such as a product list or a list of available equipment. For example, if we want to see all of the vehicles in our sample rental fleet, we can create a Cognos Report Studio list report and drag-and-drop the entire Equipment query subject onto the list.

Running the report produces a simple list:

VIN	MAKE	MODEL	YEAR	COLOR
1234ASDF	Ford	Tarus	2008	White
1234JKLM	Chevy	Truck	2005	Green
5678ASDF	Ford	Mustang	2008	Yellow

Because all of the columns in our query are being pulled from one table, this is a single table query. Although this may seem like a trivial example, it is important that you understand how this simple query was created:

```
SELECT "Equipment"."VIN" AS "VIN",
"Equipment"."MAKE" AS "MAKE",
"Equipment"."MODEL" AS "MODEL",
"Equipment"."YEAR" AS "YEAR4",
"Equipment"."COLOR" AS "COLOR"
FROM "Rentals"."dbo"."Equipment" "Equipment"
```

Our rentals Cognos Framework Manager model has a query subject called Equipment that points to a database table that is also called Equipment. A report has requested all of the query items from the Equipment query subject. To fulfill this request, the query engine examines the metadata we defined—that being the query subject itself, the joins attached to the query subject, and the cardinality of those joins. In this example, the query engine determines that all of the requested fields come from one table and all of the fields are attributes. There is nothing to aggregate—no grouping—so the query engine writes the very simple SQL statement.

Single Fact–Single Grain Queries

The complexity of our query increases when the list report uses two tables to satisfy the report request. We make a new report using [Equipment].[VIN] and [Rental Income] .[RENTAL_AMOUNT]. We add the [Rental Income].[RENTAL_AMOUNT] measure to our list report by expanding the Rental Income query subject and dragging-and-dropping RENTAL_AMOUNT to the end of our list.

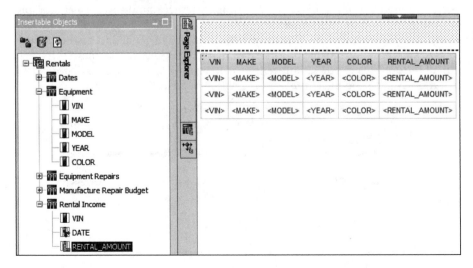

The report still looks simple; the output is a little more interesting, and the Native SQL query is more complex:

VIN	MAKE	MODEL	YEAR	COLOR	RENTAL_AMOUNT
1234ASDF	Ford	Tarus	2008	White	6,300
1234JKLM	Chevy	Truck	2005	Green	6,000
5678ASDF	Ford	Mustang	2008	Yellow	3,500

```
SELECT "Equipment"."VIN" AS "VIN",
       "Equipment"."MAKE" AS "MAKE",
       "Equipment"."MODEL" AS "MODEL",
       "Equipment"."YEAR" AS "YEAR4",
       "Equipment"."COLOR" AS "COLOR",
       SUM("Rental_Income"."RENTAL_AMOUNT") AS "RENTAL_AMOUNT"
FROM "Rentals"."dbo"."Equipment" "Equipment",
     "Rentals"."dbo"."Rental Income" "Rental_Income"
WHERE "Equipment"."VIN" = "Rental_Income"."VIN"
GROUP BY "Equipment"."VIN",
         "Equipment"."MAKE",
         "Equipment"."MODEL",
         "Equipment"."YEAR",
         "Equipment"."COLOR"
```

The IBM Cognos SQL is also more complex, but it still looks similar to the native code:

```
select
       Equipment.VIN   as   VIN,
       Equipment.MAKE   as   MAKE,
       Equipment.MODEL   as   MODEL,
       Equipment."YEAR"   as   YEAR4,
       Equipment.COLOR   as   COLOR,
       XSUM(Rental_Income.RENTAL_AMOUNT  for Equipment.VIN,Equipment.
MAKE,Equipment.MODEL,Equipment."YEAR",Equipment.COLOR )   as   RENTAL_AMOUNT
 from
       Rentals.Rentals.dbo.Equipment Equipment,
       Rentals.Rentals.dbo."Rental Income" Rental_Income
 where
       (Equipment.VIN = Rental_Income.VIN)
 group by
       Equipment.VIN,
       Equipment.MAKE,
       Equipment.MODEL,
       Equipment."YEAR",
       Equipment.COLOR
```

This query was created by the query engine using the same process as the original report. However, with more than one table required to fulfill the report request, the process was a little different. In this case, the query engine sees that two tables are required, so it looks at the cardinality of the joins on the query subjects. First, the query engine looks for a query subject with an "n" cardinality; in this case, that is Rental Income.

The query engine examines the cardinality of the other query subjects but does not find any other "n's", so it builds the SQL based on the joins it finds in the metadata we created in Cognos Framework Manager; in this case that will be [Equipment].[VIN] = [Rental_Income].[VIN]. Because the query engine found an "n" on the Rental Income query subject, the engine is expecting to find at least one query item with its usage set to Fact. The query engine examines the metadata we defined and finds that RENTAL_AMOUNT is indeed a Fact and that its Regular Aggregate property is set to Sum. Because the RENTAL_AMOUNT aggregate is set to Sum and the Cognos Report Studio query is set to the default Auto Group and Summarize, that is why we see the SUM("Rental_Income"."RENTAL_AMOUNT") AS "RENTAL_AMOUNT" and the Group By statement at the end of the SQL.

This is, again, a simple example of a single fact–single grain query. More complex variations of these queries use multiple fact and dimension tables, but the process used to generate the SQL is the same as in our single fact example because the results can be returned by a single SQL statement.

Multiple Fact–Multiple Grain Queries

On the complex end of the query spectrum, we find the multiple fact–multiple grain queries. As the name implies, these queries are requesting data from more than one fact table, where at least one of those fact tables has data stored at a different granularity (level of detail) than the other fact tables in the query. We often see this type of query when actual values are compared to budget or forecast values, because actual values are typically stored at the lowest level of detail, while budget and forecast values are typically stored at a higher level detail. In our Rental example, the RENTAL_AMOUNT from the Rental Income query subject is stored at the lowest level of detail; each RENTAL_AMOUNT is associated with a single vehicle and a single date timestamp. The BUDGET_AMOUNT from the Manufacture Repair Budget query subject is stored at a higher level of detail; each BUDGET_AMOUNT is associated with a MAKE of vehicle, which includes multiple vehicles, and YYYYMM, which contains multiple dates.

If we remove the MODEL, YEAR, and COLOR columns and add the BUDGET_AMOUNT to our current list report and check the results, we see the accurate budget amounts. (The amounts would be inflated if we did not set determinants, as discussed earlier in this chapter.)

VIN	MAKE	RENTAL_AMOUNT	BUDGET_AMOUNT
1234JKLM	Chevy	6,000	100
1234ASDF	Ford	6,300	300
5678ASDF	Ford	3,500	300
Overall - Total		15,800	400

To understand why this is so, take a look at the SQL generated by the query engine. First, we look at the Native SQL:

```
SELECT  "Equipment"."VIN"                                       AS "C0",
        "Equipment"."MAKE"                                      AS "C1",
        SUM("Manufacture_Repair_Budget"."BUDGET_AMOUNT") AS "C2"
FROM    "Rentals"."dbo"."Equipment" "Equipment",
        "Rentals"."dbo"."Manufacture Repair Budget" "Manufacture_Repair_Budget"
WHERE   "Manufacture_Repair_Budget"."MAKE" = "Equipment"."MAKE"
GROUP   BY "Equipment"."VIN",
           "Equipment"."MAKE"


SELECT  "Equipment"."VIN"                        AS "C0",
        "Equipment"."MAKE"                       AS "C1",
        SUM("Rental_Income"."RENTAL_AMOUNT") AS "C2"
FROM    "Rentals"."dbo"."Equipment" "Equipment",
        "Rentals"."dbo"."Rental Income" "Rental_Income"
WHERE   "Equipment"."VIN" = "Rental_Income"."VIN"
GROUP   BY "Equipment"."VIN",
           "Equipment"."MAKE"
```

Notice that two queries are being sent to the database. The first query returns the BUDGET_AMOUNT from the Manufacture Repair Budget query subject, and the second query returns the RENTAL_AMOUNT from the Rental Income query subject. To understand why the query is built this way, let's take a closer look at the model:

This shows the two fact tables, Rental Income and Manufacture Repair Budget, and the shared dimension table, Equipment.

When the query engine receives the request for this report, it first looks for the query subjects with the "n". In this case, two fact query subjects are found with a conformed dimension between them. What we see in this SQL is the query engine running the Manufacture Budget Repair and Equipment query followed by the Rental Income and Equipment query.

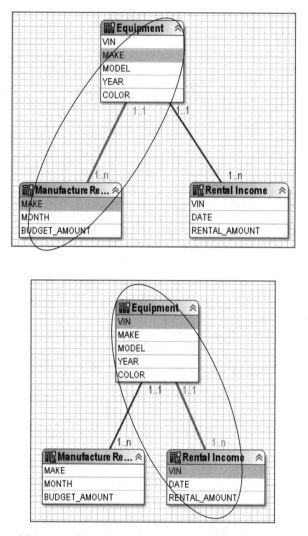

The IBM Cognos SQL provides a clear picture of what happens next:

```
1   with
2   D as
3       (select
4               Equipment.VIN   as   VIN,
5               Equipment.MAKE  as   MAKE,
6               XSUM(Manufacture_Repair_Budget.BUDGET_AMOUNT  for Equipment.VIN,Equipment.
MAKE ) as  BUDGET_AMOUNT,
7               XSUM(XSUM(Manufacture_Repair_Budget.BUDGET_AMOUNT  for Equipment.
VIN,Equipment.MAKE ) at Equipment.VIN,Equipment.MAKE )  as  Total_BUDGET_AMOUNT_
8       from
```

```
9               Rentals.Rentals.dbo.Equipment Equipment,
10              Rentals.Rentals.dbo."Manufacture Repair Budget" Manufacture_Repair_Budget
11        where
12              (Manufacture_Repair_Budget.MAKE = Equipment.MAKE)
13        group by
14              Equipment.VIN,
15              Equipment.MAKE
16        ),
17   D3 as
18      (select
19              Equipment.VIN   as   VIN,
20              Equipment.MAKE  as   MAKE,
21              XSUM(Rental_Income.RENTAL_AMOUNT   for  Equipment.VIN,Equipment.MAKE )   as
RENTAL_AMOUNT,
22              XSUM(XSUM(Rental_Income.RENTAL_AMOUNT   for  Equipment.VIN,Equipment.MAKE )
at Equipment.VIN,Equipment.MAKE )   as   Total_RENTAL_AMOUNT_
23        from
24              Rentals.Rentals.dbo.Equipment Equipment,
25              Rentals.Rentals.dbo."Rental Income" Rental_Income
26        where
27              (Equipment.VIN = Rental_Income.VIN)
28        group by
29              Equipment.VIN,
30              Equipment.MAKE
31        )
32   select
33          coalesce(D.VIN,D3.VIN)   as   VIN,
34          coalesce(D.MAKE,D3.MAKE)   as   MAKE,
35          D3.RENTAL_AMOUNT   as   RENTAL_AMOUNT,
36          D.BUDGET_AMOUNT   as   BUDGET_AMOUNT,
37          XMIN(D3.Total_RENTAL_AMOUNT_ )   as   Total_RENTAL_AMOUNT_,
38          XMIN(D.Total_BUDGET_AMOUNT_ )   as   Total_BUDGET_AMOUNT_
39      from
40          D
41            full outer join
42          D3
43            on ((D.VIN = D3.VIN) and (D.MAKE = D3.MAKE))
```

This SQL, up to line 31, looks very similar to the Native SQL. The code to which we want to pay close attention is on lines 33 and 34. The `coalesce` function plays an important role in how the query engine generates the correct results for us. The `coalesce` function accepts a list of values, query items in our case, and returns the first value in the list that is not null. After each Fact and Dimension query subject combination is run, the query engine merges the results on common (or shared) dimensional query items using the `coalesce` function. Also note lines 39 through 43; here we see the query is merging the data using a full outer join. This is done so that no data is left behind.

This is where we come back to the importance of the star schema. When we model our data using start schemas, we are providing the query engine with the information about the fact query items and the dimensional query items. The query engine then uses that information to build SQL that generated correct results.

One important rule must be followed for the star schema to work properly: Always use attributes from conformed dimensions in your report for multiple fact queries. If you do not, the `coalesce` and outer join logic in the query engine will not have enough information to merge the facts from your report.

The Model Is Not the End

Whether you love data modeling or were forced into it because no one else was willing to touch Cognos Framework Manager, it is important that you remember why you are doing this. Your organization needs accurate business analytics (BA) to be competitive, and the authors developing those analyses need correctly modeled metadata to provide timely and accurate information to the organization.

If you have not read Chapter 12, you should do so. Understanding what the report authors are trying to do with the packages you give them is critical to building successful models and deploying a successful BA implementation. There will be times when, although you have given the authors a technically correct model, the reports created from that model do not leverage the power of Cognos 10. An example of this is detailed in Chapter 12. For a quick recap, a report author who was new to Cognos Report Studio but knowledgeable in SQL wrote a report with about 32 queries. The view from the Query Explorer looked like the queries on the right.

After seeing this, an experienced Cognos Report Studio author rewrote the report. Then the new Query Explorer looked like this:

No changes were made to the model between the first report and the second, and the second report ran much faster. When you see a report with more than one or two joined queries, one of three things is happening: the report author does not understand the Cognos Framework Manager package, the package does not meet the reporting needs, or it is just a crazy report requirement. In any case, there always needs to be communication between the data modeler and the report authors.

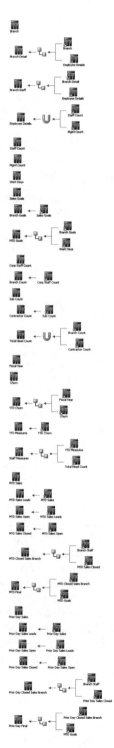

Maintaining Models in IBM Cognos Framework Manager

C hapters 16 and 17 focused on modeling relational data, which is the primary purpose of Cognos Framework Manager. But it also provides various tools and functionality that offer the metadata modeler great flexibility in the use and maintenance of both the Cognos Framework Manager model and the metadata itself.

Several often-used functions are discussed in this chapter. Several additional tools are included in Cognos Framework Manager and are not discussed here; refer to your IBM Cognos documentation for the complete list of all functionality.

Macros

The macros used in Cognos Framework Manager are similar to those found in many other applications. *Macros* are small pieces of logic or code that can be inserted into many different objects in your model, such as model query subjects, data connection definitions, filters, or just about any object that can use information that's available when the model is accessed by a report or IBM Cognos Studios.

Macros can include references to parameter maps, which you define using static values, a user's session parameters, or parameters defined by the modeler, called *model session parameters*. Model session parameters can be either static values or macros. Macros, combined with model session parameters, allow you to create session parameters that can leverage all macro functions, other session parameters, and parameter maps—in other words, you can create your own dynamic parameters.

Our customers often use macros to dynamically modify the filters being used by IBM Cognos 10 when a report is run. Here is an example of how macros work in such a scenario: Suppose a report author wants to create a sales report that returns only records belonging to the user running the report. The report author knows that one column in the Sales_Staff table is called Staff_Name, so he could add a prompt in the report asking for the user name and then use Staff_Name as a filter—something like this: *[Staff name] = ?P_Staff_name?*. Although this will limit the query results only to those records that have the sales name entered by the person running the report, a few problems could result. What if the person running the report enters someone else's name? What if someone has access to IBM Cognos Query Studio and decides to look at the sales data for all sales staff? With Cognos Framework Manager, you could use a macro to filter records directly in the query based on the user's login information.

Another use of macros is to modify the data items in a model query subject. This example is covered in detail in your IBM Cognos documentation, but it is worth mentioning here. Using macros, you can change the column names used during SQL generation. The classic example of this occurs when multilingual users use tables with multiple language columns, one for each supported locale for the users. The appropriate column would be selected at runtime based on the user's `runLocale` session parameter.

The final example we will discuss is switching database connections at runtime by using macros. Imagine that you run a service company that provides data collection and reporting to hospitals. Given the concern surrounding patient privacy, the many hospitals that use your service need to be sure that their data is kept physically separate from that of your other customers. To address the data separation issue, you create multiple databases, one for each hospital, and all of which use the same schema. At first, you decide to create a Cognos Framework Manager model for each hospital, but you quickly realize how many models, and how much maintenance, that will require. You would like to create one set of reports, and by extension one Cognos Framework Manager model, that every hospital can use. By using parameter maps combined with session parameters and some functions that come with Cognos Framework Manager, you can automate which database is used each time a report is run based on the user's logon information.

Creating a Macro

Before we go into the details of the examples, let's talk about what you use with a macro, what a macro looks like, and how you create macros.

Session Parameters

When working with macros, you can use two types of session parameters: *environment session parameters* and *model session parameters*. The environment session parameters are set when the user signs on to IBM Cognos Connection, opens a Cognos Studio, or opens Cognos Framework Manager. By default, when a user logs in through an authentication provider, the standard environment session parameters available for use include `runLocale`, `account.defaultName`, and `account.personalInfo.userName`. Depending on your authentication source, you might see additional parameters, as some authentication providers support custom session parameters. These additional environment session parameters are defined by your administrator and are made available through Cognos Configuration to Cognos Framework Manager. For example, you could have an additional attribute in your Lightweight Directory Access Protocol (LDAP) provider called City that is used to indicate the city in which a user works. This session parameter can be used in Cognos Framework Manager to filter data on the user's city.

You define model session parameters inside Cognos Framework Manager. These parameters are created using hard-coded values, macro functions, query items, and the already mentioned session parameters.

NOTE *When using a session parameter in a macro, the parameter name is preceded with a dollar sign ($).*

Accessing and modifying session parameters will be discussed in "Macro Functions," later in the chapter.

Anatomy of a Macro

In its simplest form, a macro consists of *delimiters* and *expressions*. A delimiter is a character that is used to mark the beginning and the end of the expression. In a Cognos 10 macro, the pound sign (#) is the delimiter used to mark the start and end of a macro. Therefore, a macro would look like this:

```
#expression#
```

The expression part of the macro is a little more complex. An expression can be just about anything: a macro function, a session parameter, a query item, text, and so on. What is included in the expression depends entirely upon what you want the macro to do. Table 18-1 shows a few general examples of macro expressions.

Parameter Maps

The last example in Table 18-1 makes use of a parameter map called `Language_lookup{}`. As the name implies, *parameter maps* are two-column lookups or substitution tables defined within your Cognos Framework Manager model. In our example, we passed the string `en-us` to the parameter map and the map returned the value to which `en-us` is mapped—in this case, `EN`.

Parameter maps are used when your data sources and session parameters do not contain the exact information you need in your model. In the case of the `Language_lookup` parameter map, you know that people from many different places around the world will be using this model. Each connection (or session) made to Cognos Connection could result in one of many `runLocale` values: in English alone, there are at least 15 different `runLocale` values—en, en-us, en-au, en-ca, en-gb, and so on. Each of those `runLocale` values can, for the most part, use the same base language: English.

Instead of modeling for every possible `runLocale`, you can create the `Language_lookup` parameter map to replace multiple language codes with a single common code found in

Macro	Expression	Result
`#$runLocale#`	`$runLocale`	en-us
`#sb($runLocale)#`	`sb($runLocale)`	[en-us]
`#$runLocale + ' is my preferred language'#`	`$runLocale + ' is my preferred language'`	En-us is my preferred language
`#$Language_lookup {$runLocale}#`	`$Language_ lookup{$runLocale}`	EN

TABLE 18-1 Sample Macros

the data. As shown next, parameter maps are simple structures. This parameter map has a key (the item to look up) and a return value:

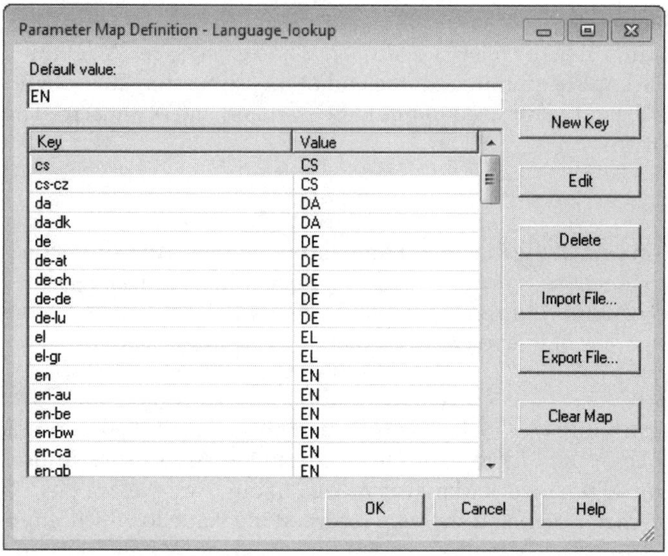

NOTE *Parameter maps can contain any key-value pair that you need, but it is important to remember that as your map becomes larger, it also becomes slower.*

Parameter maps are used in our hospital example in this chapter, so we will return to them later in the section "Create a Parameter Map."

Make a Macro

Your location within Cognos Framework Manager determines exactly how you create a macro. When you are working from the Query Subject Definition screen for a model query subject, you can use macros either in the Filters tab or in a query item from the Query Items And Calculations pane:

Filters tab

Query Items And Calculations pane

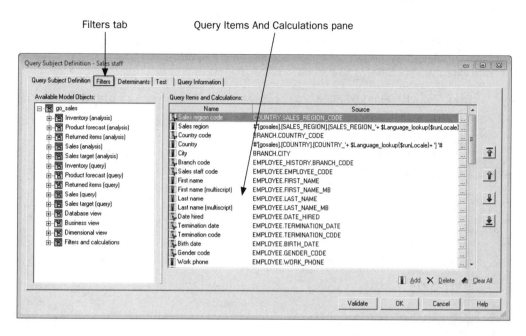

Access the Query Subject Definition screen by right-clicking a model query subject and choosing Edit Definition, or double-click the model query subject.

***

NOTE *Although you can create macros in data source query subjects, we recommend that you use macros only in model query subjects. This is in keeping with the practice of leaving data source query subjects as clean as possible for performance reasons.*

***

The Filter Definition dialog and the Calculation Definition dialog both have a Parameters tab at the bottom of the Available Components pane:

Available
Components
pane

Parameters
tab

By using one or more of the items in the Parameters tab, you can create any macro you need. We will show you an example of how to use a macro to return the records from the Sales Staff model query subject for the person running the query.

To create a macro, follow these steps:

1. Double-click the model query subject to open the Query Subject Definition screen.

2. Click the Filters tab at the top of the screen.

3. Click the Add button at the bottom of the screen:

4. Enter a name for the filter in the Name text box. Type **Staff Name Filter**.

5. On the Model tab in the Available Components pane, navigate to the data item on which you want to filter. In this example, use the Staff name from the Sales Staff model query subject.

6. In the Expression Definition pane, add the data item.

7. In the Expression Definition pane, after the data item, add the logical operator and the appropriate session parameter on which to filter. In this example use the equal sign (=) and the `account.defaultName` session parameter.

At this point, your filter definition will look something like the one shown next:

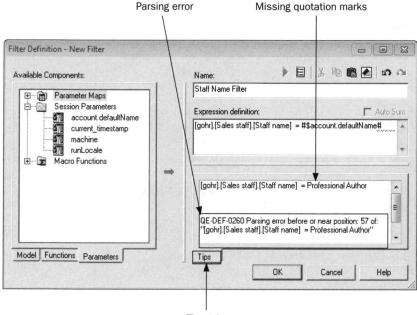

Tips tab

Note the following three items in the illustration:

- The parsing error in the Tips pane.
- The default user name is missing quotation marks.
- The user name is listed as Professional Author, which is not a name found in the Sales Staff model query subject.

The missing quotation marks present an issue, because when you use a string in a SQL statement, the string has to be enclosed in single quotation marks. We can fix the missing quotation marks using a macro function, which we will discuss in the "Macro Functions" section of this chapter coming up.

As for the user name, Cognos Framework Manager lets us set override values for any session parameter, as shown in the next section.

Override Default Session Parameter Values   Overriding the default session parameter values makes developing and testing macros much easier by removing the need to set up multiple test users.

To override default session parameter values, follow these steps:

1. From the menu bar in Cognos Framework Manager, choose Project | Session Parameters:

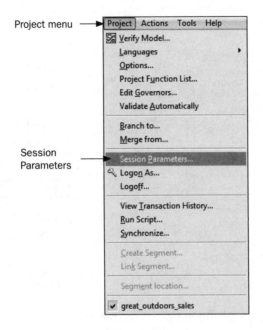

The Session Parameters dialog opens:

2. Select the parameter you want to modify and click the Edit button. The rows for the selected parameter changes to text boxes in which you can enter data.

3. In the Override Value column for the selected parameter, enter the override value. In this example, type **Sally White**, because we know that this is the name of one of our sales staff.

Override account.defaultName

4. Click OK. The override value is stored and the results of the test are changed. In this example, because we used Sally White for the override value, it now appears as the user name:

The user name looks better, but it is still missing the quotation marks. To fix that issue, we need to look at the built-in macro functions.

Macro Functions

You can use several different types of macro functions when building your macros. When you select a macro function from the Macro Functions folder, you'll see details about the function in the Tips pane, such as to what the macro can be applied, how it works with your information, and what the current results are for that macro.

NOTE *Cognos Framework Manager comes with a number of macro functions. Refer to the Cognos 10 documentation for a complete list.*

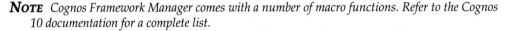
Macro Functions folder   Tips pane

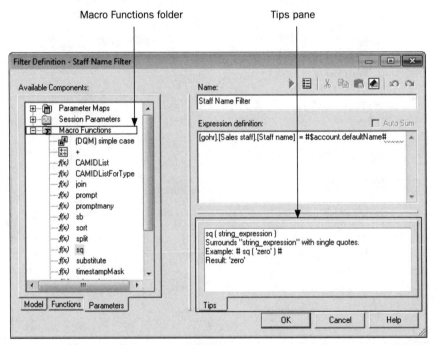

When you're working with different objects in Cognos Framework Manager, you can use delimiters to tell the application what type of object is being used. For example, when you're working with a query item or a namespace, you wrap the objects in square brackets to tell Cognos Framework Manager that this is a data item. When you need to use a string, as in our example, you use the single quotation marks macro, `#sq($account.defaultName)#`, which in our case results in 'Sally White'. If you need square brackets, use the `sb()` function.

Let's finish the user filter example that we started earlier in the chapter. We'll need to use the `sq()` macro function and a filter like the one shown next:

```
[gohr].[Sales Staff].[Staff name]  = #sq($account.defaultName)#
```

As a result, our Expression Definition information is updated, like so:

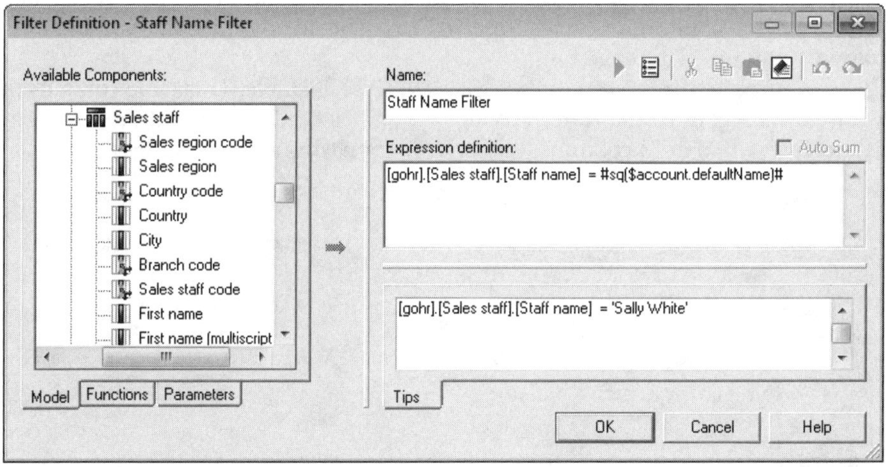

Click the Test Sample link at the lower-right to test the modified model query subject and make sure that the filter returns only records belonging to Sally White.

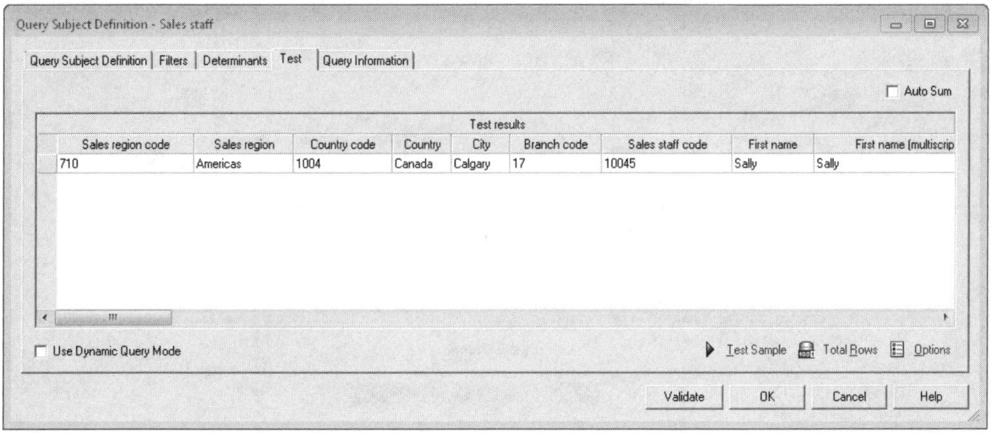

Additional Macro Examples

You can use macros in many ways; they are particularly useful when you need to determine information at runtime. In the next two sections, we will discuss two more examples to illustrate how macros can be used at runtime.

Using Macros in Multilingual Implementations

Our next example uses the `runLocale` session parameter to define a data item dynamically in a model query subject. Using the sample data that comes with Cognos 10, we continue with the Sales Staff model query subject. In this example, we will use the paragon of outdoor equipment providers, the Great Outdoors Company (GO). GO has customers in

France, Italy, and the United States, but the company does not want to maintain separate databases for each language. In this case, you, as the database administrator at GO, have decided to include a column for each supported language in any table that might hold information in multiple languages.

A good example of this is seen in the ORGANIZATION table. This table contains three pieces of information: the organization code, the organization parent, and the name of the organization presented in 23 columns, one column for each supported language.

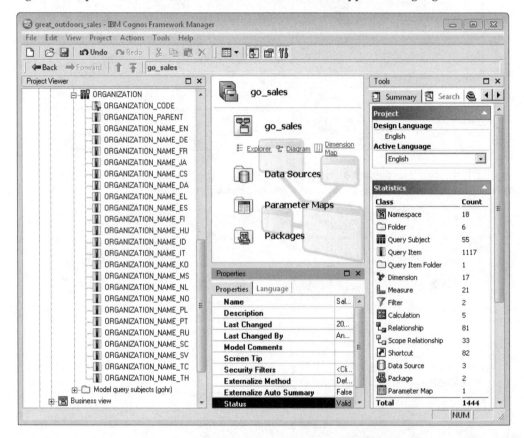

When the modeler created the Sales Staff model query subject, a macro was used to dynamically select the appropriate language for the current user based on the user's `runLocale`.

To edit the query item in the Query Subject Definition, follow these steps:

1. Using a parameter map, replace the default column, ORGANIZATION_NAME_EN, with the following macro:

```
#'[gohr].[ORGANIZATION].[ORGANIZATION_NAME_'+ $Language_
lookup{$runLocale}+ '] '#
```

When the macro is added, the Tips pane of the Calculation Definition dialog updates:

2. Click the Test button to test the macro with default session parameters to make sure that correct information has been accessed. The test results display in the Test Results pane:

3. Click the Options button to override the current session parameters to test the macro with a different `runLocale`. The Options dialog displays:

4. Click Set to open the Session Parameters dialog, where you can override the `runLocale` and set it to Italy (it):

Override value

5. Click OK and the Calculation Definition dialog displays again. The Tips pane displays the modified query item:

6. Test the new `runLocale` to make sure that the macro returns the desired results by clicking the Test icon. The results from the Organization column now display in Italian:

PART IV

NOTE *Session parameters are for the current session and remain in effect until the data modeler ends the session or manually overrides the setting.*

Using Macros to Point to the Correct Database

In our final macro example, we will use the hospital service company mentioned earlier. If you recall, we have many physically separate databases and would like to keep our number of Cognos Framework Manager models low, somewhere in the area of one. Because the schema of each database is the same, our only challenge is how to connect the right user to the right database automatically.

To do this we have to make three assumptions:

- All of the databases exist and have the exact same schema.
- All of the databases are defined as Data Sources in Cognos Connection.
- We have some way to associate the person accessing the model with the correct data source.

For simplicity's sake, let's also assume that we service three hospitals: Mercy Hospital, Lincoln Hospital, and Adams Hospital. We also have three databases, Mercy, Lincoln, and Adams, with one data source connection for each database. Our database administrator has created the databases per our request, and we have set up our data source connections, so conditions one and two are met, as shown next:

To meet our third condition, we need to know something about our users; specifically, we need to know which users can see what data. In an attempt to keep this example simple, let's assume that all the sign-on names in our authentication source are unique and that any one sign-on is permitted to see exactly one database only. For our example, we will manually create a *parameter map* to map a user to the appropriate database.

Create a Parameter Map Before we can create a parameter map, however, we need a project in which to put it. If we start from scratch using the Adams data source for our new project, our hospital project would look something like this:

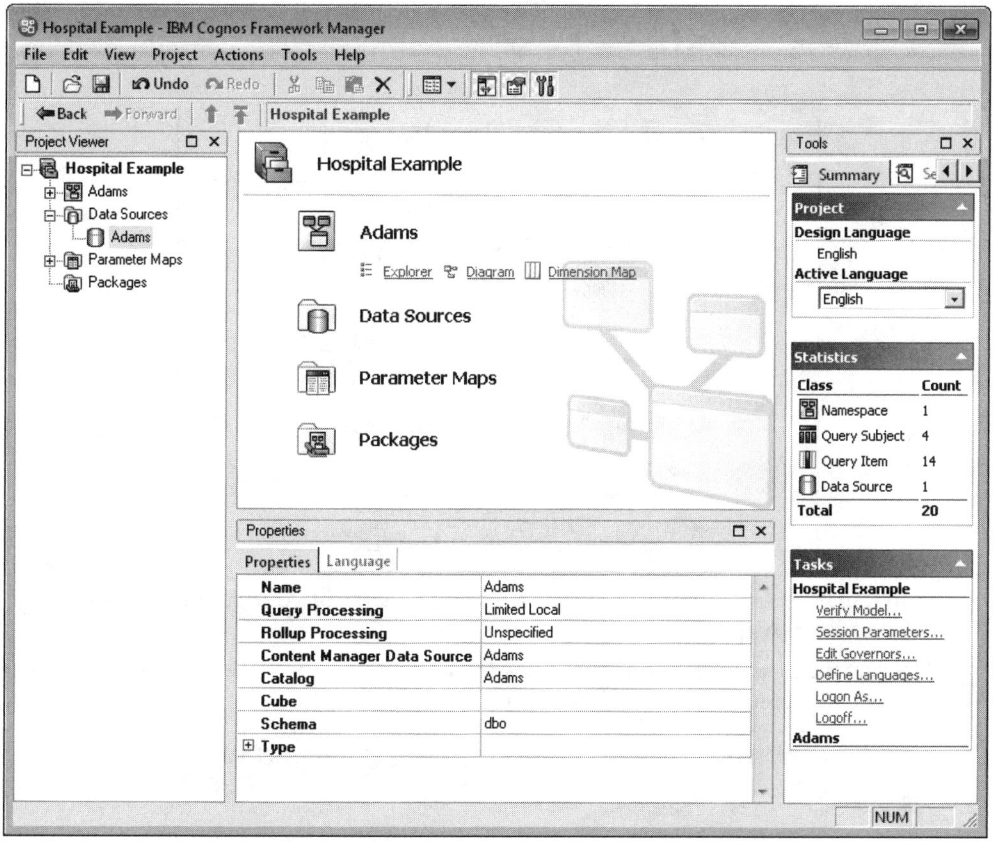

TIP *In this example, we are creating our parameter map manually. However, you can also create a parameter map from an external file or based on query items. This can be useful if an employee table contains attributes about the people in your organization and you want to supply the parameter map values based on query items. One of those employee attributes could contain the database that the employee is able to access. We could use the employee ID as the key and the database that user can access as the value to populate the parameter map. For more information on using query items to populate a parameter map, refer to the Cognos Framework Manager documentation that came with your Cognos 10 installation.*

Now that we have created a project, we can create our parameter map. The easiest way to create a parameter map is to use the Create Parameter Map Wizard.

To create a parameter map using the Create Parameter Map Wizard, follow these steps:

1. In the Project Viewer pane, right-click the Parameter Maps folder and choose Create | Parameter Map.

2. In the Select Creation Method screen, enter the name of your parameter map. In this case, enter **Hospital_Lookup**.

3. Select the method to be used to create the map. In this case, select Manually Enter The Parameter Keys, And/Or Import Them From A File:

4. Click Next. The Define Keys And Values screen displays:

5. Enter a default value. This is the value returned if no key matches what is provided to the parameter map. In this case, type **Adams**.

6. Click the New Key button.

7. Enter the keys for your map. In this example, use individual user IDs.

8. Enter the value to which the key maps. In this example, enter the name of the Content Manager data source.

9. Click Finish. You can use the parameter map to map users from your LDAP
   authentication provider to the appropriate data source connection name.

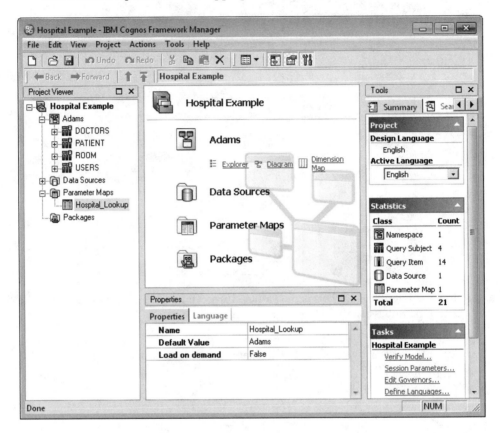

Because there are more hospitals than Adams, we need to make the name of our data
source more generic. Let's use the name "Hospital." When we rename Adams to Hospital,
the following warning displays:

This warning notifies us that Cognos Framework Manager has also updated any table query subject that was using *Adams* (this is a new feature in Cognos 10). For example, the [Adams].[DOCTORS] table is now the [Hospital].[DOCTORS] table. The objective of this example is to have one data source that can point to any data connection based on the macro. As a result, this automatic renaming works to our advantage. Cognos Framework Manager did all the heavy lifting of renaming the query subjects for us.

The table query definition for USERS displays:

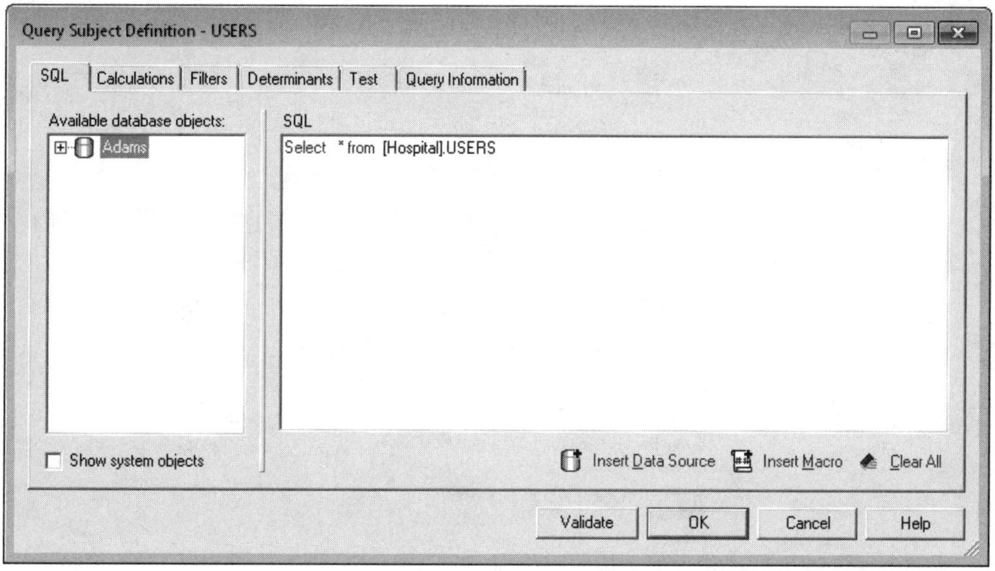

This example shows us that our query listed in the SQL pane looks correct. However, the Available Database Objects pane still displays Adams, because we renamed only the data source. We did not change the data source connection.

We have renamed the data source to a more generic name. Now we need to add our macro. This example shows the Properties pane for our Hospital data source connection:

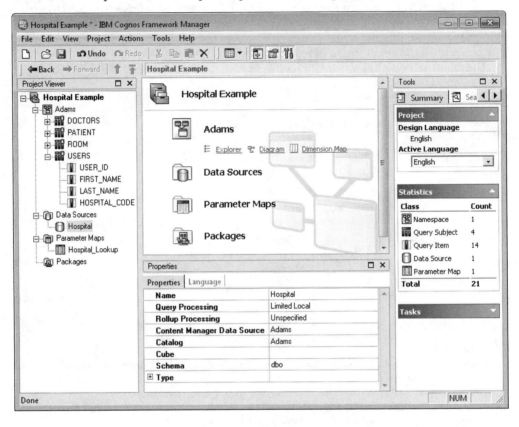

NOTE   *In this example, the Catalog property of the data source is the same name as the database. As such, we need the same macro in that field as well.*

The Content Manager Data Source is where we need to add our macro. Follow these steps:

1. Click the Content Manager Data Source field. Then click the ellipses button that displays. The Edit Property Value dialog box opens:

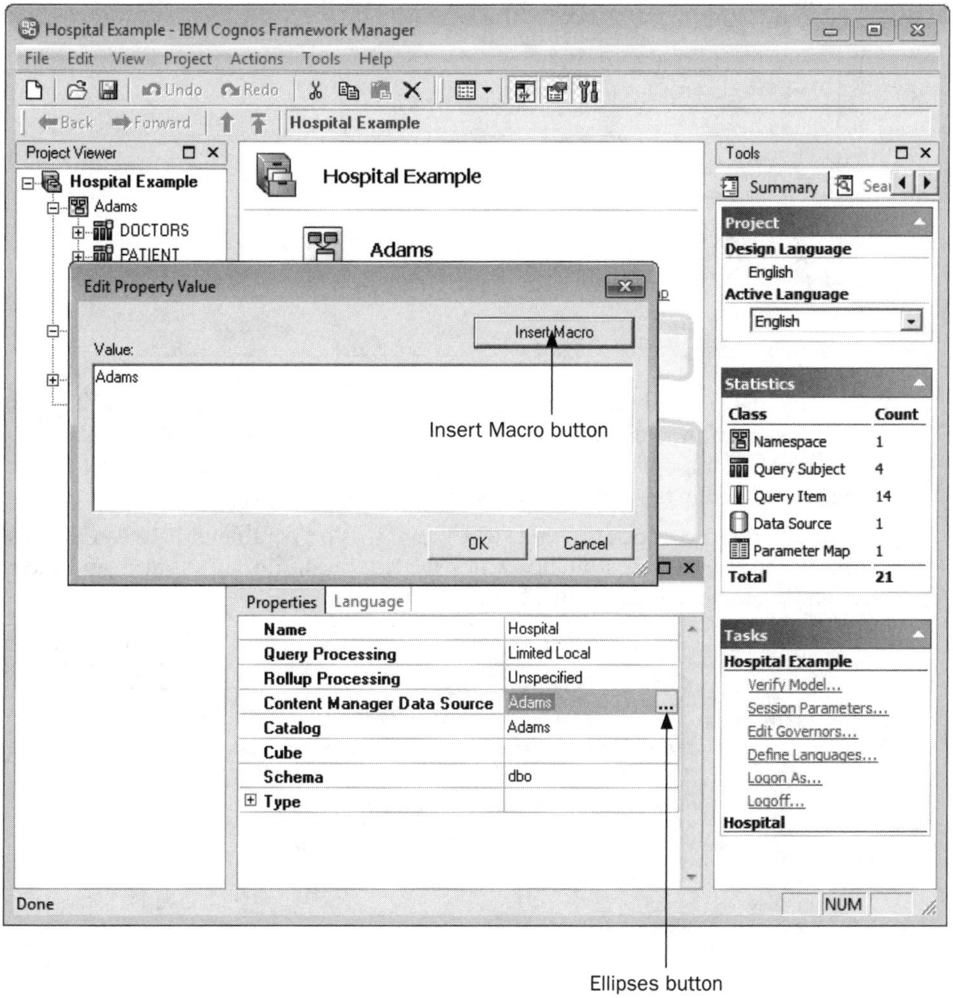

Insert Macro button

Ellipses button

2. Click the Insert Macro button to open the Macro Editor dialog to build the macro:

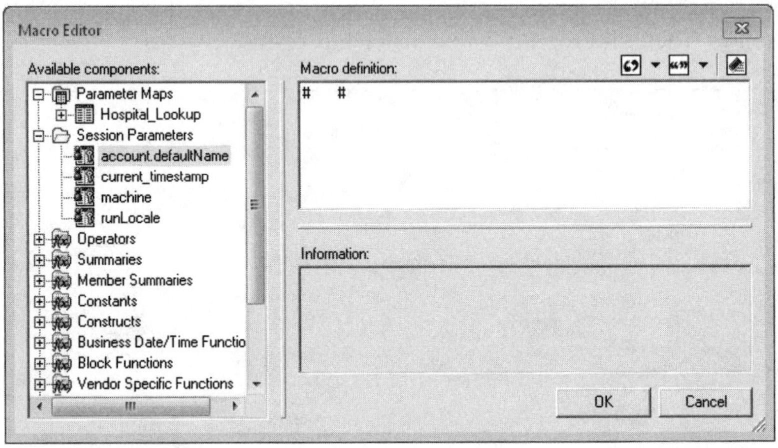

Our macro needs to determine who is trying to connect to which database. If we look at our session parameters, we see that the `account.defaultName` is available in the Available Components pane. We assume this value will be unique as all of our users are defined in the same authentication source.

3. Drag-and-drop the `account.defaultName` session parameter between the hash marks in the Macro Definition box. Click the `account.defaultName`, and the Session Parameters dialog is displayed.

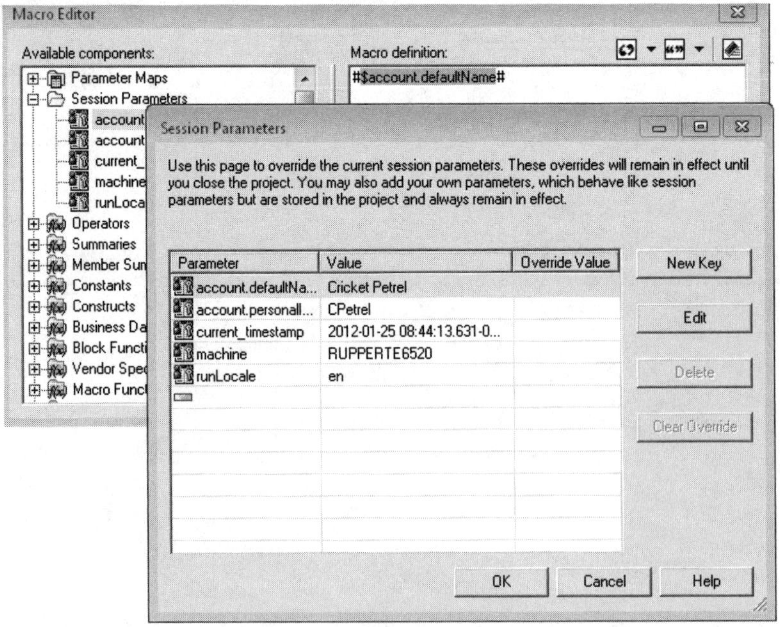

4. Click the OK button to return to the Macro Editor screen.

This example has shown the `userName` for the current session, and this gives us the key to our parameter map.

5. Using the default name as a parameter to the Hospital_Lookup parameter map, find the proper database for the current user:

The session parameter is passed to the parameter map, which returns the database value associated with CPetrel. In this example, the data source value is Adams.

You can see the SQL created when the user is CPetrel by right-clicking the USERS query subject, selecting the test option from the menu, clicking the Query Information tab, and clicking the Test Sample link at the bottom right of the screen:

Adams data source

You can test the query to make sure that each user is accessing the correct database by supplying a user name from the Lincoln hospital as the parameter override value; in this case, use WWilder. This user can access the Lincoln data source as shown next:

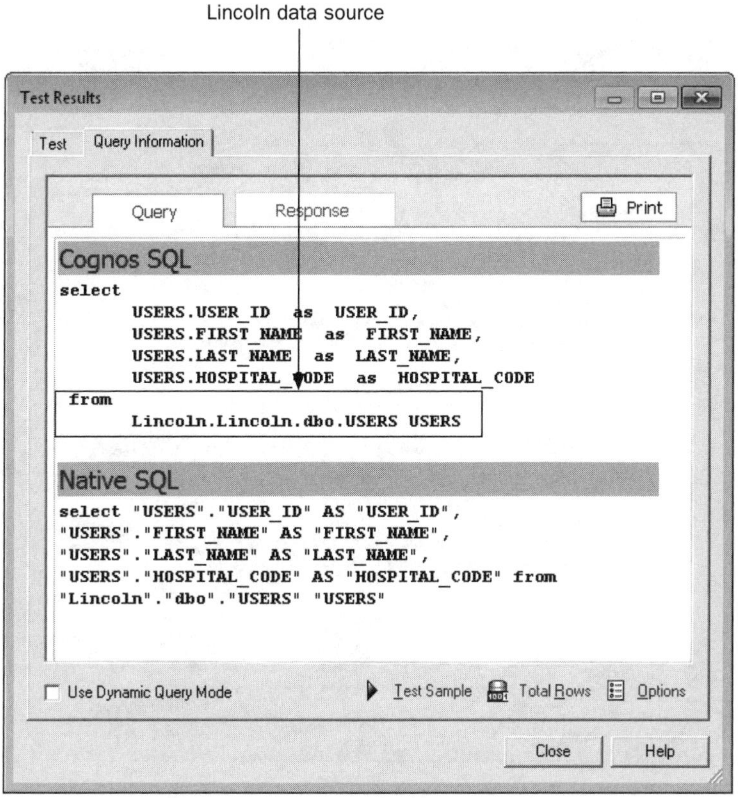

Lincoln data source

If we override the user name in our session parameter list to SKamal, that user can access the Mercy data source:

Mercy data source

```
Test Results                                                    ─  □  ✕

  Test  │ Query Information │

  ┌──────────────────────────────────────────────────────────────┐
  │        Query              Response                  🖨 Print   │
  │  Cognos SQL                                                    │
  │  select                                                        │
  │          USERS.USER_ID   as   USER_ID,                         │
  │          USERS.FIRST_NAME   as   FIRST_NAME,                   │
  │          USERS.LAST_NAME   as   LAST_NAME,                     │
  │          USERS.HOSPITAL_CODE   as   HOSPITAL_CODE              │
  │   from                                                         │
  │          Mercy.Mercy.dbo.USERS USERS                           │
  │                                                                │
  │  Native SQL                                                    │
  │  select "USERS"."USER_ID" AS "USER_ID",                       │
  │  "USERS"."FIRST_NAME" AS "FIRST_NAME",                        │
  │  "USERS"."LAST_NAME" AS "LAST_NAME",                         │
  │  "USERS"."HOSPITAL_CODE" AS "HOSPITAL_CODE" from             │
  │  "Mercy"."dbo"."USERS" "USERS"                                │
  │                                                                │
  └──────────────────────────────────────────────────────────────┘
  ☐ Use Dynamic Query Mode        ▶ Test Sample  🔢 Total Rows  ▤ Options

                                           Close        Help
```

In each case, the same query subject is referencing an entirely different database through the use of a macro that uses a parameter map and a session parameter.

Macros can be used to keep your models simple and flexible. Any time you find yourself duplicating effort, take a step back and ask yourself if a macro might be the solution.

Security

With Cognos Framework Manager, you can specify *package security* that defines who can access the package to author and run reports, and who can administer the package to publish it and set permissions for it. You can also specify *object security*, which sets explicit allow or deny access to folders, namespaces, query subjects, query items, and so on. Finally, *data security* lets you apply security filters to restrict rows returned from a query.

Configure Package Access

You can configure access permissions on a package to grant specific users, groups, or roles access to the contents of the package via the Cognos Studios. Permissions are added to a package using the users, groups, and roles found in the Cognos namespace or your authentication provider.

Package access permissions can be applied when you publish the package the first time using the Publish Wizard or at any time after that through Cognos Framework Manager or Cognos Connection. When you choose to apply package access permissions is a personal choice, although we've found it easier to apply maintain package access permissions after the package has been published, because it's easier to have power users maintain permissions through Cognos Connection that to have the modeler maintain permissions through Cognos Framework Manager. The package's properties can be accessed through Cognos Connection or in Cognos Framework Manager from the Actions menu: Choose Actions | Package | Edit Package Settings.

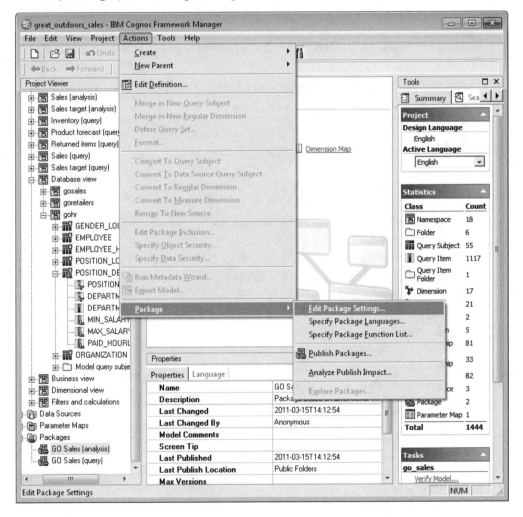

NOTE *The package properties accessed from the Edit Package Settings in Cognos Framework Manager are identical to the package properties accessed in Cognos Connection (including the Permissions tab).*

When you publish a package and do not set the access permissions from the Publish Wizard, the package inherits the permissions from the folder to which it is published. By selecting the Permissions tab on the Set Properties screen, shown next, you can see what those default settings are and how they were applied to the package, and you can modify them. To specify package access permissions, you grant Read, Write, Execute, and Traverse permissions. To specify administrator access permissions, you grant Read, Write, Set Policy, and Traverse permissions.

NOTE *Setting permissions on Cognos Connection objects is discussed in Chapter 19.*

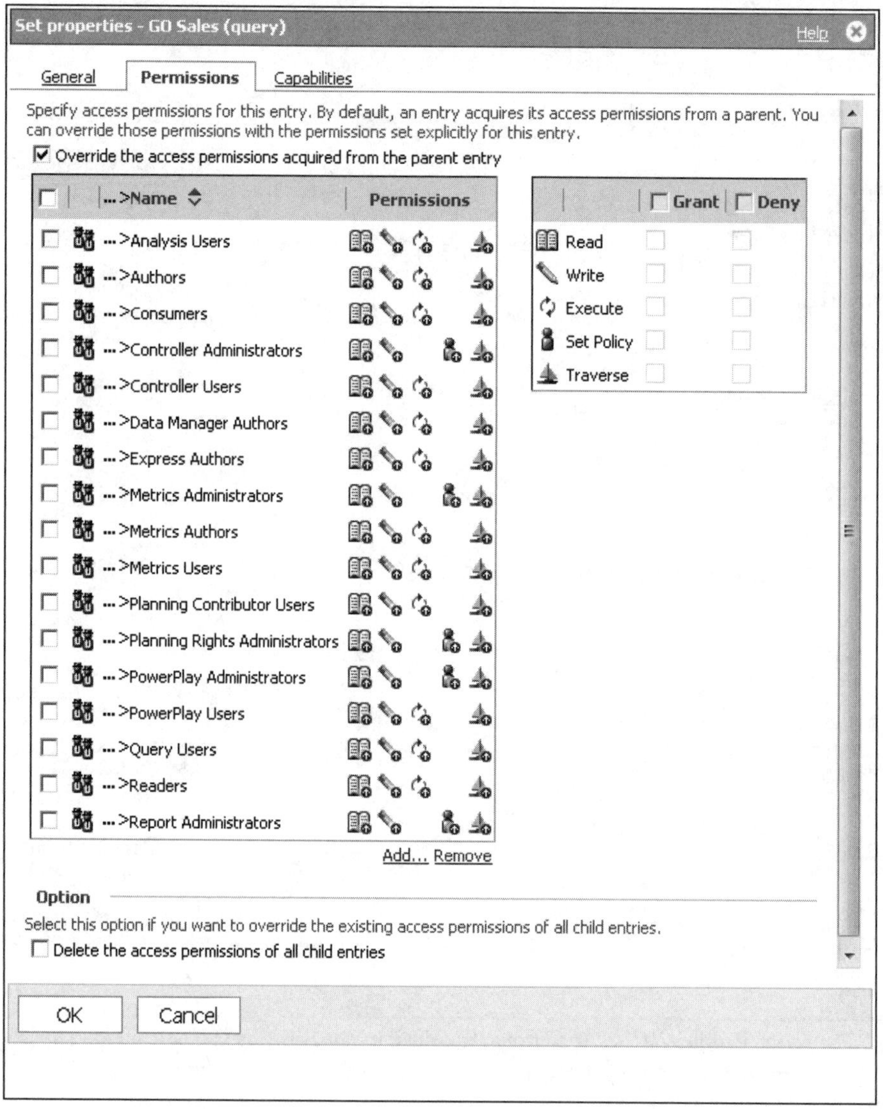

If the inherited permissions do not meet the specific needs for the package, you can easily modify them from the Permissions tab. In this example, if you wanted to restrict access on this package only to Authors, you would simply remove all the other users, groups, and roles from the permissions list.

Specify Object Security

In Cognos Framework Manager, you can apply security to individual elements, or objects, in the model. This means that for any object in the model, you can specify which users, groups, or roles can access it. If they do not have access to the object, users will not see it in any of the studios.

Object security is very strict in how it is applied. The second you secure one object, all other objects in the model are no longer visible to anyone in Cognos Studios.

To demonstrate, consider the following example. Take a few simple query subjects from the sample Cognos data and publish them as a test package called GO Sales (security). The next illustration shows the simple Sales package created in the Model Query Subjects folder:

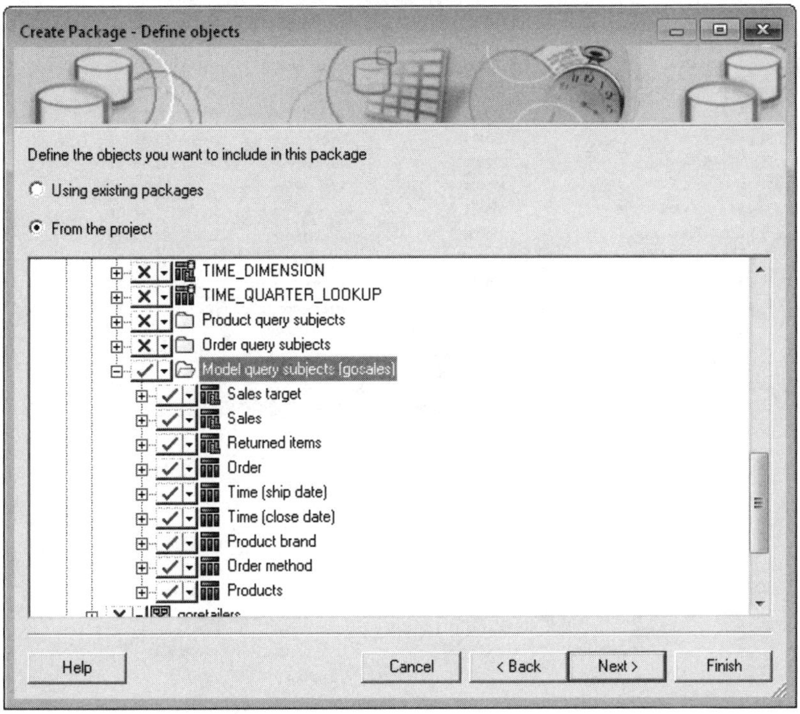

This example shows a simple report, with no object security, using the query items from the Sales Target model query subject:

Management decides that only one sales manager, Sally White, should be permitted to see the sales target. You can apply object security to the Sales Target query item in the Sales Target model query subject to accommodate this request. Follow these steps:

1. Choose Actions | Specify Object Security:

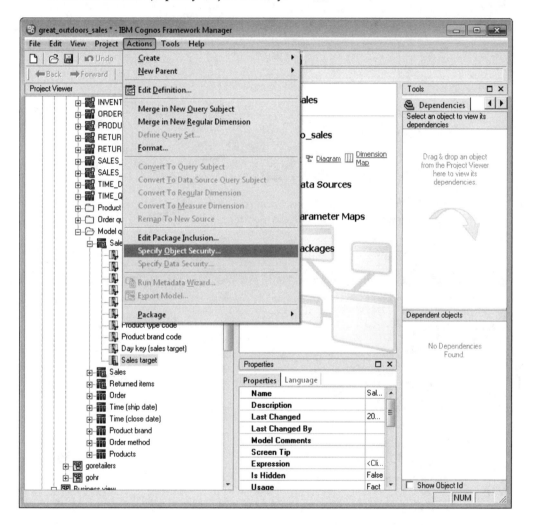

2. In the Specify Object Security dialog, click the Add button:

3. Locate Sally White in the authentication provider and add her name to the list of users permitted to access the Sales Target item:

4. Click OK. The Specify Object Security dialog displays:

5. Click OK, and Cognos Framework Manager displays a warning. Not only are you warned, but you are also given instructions on how to undo what you just did!

When you publish the package and open the report again as an administrator, you see an error:

6. Open a new report with the same package, and you see only the name of the package and nothing else:

```
┌────────────────────────────────┐
│ Menu                      ◄     │
│ ┌────────────────────────────┐ │
│ │ Insert Data                │ │
│ ├────────────────────────────┤ │
│ │ Edit Data                  │ │
│ │ Change Layout              │ │
│ │ Run Report                 │ │
│ │ Manage File                │ │
│ ├────────────────────────────┤ │
│ │ ▦ GO Sales (security)      │ │
│ │                            │ │
│ │                            │ │
│ │                            │ │
│ │                            │ │
│ │                            │ │
│ │         Insert ➡          │ │
│ ├────────────────────────────┤ │
│ │ Information            ⩘   │ │
│ └────────────────────────────┘ │
└────────────────────────────────┘
```

7. Now log on to Cognos Connection as Sally White, and you can see that the situation is not much better. Sally can see only one item in the entire package, and no one else who logs in can see any items from the package:

```
┌────────────────────────────────┐
│ Menu                      ◄     │
│ ┌────────────────────────────┐ │
│ │ Insert Data                │ │
│ ├────────────────────────────┤ │
│ │ Edit Data                  │ │
│ │ Change Layout              │ │
│ │ Run Report                 │ │
│ │ Manage File                │ │
│ ├────────────────────────────┤ │
│ │ ▦ GO Sales (security)      │ │
│ │   └ ▥ Sales target         │ │
│ │                            │ │
│ │                            │ │
│ │                            │ │
│ │         Insert ➡          │ │
│ ├────────────────────────────┤ │
│ │ Information            ⩘   │ │
│ └────────────────────────────┘ │
└────────────────────────────────┘
```

All this demonstrates an important point: *The second you secure one item in an object, all other objects in that package are no longer visible to anyone until you do something about it.*

You can quickly restore visibility by going to the root namespace or folder and allowing Everyone (or some other appropriate group or role) access to all objects. This does not undo the security you set on the Sales Target object, but all other unsecured objects inherit the security from the root level and will be available to all users:

Allow access

When applying object security, you can take one of two approaches: You can lock down everything and then grant access, which requires going through all the objects to specify the appropriate security. This happens when you specify object security on an object, as in the preceding example. The other method is to grant access to everyone at the root level and then specify object security on objects you want to hide from some users. We recommend the second method, because you typically want to hide only a select set of items from all users, not your entire model.

TIP *Use the Deny setting if you do not want a particular user or group to see an object, but they belong to another group that has access to the object. Deny overrides the Allow setting users have in the other groups to which they belong.*

Specify Data Security

In the "Macros" section of this chapter, we discussed how to build macros that can act as dynamic filters on query subjects. So far in the "Security" section, we have discussed how to set access permissions on entire packages and how to grant or deny access to individual objects in the model. In this section, you'll learn how to specify *data security*.

Data security is important, because the goal of Cognos 10 is to enable your users to create their own reports and analyses while keeping certain information confidential. For example, suppose your sales force is divided along product brands. One salesperson is responsible for each given brand, and you want to apply data security so that the salesperson running the report can see only his brand.

To make this work, you need to identify where in your model you need to apply data security. Using the sample data in Cognos 10, you see the Model Query Subjects/Products folder in the great_outdoors_sales Cognos Framework Manager project. You decide that, given the nature of your data security filter, this would be a good place to start:

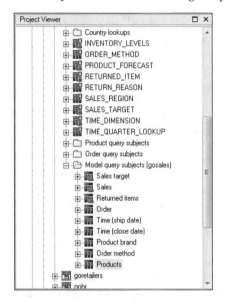

Follow these steps:

1. Choose Actions | Specify Data Security:

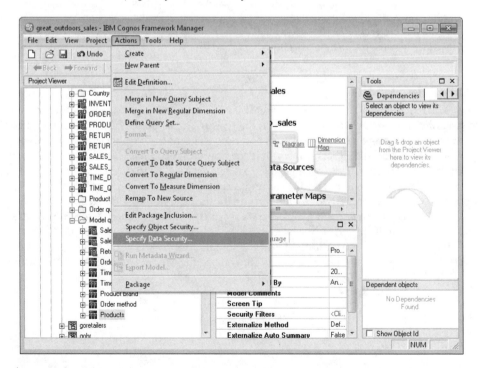

2. In the Specify Data Security dialog, you can define one or more groups. These data security groups are collections of users, groups, or roles from your authentication provider, to which you will be applying specific filters.

Sally White is responsible for the "Husky" product brand. You can restrict the data she sees by adding data security to the Product query subject, adding Sally to the data security group, and creating a filter that only returns Husky brand products. Click the Add Groups button in the Specify Data Security dialog, find Sally in the authentication provider, and add her to the selected entries:

3. Now that Sally is in a group, you can create a filter for her brand. You can create a new filter or use one that has already been defined in the model. For this example, create a new filter. In the Filter drop-down, select Create/Edit Embedded. Then click OK.

TIP *The Based On column in the Specify Data Security dialog lets you reuse groups that have already been defined and inherit their security. For example, if you added another user, Frank Bretton, to the Specific Data Security dialog, and he should see only the "Star Gazer" product brands as well as the "Husky" product brands, you can base Frank Bretton's security on Sally White's security to provide access to the "Husky" product brands. You would then create a filter for the "Star Gazer" product brands for Frank Bretton. This way, you can leverage work already done in another security filter. Refer to your IBM Cognos documentation for more details.*

4. In the Filter Definition dialog, create a simple filter that restricts product brands to Husky:

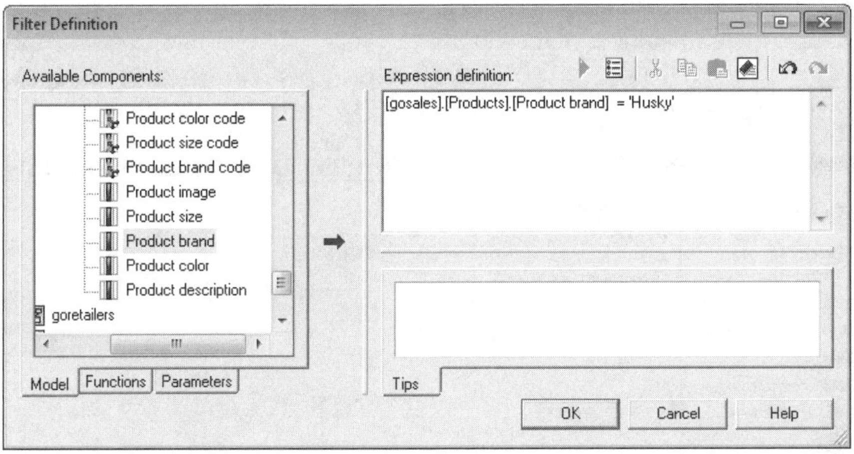

5. When you publish the package and log on as a user other than Sally, you can see all product brands:

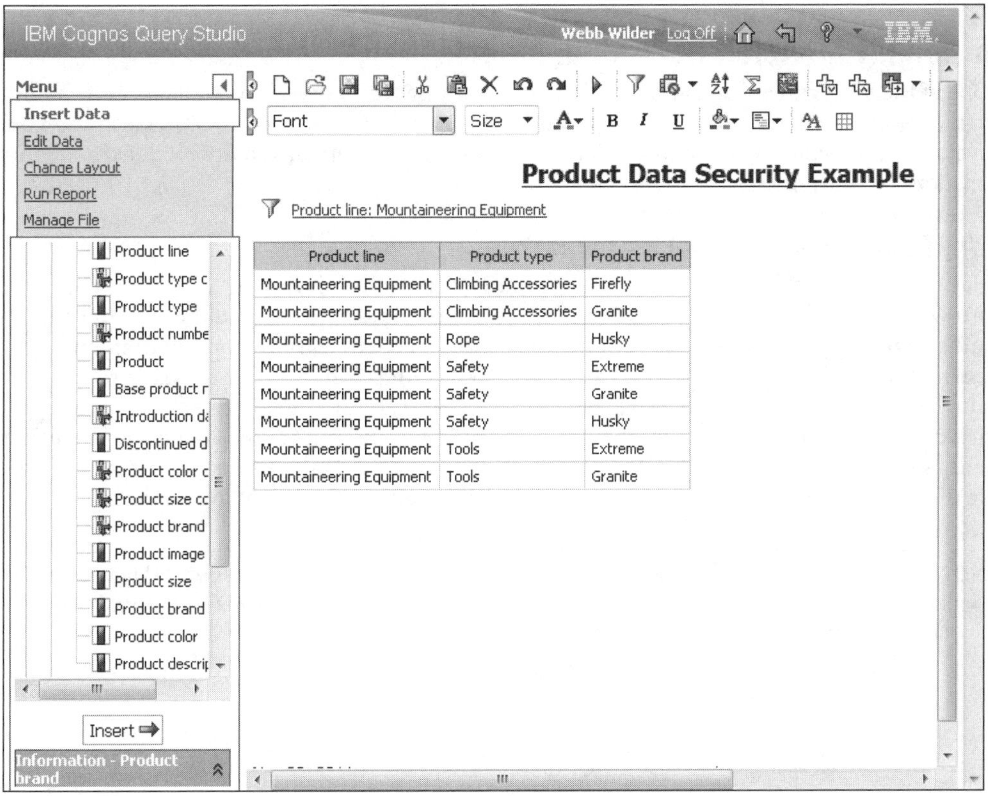

When Sally logs on and runs the exact same report, only "Husky" product brands display:

Dimensionally Modeled Relational Models

One of the most powerful, and coolest, features of Cognos Framework Manager is its ability to model relational data so that it appears dimensional to the Cognos 10 Studios and to your users. In this section, we will discuss the basics of creating dimensionally modeled relational (DMR) models.

Why Dimensionally Model Metadata?

Have you ever had a business user ask, "I want a report that shows me the gross sales of our widgets for the last month, by brand, by customer, and by region, and group the city under those regions while you are at it!" This user is not, contrary to popular opinion, asking for a smack upside the head. In fact, with this question, the user is asking for dimensional data. Anytime he says the word "by," you should hear "dimension" or a level in a dimension. The phrases "for the last…" and "for the next…" speak to a time dimension, and "show me the…" usually refers to money or some other value to be measured. We will be discussing time and measure dimensions individually in the following paragraphs.

NOTE *Dimensional data answers who, what, when, where, and why questions. Who bought something? What, exactly, did they buy? When did they buy it? Where did they get it? Why did they return it?*

When the topic of dimensional modeling is discussed, two other terms, usually, are not far behind: *OLAP* and *cubes*. OLAP, the acronym for online analytical processing, is a methodology for presenting data in an optimized dimensional manner. Cubes (also called OLAP cubes) are self-contained collections of data that have been optimized for dimensional reporting and analysis; they also contain a predefined set of data.

There is an important distinction to be made between OLAP cubes and DMR metadata. OLAP cubes are, by definition, dimensional in nature. They are self-contained, limited sets of data that have been optimized for reporting, which makes them fast. They also allow business users to look at data in smaller groups (drill-down), look at data in larger groups (drill-up), and look at data from a different perspective (slice and dice).

DMR metadata lets the user drill-up, drill-down, and slice and dice as well. The difference is that in a DMR, the data comes from a relational database, not from an optimized OLAP cube (a file).

Of course, there are pros and cons to using each. OLAP is faster, but it is only as timely as the last build. A DMR is slower but the data is up to the minute. OLAP models are usually easy to create, but DMR modeling is more complex.

Regardless of which method you use, business users think dimensionally, and if you want to be a hero in your organization, listen for the "bys" and turn them into dimensions.

TIP *IBM Cognos Transformer is the tool used to create OLAP cubes. Although Cognos Transformer is beyond the scope of this book, be sure to look into it.*

A Dimensional Primer

If you are unfamiliar with dimensional data sources, you might be wondering what the fuss is all about. Dimensional data provides the report author and analysis user with the ability to navigate quickly through large amounts of data while simultaneously exploring multiple aspects of that data.

Regular Dimensions

These "aspects of the data" are called *regular dimensions*. Regular dimensions can be things such as a product, customer, date, geography, salesperson, or anything that groups and describes your data. Regular dimensions are layered objects: they have hierarchies, hierarchies have levels, and finally levels have mandatory and optional attributes. At runtime, this information is used to generate members, which are the data entities found in multidimensional sources and, at a minimum, consist of a business key and a caption.

A *hierarchy* defines how the levels in your regular dimension relate to each other. The following illustration shows a product dimension from the Cognos 10 sample data. In this hierarchy, there are five levels. From the lowest level to the highest, these are Product, Base product, Product type, Product line, and Product(All). A veteran dimensional modeler would read that hierarchy as Products roll up to Base products, which roll up to Product types, which roll up to Product lines, and Product lines roll up to the artificial level of Product(All).

Hierarchy   Levels

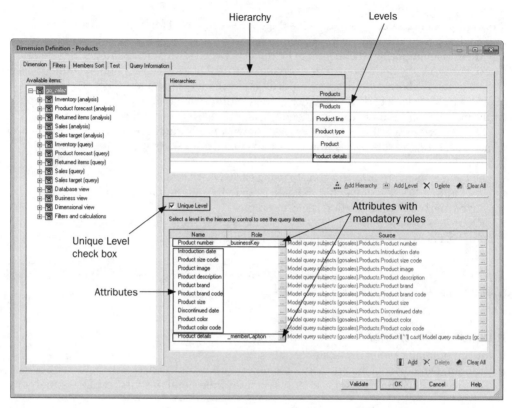

Levels in a dimension must contain an attribute that takes on the role of the `businessKey`; that is, it uniquely identifies a member for that level. In the preceding illustration, the Product level has a business key of Product number. Levels also must contain an attribute that takes on the role of labeling the members for the level. This role is called the `memberCaption`. The `memberCaption` is commonly a textual description as opposed to the business key, which is usually a code of some sort, but in some cases the `businessKey` and the `memberCaption` roles can be applied to the same attribute. Levels can also contain an attribute that uses the `memberDescription` role or attributes that simply provide additional information about the items at a given level. For the Product level, a few of the non-role attributes are product color, product size, and introduction date.

Another important concept when talking about levels is *uniqueness*. How does Cognos 10 know which items in a level consist of the unique group for that level? Later on, in the section "Build a Regular Dimension," you will see that the Dimension Definition screen contains a Unique Level check box. The Unique Level check box in regular dimensions must be checked for any level that has a business key that uniquely identifies the row of data, even if the key repeats in the data. This specifies that the level's key does not need the parent key to identify it. If it does, you leave the box cleared. If it does not, you select it. The highest level has no parent, so you do not need to select it. For example, you would clear the check box if your month key is 1 through 12, and you will also need the year keys 2005, 2006, to identify uniquely the months 1-2005, 2-2005, 3-2005,...1-2006, 2-2006, 3-2006, and so on.

Attributes are the actual data items used to define the level. Attributes can take on roles such as `businessKey`, `memberCaption`, and `memberDescription`, or they can simply provide additional details about members in a level.

Measure Dimensions

Regular dimensions provide context to the measures in which users are interested. *Measures* are the items that we count, also called facts, metrics, or key figures. Sales dollars, quantities (such as sold, shipped, bought, and broken), and inventory levels are all examples of measures, as shown here in the Dimension Definition screen:

Measure dimensions are much easier to understand than regular dimensions, because there are no hierarchies, levels, and so on. There are just numbers—plain, simple numbers.

Time (Date) Dimensions

There is no specific object for date dimensions in Cognos Framework Manager. Instead, a *time dimension* is simply a regular dimension that gives your data chronological meaning based on the data contained in the dimension—in this case, that would be calendar information.

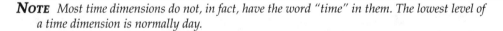

NOTE *Most time dimensions do not, in fact, have the word "time" in them. The lowest level of a time dimension is normally day.*

Time dimensions in an OLAP cube normally include levels that are useful in analyses and reports, such as month, quarter, and year. These levels are not normally found in relational data sources, but we will talk about that in a bit.

One very nice feature of a time dimension is its ability to contain multiple hierarchies. This is very useful if your organization uses more than one calendar. For example, your organization may use a fiscal calendar for the financial department that spans July to June and a standard calendar for all other departments that spans January to December.

If a business user asks for a report of all widgets sold during the first quarter, for example, what is he asking about—January or July? In this example, you can create two hierarchies within the same time dimension: a fiscal calendar hierarchy and a standard calendar hierarchy.

NOTE *If you need to report on both hierarchies at the same time, it is recommended that you create a separate dimension for each hierarchy. Currently, accessing multiple hierarchies from a single dimension is not supported.*

Why Dimensionally Model Metadata? Because of the Second Question

Earlier in this chapter we asked: "Why Dimensionally Model Metadata?" We did so because of the *second business question*—the one that the user either meant to ask in the first place, or the question he was not even aware existed until he got the answer to the first.

A hypothetical conversation leading to the second business question might go like this:

"Who bought all of our blue widgets last month?" asks Mr. Business User.

"Armin bought them all," replies the Report Author.

"What?" says Mr. Business User. "Sophia usually buys all of our blue widgets! What did Sophia buy last month since we were all out of blue widgets?"

The second business question is this: "What did Sophia buy last month?" If your data has been dimensionally modeled, the business user can quickly and easily answer the question himself using drilling, slicing, and dicing capabilities. If your data has not been dimensionally modeled, you will probably spend some time writing a second report to answer the second business question, and the third business question, and the fourth, and…?

Building the Dimensionally Modeled Relational Model

When building a DMR model, it is helpful to consider the star schema design. Star schemas are usually found in data warehouses. Simply put, star schemas are simplified data structures that have been optimized for reporting and analysis.

Star schemas are dimensional by nature because that they have one measure table and a set of dimension tables. In the following illustration, the Sales Target table would be our measure dimension and the six tables surrounding it would be regular dimensions. If you can model your relational data so that it resembles a star schema, you will have a good DMR model.

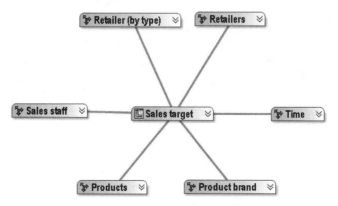

Build a Regular Dimension

Using the sample data and the great_outdoors_sales Cognos Framework Manager project, we start our DMR modeling by identifying the regular dimensions in the Database view namespace:

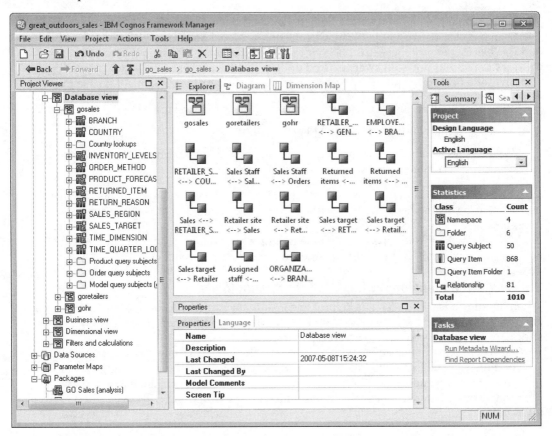

We see three measure dimension candidates: Sales target, Sales, and Returned items. The regular dimension candidates are Order, TIME_DIMENSION, Product (by brand), Order method, and Product. In this example, we'll use Sales target as our measure dimension, Product as our regular dimension, and TIME_DIMENSION as our time dimension.

After you have identified the query subjects to be used for your DMR objects, create your first regular dimension. Follow these steps:

1. Create a new namespace to contain your DMR objects. Name it DMR.

2. Right-click the new namespace and choose Create | Regular Dimension:

The Dimension Definition – New Dimension screen appears:

3. In the Available Items pane, navigate to the Products model query subject:

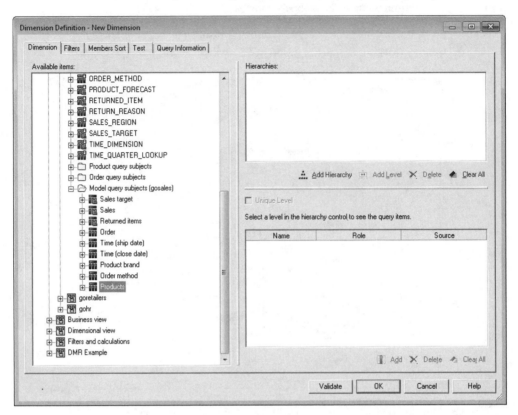

As with all of the Cognos tools, there is more than one way to get what you want, and the Dimension Definition tool is no exception. Before we start building our regular dimension, recall our discussion about what you need to make one: hierarchies, levels, and attributes. At this point, you should have a clear idea of what the new regular dimension should look like. You need answers to the following questions before you start:

- How do members roll up?
- What are the levels?
- What uniquely identifies a member in a level?
- What data describes that member?
- What additional information do we want to include about a member in the level?

Continuing with the example, we know that Products roll up to Base products, which roll up to Product types, which roll up to Product lines, and Product lines roll up to the artificial level, Product(All), which allows you to see overall totals for a hierarchy. Therefore, those are our levels. To create a level in the Dimension Definition tool, you first need a hierarchy in which to put it. With this tool, you have two options to the new hierarchy: You can click the Add Hierarchy button, or you can drag-and-drop a query item from your model query subject. The drag-and-drop option creates the hierarchy and adds the new level at the same time.

Product number is the query item that uniquely identifies a product. Because products are the lowest level of detail in our new dimension, we can assume that this query item will play the role of businessKey in the Products level. Drag the Product number query item into the Hierarchies pane of the Dimension Definition screen. After our drag-and-drop, three things happen: a new hierarchy is created, two levels are added to the hierarchy, and a member with the role of businessKey is added to the level, as shown next:

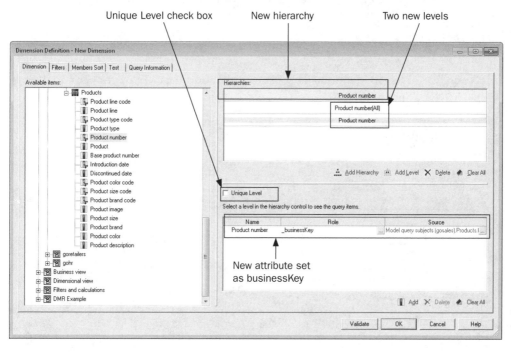

NOTE *To rename any object in the Dimension Definition screen, right-click the item and choose Rename from the contextual menu.*

The two created levels take their names from the query item itself—Product number(All) and Product number. Because we started with the lowest level of our hierarchy, we can assume that at this level the business key is unique, and we need to select the Unique Level check box.

The hierarchy takes the name of the query item that we used in the drag-and-drop; you can right-click the name of the hierarchy to rename it. It is good practice to keep your names on the generic side. Because our example dimension contains more than just the product number, it would be wise to rename the hierarchy as Product.

NOTE *The All level of a hierarchy is an automatic level that acts as a roll up of everything in the hierarchy.*

The Dimension Definition tool tries to guess what the newly added query item's role should be. If the query item is defined as an identifier in the model query subject, the Dimension Definition tool assigns it the role of businessKey. If the query item is defined as an attribute in the model query subject, the Dimension Definition tool assigns it the role of memberCaption. Remember that if the tool guesses incorrectly, you can always reassign the role manually and/or assign more than one role to the query item.

NOTE *The tool makes a guess only for the first member added to the level. For all subsequent members, you will be asked to identify the role.*

Because we added an identifier, we must manually add the memberCaption to the Product level. Follow these steps:

1. Drag-and-drop the Product from the model query subject to the appropriate level—in this case, the Product number level.

After you've added the caption, the level displays:

2. Drag-and-drop the Base product number to its proper location in the hierarchy—
in this case, between Product number and Product number(All):

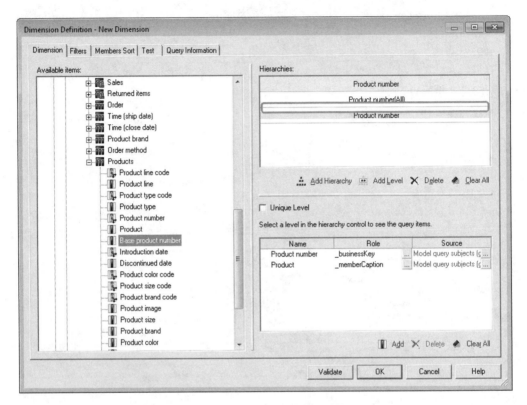

The Base product number is a bit of an exception, because it does not have any
query item that acts as a caption. Fortunately, members can be assigned multiple
roles, so for this level the Base product number acts as both businessKey and
memberCaption.

NOTE *Attributes filling the role of* memberCaption *must be character strings. If they are dates
or numbers, you must convert them to strings in the Source definition of the attribute.*

3. Now select the level you want to modify, and click the ellipses next to the role to assign. The Specify Roles dialog displays:

4. Continue building the levels in the hierarchy by adding the following:

- Product type (level name), Product type code (business key), and Product type (member caption)

- Product line (level name), Product line code (business key), and Product line (member caption)

The hierarchy displays as follows:

5. To complete this regular dimension, add query items as attribute members to the Product level without assigning them any role. Then select the Unique Level check box for all levels that meet the criteria discussed earlier.

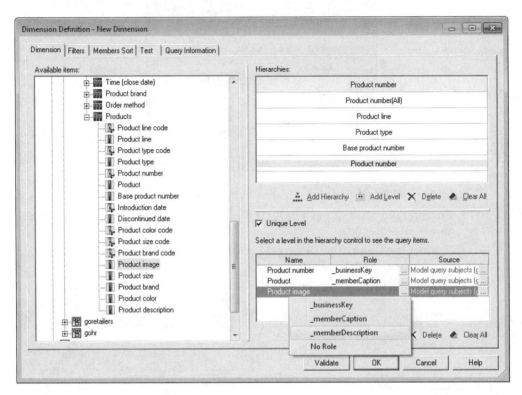

6. If available and required, you can assign an item to the memberDescription role. For example, you can specify Product description.

NOTE   *Attributes can be added to any to level except the (All) level.*

Build a Time Dimension

A *time dimension* is virtually the same as any other regular dimension. The only exception is the nature of time dimension data. Dates are often used as an example of a hierarchy because days roll into weeks, which roll into months, and so on. As discussed earlier, relational data sources often do not include a table that specifically references time, but because they are so useful, you will want to include such a table in any DMR that you design. To do so, you have two options.

- You can create a time model query subject and add calculated query items for the levels and attributes you want—items such as month, quarter, year, and so on.

- You can create a new table in your relational data source that contains these items and join the time table to your measure dimension on the date. We prefer this method, because it reduces the number of calculations that occur every time you use a date.

Date	Month	Quarter	Year	Fiscal Quarter	Fiscal Year
01/01/2011	January	Q1	2011	Q2	2010
06/12/2011	June	Q2	2011	Q4	2010

TABLE 18-2   Multiple Hierarchies in a Date Dimension

A common use of time dimensions is to make use of multiple hierarchies. A simple way to think of how a multiple hierarchy works is to consider our fiscal and standard calendars examples. One date can have different, and mutually exclusive, attributes. Table 18-2 demonstrates this ability.

The table shows that the date June 12, 2011, can be grouped in two different ways. In the standard calendar, this date is in the second quarter; in the fiscal calendar, it is in the fourth quarter.

If your data supports multiple hierarchies, you can add them to your time dimension by creating the dimension using the calendar dates, and then adding the fiscal dates as an alternate hierarchy. For example, here we added Fiscal Year and Fiscal Quarter query items to the sample data provided by IBM Cognos:

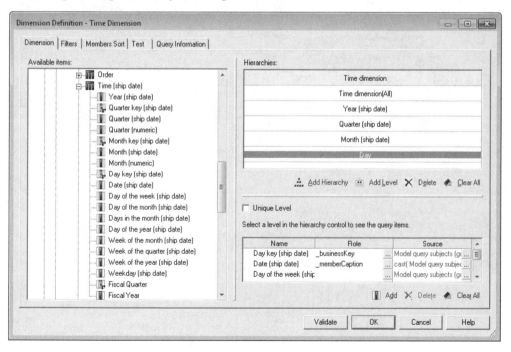

We add our alternate hierarchy by dragging-and-dropping a level of the new hierarchy to the right side of the current hierarchy in our dimension:

For our alternate hierarchy, we use Fiscal Year as the new level:

We manually set the `businessKey` and `memberCaption` for the new level and add the Fiscal Quarter, Month, and Day levels. Then we set the members and roles for each new level as appropriate:

When we save our new time dimension, it contains both hierarchies:

NOTE *Multiple hierarchies can be created in any regular dimension.*

Build a Measure Dimension

The *measure dimension* contains the answers to questions in which most business users are ultimately interested: the how many and how much. The ideal measure dimension contains only measures. If you think you need something other than measures, you should re-examine your relational model to make sure it is designed properly.

NOTE *The theory and practice of how to model data is a large area with many topics and beyond the scope of this book. If you run into trouble while modeling your data, the first place to look for help is in the "Guidelines for Modeling Metadata" documentation that comes with your Cognos 10 installation.*

To create a measure dimension, follow these steps:

1. Right-click the namespace where you would like the measure dimension to reside, and choose Create | Measure Dimension:

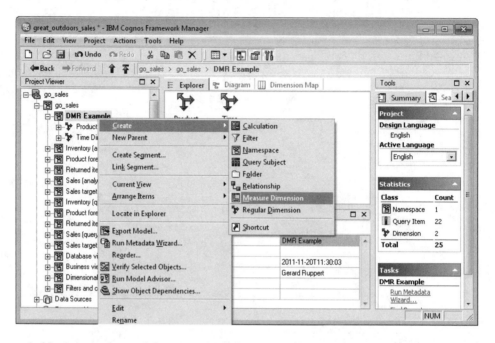

2. Navigate to the model query subject that contains the measure(s) you want to include.

3. Drag-and-drop the measure from the model query subject to the Measures pane of the Dimension Definition screen:

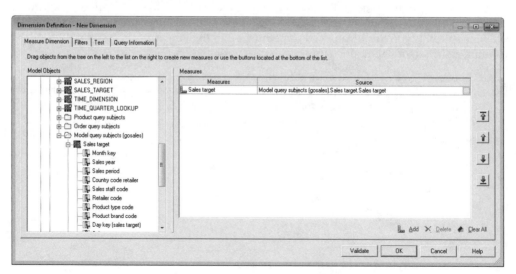

4. Click OK and examine the namespace. In this example, you now see two regular dimensions and one measure dimension:

Scope Relationships

The *scope relationship* defines which measures are in scope for which dimensions and at which levels for a hierarchy. Consider the following example as an explanation. Suppose you sell widgets every day of the year, and, of course, you are interested in how those widgets are selling. In this case, the widget sales measure is in scope down to the Day level of the time hierarchy. When you talk about widget sales per day, it makes sense. Now suppose you set a sales target for widgets and your goal is to sell 1 million widgets per month. The widget sales target measure is in scope only down to the Month level of the time hierarchy, not the Day level.

Scope is not limited to dates. Suppose the 1 million widget sales target is not for a specific type of widget, such as widget number 1337, but the target is for all widgets in the widget product line. In this case, the sales target is not only in scope to the Month level of the time hierarchy, but it is also in scope to the Product line level of the Product dimension, leaving all levels below product line out of scope.

PART IV

Cognos Framework Manager provides a visualization of scope when you double-click the namespace with your dimensions and then select the Dimension Map, as shown here:

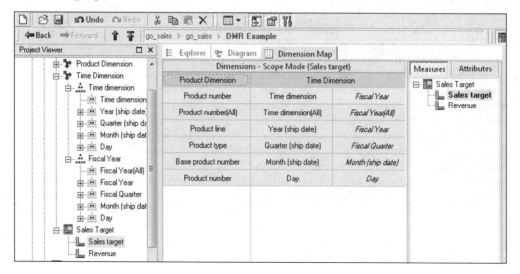

To see the scope of a measure, you'd click the measure of interest from the Measures pane.

NOTE *You can apply different levels of scope for different measures within the same measure dimension if required.*

Cognos Framework Manager will examine the metadata for the selected measure, and it will try to determine, based on the tables and joins, which levels make sense for the measure. If a level is thought to be in scope, then the background color of the level changes from white to a kind of purplish, salmon color.

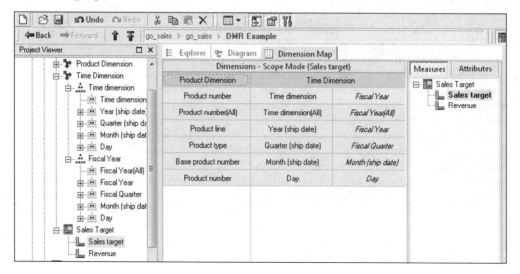

Despite its best effort, Cognos Framework Manager sometimes does not get the scope quite right. If this happens, you can change scope easily from the Dimension Map. Right-click the level of the hierarchy you want to modify and choose Set Scope. In this example, we use Month since our measure, Sales target, is valid only to the month level:

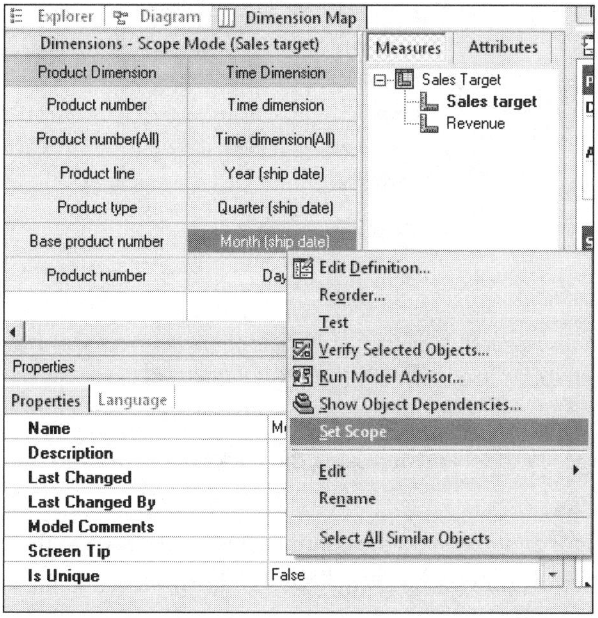

This defines the scope as ending at the selected level. All levels below the selected one are now considered to be out of scope:

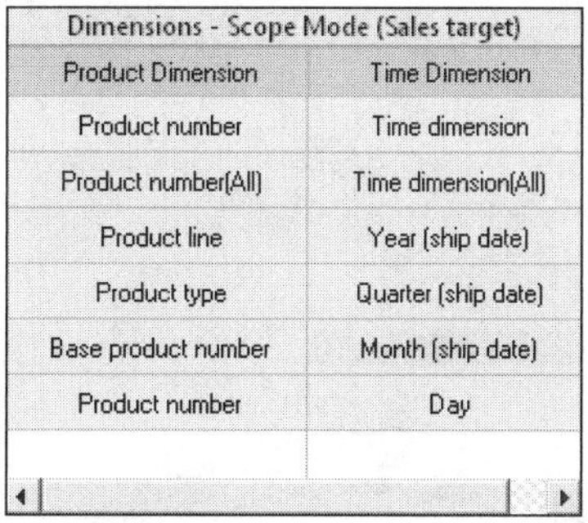

Now we can set the scope for the Base Product Number and for the Days in our Date hierarchy:

Dimensions - Scope Mode (Sales target)	
Product Dimension	Time Dimension
Product number	Time dimension
Product number(All)	Time dimension(All)
Product line	Year (ship date)
Product type	Quarter (ship date)
Base product number	Month (ship date)
Product number	Day

NOTE *When you publish a package, you must include all namespaces that are referenced in the query subjects seen by the users. Objects that are not included in the package are not available for use in any of the Cognos Studios.*

After publishing the model and accessing the package in Analysis Studio, you can follow these steps:

1. Place the Time dimension on the columns and drill-down to the month level.

2. Place the Product dimension on the rows and drill-down to the Product type.

3. Add Revenue and Sales target as the measures.

The result is an analysis showing the values for Revenue and Sales target, since they are both in scope:

Rows: Mountaineering ... ▼	Columns: Q1 ▼ Sales Target (l... ▼	
Sales target	January	
	Revenue	Sales target
Climbing Accessories	$1,852,717.44	$72,366,700.00
Rope	$2,508,982.65	$101,311,000.00
Safety	$1,945,566.04	$75,017,400.00
Tools	$2,941,485.73	$115,219,200.00
Mountaineering Equipment	**$9,248,751.86**	**$363,914,300.00**

If you drill-down on the Time dimension to the day, you can see that Sales target is null (blank). This is because Sales target *at the day level* is out of scope, as shown here:

Rows: Mountaineering ... ▼	Columns: January ▼ Sales Target (l... ▼			
Sales target	2005-01-13		2005-01-14	
	Revenue	Sales target	Revenue	Sales target
Climbing Accessories	$115,687.36		$80,801.65	
Rope	$70,926.38		$150,513.44	
Safety	$51,594.56		$130,059.88	
Tools	$113,820.40		$188,540.99	
Mountaineering Equipment	**$352,028.70**		**$549,915.96**	

If you drill-down on the Product dimension to the Base Product Number, you again lose the Sales target, because Sales target at the Base Product Number is out of scope:

Rows: 47 ▼	Columns: 2005 ▼ Sales Target (l... ▼			
Sales target	Q1		Q2	
	Revenue	Sales target	Revenue	Sales target
Husky Harness	$1,065,156.30		$981,999.20	
47	**$1,065,156.30**	**$75,017,400.00**	**$981,999.20**	

Other Interesting Features

As you become more familiar with Cognos Framework Manager, you will come across interesting features not mentioned in this chapter. It is simply not possible to discuss all the features here, but we would like to introduce you to a few that you can investigate at your leisure.

Dynamic Query Mode

A new feature found in IBM Cognos Business Intelligence v10.1 is the dynamic query mode (DQM). This feature can provide significantly increased query performance when used with supported data sources. DQM has relatively few user settings. In Cognos Framework Manager, it is either enabled for a package or it is not. DQM is enabled in Cognos configuration, configured in Cognos Framework Manager packages, and requires Java Database Connectivity (JDBC) data source connections.

A full discussion of DQM is beyond the scope of this book. However, we recommend that you explore the topic in your Cognos 10 documentation and on the IBM Cognos support web site.

Document the Project

You can create XML- or HTML-based documentation of the project or any object within the project. To do so, choose Tools | Model Report:

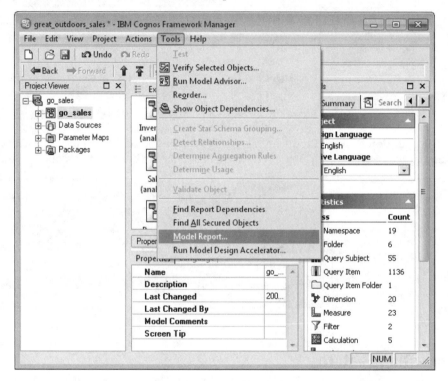

This illustration is a sample of a query subject model report:

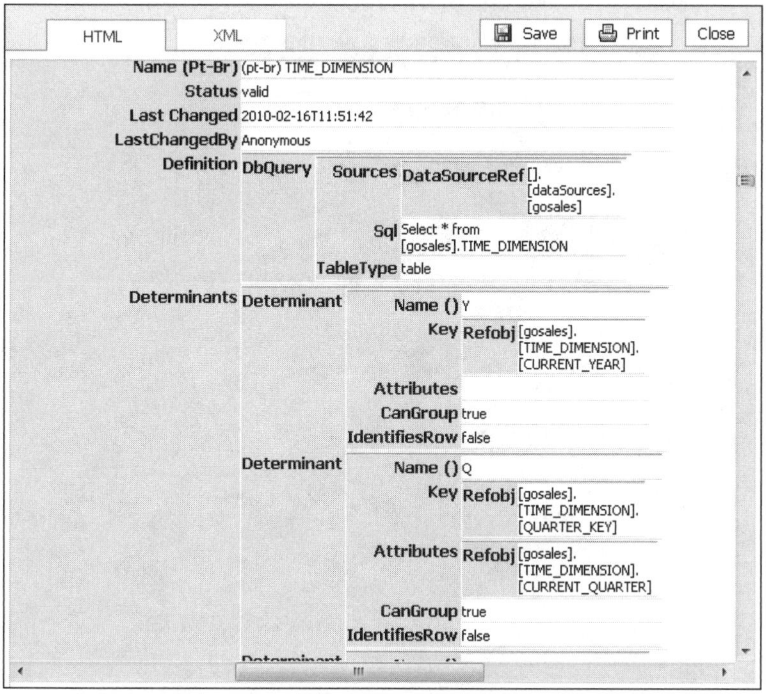

Diagram Copy and Paste

Another helpful feature, especially for those who like documentation, is the ability to save a screen copy of the model diagrams to an image file. To do so, arrange the model diagram to your liking, and choose Diagram | Screen Capture:

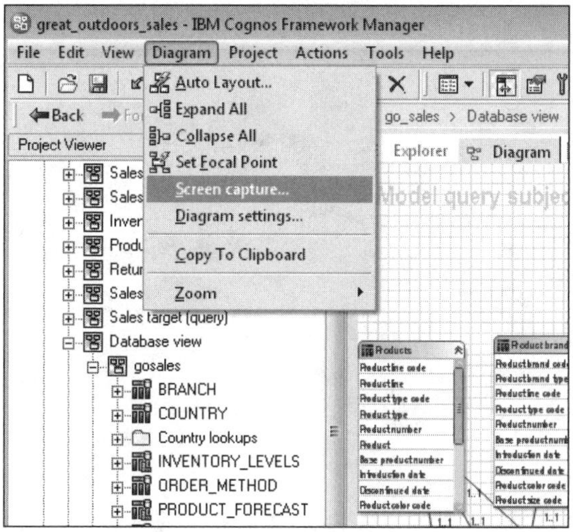

In the Save A Copy Of The Diagram In An Image File dialog, you can select the size of the image to save and the JPG, GIF, or TIF file format:

Security

Having consulted with a large number of customers since the initial release of IBM Cognos Business Intelligence v10.1, we have found that security implementations tend to fall into one of two categories: not enough or too much. Not enough security occurs when the IBM Cognos 10 default settings are left in place and security is relegated to the user logon, or when no security is implemented at all. The danger here is obvious: Anyone with access to IBM Cognos Connection can view or print any information that has been published. They can also delete any objects they find, such as reports, folders, and packages. Too much security occurs when either the system administrator does not understand the flexibility of Cognos 10 security, or, to be frank, the system administrator is paranoid. In this case, legitimate business users cannot access the information they need to make sound business decisions. The business users quickly become frustrated and the Cognos 10 installation is considered a failure by the people it is meant to help the most.

Every organization should be concerned with both information security (not allowing an unauthorized user to access information) and content integrity (not allowing someone to remove or change content). Cognos 10 lets you apply a fine level of control over all of the features and content found in the Cognos 10 environment, ensuring that you can meet both of these objectives.

Authentication

Security is disabled by default and, although you can use Cognos 10 without enabling security, it is not advised. Your Cognos 10 installation team must configure and enable security before you can restrict access to your content. If the security feature is not enabled, anyone who connects to Cognos Connection will have full access to everything in Cognos 10.

Cognos 10 security starts with *authentication*, the process of verifying that a user is who he or she claims to be, making sure that the user is an authentic user. This is accomplished through the use of user credentials (a user name and password), referred to as *basic authentication*, that are stored in a secured authentication source, or by leveraging a token or session parameter for single sign-on (SSO). Note that Cognos 10 does not provide an authentication source or any means of authenticating users out of the box; therefore, this must be implemented using a third-party authentication provider. Cognos 10 supports a variety of authentication providers that can change over time, so be sure to check the Cognos 10 "Installation Guide" for the most recent list of supported providers.

NOTE *As of this writing, the authentication providers supported in Cognos 10.1.1 are Microsoft Active Directory, IBM Cognos Series 7, eTrust SiteMinder, Lightweight Directory Access Protocol (LDAP), NT LAN Manager (NTLM), SAP, Resource Access Control Facility (RACF), and Custom Java Authentication Provider.*

Cognos 10 allows the use of more than one authentication provider, which is helpful for distributed security models. For example, if your organization is multinational, you might use one authentication provider for the United States, a different one for Central Europe, and possibly a third for the Asia Pacific region. You can log on to as many authentication sources as needed to access your application.

Cognos 10 prompts you to select the provider you want to use at logon, as shown next:

If you have a single authentication provider, you will go directly to the Log On screen with no prompting:

When a user attempts to log on to the Cognos 10 environment, the security mechanism first checks to see whether the user's credentials are valid. Does the user name and password entered match those stored in the authentication source? If the credentials are not valid, the user is prompted to try again. If the credentials are valid, the user is granted access to Cognos Connection. The next layer of security, authorization, then comes into play.

Authorization

Now that Cognos 10 knows who you are, the next question is, "What are you authorized to do?" *Authorization* defines the level of access that a user has to the Cognos 10 functionality and content. An installation of all the IMB Cognos Studios results in a large number of tools being available to users, but not all users need to have access to everything. A lot of information is likely available in Cognos Connection, and again, not every user should have permission to see everything. It is the job of the Cognos administrator to assign specific permissions to specific users.

Organization

A question new clients often ask us is, "Where should we manage our authorization information?" In our experience, maintaining your security structure in the Cognos namespace has a number of advantages over storing the structure in your authentication provider. Using the Cognos namespace allows BI administrators to maintain the security model, which is usually better than having the Active Directory administrator, who has nothing to do with BI, providing the maintenance. This type of organization allows you to optimize the security structure for your Cognos implementation; it allows for a solid security model that will more easily support changes to your security provider among others.

Users, Groups, and Roles

Managing individual user access and permissions can become extremely complex. To help simplify this effort, Cognos 10 allows you to assign users to groups and roles. *Users* are the individual people who have user names and passwords and have permission to access the application. *Groups* are a collection of users who have the same access permissions—for example, everyone in the Sales group can see content related to sales. *Roles* are a collection of users who have the same access to functionality—for example, everyone in the Authors role can create reports.

If you have defined groups and roles in your current security model and you are using that security model as your authentication provider, you can easily apply the Cognos 10 permissions directly to your existing structure. If you have multiple authentication providers or your current security model does not meet your needs, you can use the predefined groups and roles found in the Cognos 10 namespace, create your own groups and roles, or do both. A *namespace* is a unique collection of items. In this discussion, a namespace refers to a collection of users, groups, and roles. Each of the icons used to represent these items is shown in Table 19-1.

Individual users are defined in your existing security model and can become members of groups, roles, or both. For all practical purposes, groups and roles behave in the same manner. The only technical difference is that groups limit their membership to users and other groups, while roles can contain all three—users, groups, and other roles.

TABLE **19-1** User,
Group, and Role Icons

Type	Icon
User	
Group	
Role	

NOTE *For more on the difference between groups and roles, see "Groups and Roles: What Is the Difference?" later in the chapter.*

When a user belongs to more than one group or role, permissions for all of the groups and roles are merged into one set and applied to that user. So, for example, someone in the Sales group who has the Authors role will be able to see the sales content and edit reports. Another user can be in the Marketing group and have the Authors role. This user will be able to edit marketing reports but will not be able to see sales content.

The Cognos 10 namespace comes with predefined users, groups, and roles. The more frequently used default users, groups, and roles are discussed in the following sections.

NOTE *A complete list of Cognos 10 users, groups, and roles is available in the Cognos 10 documentation.*

Default Users

Anonymous is the only default user in the Cognos 10 namespace. This generic account is used when security has not been enabled or when the anonymous access option is turned on in Cognos Configuration. By default, the Anonymous user has access to any items that have not been secured and to any items that members of the Everyone group can access. To disable the Anonymous user, the Cognos 10 installation team must configure an authentication provider and set the Allow Anonymous flag to False in Cognos Configuration.

Default Groups

Cognos 10 supplies two groups by default: All Authenticated Users and Everyone. These groups are provided so that you can begin to use your Cognos 10 application as quickly as possible by allowing every user to access almost everything.

All Authenticated Users

All Authenticated Users contains any user that has been granted access by an authentication provider. This group cannot be modified or deleted; it can only be included or excluded in another group or role.

Everyone

Everyone contains any user who has been granted access by an authentication provider, as well as the Anonymous user. This group cannot be modified or deleted; it can only be included or excluded in another group and role or disabled.

Default Roles

Along with default groups, Cognos 10 supplies a number of default roles. These roles define what capabilities are available to users and groups. By assigning a user or group to a role, you are granting those users the same capabilities that the role has. Depending on your installation, you may see additional roles not listed here. If so, refer to the "Administration and Security Guide" in your Cognos documentation for details on those roles.

System Administrators

The System Administrator is the *super user*. This is the most powerful role in the Cognos 10 security model, because members of this role can access and change any item found in Cognos Connection. The System Administrator role cannot be denied access to any content and the role requires at least one member.

Consumers

Users with the Consumers role can access Cognos Connection and read and execute previously created content such as reports. Consumers cannot access any of the authoring tools.

NOTE *In Cognos BI, the Consumers role is configured to meet the definition of the license group called "Enhanced Consumers." The Consumers role as defined in Cognos 8.x is not included in Cognos 10.*

Query Users

Query Users have all the same access as Consumers. In addition, they can also use the IBM Cognos Query Studio, which lets them create and save basic reports in their personal folders and perform ad hoc queries using any published IBM Cognos Framework Manager package.

Analysis Users

Analysis Users have all the same access as Consumers. In addition, they can use the IBM Cognos Analysis Studio, which lets them "slice and dice" online analytical processing (OLAP) cubes and dimensionally modeled data and to create and save reports in their personal folders.

Authors

Authors have the same access as Query Users and Analysis Users. Authors can use Cognos Report Studio, Cognos Analysis Studio, and Cognos Query Studio as well as save reports as public content that other users can access.

Report Administrators

Report Administrators can manage the content found in Public Folders. In addition, they can also use Cognos Report Studio and Cognos Query Studio.

Server Administrators

Server Administrators can manage the inner workings of the Cognos 10 environment. They can modify the settings of servers, dispatchers, and jobs.

Directory Administrators

Directory Administrators can manage the content of Cognos 10 namespaces. They can manage groups, accounts, contacts, distribution lists, data sources, and printers.

Securing the Default Roles

The first step in securing Cognos 10 is to define the membership of the roles in your environment. A good place to start is by deleting the Everyone group from roles, which, by default, is found in a number of groups and roles. To delete this group, you must navigate to each role that includes the Everyone group by default.

To access users, groups, and roles in Cognos 10, follow these steps:

1. Log on to Cognos Connection.

2. Click Launch to display the drop-down list, and then click Cognos Administration:

IBM Cognos Administration

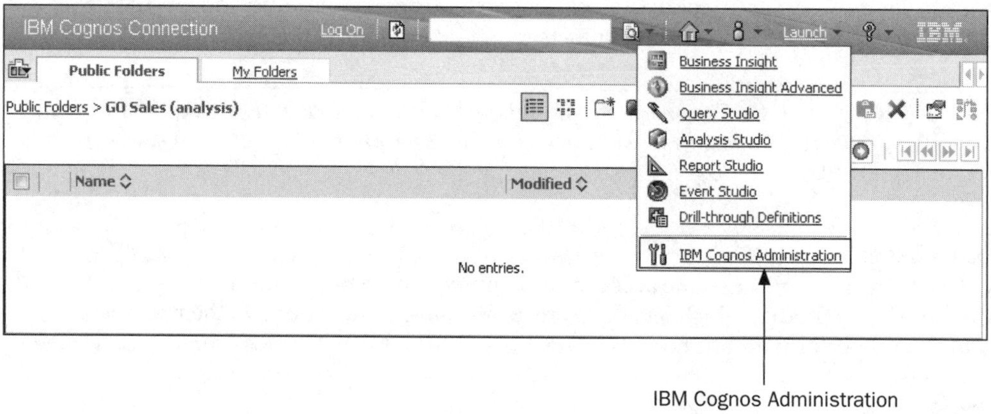

3. From the Cognos Administration screen, click the Security tab. The default Cognos 10 namespace displays, as well as any third-party authentication providers that have been configured, as shown next:

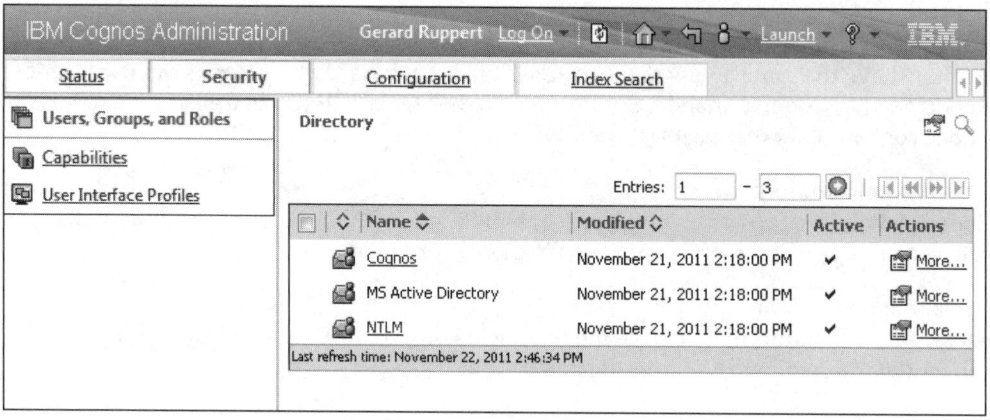

4. Click the Cognos link from the list to access the Cognos 10 namespace, shown here:

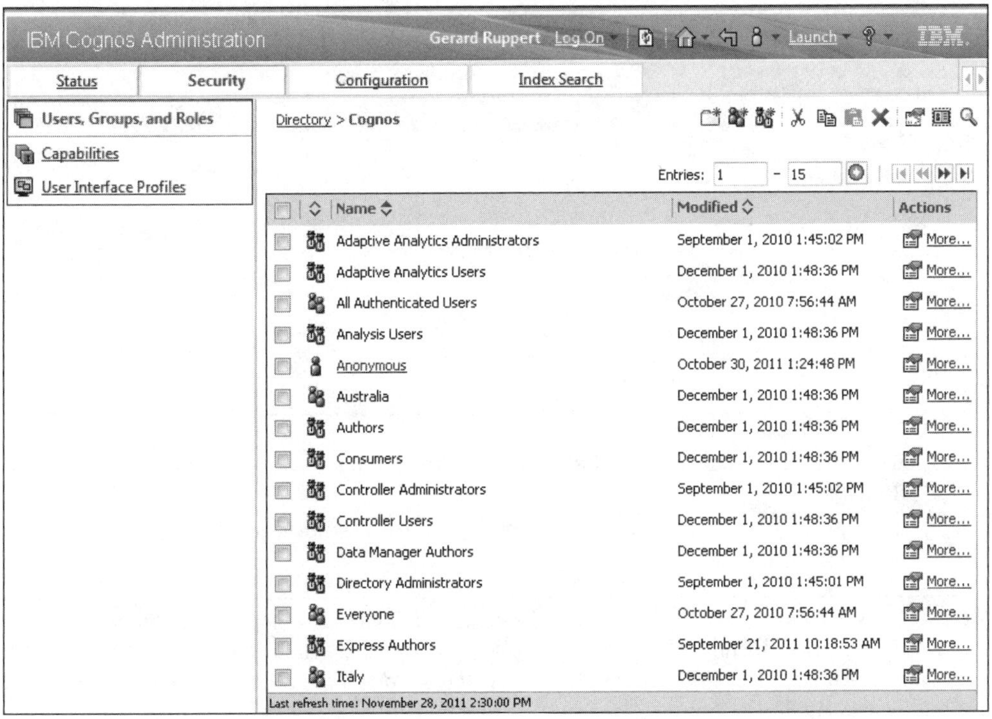

NOTE *You can log on to as many authentication sources as needed to access your application. If more than one authentication provider is configured, all will be displayed on the Security tab. To work with a namespace other than the Cognos namespace and the one by which you are currently authenticated, you must log on against the applicable namespace.*

Remove the Everyone Group

As mentioned, removing the Everyone group from your roles is a great place to start securing your Cognos 10 installation.

To remove the Everyone group from roles, follow these steps:

1. Navigate to a role. In this case, we are using the Analysis Users role.

2. Click the property icon to the right of the role.

3. Click the Members tab, as shown here:

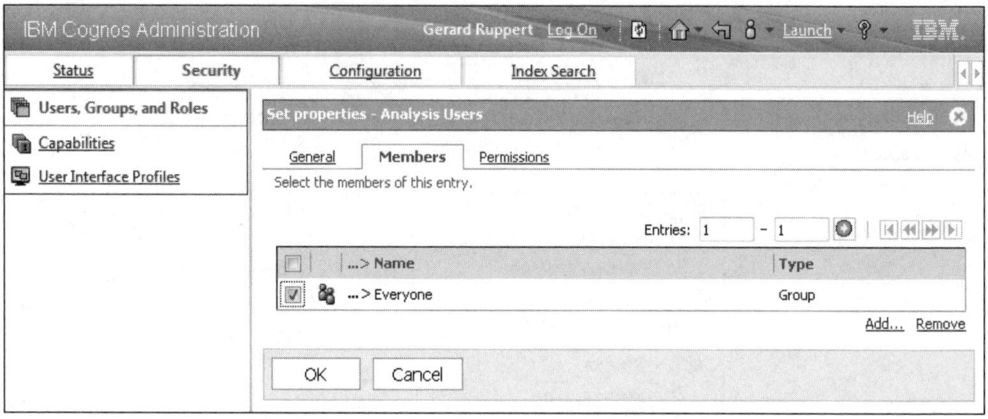

4. Select the check box next to the Everyone group, then click the Remove link, and then click OK.

5. Repeat steps 1 through 4 to remove Everyone from other roles.

NOTE *At the time of this writing, the Everyone group is included in the following groups by default: Adaptive Analytic Users, Analysis Users, Authors, Consumers, Controller Users, Data Manager Authors, Express Authors, Metrics Authors, PowerPlay Users, Query Users, Readers, and System Administrators.*

Users, Group, Roles, Capabilities, and Licensing

An important aspect of your security model is maintaining compliance with your license agreement. The Cognos 10 license groups do not always align with the default roles found in the Cognos namespace. As a result, our customers often ask how to configure security to comply with their license agreement.

Performing this alignment requires some modification to the roles found in the Cognos namespace, as well as some modifications to a few capabilities. This section of the chapter will show you to make these types of modifications. Later in the chapter we will discuss specific changes needed to align a typical IBM Cognos 10 installation with a typical set of licenses.

Customizing the Cognos Namespace

Our experience has shown that the majority of our clients use six license roles: Consumer, Enhanced Consumer, Advanced Business Author, Professional Author, Professional, and System Administrators. Of these, the System Administrators role is the only one predefined in the Cognos namespace; therefore, we must add the other four license roles to the namespace manually.

As a visual indication of custom roles, we prefix the role name with an asterisk. After adding the new roles, the Cognos namespace looks like the following:

		Name ◊	Modified ◊	Actions
☐	🎭	*Administrator	December 19, 2011 7:50:54 PM	📄 More...
☐	🎭	*Advanced Business Author	December 20, 2011 3:58:36 PM	📄 More...
☐	🎭	*Business Analyst	December 19, 2011 7:51:04 PM	📄 More...
☐	🎭	*Business Author	December 19, 2011 7:51:09 PM	📄 More...
☐	🎭	*Business Manager	December 19, 2011 7:51:16 PM	📄 More...
☐	🎭	*Consumer	December 19, 2011 7:51:21 PM	📄 More...
☐	🎭	*Enhanced Consumer	December 19, 2011 7:51:32 PM	📄 More...
☐	🎭	*Professional	December 19, 2011 8:12:12 PM	📄 More...
☐	🎭	*Professional Author	December 19, 2011 7:51:44 PM	📄 More...
☐	🎭	*Recipient	December 19, 2011 7:51:49 PM	📄 More...

Directory > **Cognos**   Entries: 1 – 15

The remaining steps required to bring your security model into alignment with a typical license scenario will be discussed at the end of this chapter in the section "User Modes and Licenses."

NOTE *The standard groups and roles found in the Cognos namespace should not be moved, deleted, or renamed. Modifying the default entries can have a negative impact on some components in Cognos BI.*

Adding Users, Groups, and Roles to the IBM Cognos 10 Namespace

As you have just seen, you will be making changes to your Cognos namespace early on. Fortunately, creating folders, groups, and roles in the Cognos namespace is similar to creating folders in any computer file system. Before you begin adding items, you should give some thought to how you would like to organize your security objects. We will be discussing a few approaches on how to organize your security model later in the chapter in the section "Using Roles, Access Permissions, and Capabilities." For now, let's create some groups and roles starting with the custom Advanced Business Author role.

Creating New Folders, Groups, and Roles

To add a new folder, group, or role to the Cognos namespace, begin by navigating to the Cognos namespace by following the steps in "Securing the Default Roles" earlier in the chapter. Then follow these steps:

1. From within the Cognos namespace, click the icon for the item you want to create. The options are shown a bit later in Table 19-2.

2. Click the New Role icon to launch the New Role Wizard.

Specify a name and description - New Role wizard		Help ⊗

Specify a name and location for this entry. You can also specify a description and screen tip.

Name:

Description:

Screen tip:

Location:
Directory > Cognos
Select another location...

| Cancel | < Back | Next > | Finish |

3. Enter the name of the role (group or folder). In this case, enter ***Advanced Business Author**. You can also enter a description of the new item and a screen tip. Then click Next. The new item will be displayed in the Cognos namespace:

Directory > Cognos

Entries: 1 – 31

	◇	Name ◇	Modified ◇	Actions
☐	🔳	* Advanced Business Author	December 3, 2011 11:23:51 AM	🖳 More...
☐	🔳	Adaptive Analytics Administrators	September 1, 2010 1:45:02 PM	🖳 More...
☐	🔳	Adaptive Analytics Users	December 1, 2010 1:48:36 PM	🖳 More...
☐	🔳	All Authenticated Users	October 27, 2010 7:56:44 AM	🖳 More...
☐	🔳	Analysis Users	November 28, 2011 2:33:36 PM	🖳 More...
☐	👤	Anonymous	December 2, 2011 10:51:50 AM	🖳 More...

TABLE 19-2 Cognos Namespace Creatable Objects

Icon	Description
	New Folder
	New Group
	New Role

Follow the same procedure to add folders and roles by first clicking the appropriate icon.

Assigning Users to Groups and Roles

Now that you have created the Advanced Business Author role, you need to add users to this role, because everyone is excited to start writing reports.

To add a user to a role in the Cognos namespace, follow these steps:

1. Navigate to the role you want to modify.

2. Click the property icon to the right of the role.

3. Click the Members tab.

4. Click the Add link at the bottom right of the members list. The Select Entries (Navigate) screen displays, listing all of the configured namespaces (authentication providers), as shown next. Only the Cognos namespace and the namespace(s) against which you are authenticated will be active (as indicated by the underline and the blue text):

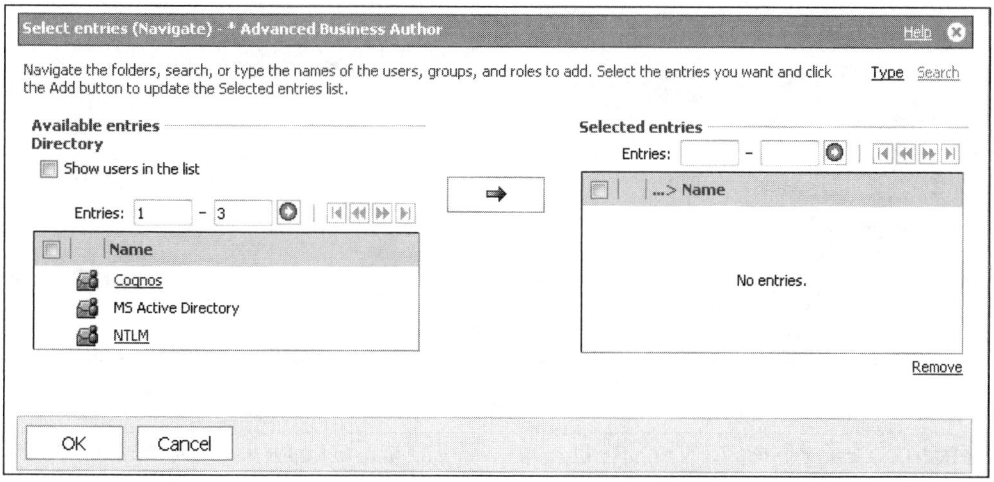

5. Because you are adding users from your authentication provider to the Cognos 10 namespace, click the namespace containing your users. In this case, click the NTLM

namespace. The authentication provider screen displays, listing the folders and
groups in the namespace, as shown next:

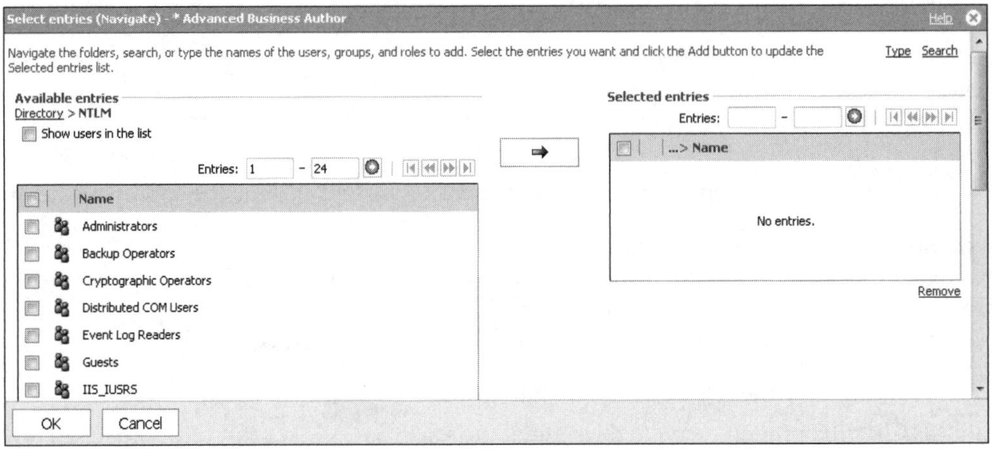

6. By default, Cognos 10 does not display the individual users within groups. To view
the members of a group, select the Show Users In The List check box and the list
will automatically refresh.

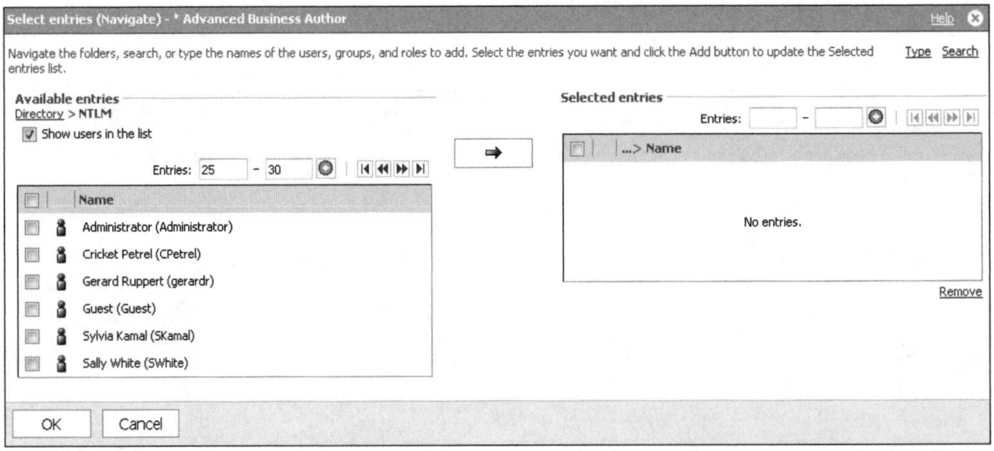

CAUTION *Groups with a large number of members can be slow to load if the authentication
provider is not indexed.*

If you have a large list of users and you do not want to scroll through the entire list,
you can use the Search feature to find a name. By default, the Search feature looks
for matches only in the names of groups and roles.

7. Click the Search link in the upper-right corner of the screen. If you are looking for a specific user, click the Advanced link in the middle of the screen.

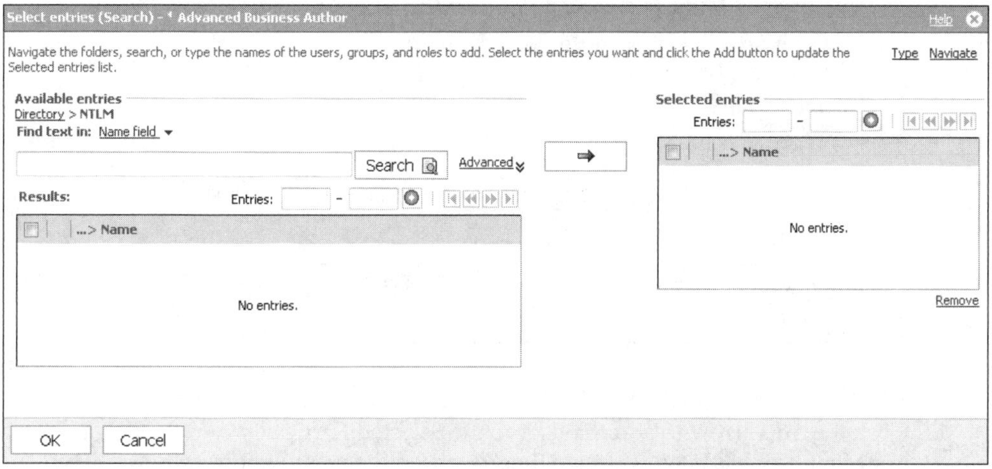

8. From the Type drop-down list, shown next, select Any, Groups And Roles, or Users to change the type of entries to search. The Find Text In string located above the input region specifies a search of just the Name Field, just the Description, or both. For this example, choose Users.

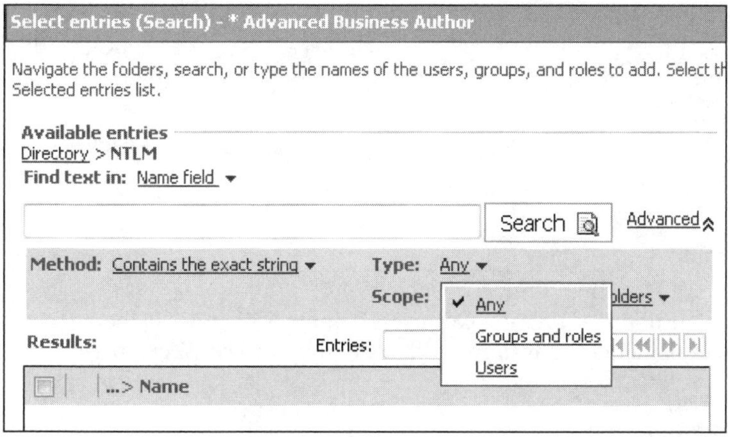

9. Let's say we're looking for a user named Webb Wilder. Type a segment of the name in the input region beneath the Find Text In text box.

PART IV

10. Click Search. The matched entries are returned.

11. To add the user to the role, select the check box next to the user name.

12. Click the Add arrow to add the user to the Selected Entries list and then click OK. Your first user has been added to the Advanced Business Author role.

The proper addition and removal of users from specific roles is the next step in bringing your Cognos implementation into compliance with your licensing agreement.

Access Permissions

Groups allow you to organize your security structure and place users with common access (for example, sales and marketing) together. Roles allow you to assign functionality (such as Advanced Business Authors, Readers, and so on) to groups and users. Access permissions allow you to define the level of interaction your users, groups, and roles can have with the objects in Cognos Connection.

All objects in Cognos 10 have five types of access permissions:

- **Read**   Allows users to view any property of the object as well as create shortcuts to the object.
- **Write**   Allows users to delete objects and modify the properties of an object, such as the name or description. When enabled on a folder, users can create new objects in that folder and save reports to that folder.
- **Execute**   Allows users to run reports and access data sources.
- **Set Policy**   Allows users to modify the security settings of an object.
- **Traverse**   Allows users to view the contents of an object and execute reports.

NOTE *Traverse permissions are needed when a drill-through report references another report in a different folder. If the report user does not have Traverse permissions on the folder that has the target report, the user will not be able to use the drill-through.*

The icons associated with each type of permission are shown in Table 19-3.

Access permissions can be set in one of three ways: Granted, Denied, or Not Set. If a user has a specific permission granted, the user can do whatever that permission allows. If the user has a specific permission denied, the user cannot do whatever that permission allows—this is called an *explicit deny*. If the user has a specific permission Not Set, the user cannot do whatever that permission allows; this is called an *implicit deny*. The Not Set and Denied permissions sound the same, but there is an important difference between the two, which will be discussed in the "Access Permissions Interaction" section a bit later in this chapter.

Setting Access Permissions

For this discussion, we assume that you have created two folders in Cognos Connection to hold content for your Sales and Marketing users and that you, cleverly, named these folders Sales and Marketing. To set the access permissions on an object, such as a report in your

TABLE 19-3
Permission Icons

Access Permission	Grant Icon	Deny Icon
Read		
Write		
Execute		
Set Policy		
Traverse		

PART IV

Sales folder, you click the properties icon of the report and then click the Permissions tab on the Set Properties screen, shown next:

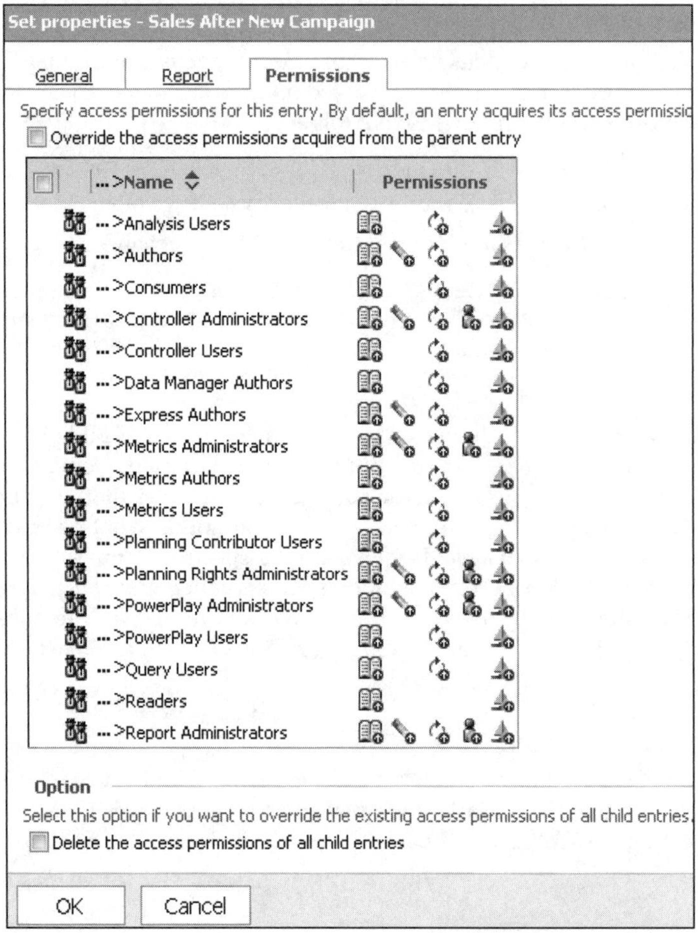

By default, the Cognos 10 access permissions of a report (or any other object) acquire the same access permissions set for the parent folder. This is a powerful tool when you're managing your security model. If the access requirements are the same for everything in a folder structure, you can set the access permissions at the top of the structure, and anything you add in the folder will automatically inherit that folder's permissions.

In this example, a report named "Sales After New Campaign" is located in the Marketing folder and was created by a user assigned the Report Administrator role. Suppose you want to give the Sales Managers group permissions to access the report even though the report is in the Marketing folder.

To change the access permissions for a specific object, follow these steps:

1. On the Permissions tab in the Set Properties screen, select the Override The Access Permissions Acquired From The Parent Entry check box, as shown next:

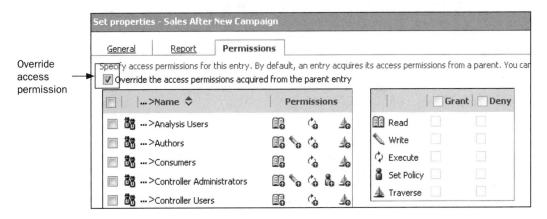

Override access permission

2. In the Access Permissions screen that displays next, check the Select All check box and click Remove Link to delete any default entries from the permissions list.

Select All check box

Add link

3. Click the Add link to add a role to the Permissions list. The Select Entries screen displays.

4. Navigate to the role in the Cognos namespace—Sales Managers, in this case.

5. Select the check box next to the role.

6. Click the Add arrow to add the role to the Selected Entries list, as shown next, and then click OK. The Permissions tab of the report displays with the Sales Managers role available, as shown here:

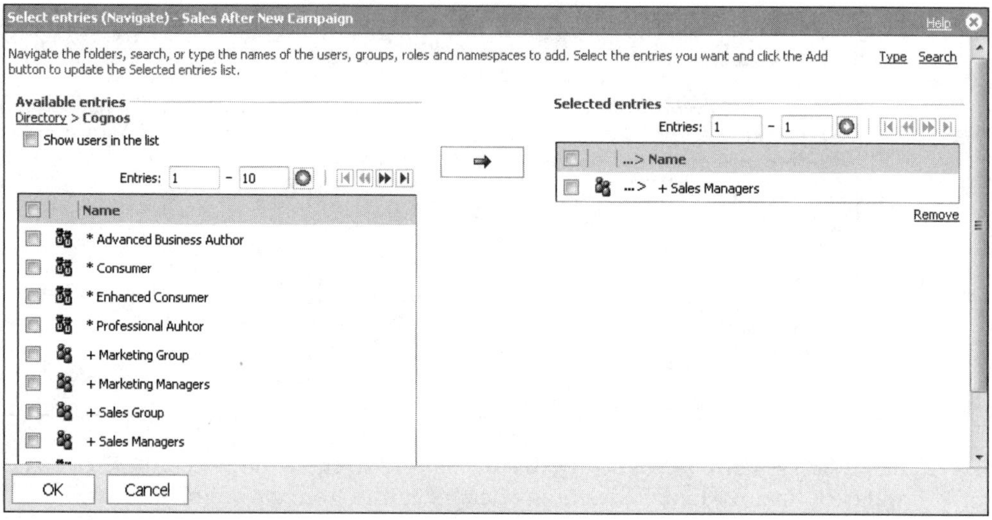

TIP *We prefix custom groups with a plus sign (+) to make visual identification of custom groups easier.*

Grant or Deny Permissions for a Role

After you have changed the access permissions for a specific object, you will need to grant or deny permissions for the roles that should be able to access that object.

To grant or deny permissions for a role, follow these steps:

1. In the Permissions tab, select the check box next to the user, group, or role name.

2. Select the Grant check box for all of the access permissions this role should be assigned.

3. Select the Deny check box for all of the access permissions this role should never be assigned.

4. Click Apply.

In this example, you want to allow members of Sales Managers to run the report, so you grant them Execute and Traverse permissions, as shown here:

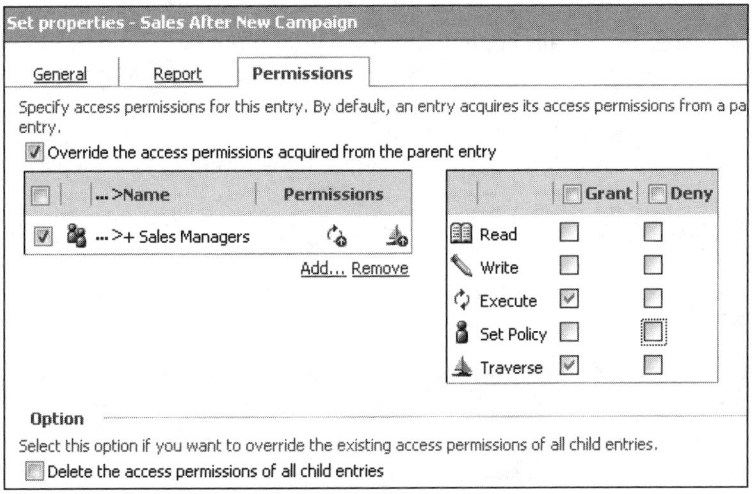

Set properties - Sales After New Campaign

| General | Report | **Permissions** |

Specify access permissions for this entry. By default, an entry acquires its access permissions from a pa
entry.

☑ Override the access permissions acquired from the parent entry

☐	...>Name	Permissions			☐ Grant	☐ Deny
☑	...>+ Sales Managers			Read	☐	☐
	Add... Remove			Write	☐	☐
				Execute	☑	☐
				Set Policy	☐	☐
				Traverse	☑	☐

Option

Select this option if you want to override the existing access permissions of all child entries.

☐ Delete the access permissions of all child entries

Because this report is in a folder, you need to confirm that Sales Managers can access the folder itself. If they cannot see the folder, they will not be able to access the report inside. View the permissions of the Marketing folder, as shown next, to determine whether the Sales Managers are in the Permissions list of the folder:

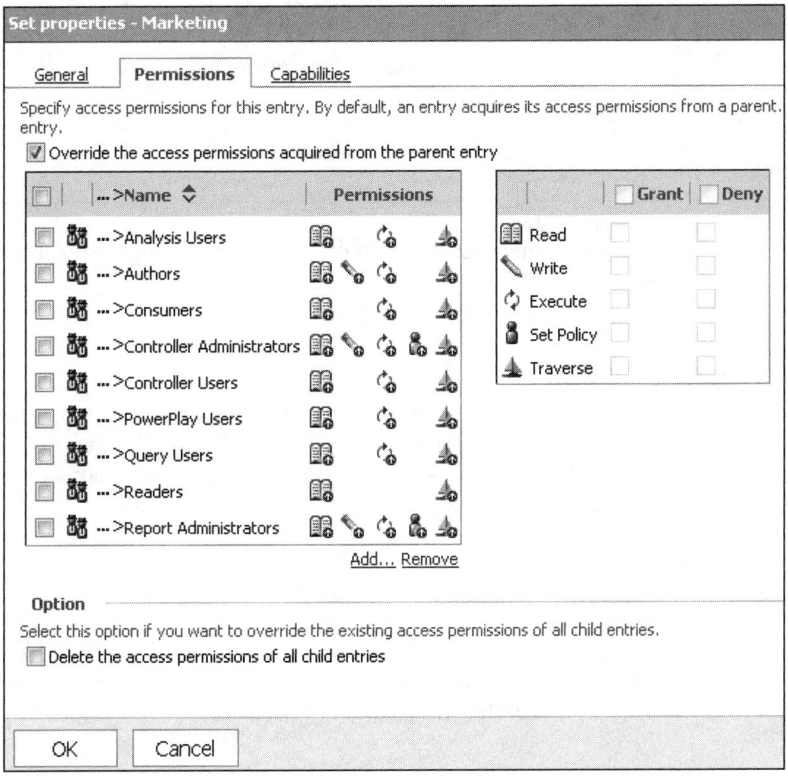

Set properties - Marketing

| General | **Permissions** | Capabilities |

Specify access permissions for this entry. By default, an entry acquires its access permissions from a parent.
entry.

☑ Override the access permissions acquired from the parent entry

☐	...>Name ⬍	Permissions			☐ Grant	☐ Deny
☐	...>Analysis Users			Read	☐	☐
☐	...>Authors			Write	☐	☐
☐	...>Consumers			Execute	☐	☐
☐	...>Controller Administrators			Set Policy	☐	☐
☐	...>Controller Users			Traverse	☐	☐
☐	...>PowerPlay Users					
☐	...>Query Users					
☐	...>Readers					
☐	...>Report Administrators					
	Add... Remove					

Option

Select this option if you want to override the existing access permissions of all child entries.

☐ Delete the access permissions of all child entries

| OK | Cancel |

Sales Managers does not appear. If someone from the Sales Managers group wanted to run the Sales After New Campaign report, they would not be able to do so. With the current permissions on the Marketing folder, members of the Sales Managers group do not have permission to view the folder. You will need to assign the Sales Managers group Traverse permissions on the Marketing folder.

To allow Sales Managers to view the Marketing folder, follow these steps:

1. On the Permissions tab of the Set Properties screen, add the Sales Managers group to the Permissions list (as discussed earlier in the chapter).

2. Click the Traverse and Execute Grant check boxes to assign the permissions, as shown here:

With this access permission, members of the Sales Managers group can access the Marketing folder and execute the Sales After New Campaign report. They cannot do anything else to the Marketing folder or to the report.

Access Permissions Interaction

Some users need to be in more than one group, and because they are in different groups, it is likely that the access permissions for the two (or more) groups will be different. If a user belongs to more than one group, the access permissions for all of their groups are merged into one set of permissions. Permissions are merged using one of two rules:

- Grant replaces Not Set.
- Deny replaces Grant and Not Set.

Suppose you have a report that allows two groups to access it. Group A has Write, Execute, and Traverse permissions. Group B has Read permissions but has been denied Execute permissions. If a user is in both groups and accesses the report, Cognos 10 grants the

Group	Read	Write	Execute	Set Policy	Traverse
A	Not Set	Granted	Granted	Not Set	Granted
B	Granted	Not Set	Denied	Not Set	Not Set
New Permissions	Granted	Granted	Denied	Not Set	Granted

TABLE 19-4 Access Permissions Interaction

following permissions to the user: Read, Write, and Traverse. The user lost the Execute permission. An example of how this works is provided in Table 19-4.

For example, suppose Cricket is a member of both the Marketing group and the Sales Managers group and she would like to access the Sales After New Campaign report. A Marketing user created the report, and he has the ability to modify the permissions of the report (Set Policy Access Permission). The author wants the Marketing group to have Read, Write, Execute, and Traverse permissions and wants the Sales Managers only to view the report. Not sure of how security works, the author decides that Read permissions should be good enough and sets the permissions in the following manner:

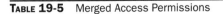

For Cricket, who is a member of both of the groups, the permissions are merged into the results shown in Table 19-5.

Group	Read	Write	Execute	Set Policy	Traverse
Marketing	Granted	Granted	Granted	Not Set	Granted
Sales Managers	Granted	Not Set	Denied	Not Set	Denied
Cricket	Granted	Granted	Denied	Not Set	Denied

TABLE 19-5 Merged Access Permissions

The author who set the permissions on these groups made two incorrect assumptions: First, the author assumed that the Read permission was needed to allow a user to run a report; however, Execute is the permission that is needed. The second assumption was that the Deny setting on the Execute permission would affect only the Sales Manager group. Because of the merge rules, Deny always takes precedence over all other permissions. The result in this example is that anyone who is in both the Marketing and Sales Manager groups has lost the ability to Execute the report. The proper permissions would be Read, Traverse, and Execute.

IBM Cognos 10 Capabilities

IBM Cognos 10 provides a fine level of control over the content users can see. Through access permissions and the ability to apply those permissions to the groups that you have defined, you are able to ensure proper access to information. Capabilities are another level of control provided by Cognos 10 that relate to what users can do as opposed to what they can see. A *capability* in Cognos 10 can have multiple functions contained within.

For example, in Cognos Report Studio, Authors can edit the SQL generated by the Cognos 10 report engine and run the report using modified SQL; they can also embed HTML code in a report. With the scheduling capability, users can schedule reports to run at any time. This capability also allows users to change the priority of their scheduled jobs and allows administrators to remove scheduling from users altogether. In both of these examples, you might not want the users to have those specific abilities within the capability.

NOTE   *The capabilities that are available in Cognos 10 can change over time. Check your Cognos BI documentation for a full list of current capabilities.*

The capabilities in Cognos 10 come with permissions assigned to default roles. In most cases, the default settings will be sufficient for your security needs. However, if you find that you need to modify the default settings, the process is the same as setting the access permissions on folders, reports, and other objects, as discussed earlier. Simply add or remove users, groups, or roles from the Permissions list of the capability or function within a capability that you would like to modify.

The capabilities in your installation of Cognos 10 will vary based on which components have been purchased and installed. Some of the more common capabilities and their additional functions are listed here.

Administration   Users are able to administer the Cognos 10 installation.

- **Adaptive Analytics administration**   Controls access to reports sourced from Adaptive Analytics.
- **Administration tasks**   Users can administer exports, imports, index updates, consistency checks, and report updates.
- **Cognos Metric Studio administration**   Users can create new metric packages with the new Metric Package Wizard in Cognos Connection and access the Tools menu in Cognos Metric Studio.
- **Configure and manage the system**   Users can configure dispatchers and services and manage the system.
- **Controller administration**   Users can use the administrative functions of Cognos 10 Controller.
- **Data source connections**   Users can add and remove data sources, as well as create sign-ins to data sources.
- **Distribution lists and contacts**   Users can create and maintain report distribution lists and contact information.
- **Execute indexed search**   Enhanced Consumers can use enhanced search functionality that uses a search index as opposed to the Content Manager.
- **Planning administration**   Users can access the Planning Contributor Administration console and the Planning Analyst to perform administration tasks.
- **PowerPlay Servers**   Users can administer PowerPlay properties.
- **Printers**   Users can add, remove, and modify printer connections.
- **Run activities and schedules**   Users can monitor the server activities and manage schedules.
- **Set capabilities and UI profiles**   Users can manage the secured functions and features and the Cognos Report Studio user interface profiles.
- **Styles and portlets**   Users can manage styles and portlets in Cognos Administration.
- **Users, groups, and roles**   Users can create, delete, and modify namespaces, users, groups, and roles.

Analysis Studio   Users can run Cognos Analysis Studio.

IBM Cognos Viewer   Users can modify the behavior of Cognos Viewer.

- **Context menu**   Users can use the context menus (submenus) in Cognos Viewer.
- **Run with options**   Users can modify the default run options of a report.
- **Selection**   Users can select and copy text from a report.
- **Toolbar**   Users can access the toolbar in Cognos Viewer.

Collaborate   Users can control access to the IBM Connections collaboration tool from within Cognos Connection.

Detailed Errors   Users can receive the full message text when they encounter an error.

Drill-Through Assistant   Users can access the Drill-Through Assistant.

Event Studio   Users can run Cognos Event Studio.

Executive Dashboard   Users can run IBM Cognos Business Insight.

Metric Studio   Users can run Cognos Metric Studio.

- **Edit view**   Users can modify the default settings of Cognos Metric Studio.

Query Studio   Users can run Cognos Query Studio.

- **Advanced**   Users can use style formatting, multilingual support, advanced calculations, and create complex filters.
- **Create**   Users can use the Save As option.

Report Studio   Users can run Cognos Report Studio.

- **Bursting**   Users can create burst reports.
- **Create/Delete**   Users can create new reports and delete existing reports.
- **HTML items in report**   Users can include embedded HTML in reports.
- **User-defined SQL**   Users can directly modify the SQL created by the report.

Scheduling   Users can schedule activities.

- **Scheduling priority**   Users can modify the priority of new or existing activities.

Accessing Capabilities

Capabilities are located on the Security tab of the Cognos Administration screen. Your list of capabilities will look similar to those shown here:

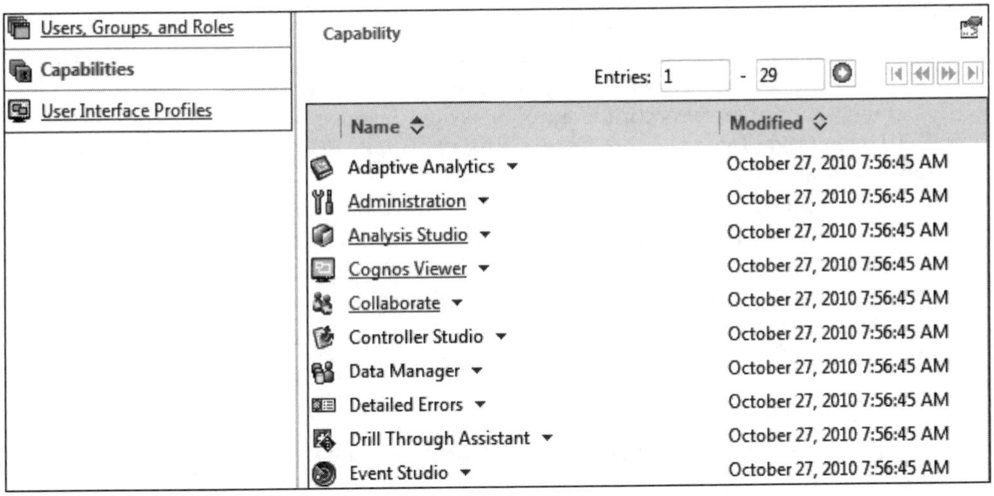

Links (underlined and in blue text) contain multiple capabilities, each of which can have its permissions set individually. For example, the Administration capability is actually made up of a dozen or so capabilities, as shown here:

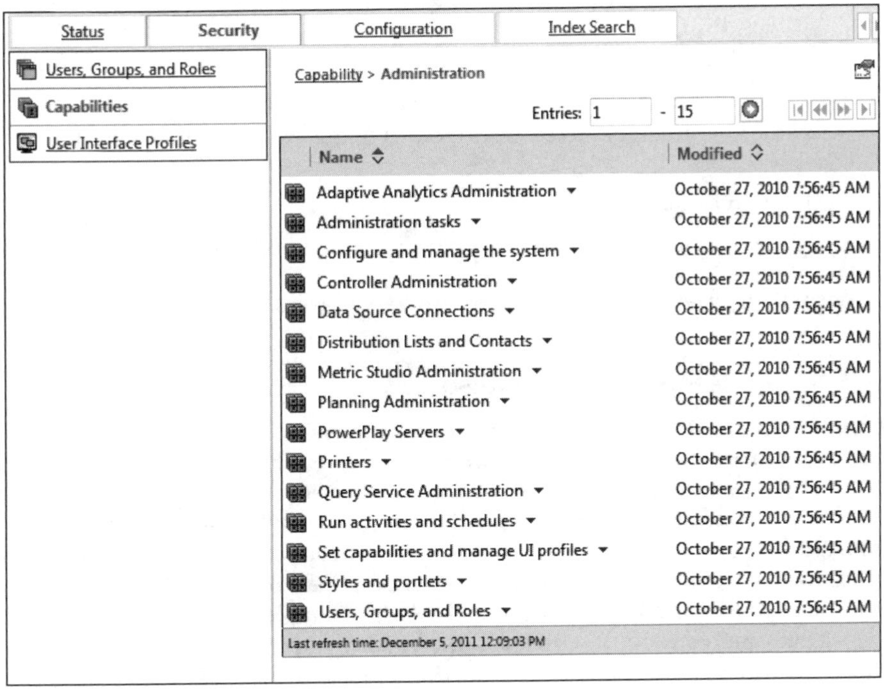

Capabilities You Might Want to Change

As mentioned earlier, in most cases, you will not need to modify any of the capabilities. The Detailed Errors capability, however, is one exception.

By default, when an error occurs, Cognos 10 writes the error to a log file in the IBM Cognos 10 installation folder on the server. This is normally a secure location that most users will not be able to access. If an error occurs during report execution, the user is presented with a message containing the location of the error details within the log file. This makes Authors dependent on someone else to assist them with troubleshooting the problem. You can configure Cognos 10 to send the complete error message to the user by adding the appropriate group or groups to the Permissions list of the Detailed Errors capability. Normally, Authors and Consumers roles are added to this capability.

To modify the Detailed Errors capability, follow these steps:

1. Navigate to the Capability screen.

2. Click the down arrow next to Detailed Errors. A text box displays the Set Properties command:

3. Click Set Properties.

4. Click the Permissions tab.

5. Select the Override The Access Permissions Acquired From The Parent Entry check box.

6. Add the Consumers role.

7. Assign the Consumers role both Execute and Traverse permissions, and then click OK.

Anyone who now encounters an error during report execution will see the full error text.

Groups and Roles: What Is the Difference?

Earlier in this chapter, we talked briefly about the differences between groups and roles. The only technical difference between a group and a role is this: A role can contain users, groups, and other roles while a group can contain *only* users and other groups. Other than that difference, groups and roles can behave the same. To keep life easier, we suggest you follow this rule of thumb: Use groups to define what Cognos 10 content a set of users can access; use roles to define what capabilities a set of users has. By following this rule, you can use groups and roles to set default functionality. As an example, if you are in the Sales Managers group and you have not been assigned a role, you cannot perform any actions in that group, because roles define what you *can* do. While in the Sales Manager group, if you are also assigned the Consumers role, you can do anything allowed by the Consumers role for any object for which the Sales Managers group has access permissions.

Once security has been applied and you have been assigned a role but not a group, you can perform the actions permitted by the role and will have limited access to the application. If you have been assigned the Authors role, for example, but you have not been placed in a group, you will be unable to access a reporting source and, even if you could, you would be unable to save the report to a global folder. You could save reports to My Folder. But because no one else can see that folder, the organization would not benefit from reports authored by you.

> **NOTE** *Membership in groups or roles is optional; however, you should use them. Otherwise, administering permissions and capabilities for each user quickly gets out of hand and maintenance becomes a nightmare.*

Using Roles, Access Permissions, and Capabilities

The success level that you achieve with your security configuration will be determined to a great degree by how well you plan your strategy before you begin. It is vital that you understand how your content will be stored, which groups will have access to what content, and which users will have which capabilities.

For most users, content is organized along functional lines. Folders are created in Cognos Connection for operational areas (such as Finance, Sales, Management, and so on). Each operational area can be divided further as needed (for example, the Sales folder could contain Regions or Product Lines). For multinational customers, a geographical organization might be displayed first, followed by a standard operational structure underneath. How your content is organized will ultimately be determined by what works best for you. No matter where you end up, you should start by mapping out on paper how you think you want your content organized and keep it handy.

When considering the access permissions you will need, start by thinking about what should be secured. In broad terms, you will need three security roles: Consumers, Authors, and Administrator. The Consumers role needs to navigate the folder structure that you have created and needs to be able to execute reports. The Consumers role will contain the largest number of users and in general will usually need Traverse, Write, and Execute access permissions. Make a list of the users who will have only these permissions and label it "Consumers."

Authors need to have the access permissions of Consumers, as well as the ability to access one or more studios. Make a new list of Authors and studios to which they will have access. Repeat this process for the roles that you will be using. You will end up with something similar to Table 19-6.

TABLE 19-6
Sample Role List

Consumer	Advanced Business Authors	Administrator
Janet	Dan	Susie
Jon	Mark	
Bryan		
Alicia		

The Administrator role can vary based on how you maintain your Cognos 10 installation. Typically, in centralized organizations, a small group of people have full administrative responsibilities. In larger organizations, individuals with a subset of the Administrator role are given responsibility for a functional area within Cognos Connection, while an overall Administrator is responsible for all of the functional areas.

You should have a clear idea of which users should be assigned to which roles, so now you can start on the content. Assuming you decide to use the functional method of organizing your content, make a list of the functional areas. This list will be the starting point of both your folder structure and, if not already defined, your groups. Assume that your functional areas, and by extension your groups, are Marketing, Research and Development (R&D), Senior Management, Sales Management, and Sales Territory. Use this list to make an Access Permissions grid. List the groups as columns and the top level Cognos Connection folders as rows. In each intersection, write what access permissions the group in the column has to the folder in that row. The resulting grid will look something like Table 19-7.

This grid provides you with a quick reference that you can use while setting up your security and for troubleshooting access permissions in the future.

How you decide to administer the security of your installation will depend on any number of factors: How many users? How much content? How widely distributed is your user base? All these factors and any others that are specific to your organization should be considered before you begin implementing a security strategy.

Business Case: Configuring Initial Security

The need for security sounds simple: Do not let people see or do things that they are not permitted to see or do. When you try to make that work with many different people having many different levels of access, however, that simple task becomes complex.

Suppose you work for a company that makes outdoor equipment, called The Really Good Outdoors Company, and you have just been given the responsibility of managing the security of the new Cognos 10 installation. You have created the following groups in the Cognos namespace: Marketing, Research and Development, Senior Management, Sales Management, and Sales Territory. Senior management has decided that your first task is to ensure that members of each group can access only content belonging to their group.

Access Permissions	Marketing	R&D	Sr. Mgmt.	Sales Mgmt.	Sales Territory
Marketing folder	RWET	ET	RET	ET	
R&D folder	ET	RWET	RET	ET	
Sr. Mgmt. folder			RWET		
Sales Mgmt. folder			RET	RWET	
Sales Territory folder			RET	RWET	RET

TABLE 19-7   Group and Folder Access Permissions Grid

Assume a directory administrator has already created the folders that each group will use. After thinking about this request, you decide that you need to take the following actions:

1. Add a user (or group of administrators) to the System Administrators role so that once security is enabled, someone has the permissions needed to make changes later on.

2. Remove the Everyone group from all of the Cognos roles and add named users and/or groups so that they will have access to default functionality provided by these roles.

3. Set access permissions on the folders so that appropriate access is provided for specific users, groups, and roles.

These actions are described in the following sections.

Add a User to the System Administrators Role

Using the same steps from the "Adding Users, Groups, and Roles to the IBM Cognos 10 Namespace" section, add a user, most likely yourself, to the System Administrators role.

To add a user to the System Administrators role, follow these steps:

1. From Cognos Connection, click the Launch link.

2. Click the Cognos Administration link.

3. Click the Security tab.

4. Click the Cognos link.

5. Scroll down to the System Administrators role.

6. Click the property icon of the System Administrators role.

7. Click the Members tab.

8. Click the Add link.

9. Follow the same navigation method to find your login ID in your authentication provider.

10. Add that ID to the Members list.

NOTE *By default, Cognos Connection shows 15 items in a list at a time. You can change that default by editing your preferences.*

Set Access Permissions

Your Cognos 10 installation is not quite secure yet. By default, all objects that are added to Cognos Connection inherit the security properties of the folder in which they are placed, which is called the *parent*, or *parent object*. Examine the properties of the Public Folders:

NOTE *By default, the Public Folders in Cognos Connection allows all the default roles to have Read and Traverse access permissions to anything in the folder. When you're creating new objects, make sure you set the access permissions to meet your needs.*

Securing the folders in the Public Folders ensures that only roles belonging to the operational area that correspond to a folder name can access the content of the folder.
To set access permissions, follow these steps:

1. Starting with the Senior Management folder, click the folder's properties icon. By default, the folder inherited the permissions of its parent (in this example, the Public Folders).

2. Select the Override The Default Access Permissions check box.

3. Delete all the roles that are defined by default.

TIP *Select the check box in the header of the list to select the entire list.*

4. Click Add.

5. Navigate to your authentication provider.

6. Select the check box of the role or group that you want to have access to this folder.

7. Click Add.

8. Click OK.

9. Because the Senior Management role owns this folder, assign the role or group Read, Write, Execute, and Traverse access permissions. When you are finished, the Senior Management permissions should look like this:

At this point, only members of the Senior Management group can access the Senior Management folder. In fact, users in other non-administrative groups and roles cannot even see the Senior Management folder. If a member of the Marketing role were to log on to Cognos Connection at this point, he or she would see a screen similar to this:

	Name ◇	Modified ◇	Actions
☐ 📁	Marketing	December 5, 2011 11:10:35 AM	🖼 More...
☐ 📁	Research and Development	December 5, 2011 1:36:31 PM	🖼 More...
☐ 📁	Sales Management	December 5, 2011 1:38:22 PM	🖼 More...
☐ 📁	Sales Territory	December 5, 2011 1:37:17 PM	🖼 More...

If a member of Senior Management were to log on, he or she would see a screen similar to this:

	Name ◇	Modified ◇	Actions
☐ 📁	Research and Development	December 5, 2011 1:36:31 PM	🖼 More...
☐ 📁	Sales Management	December 5, 2011 1:38:22 PM	🖼 More...
☐ 📁	Sales Territory	December 5, 2011 1:37:17 PM	🖼 More...
☐ 📁	Senior Management	December 5, 2011 1:41:00 PM	🖼 More...

The Cognos Connection screen displays two differences in what Senior Management sees as compared to what Marketing sees. First, Senior Management can see the Senior Management folder, which is what you would expect. However, managers cannot see the Marketing folder, because you changed the permissions on that folder earlier in this chapter.

Note   *To finish the initial security of the Public Folders, you need to repeat steps 1 through 9 for each of the subfolders found in the Public Folders.*

Business Case: Wait! That's Not What I Wanted!

You have successfully implemented the security strategy that Senior Management devised. When Senior Management members log into Cognos Connection, however, they call you in a panic because they cannot find the Marketing reports. After you reassure them that the reports have not been deleted, you ask for clarification on what they would like to see. Senior Management explains that users from each operational area should see only what is in that area's folders, but Senior Management needs to see everything.

Allowing multiple groups to have different access permissions to an object, be it a report, folder, or anything else, is common. Having a Group and Folder Access Permissions Grid (as in Table 19-7) comes in handy. Look up the Senior Management group and the Marketing folder. The Senior Management group should have Read, Execute, and Traverse access permissions on the Marketing folder. When you look at the access permissions on the Marketing folder, however, you see that is not the case:

Senior Management is not on the Permissions list. Follow the steps from the "Set Access Permissions" section earlier in this chapter to add Senior Management to the Permissions list of the Marketing folder and assign that role Read, Execute, and Traverse access permissions. Your results will look similar to this:

PART IV

User Modes and Licenses

Understanding how security in Cognos 10 works in a mechanical sense gets you halfway to having a manageable and effective security configuration. To finish the job, you need to apply your security in such a way that you (1) are sure your Cognos 10 content is available to the proper users, (2) have a system that you can manage, and (3) are in compliance with your Cognos BI licenses. Chapter 3 discussed the many licenses that are available in Cognos 10. A common question is, "How do I configure my users and groups so that I am in compliance with my licenses?" This question is best answered through the combination of groups, roles, and capabilities. Earlier in this chapter, we touched on this concept, but we will now discuss it in more detail.

To bring your default Cognos 10 installation into compliance with your licenses, you will need to create new roles, assign these roles to existing roles, and change some capabilities.

Creating License Roles

The first step in setting up your licensing is to create the new roles that align with the Cognos 10 license groups. Start by navigating to the Cognos namespace in the Security tab of the IBM Cognos Administration screen. If you have not already done so, create the following five roles:

1. * Advanced Business Author

2. * Consumer

3. * Enhanced Consumer

4. * Professional

5. * Professional Author

Modify the Default Capabilities

In order for the default roles, as well as the newly added roles, to behave as defined in the licenses, you will need to modify some of the default capabilities. The following actions are required.

Executive Dashboard Capability

Remove the Consumers role from the Executive Dashboard capability. This is required because Consumers are not licensed to use IBM Cognos Business Insight, for which access is controlled by the Executive Dashboard capability.

To remove the Consumers role, follow these steps:

1. Navigate to the Executive Dashboard capability and click the Set Properties tab.

2. Click the Permissions tab.
3. Click the Consumers role check box.

4. Click the Remove link.

Consumers role to remove

5. Click the OK button to save the change.

You will need to add the new * Enhanced Consumer role to the Executive Dashboard capability. Follow these steps:

1. From the Permissions dialog of the Executive Dashboard capability, click the Add link.
2. Navigate to the Cognos namespace.
3. From the Available Entries list, click the check box next the * Enhanced Consumer role.
4. Click the Add arrow to add the role to the Selected Entries list.

5. Click the OK button and you will return to the Permissions screen.

6. Click the check box next to the * Enhanced Consumer role and grant the Execute and Traverse permissions to the role.

Report Studio Capability

The * Professional Author role allows users access to most of the functionality found in Cognos Report Studio capability. Using the same procedure just described, add the * Professional Author role to the Cognos Report Studio capability.

NOTE *Capabilities with an active hyperlink have additional secured features.*

You will also need to add the * Professional Author role to the following Cognos Report Studio secured feature capabilities.

- Bursting
- Create/Delete
- HTML Items In Report
- User Defined SQL

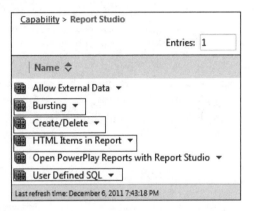

Modify the User Interface Profiles

User Interface Profiles determine which Cognos Report Studio design tools are available to report authors. The Professional Author mode grants the author all features available in Cognos Report Studio. The Express mode grants the report author a focused selection of Cognos Report Studio features aimed at dimensional data and financial reporting.

The * Professional Author role has access to the Professional Interface but not the Express Interface. You will need to add the * Professional Author role to the Professional User Interface Profile.

Modify the Custom and Standard Roles

Finally, to bring your installation into alignment with the licenses, you will need to add the following custom-created roles to the appropriate standard roles:

- *** Advanced Business Author**   Add this custom role to the Analysis Users, Express Authors, and Query Users standard roles.
- *** Consumer**   Add this custom role to the Consumers standard role.
- *** Enhanced Consumer**   Add this custom role to the Consumers standard role.
- *** Professional**   Add this custom role to the Authors standard role.
- *** Professional Author**   Add this custom role to the Express Authors and Query Users standard roles.

Troubleshooting and Testing

Applying security in Cognos 10 is not technically difficult, but it is challenging. As mentioned earlier in this chapter, the key to success is good planning. However, even the best plan will not account for every possibility. When problems are found with your security model, think about the groups and access permissions involved and start with the users and groups in question:

- If a sales person cannot see the Sales folder, make sure that user is assigned to the Sales group.
- Check the access permissions on the objects in question.
- Look for overlapping groups that might have an Explicit Deny set.
- When someone cannot execute a report, check the access permissions on the object and the roles to which the user belongs.
- If someone is trying to use Cognos Report Studio to edit a report, make sure the user is a member of the Authors role and that he or she has access permissions to the folder or report.

Finally, the best thing you can do is try it yourself. Create test users for each group and set access permissions to make sure the security is working according to plan. Nothing can replace your ability to try it and see for yourself.

IBM Cognos Connection Management

B y this point, you have packages, reports, queries, events, scheduled jobs, and more floating around your IBM Cognos Business Intelligence v10.1 (Cognos BI) installation. What do you do with it all? You could let the content become cluttered like your workshop or garage, where you can never find that one tool that you need and maintenance becomes near impossible amid the clutter. Or you could become an organizing and maintenance guru like those on TV, organizing your clutter and creating a functional workspace that operates at peak performance. IBM Cognos BI provides all the administrative tools for you. You simply need to understand your system and the needs of your organization.

IBM Cognos Administration is the area from which you can perform the majority of the functions outlined in this chapter. You can create and manage data source connections, perform some aspects of content administration, manage schedules, maintain distribution lists, perform server administration, monitor the status of activities, and specify advanced search settings.

Organize Content

An administrator can organize content from IBM Cognos Connection. When content is organized properly, it makes using IBM Cognos Connection much easier to navigate for users. With Cognos BI, administrators can create folders to house packages, content, or both. For example, an administrator can create a folder for the Accounting department that contains all the packages and content for Monthly Accounting, and another folder for Quarterly Accounting.

NOTE *The blue folders denote IBM Cognos Framework Manager packages which can also behave as a directory for other entries. A blue folder with the metric symbol on it is a Metric package, which can be used in IBM Cognos Metric Studio. The yellow folders are directories created by a user and can have content including packages (blue folders) within them.*

After you create a folder, you can organize content by moving packages, reports, jobs, or other entries into the folder. You may want to group entries by type, frequency of use, or permissions. Review the content and arrange entries according to what is most logical for the users.

To organize content into a folder, follow these steps:

1. In IBM Cognos Connection, click the New Folder button on the toolbar. The New Folder Wizard launches.

2. In the Name text box, enter a name for the folder.

3. Optionally, provide a description and a screen tip for the folder.

4. Under Location, click the Select Another Location link to specify a location for the folder that is different from the location listed, or click the Select My Folders link to save the folder in your My Folders directory.

5. Click the Finish button.

6. To set the permissions for the newly created folder, click the Set Properties button in the Actions column of the folder.

7. Click the Permissions tab. A list of users with permission to access the folder displays.

8. Modify the permissions and then click OK. (For more information on modifying permissions, refer to Chapter 19.)

9. In IBM Cognos Connection, navigate to the entries to be moved to the folder.

10. Select the check box(es) for the entries you want to relocate.

11. Click the Cut button on the toolbar.

12. Open the newly created folder.

13. Click the Paste button on the toolbar. The selected content is relocated into the new folder.

Administering Properties

In IBM Cognos Connection and IBM Cognos Administration, you can manage the properties for a variety of items, such as folders, reports, jobs, servers, groups, data sources, and distribution lists, to name a few. The general properties that can be modified include the owner, display icons, language, name, and description. Using meaningful names and detailed descriptions helps identify entries easily.

Accessing the properties is similar for all entries: click the Set Properties button in the Actions column of an entry or select the check box for an entry and click the Set Properties button on the toolbar. The properties for an item contain a General tab and a Permissions tab, as well as any number of other tabs that contain specific properties associated with the type of entry. Whether users have rights to modify properties depends on their access permissions to entries, while administrators have much more control over properties.

Status

The Status tab within IBM Cognos Administration provides a variety of functions you can use to monitor the condition of the system. From the Status tab, you can manage activities, schedules and system metrics.

Activities

Activities are entries that have been or will be processed within Cognos BI. You can view current, past, and upcoming activities. An overview of activities is shown in a bar chart by the state of the activity, with the detailed activities listed below the chart. You can apply filters to narrow down the amount of items displayed. For each entry, you can view information such as the run history and the history details.

View current activities to see what is currently happening in the IBM Cognos environment. Interactive activities are items currently being processed that are run interactively, such as a report that is requested for immediate display. Background activities are items currently being processed that are not run interactively, such as entries that are scheduled or a report executed to be saved.

View past activities to monitor the status of entries that have already been executed. Any failed entry can be examined for the cause of failure to prevent it from happening again. The execution times of an entry can also be viewed, which is useful for knowing when to expect results or whether reports are executing in a reasonable amount of time.

View upcoming activities to ensure that the appropriate planning is in place to keep the system running smoothly. For example, you could make sure that the necessary items are scheduled to occur at the proper times, and that upcoming activities are spaced out so that the system will not be overloaded with requests that would negatively affect system performance.

System

Monitoring the status of the system lets you keep an eye on the health of your installation. The System page includes three panes used for monitoring and managing system status. The Scorecard pane contains a list of entries, for which you can view a metric score and the status of each. The Metrics pane displays the metrics for the entry selected in the Scorecard pane. The Metrics pane can be filtered by selecting the desired check boxes above the metrics list. The Settings pane displays the settings for the entry selected in the Scorecard pane. System properties can be modified by clicking the Set Properties button at the top of the Settings pane.

Set Properties button

System Metrics

IBM Cognos BI makes monitoring your system easy by using metrics. The thresholds that you set define target values that show you whether your system is working as designed. If any part of your system displays a red light, you can address that portion appropriately to restore the system to peak performance. Metrics are available for the servers, server groups, dispatchers, and services.

To manage system metrics, follow these steps:

1. From the Launch menu, select IBM Cognos Administration.

2. From the Status tab, select System.

3. From the Scorecard pane, select the entry for which you want to manage metrics. The Metrics pane lists the functions that can have metrics associated with them. The left half of the pane shows the name of the function and the right half shows the metric score.

4. From the Metrics pane, click the plus sign to expand the function for which you want to modify the metrics.

5. Click the Edit button next to the metric for which you want to set thresholds. There are four options for the Performance Pattern:

- **None**   Turns off the metric
- **High values are good**   Higher values are more favorable than lower values; values above the highest threshold are Good (green), values below the lowest threshold are Poor (red), and values between the two thresholds are Average (yellow):

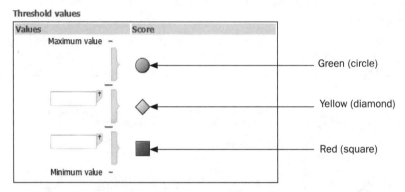

- **Low values are good**   Lower values are more favorable than higher values; values below the lowest threshold are Good (green), values above the highest threshold are Poor (red), and values between the two thresholds are Average (yellow):

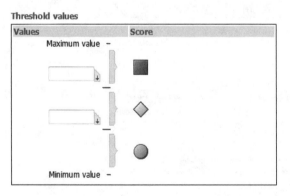

- **Middle values are good**   Values in the middle of set thresholds are favorable; values within one set of thresholds are Good (green), values between the first set of thresholds and a second set are Average (yellow), and values outside the second set of thresholds are Poor (red):

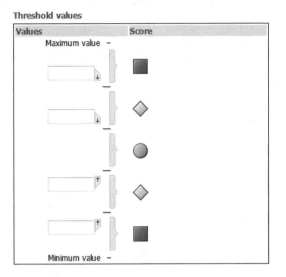

6. In the Performance Pattern area, select the desired option.

7. In the Threshold Values area, enter thresholds for the metric.

8. Click OK. The threshold values for the metric are set. You can now monitor system performance.

NOTE *Metrics and logging offer a complete view of your system. Use metrics to determine what portion of the system is running poorly. Then you can you view the logs to determine the reason.*

System Settings

Adjusting system properties allows administrators to optimize system performance. You can tweak various items in IBM Cognos BI to help your system function more efficiently. Some examples include: load balancing mode, the report size limit (governor limit), and maximum size of e-mail messages.

To modify system properties, follow these steps:

1. From the Launch menu, select IBM Cognos Administration.

2. From the Status tab, select System.

3. From the Scorecard pane, select the entry for which you want to modify settings.

4. Within the Settings pane, click the Set Properties button. The Set Properties dialog displays, with the Settings tab selected, listing the properties for the system.

5. To filter the properties by group, select the desired group from the Category drop-down.

6. Modify the value for any desired property.

7. Click OK. The Set Properties dialog closes and the modifications are saved.

NOTE *Refer to the Tune Server Performance section in the IBM Cognos Administration and Security Guide for specific details on how to tune your IBM Cognos environment.*

System Logging

Logging records system occurrences in a log file or database. For example, suppose a user logs in to Cognos Connection and then runs a report. Logging makes it possible to access information about when the user logged in to Cognos Connection, which report the user ran as well as other information such as the time the report took to execute.

Logging can occur at the following levels:

- **Minimal**   Shows system and service startup and shutdown and runtime errors.
- **Basic**   Contains the elements of Minimal plus user account management and usage, and use requests.
- **Request**   Contains the elements of Minimal and Basic, plus service requests and responses.
- **Trace**   Contains the elements of Minimal and Basic, plus requests to all components along with their parameter values and third-party queries to Cognos BI components.
- **Full**   Contains the elements of all logging levels.

As a rule, you do not want to go beyond logging at the basic level for day-to-day operations. Higher logging levels are going to impact system performance due to the amount of information being written to the log file. The more information that is being written to the log file, the slower the system runs; as a result, log levels other than Minimal or Basic should be used only for troubleshooting.

NOTE *The default logging level is set at Minimal.*

To manage logging levels, follow these steps:

1. From the Launch menu, select IBM Cognos Administration.

2. From the Status tab, select System.

3. From the Scorecard pane, select the entry for which you want to set the logging.

4. Within the Settings pane, click the Set Properties button. The Set Properties dialog displays, with the Settings tab selected, listing the properties for the selected item.

5. From the Category drop-down, select Logging to filter the properties.

Set properties - Configuration				Help	

General   **Settings**   Permissions

Specify the configuration settings for this entry. By default, an entry acquires its configuration settings from a parent.
You can override those settings with the settings set explicitly for this entry.

Category:
Logging

Reset to default value

Entries: 1   - 29

	Category ◇	Name ◇	Value	Default
☐	Logging	Audit logging level for annotation service	Minimal ▼	Yes
☐	Logging	Audit logging level for agent service	Minimal ▼	Yes
☐	Logging	Audit logging level for batch report service	Minimal ▼	Yes
☐	Logging	Audit the native query for batch report service	☐	Yes
☐	Logging	Audit logging level for the Content Manager Cache Service	Minimal ▼	Yes
☐	Logging	Audit logging level for Content Manager service	Minimal ▼	Yes
☐	Logging	Audit logging level for data integration service	Minimal ▼	Yes
☐	Logging	Audit logging level for the dispatcher	Minimal ▼	Yes

OK   Cancel

6. Modify the value for any desired Logging property.
7. Click OK. The Set Properties dialog closes and the modifications are saved.

NOTE *The logs by default are written to a log file, as flat text files, in the logs directory on the server where the application is installed. From IBM Cognos Configuration, you can configure the system to write the log information to a database. With a log database, audit reporting can be configured to report off of logged information.*

Schedules

Managing schedules is extremely important to system performance. This is especially true in organizations with a variety of people scheduling large amounts of entries (such as jobs, reports, or events). Systems have finite resources with which to function. As a result, your system can get bogged down when too many entries are scheduled to run at the same time. As administrator, you need to be able to review and modify schedules as necessary.

View Schedules

Viewing scheduled jobs is the first step in managing schedules. You need to determine what entries are scheduled, and the times for which the schedules are applied. An overview of schedules is shown in a bar chart by the state of the schedule, with the schedule details listed below the chart. The list shows the date that the schedule was last modified, who scheduled the job, the status, and the priority of each schedule.

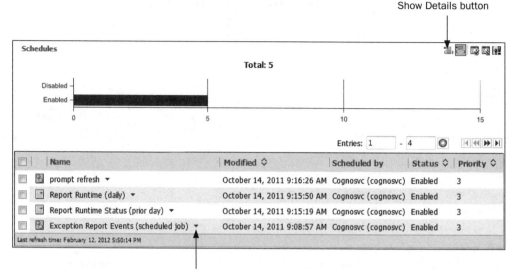

To display the location of the scheduled entries in the list, click the Show Details button on the toolbar.

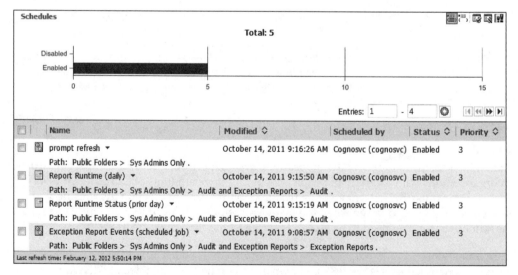

Next to each item's name in the list of scheduled entries is an Actions button. Click the Actions button to display a menu of options available for each entry:

		Name	Modified ◇	Scheduled by	Status ◇	Priority ◇
☐	▨	prompt refresh ▾	October 14, 2011 9:16:26 AM	Cognosvc (cognosvc)	Enabled	3
		Path: Public Fol ⬚ Set properties				
☐	▤	Report Runtime ▶¹ Run the schedule once...	October 14, 2011 9:15:50 AM	Cognosvc (cognosvc)	Enabled	3
		Path: Public Fol ▧ Modify the schedule...	and Exception Reports > Audit .			
☐	▤	Report Runtime ▧ Remove the schedule	October 14, 2011 9:15:19 AM	Cognosvc (cognosvc)	Enabled	3
		Path: Public Fol ◇ View run history	and Exception Reports > Audit .			
☐	▨	Exception Repo ▧ Disable the schedule	October 14, 2011 9:08:57 AM	Cognosvc (cognosvc)	Enabled	3
		Path: Public Fol ▨ Set Priority	and Exception Reports > Exception Reports .			

Last refresh time: February 12, 2012 5:50:14 PM

- **Set Properties** Displays the properties of the item—the same as navigating to Set Properties from the entry's location in Cognos Connection.
- **Run The Schedule Once** Displays options to run the scheduled entry.
- **Modify The Schedule** Displays options to make adjustments to the schedule.
- **Remove The Schedule** Deletes the schedule from the selected entry.
- **View Run History** Shows a list of the execution history for the schedule.
- **Disable The Schedule** Sets the status of the schedule to Disabled. Disabling a schedule does not delete it, but simply suspends it.
- **Set Priority** Provides a drop-down to change the priority of the schedule (the default is 3).

From the Filter pane on the left side of the IBM Cognos Administration window, the list of scheduled entries can be filtered by the user who created the schedule, status, priority, the entry's owner, type of entry, or the location of the entry.

Filter
Scheduled by:
Any
Select a user...
Status:
Any ▾
Priority:
Any ▾
Advanced options⌃
Owned by:
Any
Select a user...
Type:
Any ▾
Scope:
Any
Select a scope...
Reset to default
Apply

Modify Schedules

Users can create schedules for many different types of entries. If a lot of users are accessing resources, you can end up with a large volume of scheduled entries. Several groups of users may not necessarily communicate with one another, so a large number of entries might be scheduled to run at the same time, creating resource issues. IBM Cognos Administration allows administrators to modify schedules created by other users at a variety of levels. You can modify the frequency of a schedule, enable or disable a schedule, or change the priority of a schedule.

To modify a schedule, follow these steps:

1. From the Launch menu, select IBM Cognos Administration.

2. From the Status tab, select Schedules.

3. Next to the name of the scheduled entry you want to modify, click the Actions button.

4. Select Modify The Schedule from the context menu. The Schedule dialog displays.

5. In the Schedule dialog, modify the schedule properties as necessary.

6. To disable the schedule, select the Disable The Schedule check box.

7. To set the priority of the schedule, select the desired number from the Priority drop-down.

8. Click OK. The schedule modifications are saved.

NOTE *Changing the status or priority of a schedule can also be accomplished by selecting an entry and choosing Enable, Disable, or Set Priority from the toolbar, or from the Actions menu for an entry.*

The priority of a schedule can be set from 1 to 5: 1 is the highest priority, 5 is the lowest, and 3 is the default. Scheduled entries with a higher priority run first when executing at the same time as other scheduled entries. Issues with system resources can arise when a high priority job that takes a long time to complete is set to run at the same time as numerous smaller jobs with lower priorities. In such situations, you may want to adjust the priority of the job that takes a long time to complete so that the other jobs do not have to wait in the queue.

Security

Use the Security tab for tasks such as assigning users to groups and roles, organizing users with groups, and managing permissions and capabilities. These tasks are discussed in detail in Chapter 19. Management tasks such as accessing content in users' personal folders, setting preferences for a user, and specifying properties for the Default User Profile can also be accomplished from the Security tab.

Status	Security	Configuration	Index Search	

Users, Groups, and Roles	Directory		
Capabilities		Entries: 1 - 2	
User Interface Profiles			

	◇	Name ◇	Modified ◇	Active	Actions
		Cognos	January 17, 2012 7:37:49 PM	✔	More...
		NTLM	January 17, 2012 7:37:49 PM	✔	More...

Last refresh time: February 12, 2012 6:09:14 PM

Accessing My Folders Content

Every user has a personal area in which to save private content. This is a tab called My Folders and is accessible by each user in IBM Cognos Connection. Through IBM Cognos Administration, administrators can access this content. The ability to access this content is useful when a user has content in their My Folders area that an administrator needs to test, modify, or copy to another location.

To access My Folders content, follow these steps:

1. From the Launch menu, select IBM Cognos Administration.

2. Click the Security tab. The security menu displays at the upper-left of the screen and shows Users, Groups, and Roles.

3. In the right pane of the screen, select the namespace that contains the user whose content you want to access. In this example, click the NTLM link.

	◇	Name ◇	Modified ◇	Active	Actions
		Cognos	January 17, 2012 7:37:49 PM	✔	More...
		NTLM	January 17, 2012 7:37:49 PM	✔	More...

Last refresh time: February 12, 2012 6:09:14 PM

4. Navigate through the list of entries to locate the desired user.

TIP *You can also click the Search button on the toolbar to search for the user. This is useful if you are working with a large authentication source.*

5. In the Name column, click the user's name. The account content of the selected user displays.

Directory > NTLM > John Daniel		
	Entries: 1 - 2	
☐ ◇ |Name ◇		Modified ◇
My Folders		February 1, 2012 2:39:17 PM
My Watch Items		January 16, 2012 9:08:01 PM

6. In the Name column, click the My Folders link. The content of the user's My Folders directory is displayed. At this location, the content is read-only. To open or modify the content, you must copy it to another location.

Accessing a User's Properties

A set of properties is associated with every user's account and includes the user's preferences, personal information, and portal tabs. User preferences include items such as the number of items that appear in list view, the background style of IBM Cognos Connection, and the language and time zone in which the user views IBM Cognos Connection. Personal properties include items such as e-mail address and data source credentials. The Portal Tabs tab shows a list of the tabs the user sees when using IBM Cognos Connection. As an administrator, you may need to access these properties to view the information or to make modifications.

To access a user's properties, follow these steps:

1. From the Launch menu, select IBM Cognos Administration.

2. Click the Security tab. The security menu displays at the upper-left of the screen and shows Users, Groups, and Roles.

3. In the right pane of the screen, select the namespace that contains the user whose properties you want to access. In this example, select NTLM.

☐ ◇ |Name ◇	Modified ◇	Active	Actions
Cognos	January 17, 2012 7:37:49 PM	✔	More...
NTLM	January 17, 2012 7:37:49 PM	✔	More...
Last refresh time: February 12, 2012 6:09:14 PM			

4. Navigate through the list of entries to locate the desired user.

5. In the Actions column for the user, click the Set Properties button. The Set Properties dialog displays for the selected user.

6. Navigate to the appropriate tab and modify the desired properties.

7. Click OK to save your modifications.

Default User Profile

When a new user logs in to IBM Cognos Connection, a profile is created for the user with the default properties. You can specify the default properties, preferences, portal tabs, and permissions for new accounts.

To set properties for the Default User Profile, follow these steps:

1. From the Launch menu, select IBM Cognos Administration.

2. Click the Security tab. The security menu displays at the upper-left of the screen and shows Users, Groups, and Roles.

3. In the right pane of the screen, click the link for the Cognos namespace.

Edit Default User Profile button

4. Click the Edit Default User Profile button on the toolbar. The Set Properties dialog displays for the default user profile.

5. To set any general properties for all new user accounts, specify the desired properties on the General tab.

6. To set any preferences for all new user accounts, specify the desired properties on the Preferences tab.

7. To set the default tabs for all new user accounts, specify the desired tabs on the Portal Tabs tab.

8. Click OK upon completion of modifications. Your changes are saved.

Configuration

Use the Configuration tab for tasks such as managing data source connections, importing or exporting Cognos content, defining distribution lists and contacts, and specifying properties of dispatchers and services.

Data Source Connections

Data source connections provide the communication channel between Cognos BI and your data sources. A data source has three components: the data source, the connection that contains all of the details on how to access the external data in which you are interested, and the sign-on that contains the authentication (user name and password) for the external data source.

NOTE *When we refer to a* data source, *we are including all three components unless otherwise specified.*

Create a Data Source

Cognos BI needs to know how to communicate with your data source. The New Data Source wizard makes it easy for you to define the parameters by which this communication can occur. Cognos BI can communicate with a variety of data sources, such as XML, relational data sources, or IBM Cognos PowerCubes, to name a few.

PART IV

NOTE *You can also create a data source connection from Cognos Framework Manager. Cognos BI launches the same New Data Source wizard, and the steps are identical.*

To create a data source, follow these steps:

1. From the Launch menu, select IBM Cognos Administration.

2. Click the Configuration tab. The configuration menu displays at the upper-left of the screen and shows Data Source Connections.

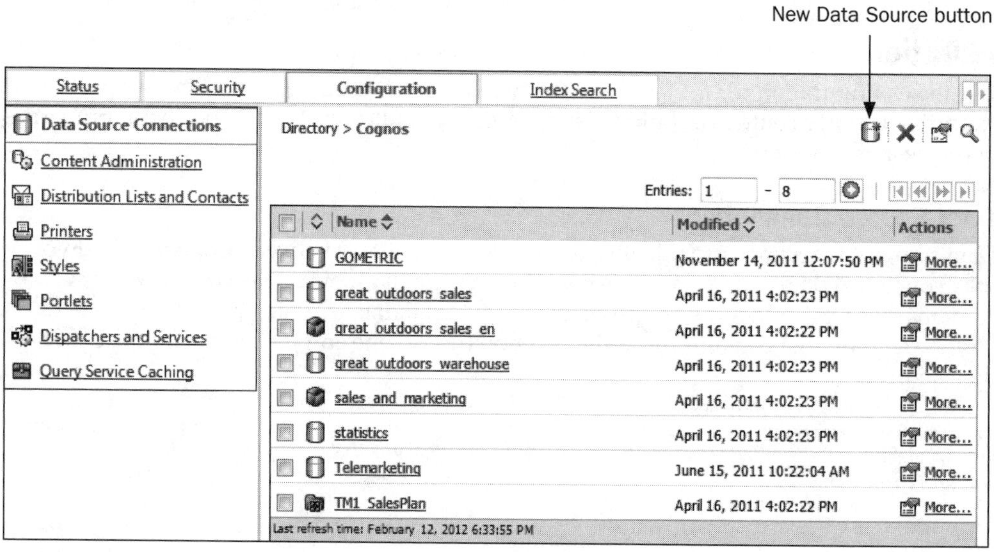

New Data Source button

3. Click the New Data Source button on the toolbar. The New Data Source wizard launches.

4. In the Name text box, enter a name for the data source.

5. Optionally, provide a description and a screen tip for the data source.

6. Click Next. The Specify The Connection screen displays.

7. From the Type drop-down list, select the type of data source to which IBM Cognos BI is connecting. The type you choose depends entirely on your data source.

8. In the Isolation Level area, select the level of isolation. The isolation level is a database attribute that defines how the database secures and keeps records consistent in its system. The Use The Default Object Gateway option uses the connection as it is defined by the database. The Specify A Value option lets you select an isolation value from a list.

TIP *Start with the default option unless otherwise instructed by your database administrator. You can modify this setting later if you decide it is needed.*

---

9. To configure the JDBC connection manually, check the Configure JDBC Connection check box.

NOTE *You need to configure the JDBC connection manually if you are using Dynamic Query mode.*

10. Click Next to continue to the connection string properties.

11. Set the necessary parameters for the data source. The following three examples show and describe parameters for three commonly used data source types.

PART IV

This example shows the parameters for an IBM Cognos PowerCube data source:

Specify the IBM Cognos PowerCube connection string - New Data Source wizard　　Help　✕

Edit the parameters to build an IBM Cognos PowerCube connection string.

Read cache size (MB):

Location

Specify the location of the cube on a Windows operating system. If the cube also resides on a Unix or Linux operating system, enter its location.

Windows location:

Unix or Linux location:

Signon

Select an authentication method.

- ● All applicable namespaces (including unsecured PowerCubes)
- ○ Restrict PowerCube authentication to a single namespace

  NTLM (Active) ▼

Select whether a cube password is needed.

- ☐ Cube password

  - ☐ Create a signon that the Everyone group can use:

    Password:

    Confirm password:

Testing

Test the connection...

[Cancel] [< Back] [Next >] [Finish]

Here are descriptions for the IBM Cognos PowerCube parameters:

- **Read Cache Size (MB)**   Specify the amount of system memory used for PowerCube access if you want to override the default value of 16MB. This memory is used for specific actions such as sorting and aggregations. We recommend starting with the default 16MB and moving up to 32MB if PowerCube access seems to be slow.

NOTE *Your system performance can be affected by many factors. Changing one setting is not guaranteed to improve your overall system performance. If your system is not performing as well as you believe it should be, the system administrator should review the Architecture and Deployment Guide that comes with the IBM Cognos BI documentation.*

- **Windows Location**   Specify the path of the PowerCube file on the server where the IBM Cognos application component is installed, if installed on a Windows server.
- **Unix or Linux location**   Specify the path of the PowerCube file on the server where the IBM Cognos application component is installed, if installed on a UNIX or Linux server.
- **Select An Authentication Method**   Specify which namespaces are available for use as authentication sources for this data source. The All Applicable Namespaces option is selected by default and uses all available namespaces. The Restrict PowerCube Authentication To A Single Namespace option allows you to confine authentication to the PowerCube to one namespace.
- **Select Whether A Cube Password Is Needed**   Specify the password for the PowerCube if it is an encrypted PowerCube.

This example shows the parameters for a Microsoft SQL Server data source:

Here are descriptions for the Microsoft SQL Server parameters:

- **Server Name**   Specify the name or IP address of the computer on which the database resides.

- **Database Name**   Specify the name of the database for which you are creating the connection. The Database name contains the following two options:
  - **Master**   Uses the Master database of the Microsoft SQL Server installation referenced by the server name.
  - **Text box**   An option to name the specific database to be accessed. This is the recommended option.
- **Signon**
  - **No Authentication**   No authentication is required to access the database.
  - **IBM Cognos Software Service Credentials**   Authentication to the data source is made with the user running the IBM Cognos service.
  - **An External Namespace**   Authenticate the data source with a namespace that has been defined in Cognos Configuration.
  - **Signons**   Authenticate with a specific user ID and specify a password, if necessary.

This example shows the parameters for an Oracle data source:

Here are descriptions for the Oracle parameters:

- **SQL*Net Connect String** The connection string as defined by Oracle for the database.
- **Signon** Authenticate with a specific user ID and specify a password, if necessary.

12. Click the Test The Connection link to ensure the accuracy of the specified parameters.

```
Test the connection - great_outdoors_sales_en                        Help  ✕

Test the parameters that make up the database connection.

Connection string:
;LOCAL;PC;WIN_PATH=d:\program files\ibm\cognos\c10_1_1
\webcontent\samples\datasources\cubes\powercubes\en\great_outdoors_sales_en.mdc;UNIX_PATH=

   ┌──────────┐
   │   Test   │
   └──────────┘

Dispatcher:
http://arches:9400/p2pd

Test the connection using:
Select a namespace to test. Select "No Authentication" to test without a namespace

 ┌───────────────────────┐
 │ No authentication  ▼  │
 └───────────────────────┘
User ID:
 ┌─────────────────────────────────────────┐
 │                                         │
 └─────────────────────────────────────────┘

Password:
 ┌─────────────────────────────────────────┐
 │                                         │
 └─────────────────────────────────────────┘

 ┌──────────┐
 │   Close  │
 └──────────┘
```

TIP *Testing the connection of a data source is a best practice to ensure that all necessary parameters have been completed correctly.*

13. Click the Test button. The results display, identifying whether the test was successful or failed. If the test fails, address the issue outlined in the error and retest the connection.

14. Click Close twice to return to the data source parameters.

15. Click Next to continue creating the data source.

16. If you chose to configure the JDBC connection, the JDBC parameters display for configuration. In the JDBC Connection String screen, set the parameters as necessary:

Specify the Microsoft SQL Server (JDBC) connection string - New Data Source wizard	Help ⊗

Edit the parameters to build a Microsoft SQL Server (driver: com.microsoft.sqlserver.jdbc.SQLServerDriver) connection string.

Server name:

Port number:

1433

Instance Name:

Database name:

Login Time Out:

0

JDBC Connection Parameters:
These optional parameters are appended to the URL and are specific to the driver.

Local Sort Options

Collation Sequence:

Level:

Primary ▾

Testing

Test the connection...

Cancel	< Back	Next >	Finish

17. Click Finish. The new data source is created.

When you create a data source for a database, you can specify commands that the database executes. See the "Database Commands" section later in this chapter for more detail.

When you create a data source connection for a Cognos PowerCube, you have the option of creating a package. To create a package for the PowerCube, select the Create A Package check box (shown next) and click OK. The New Package wizard launches.

If you have Cognos Metric Manager installed, when you create a data source using a database supported by Cognos Metric Studio, you can create a metric package. To create a metric package for the newly created data source, select the Create A Metric Package check box and click OK. The New Metric Package wizard launches.

Modify a Database Connection

Modifications can be made to existing data source specifications through Cognos Administration. This may be necessary if any parameters of the data source have changed, such as the connection string, sign-on values, database commands, or general information about the data source.

Edit the Connection String   The connection string tells Cognos BI where and how to find the data source to which you want to connect to generate reports and analyze data. If that information changes, you need to modify the parameters for the data source through IBM Cognos Administration.

To edit the connection string, follow these steps:

1. From the Launch menu, select IBM Cognos Administration.

2. Click the Configuration tab. The configuration menu displays at the upper-left of the screen and shows Data Source Connections.

3. In the name column of the right pane of the screen, click the data source you want to modify. The connection for the selected data source displays:

4. Click the Set Properties button in the Actions column of the connection.

5. Select the Connection tab. The connection properties display. The connection string is listed among the parameters for the connection.

6. Click the Edit (pencil) button at the end of the Connection String box.

7. Modify the appropriate parameters.

8. Test the connection to ensure that all necessary parameters have been completed correctly.

9. If the data source tested successfully, click OK to return to the Connection tab for the connection; otherwise, address the issues identified by the failed test.

10. Click OK on the Connection tab to return to Cognos Administration. The connection string is updated.

Database Commands   You can set database commands that execute when opening or closing a connection or session with a DB2, Oracle, or Microsoft SQL Server data source. For example, you can require that the database run a stored procedure every time Cognos BI makes a connection to a particular data source.

To set or edit database commands, follow these steps:

1. From the Launch menu, select IBM Cognos Administration.

2. Click the Configuration tab. The Configuration menu displays at the upper-left of the screen and shows Data Source Connections.

3. In the right pane of the screen, click the Set Properties button in the Actions column for the data source whose commands you want to modify.

4. Select the Connection tab. The parameters for the commands of the selected data source display:

5. Click the Set or Edit link next to the command to be modified.

NOTE *The Edit link will display only if a command has been previously set.*

6. In the XML Database Commands text box, enter the database command in XML format.

7. Click OK to return to the commands. A portion of the database command displays under the Value column.

8. Click OK to return to the list of data sources. The command is set. Test the functionality of the command the next time you access the data source with Cognos BI.

Edit the Sign-on   The sign-on for a data source contains the credentials used to authenticate the data source and the users given access to use the credentials. You may need to change the user ID or password of the credentials or modify the people accessing the data source.

NOTE *The Signon feature is not available for the XML data source.*

To edit a sign-on, follow these steps:

1. From the Launch menu, select IBM Cognos Administration.

2. Click the Configuration tab. The Configuration menu displays at the upper-left of the screen and shows Data Source Connections.

3. In the right pane of the screen, click the data source for which you want to change the sign-on. The connection for the selected data source displays:

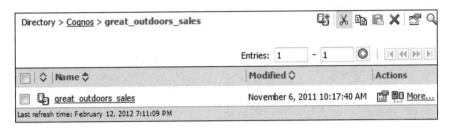

4. Click the link for the connection to access the sign-on. The sign-on displays:

5. Click the Set Properties button in the Actions column for the sign-on.

6. Select the Signon tab. The properties of the sign-on display.

7. Click the Edit The Signon link to modify the credentials used for the sign-on.

8. Update the User ID or password, and then click OK.

9. Make any necessary changes to the users, groups, or roles that have access to the sign-on.

10. Click OK. The modifications to the sign-on are saved.

Content Administration

Administrators can manage content with such tasks as creating exports for backup, moving items from one system to another (such as reports, queries, and packages), creating an index update, or creating a consistency check task. You can complete these tasks from the toolbar in Content Administration.

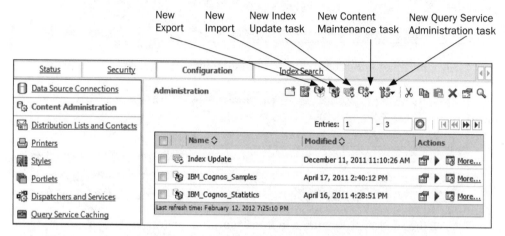

An index update task creates a task that updates the index used for index search. The index supports full-text search for Cognos BI content but requires that the index update task be run before full-text search is functional. It is a good idea to schedule an index update task at regular intervals, since the index does not automatically update when Cognos BI content changes.

Content maintenance tasks include creating a consistency check task or a report upgrade task. Consistency check tasks examine the content store for any inconsistencies or identify user accounts that exist in the content store that no longer have matching user accounts in the external namespace. The Cognos Content Manager service requires a restart to rectify identified issues. The report upgrade task is used to upgrade content from another version to the current version.

Create a Query Service administration task to schedule clearing the Query Service cache or recording the Query Service cache to a file.

The most common functions of Content Administration are exporting and importing content. These tasks are useful when users are working in more than one IBM Cognos environment, or for backing up or restoring content. For example, a large organization might have a development environment, a test environment, and a production environment; the reports are created in the development environment, validated in the test environment, and finally promoted for consumption in the production environment. Moving content between environments can be accomplished through Content Administration. Simply create an export archive of the content from the development environment and import that archive into the test environment; then repeat to go from the test environment to the production environment.

Export Content

Create an export archive of content to transfer from one installation of Cognos BI to another or to maintain a backup of content. The archive is actually a Zip file that contains all the XML definitions of the content that you have selected to export. By default, export archives are stored in the *installation path\ibm\cognos\c10\deployment* folder on the server running the export. This Zip file can then be copied to the deployment directory of another Cognos BI installation and used as a source to be imported or stored for backup.

NOTE *An administrator can customize the default archive location through the Cognos Configuration tool.*

To export a content archive, follow these steps:

1. From the Launch menu, select IBM Cognos Administration.

2. Click the Configuration tab.

3. From the Configuration menu, select Content Administration.

4. Click the New Export button on the toolbar. The New Export wizard launches.

5. In the Name text box, enter a name for the export.

6. Optionally, provide a description and a screen tip for the export.

7. Click Next. The Choose A Deployment Method screen displays with two options, as shown next. The Select Public Folders And Directory Content option allows you to choose the specific content to be exported; the Select The Entire Content Store option creates a copy of all the content. If you choose the latter option, you can also export user account information, which includes individual users' personal folders and preferences.

TIP *The Select The Entire Content Store option is a great way to create a backup of all of your content.*

8. Select a deployment method. If you are exporting the entire Content Store, skip to step 26. If not, continue with step 9.

9. Click Next. The Select The Public Folders Content screen displays.

10. Click the Add link to select the content to be exported. The Select Entries screen displays:

11. In the Available Entries area, select the check box(es) of the desired content, and then click the Add arrow (the green arrow) to add the entries to the Selected Entries area.

12. Click OK when all desired entries have been added to the Selected Entries area. The Select The Public Folders Content screen displays again, this time with entries chosen:

13. To set any entries as Disabled after importing, select the Disable After Import check box for the content that you want to disable after it has been imported to its destination.

14. To include any saved report versions of the chosen content with the export, select the Include Report Output Versions check box.

15. To include any history of execution of the chosen content with the export, select the Include Run History check box.

NOTE *Typically, when you are exporting from one environment to another, you do not want to include versions of reports or the run history from the previous environment.*

16. To include any schedules of the chosen content with the export, select the Include Schedules check box.

NOTE *For the conflict resolution options for steps 14–16, you can select Keep Existing Entries, which keeps the existing items of the destination environment, or select Replace Existing Entries, which replaces the existing items of the destination environment if a conflict occurs.*

17. Click Next. The Select The Directory Content screen displays. Include any of these options with the export if they exist in the source environment but do not exist in the destination environment.

Select the directory content - New Export wizard   Help ⊗

Select the directory content and options to include in the export.

Directory content

☐ Include Cognos groups and roles
   Conflict resolution:
   ○ Keep existing entries
   ◉ Replace existing entries

☐ Include distribution lists and contacts
   Conflict resolution:
   ○ Keep existing entries
   ◉ Replace existing entries

☐ Include data sources and connections
   ☐ Include signons

   Conflict resolution:
   ○ Keep existing entries
   ◉ Replace existing entries

[Cancel] [< Back] [Next >] [Finish]

18. To include groups and roles that are in the Cognos namespace with the export, select the Include Cognos Groups And Roles check box.

19. To include distribution lists and contacts with the export, select the Include Distribution Lists And Contacts check box.

20. To include data sources with the export, select the Include Data Sources And Connections check box. You can also include the data source sign-ons if necessary.

NOTE *If you include sign-ons with the export, you must encrypt the export archive.*

21. Click Next. The Specify The General Options screen displays.

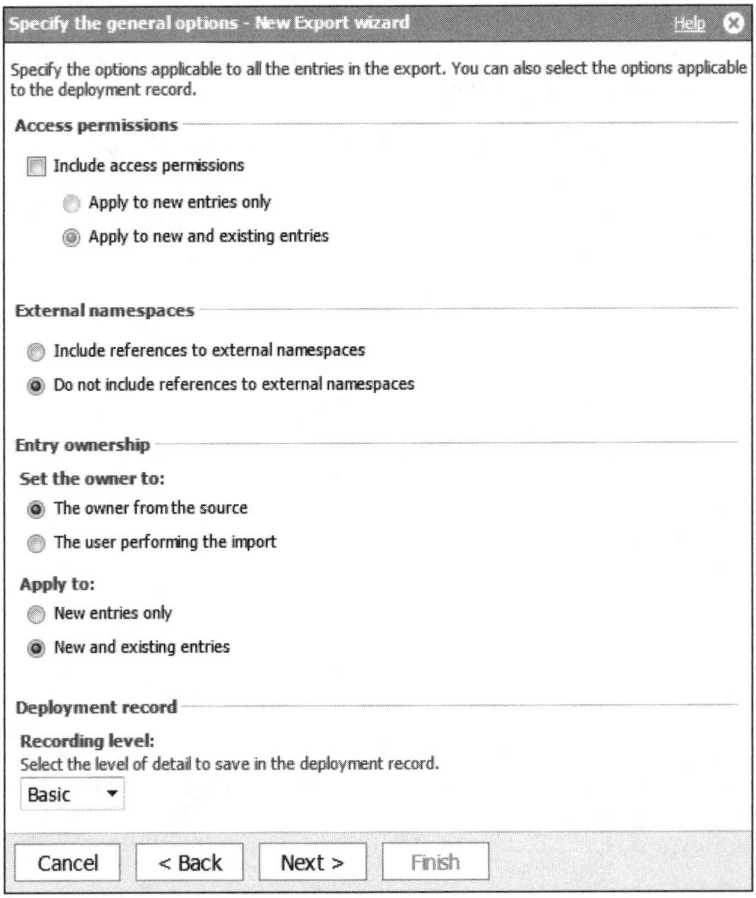

22. To include any permissions associated with the content in the export, select the Include Access Permissions check box.

23. In the External Namespaces area, select the Include References To External Namespaces option to include users that are found in a namespace other than the Cognos namespace, or choose the Do Not Include References To External Namespaces option.

NOTE *Users can be found referenced in items such as distribution lists, groups, roles, and permissions. If a user is referenced in the source environment and not available in the target environment, you will receive errors during import.*

---

24. Set the content owner to the owner from the source or to the user who will perform the import, and choose whether this applies to New Entries Only or New And Existing Entries.

25. Set the Recording Level to select the level of detail stored in the deployment record. By default, the level is set to Minimal.

TIP *If you encounter any issues with an export, you can increase the amount of detail in the deployment record and run the export again.*

26. Click Next. The Specify A Deployment Archive screen displays.

27. Select the name of an existing archive to overwrite it, or select New Archive and provide a name to create a new archive file.
28. To require a password to import the export archive, select the Encrypt The Content Of The Archive check box and set the desired password.

NOTE *Encrypting the archive is required if you are exporting the entire Content Store or if you included sign-ons in the export.*

29. Click Next. A summary of the export settings displays.
30. Review the summary of the settings.
31. To modify any settings, click Back and make any desired changes, and then return to the summary.

32. Click Next. The Select An Action screen displays.

33. Select one of the following actions:

    - **Save And Run Once** Saves the export and runs it immediately
    - **Save And Schedule** Saves the export and provides options to create a schedule to run the export
    - **Save Only** Saves the export without running it

34. Click Finish. If you chose Save Only, the export is saved and you are returned to Cognos Administration. If you chose Save And Run Once, select the desired options to run the export. If you chose Save And Schedule, select the desired options to schedule the export.

After running an export, you can view the run history to see if the content was exported successfully and how long it took to complete.

NOTE *An administrator is required to copy the Zip file from the source server to the target server before the export file can be accessed for import by the target server.*

Import Content

After an export archive has been created and made available to the archive location of the environment in which you want to import it, you are ready to import the archive, whether it be on a server different from where the export was created (common when moving between environments) or on the same server where the export was created (common when restoring from a backup).

To import a content archive, follow these steps:

1. From the Launch menu, select IBM Cognos Administration.

2. Click the Configuration tab.

3. From the Configuration menu, select Content Administration.

4. Click the New Import button on the toolbar. The New Import wizard launches.

5. From the Deployment Archive list, select the archive to be imported. The available archives are the Zip files that exist in the archive location.

6. Click Next. The Specify A Name And Description screen displays the details with which the archive was originally created.

7. Make any modifications you want to the Name, Description, or Screen Tip by entering new information in the appropriate text box(es).

8. Click Next. The Select The Public Folders Content screen displays with a list of the archive's content:

NOTE *Any options selected during export can be deselected during import, but you cannot select options in the import that were not included in the export.*

9. Select the check box(es) to the left of the content you want to import.

10. To edit the target location of any content, select the Edit (pencil) button next to the current target name of the entry.

11. To set any entries as Disabled after importing, select the Disable After Import check box for the content that you want to disable.

TIP *Disabling entries allows the content to be imported into the target environment but does not allow users to access it. This lets administrators test and validate the content before users can see it.*

12. Click Next. The Select The Directory Content screen displays with the options defined in the creation of the archive.

NOTE *The Select The Directory Content screen only displays if any of these options were included in the export archive.*

13. Make any necessary modifications to the directory content options, and then click Next. The Specify The General Options screen displays with the options defined in the creation of the archive.

14. Make any necessary modifications to the general options. Set the content owner to the owner from the source or to the user who will perform the import, and choose whether this applies to New Entries Only or New And Existing Entries. Set the Recording Level to select the level of detail to store in the deployment record. By default, the level is set to Minimal.

15. Click Next. A summary of the import settings displays.

16. Review the summary of the settings.

17. To modify any settings, click Back and make any desired changes, and then return to the summary.

18. Click Next. The Select An Action screen displays.

19. Select one of the following actions:

   - **Save And Run Once**   Saves the import and runs it immediately
   - **Save And Schedule**   Saves the import and provides options to create a schedule to run the export
   - **Save Only**   Saves the import without running it

20. Click Finish. If you chose Save Only, the import is saved and you are returned to Cognos Administration. If you chose Save And Run Once, choose the desired options to run the import. If you chose Save And Schedule, choose the desired options to schedule the import.

After running an import, you can view the run history to see if the content was imported successfully and how long it took to complete.

NOTE *When running an import, you can choose to Upgrade All Report Specifications To The Latest Version, which will attempt to update all content in the import to the newer version of IBM Cognos, or choose Keep The Existing Report Specification Versions. This option is important for users moving content from a server running an older version of the Cognos application to a server running a newer version of the Cognos application.*

PART IV

Distribution Lists and Contacts

Distribution lists allow you to create a list of recipients to which you can distribute content. A distribution list can contain users from the namespaces configured in IBM Cognos as well as individuals outside of those namespaces. To be available for distribution lists or to use as recipients of content, users outside of configured namespaces need to be defined.

New Contact   New Distribution List

	Status	Security	Configuration	Index Search		
🗄 Data Source Connections		Directory > Cognos				
🔧 Content Administration						
📇 **Distribution Lists and Contacts**				Entries: 1 – 2		
🖨 Printers		☐	◇	Name ◇	Modified ◇	Actions
🎨 Styles		☐	🆔 Person, Test		November 6, 2011 4:37:40 PM	📋 More...
🗂 Portlets		☐	📧 test distribution list		November 6, 2011 5:26:24 PM	📋 More...
🔧 Dispatchers and Services		Last refresh time: February 12, 2012 8:40:15 PM				
🗄 Query Service Caching						

Add a Contact

It might be necessary to share content with someone outside of the organization. Further, it might make sense to include that person in a distribution list if the content is shared on a regular basis. To accomplish this, Cognos BI must have some contact information about this person—specifically, a name and e-mail address. Cognos BI refers to these individuals as *contacts*.

To add a contact, follow these steps:

1. From the Launch menu, select IBM Cognos Administration.

2. Click the Configuration tab.

3. From the Configuration menu, select Distribution Lists And Contacts. The list of the namespaces configured in Cognos BI displays.

4. Click the Cognos namespace link.

NOTE *The Cognos namespace is the only namespace that you can use to store a contact.*

5. Click the New Contact button on the toolbar. The New Contact wizard launches.

6. In the Name text box, enter a name for the contact.

7. Optionally, provide a description and a screen tip for the contact.

8. In the Email Address text box, enter an e-mail address for the contact.

9. Under Location, click the Select Another Location link to specify another location for the contact within the Cognos namespace. By default, the contact is saved in the root of the Cognos namespace.

10. Click Finish. The new contact is added.

Create a Distribution List

You can distribute content to a group of users by using distribution lists.

To create a distribution list, follow these steps:

1. From the Launch menu, select IBM Cognos Administration.

2. Click the Configuration tab.

3. From the Configuration menu, select Distribution Lists And Contacts. The list of the namespaces configured in Cognos BI displays.

4. Click the Cognos namespace link.

NOTE *The Cognos namespace is the only namespace that you can use to store a distribution list.*

---

5. Click the New Distribution List button on the toolbar. The New Distribution List wizard launches.

6. In the Name text box, enter a name for the distribution list.

7. Optionally, provide a description and a screen tip for the distribution list.

8. Under Location, click the Select Another Location link to specify another location for the distribution list within the Cognos namespace. By default, the distribution list is saved in the root of the Cognos namespace.

9. Click Next.

10. Click the Add link to add recipients to the distribution list. The Select Recipients screen displays:

11. Select the check box(es) of the desired users or groups in the Available Entries area and click the Add button to add the entries to the Selected Entries area.

12. Click OK when all desired entries have been added to the Selected Entries area.

13. Click Finish. The distribution list is created.

Printers

You can provide connection settings for networked printers so that users can print Cognos BI content to configured printers. Printers can be set up through IBM Cognos Administration on the Configuration tab.

Styles

Styles define the appearance of IBM Cognos Connection. Users can change the selected style for their user account in the My Preferences area. Administrators can manage the available styles and the permissions to each through Cognos Administration on the Configuration tab.

Portlets

Portlets are used to display and organize content within portal pages. In IBM Cognos Connection, you can use Cognos portlets (such as IBM Cognos Navigator, IBM Cognos Viewer, or Image Viewer) or third-party portlets that conform to Web Services for Remote Portlets (WSRP) standards (such as Plumtree, Oracle portlets, and Sun portlets). Administrators can manage portlets with such tasks as configuring, modifying, or setting permissions through Cognos Administration on the Configuration tab.

Dispatchers and Services

Dispatchers handle user requests by routing requests to the appropriate IBM Cognos service. There is a dispatcher for each instance of the Content Manager or Application Tier components configured. Administrators can manage dispatchers and services through Cognos Administration on the Configuration tab, using tasks such as stopping or starting services, defining dispatcher routing, and setting properties for a dispatcher or a service. Environment, logging, and tuning properties can be managed from the Settings tab within the Set Properties area of each dispatcher and service.

File System Location

The location of a file system on your organization's network can be configured for use by IBM Cognos Connection. For example, you may have a shared network location that all your users access for monthly reports. If you set up a file system location through IBM Cognos Administration, reports can be run and saved to this location directly from IBM Cognos Connection.

To set up a file system location, follow these steps:

1. On the Cognos BI server, launch IBM Cognos Configuration.

2. From the Actions drop-down menu, select Edit Global Configuration.

3. Select the General tab.

4. Specify the value for the Archive Location File System Root property.

TIP *The value must be in this format:* file://(file-system-path) *for a file system relative to the server. For a Windows share, the value must be in this format:* file://\\share\folder.

5. Restart IBM Cognos BI services to update the configuration.

6. Launch IBM Cognos Administration.

7. Select the Configuration tab.

8. From the Configuration menu, select Dispatchers And Services.

9. Select the Define File System Locations button on the toolbar. The Define File System Locations screen displays.

```
Define file system locations                                    Help  ⊗

Specify a name and the URI for the location on the file system for this entry. You can also specify a
description and a screen tip.

                                       Entries:  [      ] - [      ]   ⊙  | ⏮ ⏪ ⏩ ⏭

  ☐  | Name ◇              | Location              | Actions

                                    No entries.

                                                              New....  Delete

  [ Close ]
```

10. Click the New link. The New File System Location wizard launches.

11. In the Name text box, enter a name for the file system location.

12. Optionally, provide a description and a screen tip for the file system location.

13. In the File System Location text box, enter the path for a location within the file system root.

NOTE *The file system root location was defined in Cognos Configuration in steps 1–5.*

14. Click Finish. A new file system location has been created.

Query Service Caching

Administrators can manually manage the Query Service cache by clearing the Query Service cache or recording the Query Service cache to a file through Cognos Administration on the Configuration tab. Administrators can also schedule these tasks through Cognos Administration on the Content Administration tab. These tasks apply only to the Dynamic Query Mode cache.

Index Search

Index search in Cognos Connection requires that you create and maintain the index. The index supports full-text searches for Cognos BI content. It is a good idea to schedule an index update task at regular intervals, because the index does not automatically update when Cognos BI content changes. Updating the index will index new objects and delete indexes for objects that no longer exist or are now excluded from index search. The content included and/or excluded from index search can be specified. If content is found on both the

Included Content and Excluded Content lists, it will be excluded from the search. You may want to exclude content such as archived content or content currently under development from user searches. Content can be excluded by entry type (such as folder, job, package) or by specific entries.

To create an index update task, follow these steps:

1. From the Launch menu, select IBM Cognos Administration.

2. Select the Configuration tab.

3. From the Configuration menu, select Content Administration

4. Click the New Index Update button on the toolbar. The New Index Update wizard launches.

5. In the Name text box, enter a name for the index update task.

6. Optionally, provide a description and a screen tip for the index update task.

7. Under Location, click the Select Another Location link to specify another location for the task within Administration. By default, the task is saved in the root of Administration.

8. Click Next. The Select the Content screen displays.

9. To specify the content included in the search, make modifications to the Included Content area.

10. To specify the content excluded in the search, make modifications to the Excluded Content area.

11. Click Next when you are finished modifying the selected content. The Select An Action screen displays.

12. Select one of the following actions:

    - **Save And Run Once**   Saves the index update task and runs it immediately

    - **Save And Schedule**   Saves the index update task and provides options to create a schedule to run the index update task

    - **Save Only**   Saves the index update task without running it

13. Click Finish. If you chose Save Only, the index update task is saved and you are returned to Cognos Administration. If you chose Save And Run Once, choose the desired options to run the index update task. If you chose Save And Schedule, choose the desired options to schedule the index update task.

IBM Cognos Lifecycle Manager

O ne of the tools introduced with IBM Cognos 10 is IBM Cognos Lifecycle Manager. During an upgrade of an IBM Cognos implementation, users and report authors usually express some concern over the fidelity of their reports post upgrade. Cognos Lifecycle Manager addresses that concern by allowing users and authors to compare report output before and after an upgrade. The comparison is not limited to upgrades; it can be used any time an existing report undergoes any significant change. Changes that might affect your reports include upgrading your source database version, IBM Cognos version changes, a change made to the IBM Cognos Framework Manager model that underlies the report, and so on.

Another valuable use of Cognos Lifecycle Manager is in benchmarking report performance. Tuning report performance with dynamic query mode (DQM), hardware modifications, and system settings can be tracked and verified with Cognos Lifecycle Manager.

NOTE *We strongly recommend incorporating report validation with Cognos Lifecycle Manager into your upgrade check list.*

Introduction to IBM Cognos Lifecycle Manager

Cognos Lifecycle Manager runs from an Apache Tomcat servlet, and as such, it will not be used by the average consumer. Administrators and advanced business authors stand to gain the most from using Cognos Lifecycle Manager.

Before you begin using the tool for report upgrade validation, you should be aware of two things: First, the source (or original) and the target (or upgraded) reports must be run from two different IBM Cognos installations. Second, the reports being compared must have the same name and be located in the same path on both IBM Cognos installs.

When you're using Cognos Lifecycle Manager for performance benchmarks, you should be running a report on a single sever, making adjustments to the environment, running the same report again, and comparing the run times.

Location

Cognos Lifecycle Manager is a web-based tool, which means you access it through a URL. The default URL is http://<*YourMachine*>:4797/LifecycleManager

---

NOTE *If you do not see the Cognos Lifecycle Manager welcome screen when you use the default URL, make sure the application is running and that you have the correct address.*

While Cognos Lifecycle Manager is very useful, it is not overly complex. The remainder of this chapter will walk through how to get started using the tool.

Validation Project

When using Cognos Lifecycle Manager to validate upgraded reports, you will start with a *validation project*. As a high-level overview, a validation project involves defining the source and target locations of the reports to check, setting up a login for each IBM Cognos installation, selecting the reports to validate, running both sets of reports, visually checking the output of the reports, and defining the final status of the upgraded report, either accepted or rejected.

Create a New Validation Project

To get started, go to the URL for your Cognos Lifecycle Manager application.

1. From the Welcome page, click the New Project link.

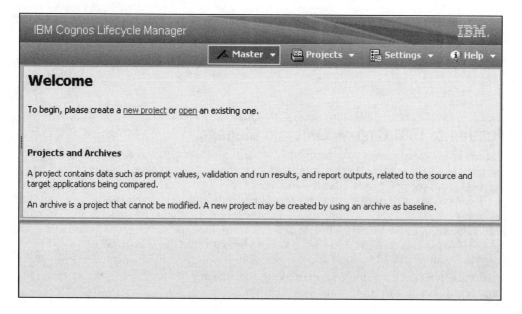

2. Choose Create Blank Project, enter a name for the project, and leave the Project Type as the default, Validation Project. For this example, name the project **New Validation**.

3. Click the Create button to create the new project.

4. Since this is the first time the project has been opened, you will be asked to configure the project. Click the Configure button.

5. In the Configure screen's Basic tab, go to the Application section. You will need to add the Gateway and Dispatcher URIs, the source and target IBM Cognos versions,

a name for each connection (optional), and the maximum number of connections available to each IBM Cognos server.

Configure				
Basic	Security	Advanced	Preferences	

Project ────────────────────────────────────

Project name: New Validation

Import Content ──────────────────────────────

Project : [▼]

Instance: [▼]

Application ──────────────────────────────────

	Source	**Target**
Name:	Source Connection	Target Connection
Gateway URI:	http://localhost/cognos/cgi-bin/cognos.cgi	http://localhost/ibmcognos/cgi-bin/cognos.cgi
Dispatcher URI:	http://localhost:9400/p2pd/servlet/dispatch	http://localhost:9300/p2pd/servlet/dispatch
Version:	8.4 ▼	10.1 ▼
Max connections:	4	4

[**Save**] [**Cancel**]

NOTE *For our example, we used a single server with two instances of IBM Cognos running.*

6. On the Security tab, provide the user credentials for each instance of IBM Cognos:

Configure				
Basic	**Security**	Advanced	Preferences	

Application credentials ───────────────────────

	Source	**Target**
Username:	gerardr	gerardr
Password:	●●●●●●	●●●●●●
Namespace ID:	NTLM	NTLM

☑ Save password in the configuration file.
(Note: Password will be saved as Clear Text.)

[**Test Connection**] [🖊 Add Parameters]

☑ Save password in the configuration file.
(Note: Password will be saved as Clear Text.)

[**Test Connection**] [🖊 Add Parameters]

ⓘ These credentials will be saved in the configuration and accessible by any user of this project. For a more secure option, leave the fields blank and Lifecycle Manager will prompt you whenever credentials are needed.

7. Click the Test Connection button for the source and the target. When your credentials have all tested successfully, click Save.

8. In the project configuration screen, click the Generate Report List button.

9. Navigate to the folder that contains the reports you want to validate. You will not select folders for the source and targets, because Cognos Lifecycle Manager assumes that the reports to validate exist in the same folder, with the same name, on both instances of IBM Cognos.

10. Click OK, and Cognos Lifecycle Manager will scan both the source and target servers for matching reports. The results can be displayed in one of three views: package, list, or tree view. The tree view is shown by default.

List View icon

11. Click on the List View icon to view all of the reports found in the source folder.

Automatic Prompt Values Generation

12. If your reports require prompt values, indicated by a status of Prompt Values Missing, change the drop-down value from Validate Models/Report to Automatic Prompt Values Generation. Then select the reports for which you want to generate prompts, and click Go.

13. Once the prompts, if required, are satisfied, select the source reports to validate by clicking the check boxes on the right, and then click the Go button.

The report selection screen displays nine columns that provide information on the following:

- **!** Sets the run priority of the corresponding report.

- **Name** The report name.

- **Status** Current report status.

- **DQM Enabled** Flag that indicates whether the report is using dynamic query mode or the default query mode.

- **Progress** Colored dots indicate where the report is in the validation process; the five dots correspond to the five tasks in the process.

- **Sticky note** Location for user notes on reports and status.

- **Options** Allows you to modify the PDF settings, select prompts, and so on.

- **Folder and lock icon** Once a report has been validated or run, the results are locked to avoid accidental overwriting. You can manually unlock reports by clicking the icon.

- **Check box** Select the report to be included in the processing for the current step.

After the validation process completes, the report list will update with the results.

Validate in Source > Samples > Models > GO Sales (query) > **Report Studio Report Samples**   1 - 7 of 7

!	Name	Status	DQM enabled	Progress		Options		
·	Briefing Book	Valid	D	● · · · ·	·			
·	Horizontal Pagination	Valid	D	● · · · ·	·			
·	No Data	Valid	D	● · · · ·	·			
·	Order Invoices - Donald Chow, Sales Person	Valid	D	● · · · ·	·			
·	PDF Page Properties	Valid	D	● · · · ·	·			
·	Singletons on Page Body	Valid	D	● · · · ·	·			
·	Table of Contents	Valid	D	● · · · ·	·			

Validate models/reports ▼   Go

14. The same process is repeated for each task: Run In Source, Validate In Target, Run In Target, and Output Comparison. After running the Output Comparison task, the results are reflected in both the Status and Progress columns.

Output Comparison > Samples > Models > GO Sales (query) > **Report Studio Report Samples**   1 - 7 of 7

!	Name	Status	DQM enabled	Progress		Options		
·	Briefing Book	No Differences	D D	● ● ● ● ●	·			
·	Horizontal Pagination	Differences	D D	● ● ● ● ●				
·	No Data	Differences	D D	● ● ● ● ●	·			
·	Order Invoices - Donald Chow, Sales Person	Differences	D D	● ● ● ● ●	·			
·	PDF Page Properties	Differences	D D	● ● ● ● ●	·			
·	Singletons on Page Body	Differences	D D	● ● ● ● ●	·			
·	Table of Contents	Differences	D D	● ● ● ● ●	·			

Compare reports ▼   Go

NOTE *If a report requires a prompt value to run, Cognos Lifecycle Manager will add a prompt icon to the Options column for the report. If you choose to ignore the prompt, Cognos Lifecycle Manager will not include that report in its processing.*

In this example, the Briefing Book report shows a status of No Differences, and all of the indicators are green. This tells us that the upgraded version of the Briefing Book output is identical to the source version.

The Horizontal Pagination report shows a status of Differences, and the last indicator is red. However, Cognos Lifecycle Manager has added a note which reads: [Auto-generated Note]:- Content same. Format Difference Only.

This note tells you that although there are differences in the source and target report output, all of the differences result from layout (format) differences, but all of the numbers are the same.

The No Data report is a little different; this report requires user input (prompts) in order to run. Because we have not provided the required input, the report has not been run.

Compare Results

After running your initial comparisons, you can start to examine the differences. Follow these steps:

1. From the output list, select the report to examine by clicking the report name. For this example, click the PDF Page Properties report. You'll see the PDF Page Properties – Properties screen.

2. Click the Status tab to open it:

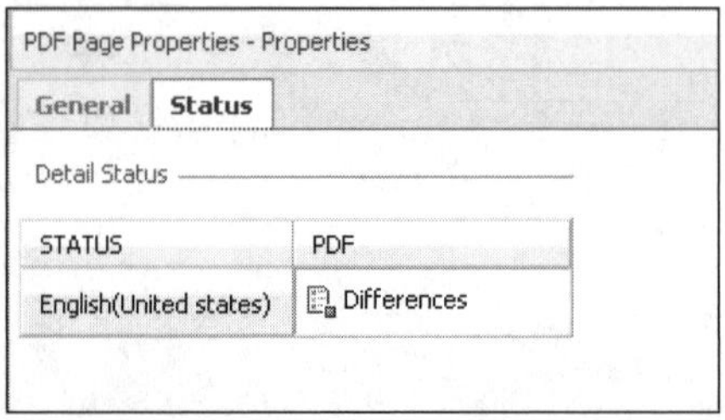

PDF Page Properties - Properties		

General | **Status**

Detail Status ————————————

STATUS	PDF
English(United states)	📄 Differences

3. Click the Differences link and you will be prompted to select one of two comparison tools:

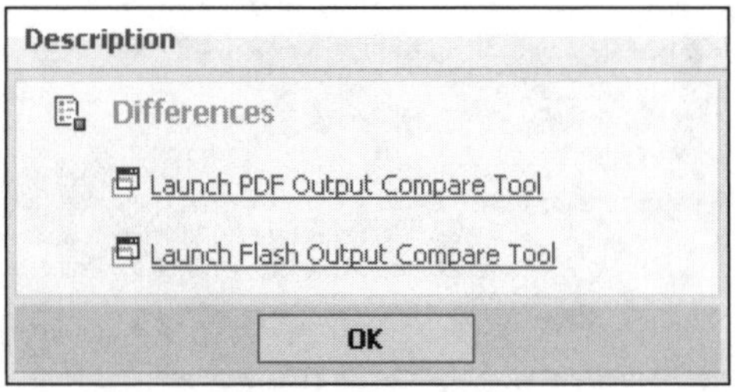

Description

📄 Differences

    📋 Launch PDF Output Compare Tool

    📋 Launch Flash Output Compare Tool

OK

Both the PDF version and the Flash version tools allow you to compare the output of the source and target reports side-by-side. Try them both to see which one you prefer.

4. Click the Launch PDF Output Compare Tool link. The report outputs are displayed:

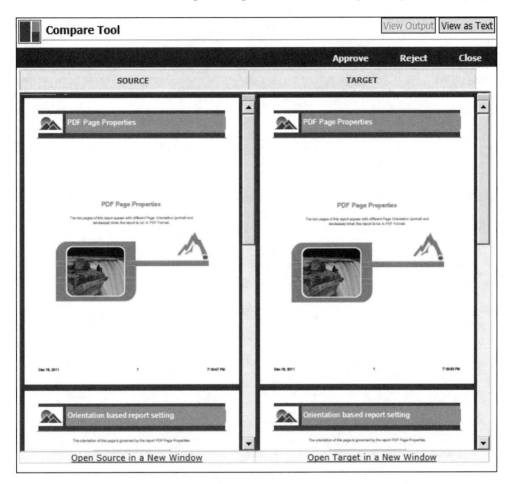

How you choose to examine the results of the output comparison depends on the size and complexity of the report. In some cases, you can "eyeball" the output side. In others, you are better off switching to the Text View.

5. To view the output as text, click the View As Text button in the upper-right corner of the Compare Tool window. After you switch to Text View, the differences between the versions are highlighted in red and become readily apparent, as shown here:

Compare Tool						View Output	View as Text

Navigation:	**| <**	**<<**	**>>**	**>|**	**Approve**	**Reject**	**Close**

SOURCE	TARGET
Page 1	
PDF Page Properties PDF Page Properties The two pages of this report appear with differ ent Page Orientation (portrait and landscap e) when the report is run in PDF Format. De c 16, 2011 1 7	PDF Page Properties PDF Page Properties The two pages of this report appear with differ ent Page Orientation (portrait and landscap e) when the report is run in PDF Format. De c 16, 2011 1 7
Page 2	
Orientation based report setting The orient ation of this page is governed by the repor t PDF Page Properties. Product line Revenue Camping Equipment $2,272,322,429.56 Golf Eq uipment $1,038,768,256.08 Mountaineering Eq uipment $585,813,990.05 Outdoor Protection $108,671,843.64 Personal Accessories $2,69 6,512,830.13 3 Dec 16, 2011	Orientation based report setting The orient ation of this page is governed by the repor t PDF Page Properties. Product line Revenue Camping Equipment $2,272,322,429.56 Golf Equ ipment $1,038,768,256.08 Mountaineering Equi pment $585,813,990.05 Outdoor Protection $10 8,671,843.64 Personal Accessories $2,696,51 2,830.1 3 Dec 16, 2011
Page 3	
Landscape set on page This page will always appear in landscape as the PDF Page Propert ies have been set on the page object. Reven ue E-mail Fax Mail Sales visit Special Tele phone Web Camping Equipment $75,899,094.63 $23,054,398.48 $21,348,644.09 $168,611,961. 87 $12,388,989.44 $153,894,892.13 $1,133,83 8,683.39 Golf Equipment $47,933,933.16 $15, 241,303.27 $12,693,287.48 $39,240,918.73 $4,964,762.97 $78,730,112.65 $527,607,049.6 3 Mountaineering Equipment $7,476,451.96 $1 1,848,370.08 $3,531,658.66 $44,616,626.64 $3,674,008.11 $22,910,827.40 $315,602,190.0 5 Outdoor Protection $5,882,477.87 $1,966,4 84.72 $2,098,391.71 $10,029,884.31 $1,136,9 31.23 $11,928,314.52 $42,951,811.89 Persona l Accessories $42,651,086.54 $17,962,985.46 $6,419,357.03 $47,695,442.45 $5,186,628.50	Landscape set on page This page will always appear in landscape as the PDF Page Propert ies have been set on the page object. Reven ue E-mail Fax Mail Sales visit Special Tele phone Web Camping Equipment $75,899,094.63 $23,054,398.48 $21,348,644.09 $168,611,961. 87 $12,388,989.44 $153,894,892.13 $1,133,83 8,683.39 Golf Equipment $47,933,933.16 $15, 241,303.27 $12,693,287.48 $39,240,918.73 $4,964,762.97 $78,730,112.65 $527,607,049.6 3 Mountaineering Equipment $7,476,451.96 $1 1,848,370.08 $3,531,658.66 $44,616,626.64 $3,674,008.11 $22,910,827.40 $315,602,190.0 5 Outdoor Protection $5,882,477.87 $1,966,4 84.72 $2,098,391.71 $10,029,884.31 $1,136,9 31.23 $11,928,314.52 $42,951,811.89 Persona l Accessories $42,651,086.54 $17,962,985.46 $6,419,357.03 $47,695,442.45 $5,186,628.50

6. Review the differences. At this point, you have three options: You can accept the upgraded report, reject the upgraded report, or cancel without changing the report status. For this example, let's accept this report. Click the Approve link at the top of the page and the Save dialog opens, shown next.

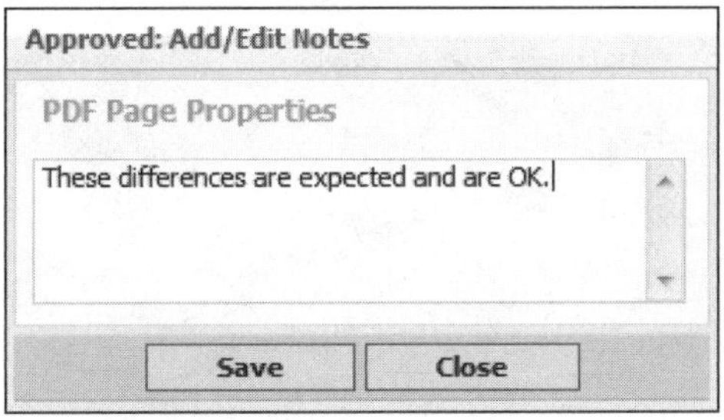

Approved: Add/Edit Notes

PDF Page Properties

These differences are expected and are OK.|

[Save]   [Close]

This changes the report status in the PDF Page Properties – Properties window from Differences to Approved:

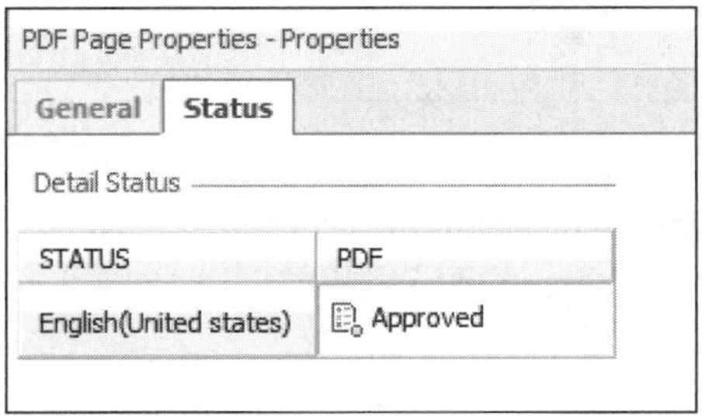

PDF Page Properties - Properties

| General | **Status** |

Detail Status

STATUS	PDF
English(United states)	Approved

NOTE *If the upgraded report output is not acceptable, select the reject button at the top of the review page, add a note describing the issue, and click the Save button. This will update the report Status from Differences to Rejected.*

Tasks Summary

During the validation process, Cognos Lifecycle Manager will track the results of each step and provide an overview on the Tasks Summary screen, shown here:

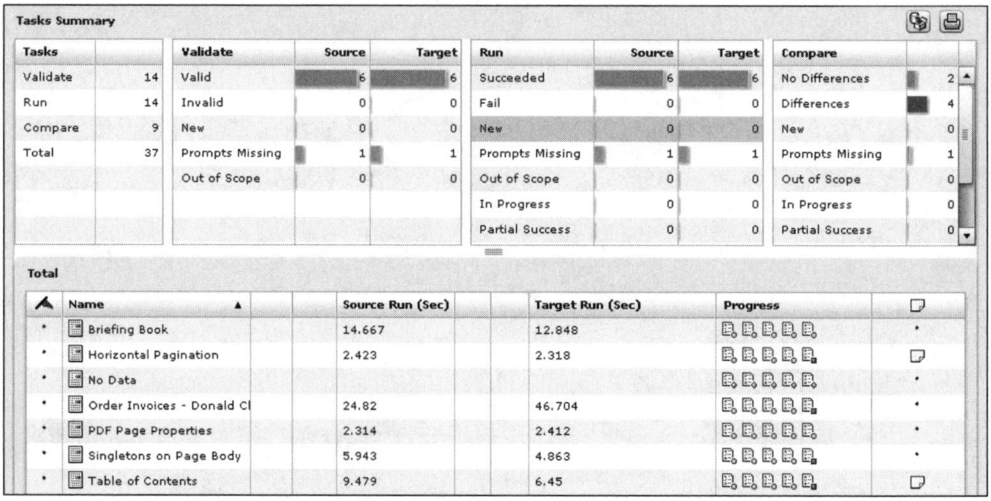

Tasks		Validate	Source	Target	Run	Source	Target	Compare		
Validate	14	Valid	6	6	Succeeded	6	6	No Differences		2
Run	14	Invalid	0	0	Fail	0	0	Differences		4
Compare	9	New	0	0	New	0	0	New		0
Total	37	Prompts Missing	1	1	Prompts Missing	1	1	Prompts Missing		1
		Out of Scope	0	0	Out of Scope	0	0	Out of Scope		0
					In Progress	0	0	In Progress		0
					Partial Success	0	0	Partial Success		0

Total

	Name	Source Run (Sec)	Target Run (Sec)	Progress	
•	Briefing Book	14.667	12.848		•
•	Horizontal Pagination	2.423	2.318		
•	No Data				•
•	Order Invoices - Donald Cl	24.82	46.704		•
•	PDF Page Properties	2.314	2.412		•
•	Singletons on Page Body	5.943	4.863		•
•	Table of Contents	9.479	6.45		

The top half of this screen provides a quick view of where you are in the validation process, including how many reports have been validated, run, and compared. The bottom half provides a view of source and target run times, the state of the validation process, and access to any notes made for a report.

Benchmark Project

Benchmark Projects in Cognos Lifecycle Manager allow the user to compare multiple run times of the same report under different report configurations.

Create a New Benchmark Project

Benchmark Projects are created in the same manner as Validation Projects. To create a new Benchmark Project, follow these steps:

1. From the New Project dialog, select the Create Blank Project radio button, name the project **New Benchmark**, and select Benchmark Project as the Project Type. Then click Create.

2. From the project screen, click the Configure button.

3. From the Configuration screen, enter the application name, the Gateway URI, and the Dispatcher URI for the server where the reports to benchmark reside.

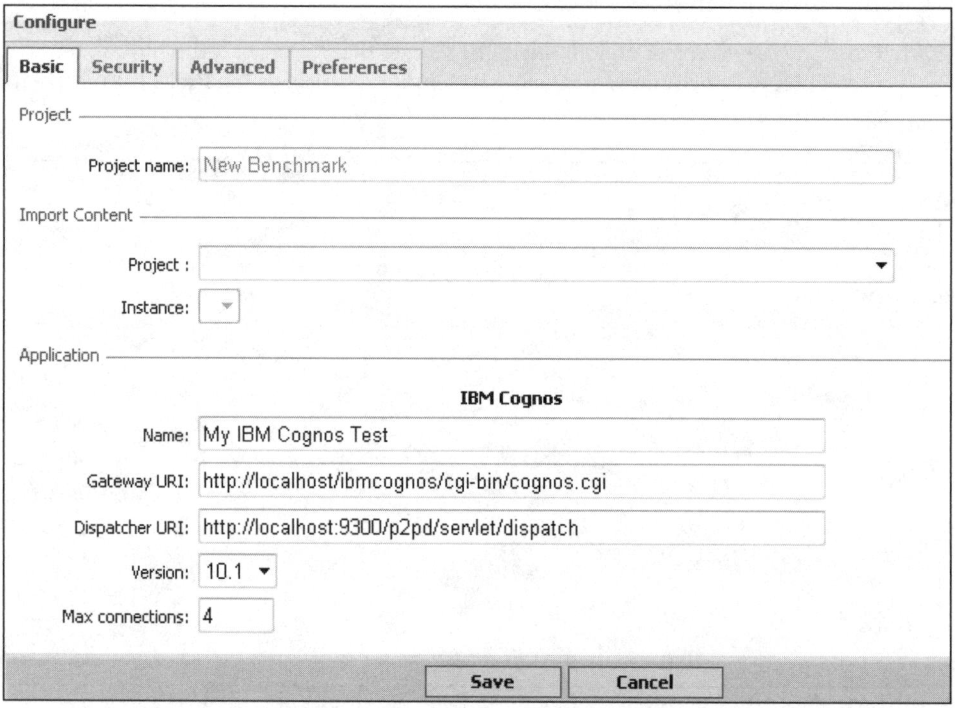

```
Configure

 Basic   Security   Advanced   Preferences

 Project ────────────────────────────────────────

        Project name:  New Benchmark

 Import Content ─────────────────────────────────

             Project :                                    ▼

            Instance:    ▼

 Application ────────────────────────────────────

                            IBM Cognos

               Name:  My IBM Cognos Test

        Gateway URI:  http://localhost/ibmcognos/cgi-bin/cognos.cgi

      Dispatcher URI:  http://localhost:9300/p2pd/servlet/dispatch

             Version:  10.1  ▼

     Max connections:  4

                                    [  Save  ]  [  Cancel  ]
```

4. On the Security tab, provide the credentials for the IBM Cognos user to run the benchmark reports. Then click Save.

5. Select the folder that contains the reports to benchmark. We will use the same reports that we used in the validation process.

6. Select the list view, and you'll see all of the reports available for benchmark testing:

7. Select all of the reports and run the Validate process.

!	Name	Status	DQM enabled	Progress		Options		
·	Briefing Book	New		·				✓
·	Horizontal Pagination	New		·				✓
·	No Data	Prompt Values Missing		··				✓
·	Order Invoices - Donald Chow, Sales Person	New		·				✓
·	PDF Page Properties	New		·				✓
·	Singletons on Page Body	New		·				✓
·	Table of Contents	New		·				✓

(Tasks panel: Validate in Run1, Run in Run1, Dashboards, Tasks Summary — Run in Run1 header, 1 - 7 of 7)

8. From the Run in Run1 task, select all reports and run the reports by clicking the Go button.

!	Name	Status	DQM enabled	Progress		Options		
·	Briefing Book	Succeeded	D	··	·			
·	Horizontal Pagination	Succeeded	D	··	·			
·	No Data	Prompt Values Missing		··	·			
·	Order Invoices - Donald Chow, Sales Person	Succeeded	D	··	·			
·	PDF Page Properties	Succeeded	D	··	·			
·	Singletons on Page Body	Succeeded	D	··	·			
·	Table of Contents	Succeeded	D	··	·			

(Launch IBM Cognos Portal — Run reports ▾ Go)

To set the initial benchmark, all the reports in the list must have a status of either Succeeded or Out Of Scope. In our example, the No Data report has a status of Prompt Values Missing.

9. To change a status to Out Of Scope, click the Status of the report you want to change, and select the Out Of Scope radio button. Then click OK.

Change Status

No Data

○ ▤ In Scope
◉ ··· Out of Scope

| OK | Cancel |

10. With all of the reports at either Succeeded or Out Of Scope, you can now set the initial benchmark by clicking the Master menu and selecting Run1.

▲ Master ▾

Run1

Run the Second Benchmark

After the initial benchmarks have been set for your reports, you can make the configuration changes that you are interested in testing. Completing the initial benchmark will add three new items to the task menu: Validate In Run2, Run In Run2, and Output Comparison.

The process for running the second benchmark is identical to the process used for the initial benchmark.

1. Click the Validate In Run2 task and select the reports to validate.

2. After the validation is complete, click the Run In Run2 task, select the reports to run with the changes you have made to your environment, and run the reports.

3. Once the reports are run, click the Output Comparison task, select the reports to compare, and then click on the Go button. This will compare the results of the initial benchmark against the results of the second benchmark. It will also update the Tasks Summary dashboard with the run results and run times for each.

4. Click the Tasks Summary tab and the run history results are displayed:

Here, you can review the results of the initial run against the second run. If the new results are acceptable, you are finished. If not, repeat the process until you get the optimal results.

NOTE *If you have problems with your reports, check the IBM Cognos documentation for troubleshooting tips.*

Index

The only official guides to
IBM® Cognos®

IBM Cognos Business Intelligence V10: The Official Guide
Dan Volitich and Gerard Ruppert

Updated for the latest release of the software, this book shows you how to develop, deploy, and maintain a complete enterprise BI solution.

IBM Cognos TM1: The Official Guide
Karsten Oehler, Jochen Gruenes, and Christopher Ilacqua

Filled with expert advice from a team of IBM professionals, this book explains how to deliver timely, accurate, and actionable performance management solutions to users across your enterprise.